West's Federal Taxation: Individual Income Taxes

West's Federal Taxation:

Individual Income Taxes

General Editors

LAWRENCE C. PHILLIPS, Ph.D., C.P.A. AND
WILLIAM H. HOFFMAN, Jr., J.D., Ph.D., C.P.A.

Contributing Authors

ROBERT W. CLARKE, Ph.D.
Associate Professor of Accounting, Rice University

D. LARRY CRUMBLEY, Ph.D., C.P.A.
Professor of Accounting, Texas A & M University

PATRICA C. ELLIOTT, D.B.A., C.P.A.
Associate Professor of Accounting, University of Washington

WILLIAM H. HOFFMAN, Jr., J.D., Ph.D., C.P.A.
Professor of Tax Accounting, University of Houston

JEROME S. HORVITZ, J.D., LL.M. in Taxation
Associate Professor of Tax Accounting, University of Houston

MARILYN PHELAN, J.D., D.B.A., C.P.A.
Professor of Law, Texas Tech University

LAWRENCE C. PHILLIPS, Ph.D., C.P.A.
Professor of Accounting, Case Western Reserve University

JAMES W. PRATT, D.B.A., C.P.A.
Associate Professor of Tax Accounting, University of Houston

W. EUGENE SEAGO, Ph.D., C.P.A.
Professor of Accounting, Virginia Polytechnic
Institute and State University

WEST PUBLISHING CO.
ST. PAUL • NEW YORK • LOS ANGELES • SAN FRANCISCO

COPYRIGHT © 1978 by WEST PUBLISHING CO.

50 West Kellogg Boulevard

P.O. Box 3526

St. Paul, Minnesota 55165

Printed in the United States of America

Library of Congress Cataloging in Publication Data

Main entry under title:

West's Federal taxation.

Includes index.

1. Income tax—United States—Law

I. Phillips, Lawrence C. II. Hoffman, William H.

KF6369.W47   343'.73'052   77–20656

ISBN 0–8299–0150–7

West's Fed.Tax.: Individuals

PREFACE

The text is intended as the basis for a first course in Federal taxation for undergraduate or graduate, accounting, business or law students. With certain modifications in the coverage of the materials, the text may be used in a survey course on Federal taxation for undergraduate or graduate students. These materials may also be valuable as a tool for self-study since they contain numerous clarifying examples which are adaptable to a self-study approach.

While primary emphasis is upon individuals, Chapter 18 includes an overview of the Federal taxation of corporations. This chapter is of particular significance for students who do not plan to take a second course in Federal taxation. For others, Chapter 18 may serve as a lead in to *West's Federal Taxation: Corporations, Partnerships, Estates, and Trusts.*

Our intent is to present a proper blend of coverage relative to the following aspects of taxation:

1. Tax policy, historical development of the tax law and rationale for a particular tax rule;
2. Tax research including coverage in the text and numerous research problems;
3. Technical tax provisions with numerous clarifying examples; and
4. Tax planning including separate tax practice suggestions at the end of most chapters.

The authors are of the opinion that any basic course in Federal taxation should offer the student the opportunity to learn and utilize the methodology of tax research. Chapters 1 and 2 and Appendix E are devoted to this topic, and each Chapter contains one or more research projects. A comprehensive case study involving the preparation of a tax return for an individual is also included in the Appendix. These materials are intended for use as special or term projects. The effectiveness of the text does not, however, depend upon the use of these research materials. They may be omitted without diminishing the presentation of all other topics.

We intend frequent revisions of this text material to accommodate statutory, judicial and administrative changes in the Federal tax law and to correct any errors or shortcomings.

Dr. LAWRENCE C. PHILLIPS and
Dr. WILLIAM H. HOFFMAN, Jr.

v *

TABLE OF CONTENTS

TABLE OF CONTENTS

CHAPTER 3. WORKING WITH THE TAX LAW—Continued

CHAPTER 4. GROSS INCOME

CHAPTER 5. GROSS INCOME—INCLUSIONS AND EXCLUSIONS

CHAPTER 5. GROSS INCOME—INCLUSIONS AND EXCLUSIONS—Continued

CHAPTER 6. DEDUCTIONS AND LOSSES— IN GENERAL

TABLE OF CONTENTS

CHAPTER 6. DEDUCTIONS AND LOSSES—IN GENERAL
—Continued

CHAPTER 7. DEDUCTIONS AND LOSSES: CERTAIN BUSINESS EXPENSES AND LOSSES

TABLE OF CONTENTS

CHAPTER 7. DEDUCTIONS AND LOSSES: CERTAIN BUSINESS EXPENSES AND LOSSES—Continued

CHAPTER 8. DEDUCTIONS: EMPLOYEE EXPENSES

TABLE OF CONTENTS

CHAPTER 8. DEDUCTIONS: EMPLOYEE EXPENSES
—Continued

CHAPTER 9. DEDUCTIONS AND LOSSES, CERTAIN ITEMIZED DEDUCTIONS

TABLE OF CONTENTS

CHAPTER 9. DEDUCTIONS AND LOSSES, CERTAIN ITEMIZED DEDUCTIONS—Continued

CHAPTER 10. STANDARD DEDUCTION, PERSONAL AND DEPENDENCY EXEMPTIONS AND DETERMINATION OF TAX

TABLE OF CONTENTS

CHAPTER 10: STANDARD DEDUCTION, PERSONAL AND DEPENDENCY EXEMPTIONS AND DETERMINATION OF TAX—Continued

CHAPTER 11. TAX CREDITS

CHAPTER 12. PROPERTY TRANSACTIONS—DETERMINATION OF GAIN OR LOSS AND BASIS CONSIDERATIONS

TABLE OF CONTENTS

CHAPTER 12. PROPERTY TRANSACTIONS—DETERMINATION OF GAIN OR LOSS AND BASIS CONSIDERATIONS—Continued

CHAPTER 13. PROPERTY TRANSACTIONS—NONTAXABLE EXCHANGES

TABLE OF CONTENTS

CHAPTER 15. PROPERTY TRANSACTIONS—SECTION 1231 AND RECAPTURE PROVISIONS

CHAPTER 16. ACCOUNTING PERIODS AND METHODS

TABLE OF CONTENTS

CHAPTER 16. ACCOUNTING PERIODS AND METHODS
—Continued

CHAPTER 17. DEFERRED COMPENSATION

TABLE OF CONTENTS

CHAPTER 17. DEFERRED COMPENSATION—Continued

CHAPTER 18. CORPORATIONS

APPENDICES

TABLE OF CONTENTS

West's Federal Taxation: Individual Income Taxes

†

Chapter 1

AN INTRODUCTION TO FEDERAL TAXATION

Before giving consideration to specific tax provisions it is desirable to review the historical development of our Federal tax law and to understand the underlying rationale for our tax system. Thus, an initial review is made of the historical, economic and social aspects of our tax law. The chapter material also includes a brief discussion of the major types of taxes and an introduction to the organizational aspects of administering the tax law. Finally, the basic tax formula is presented to provide background material for subsequent chapters.

HISTORY OF U.S. TAXATION

EARLY PERIODS

An income tax was first enacted in 1634 by the English colonists in the Massachusetts Bay Colony. In 1861, the first U.S. Federal income tax was enacted to provide revenues for the Civil War. Although these Federal income taxes were repealed after the end of the war, they proved to be a major source of revenue. Civil War income taxes provided $376 million of revenue for the Federal government during this period.[1]

1. Ray M. Sommerfeld, Hershel M. Anderson, and Horace R. Brock, *An* *Introduction to Taxation*, 1978 Ed., Harcourt, Brace, Janovich, p. 4–2.

In 1894, another Federal income tax law was enacted despite considerable political opposition and the unsettled question as to the constitutionality of an income tax during this period. The U.S. Constitution provided that " * * * No Capitation, or other direct, Tax shall be laid, unless in Proportion to the Census or Enumeration herein before directed to be taken." The question before the courts was whether an income tax was a "direct tax" and unapportioned since the Constitution required that a direct tax be apportioned among the states in proportion to their populations. In *Pollock v. Farmers' Loan and Trust Co.,* the Supreme Court held that the 1894 income tax law was unconstitutional since it was a direct tax and unapportioned.[2] In addition, the Supreme Court held that the law was invalid since it attempted to tax income from municipal obligations, i. e., that the Federal government does not have the right to levy a tax that is imposed on the borrowing power of political subdivisions.

Before the Sixteenth Amendment was ratified, Congress enacted a corporate income tax in 1909. This corporate tax was upheld by the courts since it was a special form of excise tax and not a direct tax.[3] The corporate tax was of little significance since the Revenue Act of 1913 provided for both individual and corporate taxes.

REVENUE ACTS

Due to the working in the U.S. Constitution as interpreted by the Supreme Court, it was necessary to amend the Constitution to permit the enactment of a Federal income tax. Following ratification of the Sixteenth Amendment, Congress enacted the Revenue Act of 1913. Under this Act, a flat 1 percent tax was levied upon the income of corporations. Individuals paid a normal tax rate of 1 percent on taxable income after deducting a personal exemption of $3,000 for a single person and $4,000 for a married taxpayer. Surtax rates of 1 to 6 percent were applied to high income taxpayers.

Various Revenue Acts were passed during the period from 1913 to 1939. In 1939, all of these revenue laws were codified into the Internal Revenue Code of 1939. In 1954, a similar codification of the revenue law took place. Thus, the current law consists of the Internal Revenue Code of 1954 as amended by numerous revenue laws passed since 1954.

HISTORICAL TRENDS

The income tax has proved to be a major source of revenue for the Federal government. Income taxes currently amount to approxi-

2. *Pollock v. Farmers' Loan & Trust Co.,* 3 AFTR 2602, 15 S.Ct. 912 (USSC, 1895).

3. *Flint v. Stone Tracy Co.,* 31 S.Ct. 342 (USSC, 1911).

mately 57 percent of total government receipts.[4] If FICA tax receipts are excluded, tax collections from individuals account for about 53 percent of the Federal government's budget receipts whereas corporate taxes account for approximately 24 percent.[5]

The need for revenues to finance the war effort during WW II, has converted the income tax into a "mass tax." For example, in 1939 less than 6 percent of the U.S. population was subject to the Federal income tax. In 1945, over 74 percent were subject to the Federal income tax.[6]

Certain changes in the income tax law are of particular significance in understanding the Federal income tax law. In 1943, Congress passed the Current Tax Payment Act which provided for the first "pay-as-you-go" tax system.

These changes were necessary to provide a means for raising substantial revenues in the form of a mass tax upon individuals and corporations.

ECONOMIC AND SOCIAL ASPECTS OF TAXATION

USE OF THE TAX LAW

While the primary objective of our tax policy has been to raise revenue, the Federal government has frequently used its taxing powers to foster social and economic objectives. For example, the investment tax credit provisions have been used as a fiscal policy tool to stimulate private investment in our economy. Accelerated depreciation and artificially shortened useful life classification systems for fixed assets have also been enacted to stimulate private investment. In 1971, Congress enacted (D.I.S.C.) legislation to encourage U.S. exports and, therefore, help alleviate a balance of payments problem. In 1975, Congress passed tax cuts for individuals and corporate taxpayers to help stimulate the economy.

In recent years, Congress has used the tax law to serve as an instrument for the attainment of socially desirable goals. For example, in 1969 Congress passed legislation which permits the amortization of certain pollution control facility costs over a period of 60 months.[7]

---

4. *Supra*, note 1 at p. 2–8.

5. *Tax Foundation, Inc.*, The Federal Budget for Fiscal Year 1976.

6. Goode, Richard, "The Individual Income Tax" (Washington, D.C.: Brookings Institution, 1964), pp. 2–4.

7. § 169.

In addition, a tax credit is now available for employers who hire certain new employees under work incentive programs.[8] In 1974, Congress passed a massive overhaul of our entire private pension system (ERISA). Further modifications were made in the pension area in the Tax Reform Act of 1976.

Since 1968, Congress has attempted to close specific tax provisions which permit large-scale tax avoidance by wealthy taxpayers. The attacks upon large-scale unwarranted tax privileges have resulted in the following changes:

1. Certain restrictions have been placed upon tax sheltered deductions, e. g. investment interest;

2. A 15% minimum tax is now imposed in addition to the regular Federal income tax upon certain tax deduction items which receive preferential tax treatment (note, however, that tax exempt interest is not considered to be a tax preference item under the tax law);

3. Capital gain opportunities are no longer as attractive due to the minimum tax, depreciation recapture and other limiting provisions.

The use of the tax system as a means to accomplish economic and social objectives is discussed more fully in Chapter 2 and in subsequent chapters where the rationale for specific tax rules are presented.

CRITERIA USED IN THE SELECTION OF A TAX BASE

Adam Smith first identified certain criteria or "canons of taxation" which are still being considered when questions are raised relative to the desirability of a particular type of tax or taxing structure. These "canons of taxation" are as follows: [9]

1. Equality—Each taxpayer enjoys fair or equitable treatment by paying taxes in proportion to his income level. Ability to pay a tax is the measure of how equitably a tax is distributed among taxpayers.

2. Convenience—Administrative simplicity has long been valued as an important consideration in formulating tax policy. If a tax is easily assessed, collected and the costs of administration are low, such a tax structure should be favored. The withholding "pay-as-you-go" system has been advocated because of its convenience for taxpayers. It should be noted, however, that our Federal income tax laws have become increasingly complex despite outcries from tax specialists, poli-

8. § 40.

9. *The Wealth of Nations*, Book V, Chapter II, Part II (New York: Dutton, 1910).

ticians, business executives, etc., regarding the need for administrative simplicity.

3. Certainty—A "good" tax is one in which the taxpayer can readily predict when, where, and how a tax will be levied. A business may need to know the likely tax consequences of entering into a particular type of business transaction. Some degree of certainty is built into our present tax system. For example, the Treasury Department generally issues detailed Regulations following the enactment of a tax change. In addition, the IRS issues advance rulings on the tax consequences of a proposed transaction.

4. Economy—A "good" tax is one which requires only nominal collection costs by the government and involves minimal compliance costs on the part of the taxpayer. Each year the Annual Report of the Commissioner of the IRS reports that the government's cost to collect the tax amounts to less than one-half of one percent of the revenue which is collected. On the other hand, due to the complexity of our existing tax structure, taxpayer compliance costs are probably very substantial.

TAX RATE STRUCTURE

Tax rates are applied to the tax base to determine a taxpayer's liability. The tax rates may be "proportional," "progressive" or "regressive." A tax is proportional if the rate of tax remains constant for any given income level.

Example 1. Individual X has $10,000 of taxable income and pays a tax of $2,000 or 20%. Y's taxable income is $20,000 and pays a tax of $4,000 or 20%. If the constant rate is applied throughout the rate structure, the tax is proportional.

The Federal income, Federal gift and estate tax and most state income tax rate structures are progressive. A higher percentage rate of tax is applied to increased amounts of taxable income. In the case of the Federal estate and gift tax law, a progressive rate structure is applied to transfers of wealth during life by gift and to transfers at death.

Example 2. If a married individual filing jointly has taxable income of $12,000, the tax is $1,380 plus 22% of amounts in excess of $11,200. However, if a wealthy income individual's taxable income is $110,000 the tax is $45,180 plus 62% of amounts over $103,200. The tax is progressive since higher rates are applied to greater amounts of taxable income.

A regressive rate structure applies a smaller percentage rate of tax to increasing levels of income, wealth or whatever is being used as the tax base. State sales taxes generally apply proportional rates, e. g. a 4% rate is applied to consumer purchases. To the extent that low income taxpayers spend a higher percentage of their income on consumption, the sales tax may be regarded as regressive since the flat rate is applied to a higher tax base for such lower income taxpayers.

ADJUSTMENTS TO TAX BASE AND INCIDENTS OF TAXATION

The degree to which the total tax burden is shared by our various segments of society is difficult to assess. Assumptions must be made as to who absorbs the burden for payment of the tax. For example, the corporate tax rate structure is a stair-step progression (20% for the first $25,000 of taxable income, 22% for the next $25,000 and 48% for taxable income over $50,000). Since dividend payments to shareholders are not deductible and such amounts are generally taxable income to shareholders, a form of double taxation on the same income is being levied. The double taxation argument is valid to the extent that corporations are *not* able to shift the corporate tax to the consumer through higher sales prices. In such event, the corporate tax is merely a consumption tax which is borne by consumers.

The U.S. Federal income tax rate structure appears to be highly progressive, e. g. rates range from 14 to 70%. However, if adjustments to the tax base are taken into account, a different pattern may emerge. Wealthy individuals with high incomes are more able to take advantage of certain tax benefits, e. g. tax sheltered investments, contributions of property and recognition of long-term capital gains. Recent studies have indicated that the effective tax rates for Federal and state taxes are generally proportional for almost 90 percent of the population.[10] Regressive features in state and local taxes tend to offset the slight progression in the Federal income tax.

MAJOR TYPES OF TAXES

CUSTOMS DUTIES AND EXCISE TAXES

Prior to the passage of the income tax, the U.S. relied almost exclusively upon custom duties and excise taxes to finance operations of the Federal government. Excise taxes are imposed upon selected

---

10. Joseph Pechman and Benjamin Okner, "Who Bears the Tax Burden?" (Washington, D.C., The Brookings Institution, 1974).

commodities such as alcoholic beverages, tobacco products and highway fuels. Federal excise taxes and customs duties amount to about 12% of the total Federal Budget Receipts.[11] Historically, excise taxes have been imposed upon luxury items and products whose consumption may be dangerous to society, e. g. alcohol (although there is no evidence to indicate that the excise taxes reduce the level of consumption of such products in the U.S.).

ESTATE TAX

The estate tax is levied upon the value of property transferred at death. The Revenue Act of 1916 originated the modern day version of the estate tax. The estate tax has never been a major source of revenue for the Federal government. Its original intention was to break up large concentrations of wealth among a few wealthy families. Whether this objective has been met is debatable since many wealthy individuals have been able to minimize estate taxes through the use of tax plans which comply with existing law.

Prior to 1977, each estate received an exemption of $60,000 and the estate tax rates ranged from 3 percent to 77 percent on estates in excess of $10 million. The 1976 Tax Reform Act provides a single unified transfer tax for both lifetime gift transfers and testamentary (death) transfers. The $60,000 exemption for the estate tax and a $30,000 life exemption under the former gift tax law have been replaced by a unified tax credit of $30,000 in 1977 (increasing to $47,000 in 1981). The unified transfer tax rates range from 18% to 70% for gifts or estates in excess of five million.

The estate receives a marital deduction for certain qualifying property which is left to the surviving spouse. Under the former law, the marital deduction was one-half of the adjusted gross estate. In 1977 the marital deduction is now the greater of $250,000 or one-half of the adjusted gross estate. Due to the liberalization of the marital deduction and the newly enacted tax credit, many individuals who would have been subject to estate tax under the former law, will no longer be required to pay the Federal estate tax.

Example 3. X died in 1978 leaving an estate of $300,000 to his wife. Since the marital deduction is $250,000 and the estate tax on the $50,000 is only $10,600, the $34,000 unified credit in 1978 is more than sufficient to eliminate the estate from any obligation to pay Federal estate tax assuming the credit was not previously used to reduce or eliminate gift tax on transfers made prior to death.

11. *Supra*, note 5.

GIFT TAX

The gift tax has been part of the Federal taxing system since 1932. It was enacted as a backdrop to the estate tax. To prevent widespread avoidance of the estate tax, an individual might make substantial lifetime transfers if there were no gift tax.

Prior to the passage of the Tax Reform Act of 1976, gift tax provisions, rate tables, etc., were separate and distinct from the estate tax law. It was generally preferable to make lifetime gifts instead of testamentary dispositions since the gift tax rates were substantially lower than the estate tax rates and separate exemptions and exclusions could be taken under the separate gift tax structure. The present system subjects all gratuitous transfers to a unitary taxing system and, therefore, promotes neutrality relative to life and death transfers.

EMPLOYMENT TAXES

Employers are required to pay FICA taxes (employer's share) under the Federal Insurance Contributions Act. The employer's share is 5.85% of wages paid for each employee up to a ceiling of $16,500 in 1977. A matching contribution is made by the employee through the payroll withholding system. Self-employed individuals are also required to contribute at a rate of 7.9% up to the $16,500 ceiling (in 1977).

Employers are also required to pay state and Federal unemployment taxes for their employees. For 1977, the Federal rate is 3.2% of the first $4,200 of wages paid to each employee during the year. However, the employer is allowed a credit against the Federal unemployment tax for state unemployment tax payments.

STATE AND LOCAL TAXES

State and local taxes have become of greater significance to taxpayers in recent years due to the increase in such taxes relative to total tax collections. For example, state and local taxes now comprise approximately 36 percent of the total tax receipts of Federal, state and local governments.[12]

All state governments impose a sales tax and most states levy an income tax upon individuals and corporations. Many state or county governments also impose taxes upon tangible and intangible property, e. g. intangible taxes may be imposed upon dividend and interest income or ad valorem taxes may be levied upon a taxpayer's home, automobile and other personal belongings. In addition, many local gov-

12. *Tax Foundation, Inc.,* "Facts and Figures on Government Finance," 1976.

The term "adjusted gross income" has no applicability to corporations. Trade or business expenses are merely subtracted from gross income to arrive at taxable income.

Corporations are subject to a stair-step pattern of rate progression as illustrated in the following example:

Example 5. XYZ Corporation had taxable income of $100,000 during 19X1. Its gross Federal income tax liability is computed as follows:

20 percent x the first $25,000	= $ 5,000
22 percent x taxable income from $25,000 to $50,000	= 5,500
48 percent x taxable income over $50,000	= $24,000
	$34,500

Technically, the 20 and 22 percent rates are referred to as normal taxes whereas 26 percent of the 48 percent (i. e., 48%–22%) is referred to as a surtax.

PROBLEM MATERIALS

Questions for Class Discussion

When and why was the first Federal income tax enacted in the U. S.?

Why did the Supreme Court hold that the 1894 income tax was unconstitutional?

What is the difference between the Internal Revenue Code of 1939 and the Internal Revenue Code of 1954 as amended?

Why is it that most individuals are currently subject to Federal income tax whereas in 1939 less than 6 percent of the U. S. population were required to pay Federal income taxes?

Do you feel that our Federal government could continue to collect the same amount of tax from its taxpayers if the "pay-as-you-go" system were abolished? Why?

Why is accelerated depreciation stimulating to private investment?

If a taxpayer is permitted to write off fixed assets over an artificially shortened useful life, will this practice stimulate private investment?

Give some examples of tax provisions which promote socially desirable objectives within our economy.

List Adam Smith's canons of taxation. Are these canons or criteria for a "good" tax system still appropriate in today's economy.

ernments impose flat rate income taxes upon salaries and wages and other types of earned income.

State income taxes are frequently based upon the amount of the taxpayer's Federal income tax liability, e. g. Federal adjusted gross or taxable income plus or minus certain adjustments. This permits state governments to rely more heavily upon the audit process of the Federal government and may simplify taxpayer compliance. State income taxes are usually progressive and the rates may vary significantly among states, e. g. the maximum tax rate in Ohio is 3½ percent on taxable income over $40,000 whereas the ceiling rate in North Carolina is 7 percent on taxable income over $10,000.

TAX ADMINISTRATION

INTERNAL REVENUE SERVICE

The responsibility for administering the Federal tax laws rests with the Treasury Department. Administratively, the IRS is part of the Department of the Treasury and is responsible for enforcing the tax laws.

The Commissioner of Internal Revenue is appointed by the President. His responsibilities are to establish policy and to supervise the activities of the entire IRS organization. The National Office organization of the IRS includes a Deputy Commissioner and several Assistant Commissioners who have only staff supervision over field operations.

The field organization of the IRS consists of the following:

1. Regional Commissioners (7).

2. District Directors (58).

3. Service Centers (10).

THE AUDIT PROCESS

The IRS utilizes mathematical formulae and statistical sampling techniques to select tax returns which are most likely to contain errors and to yield substantial amounts of additional tax revenues upon the audit of such returns.

While the IRS doesn't openly disclose all of its audit selection techniques, the following observations may be made relative to the probability of being selected for audit:

1. Certain taxpayers are subject to audit much more frequently than others, e. g. individuals with gross income in excess of $50,000, self-employed individuals with substantial business

income and deductions and taxpayers having prior deficiencies.

2. If information returns (form 1099) are not in substantial agreement with reported income, an audit can be anticipated.

3. If an individual's itemized deductions are in excess of norms by income levels, the probability of an audit is increased.

SETTLEMENT PROCEDURES

If an audit results in an additional assessment of tax and no settlement is reached with the IRS agent, the taxpayer may attempt to negotiate a settlement with the District Director level of the IRS. In situations involving a proposed deficiency of more than $2,500 the District Director can not settle based upon the probability of winning or losing the issue in court. Therefore, it is frequently necessary and advisable to carry the administrative appeal procedure to the Regional Appellate level of the IRS. The Appellate Division is authorized to settle all tax disputes based upon the "hazards of litigation."

If a satisfactory settlement is not reached within the administrative appeal process, the taxpayer may wish to litigate the case in the Tax Court, a Federal District Court or in the Court of Claims. It should be noted, however, that litigation should be recommended only as a last resort due to the legal costs and uncertainties relative to the final outcome. Tax administration considerations are discussed more fully in Chapter 2.

THE FEDERAL INCOME TAX SYSTEM IN BRIEF

It is necessary to acquire a basic understanding of the method used to calculate the tax liability as a first step in the study of the Federal income tax law.

TAX FORMULA FOR INDIVIDUALS

Determining an individual's income tax liability may be conveyed by the use of a simple mathematical formula as used in the following example:

Example 4. X had the following items of income, exclusions, deductions, exemptions and credits during 19X1.

1. Salary—$40,000.

2. Job related travel expenses of $2,000 which were not reimbursed by his employer.

3. Tax exempt municipal bond interest—$1,000.

4. Itemized deductions, e. g. charitable contributions, inte expense on his personal residence and state and local ta $4,200.

5. X has a wife and 2 dependent children and files a joint turn with his spouse.

6. X had $9,800 of income tax withheld during the yea entitled to tax credits of $200.

His gross and net tax liability is computed under the formula:

> Income (broadly conceived)
> — Exclusions (tax exempt interest)
>
> = Gross Income
> — Deductions for adjusted gross income e.g.
>   (unreimbursed employee expenses)
>
> = Adjusted Gross Income
> — Excess Itemized deductions:
>   Itemized deductions
>   Less: Standard deduction (zero
>   bracket amount)
> — Personal and dependency exemptions ($750x4)
>
> = Taxable Income
>
> x Applicable tax rates *
> = Gross tax on taxable income
> — Tax credits and prepayment of tax
>
> = Net tax due (refund)

* The student should check this computation by referring to the tax tabl

Individual components of the tax formula cussed in the following chapters:

> Gross income and exclusions
> Deductions for adjusted gross income
> Itemized deductions
> Tax credits
> Personal and dependency exemptions an
>   Standard Deduction

TAX FORMULA FOR CORPORATION

Corporations are subject to cert cussed more fully in Chapter 18 and porate taxpayers receive an 85 or 10(tion; special rules and limitations a capital gains and losses and to cha

10. How would you characterize the Federal income and estate and gift tax rate structure, i. e., progressive, proportional or regressive?

11. How does the shifting of tax burden from one taxpaying group to another affect the degree of progression in our tax structure?

12. Why are Federal excise taxes levied upon only a select group of products or services?

13. Are estate and gift taxes a major source of revenue for the Federal government?

14. Will a greater or lesser number of estates be subject to the Federal estate tax in 1977 than in 1976 and prior years? Why?

15. Who is primarily responsible for enforcing the operational aspects of the Federal tax laws? The Treasury Department or the Internal Revenue Service?

16. What types of taxpayers are most likely to be audited by the IRS? Why does the IRS "Pick" on these taxpayers?

17. If an IRS agent proposes a deficiency assessment and the taxpayer disagrees with the position of the agent, is it necessary to litigate the issue in court to obtain a favorable settlement?

18. What is meant by the words "hazards of litigation"? Should the IRS settle or compromise a case based upon "hazards of litigation"? Why?

19. Discuss the following tax terms as they relate to the determination of a taxpayer's tax liability:

    a. Gross income (broadly concerned)

    b. Adjusted gross income

    c. Itemized deductions

    d. Deductions for adjusted gross income

    e. Personal and dependency exemptions

    f. Tax credits and prepayments of tax

Chapter 2

UNDERSTANDING THE
FEDERAL TAX LAW

THE WHYS OF THE TAX LAW

The Federal tax law is a mosaic of statutory provisions, administrative pronouncements, and court decisions. Anyone who has attempted to work with this body of knowledge would have to admit to its disturbing complexity. For the person who has to trudge through a myriad of rule upon rule to find the solution to a tax problem, it may be of some consolation to know that the law's complexity can generally be explained. Whether sound or not, there is a reason for the formulation of every rule. Knowing these reasons, therefore, is a considerable step toward understanding the Federal tax law.

At the outset one should stress that the Federal tax law does not have as its sole objective the raising of revenue. Although the fiscal needs of the government are of obvious importance, other considerations do exist which explain certain portions of the law. Economic, social, equity, and political factors also play a significant role. Added to these factors is the marked impact the Internal Revenue Service and the courts have had and will continue to have on the evolution of Federal tax law. These matters will be treated in this chapter and, wherever appropriate, the discussion will be tied to subjects covered later in this text.

ECONOMIC CONSIDERATIONS

The use of the tax system in an effort to accomplish economic objectives appears to have become increasingly popular in recent years. Generally, it involves utilization of tax legislation to amend the Internal Revenue Code [1] and looks toward measures designed to help control the economy or to encourage certain activities and businesses.

Control of the Economy. One of the better known provisions of the tax law which purports to aid in controlling the economy is the investment tax credit. By providing a tax credit for investment in qualified property, so the logic goes, businesses will be encouraged to expand. [2] The resulting expansion stimulates the economy and generates additional employment. As a safety valve against over-expansion, the investment credit can be suspended for a period of time or completely terminated. [3]

Of more immediate impact on the economy is a change in the tax rate structure. By lowering tax rates, taxpayers are able to obtain more spendable funds. An increase in tax rates, moreover, carries the opposite effect. A recent illustration of this approach is the passage of the Tax Reduction Act of 1975, the express purpose of which was to spur economic recovery.

Encouragement of Certain Activities. Without passing judgment on the wisdom of any such choices, it is quite clear that the tax law does encourage certain types of economic activity or segments of the economy. If, for example, one assumes that technological progress is fostered, the favorable treatment allowed research and development expenditures can be explained. Under the tax law such expenditures can be deducted in the year incurred or, as an alternative, capitalized and amortized over a period of sixty months or more. In terms of timing the tax saving, such options usually are preferable to a capitalization of the cost with a write-off over the estimated useful life of the asset created. [4]

The encouragement of technological progress also can explain why the tax law places the inventor in an advantageous position.

---

1. The Internal Revenue Code is a compilation of Federal tax legislation.

2. Keep in mind that a dollar of tax credit generally means a dollar of income tax saving.

3. Since the investment tax credit first was enacted in 1962, it has been suspended once and repealed once. The credit was reinstated in 1971, and its benefits were expanded under the Tax Reduction Act of 1975. All of these changes were justified in terms of the effect they would have on the nation's economy.

4. If the asset developed has no estimated useful life, then no write-off would be available without the two options allowed by the tax law.

Not only can patents qualify as capital assets, but under certain conditions their disposition automatically carries favorable long-term capital gains treatment.

Are ecological considerations a desirable objective? If they are, this explains why the tax law permits a 60-month amortization period for costs incurred in the installation of pollution control facilities.

Encouragement of Certain Industries. No one can question the proposition that a sound agricultural base is necessary for a well-balanced national economy. Undoubtedly this can explain why farmers are accorded special treatment under the Federal tax system. Among these benefits are the following: the election to expense rather than capitalize soil and water conservation expenditures, fertilizers, and land clearing costs; the possibility of obtaining favorable long-term capital gain treatment on the disposition of livestock held for draft, breeding, or dairy purposes; and, the election to defer the recognition of gain on the receipt of crop-insurance proceeds.

Encouragement of Small Business. At least in the U.S., there exists a consensus of opinion that what is good for small business is good for the economy as a whole. Without evaluating the validity of this assumption, it has led to a definite bias in the tax law favoring small business. How else can one explain why the owner of a family business can claim bonus depreciation of up to $4,000 while General Motors Corporation is limited to a maximum of $2,000? [5]

In the corporate tax area, several provisions can be explained by their motivation to benefit small business. One provision permits the shareholders of a small business corporation to make a special election that generally will avoid the imposition of the corporate income tax.[6] Furthermore, such an election enables the corporation to pass through to its shareholders any of its operating losses.[7]

The tax rates applicable to corporations tend to favor small business in so far as size is relative to the amount of taxable income generated in any one year. Since the full corporate tax rate of 48% only applies to taxable income in excess of $50,000 (formerly $25,000), corporations that stay within the limits of the surtax exemption are subject to lower effective tax rates.

---

5. An individual filing a joint return can claim bonus depreciation of 20% on a qualifying investment of up to $20,000. Other taxpayers (including corporations) are allowed 20% of up to $10,000 of investment. See Chapter 6.

6. Known as the "Subchapter S" election, the subject is discussed in Chapter 18.

7. In general, an operating loss can only benefit the corporation incurring the loss through a carryback or carryforward to profitable years. Consequently, the shareholders of the corporation usually cannot take advantage of any such loss.

Example 1. For calendar year 1977, X Corporation has taxable income of $25,000 and Y Corporation has taxable income of $100,000. Based on this information, the corporate income tax is $5,000 for X Corporation and $34,500 for Y Corporation (see Example 5 in Chapter 1). By comparison, then, X Corporation is subject to an effective tax rate of 20% ($5,000/$25,000) while Y Corporation is subject to a rate of 34½% ($34,500/$100,000).

SOCIAL CONSIDERATIONS

Some of the tax law can be explained by looking to social considerations. This is particularly the case when dealing with the Federal income tax of individuals. Notable examples and the rationale behind each are summarized below:

—The nontaxability of certain benefits provided to employees through accident and health plans financed by employers. It would appear socially desirable to encourage such plans since they provide medical benefits in the event of an employee's illness or injury.

—The nontaxability to the employee of premiums paid by an employer for group-term insurance covering the life of the employee. These arrangements can be justified on social grounds in that they provide funds for the family unit to help it readjust following the loss of wages caused by the employee's death.

—The tax treatment to the employee of contributions made by an employer to qualified pension or profit-sharing plans.[8] The contribution and any income it generates will not be taxed to the employee until the funds are distributed. Private retirement plans should be encouraged since they supplement the subsistence income level the employee otherwise would have under the Social Security system.[9]

—The deduction allowed for contributions to qualified charitable organizations.[10] The deduction attempts to shift some of the financial and administrative burden of socially desirable programs from the public (the government) to the private (the citizens) sector.

8. These arrangements also benefit the employer by allowing it a tax deduction when the contribution is made to the qualified plan. See Chapter 17.

9. The same rationale explains the availability of similar arrangements for self-employed persons (the "H.R. 10" or "Keogh" type of plan).

10. The charitable contribution deduction is discussed in Chapter 9.

—The tax credit allowed for amounts spent to furnish care for certain minor or disabled dependents to enable the taxpayer to seek or maintain gainful employment.[11] Who could deny the social desirability of encouraging taxpayers to provide care for their children while they work?

—The disallowance of a tax deduction for certain expenditures that are deemed to be contrary to public policy. This disallowance extends to such items as fines, penalties, illegal kickbacks, and bribes to government officials.[12] Social considerations dictate that these activities should not be encouraged by the tax law. Permitting the deduction would supposedly encourage these activities.

Many other examples could be included but the conclusion would be unchanged: social considerations do explain a significant part of the Federal tax law.

EQUITY CONSIDERATIONS

The concept of equity is, of course, relative. Reasonable persons can, and often do, disagree about what is fair or unfair. In the tax area, moreover, equity is most often tied to a particular taxpayer's personal situation. To illustrate, it may be difficult for Ms. Jones to understand why none of the rent she pays on her apartment is deductible when her brother, Mr. Jones, is able to deduct a large portion of the monthly payments he makes on his personal residence in the form of interest and taxes.[13]

In the same vein, compare the tax treatment of a corporation with that of a partnership. Although the two businesses may be of equal size, similarly situated, and competitors in production of goods or services, they are not comparably treated under the tax law. The corporation is subject to a separate Federal income tax; the partnership is not. Whether the differences in tax treatment logically can be justified in terms of equity is beside the point. The point is that the tax law can and does make a distinction between these business forms.

Equity, then, is not what appears fair or unfair to any one taxpayer or group of taxpayers. It is, instead, what the tax law recognizes. Some recognition of equity does exist, however, and offers an explanation of part of the law. The concept of equity appears in tax provisions that alleviate the effect of multiple taxation, postpone the

11. See Chapter 11.

12. Recent disclosures involving large corporations with international operations have highlighted this policy.

13. The encouragement of home ownership can be justified both on economic and social grounds.

recognition of gain when the taxpayer lacks the ability or wherewithal to pay the tax, and mitigate the effect of the application of the annual accounting period concept.

Alleviating the Effect of Multiple Taxation. The same income earned by a taxpayer may be subject to taxes imposed by different taxing authorities. If, for example, the taxpayer is a resident of New York City, income might generate Federal, State of New York, and City of New York income taxes. To compensate for this apparent inequity, the Federal tax law allows a taxpayer to claim a deduction for state and local income taxes. The deduction, however, does not neutralize the effect of multiple taxation since the benefit derived depends on the taxpayer's Federal income tax bracket.[14]

Equity considerations can explain the Federal tax treatment of certain income from foreign sources. Since double taxation results when the same income is subject to both foreign and U.S. income taxes, the tax law permits the taxpayer to choose between a credit or a deduction for the foreign taxes paid.

The Wherewithal to Pay Concept. Quite simply, the wherewithal to pay concept recognizes the inequity of taxing a transaction when the taxpayer lacks the means with which to pay the tax. It is particularly suited to situations when the taxpayer's economic position has not changed significantly as a result of the transaction.

Example 2. T holds unimproved land held as an investment. The land cost T $60,000 and has a fair market value of $100,000. This land is exchanged for a building (worth $100,000) which T will use in his business.[15]

Example 3. T owns a warehouse which she uses in her business. At a time when the warehouse has an adjusted cost of $60,000, it is destroyed by fire. T collects the insurance proceeds of $100,000 and, within two years of the end of the year in which the fire occurred, uses all of the proceeds to purchase a new warehouse.[16]

In both of the above examples, T had an economic gain of $40,000 [i. e., $100,000 (fair market value of the property received) — $60,000

---

14. A tax credit, rather than a deduction, would eliminate the effects of multiple taxation on the same income.

15. The nontaxability of "like-kind" exchanges applies to the exchange of property held for investment or used in a trade or business for property to be similarly held or used. See Chapter 13.

16. The nontaxability of gains realized from involuntary conversions applies when the proceeds received by the taxpayer are reinvested within a prescribed period of time in property similar or related in service or use to that converted. Involuntary conversions take place as a result of casualty, theft losses, and condemnations by a public authority. See Chapter 7.

(cost of the property given up) |. It would seem inequitable to force the taxpayer to recognize any of this gain for two reasons. First, without disposing of the property or interest acquired, the taxpayer would be hard pressed to pay the tax. Second, the taxpayer's economic situation has not changed significantly.

Mitigating the Effect of the Annual Accounting Period Concept. For purposes of effective administration of the tax law it is necessary for all taxpayers to report to and settle with the Federal government at periodic intervals. Otherwise taxpayers would remain uncertain as to their tax liabilities and the government would have difficulty judging revenues and budgeting expenditures. The period selected for final settlement of most tax liabilities, in any event an arbitrary determination, is one year. At the close of each year, therefore, a taxpayer's position becomes finalized for that particular year. Referred to as the annual accounting period concept, its effect is to divide, for tax purposes, each taxpayer's life into equal annual intervals.

The finality of the annual accounting period concept could lead to dissimilarity in tax treatment for taxpayers who are, from a long-range standpoint, in the same economic position. Compare, for example, two individual taxpayers, C and D. Over a five-year period of time, C has annual income of $10,000 for the first four years and $100,000 in the fifth year. During the same period, D has income of $28,000 per year. Which taxpayer is better off? Considering the progressive nature of the Federal income tax, D's overall tax liability will be much less than that incurred by C. Is this a fair result in view of the fact that each taxpayer earned the same total income (i. e., $140,000) over the five-year period? It is easy to see, therefore, why the income averaging provision of the tax law can be explained on the basis of equitable considerations.[17] Keep in mind, however, that the income averaging provision does not violate the annual accounting period concept but merely operates to mitigate its effect. By income averaging, C would compute the tax on the $100,000 received in the fifth year by a special and favorable procedure without disturbing the finality of any of the returns filed or the taxes paid for the preceding four years.

The same reasoning used to support income averaging can be applied to explain the special treatment accorded by the tax law to net operating losses, excess capital losses, and excess charitable contributions.[18] Carryback and carryover procedures help mitigate the effect of limiting a loss or a deduction to the accounting period in which it was realized. With such procedures, a taxpayer might be able to salvage a loss or a deduction that might otherwise be wasted.

17. See Chapter 10.

18. The tax treatment of these items is discussed in Chapters 9 and 14.

Mitigation of the annual accounting period concept also explains in part the preferential treatment the tax law accords to long-term capital gains. Often the gain from the disposition of an asset is attributable to appreciation that has developed over a long period of time. In view of the impracticality of taxing such appreciation as it occurs, the law looks to the year of realization as the taxable event.[19] Long-term capital gain treatment, therefore, represents a rough means of achieving relief from the bunching effect of forcing gain to be recognized in the tax year of realization.[20]

The installment method of recognizing gain on the sale of property allows a taxpayer to spread tax consequences over the pay-out period.[21] The harsh effect of taxing all the gain in the year of sale is thereby avoided. The installment method can also be explained by the wherewithal to pay concept since recognition of gain is tied to the collection of the installment notes received from the sale of the property. Tax consequences, then, tend to correspond to the seller's ability to pay the tax.

POLITICAL CONSIDERATIONS

A large segment of the Federal tax law is made up of statutory provisions. Since these statutes are enacted by Congress, is it any surprise that political considerations do influence tax law? For purposes of discussion, the effect of political considerations on the tax law is divided into the following topics: special interest legislation, political expediency situations, and state and local government influences.

Special Interest Legislation. There is no doubt that certain provisions of the tax law can be largely explained by looking to the political influence some pressure groups have had on Congress. Is there any other realistic reason why, for example, prepaid subscription and dues income are not taxed until earned while prepaid rents are taxed to the landlord in the year received?

Along the same line are those tax provisions sponsored by individual Congressmen at the obvious instigation of a particularly influential constituent. In one case, for example, the effective date in proposed legislation that would reinstate the investment tax credit

19. Postponing the recognition of gain until the year it is realized is consistent with the wherewithal to pay concept. It would be difficult, for example, to pay a tax on the appreciation of an asset before its sale or other disposition has provided the necessary funds.

20. As a general rule, only one-half of long-term capital gains are subject to the Federal income tax. See Chapter 14.

21. Under the installment method each payment received by the seller represents a return of basis (the nontaxable portion) and profit from the sale (the taxable portion).

was moved back several months. It was well-known by all that the Congressman initiating the change had a constituent with substantial capital expenditures that otherwise would not have qualified for the credit.

Special interest legislation is not necessarily to be condemned if it can be justified on economic, social, or some other utilitarian grounds. At any rate, it is an inevitable product of our political system.

Political Expediency Situations. Various tax reform proposals rise and fall in favor depending upon the shifting moods of the American public. That Congress is sensitive to popular feeling is an accepted fact. There are, therefore, certain provisions of the tax law that can be explained on the basis of political expediency existing at the time of enactment.

Measures which deter more affluent taxpayers from obtaining so-called preferential tax treatment have always had popular appeal and, consequently, the support of Congress. Provisions such as the minimum tax, the imputed interest rules, and the limitation on the deductibility of interest on investment indebtedness can be explained on this basis.[22]

Other changes partially founded on the basis of political expediency include the lowering of individual income tax rates, increasing the amount of the dependency exemption and the low income allowance, and the institution of an earned income credit.

State and Local Influences. Political considerations have played a major role in the nontaxability of interest received on state and local obligations. In view of the furor that has been raised by state and local political figures every time any kind of modification of this tax provision has been proposed, one might well regard it as next to sacred.

Somewhat less apparent has been the influence state law has had in shaping our present Federal tax law. Of prime import in this regard has been the effect of the community property system employed in eight states.[23] At one point in time the tax position of the resi-

---

22. See Chapters 9 and 10.

23. The eight states with community property systems are: Louisiana, Texas, New Mexico, Arizona, California, Washington, Idaho, and Nevada. The rest of the states are classified as common law jurisdictions. The difference between common law and community property systems centers around the property rights possessed by married persons. In a common law system, each spouse owns whatever he or she earns. Under a community property system, one-half of the earnings of each spouse is considered owned by the other spouse. Assume, for example, H and W are husband and wife and their only income is the $40,000 annual salary H receives. If they live in New York (a common law state), the $40,000 salary belongs to H. If, however, they live in Texas (a community property

dents of these states was so advantageous that many common law states actually adopted community property systems.[24]   Needless to say, the political pressure placed on Congress to correct the disparity in tax treatment was considerable.   To a large extent this was accomplished in the Revenue Act of 1948 which extended many of the community property tax advantages to residents of common law jurisdictions.[25]   Thus, common law states avoided the trauma of discarding the time-honored legal system familiar to everyone.

INFLUENCE OF THE INTERNAL REVENUE SERVICE

The influence of the IRS is recognized in many areas beyond its obvious role in the issuance of the administrative pronouncements which make up a considerable portion of our tax law.   In its capacity as the protector of the national revenue, the IRS has been instrumental in securing the passage of much legislation designed to curtail the most flagrant tax avoidance practices (to close tax loopholes).   In its capacity as the administrator of the tax laws, the IRS has sought and obtained legislation to make its job easier (to attain administrative feasibility).

The IRS as Protector of the Revenue.   Innumerable examples can be given of provisions in the tax law which stemmed from the direct influence of the IRS when it was applied to preclude the use of a "loophole" as a means of avoiding the tax consequences intended by Congress.   Working within the letter of existing law, ingenious taxpayers and their advisors devise techniques which accomplish indirectly what cannot be accomplished directly.   As a consequence, legislation is enacted to close the loophole that taxpayers have located and exploited.   Some tax law can be explained in this fashion and is discussed in the Chapters to follow.

In addition, the IRS has secured from Congress legislation of a more general nature which enables it to make adjustments based upon the substance, rather than the formal construction, of what a taxpayer has done.   One such provision permits the IRS to make adjustments to a taxpayer's method of accounting when the method used by the taxpayer "does not clearly reflect income." [26]

state), the $40,000 salary is divided equally, in terms of ownership, between H and W.

24. Such states included Michigan, Oklahoma, and Pennsylvania.

25. The major advantage extended was the provision allowing married taxpayers to file joint returns and compute the tax liability as if the income had been earned one-half by

each spouse.   This result is automatic in a community property state since half of the income earned by one spouse belongs to the other spouse.   The income-splitting benefits of a joint return are incorporated as part of the tax rates applicable to married taxpayers.   See Chapter 10.

26. See Chapter 16.

Administrative Feasibility. Some of the tax law is justified on the grounds that it simplifies the IRS' task of collecting the revenue and administering the law. With regard to collecting the revenue, the IRS long ago realized the importance of placing taxpayers on a "pay-as-you-go" basis. Elaborate withholding procedures apply to wages while the tax on other types of income may be paid at periodic intervals throughout the year. The IRS has been instrumental in convincing the courts that accrual basis taxpayers should pay taxes on prepaid income in the year received and not when earned. The approach may be contrary to generally accepted accounting principles, but it is consistent with the wherewithal to pay concept.

Of considerable aid to the IRS in collecting revenue are the numerous provisions which impose interest and penalties on taxpayers for noncompliance with the tax law. Provisions such as the penalties for failure to pay a tax or to file a return that is due, the negligence penalty for intentional disregard of rules and regulations, and various penalties for civil and criminal fraud serve as deterrents to taxpayer noncompliance.

One of the keys to an effective administration of our tax system is the audit process conducted by the IRS. To carry out this function, the IRS is aided by provisions which reduce the chance of taxpayer error or manipulation and, therefore, simplify the audit effort that is necessary. An increase in the amount of the standard deduction, for example, reduces the number of individual taxpayers who will choose the alternative of itemizing their personal deductions. With less deductions to check, therefore, the audit function is simplified.[27]

The audit function of the IRS has been simplified by provisions of the tax law dealing with the burden of proof. Suppose, for example, the IRS audits a taxpayer and questions a particular deduction. Who has the burden of proving the propriety of the deduction? Except in the case of criminal fraud, the burden is always on the taxpayer.

INFLUENCE OF THE COURTS

In addition to interpreting statutory provisions and the administrative pronouncements issued by the IRS, the Federal courts have influenced tax law in two other respects.[28] First, the courts have for-

---

27. The same justification was given by the IRS when it proposed to Congress the $100 limitation on personal casualty and theft losses. Imposition of the limitation eliminated many casualty and theft loss deductions and, as a consequence, saved the IRS considerable audit time.

28. A great deal of case law is devoted to ascertaining Congressional intent. The courts, in effect, ask: What did Congress have in mind when it enacted a particular tax provision?

mulated certain judicial concepts which serve as guides in the application of various tax provisions. Second, certain key decisions have led to changes in the Internal Revenue Code. Understanding this influence helps to explain some of our tax law.

Judicial Concepts Relating to Tax. A leading tax concept developed by the courts deals with the interpretation of statutory tax provisions which operate to benefit taxpayers. The courts have established the rule that these relief provisions are to be narrowly construed against taxpayers if there is any doubt about their application. Suppose, for example, T wants to treat an expenditure as deductible for income tax purposes but has not literally satisfied the statutory requirements covering the deduction. Because income tax deductions are relief provisions favoring taxpayers, chances are the courts will deny T this treatment.

Important in this area is the arm's length concept. Particularly in dealings between related parties, transactions may be tested by looking to whether the taxpayers acted in an "arm's length" manner. The question to be asked is: Would unrelated parties have handled the transaction in the same way?

Example 4. The sole shareholder of a corporation leases property to it for a monthly rental of $500. To test whether the corporation should be allowed a rent deduction for this amount, the IRS and the courts will apply the arm's length concept. Would the corporation have paid $500 a month in rent if the same property had been leased from an unrelated party (rather than from the sole shareholder)?

Judicial Influence on Statutory Provisions. Some court decisions have been of such consequence that Congress has incorporated them into statutory tax law. One illustration of this influence appears below.

Example 5. In 19X0 T claimed a loss of $100,000 for stock in Z Corporation that had become worthless during the year. Because of the absence of any offsetting gains, the loss deduction produced no income tax saving for T either in 19X0 or in future years. In 19X5, T institutes a lawsuit against the former officers of Z Corporation for their misconduct which resulted in the corporation's failure and, thereby, led to T's $100,000 loss. In settlement of the suit, the officers pay $50,000 to T. The IRS argued that the full $50,000 should be taxed as gain to T. Because the stock in Z Corporation was written-off in 19X0 as being worthless, it had a zero value for tax purposes. The $50,000 recovery received by T on the stock was, therefore, all gain. Although the position of the IRS was logical and conformed to the tax statutes as they then existed, it was not equitable. The court stated that T should not be taxed on the recovery of an amount previously deducted unless the deduction produced a tax saving. Since the $100,000 loss deduction in 19X0 produced no tax benefit, none of the $50,000 received in 19X5 results in gain.

The decision reached by the courts in Example 5, known as the tax benefit rule, has since become part of the statutory tax law.[29]

SUMMARY

In addition to its obvious revenue raising objective, the Federal tax law has developed in response to several other factors:

—*Economic considerations.* Here, the emphasis is on tax provisions which help regulate the economy and encourage certain activities and types of businesses.

—*Social considerations.* Some tax provisions are designed to encourage (or discourage) certain socially desirable (or undesirable) practices.

—*Equity considerations.* Of principal concern in this area are tax provisions which alleviate the effect of multiple taxation, recognize the wherewithal to pay concept, and mitigate the effect of the annual accounting period concept.

—*Political considerations.* Of significance in this regard are tax provisions which represent special interest legislation, reflect political expediency situations, and exhibit the effect of state law.

—*Influence of the IRS.* Many tax provisions are intended to aid the IRS in the collection of the revenue and in the administration of the tax law.

—*Influence of the Courts.* Court decisions have established a body of judicial concepts relating to tax law and have, on occasion, led Congress to enact statutory provisions to either clarify or negate their effect.

These factors explain various tax provisions and, thereby, help in understanding why the tax law developed to its present state. The next step involves learning to work with the tax law.

PROBLEM MATERIALS

Questions for Class Discussion

1. Give examples of specific provisions of the tax law which are intended to help control the national economy.

29. See Chapter 5.

2. In what way does the tax law attempt to encourage technological progress?

3. Suppose Congress decided to use the tax laws to further encourage the installation of pollution control equipment.

    a. What type of tax benefit would you suggest?

    b. What might be more effective, a tax deduction or a tax credit? Explain.

4. In what way does the tax law encourage home ownership?

5. In what manner does the tax law favor agriculture? Why?

6. It has been suggested that Congress should enact an income tax credit for the cost of home insulation. What objective, if any, might such legislation accomplish?

7. Discuss the probable justification for the following provisions of the tax law:

    a. The surtax exemption allowed for corporate income tax purposes.

    b. The election permitted certain corporations to avoid the corporate income tax.

    c. A provision which allows railroads to amortize the cost of tunnel bores over a period of 50 years.

    d. A provision which makes nontaxable certain benefits furnished to employees through accident and health plans financed by employers.

    e. Nontaxable treatment for an employee as to premiums paid by an employer for group-term insurance covering the life of the employee.

    f. The tax treatment to the employee of contributions made by an employer to qualified pension or profit-sharing plans.

    g. The deduction allowed for contributions to qualified charitable organizations.

8. The Tax Reform Act of 1976 provided a tax credit for amounts spent to furnish care for certain minor or disabled dependents to enable the taxpayer to work or maintain gainful employment.

    a. What justification can you see for this credit?

    b. Prior to the Tax Reform Act of 1976, the child and disabled dependent care provision of the tax law merely allowed a tax deduction for such expenses. Why, do you suppose, did Congress convert the deduction into a credit?

9. T owns and operates a trucking firm. During the year his employees incur a substantial number of fines for violating the 55 mile per hour highway speed limitation. T considers these fines

as a necessary expense of running the business as he knows his firm cannot make a profit by observing the posted speed limitation. Are these fines deductible for income tax purposes? Why or why not?

10. A provision of the Code allows a taxpayer a deduction for Federal income tax purposes for state and local income taxes paid. Does the provision eliminate the effect of multiple taxation of the same income? Why or why not? In this connection, consider the following.

   a. Taxpayer, an individual, claims the standard deduction for Federal income tax purposes.

   b. Taxpayer is in the 30% tax bracket for Federal income tax purposes. The 60% tax bracket.

   c. The state imposing the income tax allows a deduction for Federal income taxes paid.

11. Provide examples of the wherewithal to pay concept operating to insulate a transaction from Federal income tax consequences.

12. Explain the annual accounting period concept. Why is it necessary?

13. State the manner in which the annual accounting period concept is mitigated by the tax provisions relating to:

   a. Income averaging.

   b. Net operating loss carrybacks and carryovers.

   c. Excess charitable contribution carryovers.

   d. Long-term capital gains.

   e. Installment sales.

14. H and W are husband and wife and live in Indiana (a common law state). During the year they earn wages as follows: $20,000 for H and $24,000 for W. If H and W file a joint return their tax will be determined by a schedule based on the tax for $22,000 multiplied by two.

   a. Why is the tax schedule applicable to married taxpayers filing a joint return determined in this manner?

   b. Suppose H and W lived in California (a community property state) and filed separate returns. How would the result compare with that reached under part a. above?

15. T, an individual taxpayer, files a Federal income tax return for the year in which he reports income on a cash basis and expenditures on an accrual basis.

   a. What was T trying to accomplish in reporting as income only the amounts actually received while claiming deductions for amounts due but unpaid?

    b.   Does the IRS have any defense against T's approach? Explain.

16.   In what way does the wherewithal to pay concept aid the IRS in the collection of tax revenue?

17.   On her income tax return for the year T claims as a deduction certain charitable contributions that she did not make. When you question her about this she responds:

    a.   "How is the IRS going to prove that I did not make these contributions?"

    b.   "Even if the IRS disallows the deductions, the worst that can happen is that I will owe the same amount of tax I would have paid anyway."

Comment on T's misconceptions about the tax law.

18.   Describe how administrative feasibility is achieved for the IRS by each of the following tax provisions:

    a.   The standard deduction allowed to individual taxpayers.

    b.   The $100 limitation on personal casualty and theft losses.

19.   Under current tax law a donor generally can make a gift of $3,000 per year to a donee without having to file a Federal gift tax return and pay a Federal gift tax. How does the provision simplify the administrative responsibility of the IRS for enforcement of the tax laws?

20.   What is meant by the concept that statutory relief provisions of the tax law are to be narrowly construed? Where did the concept originate?

21.   When does the tax benefit rule apply? With what effect?

Chapter 3

WORKING WITH THE TAX LAW

TAX SOURCES

Learning to work with the tax law involves the following three basic steps:

—Familiarity with the sources of the law;

—Application of research techniques; and,

—Effective use of planning procedures.

Statutory, administrative, and judicial sources of the tax law will be considered first.

STATUTORY SOURCES OF THE TAX LAW

Origin of the Internal Revenue Code. Prior to 1939, the statutory provisions relating to tax were contained in the individual revenue acts enacted by Congress. Because of the inconvenience and confusion that resulted from dealing with many separate acts, in 1939 Congress codified all of the Federal tax laws. Known as the Internal Revenue Code of 1939, the codification arranged all Federal tax provisions in a logical sequence and placed them in a separate part of the Federal statutes. A further rearrangement took place in 1954 and resulted in the Internal Revenue Code of 1954 which continues in effect to the present day.

Several observations are in order to help clarify the significance of the codification procedure. These are summarized below:

—With some exceptions, neither the 1939 nor the 1954 Codes substantially changed the tax law existing on the date of their enactment. Much of the 1939 Code, for example, was incorporated into the 1954 Code, the major change was the reorganization and renumbering of the tax provisions.[1]

—Statutory amendments to the tax law are integrated into the Code. The Tax Reduction Act of 1975, for example, became part of the Internal Revenue Code of 1954.

The Legislative Process. Federal tax legislation generally originates in the House of Representatives where it is first considered by the House Ways and Means Committee.[2] If acceptable to the Committee, the proposed bill is referred to the whole House of Representatives for approval or disapproval. Approved bills are sent to the Senate where they are referred to the Senate Finance Committee for further consideration.[3] The next step involves referral from the Senate Finance Committee to the whole Senate. Assuming no disagreement between the House and Senate, passage by the Senate means referral to the President for approval or veto. If the bill is approved or if the President's veto is overridden, the bill becomes law and part of the Internal Revenue Code.

When the Senate version of the bill differs from that passed by the House,[4] the Joint Conference Committee, including members of both the House Ways and Means Committee and the Senate Finance Committee, is called upon to resolve these differences. The result, usually a compromise of the two versions, is then voted on by both

---

1. This point is important in assessing judicial decisions interpreting provisions of the Internal Revenue Code of 1939. If the same provision was included in the Internal Revenue Code of 1954, the decision has continuing validity.

2. Tax bills do originate in the Senate when they are attached as "riders" to other legislative proposals.

3. Some tax provisions are commonly referred to by the number of the bill designated in the House when first proposed or by the name of the Congressman sponsoring the legislation. For example, the Self-Employed Individuals Tax Retirement Act of 1962 is popularly known as H.R. 10 (i. e.,

House of Representatives Bill No. 10) or as the Keogh Act (i. e., Keogh being one of the members of Congress sponsoring the bill).

4. This is frequently the case with major tax bills. One factor contributing to a different Senate version is the latitude each individual Senator has to make amendments to a bill when the Senate as a whole is voting on a bill referred to it by the Senate Finance Committee. Less latitude is allowed in the House of Representatives. Thus, the whole House either accepts or rejects what is proposed by the House Ways and Means Committee and changes from the floor are not commonplace.

the House and Senate. Acceptance by both bodies precedes referral to the President for approval or veto.

The typical legislative process dealing with tax bills is summarized below:

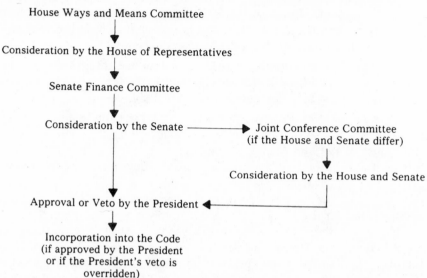

House Ways and Means Committee

↓

Consideration by the House of Representatives

↓

Senate Finance Committee

↓

Consideration by the Senate ⟶ Joint Conference Committee (if the House and Senate differ)

↓

Consideration by the House and Senate

Approval or Veto by the President ⟵

↓

Incorporation into the Code (if approved by the President or if the President's veto is overridden)

Referrals from the House Ways and Means Committee, the Senate Finance Committee, and the Joint Conference Committee are usually accompanied by committee reports. Because these committee reports often explain the provisions of the proposed legislation, they are a valuable source in ascertaining the intent of Congress. What Congress had in mind when it considers and enacts tax legislation is, of course, the key to interpreting such legislation.

The role of the Joint Conference Committee indicates the importance of compromise to the legislative process. The practical effect of the compromise process is illustrated by reviewing what happened in the Tax Reduction Act of 1975 concerning changes in the income tax rates applicable to corporations.

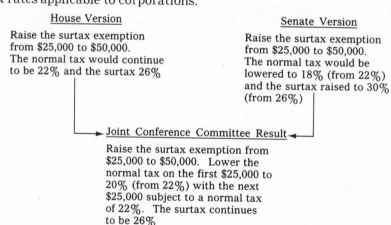

House Version	Senate Version
Raise the surtax exemption from $25,000 to $50,000. The normal tax would continue to be 22% and the surtax 26%	Raise the surtax exemption from $25,000 to $50,000. The normal tax would be lowered to 18% (from 22%) and the surtax raised to 30% (from 26%)

⟶ Joint Conference Committee Result ⟵

Raise the surtax exemption from $25,000 to $50,000. Lower the normal tax on the first $25,000 to 20% (from 22%) with the next $25,000 subject to a normal tax of 22%. The surtax continues to be 26%

Arrangement of the Code. In working with the Code it helps to understand the format followed. Note, for example, the partial table of contents reproduced below:

Subtitle A. Income Taxes
    Chapter 1. Normal Taxes and Surtaxes
        Subchapter A. Determination of Tax Liability
            Part I. Tax on Individuals
                Sections 1–5
            Part II. Tax on Corporations
                Sections 11–12

* * *

In referring to a provision of the Code, the key is usually the section number involved. In designating Section 11 (dealing with the income tax imposed on corporations), for example, it would be unnecessary to include Subtitle A, Chapter 1, Subchapter A, Part II. Merely mentioning Section 11 will suffice since the section numbers run consecutively and do not begin again with each new Subtitle, Chapter, Subchapter, or Part. However, all Code section numbers are not used. Notice that Part I ends with Section 5 and Part II starts with Section 11 (i. e., at present there are no Sections 6, 7, 8, 9, and 10).[5]

Among tax practitioners, a common way of referring to some specific area of income taxation is by Subchapter designation. More common Subchapter designations include: Subchapter C ("Corporate Distributions and Adjustments"), Subchapter K ("Partners and Partnerships"), and Subchapter S ("Election of Certain Small Business Corporations as to Taxable Status"). Particularly in the last situation, it is much more convenient to describe the effect of the applicable Code provisions involved (Sections 1371–1379) as "Subchapter S status" rather than as the "Election of Certain Small Business Corporations as to Taxable Status."

Citing the Code. Code sections often are broken down into subparts.[6] Section 11(b)(2)(A) serves as an example.

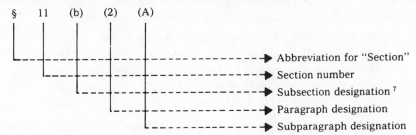

§   11   (b)   (2)   (A)

                                  → Abbreviation for "Section"
                                    → Section number
                                    → Subsection designation [7]
                                    → Paragraph designation
                                    → Subparagraph designation

5. When the 1954 Code was drafted, the omission of section numbers was intentional. This provided flexibility to incorporate later changes into the Code without disrupting its organization.

6. Some Code Sections do not necessitate subparts. See, for example, §§ 211 and 262.

7. Some Code Sections omit the subsection designation and use, in-

Broken down as to content, § 11 (b) (2) (A) becomes:

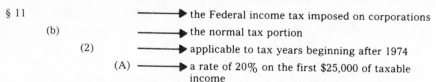

§ 11   ──────▶ the Federal income tax imposed on corporations

    (b)   ──────▶ the normal tax portion

       (2)   ──────▶ applicable to tax years beginning after 1974

          (A) ──────▶ a rate of 20% on the first $25,000 of taxable income

Throughout the remainder of the text, references to the Code sections are in the form given above. The symbols "§" and "§§" are used in place of "Section" and "Sections." Unless otherwise stated, all Code references are to the Internal Revenue Code of 1954. The format followed in the remainder of text is summarized below.

Complete Reference	Text Reference
Section 11(b)(2)(A) of the Internal Revenue Code of 1954	§ 11(b)(2)(A)
Sections 11 and 12 of the Internal Revenue Code of 1954	§§ 11 and 12
Section 13(b) of the Internal Revenue Code of 1939 [8]	§ 13(b) of the Internal Revenue Code of 1939

ADMINISTRATIVE SOURCES OF THE TAX LAW

The administrative sources of the Federal tax law can be grouped as follows: Treasury Department Regulations, Revenue Rulings and Procedures, and other administrative pronouncements. All are issued either by the U.S. Treasury Department or one of its instrumentalities [e. g., the Internal Revenue Service (IRS), or a District Director].

Treasury Department Regulations. Regulations are issued by the U.S. Treasury Department under authority granted by Congress.[9] Interpretative by nature, they provide taxpayers with considerable guidance on the meaning and application of the Code. Although not issued by Congress, Regulations do carry considerable weight and are an important factor to consider in complying with the tax law.

Since Regulations interpret the Code, they are arranged in the same sequence. Regulations are, however, prefixed by a number which designates the type of tax or administrative, procedural, or definitional matter to which they relate. For example, the prefix 1 designates the Regulations under the income tax law. Thus, the Reg-

stead, the paragraph designation as the first subpart. See, for example, § 212(1) and § 1221(1).

8.   § 13(b) of the Internal Revenue Code of 1939 is the predecessor to § 11 of the Internal Revenue Code of

1954. Keep in mind that the 1954 Code has superseded the 1939 Code. The reason why a provision of the 1939 Code may be referred to is set forth in footnote 1 of this Chapter.

9.   § 7805.

ulations under Code § 11 would be cited as Reg. § 1.11 with subparts added for further identification. The prefix 20 designates estate tax Regulations; 25 covers gift tax Regulations; 31 relates to employment taxes; and 301 refers to procedure and administration. This listing is not all-inclusive.

New Regulations and changes to existing Regulations are usually issued in proposed form before they are finalized. The time interval between the proposal of a Regulation and its finalization permits taxpayers and other interested parties to comment on the propriety of the proposal. Proposed Regulations under Code § 11, for example, would be cited as Prop.Reg. § 1.11.

Proposed and permanent Regulations are published in the *Federal Register* and are reproduced in major tax services.

Revenue Rulings and Revenue Procedures. Revenue Rulings are official pronouncements of the National Office of the IRS and, like Regulations, are designed to provide interpretation of the tax law. However, they do not carry the same legal force and effect of Regulations and usually deal with more restricted problems. Both Revenue Rulings and Revenue Procedures serve an important function in that they afford guidance to both IRS personnel and taxpayers in handling routine tax matters.

Revenue Procedures are issued in the same manner as are Revenue Rulings, but they deal with the internal management practices and procedures of the IRS. Familiarity with these procedures can increase taxpayer compliance and assist the efficient administration of the tax laws by the IRS.

Both Revenue Rulings and Revenue Procedures are published weekly by the U.S. Government in the *Internal Revenue Bulletin* (I. R.B.). Periodically, the Bulletins for a six-month period will be gathered together, reorganized by Code Section classification, and published in a bound volume designated *Cumulative Bulletin* (C.B.).[10] The proper form for citing Rulings and Procedures depends upon whether

10. Usually only two volumes of the Cumulative Bulletins are published each year. However, when major tax legislation has been enacted by Congress, a third volume may be published containing the Congressional Committee Reports supporting the Revenue Act. See, for example, the third volumes for 1974 dealing with the Employee Retirement Income Security Act of 1974 (ERISA). The 1974–3 Cumulative Bulletin contains the text of the Act itself and two House Reports plus the Conference Committee Report; 1974–3 Supp. contains additional Committee Reports and Congressional Record Excerpts relating to ERISA. This makes a total of four volumes of the Cumulative Bulletin for 1974: 1974–1, 1974–2, 1974–3, and 1974–3 Supp.

the item has been published in the *Cumulative Bulletins* or is available in I.R.B. form. Consider, for example, the following transition:

Temporary
Citation
{
Rev. Rul. 75–305, I.R.B. No. 30, 12.

Explanation : Revenue Ruling Number 305, appearing on page 12 of the 30th weekly issue of the *Internal Revenue Bulletin* for 1975
}

Permanent
Citation
{
Rev. Rul. 75–305, 1975–2 C.B. 228

Explanation : Revenue Ruling Number 305, appearing on page 228 of Volume 2 of the *Cumulative Bulletin* for 1975
}

Since the second volume of the 1975 *Cumulative Bulletins* was not published until mid-1976, the I.R.B. citation must be used until that time. After the publication of the *Cumulative Bulletin,* the C.B. citation is proper. The basic portion of both citations (i. e., Rev.Rul. 75–305) indicates that this was the 305th Revenue Ruling issued by the IRS during 1975.

Revenue Procedures are cited in the same manner, except that "Rev.Proc." is substituted for "Rev.Rul." Procedures, like Rulings, are published in the *Internal Revenue Bulletins* (the temporary source) and later transferred to the *Cumulative Bulletins* (the permanent source).

Other Administrative Pronouncements. Treasury Decisions (T. D.) are issued by the Treasury Department to promulgate new Regulations, amend or otherwise change existing Regulations, or to announce the position of the Government on selected court decisions. Like Revenue Rulings and Revenue Procedures, T. D.s are published in the *Internal Revenue Bulletins* and subsequently transferred to the *Cumulative Bulletins*.

Technical Information Releases (T.I.R.) are usually issued to announce the publication of various IRS pronouncements (e. g., Revenue Rulings, Revenue Procedures).

Individual rulings are issued upon a taxpayer's request and describe how the IRS will treat a proposed transaction for tax purposes. These apply only to the taxpayer who asks for and obtains the ruling.[11] Though this procedure may sound like the only real way to carry out effective tax planning, the IRS limits the issuance of individual rulings to restricted, preannounced areas of taxation. Thus,

11. In this regard, individual rulings differ from Revenue Rulings which are applicable to *all* taxpayers. Individual rulings may later lead to the issuance of a Revenue Ruling if the holding involved affects many taxpayers.

it is not possible to obtain a ruling on many of the problems that are particularly troublesome for taxpayers.[12]

Individual rulings are not published and, until recently, were "private" (i. e., the content of the ruling being made available only to the taxpayer requesting the ruling). However, Federal legislation and the courts have forced the IRS to modify its position on the confidentiality of individual rulings.[13] The Tax Reform Act of 1976 now requires the IRS to make individual rulings available for public inspection after identifying details are deleted.[14]

Like individual rulings, determination letters are issued at the request of taxpayers and provide guidance concerning the application of the tax law. They differ from individual rulings in that the issuing source is the District Director rather than the National Office of the IRS. Also, determination letters usually involve completed (as opposed to proposed) transactions. Determination letters are not published but are made known only to the party making the request.

The distinction between individual rulings and determination letters is illustrated below:

Example 1. The shareholders of X Corporation and Y Corporation want assurance that the consolidation of these corporations into Z Corporation will be a nontaxable reorganization. The proper approach would be to request from the National Office of the IRS an individual ruling concerning the income tax effect of the proposed transaction.

Example 2. T operates a barber shop in which he employs eight barbers. In order to properly comply with the rules governing income tax and payroll tax withholdings, T wants to know whether the barbers working for him are "employees" or "independent contractors." The proper procedure would be to request from the appropriate District Director a determination letter on the status of such persons.

JUDICIAL SOURCES OF THE TAX LAW

The Judicial Process in General. After a taxpayer has exhausted some or all of the remedies available within the IRS (i. e., no satisfactory settlement has been reached at the agent, District Confer-

---

12. Rev.Proc. 72–9, 1972–1 C.B. 719 and Rev.Proc. 73–15, 1973–2 C.B. 464 contain a complete list of areas in which the IRS will not issue advance rulings.

13. The Freedom of Information Act as interpreted by *Tax Analysts and Ad-*

vocates v. U. S., 74–2 USTC ¶ 9635, 34 AFTR2d 74–5731, 505 F.2d 350 (CA–DC, 1974) and *Tax Analysts and Advocates v. U. S.,* 75–2 USTC ¶ 9869, 37 AFTR2d 76–352, 405 F.Supp. 1065 (D.Ct.D.C., 1975).

14. Act § 1201 adding § 6110.

ence, or Appellate Division levels), the dispute can be taken to the Federal courts. The dispute is first considered by a court of original jurisdiction (known as a trial court) with any appeal (either by the taxpayer or the IRS) taken to the appropriate appellate court. In most situations the taxpayer has a choice of any of four trial courts: a Federal District Court, the U.S. Court of Claims, the U.S. Tax Court, or the Small Claims Division of the U.S. Tax Court. The trial and appellate court scheme for Federal tax litigation is illustrated in Figure 1 below.

Figure 1

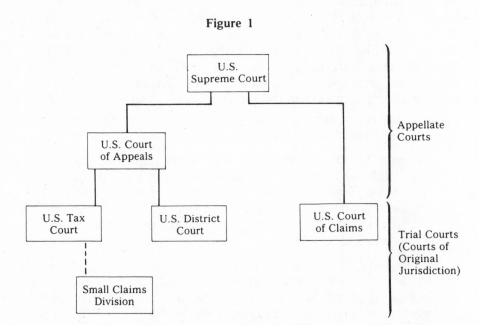

The broken line between the U.S. Tax Court and the Small Claims Division indicates that there is no appeal from the Small Claims Division. This Court hears cases involving amounts of $1,500 or less.

American law, following English law, is frequently "made" by judicial decisions. Under the doctrine of *stare decisis,* each case (except in the Small Claims Division) has precedential value for future cases with the same controlling set of facts. Most Federal and state appellate court decisions and some decisions of trial courts are published. Some 3,000,000 judicial opinions have been published in the United States; over 30,000 cases are published each year.[15] Published court reports are organized by jurisdiction (Federal or state) and level of court (appellate or trial).

15. E. H. Pollack, *Fundamentals of Le-*   N. Y.: The Foundation Press, Inc.,
     gal Research, 4th Edition (Mineola,   1973).

Trial Courts. Differences between the various trial courts (courts of original jurisdiction) are summarized below:

a) There is only one Court of Claims and one Tax Court, but there are many Federal District Courts. The taxpayer does not select the District Court which will hear the dispute but must sue in that one which has jurisdiction.

b) Each District Court has only one judge, the Court of Claims has five judges, and the Tax Court has sixteen. In the case of the Tax Court, however, the whole court will decide a case (i. e., the court sits *en banc*) only when more important or novel tax issues are involved. Most cases will be heard and decided by one of the sixteen judges.

c) The Court of Claims meets only in Washington, D. C., while a District Court meets at a prescribed seat for the particular district. Since each state has at least one District Court and many of the more populous states have more, the problem of travel inconvenience and expense for the taxpayer and his counsel (present with suits in the Court of Claims) is largely eliminated. Although the Tax Court is officially based in Washington, D. C., the various judges travel to different parts of the country and hear cases at predetermined locations and dates. While this procedure eases the distance problem for the taxpayer, it could mean a delay before the case comes to trial and is decided.

d) The Tax Court hears only tax cases; the Court of Claims and District Courts hear nontax litigation as well. This difference, plus the fact that many Tax Court justices have been appointed from IRS or Treasury Department positions, has led some to conclude that the Tax Court has more expertise in tax matters.

e) The only court in which a taxpayer can obtain a jury trial is in a District Court. But since juries can only decide questions of fact and not questions of law, even those taxpayers who choose the District Court route often do not request a jury trial. In such event, the judge will decide all issues. Note that a District Court decision is controlling only in the district in which the court has jurisdiction.

f) In order for the Court of Claims or a District Court to have jurisdiction, the taxpayer must pay the tax deficiency assessed by the IRS and sue for a refund. If the taxpayer wins (assuming no successful appeal by the Government), the tax paid plus appropriate interest thereon will be recovered. In the case of the Tax Court, however, jurisdiction is usually obtained without first paying the assessed tax deficiency. In the event the taxpayer loses in the Tax Court (and no appeal is taken or any such appeal is unsuccessful), the deficiency must be paid with appropriate interest.

g) Appeals from a District Court or a Tax Court decision are to the appropriate U.S. Court of Appeals. Appeals from the Court of Claims by-pass the Courts of Appeals and are taken directly to the U.S. Supreme Court.

Appellate Courts. Regarding appeals from a District Court or the Tax Court, the listing below indicates the Court of Appeals of appropriate jurisdiction:

First	Sixth
Maine	Kentucky
Massachusetts	Michigan
New Hampshire	Ohio
Rhode Island	Tennessee
Puerto Rico	
	Seventh
Second	Illinois
Connecticut	Indiana
New York	Wisconsin
Vermont	
	Eighth
Third	Arkansas
Delaware	Iowa
New Jersey	Minnesota
Pennsylvania	Missouri
Virgin Islands	Nebraska
	North Dakota
District of Columbia	South Dakota
Washington, D. C.	
	Ninth
Fourth	Alaska
Maryland	Arizona
North Carolina	California
South Carolina	Hawaii
Virginia	Idaho
West Virginia	Montana
	Nevada
Fifth	Oregon
Alabama	Washington
Canal Zone	Guam
Florida	
Georgia	Tenth
Louisiana	Colorado
Mississippi	Kansas
Texas	New Mexico
	Oklahoma
	Utah
	Wyoming

If the Government loses at the trial court level (i. e., District Court, Tax Court, or Court of Claims), it need not (and frequently does not) appeal. The fact that an appeal is not made, however, does not indicate that the IRS agrees with the result and will not litigate similar issues in the future. There could be a number of reasons for the Service's failure to appeal. First, the current litigation load may be heavy and, as a consequence, the IRS may decide that available manpower resources should be assigned to other, more important, cases. Second, the IRS may determine that this is not a good case to appeal. Such might be true if the taxpayer is in a sympathetic position or the facts are particularly strong in his or her favor. In such event, the IRS may wait to test the legal issues involved with a taxpayer who has a much weaker case. Third, if the appeal is from a District Court or the Tax Court, the Court of Appeals of jurisdiction could have some bearing on whether or not the decision is made to go forward with an appeal. Based on past experience and precedent, the IRS may conclude that the chance for success on a particular issue might be more promising in another Court of Appeals. The IRS will wait for a similar case to arise in a different appellate court.

District Courts and the Tax Court must abide by the precedents set by the Court of Appeals of jurisdiction. A particular Court of Appeals need not follow the decisions of another Court of Appeals. All courts, however, must follow the decisions of the U.S. Supreme Court.

Because the Tax Court is a national court (i. e., it hears and decides cases from all parts of the country), the observation made in the previous paragraph has caused problems. For many years the Tax Court followed a policy of deciding cases based on what it thought the result should be, even though the appeal of its decision may have been to a Court of Appeals that had previously decided a similar case differently. Recently this policy was changed. Now the Tax Court will still decide a case as it feels the law should be applied *only* if the Court of Appeals of appropriate jurisdiction has not yet passed on the issue or has previously decided a similar case in accord with the Tax Court's decision.[16] If the Court of Appeals of appropriate jurisdiction has previously held otherwise, the Tax Court will conform even though it disagrees with the holding.

Example 3. Taxpayer T lives in Texas and sues in the Tax Court on Issue A. The Fifth Court of Appeals, the appellate court of appropriate jurisdiction, has already decided that, based on similar facts and involving a different taxpayer, Issue A should be resolved against the Government. Although the Tax Court feels that the Fifth Court of Appeals is wrong, under its new policy it will render judgment for T. Shortly thereafter, Taxpayer U, a resident of New York, in a comparable case, sues in the Tax Court on Issue A. Assume further that the Second

16. *Jack E. Golson*, 54 T.C. 742 (1970).

Court of Appeals, the appellate court of appropriate jurisdiction, has never expressed itself on Issue A. Presuming the Tax Court has not reconsidered its position on Issue A, it will decide against Taxpayer U. Thus, it is entirely possible for two taxpayers suing in the same court to end up with opposite results merely because they live in different parts of the country!

Appeal to the U.S. Supreme Court is by Writ of Certiorari. If the Court accepts jurisdiction, it will grant the Writ (i. e., *Cert. Granted*). Most often, it will deny jurisdiction (i. e., *Cert. Denied*). For whatever reason or reasons, the Supreme Court rarely hears tax cases. The Court usually grants certiorari to resolve a conflict among the Courts of Appeals (e. g., two or more appellate courts have assumed opposing positions on a particular issue). The granting of a Writ of Certiorari indicates that at least four members of the Supreme Court believe that the issue is of sufficient importance to be heard by the full court.

The role of appellate courts is limited to a review of the record of trial compiled by the trial courts. Thus, the appellate process usually involves a determination of whether or not the trial court applied the proper law in arriving at its decision. Rarely will an appellate court disturb a lower court's fact-finding determination.

The result of an appeal could be any of a number of possibilities. The appellate court could approve (affirm) or disapprove (reverse) the lower court's finding, and it could also send the case back for further consideration (remand). When many issues are involved, it is not unusual to encounter a mixed result. Thus, the lower court could be affirmed (i. e., *aff'd*) on Issue A, reversed (i. e., *rev'd*) on Issue B, and Issue C could be remanded (i. e., *rem'd*) for additional fact-finding.

When more than one judge is involved in the decision-making process, it is not uncommon for them to disagree with one another. In addition to the majority view, there could be one or more judges who "concur" (i. e., agree with the result reached but not with some or all of the reasoning) or "dissent" (i. e., disagree with the result). In any one case it is, of course, the majority view that controls. But concurring and dissenting views may have influence on other courts or, at some subsequent date when the composition of the court has changed, even on the same court.

Having concluded a brief description of the judicial process, it is appropriate to consider the more practical problem of the relationship of case law to tax research. As previously noted, court decisions are an important source of tax law. The ability to cite a case and to locate it is, therefore, a must in working with the tax law.

Judicial Citations—The U.S. Tax Court. A good starting point is with the U.S. Tax Court. The Court issues two types of decisions: Regular and Memorandum. The distinction between the two involves both substance and form. In terms of substance, Memorandum decisions deal with situations necessitating only the application of already established principles of law; however, Regular decisions involve novel issues not previously resolved by the Court. In actual practice, however, this distinction is not always preserved. Not infrequently, Memorandum decisions will be encountered that appear to warrant Regular status and vice versa. At any rate, do not conclude that Memorandum decisions possess no value as precedents. Both represent the position of the Tax Court and, as such, can be relied upon.

Another important distinction between the Regular and Memorandum decisions issued by the Tax Court arises in connection with form. The Memorandum decisions officially are published in mimeograph form only, but Regular decisions are published by the U.S. Government in a series designated *Tax Court of the United States Reports.* Each volume of these *Reports* covers a six month period (April 1 through September 30 and October 1 through March 31) and is given a succeeding volume number. But, as was true of the *Cumulative Bulletins,* there is usually a time lag between the date a decision is rendered and the date it appears in bound form. A temporary citation may be necessary to aid the researcher in locating a recent Regular decision. Consider, for example, the temporary and permanent citations for *Pleasanton Gravel Co.,* a decision filed on June 30, 1975:

Temporary
Citation
$\left\{\vphantom{\begin{array}{c}a\\b\end{array}}\right.$ *Pleasanton Gravel Co.,* 64 T.C. —— No. 49 (1975)

Explanation : Page number left blank because not yet known

Permanent
Citation
$\left\{\vphantom{\begin{array}{c}a\\b\end{array}}\right.$ *Pleasanton Gravel Co.,* 64 T.C. 510 (1975)

Explanation : Page number now available

Both citations tell us that the case will ultimately appear in Volume 64 of the *Tax Court of the United States Reports.* But until this volume is bound and made available to the general public, the page number must be left blank. Instead, the temporary citation identifies the case as being the 49th Regular decision issued by the Tax Court since Volume 63 ended. With this information, the decision can be easily located in either of the special Tax Court services published by Commerce Clearing House or Prentice-Hall. Once Volume 64 is released, the permanent citation can be substituted and the number of the case dropped.

Before 1943, the Tax Court was called the Board of Tax Appeals, and its decisions were published as the *United States Board of Tax*

Appeals Reports (B.T.A.). These forty-seven volumes cover the period from 1924 to 1942. For example, the citation *Karl Pauli,* 11 B.T. A. 784 (1928) refers to the eleventh volume of the *Board of Tax Appeals Reports,* page 784, issued in 1928.

One further distinction between Regular and Memorandum decisions of the Tax Court involves the IRS procedure of acquiescence (i. e., "A" or "Acq.") or nonacquiescence (i. e., "NA" or "Nonacq."). If the IRS loses in a Regular decision, it will usually indicate whether it agrees or disagrees with the result reached by the Court. The acquiescence or nonacquiescence will be published in the *Internal Revenue Bulletin* and the *Cumulative Bulletin.* The procedure is not followed for Memorandum decisions or for the decisions of other courts. The IRS can retroactively revoke an acquiescence. The IRS sometimes issues an announcement that it will *or* will not follow a decision of another Federal court on similar facts.

Although Memorandum decisions are not published by the U.S. Government, they are published by Commerce Clearing House (CCH) and Prentice-Hall (P–H). Consider, for example, the three different ways that *Walter H. Johnson* may be cited:

Walter H. Johnson, T.C. Memo. 1975–245

> The 245th Memo, Decision issued by the Tax Court in 1975

Walter H. Johnson, 34 TCM 1056

> Page 1056 of Vol. 34 of the *CCH Tax Court Memorandum Decisions*

Walter H. Johnson, P–H T.C. Mem.Dec. ¶ 75,245

> Paragraph 75,245 of the *P–H T.C. Memorandum Decisions*

Notice that the third citation contains the same information as the first. Thus, ¶ 75,245 indicates the following information about the case: year 1975, 245th T.C. Memo. Decision.[17]

Judicial Citations—The U.S. District Court, Court of Claims, and Court of Appeals. District Court, Court of Claims, Court of Appeals, and Supreme Court decisions dealing with Federal tax matters are reported in both the CCH, *U.S. Tax Cases* (USTC) and the P–H, *American Federal Tax Reports* (AFTR) series.

Federal District Court decisions, dealing with *both* tax and nontax issues, also are published by West Publishing Company in their Federal Supplement Series. Examples of how a District Court case can be cited in three different forms appear below:

Simons-Eastern Co. v. U. S., 73–1 USTC ¶ 9279 (D.Ct.Ga., 1972).

---

17. In this text the Prentice-Hall citation for Memorandum decisions of the U. S. Tax Court is omitted. Thus, *Walter H. Johnson* would be cited as: 34 TCM 1056, T.C. Memo. 1975–245.

Explanation: Reported in the first volume of the *U.S. Tax Cases* (i. e., USTC) published by Commerce Clearing House for calendar year 1973 (i. e., 73–1) and located at paragraph 9279 (i. e., ¶ 9279).

Simons-Eastern Co. v. U. S., 31 AFTR 2d 73–640 (D.Ct.Ga., 1972).

Explanation: Reported in the 31st volume of the second series of the *American Federal Tax Reports* (i. e., AFTR 2d) published by Prentice-Hall and commencing on page 640. The "73" preceding the page number indicates the year the case was published but is a designation only used in recent decisions.

Simons-Eastern Co. v. U. S., 354 F.Supp. 1033 (D.Ct.Ga., 1972).

Explanation: Reported in the 354th volume of the *Federal Supplement Series* (i. e., F.Supp.) published by West Publishing Co. and commencing on page 1033.

In all of the above citations note that the name of the case is the same (Simons-Eastern Co. being the taxpayer) as is the reference to the Federal District Court of Georgia (i. e., D.Ct.Ga.) and the year the decision was rendered (i. e., 1972).[18]

Decisions of the Court of Claims and the Courts of Appeals are published in the USTCs, AFTRs, and a West Publishing Co. reporter designated as the Federal Second Series (F.2d). Illustrations of the different forms follow:

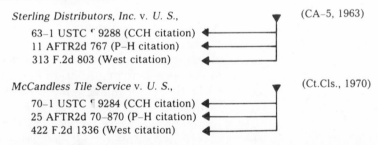

Note that *Sterling Distributors, Inc.* is a decision rendered by the Fifth Court of Appeals in 1963 (i. e., CA–5, 1963) while *McCandless Tile Service* is one rendered by the Court of Claims in 1970 (i. e., Ct. Cls., 1970).

Judicial Citations—The U. S. Supreme Court. Like all other federal tax cases (except those rendered by the U. S. Tax Court), Supreme Court decisions are published by Commerce Clearing House in the USTCs and by Prentice-Hall in the AFTRs. The U. S. Government Printing Office also publishes these decisions in the *United*

---

18. In the text the case would be cited in the following form: *Simons-Eastern Co. v. U. S.*, 73–1 USTC ¶ 9279, 31 AFTR2d 73–640, 354 F.Supp. 1033 (D.Ct.Ga., 1972).

States Supreme Court Reports (i. e., U.S.) as does West Publishing Company in its *Supreme Court Reporter* (i. e., S.Ct.) and the Lawyer's Co-Operative Publishing Company in its *United States Reports, Lawyer's Edition* (i. e., L.Ed.). An illustration of the different ways the same case can be cited appears below:

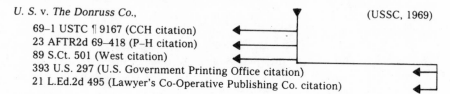

U. S. v. *The Donruss Co.*, (USSC, 1969)
    69–1 USTC ¶ 9167 (CCH citation)
    23 AFTR2d 69–418 (P–H citation)
    89 S.Ct. 501 (West citation)
    393 U.S. 297 (U.S. Government Printing Office citation)
    21 L.Ed.2d 495 (Lawyer's Co-Operative Publishing Co. citation)

The parenthetical reference (USSC, 1969) identifies the decision as having been rendered by the U. S. Supreme Court in 1969. The citations given in this text for Supreme Court decisions will be limited to the CCH (i. e., USTC), P–H (i. e., AFTR), and the West (i. e., S.Ct.) versions.

WORKING WITH THE TAX LAW — TAX RESEARCH

Tax research is the method whereby one determines the best available solution to a situation that possesses tax consequences. In other words, it is the process of finding a competent and professional conclusion to a tax problem. The problem might originate either from completed or proposed transactions. In the case of a completed transaction, the objective of the research would be to determine the tax result of what has already taken place. For example, was the expenditure incurred by the taxpayer deductible or not deductible for tax purposes? When dealing with proposed transactions, however, the tax research process is directed toward the determination of possible tax consequences. To the extent that tax research leads to a choice of alternatives or otherwise influences the future actions of the taxpayer, it becomes the key to effective tax planning.

Tax research involves the following procedures:

—Identifying and refining the problem.

—Locating the appropriate tax law sources.

—Assessing the validity of the tax law sources.

—Arriving at the solution or at alternative solutions with due consideration given to nontax factors.

—Effectively communicating the solution to the taxpayer or the taxpayer's representative.

—Following up on the solution (where appropriate) in the light of new developments.

These procedures are diagramed in Figure 2. The broken lines reflect those steps of particular interest when tax research is directed towards proposed, rather than completed, transactions.

Figure 2

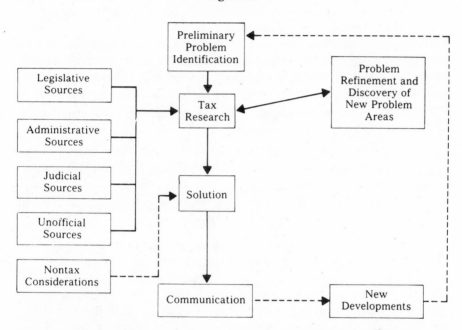

IDENTIFYING THE PROBLEM

Problem identification must start with a compilation of the relevant facts involved.[19] In this regard, *all* of the facts that may have a bearing on the problem must be gathered because any omission could modify the solution to be reached. To illustrate, consider what appears to be a very simple problem.

> **Example 4.** On December 30, 19X0, X Corporation (a calendar year and accrual basis taxpayer) declares a $20,000 bonus payable to R, one of its employees. The stock of X Corporation is held by R, S, and T, all individuals. The problem: Is the bonus deductible by X Corporation?

---

19. For an excellent discussion of the critical role of facts in carrying out tax research see Ray M. Sommerfeld and G. Fred Streuling, *Tax Research* *Techniques*, Tax Study No. 5 (New York, N.Y.: The American Institute of Certified Public Accountants, 1976), Chapter 2.

Refining the Problem. Initial reaction would be to sanction the deduction in Example 4 since it has long been accepted that salaries or other compensation represent an ordinary and necessary expense in carrying on a trade or business [see § 162(a)]. Assume, however, further fact gathering reveals the following additional information:

—The bonus was accrued on December 30, 19X0, but not actually paid until July 1, 19X1.

—R uses the cash method of accounting for income tax purposes.

—The stock in X Corporation is owned in equal proportion by R, S, and T (i. e., each owns one-third of the stock).

—R, S, and T are brothers and sisters.

With these new facts, additional research leads to a consideration of § 267(a)(2). Under this Code provision X Corporation would lose the deduction if all of the following three conditions are met:

1. X Corporation uses the accrual method of accounting while R uses the cash method;

2. The bonus is not paid within 2½ months from the end of the tax year in which accrued (in this case no later than March 15, 19X1); and

3. R owns, directly or *indirectly,* more than 50% in the value of X Corporation's outstanding stock.

Has condition 3. been satisfied since R only owns 33⅓% of the stock in X Corporation? Further research reveals that an individual is deemed, for this purpose at least, to own all of the stock owned by members of his or her family [§ 267(c)(2)]. Because members of the family include brothers and sisters [§ 267(c)(4)], R owns 100% of the stock of X Corporation [i. e., 33⅓% directly and 66⅔% indirectly].[20] All three conditions having been met, therefore, it appears X Corporation will be denied a deduction for the accrued bonus.

Further Refinement of the Problem. One of the conditions necessary for the disallowance of X Corporation's deduction under § 267 was the failure to pay the bonus to R within 2½ months from the close of the tax year in which it was accrued. Suppose, however, further investigation reveals the following:

—R had the right to receive the bonus once it was authorized (or no later than March 15, 19X1).

—X Corporation had the duty and the financial capacity to pay the bonus when it was authorized.

---

20. By virtue of the family attribution rules of § 267(c)(2), R has "constructive" ownership of the stock owned by his brothers and sisters. Thus, "indirect" ownership means "constructive" ownership.

In the light of this new information, X Corporation's deduction might not be lost. Further research indicates that if R (the payee) is in constructive receipt of the income, X Corporation (the payor) will be considered to have made a constructive payment.[21] Thus, the date of constructive payment, as opposed to the date of actual payment, will control for purposes of applying § 267. If constructive payment occurs no later than March 15, 19X1, the $20,000 bonus will be deductible to X Corporation for tax year 19X0 (the year of the accrual). Additional research would provide judicial authority setting forth guidelines on what does and does not constitute a constructive payment.[22]

Even if the deduction of the bonus is prevented by § 267, a further refinement of the problem should take into account the possible effect of § 162(a)(1). Under this provision salaries and other compensation can only be deducted if "reasonable" in amount. To properly resolve the question of reasonableness the researcher would need to gather such facts as: the nature and extent of the services performed, the amount of other compensation paid to R in the same year as the bonus, the salaries paid by similar firms for similar services, and the dividend-payment record of X Corporation. These facts, when tested by the Regulations under § 162 and court decisions on the subject, would provide the basis for assessing the reasonableness of the bonus and, consequently, its deductibility by X Corporation.

LOCATING THE APPROPRIATE TAX LAW SOURCES

Once the problem is clearly defined, what is the next step? Although this is a matter of individual judgment, most involved tax research begins with the index volume number of the tax service. If the problem is not that complex, the researcher may by-pass the tax service and turn directly to the Internal Revenue Code and the Treasury Regulations. For the beginner, this procedure saves time and will solve many of the more basic problems. If the researcher does not have a personal copy of the Code or Regulations, resorting to the appropriate volume(s) of a tax service will be necessary.[23]

---

21. Reg. § 1.267(a)–1(b)(1)(iii). The concept of constructive receipt is explained in Reg. § 1.451–2.

22. See, for example, *Fetzer Refrigerator Co. v. U. S.*, 71–1 USTC ¶ 9202, 27 AFTR2d 71–613, 437 F.2d 577 (CA–6, 1971); *F. D. Bissett & Son, Inc.*, 56 T.C. 453 (1971); and *Hender-*

shot & Smith, Inc., 34 TCM 788, T.C. Memo. 1975–183.

23. Several of the major tax services publish paperback editions of the Code and Treasury Regulations which can be purchased at modest prices. These editions are usually revised twice each year.

The major tax services available are listed below:

Standard Federal Tax Reporter, Commerce Clearing House.

Federal Taxes, Prentice-Hall.

Mertens, *Law of Federal Income Taxation,* Callaghan and Co.

Tax Coordinator, Research Institute of America.

Tax Management Portfolios, Bureau of National Affairs.

Rabkin and Johnson, *Federal, Income, Gift and Estate Taxation,* Matthew Bender, Inc.

Working With the Tax Services. In this text it is not feasible to teach the use of any particular tax service—this can only be learned by practice.[24]

There are, however, several important observations about the use of tax services that cannot be over emphasized. First, never forget to check for current developments. The main text of any service is not revised frequently enough to permit reliance on that portion as the *latest* word on any subject. Where such current developments can be found depends, of course, on which service is being used. Both the Commerce Clearing House and Prentice-Hall services contain a special volume devoted to current matters. Second, when dealing with a tax service synopsis of a Treasury Department pronouncement or a judicial decision, remember there is no substitute for the original source.

To illustrate, do not base a conclusion solely on a tax service's commentary on *Pleasanton Gravel Co.*[25] If the case is vital to the research, look it up! It is possible that the facts of the case are distinguishable from those involved in the problem being researched. This is not to say that the case synopsis contained in the tax service is wrong—it might just be misleading or incomplete.

Tax Periodicals. Additional sources of tax information are the various tax periodicals. The best means of locating a journal article pertinent to a tax problem is through Commerce Clearing House's *Federal Tax Articles.* This three-volume service includes a subject index, a Code Section number index, and an author's index. Also, the P–H tax service has a topical "Index to Tax Articles" section that is organized using the P–H paragraph index system.

24. The representatives of the various tax services are prepared to provide the users of their services with printed booklets and/or individual instruction on the utilization of such materials.

25. *Pleasanton Gravel Co.,* 64 T.C. 510 (1975).

Some of the more useful tax periodicals are listed below:

Journal of Taxation 1710 Highway 35 Asbury Park, N. J. 07712	Taxation for Accountants 1710 Highway 35 Asbury Park, N. J. 07712
The Tax Adviser 1211 Avenue of the Americas New York, N. Y. 10036	Taxes—The Tax Magazine Commerce Clearing House, Inc. 4025 West Peterson Avenue Chicago, Illinois 60646
Tax Law Review Matthew Bender & Co. 235 E. 45th Street New York, N. Y. 10017	The Tax Executive Tax Executives Institute 1111 E. Street, N.W. Washington, D. C. 20004
The Practical Accountant Institute for Continuing Professional Development 964 3rd Avenue New York, N. Y. 10022	Trusts and Estates Communication Channels, Inc. 461 Eighth Avenue New York, N. Y. 10001
National Tax Journal 21 East State Street Columbus, Ohio 43215	Monthly Digest of Tax Articles Research Documentation Corporation 14 Plaza Road Grenvale, New York 11548
Journal of Corporate Taxation Warren, Gorham and Lamont 89 Beach Street Boston, Massachusetts 02111	Oil and Gas Tax Quarterly Matthew Bender & Co. 235 E. 45th Street New York, New York 10017

ASSESSING THE VALIDITY OF THE TAX LAW SOURCE

Once a source has been located, the next procedure is to assess such source in the light of the problem at hand. Proper assessment involves careful interpretation of the tax law with consideration as to its relevance and validity. In connection with validity, an important step is to check for recent changes in the tax law.

Interpreting the Internal Revenue Code. The language of the Code can be extremely difficult to comprehend fully. For example, a subsection [§ 341(e)] relating to collapsible corporations contains *one* sentence of more than 450 words. Within this same subsection are two other sentences of 300 and 340 words. One author has noted ten common pitfalls in interpreting the Code: [26]

1. Determine the limitations and exceptions to a provision. Do not permit the language of the Code Section to carry greater or lesser weight than was intended.

2. Just because a Section fails to mention an item does not necessarily mean that the item is excluded.

26. H. G. Wong, "Ten Common Pitfalls in Reading the Internal Revenue Code," *The Practical Accountant* (July–August, 1972), pp. 30–33.

3. Read definitional clauses carefully.

4. Do not overlook small words such as "and" and "or." There is a world of difference between these two words.

5. Read the Code Section completely; do not jump to conclusions prematurely. Return to Example 4 and the bonus X Corporation accrued on behalf of R. If the analysis of § 267 stopped with subsection (b)(1) it would appear that the bonus is deductible since R owns only one-third of the stock in X Corporation and not "more than 50%." A further reading of § 267, however, reveals that R constructively owns all of the stock of his brothers and sisters (i. e., S and T). Because R is deemed to own "more than 50%" of X Corporation, the conclusion reached after only a partial examination is invalidated.

6. Watch out for cross-referenced and related provisions since many Sections of the Code are interrelated.

7. Congress is at times not careful when reconciling new Code provisions with existing Sections. Conflicts among Sections, therefore, do arise.

8. Be alert for hidden definitions; terms in a particular Code Section may be defined in the same Section *or in a separate Section.*

9. Some answers may not be found in the Code; therefore, a researcher may have to consult the Regulations and/or judicial decisions.[27]

10. Take careful note of measuring words such as "less than 50%"; "more than 50%"; "at least 80%"; and, "more than 80%."

Assessing the Validity of a Treasury Regulation. It is often stated that Treasury Regulations have the force and effect of law. This is certainly true for most Regulations, but there have been judicial decisions which have held a Regulation or a portion thereof invalid, usually on the grounds that the Regulation is contrary to the intent of Congress upon the enactment of a particular Code Section.

Keep in mind the following observations when assessing the validity of a Regulation:

—In a challenge, the burden of proof is on the taxpayer to show that the Regulation is wrong.

---

27. The Code is silent concerning the deductibility of educational expenses. Their deductibility, however, falls under the general provision of § 162(a) (the allowance for "all the ordinary and necessary expenses paid or incurred during the taxable year in carrying on any trade or business * * *"). Guidelines for their deductibility can be found in Reg. § 1.162–5.

—If the taxpayer loses the challenge, the imposition of a penalty under § 6653(a) may result. This provision deals with the "intentional disregard of rules and regulations" on the part of the taxpayer.

—Some Regulations merely reprint or rephrase what Congress has stated in its Committee Reports issued in connection with the enactment of tax legislation. Such Regulations are "hard and solid" and almost impossible to overturn because they clearly reflect the intent of Congress.

—In many Code Sections, Congress has given to the "Secretary or his delegate" the authority to prescribe Regulations to carry out the details of administration or to otherwise complete the operating rules. Under such circumstances, it could almost be said that Congress is delegating its legislative powers to the Treasury Department. Regulations issued pursuant to this type of authority truly possess the force and effect of law and are often called "legislative regulations."

Assessing the Validity of Other Administrative Sources of the Tax Law. Revenue Rulings issued by the IRS carry less weight than Treasury Department Regulations. Rulings are important, however, in that they reflect the position of the IRS on tax matters. In any dispute with the IRS on the interpretation of tax law, therefore, taxpayers should expect agents to follow the results reached in any applicable Rulings.

Revenue Rulings further tell the taxpayer the IRS's reaction to certain court decisions. Recall that the IRS follows a practice of either acquiescing (i. e., agreeing) or not acquiescing (i. e., not agreeing) with the *Regular* decisions of the U.S. Tax Court. This does not mean that a particular decision of the Tax Court is of no value if, for example, the IRS has nonacquiesced in the result. It does, however, indicate that the IRS will continue to litigate the issue involved.

Assessing the Validity of Judicial Sources of the Tax Law. The judicial process as it relates to the formulation of tax law has already been described. How much reliance can be placed on a particular decision depends upon the following variables:

—The level of the court. A decision rendered by a trial court (e. g., a Federal District Court) carries less weight than one issued by an appellate court (e. g., the Fifth Court of Appeals). Unless Congress changes the Code, decisions by the U.S. Supreme Court represent the last word on any tax issue.

—The legal residence of the taxpayer. If, for example, a taxpayer lives in Texas, a decision of the Fifth Court of Appeals means more than one rendered by the Second Court of Appeals. This is the case since any appeal from a U.S. District

Court or the U.S. Tax Court would be to the Fifth Court of Appeals and not the Second Court of Appeals.[28]

—Whether the decision represents the weight of authority on the issue. In other words, is it supported by the results reached by other courts?

—The outcome or status of the decision on appeal. For example, was the decision appealed and, if so, with what result?

In connection with the last two variables, the use of a citator is invaluable to tax research.[29] Such use is illustrated in the Appendix.

ARRIVING AT THE SOLUTION OR AT ALTERNATIVE SOLUTIONS

In Example 4 the problem was whether or not X Corporation could deduct a bonus of $20,000, declared on December 30, 19X0, and payable to R, one of its employees. A refinement of the problem added the additional information that the bonus was not paid until July 1, 19X1, and all of the stock of X Corporation was owned by R and his brother and sister. The end result was a disallowance of the deduction unless it could be shown that the bonus was constructively paid to R no later than March 15, 19X1. The solution, therefore, turned on whether the conditions for application of § 267 (i. e., disallowance of expenses involving related parties) were satisfied. But even if § 267 could be avoided, the bonus would have to pass the test of reasonableness set forth in § 162(a)(1). If, when added to the other compensation R received in 19X0 from X Corporation, some or all of the bonus is unreasonable, such amount will be disallowed as a deduction.

In summary, the solution to the problem depends upon the resolution of two questions of fact. First, has a constructive payment occurred? Second, is the compensation R received reasonable in amount? Under such circumstances, a clear-cut answer may not be possible. This, does not, however, detract from the value of the research. Often, a guarded judgment is the best possible solution that can be given to a tax problem.

COMMUNICATING TAX RESEARCH

Once satisfied that the problem has been researched adequately, the researcher may need to prepare a memo setting forth the result. The form such a memo takes could depend on a number of different considerations. For example, is any particular procedure or format

---

28. Recall that an appeal from the U. S. Court of Claims (i. e., the other trial court) is directly to the U. S. Supreme Court.

29. The major citators are published by Commerce Clearing House, Prentice-Hall, and Shepard's Citations, Inc.

recommended for tax research memos either by an employer or an instructor? Is the memo to be given directly to the client or will it first pass to the researcher's employer? But whatever form it takes, a good research memo should contain the following elements:

— A clear statement of the issue.

— In more complex situations, a short review of the factual pattern which raises the issue.

— A review of the tax law sources (e. g., Code, Regulations, Rulings, judicial authority).

— Any assumptions made in arriving at the solution.

— The solution recommended and the logic or reasoning in its support.

— The references consulted in the research process.

In short, a good tax memo should tell the reader what was researched, the results of that research, and the justification for the recommendation made.[30]

WORKING WITH THE TAX LAW—TAX PLANNING

Tax research and tax planning are inseparably linked. The primary purpose of effective tax planning is to reduce the taxpayer's total tax bill. This does not mean that the course of action selected must produce the lowest possible tax under the circumstances; the minimization must be considered in context with the legitimate business goals of the taxpayer.

A secondary objective of effective tax planning works toward a deferment or postponement of the tax to the future. Specifically, this objective aims to accomplish any one or more of the following procedures: eradicating the tax entirely; eliminating the tax in the current year; deferring the receipt of income; converting ordinary income into capital gains; proliferating taxpayers (i. e., forming partnerships and corporations or making lifetime gifts to family members); eluding double taxation; avoiding ordinary income; or creating, increasing, or accelerating deductions. However, this second objective should be accepted with considerable reservation. Although the maxim "a bird in the hand is worth two in the bush" has general validity, there are frequent cases in which the rule breaks down. For example, a tax election in one year, although it accomplishes a current reduction in taxes, could saddle future years with a disadvantageous tax position.

---

30. *Supra*, note 19, Chapter 6.

NONTAX CONSIDERATIONS

There is an honest danger that tax motivations may take on a significance that is not in conformity with the true values involved. In other words, tax considerations may operate to impair the exercise of sound business judgment by the taxpayer. Thus, the tax planning process may become a medium through which to accomplish ends that are socially and economically objectionable. Ostensibly, there exists a pronounced tendency for planning to go toward the opposing extremes of either not enough or too much emphasis on tax consider- ations. The happy medium—one that recognizes the significance of taxes, but not beyond the point at which planning serves to detract from the exercise of good business judgment, turns out to be the promised land that is seldom reached.

The remark is often made that a good rule to follow is to refrain from pursuing any course of action which would not be followed were it not for certain tax considerations. This statement is not entirely correct, but it does illustrate the desirability of preventing business logic from being "sacrificed at the altar of tax planning." In this connection, the following comment is significant:

> The lure of a quick tax dollar is often the only justification for a transaction that might have been accomplished with much sounder economic results and equivalent tax savings if more careful and deliberate consideration had been given to the prob- lem. Certainly in this atmosphere of the tax-controlled economy a very heavy obligation is cast upon the tax advisor to give seri- ous consideration as to whether a proposed action achieves a de- sirable economic result apart from tax savings or whether the immediate tax advantages may be more than offset by later eco- nomic or personal disadvantage. We cannot afford to develop successful cures that are killing our patients.[31]

TAX EVASION AND TAX AVOIDANCE

There is a fine line between legal tax planning and illegal tax planning—tax avoidance versus tax evasion. Tax avoidance is mere- ly tax minimization through legal techniques. In this sense, tax avoidance becomes the proper objective of all tax planning. Evasion, while also aimed at the elimination or reduction of taxes, connotes the use of subterfuge and fraud as a means to an end. Popular usage —probably because of the common goals that are involved—has linked these two concepts to the extent that any true distinctions

31. Norris Darrell, "Some Responsibili- ties of the Tax Adviser in Regard to Tax Minimization Devices," *Proceed- ings of the New York University* *Eighth Annual Institute on Federal Taxation* (Albany, New York, Matther Bender & Co., 1950), pp. 988–989.

have been obliterated in the minds of many. Consequently, the taint created by the association of tax avoidance and tax evasion has deterred some taxpayers from properly taking advantage of the planning possibilities. The now-classic verbiage of Judge Learned Hand in *Commissioner v. Newman* reflects the true values the individual should have. In this opinion Judge Hand declared:

> Over and over again courts have said that there is nothing sinister in so arranging one's affairs as to keep taxes as low as possible. Everybody does so, rich or poor; and all do right, for nobody owes any public duty to pay more than the law demands: taxes are enforced extractions, not voluntary contributions. To demand more in the name of morals is mere cant.[32]

FOLLOW–UP PROCEDURES

Because tax planning usually involves a proposed (as opposed to a completed) transaction, it is predicated upon the continuing validity of the advice based upon the tax research. A change in the tax law (either legislative, administrative, or judicial) could alter the original conclusion. Additional research may be necessary to test the solution in the light of current developments (see one set of broken lines depicted in Figure 2).

TAX PLANNING—A PRACTICAL APPLICATION

Returning to the facts of Example 4, what could have been done to protect X Corporation's deduction for the $20,000 bonus to R had the transaction not been completed? Concerning the § 267 issue (i. e., disallowance of accrued but unpaid expenses among certain related parties), the following steps should be taken:

—Pay the bonus to R by December 31, 19X0.

—If the payment is to be postponed, it should take place no later than March 15, 19X1. In this event, the parties should firmly establish X Corporation's liability to make the payment before the close of its tax year (i. e., December 31, 19X0).

What about any potential unreasonable compensation issue under § 162(a)(1)? One tax planning aid would be to make the amount of the bonus contingent on a predetermined formula. Bonuses arbitrarily determined at year-end are particularly suspect when paid to an employee-shareholder of a closely-held corporation.[33] Regulation § 1.162–7(2) states in part:

---

32. *Comm. v. Newman,* 47–1 USTC ¶ 9175, 35 AFTR 857, 159 F.2d 848 (CA–2, 1947).

33. The unreasonable compensation issue is essentially a problem restricted to closely-held corporations. A "closely-held corporation" can be defined as one in which only a few shareholders are in a position to manipulate corporate policy to their own advantage. Needless to say, X Corporation fits this definition since all of its stock is held by three shareholders (R, S, and T), all of whom are related to one another.

"Generally speaking, if contingent compensation is paid pursuant to a free bargain between the employer and the individual *made before the services are rendered,* not influenced by any consideration on the part of the employer other than that of securing on fair and advantageous terms the services of the individual, it should be allowed as a deduction *even though in the actual working out of the contract it may prove to be greater than the amount which would ordinarily be paid.*"   (Emphasis added.)

Thus, a contract entered into by R and X Corporation before the services are rendered (in early 19X0) establishing R's bonus as contingent on profits or some other measure of productivity will help justify a larger amount as reasonable than would otherwise be the case.

                              *   *   *

Throughout the text, most Chapters include observations on TAX PLANNING CONSIDERATIONS. Such observations are not all-inclusive but are intended to illustrate some of the ways in which the material covered can be effectively utilized to minimize taxes.

PROBLEM MATERIALS

Questions for Class Discussion

1. Trace through Congress the path usually followed by a tax bill.

2. What is the function of the Joint Conference Committee of the House Ways and Means Committee and the Senate Finance Committee?

3. Why are committee reports of Congress important as a source of tax law?

4. The Tax Reduction Act of 1975 became part of the Internal Revenue Code of 1954. Explain the meaning of this statement.

5. Judicial decisions interpreting a provision of the Internal Revenue Code of 1939 are no longer of any value in view of the enactment of the Internal Revenue Code of 1954. Assess the validity of this statement.

6. Explain the reference to "Subchapter S."

7. What is a Proposed Regulation? How would a Proposed Regulation under § 541 be cited?

8. Distinguish between:

    a. Treasury Regulations and Revenue Rulings.

    b. Revenue Rulings and Revenue Procedures.

    c. Revenue Rulings and individual (i. e., "private") rulings.

    d. Individual (i. e., "private") rulings and determination letters.

9. "Taxpayers should never run the risk of conflict with the IRS. When in doubt about a proposed transaction, they should obtain an individual (i. e., "private") ruling." Evaluate the accuracy of these remarks.

10. What is the difference, if any, between the Internal Revenue Bulletin (I.R.B.) and the Cumulative Bulletin (C.B.)?

11. Interpret each of the following citations:

    a. Rev.Rul. 77–80, I.R.B. No. 14, 9.

    b. Rev.Rul. 76–150, 1976–1 C.B. 38.

    c. Rev.Proc. 77–16, I.R.B. No. 19, 35.

    d. Rev.Proc. 76–13, 1976–1 C.B. 553.

12. What are Treasury Decisions (T.D.)?

    a. What purpose do they serve?

    b. Where are they published?

13. Summarize the trial and appellate court system for Federal tax litigation.

14. List an advantage and a disadvantage of using the U. S. Tax Court as the trial court for Federal tax litigation.

15. List an advantage and a disadvantage of using a U. S. District Court as the trial court for Federal tax litigation.

16. List an advantage and a disadvantage of using the U. S. Court of Claims as the trial court for Federal tax litigation.

17. Taxpayer lives in Michigan. In a controversy with the IRS, taxpayer loses at the trial court level. Describe the appeal procedure under the following different assumptions:

    a. The trial court was the Small Claims Division of the U. S. Tax Court.

    b. The trial court was the U. S. Tax Court.

    c. The trial court was a U. S. District Court.

    d. The trial court was the U. S. Court of Claims.

18. Suppose the U. S. Government loses a tax case in the U. S. District Court of Idaho but does not appeal the result. What does the failure to appeal signify?

19. Because the U. S. Tax Court is a national court, it always decides the same issue in a consistent manner. Assess the validity of this statement.

20. Interpret each of the citations appearing below:

    a. 54 T.C. 1514 (1970).

    b. 408 F.2d 117 (CA–2, 1969).

    c. 69–1 USTC ¶ 9319 (CA–2, 1969).

    d.   23 AFTR2d 69–1090 (CA–2, 1969).

    e.   293 F.Supp. 1129 (D.Ct., Miss., 1967).

    f.   67–1 USTC ¶ 9253 (D.Ct., Miss., 1967).

    g.   19 AFTR2d 647 (D.Ct., Miss., 1967).

    h.   56 S.Ct. 289 (USSC, 1935).

    i.   36–1 USTC ¶ 9020 (USSC, 1935).

    j.   16 AFTR 1274 (USSC, 1935).

    k.   422 F.2d 1336 (Ct.Cls., 1970).

21.   Explain the following abbreviations:

    a.   CA–2

    b.   Ct.Cls.

    c.   *aff'd*

    d.   *rev'd*

    e.   *rem'd*

    f.   *cert. denied*

    g.   *acq.*

    h.   B.T.A.

    i.   USTC

    j.   AFTR

    k.   F.2d

    l.   F.Supp.

    m.   USSC

    n.   S.Ct.

    o.   D.Ct.

22.   What is the difference between a Regular and a Memorandum decision of the U. S. Tax Court?

23.   What is a "legislative Regulation?"

24.   In assessing the validity of a court decision, discuss the significance of the following:

    a.   The decision was rendered by the U. S. District Court of Wyoming. Taxpayer lives in Wyoming.

    b.   The decision was rendered by the U. S. Court of Claims. Taxpayer lives in Wyoming.

    c.   The decision was rendered by the Second Court of Appeals. Taxpayer lives in California.

    d.   The decision was rendered by the U. S. Supreme Court.

e. The decision was rendered by the U. S. Tax Court. The IRS has acquiesced in the result.

f. Same as e. except that the IRS has issued a nonacquiescence as to the result.

PROBLEM MATERIALS

Problems

1. Using the legend provided, classify each of the statements appearing below (*Note*: more than one answer per statement may be appropriate):

Legend

D = Applies to the U. S. District Court

T = Applies to the U. S. Tax Court

C = Applies to the U. S. Court of Claims

A = Applies to the U. S. Court of Appeals

U = Applies to the U. S. Supreme Court

N = Applies to none of the above

a. Decides only Federal tax matters.

b. Decisions are reported in the F.2d Series.

c. Decisions are reported in the USTCs.

d. Decisions are reported in the AFTRs.

e. Appeal is by Writ of Certiorari.

f. Court meets only in Washington, D. C.

g. A jury trial is available.

h. Trial courts.

i. Appellate courts.

j. Appeal is to the U. S. Supreme Court and by-passes the U. S. Court of Appeals.

k. Has a Small Claims Division.

l. The only trial court where the taxpayer does not have to first pay the tax assessed by the IRS.

Research Problems

Research Problem 1. Complete the citations appearing below to the extent the research materials are available to you:

a. *Weiss v. U. S.,* —— USTC ¶ —— (D.Ct.Ohio, 1975).

b. *Weiss v. U. S.,* —— AFTR2d —— (D.Ct.Ohio, 1975).

c. —— *v. U. S.,* 72–1 USTC ¶ 9353 (CA– ——, ——).

d.   —— *v. U. S.*, 29 AFTR2d 72–917 (C.A.– —, —).

e.   *Kenneth Farmer Darrow,* 64 T.C. —— (1975).

f.   *Leck Co., Inc. v. U. S.,* 73–2 USTC ¶ —— (——, ——).

g.   *Leck Co., Inc. v. U. S.,* 32 AFTR2d —— (——, ——).

h.   *Delaware Trucking Co., Inc.,* 32 TCM 104, T.C. Memo. 1973– ——.

i.   Rev.Rul. 74–431, —— C.B. ——.

j.   Rev.Proc. ——, 1974–1 C.B. 438.

Research Problem 2. By using the research materials available to you, answer the questions posed below:

a.   Has Prop.Reg. § 1.543–6(b)(2)(ii) been finalized?

b.   What happened to Golconda Mining Corp., 58 T.C. 736 (1972) on appeal?

c.   Does Rev.Rul. 69–185 still represent the position of the IRS on the issue involved?

d.   In what areas will the IRS not issue individual (i. e., "private") rulings? See Rev.Proc. 72–9, 1972–1 C.B. 719.

Chapter 4

GROSS INCOME

This chapter includes a brief discussion of the components of taxable income (the tax formula) and the computation of tax to serve as a broad overview. This is followed by a discussion of concepts and judicial doctrines which affect the determination of gross income.

THE TAX FORMULA

The starting point in computing the income tax liability for an individual or a corporation is the determination of "gross income." § 61 provides for an "all-inclusive" definition of gross income, i. e., "gross income means all income from whatever source derived." This definition is then supplemented in the Code by a listing of items (not necessarily all inclusive) which are includible in gross income, e. g., compensation for services, rents, interest, dividends, alimony, etc. Other Code sections deal with specific rules for the tax treatment of such items.

Congress has provided that certain items are exempt from taxation, e. g., interest on governmental obligations (state and municipal bonds). These exemptions appear in §§ 101–124 of the Code. These specific items of inclusion and exclusion will be further discussed in subsequent portions of this chapter and the following chapter.

The Code also sets forth allowable deductions. Generally, trade or business expenses, unreimbursed employment related expenses and expenses attributable to rental income are deductible from gross income.[1] The allowance of these deductions results in the tax being levied upon a taxpayer's net rather than gross taxable income. In addition, individual taxpayers are allowed to deduct certain personal expenditures as itemized deductions in arriving at taxable income. Examples of these include charitable contributions,[2] medical expenses [3] (in excess of 3% of the taxpayer's adjusted gross income), certain state and local taxes,[4] interest,[5] and casualty losses.[6]

Taxpayers are also permitted certain "artificial" deductions including:

Capital gain deductions for individuals. 50 percent of the excess of net long-term capital gains over net short-term capital losses is deducted from gross income; [7]

Personal and dependency exemptions for individuals. The taxpayer may deduct $750 for himself and $750 for his spouse plus an additional $750 for each of his dependents.[8]

COMPONENTS OF THE TAX FORMULA

Figure I illustrates the tax formula for an individual. It should be noted that there are three classes of deductions: (1) "for adjusted gross income," (2) standard deduction, and (3) itemized deductions. Figure 1 also lists certain items that are "deductions *for* adjusted gross income" and those which are "deductions *from* adjusted gross income" (itemized deductions).

As illustrated in Figure I, the taxpayer may deduct *from* adjusted gross income the excess of his total itemized deductions over the standard deduction. For 1977 and subsequent years, the standard deduction is a flat $3,200 for married persons filing joint returns and $2,200 for single persons.[9] The standard deduction rules are discussed in Chapter 10.

The taxpayer is allowed a $750 exemption, an additional exemption for his or her spouse and an exemption for each dependent.[10] This exemption is allowed in addition to, and not in lieu of, the standard or itemized deductions.

1. §§ 62, 162 and 212.

2. § 170.

3. § 213.

4. § 164.

5. § 163.

6. § 165.

7. § 1202.

8. § 151.

9. Tax Reduction and Simplification Act of 1977, Act § 101(a), (b) and (d) amending §§ 1 and 3 and repealing §§ 141, 142, 144 and 145.

10. § 151.

Figure 1

TAX FORMULA FOR INDIVIDUALS*

Income (broadly conceived)		$50,000

    1. Investment income.
    2. Salaries and wages.
    3. Income from professional services.
    4. Income from a trade or business.
    5. Income from the production of rent or royalty income.
    6. Capital gains.

Less: Exclusions from income   (2,000)

    1. Tax exempt interest.
    2. Dividends received up to $100.   _____

=   Gross Income   48,000

Less: Deductions *for* adjusted gross income   (3,000)

    1. Trade or business expenses.
    2. Certain employment related expenses.
    3. Expenses incurred in the production of rent and royalty income.
    4. Alimony payments (after 1976).
    5. Moving expenses.
    6. 50 percent of the excess of net long-term capital gains over net short-term capital losses   _____

=   Adjusted Gross Income   45,000

Less: Excess of Itemized Deductions over the Standard Deduction

1. Charitable contributions	$2,000	
2. State and local taxes	1,500	
3. Interest	500	
Total Itemized Deductions	$4,000	

    Minus:

Standard Deduction (Joint return)   <u>(3,200)</u>

Amount of deduction   (800)

Less: Personal and dependency exemptions   (3,000)
        (Husband, Wife and 2 children)   _____

=   Taxable Income   41,200

×   Applicable tax rates (joint return Schedule Y)   11,240 **

Less: Tax credits and prepayments of tax   <u>(10,000)</u>

=   Net Tax Due (Refund)   <u>$ 1,240</u>

---

* Items included in the tax formula are not intended to be all inclusive. Specific provisions are discussed in subsequent chapters.

** The student should refer to Appendix A–1 to familiarize himself with the use of the tax tables.

TAX RATES

    Taxable income is defined as gross income less the allowable deductions. The next step in the process is to compute the gross tax on the taxable income. One of four tax rate schedules provided in the Internal Revenue Code must be used to compute the tax. The rate schedules are for (1) married persons filing a joint return, (2) heads of household, (3) unmarried individuals, and (4) married persons filing separate returns and estates and trusts.[11] Determining when a particular rate schedule should be used will be further discussed in Chapter 10.

The student should review the rate schedules in Appendix A–2. Note that the schedules are "progressive"; that is, as income rises, the marginal tax rate increases, and therefore, the total tax as a percent of taxable income increases. For example, the tax on $20,000 taxable income on a joint return is $3,484, or 17.4% of the income, but the tax on $40,000 is $10,700, or 26.7% of the income. The rationale for using a progressive rate schedule is that as an individual's income rises, proportionately less of it is required for his basic needs, and therefore, he can afford to pay proportionately more in taxes.

GROSS INCOME — WHAT IS IT?

GENERAL DEFINITION

Section 61(a) of the Internal Revenue Code defines the term "gross income" as follows:

Except as otherwise provided in this subtitle, gross income means all income from whatever source derived. * * *

Since the sweeping scope of the definition is apparent, the Supreme Court has frequently stated:

The starting point in all cases dealing with the question of the scope of what is included in "gross income" begins with the basic premise that the purpose of Congress was to use the full measure of its taxing power.[12]

The clause, "Except as otherwise provided in this subtitle," refers to other sections of the Code where Congress has exempted certain types of income from the tax base. These exclusions will be discussed in Chapter 5.

ECONOMIC AND ACCOUNTING CONCEPTS

The term "income" is used in the Code but is not separately defined. Thus, early in the history of our tax laws, the courts were re-

---

11. § 1.

12. *James v. U. S.*, 61–1 USTC ¶ 9449, 7 AFTR2d 1361, 81 S.Ct. 1052 (USSC, 1961).

quired to interpret "the commonly understood meaning of the term which must have been in the minds of the people when they adopted the 16th Amendment to the Constitution." [13]　The Supreme Court rejected the economist's concept of income as "the commonly understood meaning of the term" in determining the definition of income.[14]

Measuring economic income requires a determination of the fair market value of the taxpayer's net assets at the beginning and end of the year.　After this determination is made, economic income is defined as the sum of the taxpayer's change in net worth plus actual consumption of goods and services for the tax period.　Economic income also includes imputed values for such items as the rental value of an owner-occupied home and the value of food a taxpayer might grow for his personal consumption.[15]　The use of these and other market values would present difficult problems in administering the tax laws and would produce endless controversies between the taxpayer and the government.　Thus, the economist's concept of income has been rejected by the courts simply on the grounds of its impracticality.

On the other hand, the accountant's concept of income is founded on the realization principle.[16]　According to this principle, income is not recognized until there is (1) an exchange of goods and/or services between the accounting entity and some independent, external group, and (2) assets received in the exchange are capable of being objectively valued.　The mere appreciation in the market value of assets prior to a sale or other disposition is not a sufficient condition to recognize income.　Also, imputed savings arising from the self construction of assets to be used in one's own operations, is not income because there is no exchange.

The Supreme Court in *Eisner v. Macomber* [17] added the realization requirement to a judicial definition of income which had been formulated in earlier cases:

> Income may be defined as the gain derived from capital, from labor, or from both combined, provided it is understood to include profit gained through a sale or conversion of capital assets. * * * Here we have the essential matter: not a gain accruing to capital; not a *growth* or *increment* of value *in* investment;

13.　*Merchants Loan and Trust Co. v. Smietanka*, 1 USTC ¶ 42, 3 AFTR 3102, 41 S.Ct. 386 (USSC, 1921).

14.　*Ibid.*

15.　See Henry C. Simons, *Personal Income Taxation*, (University of Chicago Press, 1933) Ch. 2–3.

16.　See the American Accounting Association Committee Report on the "Realization Concept," *The Accounting Review*, April 1965, pp. 312–322.

17.　*Eisner v. Macomber*, 1 USTC ¶ 32, 3 AFTR 3020, 40 S.Ct. 189 (USSC, 1920).

but a gain, a profit, something of exchangeable value, *proceeding from* the property, *severed from* the capital, however invested or employed, and *coming in*, being *"derived"*—that is, *received* or *drawn by* the recipient for his separate use, benefit and disposal —*that* is, income derived from the property.

Thus, the early Supreme Court definition of income can simply be restated as the gain realized from capital, from labor, or from both combined.

As a result of cases subsequent to *Eisner v. Macomber*, the "from capital, from labor *   *   * " phrases can be deleted. For example, in *Glenshaw Glass Co.*,[18] the taxpayer received punitive damages from a supplier who had committed fraud and had violated federal anti-trust laws. Clearly, the damages were intended to be a punishment for the violator of the laws, and therefore, were not gain realized from capital, from labor, or from both combined. Nevertheless, the Supreme Court held that the punitive damages received by Glenshaw were income:

> Here we have instances of undeniable accessions to wealth, clearly realized, and over which the taxpayers have complete dominion.

Similarly, in other cases, the Supreme Court reasoned that embezzlement [19] and extortion proceeds [20] were income.

In summary, "income" represents an increase in wealth which is recognized for tax purposes only upon realization.

COMPARISON OF ACCOUNTING AND TAXABLE INCOME

Although income tax rules frequently parallel financial accounting measurement concepts, several differences should be noted. The following include some examples in which accounting and taxable income are different:

1. Accelerated depreciation methods used for tax purposes and straight line depreciation for accounting.

2. Product warranty reserves accrued for accounting purposes but not permitted for income tax.

3. Goodwill amortization for accounting purposes whereas no amortization is permitted under the income tax laws.

Therefore, many corporations report financial accounting income which is substantially different than the amounts reported for tax purposes.

---

18. *Comm. v. Glenshaw Glass Co.*, 55–1 USTC ¶ 9308, 47 AFTR 162, 75 S.Ct. 473 (USSC, 1955).

20. *Rutkin v. U. S.*, 52–1 USTC ¶ 9260, 41 AFTR 596, 72 S.Ct. 571 (USSC, 1952).

19. *Supra*, note 12.

Mertens includes the following discussion of the relationship between taxable and financial accounting income:

> Accounting principles are absorbed into the law of Federal income taxation where they are found to fit within the general framework of the taxing statute, or where they aid in securing uniformity of application. However, income for tax purposes is to be determined by the tax statute and not under accounting principles. The courts * * * have ordinarily accepted accounting theory only to the extent that the particular accounting principles have been shown to be reasonably well settled and where the acceptance of such principles did not require a strained construction of the statute but rather aided in its interpretation.[21]

FORM OF RECEIPT

Gross income is not limited to cash received. "It includes income realized in any form, whether in money, property, or services. Income may be realized [and recognized], therefore, in the form of services, meals, accommodations, stock or other property, as well as in cash."[22]

Example 1. An accountant prepared the tax return for a dentist in exchange for bridgework. The accountant recognizes taxable income equal to the fair market value of such bridgework.

Example 2. An employee realizes income if his employer allows him to use the company car for his vacation. The amount of the income is what the employee would have had to pay to rent a car for the trip.

Example 3. A stockholder realizes income when the corporation sells him property for less than its market value. The income is the difference between the market price of the property and the price the stockholder paid.

Example 4. A solvent debtor realizes income if his debt is discharged for less than the amount due the creditor.[23]

A transfer of property to a creditor in payment of a debt is a realizable event. The debtor must recognize income to the extent of the difference between his basis in the property he transferred and the amount of the reduction in the debt.

Example 5. The taxpayer borrowed $200,000 from a bank to build an apartment house, which served as security for the loan.

---

21. See Mertens, Law of Federal Taxation, § 5.03.

22. Reg. § 1.61–1(a).

23. Reg. § 1.61–12. See *U. S. v. Kirby Lumber Co.*, 2 USTC ¶ 814, 10 AFTR 458, 52 S.Ct. 4 (USSC, 1931).

Several years later, when the taxpayer's cost less accumulated depreciation on the apartment house was $80,000 and the balance on the debt was $120,000, the bank foreclosed, and took the apartment house in full satisfaction of the debt. The taxpayer must recognize $40,000 as income if he is solvent (fair market value of assets exceed liabilities) immediately following the cancellation of debt.

In *U. S. v. Davis* [24] the taxpayer who lived in a common law state transferred property which was held in his name to his wife pursuant to a divorce settlement. The Supreme Court held that the transfer was in satisfaction of the wife's marital rights, a realizable event, and that the husband must recognize income equal to the difference between the basis in the property and the value of the appreciated property.

EXCEPTIONS TO THE INCOME REALIZATION DOCTRINE

Over the years the Courts have provided an exception to the rule that any economic gain realized by the taxpayer is recognized as taxable income. Benefits received by the employee where the goods or services were actually provided for the benefit of the employer, and the employee had no control over their receipt, are not taxable income. An early case involved meals and lodging for a hotel manager who was required by his employer to live in the hotel and take his meals there. The Tax Court held that the value of the meals and lodging was not taxable income, reasoning as follows:

> Though there was an element of gain to the employee, in that he received subsistence and quarters which otherwise he would have had to supply for himself, he had nothing he could take, appropriate, use and expend according to his own dictates, but rather, the ends of the employer's business dominated and controlled, just as in the furnishing of a place to work and in the supplying of the tools and machinery with which to work. The fact that certain personal wants and needs of the employee were satisfied was plainly secondary and incidental to the employment. [25]

Therefore, taxable income is not realized by employees under a number of situations involving the receipt of indirect forms of economic benefit. For example:

1. An employer requires an employee to attend a convention in Hawaii and to perform significant services for the employer while there. The cost of the trip is not taxable income to the employee.

---

24. *U. S. v. Davis,* 62–2 USTC ¶ 9509, 9 AFTR2d 1625, 82 S.Ct. 1190 (USSC, 1962).

25. *Gunnar Van Rosen,* 17 T.C. 834 (1951).

2. The employee is required to have a mandatory annual physical examination the cost of which is paid by the employer.

3. The employee consumes food and beverages while entertaining a customer and the expenses are paid by the employer.

4. The employer provides $50,000 group-term life insurance coverage for the employee.

It takes very little imagination to see how it is possible to produce significant non-taxable fringe benefits for the employees. However, the expenditure must serve a business purpose of the employer, other than compensation to the employee, for the benefit to be considered a tax-free item.[26]

Return of Capital Doctrine. The gain on a transaction must be distinguished from the gross receipts or the sales price, since according to the law the tax is based upon taxable income and not upon gross receipts. This distinction is the basis for the "return of capital doctrine" succinctly expressed by the Supreme Court in *Doyle v. Mitchell Bros. Co.*[27]

    * * * We must withdraw from the gross proceeds an amount sufficient to restore the capital value that existed at the commencement of the period under consideration.

The return of capital doctrine simply means that the amount received from the sale or disposition of the property is reduced by its adjusted cost basis in arriving at the taxable gain.[28] For the sale of inventory assets, adjusted cost basis may be equated with cost of goods sold. The general rule is that gain is realized in the year of sale equal to the excess of the cash and the fair market value of property received over the adjusted basis of the disposed property. However, where the property received has no ascertainable fair market value (due to contingencies), the return of capital doctrine allows the taxpayer to defer all gain until he has collected an amount equal to the adjusted basis of the transferred assets.

This doctrine was applied in *Burnet v. Logan,*[29] where the taxpayer sold stock in a mining company for cash and for $.60 per ton of all ore to be taken from the mine. The Supreme Court concluded that "the promise to pay was so contingent, uncertain and indefinite that it cannot be considered the equivalent of cash or to have a fair market value." No gain was recognized until the total cash collected

---

26. *George D. Patterson v. Thomas,* 61–1 USTC ¶ 9310, 7 AFTR2d 862, 289 F.2d 108 (CA–2, 1960).

27. *Doyle v. Mitchell Bros. Co.,* 1 USTC ¶ 17, 1 AFTR 235, 38 S.Ct. 467 (USSC, 1916).

28. § 1001(a).

29. *Burnet v. Logan,* 2 USTC ¶ 736, 9 AFTR 1453, 51 S.Ct. 550 (USSC, 1931).

equaled the seller's basis in the stock, and subsequent collections were considered capital gain.

This doctrine is also referred to as the "open transaction" doctrine and has been applied to payments based upon a percentage of profits or gross receipts, transfers of property in exchange for a private annuity and to other situations where the promise to pay is contingent or the fair market value of the property received is indeterminable.[30] It should be noted that the IRS position is that the "open transaction" doctrine applies only in rare situations and that in most cases property received is capable of being valued.[31]

Damages awarded by a court or received in settlement of a lawsuit are often excluded from income by the application of the return of capital doctrine. Theoretically, damages awarded for a personal wrong committed against the taxpayer (e. g., alienation of affection, breach of promise to marry, invasion of privacy, slander) replace the "personal capital" destroyed by the wrongful acts.[32] Also excluded under this doctrine are damages for personal injury, such as sickness or the loss of a limb. However, damages awarded as a substitute for income are generally taxable, since the award is a restoration of lost profits or wages which would have been taxable.[33]

Where the amount received is for damages to property or damages to goodwill of a business, the taxpayer has income only to the extent the amount received exceeds the adjusted cost basis of the assets. Frequently, a business receiving a recovery of lost goodwill attributed to wrongful acts of a competitor has no cost of goodwill for tax purposes; therefore, none of the payment is a recovery of capital.[34]

YEAR OF INCLUSION

ANNUAL ACCOUNTING PERIOD

The annual accounting period is a basic component of our tax system. All taxable entities may use a calendar year to report in-

30. *U. S. v. Yerger,* 44–1 USTC ¶ 9282, 32 AFTR 855, 55 F.Supp. 521 (D.Ct.Pa.1944); *J. Darsie Lloyd,* 33 B.T.A. 903 (1936); *Clement v. U. S.,* 71–2 USTC ¶ 9519, 28 AFTR2d 71–5004, 331 F.Supp. 877 (D.Ct.N.C. 1971); But see Rev.Rul. 69–74, 1969–1 C.B. 43 and Rev.Rul. 71–492, 1971–2 C.B. 127.

31. Rev.Rul. 58–402, 1958–2 C.B. 15.

32. See Rev.Rul. 74–77, 1974–1 C.B. 33; *C. A. Hawkins,* 6 B.T.A. 1023 (1927); *L. McDonald,* 9 B.T.A. 1340 (1928).

33. *Hilda Kay,* 45 B.T.A. 98 (1941).

34. *Raytheon Production Corp. v. Comm.,* 44–2 USTC ¶ 9424, 32 AFTR 1155, 144 F.2d 110 (CA–1, 1944).

come. Those who keep adequate books and records may use a fiscal year—"a period of 12 months ending on the last day of any month other than December," or a 52–53 week year, ending on the same day of the week nearest the last day of the same month each year.[35] A retailer, choosing a 52–53 week year ending on the last Saturday in January, might choose January so that he can properly account for Christmas returns, and choose a Saturday to close the year so that inventory can be taken on Sunday. Automobile dealers often select a fiscal year ending in September so that the taxable year corresponds with their natural business year (the change in new car models).

Since the life-time earnings of a taxable entity must be divided up into these twelve-month intervals, and a tax rate schedule must be applied to the taxable income for each interval, it is often of more than just academic interest to determine the period into which a particular item of income is allocated. Determining this period is important because (1) Congress may change the rate schedule, (2) the entity's income may rise or fall between years so that placing the income in a particular year may mean that the income is taxed at a different marginal rate, or (3) the entity may undergo a change in its status, so that a different rate schedule is applied to its income (e. g., an individual might marry, or a proprietorship become incorporated.

ACCOUNTING METHODS

The year an item of income is subject to tax often depends upon which acceptable accounting method the taxpayer regularly employs. Most individuals and many businesses use the cash receipts and disbursements method of accounting whereas most corporations use the accrual method. § 1.446 of the Regulations requires the accrual method for determining purchases and sales where a taxpayer maintains inventory.[36] Therefore, some businesses employ a hybrid method which reflects a combination of the cash and accrual methods. In addition to these over-all accounting methods, under certain circumstances, a taxpayer may elect to spread his gain from the sale of property over the collection periods by electing the installment method;[37] contractors may either spread profits from contracts over the periods in which the work is done (the percentage completion method), or defer all profit until the year in which the project is completed.[38] However, the Commissioner may have the power to prescribe "the accounting method used by the taxpayer." Section 446(b) grants the Commissioner broad powers to police the "clearly reflected income" requirement of an accounting method:

35. §§ 441(a) and (d).

36. Reg. § 1.446–1(c)(2)(i).

37. §§ 453(a) and (b).

38. Reg. § 1.453–3.

[§ 446(b)]

(b) Exceptions—If no method of accounting has been regularly used by the taxpayer, or *if the method used does not clearly reflect income, the computation of taxable income shall be made under such method as, in the opinion of the Secretary or his delegate, does clearly reflect income.*

Also, a change in the method of accounting requires the consent of the Commissioner.[39]

Cash Receipts Method. Under the cash receipts method, property or services received are included in the taxpayer's gross income for the year of actual or "constructive" receipt by the taxpayer or his agent, regardless of whether the income was earned in that year.[40] The receipt of income need not be reduced to cash in the same year; rather, all that is necessary for income recognition is that property or services received have a fair market value—a cash equivalent.[41] Thus, if a cash basis taxpayer receives a note in payment for his services, he has income in that year equal to the value of the note. However, a creditor's mere promise to pay (e. g., an account receivable), with no supporting note, is not usually considered to have a fair market value.[42] Thus, the cash basis taxpayer defers the income from the services until the account receivable is collected.

The opportunity for deferring income is a major tax advantage to using the cash method of accounting. For example, a dentist who performs services in December and bills clients for such services may not receive the related cash until the following January. Therefore, in his first year in practice only 11 months income is reported. Thus, income of one month is deferred until the final year in practice, and the deferral will continue to grow as his practice grows.

Perhaps of more significance is the control to which a cash basis taxpayer has over the timing of the recognition of income and expense. For example, if the dentist were in a high income tax bracket in one particular year, he might elect to pay all outstanding bills for various expense items received prior to the end of the year since the year of payment generally determines the period in which the expenses are deductible.

Constructive Receipt. The doctrine of constructive receipt places certain limits upon the ability of cash basis taxpayers to arbitrarily shift income from one year to another so as to minimize total taxes. Regulation § 1.451–2(a) provides:

(a) *General Rule.* Income although not actually reduced to the taxpayer's possession is constructively received by him in the

---

39. § 446(e).

40. *Julia A. Strauss,* 2 B.T.A. 598 (1925).

41. Reg. §§ 1.446–1(a)(3) and (c)(1)(i).

42. *Alfred M. Bedell v. Comm.,* 1 USTC ¶ 359, 7 AFTR 8469, 30 F.2d 622 (CA–2, 1929).

taxable year during which it is credited to his account, set apart
for him or otherwise made available so that he could have drawn
upon it during the taxable year if notice of intention to withdraw
had been given. However, income is not constructively received
if the taxpayer's control of its receipt is subject to substantial
limitations or restrictions.

If the taxpayer is entitled to receive income, which is made available
to him, he cannot "turn his back" on it. The dentist is, therefore,
not permitted to defer income for December services by refusing to
accept payment until January. However, the doctrine of constructive
receipt does not reach income that the taxpayer is not yet entitled to
receive. For example, in *Cowden v. Comm.*[43] the taxpayer, while negotiating a mineral lease on property he owned, was offered a lump-
sum payment to be received in the first year of the lease. He declined the offer because of the adverse tax consequences that would
result from recognizing all of the income in one year. The prospective lessee, therefore, made another offer whereby the payments
would be spread over two years. Cowden accepted the second offer.
The Fifth Court of Appeals held that the taxpayer's refusal of the
initial offer, which included a lump-sum payment, did not result in
constructive receipt of income.

Some other examples of the application of the constructive receipt doctrine are summarized below:

Example 6. A salary check received by the taxpayer on December 31, 1946, but after banking hours, was taxable in 1946.
The check was property with a market value.[44]

Example 7. The controlling shareholder of a corporation accrued a bonus to himself on December 31, but waited until the
following year to have the check written. Since the shareholder
could control when the payment was to be made, the bonus was
constructively received on December 31st.[45]

Example 8. On December 31, the employer issued a bonus check
to an employee but asked him to hold it for a few days until the
company could make deposits to cover the check. The income
was not constructively received on December 31, since the issuer
did not have sufficient funds in his account to pay the debt.[46]

Example 9. Interest coupons which have matured and are payable, but which have not been cashed, are constructively received
in the taxable year during which the coupons mature, unless it

43. *Cowden v. Comm.*, 61–1 USTC ¶
9382, 7 AFTR2d 1160, 289 F.2d 20
(CA–5, 1961).

44. *C. F. Kahler,* 18 T.C. 31 (1952).

45. *W. C. Leonard & Co. v. U. S.*, 71–1
USTC ¶ 9290, 27AFTR2d 964, 324 F.
Supp. 422 (D.Ct.Miss.1971).

46. *L. M. Fischer*, 14 T.C. 792 (1950).

can be shown that there are no funds available for the payment of the interest.[47]

Example 10. Interest on bank savings accounts, and dividends on savings and loan deposits (treated as interest for tax purposes), is income to the depositor for the tax year when credited to his account.[48]

Example 11. Dividends on stock are not taxed until the check is received if the corporation, as a regular business policy, mails year-end dividends so that they cannot be received by the shareholder until January.[49]

Also, a partner,[50] Subchapter S Corporation shareholder,[51] and beneficiary of a trust,[52] are considered to constructively receive their shares of the partnership, corporation or trust income as of the last day of its tax year.

EXCEPTIONS APPLICABLE TO CASH BASIS TAXPAYERS

Certain U.S. Government savings bonds ("Series E") are issued at a discount and are redeemable for fixed amounts which increase at stated intervals. No interest payments are actually made; rather, the difference between the purchase price and the amount received upon redemption is the bond holder's income from the investment.

Under the general rules of tax accounting, a cash basis taxpayer does not recognize income until the bonds are actually redeemed. This deferral of income may be advantageous for taxpayers who are in high tax brackets and are approaching retirement. The redemption and subsequent recognition of taxable income during retirement years may produce favorable tax consequences if the taxpayer's effective rate of tax is lower.

The Code provides for a special election whereby the owner can include in his gross income the annual increment in redemption value.[53] The election may be advisable to avoid the "bunching" of income in the year of redemption. Also, tax savings can be achieved by making gifts of these bonds to children who then elect to report the annual increments in redemption price in gross income. If the children have no other source of income during these years, the bond interest can be offset by the child's personal exemption. When the election is made to report the income from the bonds on an annual basis, it applies to all such obligations the taxpayer owns at the time

47. Reg. § 1.451–2(b).

48. Ibid.

49. Ibid.

50. § 702(a).

51. § 1373(a).

52. § 652(a).

53. § 454(a).

of the election, and all such securities acquired subsequent to the election. A change in the method of reporting the income from the bonds requires permission of the Commissioner of Internal Revenue.[54]

Another exception to the general rules of cash basis accounting is a provision which allows farmers to defer the recognition of the crop insurance proceeds until the tax year following the tax year in which the crops were destroyed.[55] This provision protects the farmer from having to report two years income in one tax year.

> **Example 12.** The cash basis farmer completes his harvest in October 19X1 but does not collect his sales proceeds until the following January 19X2. In March 19X2 he plants a crop which is destroyed in August 19X2. He collects the crop insurance proceeds in September 19X2. Under the usual applications of accounting, the income from 19X1 harvest and the 19X2 crop insurance would be reported in 19X2. However, the farmer can elect (under Section 451(d)) to defer the 19X2 income from the insurance until 19X3.

Accrual Method. Under accrual accounting, an item is generally included in the gross income for the year in which it is earned, regardless of when the income is collected. The income is earned when (1) all the events have occurred which fix the right to receive such income and (2) the amount thereof can be determined with reasonable accuracy.[56]

The "all events" test is technically satisfied in the case of sales of property when title to the property passes to the buyer.[57] However, for inventories, the Regulations do not require the taxpayer to recognize income upon the passage of title. Rather, the income from these recurring sales may be accrued either (1) when the goods are shipped, (2) when the product is delivered or accepted, or (3) when the title to the goods actually passes, provided the method selected is consistently applied.[58]

Where the taxpayer's rights to the income are contested (e. g., a contractor who fails to meet specifications), the year in which the income is subject to tax depends upon whether payment has been received. According to the claim of right doctrine (discussed below), income cannot be deferred beyond the year of receipt of the payment. However, income does not accrue until a settlement of the claim is reached; only then is the right to receive income established.[59]

---

54. Ibid.

55. § 451(d).

56. Reg. § 1.451–1(a).

57. *Lucas v. North Texas Lumber Co.,* 2 USTC ¶ 484, 8 AFTR 10276, 50 S. Ct. 184 (USSC, 1929).

58. Reg. § 1.446–1(c)(1)(ii).

59. *Burnet v. Sanford and Brooks,* 2 USTC ¶ 636, 9 AFTR 603, 51 S.Ct. 150 (USSC, 1931).

If a taxpayer has the right to receive the income as of a particular date, it is not necessary that the exact amount of income be known at the date of accrual. The Regulations merely require a reasonably accurate estimate. If, in a later year, the exact amount of the income (previously accrued on the basis of an estimate) is determined, the difference is to be taken into account by adjusting the income of the later year.

Accrual of the income cannot be postponed simply because a portion of the income may have to be returned in a later year. In *Brown v. Helvering*,[60] the taxpayer earned commissions on insurance policies in the year of sale, but was required to return a portion of the premiums if a policy was cancelled in a later year. The Supreme Court ruled that all commissions were taxable in the year of sale, and the repayments were not deductible until actually paid.

Claim of Right Doctrine. This doctrine has evolved from court decisions which have held that an amount is includible in income upon actual or constructive receipt if the taxpayer has an unrestricted claim to such amounts. The fact that the claim is subsequently found to be invalid by a court does not change the fact that the claim did exist.[61] This doctrine applies to both cash-basis and accrual-basis taxpayers. The claim of right doctrine was set forth by the Supreme Court in *North American Oil Consolidated Co. v. Burnet*,[62] and has often been used to settle disputes as to the year taxpayers must report income from transactions involving claims.

In *North American Oil,* a dispute arose between the company and the Federal government as to who had title to certain oil producing land. Because of the dispute, the income from the property for the year 1916 was collected by a court appointed receiver. Although the receiver paid the money to North American in 1917, it was not until 1922 when the litigation was settled, and the court ruled that the oil company was actually entitled to the funds. The question before the Court in the tax case was: should the income be taxed when actually earned (1916), when released from escrow (1917), or when the dispute was finally resolved in 1922? The Supreme Court held that the income was taxable when the funds were released from escrow.

If a taxpayer received earnings under a claim of right without restrictions as to its disposition, he has received income which he is required to return [report on his tax return], even though it

60. *Brown v. Helvering*, 4 USTC ¶ 1223, 12 AFTR 128, 54 S.Ct. 356 (USSC, 1933).

61. *Healy v. Comm.*, 53–1 USTC ¶ 9292, 43 AFTR 382, 73 S.Ct. 671 (USSC, 1953).

62. *North American Oil Consolidated v. Burnet*, 3 USTC ¶ 943, 11 AFTR 16, 52 S.Ct. 613 (USSC, 1932).

may still be claimed that he is not entitled to retain the money, and even though he may be adjudged liable to restore its equivalent.

The claim of right doctrine has also been used to decide the year of inclusion where the taxpayer receives income that must later be returned. In *U. S. v. Lewis*,[63] the taxpayer received a bonus of $22,000 in 1944. In a later year, it was determined that the bonus had been improperly computed and Lewis had to repay the $11,000 to his employer. The Supreme Court ruled that a claim of right existed when the bonus was received:

> Until payment of the judgment in 1946, respondent Lewis had at all times claimed and used the full $22,000 unconditionally as his own, in the good faith though "*mistaken*" belief that he was entitled to the whole bonus.

Thus, the bonus was taxable in 1944, and the taxpayer was allowed to deduct an $11,000 loss on his 1946 return. Similarly, embezzlement proceeds are taxed in the year of receipt, even though in a later year the taxpayer is "caught" and liable for the amount taken.

The underlying rationale for the claim of right doctrine was developed in an earlier case where the Supreme Court stressed the relationship of the annual accounting requirement to the federal fiscal system:

> It is the essence of any system of taxation that it should produce revenue ascertainable and payable at regular intervals. Only by such a system is it practicable to produce a regular flow of income and apply methods of accounting, assessment and collection capable of practical operation.[64]

Thus, the claim of right doctrine serves to insure a steady flow of Federal revenues by levying tax on income in the period the taxpayer receives the benefits and has the cash to pay the tax, rather than deferring the tax until all possible claims have been settled.

For a cash basis taxpayer, there must be a receipt of cash or property, whereas an accrual basis taxpayer must merely have the right to receive the income during the tax year.[65] Thus, if an accrual basis taxpayer sells goods on account which are uncollected at the end of the year and the seller is liable under a guarantee that lapses in the following year, he cannot defer income from the sale until the end of the period covered by the guarantee. The income is taxed in the year of sale when the right to payment was established.

However, the claim of right doctrine generally does not reach uncollected income that is contested at the end of the particular tax year; nor does it apply if, at the time of receipt, the taxpayer knew

63. *U. S. v. Lewis*, 51–1 USTC ¶ 9211,   64. *Supra*, note 59.
     40 AFTR 258, 71 S.Ct. 522 (USSC,
     1951).   65. Reg. § 1.451–1(a).

he was under an absolute obligation to make repayment.[66] For example, a contractor who, allegedly, did not meet specifications, may be able to defer income from the contract until the claim is settled. If a customer erroneously paid a bill twice, the seller would have a liability to the buyer for the overpayment, and thus the overpayment is not income. Also, a lessor who receives a deposit from the lessee to secure performance, generally has an obligation to repay, and thus has no income until a lessee violates the terms of the lease.[67] (However, if the deposit is in fact a prepayment of rent, it is taxed in the year of receipt, as discussed below.)

Prepaid Income. For financial reporting purposes, payments received from customers prior to being earned are reflected as prepaid income and as a liability to the customer. However, for tax purposes, the prepaid income is often taxed in the year of receipt. For example, if a tenant pays the January rent in the preceding December, an accrual (or cash) basis landlord must report the income for tax purposes as earned in December.

The Commissioner has often justified taxing prepaid income in the year of receipt by applying the claim of right doctrine to tax income in the year the recipient has unrestricted use of the funds. The Commissioner has been especially successful in using the doctrine to tax prepayments for services in the year of receipt.[68] Taxpayers have argued that taxing prepaid income in the year of receipt violates the "clearly reflect income" requirement since expenses related to earning the income are deductible only in later years. Therefore, income and expenses are not properly matched. However, the taxpayer has had only limited success with this argument.[69]

The Commissioner has won in some cases involving prepaid dues because the taxpayer could not demonstrate that prorating income over the period covered by the dues would clearly reflect income. In *Automobile Club of Michigan,*[70] the Commissioner argued that the Association's annual membership dues were taxable in the year of receipt under the claim of right doctrine. The Association argued that the Commissioner's method did not clearly reflect income; that is, under generally accepted accounting principles, the income should be

---

66. *Comm. v. W. W. Turney,* 36–1 USTC ¶ 9168, 17 AFTR 679, 82 F.2d 661 (CA–5, 1936).

67. *John Mantell,* 17 T.C. 1143 (1952).

68. *South Dade Farms, Inc. v. Comm.,* 43–2 USTC ¶ 9634, 31 AFTR 842, 138 F.2d 818 (CA–5, 1943).

69. In a recent case, a District court held in favor of the taxpayer where

he argued that deferring the recognition of prepaid income was necessary to have a proper matching of revenues and expenses. See *Automated Marketing Systems, Inc. v. Comm.,* 74–2 USTC ¶ 9711, 34 AFTR2d 74–5427 (CA–7, 1975).

70. *Automobile Club of Michigan v. Comm.,* 57–1 USTC ¶ 9593, 50 AFTR 1967, 77 S.Ct. 707 (USSC, 1957).

prorated over the period covered by dues. The Supreme Court rejected the taxpayer's position on the basis that the Association's accounting method was "artificial." The Court reasoned that substantially all the services rendered were performed on the demand of the members and since such performance had no fixed future dates, the mere passage of time was no better basis for recognizing income than the Commissioner's method. Furthermore, the Association could not predict in which period it would incur costs (and the amount) for a particular member; therefore, it could not justify proration on the basis of matching costs and revenues.[71]

In *Artnell Company v. Comm.*,[72] the Seventh Court of Appeals distinguished season ticket sales to Chicago White Sox baseball games from the collection of auto association membership dues. The baseball team played its games on definite dates. Thus, the taxpayer could demonstrate when the income would be earned and the taxpayer was, therefore, permitted to defer the income until the games were played.

The Commissioner has also lost on other grounds. In some cases involving sales of unascertained goods, the sales proceeds received prior to the time the goods were set aside for the customer were held to be a mere deposit and no income was recognized until the goods were set aside.[73] In *Consolidated-Hammer Dry Plate & Film Co. v. Comm.*,[74] the taxpayer received partial payment from the government on a contract. The government had not yet accepted the finished product. Therefore, the court held the partial payments "were attributes of a financing arrangement in the nature of a loan and the proceeds of a loan do not constitute taxable income." Also, Congress has intervened in the controversy. In 1958 and 1961 Sections 455 and 456 were enacted. Section 455 allows the taxpayer to prorate subscriptions income over the subscription period, and Section 456 allows certain membership organizations to prorate dues over the membership period.

Deferral of Advance Payments. Finally, in 1971, the IRS modified its position on certain types of prepaid income, and issued new Regulations and Procedures.[75]

71. See also *American Automobile Association v. U. S.*, 61–2 USTC ¶ 9517, 7 AFTR2d 1618, 81 S.Ct. 1727 (USSC, 1961); *Schlude v. Comm.*, 63–1 USTC ¶ 9284, 11 AFTR2d 751, 83 S.Ct. 601 (USSC, 1963).

72. *Artnell Company v. Comm.*, 68–2 USTC ¶ 9593, 22 AFTR2d 5590, 400 F.2d 981 (CA–7, 1968).

73. *Veenstra & DeHavaan Coal Co.*, 11 T.C. 964 (1948).

74. *Consolidated Hammer Dry Plate & Film Co. v. Comm.*, 63–1 USTC ¶ 9494, 11 AFTR2d 1518, 317 F.2d 829 (CA–7, 1963).

75. Rev.Proc. 71–21, 1971–2 C.B. 549.

Reg. § 1.451–5 applies to advance payments for goods and long-term contracts. In summary, the regulation permits accrual basis taxpayers to defer the recognition of income from advance payments:

(1) For the future sale of inventories that are not on hand on the last day of the year, and the amount collected is less than the seller's cost of the goods.

(2) For the building, installation, or construction of an item which will not be completed within the same taxable year.

Deferral of such advance payments is permitted if the taxpayer's method of accounting is not at variance with the method used for financial reporting purposes.[76] An exception applies where substantial advance payments have been received and the goods are either available through normal supply channels or are included in the taxpayer's inventory. If these conditions exist, all advance payments received must be included in income by the end of the second taxable year following the year substantial advance payments (receipts equal to or in excess of the estimated cost of goods sold) are received.[77]

Revenue Procedure 71–21 permits an accrual basis taxpayer to defer advance payments for services to be performed by the end of the tax year following the year of receipt. No deferral is allowed if the taxpayer may be required to perform the services, under the agreement, after the tax year following the year of receipt of the advance payment.

> **Example 13.** The Best Pest Control Co. sells its services under 12, 18 and 24 month contracts. The company services each customer every month. In April of the current year, the company sold customer contracts as follows:

Length of Contract	Total Proceeds
12 months	$6,000
18 months	3,600
24 months	2,400

Fifteen hundred dollars of the $6,000 may be deferred, $\frac{3}{12} \times$ $6,000, and $1,800 of the $3,600 may be deferred since it will not be earned until the next year. However, the entire $2,400 received on the 24 month contracts is taxable in the year of receipt, since a part of the income will still be unearned by the end of the tax year following the year of receipt.

The Revenue Procedure does not apply to prepaid rent, prepaid interest, or amounts received under guarantee or warranty contracts. Thus, the income will still be taxed in the year of receipt "if collected prior to the time the income is actually earned." However, in the case of "rents" there is a special definition of the term:

---

76. Reg. § 1.451–5(b)(2).   **77.** See Reg. § 1.451–5(c)(4), Example.

> "Rent" does not include payments for the use of occupancy of rooms or other space where significant services are also rendered to the occupant * * *.

The effect of the definition is to allow hotels, motels, tourist homes, and convalescent homes to defer the recognition of income under the rules discussed above.

In summary, Revenue Procedure 71–21 will result in conformity of tax and financial accounting in a very limited number of prepaid income cases. It is not apparent why prepaid rents and interest cannot be deferred, why revenues under some service contracts may be spread over two years, and why revenues under longer service contracts must be reported in one year. Revenue Procedure 71–21 will lessen the number of controversies involving prepaid income, but a logically consistent policy has not yet evolved.

INCOME SOURCES

PERSONAL SERVICES

It is a well established principle of taxation that the income from personal services must be included in the gross income of the person who performs the services. This principle was first established in a Supreme Court decision, *Lucas v. Earl*.[78] Mr. Earl had entered into a binding agreement with his wife whereby she was to receive one-half of his salary. Justice Holmes used the celebrated "fruit and tree" metaphor to explain that the fruit (income) must be attributed to the tree from which it came (Mr. Earl's services). Thus, a mere assignment of the income did not shift the liability for the tax.

In the case of a child, the Code specifically provides that amounts earned from his personal services must be included in the child's gross income, even though the income is paid to other persons such as parents. However, if the income is used by the parents to satisfy their legal obligation to support the child, the parents must recognize taxable income from the discharge of that obligation.[79]

ASSIGNMENT OF INCOME FROM PROPERTY

Income from property (e. g., interest, dividends, rent) must be included in the gross income of the owner of the property.[80] Thus, where the father clipped interest coupons from bonds shortly before the interest payment date and gave the coupons to his son, the inter-

78. *Lucas v. Earl*, 2 USTC ¶ 496, 8   **80.** *Galt v. Comm.*, 54–2 USTC ¶ 9457,
    AFTR 10287, 50 S.Ct. 241 (USSC,   46 AFTR 633, 216 F.2d 41 (CA–7,
    1930).   1954).

79. Rev.Rul. 56–484, 1956–2 C.B. 23.

est was taxed to the father.[81] Also, a father who assigned rents from rental property to his son, was taxed on the rent since the father retained ownership of the property.[82] Taxpayers have attempted to assign the income from property while maintaining well disguised controls that approximate actual ownership of the property. In *Helvering v. Clifford*,[83] the grantor transferred common stocks to a trust. The stock was to remain in the trust for five years, at which point complete ownership would revert to the grantor. While the property was in trust, the grantor had absolute discretion over the amount of income that was to be distributed to the income beneficiary. Also, he retained the right to vote the stock and could sell the stock and reinvest the proceeds. The Supreme Court upheld a lower court decision that the grantor had retained so many of the benefits of ownership of the property that the "transfer" would not be recognized for tax purposes; hence, the grantor was taxed on the income from the property. In cases such as *Clifford*, the courts usually look to the substance of the transaction rather than its form, to determine who is the equitable owner of the propery.

Other questions associated with transfers of income-producing property are: who is to pay the tax on income accrued at the time of the transfer and when does the income accrue? The position of the Internal Revenue Service is that in the case of a gift, interest accrues on a daily basis, but that the cash basis donor does not recognize the income until it is collected by the donee.[84]

> **Example 14.** Father, a cash basis taxpayer, gave son $10,000 face amount bonds with an 8% stated rate of interest. The gift was made on November 30th and the interest is payable each January 1. When the son collects the interest in the following January, Father must recognize (.08) (10,000 × 334/365 = $732 interest income. The son will recognize $68 interest income.

Where there is a sale of property with accrued interest, a portion of the selling price is treated as interest and is taxed to the seller in the year of sale.

Tax on Dividends. Dividends do not accrue on a daily basis since the declaration of the dividend is at the discretion of the corporation's board of directors; but once the dividend is declared, the Tax Court has held that a donor does not shift the tax liability to the donee even though the gift is made before the "record date," which is the date the corporation looks to its stockholder's ledger to determine who should receive the dividend check.[85] The Court reasoned that the

---

81. *Helvering v. Horst*, 40–2 USTC ¶ 9787, 24 AFTR 1058, 61 S.Ct. 144 (USSC, 1940).

82. *Supra*, note 80.

83. *Helvering v. Clifford*, 40–1 USTC ¶ 9265, 23 AFTR 1077, 60 S.Ct. 554 (USSC, 1940).

84. Rev.Rul. 72–312, 1972–3 C.B. 22.

85. *M. G. Anton*, 34 T.C. 842 (1960).

"fruit" had sufficiently ripened at the date of declaration to tax the dividend to the donor of the stock.

Upon the sale of stock, dividends are generally taxed to the person who is entitled to receive the dividend. Thus, if the stock is sold after the declaration date but before the date of record, the purchaser will be taxed on the dividends since he will receive the income.[86] This rule can cause some inequities. The purchaser of stock during the post declaration and pre-record date interval will in effect pay for the right to collect the dividend, and thus it would seem that the collection of the declared dividend should be treated as a return of capital, i. e., an adjustment of the purchase price. Since the tax law does not provide for an adjustment of the purchase or selling price, the seller's basis for determining capital gain or loss is similarly affected.

Example 15. On June 20th Father owned 200 shares of XYZ, Inc., common stock with a cost and market value of $50 per share. On June 21, the corporation declared a $1 per share dividend payable on July 6 to stockholders on record June 30. The price of the stock increased by $1 per share following the declaration of the dividend and on June 22, Father sold 100 shares for $5,100 and gave 100 shares to his son. Father would report a $100 capital gain on the sale of the stock on June 22 and $100 dividend income on July 6 when son collected the dividend.

INCOME FROM PARTNERSHIPS, SUBCHAPTER S CORPORATIONS, TRUSTS AND ESTATES

Each partner must report his distributive share of the partnership's income and deductions for the partnership's tax year ending within or with his tax year.[87] The income must be reported by each partner as if earned even if such amounts are not actually distributed.

A shareholder in a Subchapter S Corporation, a corporation that has elected to be treated in most respects as a partnership, must report his share of the corporation's "undistributed taxable income" for the corporation's tax year ending with or within his tax year.[88] In addition, the shareholder must include in income for the tax year received actual distributions by the corporation out of its current year's income.

Example 16. Subnormal Inc., a Subchapter S Corporation, earned taxable income of $60,000 during its fiscal year ended June 30th, 19X2. The corporation distributed as a dividend to each of its fifty percent shareholder's $20,000 on December 15, 19X1.

---

86. Reg. § 1.61–9(c).   **88.** Reg. § 1.1373–1(a).

87. Reg. § 1.706–1(a)(1).

Each calendar year shareholder must report $20,000 income in 19X1 as a distribution out of the corporation's current year's income, and $10,000 in 19X2 as his share of the corporation's "undistributed taxable income." If the business had been operated as a partnership, the calendar year partners would recognize no income until 19X2, at the close of the partnership tax year.

The beneficiaries of estates and trusts are generally taxed on the income earned by the estates or trusts that is actually distributed or required to be distributed to them.[89] Any of the income not taxed to the beneficiaries is taxed to the estate or trust.

INCOME IN COMMUNITY PROPERTY STATES

State law in Louisiana, Texas, New Mexico, Arizona, California, Washington, Idaho and Nevada is based upon a community property system. The basic difference between common law and community property systems centers around the property rights possessed by married persons.

Property may be held separately in a community property state if it is acquired prior to marriage or property is received by gift or inheritance following marriage. Otherwise, any property held is deemed to be owned in equal shares by the married persons.

Income from personal services, e. g. salaries and wages and income from community property is treated as being earned equally by both spouses in all of the community property states. However, in Texas and in certain other community states, income from separate property is deemed to be community property. In other community property states such as California, income from separate property is treated as separate property.

> **Example 17.** H and W (spouses) live in Texas, a community property state. W inherited 1,000 shares of XYZ Company stock from her father which paid $2,000 of taxable dividends during the year. H earned $20,000 salary from his employer.
>
> 1. W's income is $1,000 from the stock and $10,000 salary or $11,000.
>
> 2. H's income is $1,000 from the stock and $10,000 salary or $11,000.
>
> 3. If H and W lived in California, H's income would be only $10,000 from the salary and W's income would be $2,000 from the dividends on the stock and $10,000 salary or $12,000.
>
> 4. In a common law state, W's income would consist solely of $2,000 dividend income whereas the $20,000 salary would be deemed to be earned by H.

89. §§ 652(a) and 662(a).

TAX PLANNING CONSIDERATIONS

Despite restrictions which are placed upon an individual's ability to shift income among family members, i. e., restrictions upon the assignment of income to others, various tax planning opportunities are still available to accomplish these objectives. For example, the tax liability of a family can be minimized by shifting income among members of the family—from higher to lower bracket family members. This can be accomplished through gifts of income producing property.

The deferral of taxes is also a worthy goal of the tax planner since tax deferrals are tantamount to interest free loans from the government. The taxpayer can often defer the recognition of income from appreciated property by postponing the realizable event, i. e., a sale or exchange of the property. If the taxpayer needs cash, obtaining a loan by using the appreciated property as collateral may be the least costly alternative.

In the case of the accrual basis taxpayer receiving advance payments from customers, the transactions should be structured so as to avoid paying a tax on income prior to the time the income is actually earned. Revenue Procedure 71–21 provides the guidelines for deferring the tax on prepayments for services, and Reg. § 1.451–5 provides the guidelines for sales of goods. Also, with both the cash and accrual basis taxpayer, income can sometimes be deferred by providing that advance payments are to be treated as deposits rather than prepaid income.

PROBLEM MATERIALS

Questions for Class Discussion

1. Our income tax system for individuals is sometimes described as "progressive." What is meant by the term progressive?

2. What difference does it make whether a deduction is classified as "for adjusted gross income" or as an itemized deduction?

3. What are some of the differences between accounting tax and economic concepts of income?

4. Which of the following would be considered "income" for the current year by an economist, but would not be gross income for tax purposes? Explain the reasoning for each difference.

   (a) Securities acquired two years ago for $10,000 had a value at the beginning of the current year of $12,000, and a value at the end of the year of $13,000.

(b) An individual lives in the home he owns.

(c) A corporation obtained a loan from a bank.

(d) A stockholder paid the corporation $3,000 for property valued at $5,000.

(e) An individual owned property which was stolen. The cost of the property three years ago was $2,000 and his insurance company paid him $6,000, the value of the property on the date of theft.

(f) At the end of the current year a shareholder sold his stock for 200% of all dividends to be paid on the stock from the date of sale until his death.

(g) An individual was involved in an automobile accident and lost the use of his left foot. He sued the other party involved in the accident, and was awarded $25,000 for physical damages.

(h) An individual found a box of seventeenth century Spanish coins while diving in international waters.

(i) An employer provides free coffee for all of his employees.

(j) An individual received a $200 price rebate from the manufacturer when he purchased a new car.

5. In 19X1 a farmer incurred costs of $15,000 to raise corn with a market value of $21,000. In 19X2 he fed the corn to his hogs and they gained 80,000 pounds. At the end of 19X2 he sold the hogs for $.50 per pound. When did the farmer realize income from the above?

6. Does a taxpayer realize income when he makes a gift?

7. What are some nontaxable fringe benefits an employer can provide employees?

8. Does an attorney realize income if he writes a medical doctor's will in exchange for a "free" physical examination? Explain.

9. Does a taxpayer realize income from an award received from the court as a result of a slander suit? Explain.

10. If an item of income is subject to tax, what difference could it make as to whether the income is taxed in this year or next year?

11. Under what conditions must the taxpayer use the accrual method of accounting?

12. Can a taxpayer use the cash method to report his salary income, and the accrual method to report his interest income?

13. A corporation pays all of its monthly salaried employees on the last Friday in each month. What would be the tax consequences to the employees if the date of payment were changed to the first Monday of the following month?

14. What are some possible tax advantages from the use of the cash method of accounting?

15. What is the constructive receipt doctrine?

16. When is income received, that is being contested, subject to tax?

17. What alternatives are available for reporting interest income from Series E–U.S. Government bonds?

18. Compare the accounting and tax treatments of income collected by an accrual basis taxpayer prior to the time it is earned.

19. Compare the facts and issues in North American Oil Consolidated Company with a case involving prepaid rent income. Are they similar enough to warrant the application of the claim of right doctrine (as developed in the former) to the prepaid rent income case?

20. On what grounds did the Supreme Court reject the Automobile Association of Michigan's argument that prorating the income from dues over the period covered by the dues was necessary to "clearly reflect" the Association's income?

21. The taxpayer is in the wholesale hardware business. His customers pay for the goods at the time they place the order. Often the taxpayer is out of stock on particular items and must back-order the goods. When this occurs, the taxpayer usually retains the customer's payment, orders the goods from the manufacturer, and ships them to the customer within a month. At the end of the year there were several unfilled orders. Is it possible to defer the recognition of income from the receipt of advance payments on the unfilled orders?

22. Under what conditions can the tax on income from property be shifted between individuals?

23. What difference does it make relative to the reporting of income from property and personal services if married taxpayers reside in a community property state?

24. Contrast the Texas community property rules with the California community property system for reflecting income from separate property.

Problems

1. Mr. and Mrs. A file a joint return and have two dependent children. During the current year Mr. A received salary and interest totaling $10,500, and his wife earned $3,000 in a part-time job. He had $380 in non-reimbursed travel expenses in connection with his job, and had other allowable deductions as follows:

Charitable contributions	$ 600
State and local income, property and sales tax	1,400
Interest paid	2,000

Mr. and Mrs. A had $1,700 federal income taxes withheld from their wages.

Compute Mr. and Mrs. A's (1) adjusted gross income, (2) taxable income (3) gross tax, and (4) net taxes payable or refund due.

2. Mr. B is married, files a joint return and has $5,000 in itemized deductions and exemptions. He owns an unincorporated business which earns $80,000 per year. Mr. B also receives $2,000 interest per year. Assuming the business is incorporated, and Mr. B receives a salary of $55,000 per year, compare the total taxes on the $80,000 income from the unincorporated business with the total tax on his income and the Corporation's taxable income of $25,000.

3. Which of the following payments for damages would be taxable?

   (a) A corporation received $100,000 from a competitor for infringement upon its patent rights.

   (b) A woman of ill repute is paid $60,000 because her personal files were incorporated in a biography without her consent.

   (c) A client is paid $12,000 by his investment counselor as reimbursement for a loss resulting from the adviser's poor advice.

4. Determine the taxpayer's income for tax purposes in each of the following cases:

   (a) In the current year the RST Corp. purchased in the market $1,000,000 par value of its bonds, and paid the bondholders $980,000 plus accrued interest. The bonds had been issued 10 years ago at par, and were to mature in 25 years from the date of issue. Does the corporation recognize income from the purchase of the bonds?

   (b) A stockholder of a corporation sold property to that corporation for $60,000, which was his cost. The value of the property on the date of sale was $50,000. Does the taxpayer have any taxable income from the sale?

   (c) Tom Brown was a football coach at a state university. Because of his disappointing record, he was asked to resign and accept one-half of his pay for the remaining three years of his contract. The coach resigned accepting $30,000.

   (d) Joe Smith transferred some farm land with a cost of $10,000 to a creditor in satisfaction of Joe's $15,000 debt.

5. Ed Black sold his business for $50,000 plus 5% of gross sales from the business for the 3 years following the sale. His collections under the 3 year agreement were:

Year 1	$ 8,000
Year 2	12,000
Year 3	6,000

Ed's basis in the business was $60,000. What is Ed's gross income from the sale in the year of the sale, in Year 1, Year 2, and Year 3?

6. Dr. Dooalot is a very successful neuro-surgeon. The charge for an office visit is either paid on the date of visit or within one month. However, surgery patients often issue a 60 day note in payment of his fee, and the notes have a value equal to their face amount. Most of these patients are covered by insurance so they bill the insurance company, collect the cash, and then pay off the note. From the information below compute Dr. Dooalot's gross income by (1) the cash basis and (2) the accrual basis of accounting.

Office visits

Cash received at the time of visits	$15,000
Collections on accounts receivable	40,000
Accounts receivable, beginning of the year	6,000
Accounts receivable, end of the year	10,000

Surgery

Collections on notes	$50,000
Notes receivable, beginning of year	8,000
Notes receivable, end of the year	14,000

7. When would a cash basis taxpayer recognize the income in each of the following situations?

(a) The taxpayer's payroll check is mailed from the home office on December 31 and is delivered to him in a local office on January 3 of the following year.

(b) The taxpayer who was entitled to a $10,000 bonus on December 15 of the current year asked his employer to place it in an escrow account on his behalf with the agreement that he would not withdraw it until age 65 (in 10 years). If he died before age 65, the $10,000 would be paid to his heirs.

(c) A medical doctor had several Blue Cross claims which, if mailed in by the end of November, would be paid in December. However, he told his office manager not to process the claims until December 1 so payment would not be received until January of the following year.

8. What would be the tax effects of the following transactions to employees, using the cash method of accounting?

(a) An employee was awarded a bonus based on 10 percent of the corporation's profits. The following year it was discovered that the profits had been overstated due to an arithmetical error. As a result the employee was required to refund $2,000 of the amount received in the previous year.

(b) On December 31, an employee received a $500 advance for his estimated traveling expenses for the following January. He actually spent $480 in January, and retained the $20 to apply to February expenses.

9. (a) On December 27, Ed White agreed to buy land from Joe Green for $75,000 but Green's lawyer was out of town, and the sale could not be formally closed until the following January. Does Green, an accrual basis taxpayer, report his gain as accruing in December, or should the gain be reported in January of the following year?

(b) Jim Morris owned an office building which was leased to tenants under long-term leases yielding annual rents of $100,000. He sold the building for a price based on three times the annual rents, and collected $300,000 on the date of sale. Under the sale agreement, Morris was to reimburse the buyer for all rents lost during the three year period due to lease cancellations or non-payments by tenants. Since the exact amount of the gain will not be known until the third year following the sale, can Morris postpone the recognition of his gain until that year?

10. The Serenity Garden Apartments, an accrual basis taxpayer, requires each new tenant to make a $200 deposit upon signing a lease. If the tenant breaks the lease, he forfeits the deposit. Also, when a tenant moves (upon expiration of his lease), his apartment is inspected, and any damages are deducted from the deposit. During the current year Serenity collected $15,000 in deposits from new tenants, withheld $9,000 for damages and forfeitures from old tenants, and refunded $5,000. (a) What are the effects of these items on Serenity's taxable income? (b) Assume the $15,000 collected was for a payment of the last month's rent under the lease. Would the $15,000 be taxable in the year of receipt?

11. (a) An automobile dealer has several new cars in his inventory, but often he does not have the right combination of body style, color, and accessories. For some customers he makes an offer to sell a car at a certain price, accepts a deposit, and then orders the car from the manufacturer. When the car is received from the manufacturer, the deal is closed and the dealer receives the balance of the sales price. At the end of the current year, the dealer has deposits totaling $8,200 for cars that have not been received from the manufacturer. When is the $8,200 subject to tax?

(b) The Peace of Mind Exterminating Company, a calendar year taxpayer, contracts to service homeowners once a month under a one or two year contract. On April 1 of the current year, the company sold a customer a one year contract for $60. How much of the $60 is taxable in the current year if you assume the company is an accrual basis taxpayer? If the $60 were a payment on a 2 year contract, how much would be taxed in the year the contract was sold?

(c) The taxpayer owns an amusement park whose fiscal year ends September 30. To increase business during the fall and winter months, he sold passes that would allow the holder to ride "free" during the months of October through March. During the month of September he collected $6,000 from the sale of passes for the upcoming Fall and Winter. When will the $6,000 be taxable to the accrual basis taxpayer?

(d) The taxpayer is in the office equipment rental business and uses the accrual basis of accounting. In December he collected $5,000 in rents for the following January. When is the $5,000 taxable?

12. On November 30, Father gave Son a $10,000 face amount corporate bond. Six percent interest was payable on the bond each January 1. Also on November 30, he gave common stock of ABC Corp. to his son. On November 29, a dividend had been declared on the stock payable on December 10 to stockholders of record as of December 5. Son collected $600 in dividends on the stock on December 10. How much interest and dividend income must Father report and in which year must the Father report his interest income (if any)?

13. Father owned the controlling interest in a corporation. Son was a minority shareholder in the same corporation. Son was a sailing enthusiast but could not afford a boat, so Father had the corporation purchase a boat, which would be available to Son at all times. What are the possible tax consequences of the Son's use of the corporation's boat?

14. H and W were divorced on December 31, 19X1. H earned $30,-000 salary from his employer during the year whereas W's salary was $16,000. W also received $8,000 taxable dividends from stock which is held as separate property.

a. If H and W reside in Texas, how much income should be reported by each on their separate tax returns for 19X1?

b. If amounts are withheld from their salaries, how are these amounts reported on H and W's separate returns?

c. If H and W reside in a common law state, how much income should be reported by each on their separate returns?

Research Problems

1.   K. E. Man is the Vice-President of a large publicly held corpo-
     ration. As an officer he has participated in the company's bonus
     plan for several years. In a previous year the bonuses given
     were in the form of annuity contracts purchased from an insur-
     ance company. The contracts were non-transferable, and pay-
     ments did not begin until the employee reached age 65.

     Mr. Man's return was examined and the revenue agent contends
     that Mr. Man should include the purchase price of the annuity
     in his income for the year he received the contract. Since the
     annuity is nontransferable and Mr. Man did not have the option
     to receive cash, Mr. Man does not think he should have to recog-
     nize any income until he begins collecting on the annuity con-
     tract.

     The taxpayer asks your opinion on the matter.

2.   The taxpayer won $160,000 in the Irish Sweepstakes. However,
     because he is a minor (14 years old) local law requires that the
     winnings be placed in escrow and not be withdrawn until he is
     18 years old.
     When is the income subject to tax?

3.   Your client purchased convertible preferred stock in RST, Inc.
     several years ago. His original purchase price of the stock
     was $1,000, and the preferred stock is convertible into common
     stock with a value of $2,500. He would like to know the tax
     consequences of converting the preferred into common stock.

4.   Mr. White is a commissioned agent for a large insurance com-
     pany. During the year he purchased a policy on his life and the
     lives of his children and received a commission. White treated
     the commissions on these policies as a reduction in cost rather
     than income. However, the Internal Revenue Service Agent says
     White must include the commissions in his gross income. The
     taxpayer seeks your assistance in resolving the matter with the
     agent.

Chapter 5

GROSS INCOME—INCLUSIONS AND EXCLUSIONS

ITEMS SPECIFICALLY INCLUDED IN GROSS INCOME

The previous chapter discussed the concepts and judicial doctrines which affect the determination of gross income. At this point it is necessary to focus upon specific items which are either inclusions or exclusions from gross income.

ALIMONY AND SEPARATE MAINTENANCE PAYMENTS

Alimony and separate maintenance payments made by one spouse to another result in a shifting of income from the paying to the receiving spouse. Prior to 1942 there was no provision for alimony in the Code. In addition, a 1917 Supreme Court decision held that the wife was not taxed on the alimony she received and the husband was not allowed a deduction for the alimony payment.[1] Thus, the husband was required to bear the tax burden for amounts which were effectively shifted to his former spouse. In 1942 the Code was amended to alleviate this inequitable condition by making the alimo-

1. *Gould v. Gould*, 1 USTC ¶ 13, 3 AFTR 2958, 38 S.Ct. 53 (USSC, 1917)

ny taxable to the recipient and deductible by the payor. For years beginning after December 31, 1976 the person making the alimony payments is allowed a deduction *for* adjusted gross income.

Since 1942 the Code has been further amended to establish an overriding "Federal concept" of what constitutes alimony so that legal definitions under state law are not controlling. Under current law, alimony payments are taxable to the wife and deductible by the husband where such payments are periodic payments: (1) made pursuant to a decree of divorce or separate maintenance, (2) made pursuant to a written separation agreement or, (3) pursuant to a decree of support.[2] The payments must be in "discharge of a legal obligation arising from the marital or family relationship."[3]

Example 1. The terms of the divorce decree require S to make monthly alimony payments of $1,000 to W. If S makes *voluntary* payments of $2,000 per month, the $1,000 excess is not deductible by S or includible in W's gross income.

Property Settlements. The divorce or separation agreement often includes a division of the property accumulated during marriage as well as a provision to provide for future support. The property division is not considered to be alimony since a property settlement is a mere redistribution of property rights between the individual spouses. Conversely, payments for future support are in discharge of the husband's legal obligation and, therefore qualify as alimony. Despite the fact that property settlements do not qualify as alimony, a transfer of property owned by a husband to his wife (or vice versa) is a taxable event. If the value of the transferred property exceeds its basis, the transferor (husband) recognizes gain on the exchange.[4]

Often, the property settlement provides for a lump-sum payment of the principal amount. Since a lump-sum is not a "periodic payment," none of it can be considered alimony. However, § 71 specifies that if the principal sum is paid in installments, it will still be treated as alimony provided (1) the principal sum is paid over a period ending more than 10 years from the date of the agreement; or, (2) the payments are subject to a contingency such as the death of either spouse, remarriage of the wife, or change in the economic status of either spouse; and (3) the payments are in the nature of alimony or an allowance for support.[5]

Example 2. The divorce decree provides that the husband is to pay the wife a principal sum of $60,000 payable in the amount of $1,000 per month for five years. If she dies before the end of

2. § 71; § 215 provides for the inclusion of alimony in the gross income of the recipient spouse.

3. § 71(a).

4. *U. S. v. Davis*, 62–2 USTC ¶ 9509, 9 AFTR2d 1625, 82 S.Ct. 1190 (USSC, 1962).

5. § 71(c); Reg. § 1.71–1(d)(1)–(3).

the fifth year, her estate is to receive the balance of the payments. The payments are not "periodic," and therefore are not income to the wife nor deductible by the husband.

Example 3. The separation agreement requires the husband to pay the wife a principal sum of $108,000 payable in the amount of $1,000 per month for nine years or until her death, whichever occurs first. The payments are subject to a contingency and therefore qualify as "periodic."

Example 4. The separation agreement provides that the wife will receive $1,000 per month for five years in satisfaction of her husband's obligation to support her. The payments are treated as alimony since they are in the nature of alimony.

Where the installment payments are to extend over more than ten years, only payments of up to 10 percent of the principal sum can be considered alimony in any one year.[6]

Example 5. The decree of divorce provides that the husband is to pay the wife a principal sum in installments of $15,000 per year for five years and $5,000 per year for the next 10 years. The total amount the wife is to receive, $125,000, is considered a principal sum. Therefore, in each of the first five years the wife must include in income $\frac{1}{10}$ x $125,000 = $12,500. She must include the entire $5,000 per year for the sixth through the fifteenth year.[7] Comparable treatment is accorded to the husband.

Child Support. Amounts expended for the support of a child represent a non-deductible personal expense, regardless of whether the payments are made in the typical family setting or pursuant to a decree of divorce or a separation agreement.[8] Undoubtedly, the need for funds to support a child must enter into the bargaining between a husband and wife contemplating divorce or separation. The Supreme Court has held that unless the decree or agreement specifically calls for child support payments, none of the payments will be regarded as such.[9] Therefore, the agreement should specifically identify the portion of the payment which is for child support.

Example 6. The divorce decree provides that the former husband is required to pay periodic alimony payments of $300 per month and $200 child support. Since the decree specifically calls for child support payments, only $300 qualifies as alimony and is includible in the income of the wife and deductible by the former husband.

6. § 71(c)(2).

7. Reg. § 1.71–1(d)(5) Ex. (4).

8. § 71(b).

9. *Comm. v. Lester,* 61–1 USTC ¶ 9463, 7 AFTR2d 1445, 81 S.Ct. 1343 (USSC, 1961).

INCOME FROM ANNUITIES

An annuity is a type of investment in which an individual pays a fixed amount in exchange for the right to receive periodic payments for life or for some definite period. If the annuity payments are based upon the life of an individual, the amount of such payments are determined through the use of standard mortality tables. Therefore, if an individual lives to exactly his expected age of death, the annuitant will recover his investment in the contract as a return of capital plus interest on the amount of the capital invested. Individuals who die prematurely do not fully recover their capital contributions whereas other individuals who outlive their expected mortality fully recover the investment, earn interest and enjoy mortality gains.

The tax accounting problem associated with annuities is one of apportioning the amounts received between recovery of capital and income. Under prior tax laws, the annuitant was allowed to recover his entire investment in the annuity contract before recognizing any income. After some experience with other formulas, in 1954 Congress adopted the present approach which allows an annuitant to exclude (as a return of capital) from income the proportion of each payment that his investment in the contract bears to the expected return under the contract.[10] The expected return is the annual amount to be paid to the annuitant multiplied by the number of years of life using the mortality tables in the Regulations.[11]

> **Example 7.** The taxpayer purchased an annuity from an insurance company for $60,000. He was to receive $500 per month for life and his life expectancy was 15 years from the annuity starting date. In the first year he collects $6,000.
>
> $$\frac{\text{Investment in contract (\$60,000)}}{\text{Expected return (\$500} \times 12) \times 15 \text{ years}} \times \$6,000 = \$4,000$$

The $4,000 is a return of capital and $2,000 is taxable income.

The exclusion ratio remains the same and continues to be applied to annuity payments even if the annuitant outlives his life expectancy.[12] Thus, if in the above example, the taxpayer lived 20 years after the payments began, he could still exclude two-thirds of each payment from income even though the entire investment was recovered after 15 years. On the other hand, if he lived less than 15 years, the annuitant would be taxed on some amounts which were actually a return of capital.

Employee Annuities. An exception is provided in § 72(d) for employee annuities. Under a qualified pension or profit sharing plan, amounts contributed by the employer to a retirement fund may subse-

---

10. § 72.

11. § 72(c)(3); Reg. § 1.72–5(a).

12. Reg. § 1.72–4(a)(4).

quently be used to acquire annuity contracts for retired employees. The employer contributions to the retirement fund are not included in the employee's income and are not, therefore, considered as part of the employee's investment in the contract.[13] Thus, for noncontributory plans, the entire amount received by the employee from the retirement annuity is taxable income. However, if the plan is contributory, i. e., the employee contributes some of his after-tax salary to the cost of the annuity, such amounts represent a return of capital and are included in the employee's investment in the contract. In situations where the employee contributions are insignificant relative to the value of the annuity, Congress has provided a substitute approach to the regular recovery exclusion ratio. If an employee will receive retirement amounts during the first 3 years which are equal to or exceed his investment, such amounts are treated as a tax-free return of capital until the investment is reduced to zero. Subsequent amounts received are fully taxable.[14]

> **Example 8.** S, an employee of XYZ Company made contributions of $10,000 to a qualified pension plan. Upon retirement S is to receive annual pension benefits of $5,000.
>
> Since the amounts which will be received during the first 3 years ($15,000) exceed S's contributions to the plan ($10,000), the 3 year return of capital special rule applies. Thus, all amounts received during the first 2 years of $10,000 are treated as a tax-free return of capital. All subsequent pension payments are fully taxable to S.
>
> **Example 9.** Assume the same facts as in example 8 except that S's total contributions are $30,000.
>
> Since the amounts received in the first 3 years ($15,000) do not equal or exceed the employee contributions ($30,000), the 3 year rule does not apply. Instead, the regular annuity rules must be used as illustrated in Example 7.

PRIZES AND AWARDS

Prior to 1954 there was uncertainty relative to the taxability of prizes and awards. Taxpayers often sought to treat prizes and awards as nontaxable "gifts." In many situations it was difficult to determine whether the "prize or award" was in the nature of a gift. In 1954 Congress added § 74 which was intended to eliminate the uncertainty relative to the tax status of prizes and awards.

Under § 74, the fair market value of prizes and awards (other than fellowships and scholarships that are exempted under § 117, discussed below) are includible in income. Therefore, TV giveaway prizes, door prizes as well as awards from an employer to an em-

---

13. See §§ 401–404.   **14.** § 72(d).

ployee in recognition of achievement are fully taxable to the recipient.[15]

An exception is provided if: (1) the award is received in recognition of religious, charitable, scientific, educational, artistic, literary or civic achievement; (2) the recipient must be selected without any action on his part to enter a contest or proceedings; and (3) the recipient must not be required to render substantial future services as a condition to receiving the prize or award.[16] Thus, awards such as the Nobel prize and the Pulitzer prize will qualify for the exclusion.[17]

"Aristic" has been narrowly construed by the Courts. Thus, athletes have been unsuccessful in their attempts to exclude "outstanding player awards" as being in recognition of "artistic" achievement.[18]

GROUP–TERM LIFE INSURANCE

Prior to the passage of § 79 in 1964, the premiums paid by employers for group-term life insurance on the life of employees were totally excluded from the employee's income. Some companies took undue advantage of the exclusion by providing large amounts of group-term insurance for executives. Current law, therefore, sanctions an exclusion for only the premiums paid on the first $50,000 of group-term life protection. For each $1,000 of coverage in excess of $50,000, the employee must include the following amounts of premiums paid by the employer in gross income: [19]

Uniform Premiums for $1,000 of Group-Term Life Insurance Protection

Attained Age Last Day of the Employee's Tax Year	Cost Per $1,000 of Protection for 1-Month Period
Under 30	8 cents
30–34	10 cents
35–39	14 cents
40–44	23 cents
45–49	40 cents
50–54	68 cents
55–59	$1.10
60–64	$1.63

Example 10. The A Corporation has a group-term life insurance policy with coverage equal to the employee's annual salary. Mr. A, age 52, is president of the Corporation and receives an an-

---

15. Reg. § 1.74–1(a)(1).

16. § 74(b).

17. Reg. § 1.74–1(b).

18. *P. V. Hornung,* 47 T.C. 428 (1967).

19. Reg. § 1.79–3(d)(2).

nual salary of $75,000. Mr. A must include $204 in gross income from the insurance protection for the year.

$$\frac{(\$75,000-\$50,000)}{\$1,000} \times (.68) \times (12 \text{ months}) = \underline{\$204}$$

Generally, the amount that must be included in income, computed from the above table, is much less than the price an individual would have to pay for the same amount of protection. Thus, even the excess coverage provides some tax favored income for employees where group-term life coverage in excess of $50,000 is desirable.

The benefits under § 79 are only available to "employees." Proprietors and partners are not "employees" and, therefore, the premiums paid on the life of the proprietor or a partner are not deductible by the partner or proprietor. Also, to prevent a company from providing coverage solely to a selected few highly paid officers or shareholders, the Regulations generally require broad scale coverage of employees to satisfy the "group" requirement.[20] For example, limiting coverage to shareholder-employees would not constitute a qualified group. Therefore, if premium coverage were confined solely to this group, the $50,000 exclusion on group-life insurance coverage for each employee would not apply.

EXCLUSIONS FROM GROSS INCOME

STATUTORY AUTHORITY

§§ 101 through 123 provide the authority for excluding specific items from gross income. In addition, other exclusions are scattered throughout the Code. Each exclusion has its own legislative history and reason for enactment. Certain exclusions are intended as a form of indirect welfare payments. Other exclusions were intended to prevent double taxation of income or to provide incentives for socially desirable activities such as making scholarships nontaxable for educational activities. In some cases exclusions have been enacted by Congress to rectify the effects of judicially imposed decisions. For example, § 109 was enacted to exclude improvements made by a lessee from the lessor's income upon the termination of the lease. Previously, the Supreme Court held that such amounts were taxable income.[21] In this court decision, the lessor was required to include the fair market value of the improvements in income upon the termination of the lease despite the fact that there had been no sale or disposition of the property. Congress provided relief for this situation by deferring the value of the improvements from the lessor's income until the proper-

20. Reg. § 1.79–1(b)(1)(iii)(b).

21. *Helvering v. Bruun*, 40–1 USTC ¶ 9337, 24 AFTR 652, 60 S.Ct. 631 (USSC, 1940).

ty is sold unless the improvements are made by the lessee in lieu of paying rent.[22]

ADMINISTRATIVE POLICY

Administrative actions of the Internal Revenue Service, which are expressed through the issuance of interpretive Rulings and Regulations, have occasionally resulted in the exclusion of an item from gross income. For example, the Code does not specifically exclude Social Security benefits. However, in a Revenue Ruling the Commissioner has announced that the benefits are not subject to tax.[23] Apparently, in the view of the Commissioner, these payments are in part a return of the after-tax contributions of the individual and in part a welfare or annuity payment from the government.

INFLUENCE OF JUDICIAL DECISIONS

In *Arnold v. U. S.*, the Court summarized the Commissioner's attitude toward taxing payments made under government programs and the possible redress as follows: [24]

> Where a governmental body makes a payment to a taxpayer, the Commissioner tends to exclude it from income, even though similar payments from a private source would be taxable. . .

> There being no Court review of rulings favorable to the taxpayer, such rulings cannot be tested, except by Congressional amendment to the statute.

These court cases and the position of the IRS highlight the roles and responsibilities of the administrative, legislative and judicial branches of our government in formulating tax law. For example, in *Arnold v. U. S.*, the taxpayers attempted to exclude from income, insurance proceeds paid to them as a reimbursement for added expenses of temporary living quarters following a fire in their home. Similar payments made by a government agency to families displaced by urban renewal projects had been held non-taxable in a Revenue Ruling.[25] Nevertheless, the court held that the insurance proceeds were includible in income under the "all inclusive" definition provided under § 61 of the Code. Further, the court implied that the Commissioner's ruling may have been in error. Because of Congressional dissatisfaction with the *Arnold* decision and earlier cases on the same issue, § 123 was enacted. This section provides (subject to limitations) for the exclusion of such insurance proceeds from income.

---

22. § 109.

23. Rev.Rul. 70–217, 1970–1 C.B. 12; I.T. 3447, 1941–1 C.B. 191.

24. *Arnold v. U. S.*, 68–2 USTC ¶ 9590, 22 AFTR2d 5661, 289 F.Supp. 206 (D.Ct.N.Y.1968).

25. Rev.Rul. 60–279, 1960–2 C.B. 11.

SUMMARY OF PRINCIPAL EXCLUSIONS

Table 1 contains a listing of the principal exclusions from gross income.

Table 1

PRINCIPAL EXCLUSIONS FROM GROSS INCOME

1. Donative items:

    Gifts, bequest, inheritances and employee death benefits (§§ 102 and 101(b))
    Life insurance proceeds paid by reason of death (§ 101)
    Scholarships and fellowships (§ 117)
    Certain prizes and awards (§ 74(b))

2. Personality and welfare items:

    Injuries or sickness payments (§ 104)
    Public assistance payments (Rev.Rul. 71–425, 1971-2 C.B. 76)
    Amounts received under insurance contracts for certain living expenses (§ 123)

3. Wage and salary supplements:

    (a) Fringe benefits:

    Accident and health benefits (§§ 105 and 106)
    Disability pay (§ 105)
    Lodging and meals furnished for the convenience of the employer (§ 119)
    Unemployment compensation (Rev.Rul. 55–652)
    Rental value of parsonages (§ 107)
    Employer contributions to employee group term life insurance (§ 79)
    Employee discounts and the use of the employer's facilities and services (Prop.Reg. § 1.61–16)

    (b) Military benefits:

    Combat pay (§ 112)
    Mustering-out pay (§ 113)

    (c) Foreign earned income (§ 911)

4. Investor items:

    Interest on state and local government obligations (§ 103)
    Dividend exclusion (§ 116)

5. Old-age items:

    Social Security benefits (Rev.Rul. 70–217, 1970–7 C.B. 12)
    Gain from the sale of personal residence for elderly taxpayers (§ 121)

6. Other

    Recovery of a prior year's deduction which yielded no tax benefit (§ 111)

GIFTS AND INHERITANCES

Since the enactment of the income tax law in 1913 Congress has allowed the recipient of a gift or inheritance to exclude the value of the property from gross income.[26]   However, the recipient of a gift is subject to income tax upon income which is subsequently earned.

In numerous cases "gifts" are made in a business setting.   For example, a salesman gives a purchasing agent free samples; an employee receives cash from his employer upon retirement; a corporation makes payments to employees who were victims of a natural disaster; a corporation makes a cash payment to a former employee's widow.   In these and similar instances, it is frequently not clear whether a gift was made or the payments represent compensation for past, present or future services.

The courts have defined a gift as "a voluntary transfer of property by one to another without any [valuable] consideration or compensation therefrom." [27]   If the payment is intended to be for services rendered, it is not a gift even though the payment is made without legal or moral obligation and the payor receives no economic benefit from the transfer.   To qualify as a gift, the payment must be made "out of affection, respect, admiration, charity or like impulses." [28]   Thus the cases on this issue have been decided on the basis of the donor's intent as determined by all the facts and circumstances in the particular case.

In a landmark case, *Comm. v. Duberstein*,[29] the taxpayer, (Duberstein) received a Cadillac from a business acquaintance.   Duberstein had gratuitously supplied the business man with the names of potential customers with no expectation of compensation.   The Supreme Court concluded:

> *   *   *   despite the characterization of the transfer of the Cadillac by the parties [as a gift] and the absence of any obligation, even of a moral nature, to make it, it was at the bottom a recompense for Duberstein's past service, or an inducement for him to be of further service in the future.

Therefore, Duberstein was required to include the fair market value of the automobile in gross income.

Similarly, a bequest may be taxable if it represents a disguised form of compensation for services.   In *V. R. Wolder v. Comm.*, an attorney entered into an agreement whereby the client would bequeath to the attorney certain securities in consideration for services rendered during the client's life.[30]   The value of the securities on the date of the client's death was held to be taxable income to the attorney.

26. § 102(a).

27. *Estate of D. R. Daly*, 3 B.T.A. 1042 (1926).

28. *Robertson v. U. S.*, 52–1 USTC ¶ 9343, 41 AFTR 1053, 72 S.Ct. 994 (USSC, 1952).

29. *Comm. v. Duberstein*, 60–2 USTC ¶ 9515, 5 AFTR2d 1626, 80 S.Ct. 1190 (USSC, 1960).

30. *V. R. Wolder v. Comm.*, 74–1 USTC ¶ 9266, 33 AFTR2d 74–813, 493 F.2d 608 (CA–2, 1974).

EMPLOYEE DEATH BENEFITS

Frequently an employer will make payments to a deceased employee's widow, children or other beneficiaries even though there is no legal or moral obligation to make such payments. Thus, the question arises as to whether the employer's payments may be treated as a gift by the recipient. Generally, the IRS's position is that such payments are compensation for prior services rendered by the former deceased employee rather than a gift.[31] However, some courts have held that payments to an employee's widow or other beneficiaries are gifts where: [32]

(1) the payments were made to the widow and/or children, rather than to the employee's estate;

(2) there was no obligation on the employer's part to pay any additional compensation to the deceased;

(3) the employer derived no benefit from the payment;

(4) the widow and/or children performed no services for the employer;

(5) the decedent had been fully compensated for his services;

(6) compensation payments were made pursuant to a Board of Directors' resolution which followed a general company policy of providing such payment for families of deceased employees.

The widow's case for exclusion is greatly strengthened if the payment is made in "light of her financial needs".[33] These factors, together, tend to indicate whether the payment was made as an act of "affection or charity".

§ 101(b) attempts to eliminate or reduce controversy in this area by providing for an automatic exclusion of the first $5,000 paid by the employer to the employee's beneficiaries "by reason of the death of the employee." The $5,000 exclusion must be apportioned among the beneficiaries on the basis of each beneficiary's percentage of the total death benefits received.[34] Where the employer's payments exceed $5,000, the beneficiaries may still be able to exclude the entire amount received as a gift if they are able to show gratuitous intent on the part of the employer.

The exclusion is not applicable to amounts that the employee had a nonforfeitable right to receive immediately before his death such as accrued salary or commissions.[35] Since such nonforfeitable amounts

31. Rev.Rul. 62–102, 1962–2 C.B. 37.

32. *Estate of Sydney J. Carter v. Comm.*, 71–2 USTC ¶ 9129, 29 AFTR2d 332, 453 F.2d 61 (CA–2, 1972) and cases cited therein.

33. *Simpson v. U. S.*, 58–2 USTC ¶ 9923, 2 AFTR2d 6036, 261 F.2d 497 (CA–7, 1958), *cert. denied*, 79 S.Ct. 724 (USSC, 1958).

34. Reg. § 1.101–2(c)(1).

35. § 101(b).

would be payable regardless of the employee's death, the payments are not considered to be made "by reason of the death of the employee." However, lump-sum distributions to an employee's beneficiaries from a qualified pension, profit-sharing, or stock bonus plan are not treated as nonforfeitable for purposes of the death benefit exclusion.[36] In the case of a nonlump-sum distribution from a qualified plan, the $5,000 exclusion applies only if the employee's rights to such amounts are forfeitable at his death.

> **Example 11.** The X Corporation has a profit-sharing plan for the benefit of its employees. For each year of the employee's service to the firm, 10 percent of his accumulated share of the profit-sharing trust becomes nonforfeitable. If he dies prior to completing 10 years of service, the employee's beneficiaries receive 100% of the accumulated benefits in a lump-sum distribution.
>
> At the time of his death Mr. Y had completed six years of service with the firm. His accumulated share of the profit-sharing trust was $10,000, of which $6,000 (6 years x .10 x $10,000) was nonforfeitable.
>
> If the plan were not "qualified," the beneficiaries would be entitled to exclude only $4,000, the $10,000 they received less the $6,000 that was nonforfeitable at the time of the employee's death. However, if the profit-sharing plan were qualified, $5,000 could be excluded if payment were made in the form of a lump-sum.

If payments in excess of $5,000 are treated as compensation and are therefore taxable income of the beneficiaries, such amounts are deductible by the employer as ordinary and necessary business expenses.[37] However, if such excess amounts represent gifts, the employer is entitled to a maximum deduction of only $5,025 ($5,000 death benefit plus a $25 ceiling amount for a business gift).[38]

LIFE INSURANCE PROCEEDS

The general rule is that insurance proceeds paid to the beneficiary upon the death of the insured are exempt from income tax.[39] The rationale for excluding insurance proceeds from income is based upon the fact that the premium payments are a nondeductible personal expenditure of the insured. In addition, social policy considerations suggest that favorable tax treatment should be granted to the beneficiaries of life insurance following the death of the insured who is frequently the sole provider for the family. It should be noted,

36. *Ibid.*

37. Reg. § 1.404–(a)(12).

38. § 274(b).

39. § 101(a).

however, that life insurance proceeds are generally subject to the Federal estate tax.

§ 101 provides an exception to the general rule that life insurance proceeds are excluded from income. This exception is applicable where a life insurance contract has been transferred for valuable consideration to another individual who assumes ownership rights. The insurance proceeds are income to the assignee to the extent that the proceeds exceed the amount paid for the policy plus any subsequent premiums paid.[40]

> **Example 12.** A pays premiums of $500 for an insurance policy in the face amount of $1,000 upon the life of B, and subsequently transfers the policy to C for $600. C receives the proceeds of $1,000 upon the death of B. The amount which C can exclude from his gross income is limited to $600 plus any premiums paid by C subsequent to the transfer.[41]

The Code, however, provides for exceptions to the exception rule whereby the proceeds from certain transfers are excluded from income under the general rule. The four exceptions to the exceptions are transfers to:[42]

(1) a partner of the insured,

(2) a partnership in which the insured is a partner,

(3) a corporation in which the insured is an officer or shareholder,

(4) a transferee whose basis in the policy is determined by reference to the transferor's basis.

The first three exceptions facilitate the use of insurance contracts to fund buy-sell agreements.

> **Example 13.** R and S are equal partners who have an agreement that allows either partner to purchase the interest of a deceased partner for $50,000. Neither partner has sufficient cash to actually buy the other partner's interest, but each has a life insurance policy on his own life for $50,000. R and S could exchange their policies (usually at little or no taxable gain) and upon the death of either partner, the surviving partner could collect tax free insurance proceeds which could then be used to purchase the decedent's interest in the partnership.
>
> Similarly, if R and S incorporate their business, they could transfer their insurance policies to the corporation for valuable consideration and the corporation could use the tax exempt death proceeds to redeem the deceased shareholder's stock.

---

40. § 101(a)(2).   **42.** § 101(a)(2)(A) and (B).

41. Reg. § 101–1(b)(5) Ex. 1.
West's Fed. Tax: Individuals—5

The fourth exception applies to policies that were transferred pursuant to a tax-free exchange, e. g., (1) a transfer of insurance policies to a corporation by its controlling (owning 80% of the stock) shareholders in exchange for the corporation's stock or securities; [43] or (2) a transfer resulting from a corporate reorganization. [44]

INTEREST ON LIFE INSURANCE PROCEEDS

Investment earnings arising from the reinvestment of life insurance proceeds are generally subject to income tax. However, § 101(d) provides favorable tax advantages for a surviving spouse who elects to receive the insurance proceeds in installments. The surviving spouse may exclude the first $1,000 of interest income collected on the proceeds each year.

Example 14. Mrs. T was the beneficiary of her husband's $100,-000 life insurance policy. She elected to receive the principal in ten installments of $10,000 each plus interest on the unpaid principal. The first year she received $13,600 which included $3,600 interest. She must recognize interest income of $2,600.

While the $1,000 interest exclusion offers an attractive tax advantage if the election is made to receive the proceeds in the form of installment payments, it may be possible to earn a greater after-tax return from investing the lump-sum proceeds in other types of investments, e. g., stocks or tax-free municipal bonds.

SCHOLARSHIPS AND FELLOWSHIPS

Prior to 1954, there was no specific provision in the Code concerning scholarships and fellowships. Generally, a grant was considered taxable unless the taxpayer could show that such amounts were nontaxable gifts. The enactment of § 117 was intended to provide some general rules for determining the taxability of scholarships and fellowships. However, the new section did little more than codify existing case law and treasury decisions and has left many issues unresolved. [45] Thus, each year there are several cases before the courts involving scholarships and fellowships.

The Regulations define a scholarship as "an amount paid or allowed to, or for the benefit of, a student, whether an undergraduate or a graduate, to aid such individual in pursuing his studies." [46] A fellowship is "an amount paid or allowed to, or for the benefit of, an individual in the pursuit of study or research." [47] The term fellowship includes amounts received to cover the expenses of travel, re-

---

43. § 351.

44. § 368(a).

45. See *Elmore L. Reese, Jr.*, 45 T.C. 407 (1966) for a discussion of the history of the scholarship provisions.

46. Reg. § 1.117–3(a).

47. Reg. § 1.117–3(c).

search, clerical help, and equipment as well as the individual's general living expenses, provided the expenses are related to his studies.[48] However, the payments are compensation and are therefore taxable if such amounts represent payments for past, present, or future services, or are primarily for the benefit of the grantor.[49]

Often the payments are made for dual motives, i. e., to aid the recipient and to benefit the grantor. The courts have also adopted a "purpose of the expenditure" test to decide such cases.

> It is apparent from the above cited regulations and rulings that whether a payment qualifies as a scholarship or fellowship grant excludable from gross income under Section 117 of the 1954 Code depends upon whether the primary purpose of the payment is to further the education and training of the recipient or whether the primary purpose is to serve the interest of the grantor. The problem is usually somewhat difficult of solution because of the fact that in most of the situations there is a dual or mutual benefit involved. The question of necessity must be resolved on a factual basis and depends upon the facts and circumstances in each particular case.[50]

Many graduate students receive payments for teaching or assisting in research. Generally, the payments are compensation for services and therefore taxable. However, in some degree programs all students are required to do some teaching or research (e. g., an internship in education, or research in the physical sciences). In these cases, the requirements to perform services will not prevent the payment from being excluded as a scholarship;[51] but an institution can not bring all of its payments to graduate students under the scholarship exclusion by simply making some teaching or research a requirement for a degree. The primary purpose of the payment must be to further the education and training of the recipient rather than "to serve the interest of the grantor." Whether this test is satisfied is "basically a question of fact."[52]

A hospital's payments to medical interns and residents are often the subject of litigation under the fellowship provision. Generally, the payments are considered compensation where the interns' duties are geared to the operational needs of the hospital rather than the intern's research and study needs.[53] However, in some cases the courts have ruled that the payments were primarily to further the educational needs of the student where:[54]

48. § 117(a)(2).

49. Reg. § 1.117–4(c).

50. *C. P. Bhalla,* 35 T.C. 13 (1960).

51. § 117(b)(1).

52. *Ussery v. U. S.,* 61–2 USTC ¶ 9740, 8 AFTR2d 5727, 296 F.2d 582, (CA–5, 1961).

53. *A. J. Prosky,* 51 T.C. 918 (1969).

54. *Wrobleski v. Bingler,* 58–2 USTC ¶ 9556, 1 AFTR2d 1987, 161 F.Supp.

(1) The principle purpose of the institute was training medical specialists rather than providing patient care; and

(2) The recipient of the funds did not replace personnel who otherwise would have been employed for the care of patients.

There is also a special provision in the Code for an individual who receives a fellowship or scholarship where he or she is *not* a candidate for a degree. The "non-candidate" must meet the same requirements as the degree candidate; the payments cannot be made for services of the recipient nor be primarily for the benefit of the grantor. In addition, the payments must be received from a government or other non-profit organization.[55] If these requirements are satisfied, the exclusion for the non-degree candidate is limited to $300 times the number of months during which the recipient received amounts in the taxable year, subject to a maximum of 36 total months.[56]

Some employers have made scholarships available solely to the children of key employees. The tax objective of these plans was to provide a nontaxable fringe benefit to the executives by making the payment to the child in the form of an excludable scholarship. However, the IRS has ruled that the payments are generally taxable income to the parent-employee.[57]

Amounts paid to or for the benefit of employees which do not qualify as scholarships or fellowships under § 117 are includible in income under § 61. However, such amounts may still qualify as expenses incurred in the trade or business of an employee (rather than a personal expense).[58] In such event, the employee receives an offsetting deduction against the income which is taxable. Many employers provide for tuition reimbursements for their employees. The IRS has ruled (under certain conditions) that such expenditures are deductible by the employee as educational expenditures and, therefore, it is not necessary for the employer to report the tuition reimbursements as wages for purposes of Federal employment taxes or for inclusion in the employee's W–2 form.[59]

COMPENSATION FOR INJURIES AND SICKNESS

§ 104 excludes from gross income, compensation for personal injuries and sickness whether received as (1) workmen's compensation

901 (D.Ct.Pa.1958); to the contrary, Rev.Rul. 57–386, 1957–2 C.B. 105; but under facts similar to the above, payments to student nurses and anesthetists were excludable according to the IRS in Rev.Rul. 58–338, 1958–2 C.B. 54; Rev.Rul. 72–568, 1972–2 C.B. 48.

55.　§ 117(b)(2).

56.　§ 117(b)(2)(B).

57.　Rev.Rul. 75–448, 1975–2 C.B. 55.

58.　Reg. § 1.162–5.

59.　Rev.Rul. 76–71, 1976–1 C.B. 308.

benefits, (2) by suit or agreement, or (3) amounts received through accident or health insurance.

State laws require the employer to compensate employees for job related injuries. Although these payments are a partial substitute for lost wages, Congress has excluded workmen's compensation benefits from gross income.

Also, excluded by § 104 are damages received (whether by suit or agreement) on account of personal injuries or sickness. The damages for personal injury or sickness may be received from the actual prosecution of a law suit or such amounts may be received through a legal settlement in lieu of prosecution.[60] Congress has granted an exclusion for such amounts to offset the personal hardships arising from such injuries or sickness.

Benefits collected under an accident and health insurance policy are excluded from income if the premiums are paid by the employee or by someone other than the employer. The benefits are treated as a recovery of premiums paid on the policy, a return of capital. However, if the taxpayer's employer pays the premiums, the taxation of the benefits is governed by § 105(d), the "disability pay" provision, discussed below.

> **Example 15.** Employee A acquired and paid the premiums on a medical and disability insurance policy. The insurance company paid $100 per week to A for disability benefits during the year. Such payments are nontaxable under § 104(a)(3).

> **Example 16.** Employee B was injured in a job related accident and collects $80 per week workmen's compensation benefits from the state. Such benefits are excluded from income under § 104 (a)(1).

> **Example 17.** C was injured in an automobile accident. He received a settlement amounting to $50,000 from the insurance company for personal injury damages. Such amounts are excluded from income under § 104(a)(2).

The IRS has ruled that state welfare payments are not income to the recipient since such amounts represent nontaxable gifts made on the basis of need.[61]

ACCIDENT AND HEALTH BENEFITS

Employers frequently provide their employees with accident and health insurance plans. If the premiums are paid by the employer, the employees are not required to include such amounts in income.[62] Since employees receive these "tax-free" fringe benefits, § 105(a)

60. Reg. § 1.104–1(c).   **62.** § 106.

61. Rev.Rul. 71–425, 1971–2 C.B. 76.

provides the general rule that amounts received by the employee are includible in gross income. However, §§ 105(b) through (d) provide exceptions which permit the employee to exclude specific benefits which would otherwise be taxable under the general rule of § 105(a).

§ 105(b) Excludes payments received for medical care of the employee, his spouse and his dependents except to the extent such amounts relate to medical expenses which were deducted by the taxpayer in a prior year.

§ 105(c) Excludes payments for the permanent loss or loss of the use of a member or function of the body, or the permanent disfigurement, of the taxpayer, his spouse or a dependent.

§ 105(d) Excludes "disability pay" subject to limitations.

Example 18. Employee D incurred $2,000 of medical expenses in 19X1. However, only $500 of such expenses were deductible due to the 3% limitation rules. In 19X2, D received a $2,000 reimbursement from the insurance company relating to the 19X1 expenses. $1,500 is excluded from income. However, $500 must be included in 19X2 income since D received a corresponding tax benefit in 19X1. This rule applies regardless of whether the employee pays any portion of the cost of the policy.

Example 19. Employee E lost an eye in an automobile accident that was unrelated to his work and collected $10,000 from an insurance policy carried by his employer. As a result of the accident he incurred $2,000 of medical expenses which were deducted as medical expenses. If the payments are computed with reference to the nature of the injury and are not related to the time period the employee is absent from work, the entire $10,000 is excluded from income despite the $2,000 tax benefit from the injury related medical expenses.

MEDICAL REIMBURSEMENT PLANS

It may be possible for an employer to provide an uninsured medical reimbursement plan solely for its key employees. The Regulations provide that "a plan may cover one or more employees and there may be different plans for different employees. * * *" [63] In the case of a closely held corporation the plan is often structured so that the shareholder-employees receive a substantial percentage of the benefits. However, if the plan covers only shareholders, the benefits may be construed as a disguised dividend and would be fully taxable to the recipient.[64]

---

63. Reg. § 1.105–5(a).

64. *Larkin v. Comm.*, 68–1 USTC ¶ 9362, 21 AFTR2d 1307, 394 F.2d 494 (CA–1, 1968).

The Regulations require that the accident and/or health benefits be made under a "plan" which implies that there must be a consistent pattern as to who is to receive the benefits and how the benefits will be determined. However, the plan need not be in writing, nor is it necessary that the employee's benefits be enforceable; but at the time the employee becomes sick or injured the employer must have a "program, policy or custom" of providing the benefits. Knowledge of the plan and its rules must be made available to the employees.[65]

SICK AND DISABILITY PAY

The Tax Reform Act of 1976 generally limits the exclusion for sick pay to taxpayers under age 65 who have retired on disability and are permanently and totally disabled.[66] To be permanent, the physical or mental impairment must be expected to result in death, or the disability must have lasted or be expected to last for a continuous period of not less than 12 months.[67] For years prior to 1977 the exclusion applied to all employees who received wages for a period of absence from work because of personal injury or sickness. Under the new rules, the exclusion for amounts received under wage continuation plans due to disability is limited to $100 per week.[68] In addition, if the taxpayer's adjusted gross income is more than $15,000, the excludible amount is reduced on a dollar for dollar basis.[69]

> **Example 20.** Joe Jones, age 58, is totally and permanently disabled in 1977. His retirement disability pension from his company amounted to $200 per week. In addition, Mr. Jones had $8,000 gross income from other sources, e. g. taxable dividends, interest, etc.

Gross Income:

Disability pension $200 × 52 weeks	$10,400
Other taxable income	8,000
	18,400
Adjustments from gross income	–0–
Adjusted gross income	18,400
Excluded amount – Limit $100 per week	5,200
Less $18,400 – $15,000 ceiling amount	(3,400)
Allowable exclusion from income	$ 1,800

The employer may report excludible disability pay on the employee's W–2 form. However, the employee should attach a separate

---

65. Reg. § 1.105–5(a).   **68.** § 105(d)(2).

66. § 105(d)(1).   **69.** § 105(d)(3).

67. § 105(d)(5).

statement to the tax return showing the calculation of the excluded amount. An employer is not required to withhold Federal income tax on the exempt portion of the disability pay.[70]

MEALS AND LODGING FURNISHED FOR THE CONVENIENCE OF THE EMPLOYER

In general, the value of meals and lodging furnished to an employee is includible in the employee's income. However, § 119 provides that the value of meals furnished to an employee by his employer is excluded from income under the following conditions:

1. The meals are furnished on the business premises of the employer, and

2. The meals are furnished for the convenience of the employer.[71]

Reg. § 1.119–1(d) gives the following examples of where these conditions are satisfied.

(1) A waitress is required to eat her meals on the premises during the busy lunch and breakfast hours.

(2) A bank furnishes a teller meals on the premises to limit the time he is away from his booth during the busy hours.

(3) A worker is employed at a construction site in a remote part of Alaska. The employer must furnish meals and lodging due to the inaccessibility of other facilities.

(4) A hospital provides a free cafeteria for its staff. The employees are not required to eat on the premises, but the hospital's business purpose in providing the meals is to induce employees to stay on the premises in case an emergency arises.

Some of the important considerations in regard to meals are: (1) the need to have the employee available in emergency situations, (2) the length of the meal period allowed by business operations, (3) the ability to find meals elsewhere in a reasonable period.

The value of lodging furnished to an employee is excluded from income if the following three tests are met:[72]

1. The lodging is furnished on the *business premises* of the employer,

2. The lodging is furnished for the *convenience* of the employer, and

3. The employee is *required* to accept the lodging as a condition of employment.

The "on the business premises of the employer" requirement, applicable to both meals and lodging, has resulted in much litigation.

70. Prop.Reg. § 31.3401–(b)(8).   **72.** Reg. § 1.119–1(b).
71. Reg. § 1.119–1(a)(1).

The Regulations define business premises as simply "the place of employment of the employee".[73] Thus, in *Comm. v. Anderson* [74] the Sixth Court of Appeals held that a residence owned by the employer and occupied by Anderson, that was two blocks from the motel which Anderson managed, was not part of the business premises. However, in *J. B. Lindeman*,[75] the Tax Court considered an employer-owned house across the street from the hotel that was managed by the taxpayer to be on the business premises of the employer.

The exclusion of meal allowances has been litigated several times by state highway patrolmen. The patrolmen have reasoned that they must eat their meals in the area they serve because they are on call for emergency duty throughout the eight-hour shift. Furthermore, the patrolmen have contended the business premises of the state extends to the entire state. Some district courts and appellate courts have ruled in favor of the patrolmen, but the Tax Court agrees with the Commissioner.[76]

FOREIGN EARNED INCOME

A U. S. citizen is generally subject to U. S. tax on his total income regardless of the geographic origin of the income. § 911 provides an exception in the case of "foreign earned income". An individual, who has either established a bona fide foreign residence or is present in a foreign country for 510 days (17 months) during a period of 18 consecutive months, may exclude up to $15,000 per year of foreign earned income computed on a daily basis.[77] An exception is provided for employees of domestic charities located overseas. Such individuals are entitled to exclude $20,000 of their foreign earned income.[78]

The exclusion was originally intended to stimulate trade between the U. S. and foreign countries by effectively increasing the after-tax compensation of employees who work abroad and thus encouraging qualified employees to relocate. For years beginning after 1976, however, U. S. citizens employed in foreign countries are denied a tax credit or deduction for foreign income taxes paid on the amount, e. g. $15,000 of income which is excluded from U. S. tax.[79] Therefore,

73. Reg. § 1.119–1(c)(1).

74. *Comm. v. Anderson*, 67–1 USTC ¶ 9136, 19 AFTR2d 318, 371 F.2d 59 (CA–6, 1966).

75. *J. B. Lindeman*, 60 T.C. 609 (1973).

76. See cases for the taxpayer: *U. S. v. Keeton*, 67–2 USTC ¶ 9675, 20 AFTR2d 5688, 383 F.2d 429 (CA–10, 1967); *Saunders v. Comm.*, 54–2 USTC ¶ 9589, 46 AFTR 600, 215 F.2d 768 (CA–3, 1954). For the IRS: *C. H. Hyslope*, 21 T.C. 131 (1953); *Wil-* *son v. U. S.*, 69–2 USTC ¶ 9490, 24 AFTR2d 69–5011, 412 F.2d 694 (CA–1, 1969).

77. § 911(a)(1) and Act § 1011(a) amending § 911(c)(1). For years prior to 1977, individuals who were bonafide residents could exclude $25,000 and those present in a foreign country could exclude $20,000 of foreign income.

78. Act § 1011 amending § 911(c)(1).

79. Act § 1011(b) amending § 911(a).

the tax advantages which accrue to U. S. citizens working in foreign countries have been curtailed by the 1976 Tax Reform Act. The computation of the foreign tax credit is discussed in Chapter 11.

The $15,000 upper limit was intended to curb "abuses" of the law. Before any ceiling limitation was imposed, high salaried non-technicians (e. g., movie stars) were performing services abroad and were obtaining the full benefits from the exclusion.[80]

The exclusion applies to "foreign earned income". The income is "foreign" if it is earned outside of the United States, its territories or possessions.[81] Earned income includes wages, salaries, professional fees and other amounts received as compensation for personal services actually rendered in a foreign country. If the income is derived from the taxpayer's share of the profits from an unincorporated business and capital is a material income-producing factor to the business, the taxpayer's earned income cannot exceed 30 percent of his share of the profits.[82]

Some of the factors considered in determining whether the taxpayer is a bona fide resident of a foreign country are:[83] (1) Does he expect to be there for an indefinite or extended period? (2) Does his family reside in the foreign country? (3) Do he and his family reside in permanent quarters (e. g., a house rather than a hotel)? (4) Does he take part in the local activities where he resides? If the residence requirement is satisfied for an uninterrupted period that includes an entire tax year, the exemption applies to that year and to any partial year in which he was a bona fide resident. Even though the taxpayer may not be able to satisfy the residence requirement, he may still be able to obtain the exclusion if he is physically present in the foreign country for 510 days during a period of 18 consecutive months.

> **Example 21.** T was employed by a U. S. Corporation working in Mexico City from December 1, 19X1 to March 30, 19X3, and was paid less than $15,000 per year. T did not establish residence in Mexico since his family remained in the U. S. and he was living in temporary quarters. None of T's income is excludable since he does not satisfy the "bona fide resident" nor 510 days in 18 consecutive months test.
>
> If T had established residence in Mexico, all of the income would be excludable.
>
> If T did not establish residence in Mexico, but remained there until June 30, 19X3, his income would be excludable under the 510 days in 18 consecutive months test.

---

80. Rep.No.685, 83rd Cong., 1st Sess., 1953–2 C.B. 458.

81. Reg. § 1.911–2(f).

82. § 911(b).

83. *Marilyn Fugit,* 34 TCM 646, T.C. Memo. 1975–140.

INTEREST ON CERTAIN STATE AND LOCAL GOVERNMENT OBLIGATIONS

At the time the 16th amendment was ratified by the states there was some question as to whether the Federal government possessed the constitutional authority to tax interest on state and local government obligations. Taxing the interest on these obligations was thought to violate the doctrine of intergovernmental immunity in that the tax would impair the state and local government's ability to finance its operations.[84] Thus, interest on state and local government obligations was specifically exempted from Federal income tax. The exemption is still part of our tax laws but most commentators agree that the exclusion of such interest is based upon political rather than constitutional requirements.

Obviously, the exclusion of the interest reduces the cost of borrowing for the state and local governments since a taxpayer in the sixty percent marginal tax bracket requires only a four percent yield on a tax exempt bond to obtain the same after-tax income as a taxable bond paying ten percent interest $[4\% \div (1 - .6) = 10\%]$.

However, the lower cost for the state and local government is more than offset by the revenue losses for the Federal government. Also, tax exempt interest is considered to be a substantial "loophole" for the very wealthy. Thus, bills have been proposed to Congress calling for Federal government subsidies to those state and local governments which voluntarily choose to issue taxable bonds. Under these proposals, the tax exempt status of existing bonds would not be eliminated.

The current tax exempt status applies solely to the obligations of state and local governments, e. g., interest on bonds and notes. Thus, income received from the accrual of interest on an overpayment of state income tax is fully taxable.[85] Neither does the exemption apply to gains on the sale of tax exempt securities.

During recent years, state and local governments have developed sophisticated financial schemes to attract new industry. For example, local municipalities have issued bonds to finance the construction of plants to be leased to private enterprise. Because the financing could be arranged with low interest rate municipal obligations, the plant could be leased at a lower cost than the private business could otherwise attain. The state and local governments have also issued tax exempt bonds and have invested the proceeds in higher yielding

---

84. *Pollock v. Farmer's Loan & Trust Co.*, 3 AFTR 2557, 15 S.Ct. 912 (USSC, 1895).

85. *Kieselbach v. Comm.*, 43–1 USTC ¶ 9220, 30 AFTR 370, 63 S.Ct. 303 (USSC, 1943). *U. S. Trust Co. of New York v. Anderson*, 3 USTC ¶ 1125, 12 AFTR 836, 65 F.2d 575 (CA–2, 1933).

federal and corporate bonds (so-called "arbitrage transactions"). §§ 103(c) and (d) were enacted in 1969 to place limitations upon the use of industrial development and arbitrage bonds by state and local governments.

Under § 103(c), the tax exemption does not apply to interest on bonds whose proceeds will be used directly or indirectly by a business. However, exemptions are provided in the Code for (1) small issues, $1,000,000 or less, and (2) obligations whose proceeds are used to finance an industrial park, and (3) obligations whose proceeds are used to finance certain public goods and services such as public transportation, airports, water, sewage, sports facilities, parks, conventions or trade show facilities, and public housing projects.[86]

DIVIDEND EXCLUSION FOR INDIVIDUALS

§ 116 provides some relief from the double taxation of corporate income, i. e., the income is initially subject to the corporate income tax and the subsequent dividend distributions are taxed to the shareholders. An individual may exclude the first $100 of dividends received from domestic (U. S.) corporations during the year. On a joint return a maximum of $100 of the husband's dividends and $100 on the wife's dividends may be excluded. Dividends received on jointly owned stocks are treated as though the husband and wife each receive one-half.

Example 22. Mr. and Mrs. A received dividends in the current year as follows:

Dividends Received on Stock Owned by

	Mr. A	Mrs. A	Jointly	Total
X Corp.	$150	$ 40		$190
Y Corp.	90	40		130
Z Corp.			$30	30
	$240	$ 80	$30	$350

On a joint return Mr. and Mrs. A would report $350 less a $100 exclusion for the husband's dividends and a $95 exclusion for Mrs. A's dividends. The exclusion for Mrs. A is the $80 she received on her stock plus one-half of the dividends from the jointly owned shares.

For taxpayers residing in community property states, the general rule is that the income is deemed to be earned equally by the married persons. An exception is provided in California and in certain other community property states for income from separate property. In these states income from separate property accrues to the separate property owner.

86. §§ 103(c)(4), (5) and (6).

Example 23.

	Mr. A	Mrs. A	Community Property	Total
X Corp.	$150	$40		$190
Y Corp.	90	40		130
Z Corp.			$30	30
	$240	$80	$30	$350

In Texas and in other states following the "Texas Rule", the $320 of dividends from separate property is deemed to be community income. Therefore, Mr. A's income for purposes of the $100 dividend exclusion would be $160 plus $15 or $175. Mrs. A's income would include one-half of the separate property income of $160 plus one-half of the community property dividends of $15 or $175.

In California and in other states following the California rule, Mr. A's income would be $240 from his separate property plus $15 from his share of the community property or $255. Mrs. A, however, would report $80 plus $15 or a total of $95 and her dividend exclusion would be limited to this amount.

The dividend exclusion does not apply to dividends received from deposits with savings and loan associations and savings banks (treated as interest) and patronage dividends from cooperatives. Dividends on unmatured life insurance policies are generally treated as a reduction in the cost of the premium payments and, therefore, are not income.

TAX BENEFIT RULE

Generally, if a taxpayer obtains a deduction for an item in one year and later recovers the portion of the prior deduction, the recovery produces taxable income in the year of recovery.[87]

Example 24. A taxpayer who uses the direct charge-off method for bad debts, deducted as a loss a $1,000 receivable from a customer when it appeared the amount would never be collected. The following year the customer paid $800 on the receivable. The taxpayer must report as income the $800 in the year it is received.

However, § 111 provides that the taxpayer must report income from the recovery of a bad debt, prior tax or delinquency amount only to the extent a tax benefit was realized from the deduction in the year it was taken. Thus, if the taxpayer in the above example had no taxable income in the year of the deduction (e. g., his itemized deductions and personal exemptions exceeded his adjusted gross income), the re-

---

87. § 111(a).

covery would be partially or totally excluded from income in the year of the recovery.

> **Example 25.** The taxpayer in the above example had $2,200 adjusted gross income after dedutcing the $1,000 uncollectible receivable. His itemized deductions and personal exemptions for that year were $3,000. $800 would not be taxable income in the year it was collected since the taxpayer would not have received any tax benefit for this amount in the year of the write-off. (2,200 + 800 − 3,000 = 0). However, if he collected $1,000 on the account he would have to report $200 income in the year of collection ($2,200 + 1,000 − 3,000 = $200).

This example assumes that the taxpayer received no benefit from the carryback or carryover of the $800 loss under the net operating loss provisions.[88]

The Code specifically mentions "bad debts, prior taxes and delinquency amounts" as items subject to the tax benefit rule. However, due to the Supreme Court decision in *Dobson v. Commissioner*,[89] which involved the recovery of a prior year's loss on the sale of common stocks, the Regulations have been expanded to make § 111 applicable to recoveries "with respect to all losses, expenditures, and accruals made the basis of deductions from gross income for prior taxable years." [90]

INCOME FROM DISCHARGE OF INDEBTEDNESS

A transfer of appreciated property in satisfaction of a debt is a realizable event. The transaction is treated as a taxable sale of the appreciated property followed by a payment of the debt.[91] A corporation also realizes income if its bonds are repurchased at a discount.

> **Example 26.** X Corporation issued bonds for $1,000,000. Two years later the corporation repurchased the bonds on the open market for $900,000. X Corporation realizes a $100,000 gain on the retirement of the debt.

However, there are six situations where the income realized from the discharge of indebtedness will not be recognized.

(1) A reduction in the debt is the result of a gift by the creditor to the debtor; [92]

---

88. See Reg. 1.111–1(b)(3) Example for the computation of tax benefit arising from the utilization of net operating losses.

89. *Dobson v. Comm.*, 44–1 USTC ¶ 9108, 31 AFTR 773, 64 S.Ct. 23ξ (USSC, 1944).

90. Reg. § 1.111–1(a).

91. *Peninsula Properties Co., Ltd.*, 47 B.T.A. (1942).

92. *Helvering v. American Dental Co.*, 43–1 USTC ¶ 9318, 30 AFTR 397, 63 S.Ct. 577 (USSC, 1943).

(2) the liability is discharged under bankruptcy proceedings;[93]

(3) the debtor is insolvent both before and after the discharge;[94]

(4) a shareholder cancels the corporation's indebtedness to him;[95]

(5) the cancellation of certain student loans;

(6) the taxpayer makes an election under § 108 to defer the gain.

The first exception is rarely applicable to a business setting since businessmen generally do not gratuitously forgive debts. While a businessman may settle debts for less than the original amount, the settlement is usually due to the debtor's adverse financial condition or due to a dispute as to the correct amount of the liability rather than from "love, affection or generosity."[96]

The second exception only applies where the debtor has entered into formal bankruptcy proceedings under Federal laws. However, the third exception, insolvency before and after the discharge, will be applicable to a troubled business that has not actually entered formal bankruptcy. If the taxpayer is insolvent before but solvent after the discharge, income is recognized by the insolvent taxpayer in an amount equal to the excess of the fair market value of his assets over liabilities immediately prior to the discharge of the indebtedness.

A shareholder's cancellation of the corporation's indebtedness to him, the fourth exception, is considered a contribution of capital to the corporation. Under § 118, the corporation recognizes no income from the shareholder's contribution.

In 1976 the tax law was amended to provide an exception (item 5 above) for certain student loans whereby the cancellation of such loans will not produce taxable income to the debtor.[97] The cancellation must result from the former student satisfying a condition of the loan, e. g. that he work in a particular geographical location or for certain classes of employers such as an M.D. agreeing to practice in a rural area.

The sixth exception is a relief provision for a corporation or individual engaged in a business which has realized income from a discharge of its indebtedness; e. g. retirement of bonds or mortgages. Under § 108, if the debt is owed by (1) a corporation, or (2) an individual who incurred the debt in connection with his trade or business, the income realized from the discharge of the debt may be excluded from income and used to reduce the debtor's basis in its business

93. Reg. § 1.61–12(b).

94. Rev.Rul. 58–600, 1958–2 C.B. 29.

95. Reg. § 1.61–12(a).

96. *Comm. v. Jacobson*, 49–1 USTC ¶ 9133, 37 AFTR 516, 69 S.Ct. 358 (USSC, 1949).

97. Act § 2117 amending § 61.

property. The election to exclude such gains from income may be of limited benefit since the basis of the property is adjusted downward and may result in lower depreciation deductions or a larger realized gain upon the eventual sale of the property. Thus, the income is merely deferred rather than completely excluded from income.

The taxpayer must make an election to exclude the income and adjust the basis of the properties. A special form (Form 982) is available for making the election and should be completed and filed with the tax return for the year the income was realized. § 1.1017–1 of the Regulations sets forth procedures for adjusting the basis of specific assets.

TAX PLANNING CONSIDERATIONS

Our tax laws exclude certain types of economic gains from tax. Therefore, tax planning techniques may be useful to assist taxpayers in obtaining the maximum benefits from the exclusion of such gains. Below are some of the tax planning opportunities made available by the exclusions.

ALIMONY

The person making the payments favors a divorce settlement where the payments will qualify as deductible alimony. On the other hand, the recipient prefers that the payments do not qualify as alimony. If the payor is in a higher tax bracket than the recipient, both parties may benefit, after-tax, by increasing the payments but setting the terms so that they qualify as "periodic".

Example 27. H and W are in the process of reaching a divorce agreement. W has asked for $100,000 to be paid in four equal annual installments of $25,000 each. W is in a 30 percent marginal tax bracket. H, who is in a 50 percent marginal bracket, agrees on the total amount but would like to add to the agreement that the payments cease in the event she remarries prior to the end of the four years, so that the payments will qualify as alimony. W agrees to accept the remarriage contingency provided she receives $40,000 each year for four years.

Under the $25,000 per year alternative, W would have $25,000 per year in non-taxable income at an after-tax cost to H of $25,000 per year. Under the $40,000 per year alternative, she would receive $(1 - .3)\ (\$40,000) = \$28,000$ at an after-tax cost to H of $(1 - .50)\ (\$40,000) = \$20,000$.

GROUP–TERM LIFE INSURANCE

This is a tax-favored employee fringe benefit in that the employer may deduct the premiums while the employee may exclude from taxable income the premium payments on up to $50,000 of coverage per year. If the corporation pays $300 in premiums for an employee in the 40 percent marginal tax bracket, this is equivalent (after-tax) to $500 in salary. Even though the employee must pay tax on his coverage in excess of $50,000 per year, the rates used by IRS to compute the employee's income are usually much lower than he would have to pay to obtain similar coverage under an individual term policy.

EMPLOYEE DEATH BENEFITS

An employer can make arrangements to transfer up to $5,000 of tax-free income to each of his employee's beneficiaries. It may be advisable to establish a formal plan which authorizes such payments to beneficiaries of former employees. Where the death benefits exceed $5,000, the tax advisor should ascertain if the payments are excludible as a gift instead of being taxable as compensation for services rendered by the decedent.

INTEREST ON LIFE INSURANCE PROCEEDS PAID TO A SURVIVING SPOUSE

A $1,000 annual interest exclusion is available to a surviving spouse who collects life insurance proceeds in installments. These attractive tax benefits should be considered in the selection of a settlement option (e. g., lump-sum, installments, annuity) under the policy.

FOREIGN EARNED INCOME

An employee who must work abroad should usually seek to establish residency in the foreign country so as to obtain the benefits of the foreign earned income exclusion. A bona fide foreign residence can usually be established if the employment period is indefinite or for an extended period and involves a family move into permanent type quarters.

Where residency can not be established, the taxpayer will still qualify for the foreign income exclusion if he meets the 18 consecutive month and 510 day physical presence tests. Thus, he should be careful in planning leave time away from the foreign country.

Consideration should be given to the effective rate of tax that will be levied by the foreign country since a portion of the foreign income is no longer eligible for use in computing the foreign tax credit.

MEALS AND LODGING PROVIDED FOR THE CONVENIENCE OF THE EMPLOYER

Where a business need can be served by the employee living on or near the employer's premises, the employer can provide the employee with non-taxable income in the form of meals and lodging by requiring that he live on the employer's premises. In addition, certain non-taxable meals may be provided to employees if the meals are business related, e. g. entertainment of customers by company sales personnel.

ACCIDENT AND HEALTH BENEFITS

An employer can provide employees with non-taxable income in the form of disability and accident insurance coverage. Also, the employer may provide medical expense protection (hospital, doctors, dentists) for the employee, his spouse and dependents. The medical protection may be solely in the form of insurance coverage for the employee and his spouse and dependents. It is also possible to provide a medical reimbursement plan to cover medical expenses. In addition, the employer may provide a salary continuation plan which permits employees who become totally disabled to exclude such amounts. In the case of the medical reimbursement and disability pay, the employer may have different plans for different classes of employees. Thus, the plan may discriminate in favor of owner-employees. However, to insure that the exclusion will be allowed, it may be desirable to distribute a description of the plan to the employees and it is generally advisable to include one or more non-shareholders in the plan.

OTHER EMPLOYEE FRINGE BENEFITS

Other employee benefits that are not generally includable in gross income include: discounts on the employer's merchandise; free parking; payment of the employee's dues in vocational or professional organizations; supper money; and non-business use of the employer's facilities where no additional cost is incurred by the employer.

INVESTOR ITEMS

The tax exemption granted on state and local government bonds is particularly attractive for taxpayers who are in high marginal tax brackets. A five percent yield on these securities is equivalent to a sixteen percent before tax yield on taxable securities for an individual who is in a 70% tax bracket.

PROBLEM MATERIALS

Questions for Class Discussion

1. What are the possible income tax consequences of a divorce agreement for the husband and wife?

2. What special tax treatment is afforded an individual who collects on an "employee annuity"?

3. Under what conditions may an award be excluded from gross income?

4. What are the tax consequences to an individual who pays a debt by transferring appreciated property to a creditor?

5. What are the possible tax consequences to an owner of land when the tenant constructs a permanent type building on the property?

6. Who pays the tax on a gift of the income from a certain piece of property? The donee or donor?

7. What is a gift?

8. Mr. A served as chairman of the local school board campaign. Upon completion of his term in office, the organization awarded him a silver serving tray in recognition of his outstanding service to the organization. The value of the tray was $200. Is Mr. A required to include the value of the tray in his income?

9. Does the employee death benefits provision generally reduce the tax problems of the family of a deceased employee?

10. What types of payments made by the employer to the family of a deceased employee would not be eligible for the employee death benefits exclusion?

11. Under what conditions are life insurance proceeds subject to taxation?

12. How do the tax laws influence a survivor's choice of a settlement option under a life insurance policy on the life of the deceased spouse?

13. In cases involving doctors serving an internship or residency in a hospital, what criteria are used to determine whether the pay received by the doctor is an excludable scholarship or fellowship?

14. Under what conditions can a person who is not a candidate for a degree exclude an amount received as a scholarship or fellowship?

15. If a taxpayer receives an award for damages to his leg he suffered in an automobile accident, the payment is generally excludable from taxable income. Are the tax treatments of pay-

ments for personal injury and damages to property logically consistent?

16. What non-taxable fringe benefits are available to employees that are not available to partners and proprietors?

17. What are the possible tax consequences for a corporation that establishes a medical expense reimbursement plan that covers only one employee who also owns all of the corporation's outstanding stock?

18. What can an employer do to assure that the employees will receive favorable tax benefit for disability pay benefits?

19. Fred Smith earned $400 for the month of June. John Jones received $400 in disability pay. If the tax formula is supposed to reflect the taxpayer's "ability to pay" why should Fred pay taxes on his income while John pays no tax on his income?

20. How do you determine if the meals and lodging supplied by the employer is to serve a business purpose of the employer? Is the tax treatment of meals and lodging affected if the employer advertises that the meals and lodging provided are one of the benefits of working for him?

21. What special tax treatment is available to U. S. citizens who work abroad?

22. How do you determine whether a person is a "bona fide resident" of a foreign country?

23. What would be the social and economic consequences of eliminating the tax exemption now granted for interest on state and local government bonds?

24. What is the purpose of the dividend exclusion?

25. What are the tax consequences of recovering an amount deducted on a previous year's tax return?

26. How does the tax treatment of a corporation's income from retiring bonds for less than book value (issue price, plus amortized discount or less amortized premium) differ from the income from a shareholder's forgiveness of the corporation's indebtedness to him?

Problems

1. Which of the following items may be excluded from gross income?

   (a) Interest on U. S. government bonds.

   (b) Gain on the sale of State of New York bonds.

   (c) Interest on a state income tax refund.

   (d) A cash award for being selected the outstanding teacher. The selection is made on the basis of student nominations.

   (e) The Nobel Peace Prize.

(f) Meals and lodging furnished a forest warden in the Yosemite National Park.

(g) Insurance to reimburse the taxpayer for additional living expenses the taxpayer incurred as a result of a fire in his home.

(h) Social Security benefits.

(i) Employee's group hospitalization insurance premiums paid by the employer.

(j) A financial assistantship which requires the student to work 20 hours per week in a laboratory. Only students with a B+ average or better are eligible for the assistantship.

(k) Interest earned on a cash gift.

(l) A $10,000 prize received by the taxpayer when his name was selected at random from a telephone book.

(m) Securities received as a bequest from the taxpayer's deceased father.

2. Mr. and Mrs. X are in the process of negotiating their divorce agreement. What would be the tax consequences to Mr. X and Mrs. X if the following, considered individually, become part of the agreement:

(a) Mrs. X is to receive $1,000 per month until she dies or remarries and these payments are not to be alimony but part of the property settlement. Under state law the payments are considered a part of a property settlement.

(b) Mrs. X is to receive a principal sum of $50,000 plus $1,600 per month until she dies or remarries.

Mr. X transferred common stocks with a value of $50,000 which had an adjusted cost basis of $30,000 in payment of the principal sum.

(c) Mrs. X is to receive a principal sum of $100,000, with $50,000 to be paid in the year of the divorce and $5,000 per year to be paid to her in each of the following 10 years.

3. The taxpayer purchased an annuity from an insurance company for $15,000 on January 1, 19X1. The annuity was to pay him $1,200 per year for life. At the time he purchased the contract his life expectancy was 16 years.

(a) Determine his taxable income from the annuity in the first year.

(b) Assume he lives 20 years after purchasing the contract, what would be his taxable income in the 19th year?

(c) Same as (a) except the annuity was received under a settlement option of an insurance policy on the life of his wife.

(d) Same as (a) except the annuity was received from a qualified pension plan and the employee had contributed $3,000 toward the cost of the annuity.

4. Indicate whether the following results in taxable income to the recipient. If the item is not taxable, explain why.

(a) Sweet Sue Blue won the Miss Centerville beauty contest, and received a $1,000 college scholarship.

(b) Larry Longstride won the master's mile run held in his home town. As the winner he received a $1,000 cash prize paid by a philanthropist who sponsored the race to encourage running for health purposes.

(c) Carl Adkins received a $500 award from his employer for making the Dean's list at a college where Carl was a part-time student. The employer frequently makes such payments to encourage employees to further their education.

5. The LMN Corp. carries an ordinary life insurance policy on its key employees, one of whom is 45 year old Mr. L. The annual premiums are $1,800 and the face amount of the policy is $30,000. The corporation also covers Mr. L. for $25,000 under a group-term policy that applies only to shareholder employees. Mr. L. also has $100,000 in protection under the employer's group policy that applies to all employees and coverage of $2\frac{1}{2}$ times the employee's annual salary. Mr. L. has the right to name the beneficiary on all policies. Determine Mr. L.'s taxable income from the above.

6. Does the individual recognize income in the following cases?

(a) Mr. Brown was an attorney. His uncle bequeathed certain property to Brown on the condition that Brown serve as executor of the uncle's estate. Brown served as executor and received securities with a value of $15,000.

(b) On his last day at work, after 36 years of working for the same firm, Robert Cranford received a gold watch from his employer "in appreciation of his long and loyal service to the firm."

(c) Les Linard was employed as a maintenance man for the Ajax Manufacturing Company for several years when he became a victim of a terminal illness. His medical bills far exceeded his insurance and savings. Recognizing Les' dire financial and physical circumstances, his employer gave him $3,000.

(d) Daniel Abbot cashed in his endowment life insurance policy and collected $10,000. He had paid premiums totaling $7,-000.

7. Sam Elliot died during the current year. At the time of his death his accrued salary and commissions totaled $1,500 and were paid to his wife. She collected his interest in the employer's qualified

profit sharing plan amounting to $24,000. Sam's non-forfeitable interest in the plan at the time of his death was $22,000. The employer also paid her $28,000 which represented an amount equal to Sam's salary for the year prior to his death. The employer had a policy of making the salary payments to "help out the family in the time of its greatest need." As beneficiary of her husband's life insurance policy, she elected to collect the proceeds in installments. In the year of death she collected $8,000 which included $1,500 interest income. What is Mrs. Elliot's taxable income from the above?

8. Several years ago, Red Sails transferred his life insurance policy to a partnership in which he was a partner. The partnership was to receive the proceeds of the policy at the time of his death. At a time when the partnership's basis in the policy was $25,000 and after Red had ceased to work in the partnership on a full-time basis, the partnership was incorporated. The incorporation was a non-taxable event and in exchange for his interest in the partnership, Red received interest bearing long-term notes (due in 10 years) and did not participate in the corporation's business affairs. Several years later when the corporation's basis in the policy was $35,000, Red died and the corporation used the proceeds of the policy ($60,000) to retire Red's notes for $5,000 less than their face amount. What are the tax consequences to the corporation of collecting on the policy and retiring the notes?

9. Ron Ready received a State Medical Education Assistance loan while he was working towards his degree. To qualify for the loan the student must be in the top 25% of his class. Under the terms of the loan he received $4,000 per year during his last 2 years of medical school. However, if he practiced in a rural area for three or more years, he was not required to repay the loan. Ron fulfilled the practice requirements in the current year. Does he realize taxable income from the above? If so, when would the income be considered realized?

10. The taxpayer was a chemist working for a large corporation when he decided to return to the University to earn a Ph.D. He discussed his plans with his supervisor who encouraged him to pursue his studies, but said the company could not pay him, nor hold his job while he was gone. However, the supervisor said the company was interested in any type of research concerned with controlling air pollutants because of the potential commercial markets and the company would sponsor his dissertation if it were in the area of pollution. The taxpayer wrote a dissertation proposal; the company reviewed it and they awarded him a $10,000 scholarship. Under the agreement, the company had no rights to the taxpayer's research effort. Because of the taxpayer's new area of expertise, the employer offered him a new higher paying job when

he completed his degree requirement. His first assignment was to develop his dissertation into a new product. Is the $10,000 an excludable fellowship?

11. Billy Dervall was a partner in a very successful law firm when he contracted emphysema and was not able to work after Friday, April 1. He died October 1 after collecting his full share of the partnership profits totaling $40,000 for the period April through September. What is Dervall's disability pay exclusion?

12. Does the taxpayer recognize taxable income from the following?

   (a) Florence Flightingale is a registered nurse working in a community hospital. She is not required to take her lunch on the hospital premises, but she can eat in the cafeteria at no charge. The hospital adopted this policy to encourage employees to stay on the premises and therefore be available in the case of emergencies. During the year, Florence ate most of her meals on the premises and the total value of those meals was $750.

   (b) Joe Goldman is the manager of a hotel. His employer will allow him to live in one of the rooms rent free or receive a $200 per month cash allowance for rent. Joe elected to live in the hotel.

   (c) Smokey Joe Jones is a forest ranger and lives in his employer's cabin in the forest. He is required to live there and because there are no restaurants near the forest, the employer supplies Smokey with groceries that he cooks and eats on the premises.

   (d) Tom Kooky is a partner in the Rocking R Ranch partnership. He is the full-time manager of the ranch and there is a business purpose for his living on the ranch.

13. Sam Brown, a U. S. citizen, began work on an American oil construction site in Peru on March 1 of the previous year, earning a salary of $700 per week. He and his wife became bona fide residents of Peru in March and he continued to work there until December of the current year when his wife became seriously ill and they had to return to the U. S. During the 21-month period from March 1 of the previous year to December 1 of the current year, Sam worked for his employer in Columbia for three weeks in January and he and his wife were on a paid vacation in the U. S. for two weeks in February. Mrs. Brown operated a dress shop as a proprietorship from March 1 to August 31 of the current year. She worked in the shop on a full-time basis, and her profits for the period was $4,000. Compute Mr. and Mrs. Brown's taxable income, for the current year, from the above.

14. (a) If state government bonds are yielding 5%, what rate of interest would have to be paid on a taxable bond of compar-

able risk in order to attract investors who are in the sixty percent marginal tax bracket?

(b) Mr. Jones' home was condemned by the state for a highway right-of-way. Jones contested the valuation placed on his property and it took two years to settle the case. Upon settlement, Jones received $40,000 for his property and $3,000 interest on the condemnation award. He also collected $4,000 interest on the city's industrial development bonds. The proceeds were used to finance construction of a municipal airport. What is Jones' taxable income from the above?

15. During the current year Al Adams received $60 in dividends on stock he owned in American Telephone Co. His wife also owned shares in the same corporation and received $120 in dividends. They jointly owned stock in another domestic corporation which paid $50 in dividends and stock in a French corporation which paid $40 in dividends. They also have a joint account with a savings and loan association which paid $80 in dividends and Mr. Adams collected a $30 dividend on his life insurance policy.

(a) Calculate the dividend exclusion for Mr. and Mrs. Adams on their joint tax return assuming they reside in a common law state.

(b) Calculate the dividend exclusion if Mr. and Mrs. Adams reside in Texas.

16. In a previous year, the cash basis taxpayer took a deduction for an $8,000 commission paid to a broker who supposedly located a customer for the taxpayer's products. Actually, the customer did not have the necessary capital to buy the taxpayer's product and the broker knew this at the time he collected his commission. So, in the current year, the taxpayer threatened to sue the broker who then refunded the commission. The taxpayer is in a higher marginal tax bracket in the current year than he was in the year the commission was deducted. Can he obtain any relief under § 111?

17. The UPZ Corporation, an accrual basis taxpayer, was experiencing trouble in paying its bills because of a shortage in working capital. The corporation had to pay for most of the materials it acquired soon after delivery, but UPZ sold its finished products on long-term contracts. The corporation tried to borrow money from a bank, but the loan officer said the loan could not be granted until UPZ reduced its short-term debt. Accrued rent totaling $12,000 was part of the short-term debt. The rent had been deducted on the previous year's tax return. The landlord was anxious for UPZ to stay in business because he thought it would be difficult to obtain a new tenant, so he cancelled the debt. The

corporation also owed a shareholder $30,000 on a short-term note, which he agreed to cancel. The corporation's balance sheet prior to the debt cancellation was as follows:

Cash	$40,000	Current Liability	$200,000
Accounts receivable	150,000	Long-term debt	50,000
Inventory	90,000	Paid in Capital	320,000
Fixed assets (net)	220,000	Retained earnings	(70,000)
	$500,000		$500,000

The fair market value of the company's assets is equal to its book value.

(a) Is the cancellation of the debt to the shareholder a taxable event to the corporation?

(b) Is the cancellation of the $12,000 accrued rent taxable to the company?

Research Problems

1. The taxpayer, a U. S. Citizen, is a statistician and has devoted several years to studying the game of Black-Jack. He developed a probability based fool-proof system to beat the house which he used in a European country and won over $40,000 from an initial investment of $2,000. The taxpayer satisfied the foreign residency test for the foreign earned income exclusion; however, the IRS agent has disallowed the exclusion on the basis that the income does not qualify as "earned" since it was not received for "personal services actually rendered."

    Does the taxpayer's income qualify for the exclusion?

2. Mr. and Mrs. Brown are in the process of reaching a divorce settlement. Mr. Brown has agreed to pay Mrs. Brown $1,000 per month for the remainder of her life or until remarriage. However, Mrs. Brown is concerned about the possibility of Mr. Brown pre-deceasing her and that the assets in his estate will not be sufficient to continue paying her alimony. Therefore, she has requested that Mr. Brown continue to pay the premiums on an insurance policy on his life with Mrs. Brown the beneficiary.

    Would Mrs. Brown be required to include the insurance premiums in her income as alimony?

Chapter 6

DEDUCTIONS AND LOSSES—
IN GENERAL

GENERAL TESTS FOR
DEDUCTIBILITY

After having discussed what constitutes gross income, and inclusions and exclusions from gross income, it is necessary to review deductions and losses. Understanding how expense items are classified is a necessary prelude to the discussion of specific tax rules. Therefore, Chapter 6 includes an initial discussion of how expenses are classified under the tax law.

As previously discussed, § 61 provides an "all inclusive" definition of what constitutes items of gross income. Deductions and exemptions, however, must be specifically provided for in the statute.[1] The courts have established the doctrine that an item is not deductible unless a specific Code section provides for its deduction, i. e., "deductions are a matter of legislative grace."[2]

---

1. § 63(a).

2. *New Colonial Ice Co. v. Helvering,* 4 USTC ¶ 1292, 13 AFTR 1180, 54 S. Ct. 788 (USSC, 1934).

CLASSIFICATION OF DEDUCTIBLE EXPENSES

For individual taxpayers deductions are either (1) *for* adjusted gross income or (2) *from* adjusted gross income (itemized deductions). Corporations are not subject to this separate classification scheme since the term "adjusted gross income" does not appear in the corporate tax formula. In the computation of taxable income for corporate taxpayers, items of expense are either deductible or are not deductible, e. g. certain corporate expenses which are unreasonable would not be deductible.

The most frequently encountered deductions *for* adjusted gross income of individual taxpayers include:

1. Expenses of a trade, business or profession;
2. Expenses attributable to the production or collection of income or for the management, conservation, or maintenance of property held for the production of income, e. g. rent and royalty expenses;
3. Certain employment related expenses such as traveling, i. e., meals and lodging while away from home, transportation, moving and employee expenses which are reimbursed by the employer; and
4. Alimony payments for taxable years beginning after 1976.

Some of the more frequently encountered deductions *from* adjusted gross income (itemized deductions) include the following:

1. Contributions to qualified charitable organizations;
2. Medical expenses in excess of 3 percent of adjusted gross income;
3. State and local taxes, e. g. sales, real estate, and state and local income taxes;
4. Investment related expenses, e. g. safe deposit box rental and investment counsel or custodian fees.

The distinction between *for* and *from* adjusted gross income is significant since many tax calculations are based upon adjusted gross income, e. g. medical expenses and contribution deduction limitations. Further, if an item is deductible *from* adjusted gross income as an itemized deduction, a taxpayer may be prevented from using the standard deduction which would otherwise be available.

Example 1. John Jones is married and files a joint return with his spouse in 1977. He and his wife have adjusted gross income of $30,000 and have incurred $2,400 of itemized deductions during the year. In December, John asks you whether he should pay his real estate taxes of $400 in December or wait until the following January. Since the allowable standard deduction for 1977 is a flat $3,200 and the real estate taxes are deductible only as itemized deductions, John would obtain no tax benefit from paying the real estate taxes in December and should, therefore, make the payment in January of the following year.

Trade or Business Expenses. § 162(a) permits a deduction for all "ordinary and necessary" expenses paid or incurred in carrying on a trade or business including reasonable salaries paid for personal services, traveling expenses while away from home overnight in the pursuit of a business and expenses for the use of business property.

The term "trade or business" is not defined in the Code or Regulations and the courts have not provided a satisfactory definition. Therefore, it is usually necessary to ask some of the following questions to determine whether an item qualifies as a trade or business expense:

1. Was the use of the particular item related to a business activity, e. g. if funds are borrowed for use in a business, the interest should be deductible as a business expense? However, if the funds were used to acquire passive investments, e. g. stocks and taxable bonds, the interest expense is an itemized deduction.

2. Was the expenditure incurred with the intent to realize a profit or to produce income, e. g. expenses in excess of the income from raising horses would not be deductible if the activity were conducted as a personal hobby.

3. Were the taxpayer's activities, i. e., operation and/or management activities extensive enough to warrant the carrying on of a trade or business?

§ 162 excludes the following items from classification as a trade or business expense:

1. Charitable contributions or gifts;

2. Bribes, illegal kickbacks and certain treble damage payments; and

3. Fines and penalties.

Expenses Attributable to the Production or Collection of Income. § 212 provides for the deductibility of ordinary and necessary expenses which are paid or incurred:

1. For the production or collection of income;

2. For the management, conservation or maintenance of property held for the production of income; and

3. In connection with the determination, collection, or refund of any tax.

Thus, under this definition the following items would not be deductible:

1. Expenses related to the management, conservation, or maintenance of a personal residence; [3]

2. Expenses related to tax exempt income; [4] and

3. Hobby, sport or recreation related expenses.[5]

Investment related expenses, e. g. safe deposit box rentals are deductible under § 212 [6] as deductions attributable to the production of investment income. However, investment related expenses are treated as itemized deductions whereas rent and royalty expenses are deductible for adjusted gross income.[7]

To obtain a deduction under § 212, it is not necessary for the property to be currently producing taxable income.[8] For example, a taxpayer who holds a former residence with the expectation of realizing appreciation in the market value may be entitled to expense deductions such as maintenance and depreciation even though the property is not held for rental purposes.[9]

ORDINARY AND NECESSARY EXPENSES

Inclusion in the Code. The terms "ordinary" and "necessary" are found in both §§ 162 and 212. § 162 governs the deductibility of trade or business expenses. To be deductible under this section of the Code, a trade or business expense must be not only "ordinary and necessary" but "reasonable" in amount. The Regulations under § 212, in addition, state that expenses must bear a reasonable and proximate relation to the production or collection of income or to the management, conservation, or maintenance of property held for the production of income.[10]

Definition and Meaning of the Terms. The words "ordinary and necessary" are not defined in the Code or Regulations. An expenditure must be both "ordinary and necessary." The problem is that many expenses which are necessary are *not* ordinary. The courts have held that an expense is necessary if a prudent businessman would incur the same expense the payment of which is appropriate and helpful in the taxpayer's business.[11]

An expense is ordinary if it has the connotation of being normal, usual, or customary in the type of business conducted by the taxpay-

---

3. Reg. § 1.212–1(h).

4. Reg. § 1.212–1(e).

5. Reg. § 1.212–1(c).

6. Reg. § 1.212–1(g).

7. § 62(5).

8. Reg. § 1.212–1(b).

9. *Frank A. Newcombe,* 54 T.C. 1298 (1970).

10. Reg. § 1.212–1(d).

11. *Welch v. Helvering,* 3 USTC ¶ 1164, 12 AFTR 1456, 54 S.Ct. 8 (USSC, 1933).

er and is not capital in nature.[12] However, the courts have also held that an expense does not have to be recurring to be deductible as "ordinary." [13]

> **Example 2.** T purchased a manufacturing concern which has just been adjudged bankrupt. Because the concern has a poor financial rating, T satisfies some of the obligations incurred by its former creditors. Although he had no legal obligation to pay these debts, T felt that this is the only way he could reestablish a source of credit for future inventory purchases.
>
> (1)   Were the payments necessary? The Supreme Court found that the payments were necessary in that they were both appropriate and helpful.[14]
>
> (2)   Were the payments ordinary? The court held that the payments were *not* ordinary but were in the nature of capital expenditures to build a reputation (goodwill).

> **Example 3.** W, a widow, owned a small portfolio of investments left to her by her late husband. Part of this portfolio included 100 shares of Texaco, Inc., common stock. W incurred $350 in travel expenses to attend the annual shareholders' meeting of Texaco at which she voted her 100 shares against the current management group. Were W's expenses deductible under § 212? No deduction would be permitted since the expenses must bear a reasonable and proximate relation to the value of the property investment.[15]

REASONABLENESS REQUIREMENT

Requirements in the Code and Judicial Interpretations. The Code refers to reasonableness solely with respect to salaries and other compensation for personal services.[16] The courts, however, have held that for a business expense to be "ordinary and necessary" it must also be "reasonable" in amount.[17]

What constitutes reasonableness is a "question of fact." If an expense is unreasonable, the excess amount is not allowed as a deduction. The question of reasonableness generally arises in closely-held corporation situations where there is no separation of ownership and management. In such cases, transactions between the shareholders

12. *Deputy v. DuPont,* 40–1 USTC ¶ 9161, 23 AFTR 808, 60 S.Ct. 363 (USSC, 1940).

13. *Dunn and McCarthy, Inc. v. Comm.,* 43–2 USTC ¶ 9688, 31 AFTR 1043, 139 F.2d 242 (CA–2, 1943).

14. *Supra,* note 11.

15. *J. Raymond Dyer,* 36 T.C. 456 (1961); Reg. § 1.212–1(d).

16. § 162(a)(1).

17. *Comm. v. Lincoln Electric Co.,* 49–2 USTC ¶ 9388, 38 AFTR 411, 176 F.2d 815 (CA–6, 1949).

and the company may result in the disallowance of excessive salaries, rent expense, etc. to the corporation. If the excessive payments for salaries, rents, etc. bear a close relationship to the stockholdings of the recipients, such amounts are treated as dividends to the shareholders and are nondeductible by the corporation.[18]

Example 4. XYZ Corporation is closely-held in equal ownership interests by X, Y and Z. The company has been highly profitable for several years and has not paid dividends. X, Y and Z are key officers of the company and each receive salaries of $200,000. Salaries for similar positions in comparable companies are only $100,000.

1. Amounts paid to X, Y and Z in excess of $100,000 may be deemed unreasonable and a total of $300,000 excessive salaries may be disallowed to the company.

2. The excess amounts may be treated as dividends rather than salary income to X, Y and Z since such excess amounts are proportional to the stock ownership percentages.

DEDUCTIONS AND LOSSES—TIMING OF EXPENSE RECOGNITION

Importance of Taxpayer's Method of Accounting. A taxpayer's method of accounting is important in determining taxable income because the method used determines when an item is includible in income and when an item is deductible on the tax return. Usually the taxpayer's regular method of record-keeping is used for income tax purposes.[19] The taxing authorities do not require uniformity among all taxpayers, but they do require that the method used clearly reflects income and that a taxpayer must handle items consistently.[20] The most common methods of accounting are the cash method and the accrual method. In most instances, individuals and professional service organizations use the cash method whereas most corporations use the accrual method.

Restrictions Upon the Cash Method. For cash basis taxpayers, expenses are usually deductible only when they are actually paid. For example, rent expense is not deductible by a cash basis taxpayer until the rent payment is made.

Since the cash basis method would allow a taxpayer almost unlimited discretion to affect the timing for recognizing income and expense items, (e. g. buying assets, supplies, etc., on December 31 to reduce that year's income), certain restrictions have been imposed. Where inventories are an income producing factor, the accrual method must be used for the computation of sales and cost of goods sold

18. Reg. § 1.162–8.

19. § 446(a).

20. §§ 446(b) and (e); Reg. § 1.-446(a)(2).

unless the Internal Revenue Service agrees to another method.[21] Likewise, assets with a useful life of more than one year must be capitalized subject to depreciation or amortization even though the taxpayer is using the cash method.

Generally, a cash basis taxpayer can deduct expenses when they are paid. However, prepayments of expenses are required to be capitalized. The Tax Reform Act of 1976 has now effectively placed cash basis taxpayers on the accrual basis with respect to the deductibility of prepaid interest.[22]

Prepaid rent is not allowed as a deduction when paid but must be deducted ratably over the prepayment period.[23]

Example 5. On July 1 of the current year, T leases a building for one year for use in his business. Under the terms of the lease, T pays the full annual rental of $6,000 in advance. Assuming T uses the cash method of accounting, $3,000 can be deducted in the current year and the remainder can be deducted in the subsequent year.

Prepaid medical expenses are not allowed as a deduction when paid by a cash basis taxpayer either.[24] The payment must be made in the same (or later) year in which the medical services are performed.

Example 6. On December 30 of the current year, T pays a physician $2,000 for an operation to be performed in February of the next year. The physician did not require the prepayment and regarded the procedure as highly irregular. T cannot deduct the $2,000 in the current year since it is a prepaid medical expense. If T had the operation in the current year and paid for it in the following year, a deduction in the subsequent year could have been taken.

Restrictions upon the cash method of accounting are discussed more fully in Chapters 4 and 16 of this text.

Accrual Method Requirements. A taxpayer using the accrual method of accounting includes income when it is earned (whether or not it is actually received) and deducts expenses when they are incurred (regardless of when they are paid). Income is earned when the right to receive it is established and the amount can be determined with reasonable accuracy.[25] Usually this means when the service is performed or the product is delivered. Likewise, expenses

---

21. Reg. § 1.446–1(c)(2).

22. § 461(g).

23. *Baton Coal Co. v. Comm.,* 2 USTC ¶ 788, 10 AFTR 270, 51 F.2d 469 (CA–3, 1931).

24. *Robert S. Basset,* 26 T.C. 619 (1956).

25. Reg. § 1.451–1(a).

are incurred when the liability is fixed by performance, completion or delivery of services and goods. As previously discussed in the text, taxpayers must use the accrual method of accounting for sales and cost of sales (if inventories are a material income producing factor) and assets of a fixed, or long term nature must be capitalized subject to depreciation.

Items which accrue ratably over a period of time (such as rent, interest and insurance premiums) are deducted by both cash and accrual basis taxpayers ratably over the time period involved. However, income received in advance (e. g. prepaid rent) must generally be included in income upon the receipt of such amounts. This treatment applies to both cash and accrual basis taxpayers.

A charitable contribution can be deducted only in the year paid by an individual, regardless of whether the cash or accrual basis is used.[26] An accrual basis taxpayer cannot deduct a charitable contribution when it is pledged unless the taxpayer is an accrual basis corporation, the payment is actually made on or before the fifteenth day of the third month following the close of the taxable year (i. e., by March 15 for calendar-year taxpayers); and the board of directors has authorized the contribution.[27]

> **Example 7.** In the current year T, an accrual basis individual, pledges $5,000 to his church—such pledge not being paid until next year. T cannot deduct the contribution until next year when it is actually paid. If T were an accrual basis corporation, the pledge could be deducted in the current year provided it was properly authorized by the board of directors, paid by March 15 of the next year, and the election to do so was made on this year's return.

DISALLOWANCE POSSIBILITIES

The tax law includes several provisions which provide for the disallowance of certain types of expenses. Without specific restrictions in the tax law, taxpayers might be able to deduct certain items which in reality are personal nondeductible expenditures. For example, specific tax rules are provided to determine whether an expenditure is for trade or business purposes or is related to a personal hobby and is, therefore, not deductible.

Certain disallowance provisions represent a codification and/or extension of prior court decisions e. g. the courts had denied deductions for payments which were deemed to be in violation of public

---

26. Reg. § 1.170–1(a)(1).   **27.** § 170(a)(2); Reg. § 1.170–3(b).

policy. Thus, the tax law was changed to provide specific authority for the disallowance of such deductions.

The following text material includes a detailed discussion of specific disallowance provisions in the tax law.

PUBLIC POLICY LIMITATION

Justification for Denying Deductions. The courts have developed the principle that a payment which is in violation of public policy is not a necessary expense and is, therefore, not deductible.[28] If the law were to permit such deductions, the government would, in effect, be subsidizing a taxpayer's wrongdoing. As a result of these judicial interpretations, § 162 now denies a deduction for bribes or kickbacks; for fines and penalties paid to a government for violation of law; and two-thirds of the treble damage payments made to claimants under violation of the antitrust law.[29]

> **Example 8.** During the year T, an insurance salesman, paid $5,000 to U, a real estate broker. The payment represented 20 percent of the commissions earned by T from policies referred to him by U. Under state law the splitting of commissions by an insurance salesman is an act of misconduct which could warrant a revocation of the salesman's license.
>
> § 162(c) states that no deduction is permitted for a kickback which is illegal under state law (if such state law is generally enforced), and which subjects the payor to a criminal penalty or the loss of license or privilege to engage in a trade or business. Thus, the payments of $5,000 by T to U are not deductible if the state law is generally enforced.

Legal Expenses Incurred in Defense of Civil or Criminal Penalties. Generally, legal expenses (assuming reasonableness) are deductible as ordinary and necessary business expenses if incurred in connection with a trade or business activity. Legal expenses may also be deductible under § 212, e. g. legal expenses incurred in conjunction with rental property which is held for the production of income or tax counsel relative to the preparation of the taxpayer's income tax returns. If legal expenses are incurred for personal reasons, e. g. to obtain a divorce (non-tax aspects), the expenses are not deductible.

Legal fees pursuant to a criminal defense are deductible if the crime is associated with the taxpayer's trade or business activity.[30]

---

28. *Tank Truck Rentals, Inc. v. Comm.*, 58–1 USTC ¶ 9366, 1 AFTR2d 1154, 78 S.Ct. 507 (USSC, 1958).

30. *Comm. v. Tellier*, 66–1 USTC ¶ 9319, 17 AFTR2d 633, 86 S.Ct. 1118 (USSC, 1966).

29. §§ 162(c), (f), and (g).

Previously, the IRS' position was that the legal fees were deductible only if the taxpayer was successful in the criminal suit.

In determining whether legal expenses are deductible, the taxpayer must be able to show that the origin and character of the claim is directly related to his trade or business or an income producing activity. Otherwise, the legal expenses are personal and nondeductible. For example, where a Secretary-Treasurer, who was responsible for the corporation's tax matters, incurred legal expenses in connection with his defense of criminal indictments for evasion of the corporation's income taxes, such legal expenses were deductible by the officer.[31] The court reasoned that the executive was in the trade or business of being an executive and that the court action would impair his ability to conduct this business activity.

POLITICAL CONTRIBUTIONS MADE BY INDIVIDUALS

Generally, no business deduction is permitted for direct or indirect payments for political purposes.[32] Historically, the government has been reluctant to grant favorable tax treatment to business expenditures for political purposes because of the possible abuses and the need to prevent undue influence upon the political process. However, the Revenue Act of 1971 enacted legislation which permits either a tax credit or a deduction for political contributions made by individual taxpayers. The credit is equal to one-half of the contribution but is limited to $25.00 or $50.00 on a joint return.[33] Instead of taking the tax credit, an individual may elect an itemized deduction for amounts up to $100 (or $200 on a joint return).[34] Generally, the deduction is preferable for high income tax bracket individuals who itemize their deductions. Tax credits are discussed in Chapter 11.

Qualifying Political Contributions. Political contributions of cash can be made to a candidate for election to a Federal, state or local office or to a political committee.[35] The term "political contribution" does not include any of the following: [36]

1. Contributions of property or services;

2. Amounts paid for raffle tickets; and

3. Amounts paid for advertising.

Example 9. During 19X2, T contributed $400 to the Republican National Campaign Committee to Reelect the President. Assuming the funds were properly used, T is entitled to a deduction of $100 ($200 on a joint return) if he itemizes his deductions. Otherwise, T may elect to take a tax credit of $25.00 ($50.00 on a

31. Rev.Rul. 68–662, 1968–2 C.B. 69.   34. § 218.

32. § 276.   35. § 41(c).

33. § 41(b)(1).   36. Prop.Reg. § 1.41–(d).

joint return). In this instance, the deduction is preferable if T's marginal tax rate is greater than 25 percent.

INVESTIGATION OF A BUSINESS

Taxpayers frequently incur expenses in the process of exploring new business opportunities. Expenses incurred in such investigations do not qualify as ordinary and necessary business expenses (§ 162) nor are they deductible under § 212 as expenses incurred in the production of income.[37] Business investigation costs are nonamortizable intangible capital costs which are generally deductible only as a loss in the year of abandonment or sale of the new business.[38]

If the taxpayer decides not to acquire or enter into the new business activity, the position of the IRS is that no deduction for a loss is permitted to individuals since the taxpayer is not actively engaged in a trade or business activity.[39] The courts, however, have permitted a loss deduction to individuals where the activities were specific in nature and involved more than a general investigation.[40]

Example 10. T, a disgruntled middle management executive for a large corporation, desires to go into business for himself. He conducted a general investigation of a motel in Florida and incurred $350 of travel expenses. In addition, T paid a CPA $300 to conduct a financial analysis of the motel's financial condition.

1. If T acquires the motel, the investigation expenditures are capital expenditures which are recoverable only upon the abandonment or sale of the business. Such expenses are not trade or business expenses under § 162 and would be deductible only as a loss under § 165(c)(2).

2. If T decides not to make the investment, it is the position of the IRS that the expenditures are not deductible. Since the investigation was general in nature it would be difficult to qualify such expenditures as losses under existing judicial authority.

Example 11. Assume the same facts as in the prior example except that T already owns and manages several motels.

Since T is in the trade or business of owning and managing motels and is merely investigating the possibilities of expansion of his business, the investigation expenses are deductible if T decides not to acquire the motel. If T acquires the motel, the expenses are capital expenditures which are recoverable only upon the abandonment or sale of the motel in Florida.

---

37. *Morton Frank*, 20 T.C. 511 (1953); *Dwight A. Ward*, 20 T.C. 332 (1953).

38. Rev.Rul. 57–418, 1957–2 C.B. 143.

39. *Ibid.*

40. *Harris W. Sneed*, 52 T.C. 880 (1969).

HOBBY LOSSES

Rationale for § 183. Deductions under § 162 for business expenses and § 212 for expenses attributable to the production of income are permitted only where the taxpayer can show that the business or investment activity was entered into for the purpose of making a profit and not for personal pleasure (i. e., recreation). Certain activities may have profit-seeking or personal attributes depending upon individual circumstances, e. g. raising horses and operating a farm which is used as a weekend residence. Since personal losses are not deductible whereas losses attributable to profit-seeking activities may be deducted and used to offset a taxpayer's other income, e. g. salary of an executive, it was necessary to develop tax rules to prevent possible tax avoidance.

General Rules. If a taxpayer (an individual or Subchapter S Corporation) can show that an activity has been conducted with the intent to earn a profit, any losses from the activity are fully deductible and § 183 is not applicable. The hobby loss rules apply only if the activity is not engaged in for profit. § 183 provides that hobby expenses are deductible only to the extent of hobby income.[41]

The Regulations stipulate the following relevant factors which are to be considered in making the determination if the activity is a hobby: [42]

1. The manner in which the activity is carried on, e. g., if the activity is conducted in a businesslike manner;

2. The expertise of the taxpayer or his advisors;

3. The time and effort expended;

4. The expectation that the assets of the activity will appreciate in value;

5. The previous success of the taxpayer in the conduct of similar activities;

6. The history of income or losses from the activity;

7. The relationship of profits earned to losses incurred;

8. The financial status of the taxpayer, e. g. if the taxpayer does not have substantial amounts of other income, this fact may indicate that the activity is engaged in for profit; and

9. Elements of personal pleasure or recreation in the activity.

Presumptive Rule of § 183. The Code provides a rebuttable presumption that an activity is profit-seeking if it shows a profit in at least two of any five (seven for horses) consecutive years ending with the taxable year in question.[43] For example, if these profitabili-

---

41. § 183(b).   **43.** § 183(d).

42. Reg. §§ 1.183–2(b)(1) through (9).

ty tests have been met, the activity is presumed to be a trade or business rather than a personal hobby. In effect, the burden of proof is shifted to the IRS to show that the activity is personal rather than trade or business related. A taxpayer can elect to postpone the application of this test by electing to wait until he has conducted the activity for five years or until the activity has generated two profitable years.[44]

> **Example 12.** Nathan Jones is an executive for a large corporation and is paid a salary of $200,000. His wife is a collector of antiques. Several years ago she opened an antique shop in a local shopping center and spends most of her time buying and selling antiques. She occasionally earns a small profit from this activity but more frequently incurs substantial losses. If such losses are business related, they are fully deductible against Nathan's salary income if a joint return is filed.
>
> 1. As a tax advisor you should initially see if the antique "business" has met the 2 of 5 years profit test in § 183.
> 2. If the presumption is not met, the activity may nevertheless qualify as a business if the taxpayer can show that the intent is to engage in a profit-seeking business. It is not necessary to show actual profits.
> 3. Attempts should be maintained to fit the operation within the nine criteria which are prescribed in the Regulations, e. g. that the activity is conducted in a businesslike manner; that the taxpayer devoted extensive time and effort to the business, etc.

If an activity is deemed to be a hobby, the expenses are deductible only to the extent of the income from the hobby. However, certain expenses may be allowable under other sections of the Code without regard to whether the activity is a hobby or not. For example, interest expense is deductible under § 163. Since the total expense deductions of the hobby cannot exceed the income, the Code provides that the otherwise deductible items, e. g. interest must be deducted first in computing the overall limitation.[45]

> **Example 13.** T, the vice-president of an oil company, decides that in his spare time he wants to become an artist. Pursuant to this desire during the current year he incurs the following expenses:
>
> | | |
> |---|---|
> | Correspondence study course on figure painting | $ 350 |
> | Art supplies | 200 |
> | Cost of converting attic in family residence to a studio | 3,000 |
> | Interest on $3,000 borrowed from a bank—the proceeds were used to convert the attic to a studio | 240 |
> | Fees paid to female models who posed for figure studies | 450 |

44. § 183(e).   **45.** § 183(b)(2).

During the year T sold three paintings to close friends for $100 each.

In the event the activity is deemed a hobby, the $240 of interest expense (which is fully deductible without regard as to whether the activity is a hobby) must first be offset against the $300 of income. Thus, only $60 of other hobby expenses are deductible. The net result is that T must include $300 of income in his gross income and receives deductions of $240 for interest and $60 for other expenses. The remaining expenditures are disallowed.

If the interest expenses exceeded the amount of hobby income, such excess amounts would be deductible *from* adjusted gross income (as itemized deductions) if the activity were deemed a hobby.

Rental of Vacation Homes. The Tax Reform Act of 1976 added § 280A which places restrictions upon taxpayers who rent their vacation homes for part of the tax year. The following rules apply depending upon the extent to which the vacation home is rented during a particular year:

1. If the home is rented for less than 15 days, all rentals are excluded from gross income and rent expenses are disallowed.[46] However, the taxpayer may still claim deductions for real estate taxes, interest, etc., which would otherwise be deductible as deductions *from* adjusted gross income (itemized deductions).

2. If the vacation home is not used more than 14 days for personal use (or more than 10% of the total days rented), § 280A limitations do not apply.[47] In this case, rental expenses may or may not be allowed under the hobby loss deductibility rules of § 183.

3. If the vacation home is rented for 15 or more days and is used for personal purposes for (1) more than 14 days or (2) more than 10% of the rental days, (the usual case) deductions are applied against gross income and may be scaled down in the same manner as is applied to hobby loss expenses.

Example 14. Sam Jones rents his vacation home for 4 months and lives in the home for 1 month. Rules outlined in No. 3 above, therefore, apply. His gross income from rent is $3,000;

---

46. § 280A(g).   **47.** § 280A(d).

real estate taxes, $800; $1,500 mortgage interest; $800 for utilities and maintenance and $1,000 depreciation.[48]

	Taxable and Deductible	Not Deductible
Gross Income	$ 3,000	
Apportioned to:		
(1) Taxes and Interest (otherwise deductible items)	(2,300)	
(2) Utilities and maintenance	(700)	$ 100
(3) Depreciation	(–0–)	1,000
	$ –0–	$1,100

Taxes and interest are itemized deductions which are deductible regardless of whether the vacation and/or hobby loss rules apply. Thus, $2,300 of such expenses must be deducted and used as an offset against the $3,000 gross income. Therefore, only $700 of additional expenses may be deducted under the vacation home limitation rules.

EXPENDITURES INCURRED FOR TAXPAYER'S BENEFIT OR TAXPAYER'S OBLIGATION

Generally, an expense must be incurred for the taxpayer's benefit or arise from the taxpayer's obligation; an individual cannot claim a tax deduction by paying the expenses of another individual. One exception to this rule is the payment of medical expenses for a dependent. Such expenses are deductible by the payor.[49]

Example 15. During the current year, F pays the interest on his son's home mortgage. Neither F nor the son can take a deduction for the interest paid because the obligation is not F's and the son did not pay the interest.

The tax result might have been more favorable if F had made a cash gift to the son and let the son pay the interest. Then the interest could have been deducted by the son and (depending upon other gifts and the amount involved), F may not have been liable for any gift taxes on the cash gift to the son. A deduction would have been created with no cash difference to the family.

Example 16. Taxpayer's daughter, D, married in January. Her husband was in the Army and was shipped overseas in February. D lived with T for the entire year except for a short honeymoon. She was supported by T and T paid her medical bills. D filed a joint return with her husband who had a gross income of $3,000. T cannot claim D as a dependent (because she filed jointly with her husband) and, as a consequence, T cannot deduct the medical bills paid for D.

---

48. See Reg. § 1.183–1(d)(3) Ex. (i) and (ii).   **49.** § 213(a)(1).

D should not have filed jointly with her husband, or as an alternative, T should have made a gift to her and she should have paid her own medical expenses.

One business cannot deduct the expenses of another business. For example, if two businesses (whether or not incorporated) are controlled by the same interest, the IRS may redistribute or reallocate any items of income, expense or credit where such reallocation is required either to prevent the evasion of taxes or to clearly reflect income of any such businesses.[50]

Example 17.   R Corporation and S Corporation are owned by the same shareholders. During the year S Corporation pays $50,000 for certain research and development expenditures which also benefit R Corporation. The payment was made by S Corporation because it alone has enough income to offset the deduction. The IRS may disallow part of the $50,000 expense on the return of S Corporation.

DISALLOWANCE OF PERSONAL EXPENDITURES

§ 262 states that "except as otherwise expressly provided in this chapter, no deduction shall be allowed for personal, living, or family expenses." Thus, an individual must be able to identify a particular section of the Code which sanctions the deductibility of an otherwise personal nondeductible expenditure, e. g. charitable contributions—§ 170, medical expenses—§ 213, moving expenses—§ 217. In addition, an individual may deduct "ordinary and necessary" expenses paid or incurred (1) for the production or collection of income, (2) for the management, conservation, or maintenance of property held for the production of income, or (3) expenses in connection with the determination, collection, or refund of any tax.[51]

Sometimes the personal and deductible character of a particular expenditure are not easily separated or determined.

Example 18.   During the current year H pays $1,500 in legal fees and court costs in order to obtain a divorce from his wife, W. Involved in the divorce action was a property settlement which concerned the disposition of income producing property owned by H.

The Tax Court[52] held in a similar case that H could not deduct any of the $1,500 costs. "Although fees primarily related to property division concerning his income-producing property, they weren't ordinary and necessary expenses paid for conservation or maintenance of property held for production of income. Legal fees incurred in defending against claims that arise from taxpay-

50.   § 482.

51.   § 212.

52.   *Harry H. Golberg,* 29 TCM 74, T. C. Memo., 1970–27.

er's marital relationship aren't deductible expenses regardless of possible consequences on taxpayer's income-producing property."

The IRS has clarified the issue of when legal fees incurred in connection with a divorce are deductible.[53] Their position is that an expense must relate solely to tax counsel in a divorce proceeding. For example, legal fees attributable to the determination of dependency exemptions of children, setting up a trust to make periodic alimony payments or to determine the tax consequences of a property settlement are deductible if the fees are distinguishable from the general legal fees of obtaining a divorce.

DISALLOWANCE OF DEDUCTIONS FOR UNREALIZED LOSSES

One of the basic ideas in tax law is that a deduction can be taken only where a loss has actually been realized. For example, a drop in the market price of securities held by the taxpayer does not result in a loss until the securities are actually sold or exchanged at the lower price. Furthermore, any deductible loss is limited to the taxpayer's cost basis in the asset.

> **Example 19.** Early this year T purchased a house for $50,000 in a new residential subdivision. Shortly thereafter heavy spring rains led to severe flooding which indicated that the subdivision's drainage facilities were inadequate. Because the subdivision now has a reputation of poor drainage, T estimates that the most he could receive on the resale of his home would be $30,000. He has the written appraisal reports of several reputable real estate brokers to support the $20,000 loss in value.
>
> Although § 165 allows a deduction for casualty losses, the loss is based on actual physical loss, not decline in value that may be a "fluctuation in market value not attributable to any actual physical depreciation."[54]
>
> If T later sells his house for $30,000, he will have a $20,000 loss which is not deductible because the house is a personal asset and the decline in value is not the result of a casualty. Casualty losses are discussed in Chapter 7.

DISALLOWANCE OF DEDUCTIONS FOR CAPITAL EXPENDITURES

The Code specifically disallows a deduction for "any amount paid out for new buildings or for permanent improvements or betterments made to increase the value of any property or estate."[55] The Regulations further define capital expenditures to include those expenditures which (1) add to the value or prolong the life of property or (2) adapt the property to a new or different use.[56] Incidental repairs

---

53. Rev.Rul. 72–545, 1972–2 C.B. 179.   **55.** § 263(a).

54. *Joe B. Thornton*, 47 T.C. 1 (1966).   **56.** Reg. § 1.263(a)–1(b).

and maintenance of the property are not capital expenditures and can be deducted as ordinary and necessary business expenses.[57] Thus, repairing a roof is a deductible expense whereas replacing a roof is a capital expenditure subject to depreciation deductions over its useful life. The tune-up of a delivery truck is an expense; a complete overhaul is probably a capital expenditure.

Exceptions. There are several exceptions to the general rule regarding capitalization of expenditures. Taxpayers can elect to expense certain mineral developmental costs and intangible drilling costs.[58] In addition, certain farm capital expenditures (such as soil and water conservation, fertilizer and land clearing costs) and certain research and experimental expenditures may be immediately expensed.[59]

Capitalization Versus Expense. When an expenditure is capitalized (rather than expended) the deduction is, at best, deferred and, at worst, lost forever. If the expenditure is for some improvement that has an ascertainable life, the expenditure can be depreciated or amortized over that life. Although an immediate tax benefit for a large cash expenditure is lost, the cost can be deducted in increments over a longer period of time. For example, the new roof mentioned previously can be depreciated. Costs that can be amortized include copyrights and patents. However, there are many other expenditures (such as land and payments made for goodwill) that cannot be amortized or depreciated. Goodwill has an indeterminate life whereas land is not a depreciable asset since its value does not generally decline.

Example 20. T purchased a prime piece of land located in an apartment zoned area. T paid $500,000 for the property which had an old (but usable) apartment building on it. T immediately had the building demolished at a cost of $100,000. The $500,000 cost and $100,000 demolition costs must be capitalized and the basis of the land becomes $600,000. Since land is a nondepreciable asset, no deduction is allowed.

More favorable tax treatment might result if T rented the apartments in the old building for a period of time to establish that there was not an intention to demolish the building. In that case, it might be possible to allocate a substantial portion of the original purchase price of the property to the building (a depreciable asset). When the building was later demolished, any remaining adjusted cost basis of the building could be taken as an ordinary (§ 1231) loss and the $600,000 would not have been frozen into the land with no deduction until it was sold.

57. *Ibid.*

58. §§ 263(c) and 616.

59. §§ 175, 180, 182 and 174.

Example 21. During the year T pays $3,000 in legal fees incurred in connection with the defense of a will contest suit. In an action brought by her brothers, T was successful in protecting the inheritance left to her by her mother. T must capitalize the $3,000 of legal fees unless the contested items were income items that must be included in her gross income when received (a highly unlikely event). The capitalized fees are, of course, not deductible by her.[60]

In some cases a taxpayer (given the choice) might prefer to capitalize rather than expense a particular item if the property is depreciable. In some instances an immediate deduction may create a net operating loss which (unless used up) expires in seven years. Thus, no tax benefit (or a smaller tax benefit) would be derived from an immediate deduction. The same expenditure, if capitalized and depreciated over a longer future period, could be offset against taxable income later (or against higher tax bracket income in future years) which results in a greater tax benefit.

Capitalization Elections. Because of the tax avoidance possibilities inherent in allowing elective "capitalize or expense" decisions, most expenditures are, by law, not elective. They are generally either—or decisions based on the nature of the expenditure. However, in certain cases it is permissible to elect whether to capitalize or to immediately expense a particular item. For example, § 266 allows taxpayers to elect to capitalize certain "taxes and carrying charges." This election applies to carrying charges, interest or indebtedness and certain taxes (such as property and employer paid payroll taxes) paid during the construction period on real (buildings and land) or personal property (such as machinery and equipment) whether the property is business or nonbusiness in nature.[61] A taxpayer may elect to capitalize some expenditures and not others. For example, one could elect to capitalize property taxes and expense interest on the construction indebtedness. A new election may be made for each project. For example, one could elect to capitalize expenditures on a factory being constructed and expense the same type of items on a constructed machine. On unimproved and unproductive real estate (land held for later sale, for example) a new election may be made for each year.

§ 189, which was added in 1976, now requires individuals, Subchapter S corporations, and personal holding companies to capitalize construction period interest and taxes subject to specific rules for amortizing such amounts. Special transitional rules are provided in the law. This change was intended to restrict tax shelter opportunities for individuals.

---

60. Reg. §§ 1.212–1(k) and 1.263(a)–2(c).

61. Reg. §§ 1.266–1(a) through 1.266–1(e).

TRANSACTIONS BETWEEN RELATED PARTIES

The Code places restrictions upon the recognition of gains and losses between related parties. Because of relationships created by birth, marriage and business there would be endless possibilities for engaging in various types of financial transactions which would produce tax savings with no real economic substance or change. For example, a wife could sell property to her husband at a loss, deduct the loss on their joint return and her husband could hold the asset indefinitely and, therefore, create an artificial loss. Such "sham" transactions have resulted in a complex set of laws designed to eliminate such abuses.

Losses. § 267 provides for the disallowance of any "losses from sales or exchanges of property * * * directly or indirectly," between related persons.[62] Upon the subsequent sale of such property to a nonrelated party, any gain recognized is reduced by the loss which was previously disallowed.

Example 22. A father sells common stock with a basis of $1,000 to his son T for $800. T sells the stock several years later for $1,100. The $200 loss is disallowed upon the sale to T, and only $100 of gain is taxable upon the subsequent sale.

Example 23. A father sells common stock with a basis of $1,000 to his son T for $800. T sells the stock for $900. T's gain of $100 is eliminated due to the $200 previously disallowed loss. Note that the offset may result in only partial tax benefit upon the subsequent sale. If the property had not been transferred to T, his father could have recognized a $100 loss upon the subsequent sale ($1,000 basis − $900 selling price).

Unpaid Expenses and Interest. § 267 also operates to prevent related taxpayers from engaging in tax avoidance schemes in situations where one related taxpayer uses the accrual method and the other is on a cash basis. An accrual basis closely-held corporation could borrow funds from a cash basis individual shareholder. At the end of the year the corporation would accrue and deduct the interest but the cash basis lender would not recognize interest income since no interest had been paid. § 267 specifically disallows a deduction to the accruing taxpayer unless the expense, e. g. interest, salaries or bonus, etc., is paid within 2½ months after the end of the lender's taxable year.[63] This section is particularly burdensome for owner-employees of closely-held corporations since the accrual basis corporation is never entitled to the deduction for such amount if the payment is not made within the 2½ month period.[64] This is the case even if the pay-

---

62. § 267(a)(1).

63. § 267(a)(2).

64. Reg. § 1.267(a)–1(b)(2).

ment is made during a subsequent period and the cash basis individual is, therefore, required to include the payment in income.

Relationships and Constructive Ownership. § 267 operates to disallow losses and deductions only between related parties. Losses or deductions generated by similar transactions with a stranger or an unrelated party are allowed. Related parties include the following: [65]

(1) Brothers and sisters (including half-blood), spouse, ancestors and lineal descendents of the taxpayer;

(2) A corporation owned more than 50% (directly or indirectly) by the taxpayer;

(3) Two corporations owned more than 50% (directly or indirectly) by the taxpayer if either corporation is a personal holding company or a foreign personal holding company; and

(4) A series of other complex relationships between trusts, corporations and taxpayers.

The law provides that constructive ownership rules are applied in determining whether the taxpayers are "related." [66] Constructive ownership rules state that stock owned by certain relatives or related entities is deemed to be owned by the taxpayer for loss and expense deduction disallowance purposes. Thus, for example, a taxpayer owns not only his stock but the stock owned by his lineal descendants, ancestors, brothers and sisters or half-brothers or sisters and his spouse. He also owns his proportionate share of stock owned by any partnership, corporation, estate or trust of which he is a member.

Example 24. The stock of V Corporation is owned 20% by T, 30% by T's father, 30% by T's mother, and 20% by T's sister. On July 1 of the current year T loaned $10,000 to V Corporation at 7% annual interest, principal and interest payable on demand. V Corporation uses the accrual basis and T uses the cash basis for tax purposes. Both are on a calendar year. Since T owns the 80% owned by her parents and sister, she constructively owns 100% of Corporation V. If the corporation accrues but does not pay the interest within the taxable year or within 2½ months thereafter (i. e., by March 15 of next year) no deduction is allowed to V. If T were an accrual basis taxpayer or if payment were actually or constructively received by T, the deduction would be allowed.

SUBSTANTIATION REQUIREMENTS

The tax law is built upon a voluntary system: taxpayers file their tax returns; report income and take deductions to which they

65. § 267(b).   **66.** § 267(c).

are entitled and pay their taxes through the withholding method (on salaries and wages) and/or by making estimated tax payments throughout the year. All of the transactions shown on the return require records and substantiation. A W-2 form, for example, substantiates the wages earned and the Federal income tax withheld. Some events throughout the year have to be documented as they occur. For example, it is generally advisable to receive a pledge payment statement from one's church in addition to a cancelled check to properly document a charitable contribution. Other types of deductible expenditures may require receipts or some other type of documentation.

Some areas of deductible expenditures such as business entertainment, gifts and travel have been subject to abuse. Prior to 1962, taxpayers could rely upon the so called "Cohan rule" which provided that a taxpayer could deduct travel or entertainment expenses based upon an approximation of the actual amounts where the exact amount was not determinable. In *Cohan v. Comm.*, the court permitted a partial deduction for entertainment expenses of a playwright who kept no records.[67]

The law now provides that no deduction will be allowed for any travel, entertainment or business gift expenditure unless properly substantiated by "sufficient evidence corroborating [the taxpayer's] own statements" of the following information: [68]

1. Amount of the expense;

2. Time and place of travel or entertainment (or date of gift);

3. The business purpose of such expense;

4. The business relationship of the taxpayer to the person entertained (or receiving the gift).

"Adequate records" can be a diary, account book or other expense record, provided the record is made at or near the time of the expenditure.[69] Furthermore, documentary evidence (receipts, paid bills, etc.), is required for lodging and any other expenditure of $25 or more.[70]

Specific rules for deducting travel and entertainment expenses are discussed in Chapter 7.

EXPENSES AND INTEREST RELATING TO TAX-EXEMPT INCOME

Since certain income is tax exempt (such as interest on municipal bonds) and § 212 allows one to deduct expenses incurred for the production of income, it might be possible to borrow money at 9%

---

67. *Cohan v. Comm.*, 2 USTC ¶ 489, 8 AFTR 10552, 39 F.2d 540 (CA-2, 1930).

68. § 274(d)(1).

69. Reg. § 1.274-5(c)(2)(ii)(a).

70. Reg. § 1.274-5(c)(2)(iii)(a) and (b).

and reinvest it in municipal bonds paying 7%; to deduct the interest paid while excluding the interest earned and (due to a tax bracket as high as 70%) actually profit from the transaction.

Specific Disallowance Under the Law. In order to eliminate this possibility, § 265 specifically disallows as a deduction any expense of producing tax-exempt income. Interest on any indebtedness incurred or continued to purchase or carry tax exempt obligations is disallowed under § 265.[71]

Judicial Interpretations. The courts have generally applied a liberal interpretation so that it is not always necessary for the IRS to show that the borrowings were directly invested in tax exempt securities. In one case, the court held that because of the taxpayer's use of municipal bonds as collateral for short-term loans to meet operating expenditures, he could not deduct the interest paid on the short-term loans.[72] However, the court did not require that existing municipal bonds be sold to finance the building of a factory (i. e., the interest on the factory mortgage would be deductible) since the liquidity of the business would be threatened. However, in another case, an interest expense deduction was denied to a taxpayer who was able to show a valid business purpose for continuing an indebtedness which was being used to "continue or carry" tax exempt securities.[73]

> **Example 25.** In January of the current year, T borrows $100,-000 at 8% interest which he uses to purchase 5,000 shares of stock in P Corporation. In July of the same year he sells the stock for $120,000 and reinvests the proceeds in City of Houston bonds, the income from which is tax-exempt. Assuming the $100,000 loan remained outstanding throughout the entire year, the interest attributable to the period in which the bonds were held cannot be deducted.

PROBLEM MATERIALS

Questions for Class Discussion

1. Why is it important to distinguish between deductions *for* and *from* adjusted gross income for individual taxpayers?

2. Are the following items deductible *for* adjusted gross income, *from* adjusted gross income or nondeductible personal items?

    a. Unreimbursed travel expenses of an employee.

    b. Alimony payments.

    c. Charitable contributions.

71. § 265(2); Reg. § 1.265–2.

72. *The Wisconsin Cheeseman, Inc. v. U. S.*, 68–1 USTC ¶ 9145, 21 AFTR2d 383, 388 F.2d 420 (CA–7, 1968).

73. *Illinois Terminal Railroad Co. v. U. S.*, 67–1 USTC ¶ 9374, 19 AFTR2d 1219, 375 F.2d 1016 (Ct.Cls., 1967).

    d.   Medical expenses.

    e.   Safe deposit box rentals.

    f.   Repairs made on personal residence.

    g.   Expenses related to tax exempt municipal bonds.

3. How is it possible for an expense to be necessary but not ordinary?

4. Is a business expenditure deductible if it is ordinary and necessary but not reasonable in amount?

5. Is a taxpayer permitted to deduct bribes, kickbacks or fines and penalties paid to a government for violation of law? Why?

6. Are legal expenses deductible if they are incurred to obtain a divorce? If they are incurred in connection with a trade or business? Why is this distinction made?

7. When is it preferable to claim a deduction for a political contribution in lieu of a credit?

8. If a taxpayer incurs expenses (e. g., travel, meals and lodging) in connection with the investigation of a new business opportunity, how are expenses treated if the new business is acquired? If the new business is *not* acquired?

9. What factors should be considered to determine whether an activity is a legitimate business activity or is a hobby?

10. If a taxpayer is unable to meet the requirements of § 183 relative to earning a profit in at least two of five consecutive years, is it possible to qualify the activity as a business? Why?

11. Why has the Code placed restrictions upon deductions relative to the rental of vacation homes?

12. Is there such a thing as a "pure" cash basis allowable for tax purposes? Explain.

13. When can prepaid expenses be taken by a cash basis taxpayer? Explain.

14. Contrast the accrual method and cash method as they are defined for tax purposes. What are their differences? What are the similarities?

15. Why do you suppose a church pledge cannot be deducted by an individual on the accrual basis?

16. What would be the tax manipulation possibilities if a taxpayer could deduct items paid by him but for the benefit of (say) a parent who does not qualify as his dependent?

17. List five personal type expenses that are "expressly provided" as deductions in the Code.

18. Are the legal fees paid in connection with a divorce ever deductible? Explain.

19. Why is a loss limited to a taxpayer's basis (even where the fair market value is much higher) or actual outlay?

20. Distinguish between deductible repairs and capital expenditures. Is the distinction dependent upon the dollar amount involved?

21. Would anyone ever *want* to capitalize (rather than expense) an item? Explain.

22. Discuss the reasons for the disallowance of losses between related parties. Would it make any difference if the parent sold stock to an unrelated third party and the child re-purchased the same number of shares of the stock in the market the same day?

23. What is constructive ownership? Discuss.

24. Discuss the substantiation requirements for deductible expenditures, particularly those for travel and entertainment.

25. If a taxpayer borrows funds which are used to acquire tax exempt securities, is a deduction permitted for the interest payments on the borrowed funds? Why?

26. Discuss the tracing problems which are encountered in the enforcement of the restrictions in § 265 which disallows a deduction for expenses of producing tax exempt income.

Problems

1. Jones is a controlling shareholder and president of the Jones Bay Construction Company. The company is privately held and has never paid dividends due to the need for internally generated funds to finance its business expansion. The remaining shareholders are members of Mr. Jones' immediate family. The company paid Mr. Jones a salary of $60,000 and a bonus of $40,000 which was calculated as a fixed percentage of the company's net income. Comparable salaries for presidents of similar companies are only $60,000–$80,000.

   a. Is the salary payment and/or bonus deductible by the company as an ordinary, necessary and reasonable business expense?

   b. How would the payments be treated by Mr. Jones if the company is not permitted to deduct a portion of the payments?

2. XYZ Construction Company made payments (kickbacks) of $60,-000 to various Government officials during 19X1. The president of the company argues that the payments are ordinary, necessary and reasonable business expenses which if not made would force the company into bankruptcy. The kickbacks are illegal and subjects the company and its officers to possible criminal and civil penalties.

   a. Is the company permitted to deduct any portion of the $60,-000?

    b.   If the company elected to treat the $60,000 as manufacturing overhead and, therefore, allocate such amounts to its inventory and cost of sales, would the tax treatment of the payments be any different? Would you suggest this treatment to XYZ company?

3.   In the current year T contributed $110 to the campaign of George Forbes who ran successfully for a position on the Cleveland City Council.

    a.   If T is married and files a joint return, how much, if any, may be claimed as a deduction?

    b.   Would it matter if T did not itemize his deductions but claimed the standard deduction?

    c.   May T claim a tax credit in lieu of any deduction? If so, how much?

    d.   Would it matter if T and his wife file separate returns?

4.   T, the owner of a chain of motels in Ohio, travels to Florida to investigate a possible acquisition of a motel chain located in the South. He incurred travel, legal and financial expenses of $2,000 in the course of the investigation.

    a.   Discuss the tax treatment of T's expenses in the event he decides to make the investment.

    b.   In the event he decides not to make the investment.

5.   T, the vice-president of an oil company, decides that in his spare time he wants to become a writer. Pursuant to this desire during the current year he incurs the following expenses:

1.	Correspondence study course on creative writing	$ 600
2.	Writing supplies and typing costs	500
3.	Cost of converting a former bedroom in the family residence to an office	3,000
4.	Interest on $3,000 borrowed from a bank—the proceeds were used to convert the bedroom into an office	200

During the year T sold one of his books to a publisher and received a royalty check for $100.

    a.   Discuss T's tax position in the event the activity is deemed a hobby.

    b.   In the event the activity is not a hobby.

    c.   What tax planning considerations would you recommend for T to help avoid hobby loss treatment?

6.   During the year Jones rents his vacation home for three months and spends one month of his vacation at the home. His gross rental from the property was $3,300. He incurred the following

expenses: mortgage interest $1,500, real estate taxes $1,000. The following expenses are specifically allocable to the rental use of the home: utilities $400, maintenance $300 and depreciation of $800. Compute Mr. Jones' allowable deductions for the vacation home.

7. T, a cash basis taxpayer, rented a building from J on October 1, 19X6, paying $12,000 (one full year's rent) in advance. How much can T deduct in 19X6? How much does J include in income if he is an accrual basis taxpayer? A cash basis taxpayer?

8. B, a single, cash basis taxpayer, had a serious illness in December, 19X6, which resulted in medical bills of $3,500. She earned $20,-000 in 19X6 and expects the same income in 19X7. She has pledged $1,500 to the church in 19X6 (to be paid in 19X7) and bought a home in November, 19X6, which will result in interest and property taxes in 19X7 of $3,000. In 19X6, she had other itemized deductions of $1,500, and in 19X7 she expects to have other deductions of $1,800. She asks your advice as to when she should pay the medical bills so as to maximize her tax benefit.

9. J, a single taxpayer, owns a sizable tract of land that he is holding for possible future long term capital appreciation. Annually his property taxes and interest on this real estate amount to $2,000. In some years, J itemizes his deductions and in other years, he uses the standard deduction. Does the § 266 election to capitalize property taxes and interest have any tax saving possibilities for J? Illustrate.

10. Indicate whether each expenditure below is deductible by F who paid the items in question:

    a. Interest on his dependent son's auto loan;

    b. Medical expenses of his mother. (She is not F's dependent);

    c. Property taxes on his wife's summer home. They are filing a joint return;

    d. Business lunches for F's clients;

    e. Money given to F's 10 year old dependent daughter to put into the Sunday School collection plate at church.

11. H obtained a divorce in 19X6, and paid the following fees:

Court costs and legal fees of obtaining divorce	$ 200
Rewriting of will	150
Detective fees paid for obtaining evidence of infidelity	500
Legal fees of determining who gets the children as dependents	200
Legal fees in determining the basis of settlement property	1,000
Expense of changing locks on the family home	100

How much can H deduct on the 19X6 return?

12. X borrowed $100,000 from a bank in December, 19X1. He prepaid the interest of $1,000 per month for the period from Decem-

ber 1, 19X1 through September 30, 19X2. The prepayment of 10 months interest of $10,000 was deducted on his 19X1 tax return.

    a. How much of the interest is deductible in 19X1?

    b. How much is deductible in 19X2?

    c. Would your answer be different if the prepayment resulted in a material distortion of income during the two years?

13. P made the following expenditures in 19X6 in connection with her business property. Assuming all depreciation is straight line with a 10 year life and no salvage value and that she takes a full year's depreciation on all 19X6 capital expenditures, compute her deductions in 19X6:

Purchase of 10 acres for a parking lot	$10,000
Paving of parking lot	4,000
Overhaul of delivery truck	800
Tune-up of second delivery truck	120
Purchase of goodwill	2,000
Interest on loan on 10 acres	600
Replacement of furnace in factory	3,000
Repair of hail-damaged roof tiles	900

14. What is R's constructive ownership of X corporation, given the following information?

Shares owned by R	300
Shares owned by S, R's uncle	200
Shares owned by T, R's partner	10
Shares owned by U, a partnership owned by R & T equally	100
Shares owned by V, R's granddaughter	190
Shares owned by outsiders	200

15. In January, 19X6, D borrows $50,000 and invests it in E Company stock. On September 1, 19X6, D sells the stock for $55,000 and reinvests in municipal bonds. Assuming the loan is outstanding the entire year, how much interest can D deduct?

Research Problems

1. Dr. Smith's office is in a building owned by the Medical Properties Corporation (MPC). Dr. Smith uses the cash method of accounting while MPC uses the accrual method. Both file their returns on a calendar year basis. The monthly rent is $200 payable on the first day of each month. Smith must give three months notice if he wishes to move out.

Smith moves in on July 1, 19X1. Under the contract with MPC, he pays $1,000 at that time, of which $200 is a refundable damage deposit, $600 is rent for the last three months of his occupancy (i. e., the three months after he gives notice), and $200 is rent for July, 19X1. Smith pays the rent on time each month through July, 19X2.

In July, 19X2, Smith loses a malpractice suit. The litigation exhausts his funds. He fails to pay the August and September rent. On October 1, 19X2, he gives notice to MPC, proceeds to sell his equipment, gives up his practice, and goes to work in the research laboratory of a drug company. MPC uses $75 of Smith's damage deposit against repair costs to the premises and applies the remaining $125 to the August rent. Thus, Smith still owes MPC $275.

In April, 19X3, Smith pays MPC the $275 he owes.

a. What rent deductions, if any, can Smith claim on his 19X1, 19X2, and 19X3 returns?

b. How are these amounts reported for MPC in 19X1, 19X2, and 19X3?

2. Dr. Smith and his wife file joint tax returns. Mr. and Mrs. Smith jointly own a personal residence and an apartment building which are *not* subject to a mortgage. During 19X1, Mrs. Smith mortgaged the personal residence and received $100,000 from the bank. These funds were invested in tax free municipal bonds earning 7% interest. The mortgage interest on the home was 8% or $8,000.

The apartment was also mortgaged during the year and the funds ($200,000) were invested in Dr. Smith's medical clinic. The interest on this mortgage was $15,000 in 19X2.

How much interest, if any, can be deducted in 19X1? (Ignore any potential gift tax consequences.)

Chapter 7

DEDUCTIONS AND LOSSES: CERTAIN BUSINESS EXPENSES AND LOSSES

Working with the tax formula for individuals requires the proper classification of items which are deductible *for* adjusted gross income and items which are deductions *from* adjusted gross income (itemized deductions). Business expenses and losses, which are discussed in this chapter, are deductions *for* adjusted gross income to arrive at the taxpayer's adjusted gross income.

Itemized deductions (in excess of the flat amount of standard deduction) and a taxpayer's personal and dependency exemptions are subtracted *from* adjusted gross income in the determination of taxable income. Itemized deductions are discussed in Chapter 9 whereas the standard deduction and the personal and dependency exemptions are discussed in Chapter 10. A brief summary of the tax formula is as follows:

Gross Income			$50,000
Less:	Deductions <u>for</u> adjusted gross income		(2,000)
=	Adjusted Gross Income		48,000
Less:	Excess itemized deductions:		
	Itemized deductions	$8,200	
	Minus: Standard Deduction (zero bracket amount)	(3,200)	(5,000)
Less:	Personal and Dependency Exemptions ($750 x 4)		(3,000)
=	Taxable Income		$40,000

BAD DEBTS

If a taxpayer sells goods or provides services on credit and the account receivable subsequently becomes worthless, a bad debt deduction is permitted providing income arising from the creation of the debt (accounts receivable) was previously included in income.[1] No deduction is allowed, for example, for a bad debt arising from the sale of a product or service where the taxpayer is on the cash basis since no income is reported until the cash has been collected.

A deduction is allowed for any debt which becomes worthless or partially worthless within the taxable year.[2] The taxpayer must be able to demonstrate to the satisfaction of the IRS, the amount which is worthless and the amount charged off.[3] If the debt becomes totally worthless in a future year, only the remainder not previously deducted can be written off.

One of the more difficult tasks is determining if and when a bad debt is, in fact, worthless since the loss is deductible solely in the year of partial or total worthlessness. Legal proceedings need not be instigated where the facts surrounding the individual case indicate that such action will not result in collecting the debt.[4]

Example 1. In 19X1 taxpayer J loaned $1,000 to K, who agreed to repay the loan in two years. In 19X3 K disappeared after the note became delinquent. If a reasonable investigation by J indicates that he would not be able to find K or a suit against her would not result in collection, he can deduct the $1,000 in 19X3.

Bankruptcy is generally an indication of at least partial worthlessness of a debt. Sometimes bankruptcy will cause a debt to become bad before the settlement date. If this is the case, the deduction must be taken in the year of worthlessness, not in the later year upon settlement.

Example 2. In Example 1 above, assume K filed for personal bankruptcy in 19X2. At that time J learned that unsecure creditors were expected to ultimately receive 20¢ on the dollar. In 19X3 settlement is made and he receives only $150. He should deduct $800 ($1,000 loan less $200 expected settlement) in 19X2 and deduct $50 in 19X3 ($200 balance less $150 proceeds). He is not permitted to wait until 19X3 to deduct the entire $850.

A taxpayer may use the reserve for bad debts method or the specific charge-off method in accounting for bad debts. However, a de-

---

1. Reg. § 1.166–1(e).

2. § 166(a); Reg. § 1.166–3.

3. Reg. § 1.166–3(a)(iii).

4. Reg. § 1.166–2(b).

duction for partial worthlessness of a bad debt is permitted only where the specific charge-off method is being used.[5] Under the reserve for bad debts method, a deduction is allowed for a reasonable addition to the reserve.[6]

ALLOWABLE METHODS

Under the specific charge-off method, a taxpayer receives a deduction when a specific debt becomes either partially or wholly worthless. The taxpayer must satisfy the District Director that a debt is partially worthless and the amount of worthlessness. In the case of total worthlessness, a deduction is allowed for the entire amount in the year of worthlessness. The amount of the deduction depends upon the taxpayer's basis in the bad debt. If the debt arose from the sale of services or products and the face amount was previously included in income, this amount is deductible. If the taxpayer purchased the debt, the deduction is equal to the amount the taxpayer paid for the debt instrument.

Under the reserve method of accounting for bad debts, the taxpayer's deduction is based upon a "reasonable addition" to the reserve. This may be contrasted with the direct-charge-off method where the amount of the bad debt deduction is based upon the actual write-off of specific accounts. What constitutes a "reasonable addition" to the reserve is largely a matter of judgment and depends upon individual facts and circumstances. The Regulations recognize that the reasonableness of an addition to the bad debt reserve is dependent upon such conditions as business prosperity and individual differences among classes of businesses.[7] The determining factors are the total amount of debts outstanding and the balance in the reserve account at the end of the year. If the taxpayer's estimated bad debts are more (or less) than the actual losses later, the reserve must be adjusted downward (or upward) in the future year; i. e., each current year must be adjusted based upon that year's experience.

DETERMINING RESERVE ADDITIONS

The courts have generally applied a formula approach for determining a "reasonable addition" to the bad debt reserve. The IRS frequently uses an approach which was derived from the Black Motor Co. case.[8] The formula approach is based upon a weighted average of the ratio of bad debts to accounts and notes receivable for the current and preceding five years. This percentage is then applied to the ending balance of accounts and notes receivable to determine the

5. Reg. § 1.166–3(a).

6. Reg. § 1.166–4(a).

7. Reg. § 1.166–4(b)(1).

8. *Black Motor Co. v. Comm.*, 42–1 USTC ¶ 9265, 28 AFTR 1193, 125 F. 2d 977 (CA–6, 1942).

required amount in the reserve at the end of the year. The bad debt deduction represents the amount necessary to bring the reserve up to its required balance at the end of the year.

Example 3.   Black Motor Co. formula approach

1. $\dfrac{\text{Bad debts—current year plus five preceding years}}{\substack{\text{Total accounts and notes receivable at the end} \\ \text{of each of these years}}}$ $\dfrac{20,000}{500,000} = 4\%$

2. 4% x Accounts and notes receivable at the end of
   the current year ($80,000)   = $ 3,200*

       * This amount represents the required balance in the reserve at
         the end of the year.

3. Beginning balance in the reserve for doubtful
   accounts $ 3,000

      + Recoveries of previous accounts written off   200

      − Write off of specific accounts during the year   (600)

      + Bad debt deduction (addition to reserve)   600

      = Ending balance in the reserve $ 3,200

It should be noted that the formula approach is not mandatory since individual facts and circumstances need to be taken into account. In addition, the IRS now agrees that the Black Motor formula is not controlling and that the bad debt addition may be more or less depending upon the facts and circumstances.[9]

FILING REQUIREMENTS

The taxpayer using the reserve method must attach a statement to every return with the following information:[10]

(1) The volume of charge sales during the year and the percentage of the reserve to such amount;

(2) The total amount of notes and accounts receivable at the beginning and close of the taxable year;

(3) The amount of debts which have been charged against the reserve;

(4) The computation of the addition to the reserve for bad debts.

ELECTION OF METHODS

Subject to the approval of the IRS, a taxpayer may elect to use either method of accounting. However, the taxpayer can elect the reserve method without the consent of the IRS if the election is made

---

9. Rev.Rul. 76–362, I.R.B. 1976–39, 5,   10. Reg. § 1.166–4(c).
   9/29/76.

in the first taxable year that a bad debt occurs.[10.1]   Once an election is made, that method must be followed in all future years unless the taxpayer receives permission to change.   A request for a change in methods must be made within 180 days from the start of the tax year for which the change is sought.[11]

If a taxpayer desires to change to the reserve method, only 10 percent of the initial reserve amount is deductible in the year of change.   The remaining 90 percent of the initial reserve deduction must be spread over the next succeeding 9 years.[12]   The spreading of the deduction over a 10-year period is required to prevent the "bunching" of deductions in one year.

BUSINESS VERSUS NONBUSINESS BAD DEBTS

A nonbusiness bad debt is a debt that is not related to the taxpayer's trade or business when it was created or became worthless. The determination of whether a debt is business or nonbusiness related depends upon whether the lender was engaged in the business of lending money and/or if there is a proximate relationship between the creation of the debt and the lender's trade or business.   The use to which the borrowed funds are put by the debtor is of no consequence.[13]   Loans to relatives or friends are the most common type of nonbusiness bad debt.

> **Example 4.**   Joe loaned his friend, Sara, $1,500.   Sara used the money to start a business which failed.   Even though the money was used in a business, to Joe it is a nonbusiness bad debt because the business was Sara's, not Joe's.

> **Example 5.**   Joe loaned another friend, Sam, $500.   Sam was unable to repay Joe due to financial difficulties.   The loss is a nonbusiness bad debt to Joe.

The distinction between a business bad debt and a nonbusiness bad debt is important because a business bad debt is deductible as an ordinary loss in the year incurred while a nonbusiness bad debt is always treated as a short-term capital loss.[14]   Thus, regardless of the age of a nonbusiness bad debt, a nonbusiness bad debt deduction is of limited benefit due to the capital loss limitations upon deductibility in any one year.   Capital loss limitation rules are discussed in Chapter 14.   In addition no deduction is allowed for the partial worthlessness of a nonbusiness bad debt and no deduction is permitted if the lender receives a partial recovery of the debt.[15]

10.1   Reg. § 1.166–1(b).

11.   § 446(e); Reg. § 1.446–1(e)(3).

12.   Rev.Proc. 70–27, 1970–2 C.B. 509.

13.   Reg. § 1.166–5(b)(2).

14.   § 166(d)(1)(B).

15.   Reg. § 1.166–5(a)(2).

The following are illustrations of business bad debts which were adapted from the Regulations.

Example 6.[16] In 19X1 A sold his business but retained a claim (i. e., note or account receivable) against B. The claim became worthless in 19X2. A's loss is treated as a *business* bad debt since the debt was created in the conduct of A's former trade or business. Business bad debt treatment is accorded to A despite the fact that he was holding the note as an investor and was no longer in a trade or business when the claim became worthless.

Example 7.[17] In 19X1 A died and left his business assets to his son C. One of the business assets inherited by C was a claim against B which became worthless in C's hands in 19X3. C's loss is a *business* bad debt since * * * "the loss is sustained as a proximate incident to the conduct of the trade or business in which he is engaged at the time the debt becomes worthless."

The nonbusiness bad debt provisions are not applicable to corporations—it is assumed that any loans made by a corporation are related to its trade or business.

LOANS BETWEEN RELATED PARTIES

Loans between relatives always raise the issue as to whether the loan was bona fide or was a gift. The Regulations state that a bona fide debt is a debt which arises from a debtor-creditor relationship based upon a valid and enforceable obligation to pay a fixed or determinable sum of money.[18] Thus, a gift is not a loan where advances between relatives occur. Thus, the individual circumstances must be examined. Some considerations are: Was a note properly executed? Is there collateral? What collection efforts were made? What was the intent of the related parties?

Example 8. T loans $2,000 to his widowed mother in order that she may obtain an operation. The mother owns no property, is not employed, and her only means of subsistence consists of the Social Security benefits. No note is issued for the loan; no interest provided for, or repayment date mentioned. In the current year the mother dies leaving no estate.

Assuming the loan is not repaid, T cannot take a deduction for a nonbusiness bad debt because the facts indicate that no debtor-creditor relationship existed.

---

16. Reg. § 1.166–5(d), Example 1.   18. Reg. § 1.166–1(c).

17. Reg. § 1.166–5(d), Example 3.

WORTHLESS SECURITIES

A loss is allowed under § 165 for a security that becomes worthless during the year.[19] Such securities are usually shares of stock or some form of indebtedness. Such losses are generally treated as capital losses. The loss is deemed to have occurred on the last day of the taxable year. Capital losses may be of limited benefit due to the capital loss limitation provisions. Chapter 14 discusses the capital loss limitation rules.

SECURITIES IN AFFILIATED CORPORATIONS

Special treatment is provided for corporations who own securities in affiliated companies.[20] Ordinary loss treatment is granted for such worthless securities if the corporate holder owns 80 percent of the voting power of all classes of stock and at least 80 percent of each class of nonvoting stock of the affiliated company.

SMALL BUSINESS STOCK

The general rule is that shareholders receive capital gain or loss treatment upon the sale or exchange of stock. However, it is possible to receive an ordinary loss deduction in the case of a loss sustained on small business stock—"§ 1244 Stock." Only individuals are eligible to receive the ordinary loss treatment under § 1244 and the loss is limited to $25,000 ($50,000 for married individuals filing jointly) per year. Several qualifications have to be met (such as a capitalization not exceeding $500,000, a domestic corporation, common stock only, etc.) in order for the worthlessness of § 1244 stock to be treated as an ordinary—rather than a capital—loss.[21]

CASUALTY AND THEFT LOSSES

An individual may deduct a loss under § 165(c) under the following circumstances: (1) The loss is incurred in a trade or business; (2) The loss is incurred in a transaction entered into for profit; and (3) A loss arising from fire, storm, shipwrecks, or other casualty or from theft.[22] A casualty is defined as "the complete or partial destruction of property resulting from an identifiable event of a sudden, unexpected or unusual nature."[23] Examples would include such

---

19. § 165(g).

20. § 165(g)(3).

21. Reg. § 1.1244.

22. § 165(c).

23. *Matheson v. Comm.,* 2 USTC ¶ 830, 10 AFTR 945, 54 F.2d 537 (CA–2, 1931).

events as hurricanes, tornadoes, floods, storms, shipwrecks, fires, auto accidents, mine cave-ins, sonic booms and vandalism. In the case of weather, the damage causing weather (drought, for example) must be unusual and severe for the particular region. Damage must be to the taxpayer's property in order to qualify as a casualty loss.

In an automobile accident, a deduction can be taken only where the damage was not caused by the taxpayer's willful act or willful negligence.[24]

> **Example 9.** T parks his car on a hill and fails to properly set the brake or curb the wheels. As a result of T's negligence, the car rolls down the hill, damages U's front porch, injures U who was sitting on the porch, and damages T's car. Due to the accident T is forced to pay the following amounts:

Medical expenses for U's injuries	$350
Repairs to T's car	400
Repairs to U's porch	300
Fine for moving traffic violation	30

> The $400 repairs to T's car should qualify for casualty loss treatment since T's act of negligence appears to be simple rather than willful. The other expenses are not to T's property and are, therefore, not deductible by T.

EVENTS THAT ARE NOT CASUALTIES

Not all "acts of God" are treated as casualty losses for income tax purposes. A casualty must be sudden, unexpected or unusual. Progressive deterioration (such as erosion due to wind or rain) is not a casualty because it does not meet the "suddenness" test.

One prime example of non-sudden events is in the area of disease and insect damage. In the past, some courts have held that termite damage over periods of up to 15 months after infestation constituted a "sudden" event and was, therefore, deductible as a casualty loss.[25] On the other hand, where the damage was caused by termites over periods of several years, some courts have disallowed a casualty loss deduction.[26] Despite the existence of some judicial support for the deductibility of termite damage as a casualty loss, the current position of the IRS is that termite damage is not deductible.[27]

---

24. Reg. § 1.165–7(a)(3)(i).

25. *Rosenberg v. Comm.*, 52–2 USTC ¶ 9377, 42 AFTR 303, 198 F.2d 46 (CA–8, 1952); *Shopmaker v. U. S.*, 54–1 USTC ¶ 9195, 45 AFTR 758, 119 F.Supp. 705 (D.Ct.Mo., 1953).

26. *Fay v. Helvering*, 41–2 USTC ¶ 9494, 27 AFTR 432, 120 F.2d 253 (CA–2, 1941); *U. S. v. Rogers*, 41–1 USTC ¶ 9442, 27 AFTR 423, 120 F.2d 244 (CA–9, 1941).

27. Rev.Rul. 63–232, 1963–2 C.B. 97.

THEFT LOSSES

Theft includes but is not necessarily limited to larceny, embezzlement and robbery.[28] "Theft" does not include misplaced items.[29]

Theft losses are computed like other casualty losses (discussed below) but the timing for recognition of the loss differs. A theft loss is taken in the year of discovery, not the year of the theft (unless, of course, the discovery occurs in the same year as the theft). If, in the year of the discovery, a claim exists (e. g. against an insurance company) and there is a reasonable expectation of recovering the fair market value of the asset from the insurance company, no deduction is permitted.[30] If, in the year of settlement, the recovery is less than the assets' fair market value, a partial deduction may be available in the year of settlement.

> **Example 10.** J's new sailboat was stolen from the storage marina in December, 19X1. He discovered the loss on June 3, 19X2 and filed a claim with his insurance company who settled on January 30, 19X3. Assuming there was a reasonable expectation of full recovery, no deduction is allowed in 19X2. A partial deduction may be available in 19X3 if the actual insurance proceeds are less than the fair market value of the asset. Loss measurement rules are discussed in a later section of this chapter.

WHEN TO DEDUCT CASUALTY LOSSES

Disaster Losses. Generally, a casualty loss is deducted in the year the loss occurred. An exception is allowed for casualties sustained in an area designated as a disaster area by the President of the United States.[31] In those cases, the taxpayer may elect to treat the loss as having occurred in the taxable year immediately preceding the taxable year in which the disaster actually occurred. The law was amended in 1972 to provide immediate relief to flood victims in the form of immediate tax benefits, e. g. the tax benefits are accelerated due to being deductible in the earlier year.

The taxpayer makes this election by claiming the disaster loss on his tax return for the prior year (i. e., if the due date—plus extensions—for the prior year's return has not passed). If the disaster occurs after the prior year's return has been filed, it is necessary to either file an amended return or a refund claim. In any case, the taxpayer must clearly show that such an election is being made.[32] The

---

28. Reg. § 1.165–8(d).

29. *Mary Francis Allen,* 16 T.C. 163 (1951).

30. Reg. § 1.165–8(a)(2).

31. § 165(h).

32. Reg. § 1.165–11(e).

election should show the date(s) of the disaster, the location of the property destroyed, and other pertinent facts. The election must be made by the later of (1) the due date of the income tax return for the year in which the disaster occurred or (2) the due date (including extensions) of the income tax return for the year immediately preceding the year in which the disaster occurred.

> **Example 11.** During the first week in April 19X2 unusually heavy rainfall caused severe flooding in a large region of Southeast Louisiana. Shortly thereafter the region was designated by the President of the United States as a disaster area and, therefore, eligible for assistance by the Federal government under Chapter 15, Title 42 of the U. S. Code. T, a resident of the affected area, suffered $3,000 in damage to his property due to the flooding. T is a calendar year taxpayer and has already filed his income tax return for the prior year (19X1).
>
> T can file an amended return or refund claim for 19X1 or he can wait until filing the 19X2 return in 19X3 and claim a loss on his 19X2 return.

Other Casualty Losses. No casualty loss is permitted if there exists a reimbursement claim with a "reasonable prospect of [full] recovery." [33] If the taxpayer has a partial claim, only part of the loss can be claimed in the year of the casualty and the remainder is deducted in the year the claim is settled.

> **Example 12.** G's new sailboat was completely destroyed by fire in 19X3. Its cost and fair market value was $10,000. Her only claim against the insurance company was on a $7,000 policy which was not settled by year-end. The following year, 19X4, G settled with the insurance company for $6,000. G is entitled to a $3,000 deduction in 19X3 and a $1,000 deduction in 19X4. If the sailboat were held for personal use, the $3,000 deduction in 19X3 would be reduced by $100 (see discussion below).

If a taxpayer receives subsequent reimbursement for a casualty loss previously sustained and deducted, an amended return is not filed. Instead, the taxpayer must include the reimbursement in gross income on the return for the subsequent year (provided the previous deduction resulted in tax benefit).[34]

MEASURING THE AMOUNT OF LOSS

The computation of a casualty loss deduction depends upon whether the property is held for personal use or is business property. Property which is held for the production of income (e. g. rental property) is treated similarly to business use property. After the loss is computed on property held for personal use, a $100 statutory

---

33. Reg. § 1.165–1(d)(2)(i).   **34.** Reg. § 1.165–1(d)(2)(iii).

floor is used to reduce the allowable deduction.[35]   To the extent of $100 of loss, the taxpayer receives no relief for casualty losses relative to property which is held for personal use.   The $100 statutory floor does not apply to casualty losses on business property.

Any insurance recovery reduces the loss for both business and personal use casualties.   In fact, a taxpayer may realize a gain on a casualty if the insurance proceeds exceed the cost basis of the property.   Chapter 15 discusses the treatment of net casualty gains and losses.

The general rule for partial losses to both business and personal use property and the complete destruction of personal use property is: Use the lower of (1) the adjusted basis of the property or (2) the difference between the fair market value before the casualty and the fair market value immediately after the casualty.[36]   If business property or property which is held for the production of income (e. g. rental property) is completely destroyed and if the fair market value before the casualty is less than the adjusted basis, the loss is limited to the adjusted basis of the property.[37]   Any property that is part business and part personal must be allocated and computed separately. The $100 floor is then deducted from the personal use portion only. The $100 floor applies separately in respect to each casualty and applies to the entire loss from each casualty, e. g. if a storm damages a taxpayer's residence and his automobile is also damaged by the storm, only $100 is subtracted from the total amount of the loss.[38]

Example 13.   This year T had the following casualty losses:

Asset	Adjusted Basis	Fair Market Value of Asset Before the Casualty	After the Casualty
A	$500	$300	$ 0
B	800	600	500
C	900	200	0
D	100	700	400

Assets A and B are held for personal use while C and D were used in T's business at the time of the casualty.   Assume no insurance recovery is expected and that the losses to Assets A and B are from different casualties.

The following losses are allowed:

Asset A: $200 ($300—the lesser of adjusted basis or loss in value—minus the $100 floor).   Such casualty losses are generally treated as an itemized deduction.

35. § 165(c)(3).   37. Reg. § 1.165–7(b)(1)(ii).

36. Reg. § 1.165–7(b)(1).   38. Reg. § 1.165–7(b)(4)(ii).

Asset B: $–0– ($100—the lesser of adjusted basis of $800 or the $100 loss in value, minus the $100 floor.)

Asset C: $900. The complete destruction of a business asset results in a deduction of the adjusted basis since the adjusted basis is greater than the fair market value.

Asset D: $100. (The lesser of adjusted basis of $100 or the $300 loss in value). Both Asset C and D losses are deductions *for* adjusted gross income and no $100 floor applies because they are business assets.

Generally, an appraisal before and after the casualty is needed to measure the amount of the loss. However, the cost of repairs to the damaged property is acceptable as a method of establishing the loss in value provided the following criteria are met:

(1) The repairs are necessary to restore the property to its condition immediately before the casualty,

(2) The amount spent for such repairs is not excessive,

(3) The repairs do not care for more than the damage suffered, and

(4) The value of the property after the repairs does not as a result of the repairs exceed the value of the property immediately before the casualty.[39]

RESEARCH AND
EXPERIMENTAL EXPENDITURES

§ 174 sets forth the treatment of "research and experimental expenditures." The Regulations define research and experimental expenditures as:

All such costs incident to the development of an experimental or pilot model, a plant process, a product, a formula, an invention, or similar property, and the improvement of already existing property of the types mentioned. The term does not include expenditures such as those for the ordinary testing or inspection of materials or products for quality control or those for efficiency surveys, management studies, consumer surveys, advertising, or promotions.[40]

Expenses in connection with the acquisition or improvement of land or depreciable property are not research and experimental expenditures; they increase the basis of the land or depreciable property. However, depreciation on a building (for example) used for research may be a research and experimental expenditure.[41]

---

39. Reg. § 1.165–7(a)(2)(ii).   **41.** Reg. § 1.174–2(b)(1).

40. Reg. § 1.174–2(a)(1).

The law permits three alternatives for the handling of research and experimental expenditures. These expenditures may be expensed in the year paid or incurred or they may be deferred and amortized. If neither of these two methods are elected, the research and experimental costs must be capitalized.[42] In such case a deduction may not be available until the research project is abandoned or is deemed worthless. Since many products resulting from research projects do not have a definite and limited useful life, a taxpayer should ordinarily elect to write off the expenditures immediately or to capitalize such costs subject to amortization. Otherwise, tax benefit will be delayed for an indefinite period. It is generally preferable to elect an immediate write-off of the research expenditures due to the time value of the tax deduction. Therefore, most taxpayers elect the immediate write-off method.

EXPENSE METHOD

A taxpayer can elect to expense all of the research and experimental expenditures incurred in the current year and all subsequent years.[43] The consent of the IRS is not required if the method is adopted for the first taxable year in which such expenditures were paid or incurred. Once such an election is made, the taxpayer must adhere to it from that time forward unless a request for change is made to the IRS.[44] In certain instances a taxpayer may incur research and experimental expenditures prior to actually engaging in any trade or business activity. In such instances the Supreme Court has applied a liberal standard of deductibility and permitted a deduction in the year of incurrence.[45]

DEFERRAL AND AMORTIZATION METHOD

The deferral and amortization method is allowed for the treatment of research and experimental expenditures, providing that the taxpayer makes a binding election [46] (permission to change must be obtained from the IRS) to treat such expenditures as a deduction ratably over such period of not less than 60 months as may be selected by the taxpayer (beginning with the month is which the taxpayer first realizes benefits from such expenditures).[47]

The option of treating research and experimental expenditures as deferred expense is usually employed in situations where a company does not have sufficient income in experimental years to offset the R&D expenses. Rather than create net operating loss carryovers

42. Reg. § 1.174–1.

43. § 174(a)(1).

44. § 174(a)(3).

45. *Snow v. Comm.*, 74–1 USTC ¶ 9432, 33 AFTR2d 74–1251, 94 S.Ct. 1876 (USSC, 1974).

46. § 174(b)(2).

47. Reg. § 1.174–4(b)(2); § 174(b)(1).

which may not be utilized due to the seven year limitation on such carryovers, the deferral and amortization method may be used.

Example 14. R Corporation, a manufacturer of plastic products, uses the accrual method and files its return on a calendar year basis. In January 1, 19X1, work is started on a special research project which, if successful, would result in a "process" that would streamline the manufacturing activity for plastic products and effect a considerable cost saving. On this same day a building is acquired for $60,000, 30% of which will be used in connection with the research project. Assume the building is to be depreciated under the straight-line method over a fifteen year period with no estimated salvage value. During the year the following additional expenditures are incurred in connection with the research project:

Salaries	$12,000
Heat, light, and power	1,000
Drawings	2,500
Models	7,500
Lab materials	9,000

The project is successfully concluded on December 30, 19X1 and results in a process which is marketable (but not patentable) and which possesses an indefinite useful life. R Corporation first realizes the benefits from the new process in 19X2.

The R Corporation can (1) capitalize all the expenses and leave them on the balance sheet as an asset indefinitely; (2) elect to expense all the expenditures under § 174 (including the depreciation) in year 19X1 or (3) Elect to capitalize all expenditures under § 174 (including the depreciation attributable to the project) and amortize it as follows:

Depreciation (30% of 1 year's depreciation of $4,000)	$ 1,200
Salaries	12,000
Heat, light and power	1,000
Drawings	2,500
Models	7,500
Lab Material	9,000
Total	$33,200
Monthly Amortization:	

$$\frac{\$33200}{60} = \qquad \underline{\$553.33}$$

Amortization starts January 1, 19X2.

NET OPERATING LOSSES

The requirement that every taxpayer file an annual income tax return (whether on a calendar year or on a fiscal year) may result in certain inequities for taxpayers who experience cyclical patterns of income or expenses. Inequities result from the application of a progressive rate structure to amounts of taxable income applied on an annual basis. In addition, a net operating loss in a particular tax year would produce no tax benefit if the Code did not include provisions for the carryback and carryforward of such losses to profitable years.

> **Example 15.** J has a business which realizes the following taxable income or (loss) over a five-year period; 19X1, $50,000; 19X2, ($30,000); 19X3, $100,000; 19X4 ($200,000); and 19X5, $356,000. She is married and filing jointly.
>
> P, on the other hand, has a taxable income pattern of $55,200 every year. He, too, is married filing jointly. A comparison of their 5 year tax bills is as follows:

Year	J's Tax	P's Tax
19X1	$15,460	$18,060
19X2	–0–	18,060
19X3	43,260	18,060
19X4	–0–	18,060
19X5	217,940	18,060
	$276,660*	$90,300*

> *The computation of tax is made without regard to any tax credits, maximum tax on earned income, or net operating loss benefits.

Even though J and P realized the same total income ($276,000) over the 5-year period, J had to pay taxes of $276,660 while P paid taxes of $90,300.

To provide partial relief from this inequitable tax treatment, a deduction is allowed for net operating losses.[48] This provision permits the offsetting of net operating losses for any one year against taxable income of other years. A net operating loss is intended as a relief provision for business income and losses; therefore, only losses from the operation of a trade or business (or profession), casualty losses, or losses from the confiscation of a business by a foreign government can create a net operating loss. In other words, a salaried individual with itemized deductions and personal exemptions in excess of income is not permitted to deduct such excess amounts as a net operating loss. On the other hand, a personal casualty loss may

48. § 172.

be treated as a business loss and can, therefore, create (or increase) a net operating loss.[49]

COMPUTATION OF THE NET OPERATING LOSS

Since the net operating loss provisions apply solely to business related losses, certain adjustments must be made to reflect a taxpayer's "economic" loss. The required adjustments for corporate taxpayers are usually insignificant since a corporation's taxable loss is quite often similar to its economic loss.[50] However, individual taxpayers are allowed deductions for such items as personal and dependency exemptions, itemized deductions, long term capital gains deductions etc., which do not reflect actual business related economic losses.

To arrive at the net operating loss (economic loss) for an individual, taxable income must be adjusted for the following items:[51]

(1) The net operating loss carryover or carryback from another year is not allowed in the computation of taxable income (loss) for the year. The net operating loss for each year must be kept separate for purposes of the carryback and carryforward provisions discussed below;

(2) Capital losses may not exceed the amount of capital gains included in income. Since capital losses can be carried forward for individuals under another section of the law, these losses cannot be "mixed" with net operating losses;

(3) Nonbusiness capital losses may not exceed nonbusiness capital gains. Business capital gains and losses are granted § 1231 treatment (described in Chapter 15) and are allowed 100% since they reflect the business, or economic, loss. In other words, a nonbusiness capital loss cannot be used to offset a business capital gain;

(4) No deduction is' allowed for 50 percent of the excess of long-term capital gains over short-term capital losses. This 50 percent deduction does not require an outlay of assets, so it does not reflect an economic loss;

(5) No deduction is allowed for personal and dependency exemptions. These $750 amounts do not reflect economic, or business, outlays;

(6) Nonbusiness deductions (itemized deductions less personal casualty losses) may not exceed nonbusiness income. The theory is that nonbusiness income may be offset by nonbusi-

---

49. § 172(d)(4)(c);   Reg.   §   1.172–3(a)(3)(iii).

50. Reg. § 1.172–2.

51. § 172(d); Reg. § 1.172–3(a).

ness deductions, but that nonbusiness deductions cannot offset business income. Nonbusiness deductions such as medical expenses, charitable contributions, etc. are really items of personal consumption; not business expenses or losses. Nonbusiness income is limited to such passive items as dividends and interest. Business income (or losses) include salaries, rents, trade or business, and gains and losses on the sale or exchange of business assets;

(7) No deduction for contributions to a self-employment retirement plan is allowed. Since the taxpayer has put aside amounts that will provide future benefits, there is no real economic loss, merely a deferral of the benefit.

Example 16. T began the operation of a retail store in 19X4 and had a NOL of $185 for that year. T had no taxable income for 19X1, 19X2, or 19X3. During 19X5 he had the following income and deductions:

Income

Gross income from the business	$67,000	
Salary from a part-time job	875	
Interest on savings account	525	$68,400

Deductions

NOL carryover from 19X4	$ 185	
Business expenses	71,000	
Net short-term capital loss—sale of stock	500	
Net loss on rental property	100	
Personal exemptions (two)	1,500	
Itemized deductions	3,900	77,185
Taxable income		$(8,785)

T's Net Operating Loss is computed as follows:

Taxable Income			$(8,785)
Add:			
Net operating loss from 19X4		$ 185	
Net STCL from sale of stock		500	
Personal exemptions		1,500	
Itemized Deductions	$3,900*		
Less Nonbusiness income	525	3,375	5,560
Net Operating Loss			$ 3,225

Note: The economic loss can be thought of as follows:

Business loss:		
Income	$67,000	
Expenses	(71,000)	$(4,000)
Rental loss		(100)
Salary income		875
Net economic (operating) loss		$(3,225)

* If a taxpayer does not itemize his deductions, the standard deduction may be used to offset nonbusiness income.

CARRYBACK AND CARRYOVER PERIODS

A net operating loss must be applied initially to the three taxable years preceding the year of the loss.[52] It is carried first to the third prior year, then the second prior year, then the immediately preceding tax year (or until used up). If the loss is used up in any year, nothing is left to carry over. If the loss is still not used up, it must be carried forward to the first year after the loss year, and then forward to the second, third, fourth, and fifth year after the loss year. For years ending after 1975 the carryover period is generally seven years.[53] If a loss is sustained in 1978, it is used up in this order: 1975, 1976, 1977, 1979, 1980, 1981, 1982, 1983, 1984, and 1985.

For taxable years ending after December 31, 1975 a taxpayer can elect not to carryback a net operating loss to any taxable year.[53.1] In such case, the loss is available as a carryback or carryforward to the next year.

If the loss is being carried to a preceding year, an amended return is filed on Form 1040X, or a quick refund is filed on Form 1045. In any case, a refund of taxes previously paid is requested. When the loss is carried forward, the current return shows a net operating loss deduction for a prior year's loss.

Where there are net operating losses in two or more years, the rule is to always use the earliest loss first until it is completely absorbed; then the later loss(es) can be used until they are also absorbed or lost. Thus, one year's return could show net operating loss carryovers from two or more years; each loss is computed and applied separately.

RECOMPUTATION OF TAX LIABILITY FOR YEAR TO WHICH NOL IS CARRIED

When a net operating loss is carried back to a non-loss year, the taxable income and income tax must be recomputed. Several deductions such as medical expenses are based on the amount of adjusted gross income. When a net operating loss is carried back, all such deductions except the charitable contribution deduction must be recomputed on the basis of the new adjusted gross income after the net operating loss has been applied.[54] Furthermore, any tax credits limited by or based upon the tax must now be recomputed, based on the recomputed tax.

---

52. § 172(b)(1) and (2).

53. Act § 806(a) amending § 172(b)(1)(B).

53.1 Act § 806(c) amending § 172(b)(3).

54. Reg. § 1.172–5(a)(3)(ii).

Example 17. J sustained a net operating loss of $9,000 in 1977. For 1974 his income tax return was as follows:

Salary income		$10,000
Dividends (net of exclusion)		2,000
Net long-term capital gain	$1,400	
Less: 50% exclusion	(700)	700
Adjusted gross income		12,700
Itemized deductions:		
Charitable contributions	$1,700	
Medical expenses	$ 900	
Less: 3% of AGI	(351)	569
Interest		800
Taxes		420
Other		100
		(3,589)
		$ 9,111
Exemptions (two)		(1,500)
Taxable Income		$ 7,611
Tax (Married filing jointly)		$ 1,306

J's new tax liability for the carryback year is computed as follows:

Adjusted gross income		$12,700
Less: net operating loss		9,000
Recomputed AGI		3,700
Itemized deductions:		
Charitable contributions	$1,700	
Medical expenses	$ 900	
Less: 3% of AGI ($2,700)	81	819
Interest		800
Taxes		420
Other		100
		(3,839)
		(139)
Personal and Dependency Exemptions ($750 × 2)		(1,500)
Taxable income (Loss)		$(1,639)
Tax		–0–
Tax originally paid and refund claim		$ 1,306

After determining the amount of refund claim for the initial carryback year, it is necessary to determine the extent to which the remaining loss (if any) is available for carryover to future years. Since the economic loss is all that may be carried back, the economic (net operating) loss can only be used to offset economic gains. In determining if any net operating loss is left over to carry forward, the following adjustments must be made to the recomputed taxable income of the year to which the loss was carried: [55]

(1) Personal exemptions must be added back;

(2) The long-term capital gain deduction must be added back;

---

55. § 172(b)(2); Reg. § 1.172–5(a)(3).

(3) The net capital loss must be added back;

(4) An adjustment for the percentage limitation, if any, based on the new adjusted gross income. This adjustment is computed as follows:

    A. Compute a new AGI based on the old AGI plus the capital gain or loss adjustment (2 or 3 above) and any other adjustments toward AGI.

    B. Compute the new medical (or other) deduction limitation based on the new AGI. This figure is the adjustment to add to the recomputed taxable income.

Since the figure to which the above adjustments are being added is a negative figure (i. e., there is no net operating loss or net operating loss carryover if there is a positive taxable income), these adjustments serve to reduce the net operating loss available for carryover to the next year.

> **Example 18.** The adjustments necessary to determine if there is a net operating loss carryover available for future years are as follows:

New Taxable Income (loss)—1974 initial carryback year		$(1,639)
Add:		
Exemptions		$1,500
Net LTCG deduction		700
Medical Expense Deduction:		
Old AGI	$11,700	
Plus LTCG deduction	700	12,400
3% limitation. 3% of $12,400 less $81		
(previous amount allowed)	251	2,451
		+ $ 812

Since the ending figure is positive, there is no net operating loss left to carry over to 1975.

DEPRECIATION AND AMORTIZATION

§ 167 permits a depreciation deduction in the form of a reasonable allowance for the exhaustion, wear and tear, and obsolescence of business property and property which is held for the production of income, e. g. rental property held by an investor.[56] Obsolescence refers to normal or gradual technological change due to reasonably foreseeable economic conditions. If rapid or abnormal obsolescence occurs, a taxpayer may change to a shorter estimated useful life if there is a "clear and convincing basis for the redetermination." [57]

---

56. § 167(a); Reg. § 1.167(a)–1(a).   **57.** Reg. § 1.167(a)–1(b).

The taxpayer must adopt a reasonably consistent plan for depreciating the cost or other basis over the estimated useful life of the property, e. g. the taxpayer cannot arbitrarily defer or accelerate the amount of depreciation from one year to another.[58]   In addition, the basis of the depreciable property must be reduced by the depreciation allowed but not less than the allowable amount,[59] e. g. if the taxpayer does not claim any depreciation on his depreciable property during a particular year, the basis of the property is nevertheless reduced by the amount of depreciation which should have been deducted.

Example 19.   On January 1, 19X1 X paid $6,000 for a truck which was used in his business.   He used a 4 year life; no salvage value and straight line depreciation.   Thus, the allowable depreciation was $1,500 per year.   However, depreciation actually taken was as follows:

19X1	$1,500
19X2	–0–
19X3	–0–
19X4	1,500

The adjusted basis of the truck must be reduced by the full amount of allowable depreciation of $6,000 ($1,500 x 4 years) despite the fact that X claimed only $3,000 depreciation during the four-year period.   Therefore, if X sold the truck at the end of 19X4 for $1,000, a $1,000 gain would be recognized since the adjusted cost basis of the truck is 0.

The depreciation rules have been revised significantly during the past several years to reflect fiscal and social policy objectives of Congress.   For example, a rapid recovery of capital is accomplished by allowing accelerated depreciation methods or by permitting taxpayers to use artificially shortened useful life estimates.   In certain periods, Congress has deemed it necessary to stimulate private investment in capital assets and has, therefore, permitted businesses to use methods which assure a rapid recovery of capital.   For example, in 1971 the Asset Depreciation Range (ADR) System was enacted into law which permits the use of shorter estimated lives than would otherwise be allowed.[60]   In addition, Congress has attempted to stimulate increased investment in low income housing by permitting rapid amortization of certain rehabilitation expenditures.[61]

QUALIFYING PROPERTY

The use rather than the character of property determines whether a depreciation deduction is permitted.   Property must be used in a trade or business or held for the production of income.

58.   *Supra*, note 56.

59.   § 1016(a)(2); Reg. § 1.167(a)–10(a).

60.   § 167(m); Reg. § 1.167(a)–11.

61.   § 167(k).

Example 20. X is a self employed CPA who uses his automobile for both personal and business purposes. A depreciation deduction is permitted only for the portion of the property which is used in his business. If the automobile were acquired at a cost of $5,000 and X's mileage during the year was 10,000 miles (3,000 miles for business) only 30% of the cost or $1,500 would be subject to depreciation.

The basis for depreciation is generally the adjusted cost basis for determining gain if the property were sold or disposed of.[62] However, if personal use type assets are converted to business or income producing use, the basis for depreciation is the lower of the adjusted basis or fair market value when the property is converted.[63]

Example 21. X acquires a personal residence in 19X1 for $30,000. In 19X4 he converts the property to rental use when the fair market value is only $25,000. The basis for depreciation is $25,000 since the fair market value is less than the adjusted basis. The $5,000 decline in value is deemed to be personal and, therefore, nondeductible.

The Regulations provide that tangible property is depreciable only to the extent that the property is subject to wear and tear, to decay or decline from natural causes, to exhaustion, and to obsolescence.[64] Thus, land and inventory are not depreciable whereas land improvements are depreciable, e. g., paved surfaces, fences, landscaping, etc.

Depreciation or amortization of intangible property is not permitted unless the property has a definite and limited useful life.[65] For example, patents and copyrights have a definite and limited legal life and are, therefore, eligible for amortization. Goodwill is not amortizable since its life extends for an unlimited period.[66]

The terms "depreciation" and "amortization" are often used interchangeably. However, amortization generally refers to the allocation of the cost of an intangible asset whereas depreciation is used with respect to tangible assets.

Other types of intangible assets which may or may not be subject to amortization include the cost of acquiring customer and subscription lists. The IRS has held that such assets are indistinguishable from goodwill and are, therefore, not subject to amortization.[67] However, the courts have permitted a deduction for amortization where the taxpayer has been able to establish an ascertainable life separate and distinct from goodwill and that the asset had a limited useful life which could be ascertained with reasonable accuracy.[68]

62. § 167(g).

63. Reg. § 1.167(g)–1.

64. Reg. § 1.167(a)–2.

65. Reg. § 1.167(a)–3.

66. *Ibid.*

67. Rev.Rul. 74–456, 1974–2 C.B. 65.

68. *Manhattan Co. of Virginia, Inc.,* 50 T.C. 78 (1968); *Houston Chronicle*

SALVAGE VALUE

The Regulations define salvage value as follows:

" * * * the amount (determined at the time of acquisition) which is estimated will be realizable upon sale or other disposition of an asset when it is no longer useful * * * and is to be retired from service by the taxpayer." [69]

Salvage value is not changed merely because of fluctuations in price levels. However, if a redetermination is made of an asset's useful life, its salvage value can be redetermined based upon the subsequent facts and circumstances. The amount of salvage value depends upon the individual practices of each taxpayer rather than the inherent quality of the asset.[70] In general, however, if a taxpayer uses a short useful life with the practice of early disposal of assets, a higher salvage value is warranted.

An asset may not be depreciated below its salvage value.[71] However, the Code permits a taxpayer to disregard salvage value for amounts up to 10 percent of the basis in the property.[72] This rule applies to tangible personal property (other than livestock) with an estimated useful life of three years or more.

> **Example 22.** The XYZ Company acquires a machine for $10,000 in 19X1 with an estimated salvage value of $2,000 after 10 years. The company may disregard salvage value to the extent of $1,000 and compute its depreciation based upon a cost of $10,000 less $1,000 salvage. The adjusted basis may be reduced to $1,000 (depreciation of $9,000 may be taken) despite the fact that the actual salvage value is $2,000. This rule was incorporated into the law to reduce the number of IRS and taxpayer disputes relative to the amount of salvage value which should be used.

DEPRECIATION METHODS

The Code provides for the following alternative depreciation methods: [73]

1. The straight-line method (cost basis less salvage ÷ the estimated useful life).

2. The declining-balance method, using a rate not to exceed twice the straight-line rate (common methods include 200% DB, 150% DB and 125% DB.) Salvage value is not taken

Publishing Co. v. U. S., 73–2 USTC ¶ 9537, 32 AFTR2d 5312–A, 481 F.2d 1240 (CA–5, 1973).

69. Reg. § 1.167–(a)–1(c).

70. Reg. § 1.167–(a)–1(b); *Hertz Corp. v. U. S.*, 60–2 USTC ¶ 9555, 5

AFTR2d 1792 (1960) 80 S.Ct. 1420 (USSC, 1960).

71. *Supra*, note 69.

72. § 167(f).

73. § 167(b).

into account under any of the declining balance methods since a built-in residual is assured, i. e., a fixed percentage rate is applied to the cost less accumulated depreciation which leaves a residual balance at the end of the asset's useful life.

3. Any other consistent method, which does not result in greater total depreciation being claimed during the first two-thirds of the useful life, than would be allowable under the double-declining balance method. Permissible methods include sum-of-the-year's-digits-SYD, machine-hours and the unit-of-production method.

Example 23. X acquires a new automobile on 1/1/19X1 to be used in his business. The asset cost $10,000 with an estimated salvage value of $2,000 and a 4-year useful life. The following amounts of depreciation could be deducted depending upon the method of depreciation which is used:

	19X1	19X2	19X3	19X4
1. Straight-line: $10,000 cost less ($2,000 salvage reduced by 10% of cost) ÷ 4 years	$2,250	$2,250	$2,250	$2,250
2. Double-declining balance:				
a. $10,000 × 50% (twice the SL rate)	$5,000			
b. $10,000–$5,000 × 50%		$2,500		
c. $10,000–$5,000–$2,500 × 50%			$1,250	
d. $10,000–$5,000–$2,500– $1,250 × 50%				$ 625
3. Sum-of-the-year's-digits: $10,000 cost less ($2,000 salvage reduced by 10% of cost) or $9,000				

Cost or Basis

$10,000 – salvage $1,000 $\times$ $\dfrac{\text{remaining life at beginning of the year}}{\text{sum of year's-digits for estimated life}}$ $\left(\dfrac{4}{10}\right)$ *

	19X1	19X2	19X3	19X4
A. $9,000 × ⁴/₁₀	$3,600			
B. $9,000 × ³/₁₀		$2,700		
C. $9,000 × ²/₁₀			$1,800	
D. $9,000 × ¹/₁₀				$ 900

* The sum-of-the-year's-digits method may be computed by the following formula: $\text{SYD} = \dfrac{Y(Y+1)}{2}$

Y = estimated life in years

$$\text{SYD} = \frac{4(4+1)}{2}$$

$$\text{SYD} = 10$$

An alternative method of calculating depreciation under the sum-of-the-year's-digits method is sanctioned by the Regulations. This method is required to be used for multiple asset accounts and may be used for single asset accounts: [74]   This method of calculating SYD depreciation is as follows:

Uncovered cost or basis—salvage $\times$ remaining life at beginning of year
sum-of-year's-digits for the remain-
ing estimated life

Example 24.   Using the depreciation calculations in the prior example, the following is a comparison of the depreciation reserve at the end of 19X4.

	Cost	– Depreciation	Book Value = of Residual
1. Straight-line	$10,000	$9,000	$1,000
2. Double-declining balance	$10,000	$9,375	$ 625
3. Sum-of-the-year's digits	$10,000	$9,000	$1,000

RESTRICTIONS UPON DEPRECIATION METHODS

The Tax Reform Act of 1969 placed certain restrictions upon the use of accelerated methods for new and used real property.   These restrictions were imposed to reduce the opportunities for using real estate investments as a tax shelter since the use of accelerated depreciation frequently resulted in the recognition of ordinary tax losses on economically profitable real estate ventures.[75]

The following methods are now permitted for commercial and residential real property: [76]

	Nonresidential Real Property (commercial and industrial buildings, etc.)	Residential Real Property (two family houses, etc.)
1. New property acquired after 7/24/69	150% DB, SL	200% DB, SYD, 150% DB or SL
2. Used property acquired after 7/24/69	SL	125% DB if useful life is 20 years or greater, SL

Restrictions upon the use of accelerated methods have not been imposed upon new tangible personal property, e. g., machinery and equipment and automobiles.   However, 200% DB and SYD are not permitted for used tangible personal property.   Since the acquisition of used property does not result in any net addition to gross private investment in our economy, Congress has chosen not to provide rapid

74.   Reg. § 1.167(b)–3(a)(2)(ii).

75.   S.Rep. 91–552, 91st Cong., 1st Sess., 1969, p. 212.

76.   § 167(j).

accelerated depreciation for used property. It should be noted that accelerated methods, i. e., 200% DB and SYD are permitted for new residential real property. Presumably, our needs to stimulate construction of new housing units justifies the need for such accelerated methods.

ADDITIONAL FIRST–YEAR DEPRECIATION

§ 179 permits taxpayers to elect to take an additional amount of depreciation in the year of acquisition equal to 20 percent of the cost of new or used tangible depreciable property. The qualifying property must have a useful life of 6 or more years. The deduction is limited to the first $10,000 of qualifying property in any one year ($20,000 if a joint return is filed). If a partnership acquires the property after 1975, a $10,000 aggregate limitation applies at the partnership level so that the partners must include only their pro rata share of the $10,000 ceiling amount on their individual returns.[77]

Salvage value is ignored in computing the amount of "bonus" depreciation. However, the basis of the property used in computing the ordinary depreciation must be reduced by the amount of additional or "bonus" depreciation.

> **Example 25.** X is a self-employed individual who acquires equipment costing $30,000 in 19X1. Since X files a joint return she may elect to deduct $4,000 of additional depreciation in 19X1 (20% x $20,000). The basis for computing regular depreciation is reduced to $26,000 if the election is made.

The additional depreciation election is of primary benefit to small businesses since the ceiling amounts reduce the importance of the additional depreciation for large companies.

REHABILITATION EXPENDITURES FOR LOW–INCOME HOUSING

The Code provides a special five-year amortization election for rehabilitation expenditures on low income housing.[78] The rehabilitation expenditures must exceed $3,000 per dwelling unit over two consecutive years and in the aggregate may not exceed $20,000 per dwelling unit.[79] Any cost in excess of the $20,000 ceiling is subject to the regular depreciation rules.

> **Example 26.** In 1977 X incurred $30,000 of rehabilitation expenditures to fix up an old home which qualifies as low income housing. $20,000 may be depreciated on a straight-line basis over 60 months using the elective provisions of § 167(k) whereas $10,000 must be depreciated under § 167 regular depreciation rules.

77. Act § 213(a) amending § 179(d).   **79.** Act § 203 amending § 167(k).

78. § 167(k).

ACCOUNTING AND USEFUL LiFE SYSTEMS

Each depreciable asset may be treated separately or various asset groupings are permitted including the following: [80]

1. A "group account," i. e., similar types of assets with approximately similar useful lives are depreciated as a unit;

2. A "classified account," i. e., similar assets such as furniture and fixures are aggregated without regard to their useful lives;

3. A "composite account," i. e., assets are grouped without regard to their character or useful lives.

If property is treated as a separate item, gain or loss upon its sale or other disposition is recognized. However, if a retirement is from a multiple-asset account, gain is not recognized and loss is generally recognized only if the retirement is "abnormal." [81]

One of the problems in computing the amount of depreciation is the determination of useful life. One source of information is the company's previous experience and policy with respect to asset maintenance and utilization. Another source is the IRS guideline lives.[82] The adoption of lives which are comparable to the IRS guide may help to reduce or eliminate disputes with agents.

In 1971, the IRS guideline life system was modified and liberalized by the enactment of the Asset Depreciation Range System (ADR) which permits the use of lives within a range of 20% below or above the IRS guideline lives.[83]

The ADR rules are extremely complex and the Regulations should, therefore, be carefully reviewed. However, the following general characteristics may be noted:

1. The ADR is an election which is made on an annual basis.

2. Assets are grouped into guideline classifications as set forth in Rev.Proc. 72–10.[84]

3. The election generally applies to all eligible assets placed in service during the year of election.

4. Certain half year conventions are provided for asset additions and retirements.

5. Certain repairs may be capitalized under a special repair allowance convention.

---

80. Reg. § 1.167(a)–(7)(a).

81. Reg. § 1.167(a)–(8).

82. Rev.Proc. 62–21, 1962–2 C.B. 418 as amended and supplemented; Rev. Proc. 65–13, 1965–1 C.B. 759.

83. Reg. § 1.167(a)–(11).

84. Rev.Proc. 72–10, 1972–1, C.B. 721.

CHANGE IN DEPRECIATION METHOD

A taxpayer may change from the declining balance method to straight-line without the consent of the Commissioner.[85] To make any other change in depreciation methods the taxpayer must file a request for change on Form 3115 within the first 180 days of the year. Currently, the IRS grants automatic approval of the change if certain conditions are met. See Chapter 16 for an expanded discussion of accounting method changes.

AVERAGING CONVENTIONS

To simplify recordkeeping, taxpayers are allowed to select an averaging convention for asset additions and retirements during the year. One method is to assume that all additions and retirements during the first half of the year occurred on the first day of the year and that additions and retirements in the last half occurred on the last day of the year. An averaging convention must be consistently followed and may not be used in any year in which it results in a material distortion of income.[86]

TAX PLANNING CONSIDERATIONS

BAD DEBTS

It is generally preferable to elect the reserve method for bad debts since the taxpayer is permitted a deduction (in the calculation of the addition to the reserve) for amounts which would not be deductible until subsequent periods if the specific charge-off method were used. In addition, the reserve method may mitigate conflicts with the IRS as to the exact year of worthlessness since, under the specific charge-off method, a deduction is available only in such year. The IRS may determine that the loss took place during periods prior to which the deduction was claimed and a refund adjustment may be barred by the statute of limitations.

If the reserve method is used, the taxpayer should generally use an approach similar to the Black Motor Company formula which is based upon previous history of bad debt losses. If an alternative approach is used, the taxpayer should be prepared to justify this method by providing specific documentation relative to the nature and risks of the business and the character of the receivables.

If a taxpayer is starting a new business and initial net operating losses are anticipated, the direct charge-off method may be preferable during the initial years. Otherwise, the additional bad debt expense

---

85. § 167(e)(1).   **86.** Reg. § 1.167(e)–1(b).

deductions allowed under the reserve method may operate so as to increase the taxpayer's net operating losses. Since net operating losses may be carried forward for only seven years, the tax benefits may be lost. The reserve method may then be elected after the business has become profitable.

NET OPERATING LOSSES

In certain instances it may be advisable for a taxpayer to elect not to carryback a net operating loss to a particular year. For an individual, the benefits from the loss carryback may be scaled down or lost due to the "economic" adjustments which are required to be made to taxable income for the year to which the loss is carried. For corporate taxpayers the election not to carryback the loss to a particular year may be advantageous in certain circumstances. For example, where a corporation has substantial net long-term capital gains and insignificant amounts of ordinary taxable income in the year to which the loss is carried, the loss carryback may result in limited tax benefit due to the application of the alternative tax computation for corporations. The alternative tax for corporations is discussed in Chapter 18.

DEPRECIATION AND AMORTIZATION

If a taxpayer is starting a new business and initial losses are anticipated (or if the taxpayer expects to be in a relatively low tax bracket during the next few years), consideration should be given to the use of depreciation and amortization methods which produce smaller deductions in the early years. Thus, the taxpayer might elect under § 174 to capitalize and amortize research and experimental costs over a period of not less than 60 months instead of electing the expense method. In addition, it may be preferable to elect straight-line depreciation instead of an accelerated method and not elect additional or "bonus" depreciation during the early years. The choice of estimated useful lives should also reflect estimates of future amounts of taxable income or loss and effective tax rates during such periods.

DOCUMENTATION OF RELATED TAXPAYER LOANS, CASUALTY AND THEFT LOSSES

Since non-bona fide loans between related taxpayers may be treated as gifts, adequate documentation is needed to substantiate a bad debt deduction if the loan subsequently becomes worthless. Documentation should include proper execution of the note (legal form), and the establishment of a bona fide purpose for the loan. In addition, it is desirable to provide for a reasonable rate of interest on the loan and a fixed maturity date.

Since a theft loss is not permitted for "misplaced" items, a loss should be documented by a police report and evidence of the value of the property, e. g. appraisals, pictures of the property, newspaper clippings, etc. Similar documentation of the value of property should be provided to support a casualty loss deduction since the amount of loss is measured by the decline in fair market value of the property.

PROBLEM MATERIALS

Questions for Class Discussion

1. Why can't a *cash* basis taxpayer deduct a bad debt arising from the sale of a product or service?

2. Is a deduction for partial worthlessness of a bad debt permitted for taxpayers who use the reserve method? Explain.

3. Why it is important to determine the exact year of worthlessness for a bad debt?

4. Compare and contrast the "reserve method" and the "direct charge-off" methods. Which method is generally preferred by most businesses? Why?

5. Is it necessary for the taxpayer to strictly adhere to the Black Motor formula approach in computing the addition to the bad debt reserve? Explain.

6. Discuss the difference(s) between business and non-business bad debts? How is the distinction determined? How is each treated on the return?

7. What are the considerations to be taken into account in determining if a bad debt arising from a loan between related parties is, in fact, a bad debt?

8. Under what circumstances can a worthless security be treated as an ordinary loss?

9. What "Acts of God" give rise to a casualty loss? Which ones do not? Discuss.

10. How are thefts treated differently from "Acts of God" for casualty losses?

11. When is a casualty loss deductible? What is the exception? How is the election made? Discuss.

12. How is a personal casualty loss computed? A business casualty loss? What effect do insurance proceeds have on both types of losses?

13. Is it possible to have a casualty gain? How is it taxed?

14. Discuss the ways a partial casualty loss can be measured.

15. What is a disaster loss? Why might a taxpayer benefit from making the disaster loss election?

16. What are "research and experimental" expenditures? Discuss the alternative ways they may be handled for tax purposes.

17. Why do most taxpayers elect to write off research and experimental expenditures rather than capitalize and amortize such amounts? Are there some situations where the capitalization approach would be preferable?

18. What is the rationale behind the net operating loss deduction? Who benefits from this provision?

19. Why is a personal casualty loss allowed in computing a net operating loss? Why aren't other personal expenditures allowed such as mortgage interest and charitable contributions?

20. Why aren't such things as nonbusiness deductions, the long-term capital gains exclusion, etc., allowed in computing the net operating loss?

21. Discuss the periods to which net operating losses may be carried. Can the taxpayer elect not to carry a net operating loss back to any one year. What possible benefit might result from not carrying a loss back to a particular year?

22. Is it necessary to recompute the tax liability for the year to which the net operating loss is carried? Why?

23. If a taxpayer does not claim depreciation in one year, can he claim an excess amount during a subsequent year? How is the basis for depreciable property affected by the failure to claim depreciation during any one year?

24. Why is accelerated depreciation and/or the use of short estimated lives stimulating to our economy?

25. If a personal use type asset is converted to business use, why is it necessary to compute depreciation upon the lower of fair market value or adjusted basis at the date of conversion? i. e., what is the rationale for this requirement?

26. Why is a patent subject to amortization whereas goodwill is not amortizable?

27. What is the difference between the terms depreciation and amortization?

28. Is it possible to depreciate an asset below its salvage value?

29. When can a taxpayer disregard salvage value?

30. What types of property are not depreciable under the 200% DDB or SYD methods? Why were restrictions placed upon these types of assets?

31. What types of depreciation or amortization methods are available for rehabilitation expenditures on low-income housing?

32. Is gain or loss recognized if an asset is retired from a multiple asset account? From a separate asset account?

33. Why would a taxpayer elect to use the Asset Depreciation Range (ADR) System and/or the IRS guideline lives?

34. Is it possible to change depreciation methods without obtaining the consent of the Commissioner?

Problems

1. M loaned T $5,000 on April 1, 19X4. In 19X5 T filed for bankruptcy. At that time it was revealed that T's creditors could expect to receive 50¢ on the dollar. In February 19X6 final settlement was made and M received $2,000. How much loss can M take in which year? How is it treated on his return?

2. F borrowed $1,000 from G on March 18, 19X6 to buy a motorcycle. F gave G his personal note payable on that date. In July, F had an accident and totalled the motorcycle (to say nothing of what he did to himself). On December 31, 19X6, the note was worth $800. What is G's bad debt deduction in 19X6? Would your answer be different if the note was completely worthless on 12/31/19X6?

3. In (2) above, would your answer be different if G had been in the business of selling motorcycles and had sold the bike to F, taking the note in return?

4. X loaned Y $1,000 (secured by a note) on January 3, 19X6. X sold the note to Z for $900 on June 1, 19X6. Y went bankrupt on December 31, 19X6. Determine what bad debt deduction (if any) X and Z had in 19X6.

5. Determine the amount of addition to the Reserve for Bad Debts for the J Company as of December 31, 19X6 under the Black Motor Co. formula, given the following information:

   1. Net bad debts for the current year and five preceding years—$60,000

   2. Total accounts and notes receivable outstanding at the end of the Year

19X1	$100,000
19X2	110,000
19X3	90,000
19X4	80,000
19X5	120,000
19X6	100,000

   3. Beginning balance in the reserve for doubtful accounts in 19X6 = $12,000

4. 19X6 recoveries of previous accounts written off = $2,000
5. Specific writeoffs during 19X6 = $8,000

6. L ran a red light and was hit broadside by a dumptruck loaded
    with kumquats. The following amounts for damages were paid
    by L:

Moving violation citation	$ 25
Damages to L's car	600
Medical expenses of L's passenger	900
Damages to dumptruck	350
Medical bills of L (the truckdriver broke his nose in the discussion following the accident)	120
Replacement of ruined kumquats	1,000

How much can L deduct on his income tax return as a casualty
loss?

7. If the red light had been run by the dumptruck in problem (6)
    above, would your answer be different?

8. When J returned from a vacation in Hawaii on November 8,
    19X6, she discovered that a burglar had stolen her silver, stereo
    and color television. In the process of removing these items,
    the burglar damaged her Chippendale china cabinet, which had
    cost her $1,000. Her silver had cost $2,600 and was valued at
    $4,500; the stereo system had cost $6,000 and was valued at
    $4,500; the television had cost $600 and was worth $400. She
    filed a claim with her insurance company and was reimbursed
    as follows on December 20, 19X6:

Silver	$2,000
Stereo	4,000
Television	350

The insurance company refused to reimburse her for the damaged china cabinet, but she protested and was finally paid $200
toward the repair bill of $320 on January 30, 19X7.

How much, and in what year, can J take a casualty loss?

9. K owned an acre of land in Kansas upon which he had his home,
    two rental houses, an apartment building and his construction
    company. A twister hit the area and destroyed one of the rental
    houses, damaged the apartment building and destroyed some of
    his construction equipment. The renter of his other rental house
    moved out for fear of another tornado and K lost $300 in rent.
    The town real estate appraiser told him his house (adjusted
    basis of $35,000) had been worth $50,000 until the disaster and
    was now worth only $30,000 (although it was undamaged) be-

cause it had been established that his house was in a well-known tornado path. Other losses were as follows:

Item	Adjusted Basis	FMV Before	FMV After	Insurance Proceeds
House #1	$ 23,000	$ 29,000	$ -0-	$25,000
Apartment house	100,000	150,000	120,000	21,000
Equipment	60,000	75,000	-0-	50,000

     a.   What is the amount of the casualty loss K can take on his tax return?

     b.   Assuming the loss occurred on March 3, 19X7 and that the area was designated by the President as a disaster area, what options were open to K as to when to take the loss?

10.   X Corporation started developing a new process for gold plating conductor wires in 19X7. A workable process (no useful life can be determined) was developed by June 30, 19X7. The following expenses were incurred:

Cost of research equipment used in developing the process—the equipment has an estimated life of 10 years	$ 50,000
Materials and supplies	100,000
Salaries	60,000
Other	40,000

Compute the alternative methods available to X Corporation and the year(s) in which the costs are deductible.

11.   S had a net operating loss in 19X6 of $100,000. Assuming she had taxable income (after necessary adjustments) as follows, show how and in what sequence her loss would be absorbed assuming she elects to carryback the loss to each year:

19X3	$8,000	19X8	$ 8,000
19X4	4,000	19X9	12,000
19X5	6,000	19X10	15,000
19X7	3,000	19X11	40,000

Which years would she file a claim for refund for?

12.   G owns a grocery store. In 19X6 his gross sales were $286,000 and operating expenses were $310,000. Other items on his 19X6 return were as follows:

Nonbusiness capital gains	$ 6,000
Nonbusiness capital losses	9,000
Itemized deductions	10,000
Ordinary nonbusiness income	4,000
Salary from part-time job	2,000
Personal exemption	750

In 19X3 his taxable income was $16,000. There was a long-term capital gain deduction of $2,000; he used the standard deduction and had one personal exemption.

a. What is his 19X6 net operating loss?

b. What amount of the net operating loss for 19X6 may be carried back to 19X3?

c. What is his 19X3 taxable income?

d. What is the carryover to 19X4?

e. What is the last year to which the loss can be carried?

13. X Company acquired an automobile for use in the business on 1/1/19X1 for $6,000. No depreciation was taken in 19X1 or 19X2 since the company had net operating losses and wanted to "save" the deductions for later years. In 19X3 the company claimed a three year life for the automobile and no salvage value and deducted $2,000 of depreciation using a straight-line rate. On 1/1/19X4 the automobile was sold for $3,000.

Calculate the gain or loss on the sale of the automobile in 19X4.

14. What depreciation methods can be used for the following assets which were acquired after 1969:

a. Used machinery and equipment used in business.

b. New apartment building held for investment.

c. Land held for business use.

d. Used apartment building held for investment.

e. New factory building used for business.

f. New automobile used in business.

15. X acquired a personal residence in 19X1 for $30,000. In January, 19X3 he converted the residence to rental property when the fair market value was $32,000.

a. Calculate the amount of depreciation which can be taken in 19X3 assuming that the straight-line rate is used with 0 salvage and a 30 year life.

b. What would your answer be if the property was worth only $20,000 in 19X3?

16. XYZ Corporation acquired the assets of ABC Company for $1,-000,000 in cash. The book value of the tangible assets was $400,-000 whereas their fair market value was $600,000. XYZ was willing to pay $400,000 for ABC's goodwill since the company's operations have been extremely profitable.

For accounting purposes, XYZ has amortized the goodwill over a period of 40 years as prescribed by Accounting Principles Board Opinion No. 17. Is this procedure acceptable for income tax purposes? Explain.

17. X acquires a machine for $10,000 with a $1,500 salvage value. What is the least amount of salvage value which must be used if the following depreciation methods are used:

    a. 200% DDB—double declining balance

    b. SYD—Sum-of-the-year's-digits

    c. 150% DB

    d. SL—Straight-line

    e. Additional first year depreciation

18. X acquired new business equipment for $40,000 on 1/1/19X1. The equipment has a $2,000 salvage value and a 10 year useful life. X files a joint return with his spouse.

    a. Calculate the amount of "bonus" depreciation.

    b. Calculate the amount of depreciation for 19X1 using the following

       1. 200% DDB

       2. SYD

       3. SL

19. X acquired a low-income housing apartment in January 19X1 and incurred the following rehabilitation expenditures for each of the 10 housing units: $24,000 times 10 units or $240,000. These expenditures have a useful life of 20 years with no salvage value.

    Calculate the amount of amortization which may be claimed if the rapid amortization election is made.

Research Problems

1. T, a stockbroker, went to Las Vegas to celebrate New Year's Eve in 19X1. He was shooting craps and did quite well until midnight. He won a total of $40,000. After a midnight brunch, he returned to the tables and lost $50,000. He decided this was no way to celebrate the arrival of 19X2 and went home after losing a net amount of $10,000.

    a. How much must T include in his income in 19X1 and 19X2? How much is reported in each year?

    b. Suppose that T was a professional gambler and incurred the following expenses in 19X1 in addition to his winnings and losing above:

Transportation to Vegas	$ 750
Cash gifts to the dealer for luck	500
Fees paid to police in Iowa to "look the other way"	3,000
Motel and meals on gambling trip	300
Clothes to give him the appropriate "look"	5,000

    What can T deduct on his 19X1 return?

2. X acquired an old apartment building and land for $100,000 in 19X1. The land was appraised at $50,000 and the apartment was worth $50,000. X demolished the apartment building at a cost of $20,000 and constructed a new apartment for $300,000.

   a. Calculate the cost basis for depreciation relative to the new apartment.

   b. Would your answer be different if X had rented the old apartment for a period of 5 years prior to its demolition and the construction of the new apartment?

DEDUCTIONS: EMPLOYEE EXPENSES

After completing our discussion of business expenses and losses in the previous chapter, it is now appropriate to discuss employment related expenses. The Code provides that certain employee expenses are deductible for adjusted gross income and treated as if they were expenses incurred in a trade or business. Other types of employee expenses are deductible *from* adjusted gross income (itemized deductions). Chapter 8 first gives consideration to the proper classification of employee expenses before discussing specific items.

CLASSIFICATION OF EMPLOYMENT RELATED EXPENSES

SELF–EMPLOYED VERSUS EMPLOYEE STATUS

In many instances it is difficult to distinguish whether an individual is self-employed or is performing services as an employee. Expenses of self-employed individuals are deductible as trade or business expenses (*for* adjusted gross income). However, if the expenses are incurred as the result of an employment relationship, they are deductible subject to the limitations in the Code relative to employee expenses.

Generally, an employer-employee relationship exists when the employer has the right not only to specify the end result, but also to specify the ways and means by which the end result is to be attained. Thus, an employee is subject to the will and control of the employer not only as to what shall be done but how it shall be done.[1] If the individual is subject to the direction or control of another only to the extent of the end result (i. e., the preparation of a taxpayer's return by an independent CPA) but not as to the means of accomplishment, an employee relationship does not exist. Other factors may exist which indicate an employer-employee relationship such as the right to discharge the person performing the service without legal liability; the furnishing of tools or a place to work, payment based upon time spent rather than the task performed, etc. However, each case is tested upon its own merits and the right to control the means and methods of accomplishment is the definitive test. Generally, physicians, lawyers, dentists, contractors, subcontractors, etc. who offer services to the public, are not classified as employees.[2]

Example 1. D is a lawyer whose major client accounts for 60 percent of her billings. She does the routine legal work, income tax returns and other legal work at their request. She is paid a monthly retainer in addition to amounts charged for extra work. She is a self-employed individual. Even though most of her income is from one client, she still has the right to determine how the end result is attained.

Example 2. E is a lawyer who D hired to assist her in the performance of legal services for the client mentioned in Example 1. He is under her supervision; she reviews his work, and pays him an hourly fee. He is an employee of D.

Example 3. F is a practical nurse who works as a live-in nurse. She is under the supervision of the patient's doctor and is paid by the patient. She is not an employee of either the patient (who pays her) or the doctor (who supervises her) because the ways and means of attaining the end result (care of the patient) is under her control.

A self-employed individual is required to file Schedule C of Form 1040 and all allowable expenses related to that activity are deductions *for* adjusted gross income (AGI).[3]

DEDUCTIONS FOR OR FROM AGI

The Code specifies those employee expenses which are deductible *for* adjusted gross income.[4] All other employee expenses must be deducted *from* adjusted gross income and cannot be deducted unless the

1. Reg. § 31.3401(c)–(1)(b).

2. Reg. § 31.3401(c)(1)(c).

3. §§ 62(1) and 162(a).

4. § 62(2).

employee-taxpayer itemizes his or her deductions. The deductions *for* adjusted gross income include travel, transportation, moving expenses, expenses of an outside salesman and other reimbursed employment related expenses. All other employee expenses are deductible *from* adjusted gross income (itemized deductions). Certain activities require an apportionment of expenses among these two categories (*for* and *from* AGI).

The distinction between *for* and *from* AGI is important since no benefit is received for an item which is deductible *from* adjusted gross income if a taxpayer's itemized deductions are less than the standard deduction (referred to as the zero bracket amount). In addition, certain deductions are based upon the amount of adjusted gross income, e. g. medical expenses.

SPECIAL TREATMENT FOR OUTSIDE SALESMEN

If an employee qualifies as an "outside salesman", *all* employment related expenses are deductible *for* adjusted gross income and may be deducted even if the taxpayer uses the standard deduction.[5]

Congress apparently felt that an outside salesman's activities resembled those of a self-employed individual more than those of an employee and, therefore, should receive favorable treatment.

Definition of an Outside Salesman. An "outside salesman" is one who solicits business away from the employer's place of business on a full-time basis.[6] An employee who performs service or delivery functions from an employer's place of business is not an outside salesman. However, "outside salesman" status is not lost if the employee performs incidental tasks (such as writing up orders, picking up mail or phone messages, etc.) at the employer's office.

The question of whether an employee is an "outside salesman" has been the subject of extensive litigation. Each case has been decided on its own merits and quite often different interpretations have been given to similar fact patterns.

Example 4. The following are illustrations of employees who qualify as "outside salesmen" since the performance of office duties is incidental to their primary outside sales job:

1. G is a real estate agent who reports to his office on a daily basis to check new listings, current sales, etc.

2. R is an employee who sells burglar alarm systems to local businesses. He checks in to his office periodically to obtain new leads and to write up orders.

The following are illustrations of employees who are *not* "outside salesmen" since the nature of their job is primarily service or delivery rather than a selling function:

5. § 62(2)(D).   6. Reg. § 1.62–1(h).

1. B is a bread deliveryman who makes regular rounds after picking up fresh bread at his employer's bakery. He uses the company office to do his daily accounting and cash check-out.

2. Q is a television repairman who is dispatched from his employer's shop to perform service repair calls for customers.

REIMBURSED EXPENSES

It has been stressed in this chapter that certain expenses of an employee are deductions *for* adjusted gross income: travel, transportation, moving expenses, and the expenses of an "outside salesman". Other expenses of an employee such as professional dues and subscriptions, entertainment, uniforms, etc., must be deducted *from* adjusted gross income. The exception to this rule is where reimbursements from the employer are received.

Reimbursements are included in an employee's gross income. Congress apparently felt that, since the reimbursements were income, an offsetting procedure should be allowed. Therefore, the law in effect allows an employee to deduct any bona fide employee expense *for* adjusted gross income if that expense is reimbursed by the employer.[7] Thus, an employee who has reimbursed employee expenses is allowed to offset the expenses incurred against the reimbursement (income) whether or not the election to itemize is made.

When reimbursements are present, there are three distinct possibilities: (1) the expenses and the reimbursements are equal; (2) the reimbursement exceeds the expenses; and (3) the expenses exceed the reimbursement. The treatment of the first two possibilities depends upon whether the employee has made an "adequate accounting" to the employer.

Record-keeping Requirements. An "adequate accounting" means that the employee has submitted a record (with receipts and other substantiation) to the employer with the following pertinent facts: amount, place and date of expenditure, and the business purpose and business relationship of the expenditure.[8] The use of reasonable per diem (currently $44 per day unless to an area the U. S. government allows its employees a higher per diem), rates and mileage (currently 15 cents per mile) can constitute an "adequate accounting" unless the employer and employee are related. Any employee who does not adequately account to his employer, must submit a detailed statement to his return showing expense categories, reimbursements, etc.[9] The following situations may be encountered:

(1) Expenses and reimbursements are equal. If an adequate accounting has been made, the employee may omit both the

7. § 62(2)(A).   9. Reg. § 1.162–17(c).
8. Reg. § 1.162–17(b)(4).

reimbursement and the expenses from the tax return.[10]   If an adequate accounting has not been made, then a complete statement of all expenses (by category) and all reimbursements must be attached to the return.

(2) Reimbursements exceed expenses.   If an adequate accounting has been made, the employee may report the excess as miscellaneous income and ignore the expenses and reimbursements up to the amount of the expenses.[11]

(3) Expenses exceed reimbursements.   Regardless of whether an adequate accounting is made to the employer, if the employee deducts the excess expenses, the statement described above must be attached to the income tax return.[12]

Allocation Problems.   A further problem exists where reimbursements are intended to cover all employee expenses and where the total reimbursement is less than the total expense.   Travel and transportation are deductible *for* adjusted gross income, whether or not they are reimbursed.   Other expenses of an employee (unless an "outside salesman") are deductible *for* adjusted gross income only to the extent that they are reimbursed.   Where all expenses are partially reimbursed the whole problem is solved by using a simple pro rata procedure; All travel and transportation expenses are deductible *for* adjusted gross income and only the pro rata share of other expenses that have been reimbursed are deductible *for* adjusted gross income. The remainder (which represents the unreimbursed other expenses) is an itemized deduction.   The formula for computing the other expenses deductible *for* adjusted gross income is: [13]

$$\frac{\text{Total other expenses}}{\text{Total expenses (including travel + transportation)}} \times \text{Reimbursement}$$

Example 5.   Assume an employee incurs a total of \$3,750 in business expenses consisting of transportation expenses of \$500; meals and lodging away from home of \$2,500; and dues, subscriptions, and entertainment expenses amounting to \$750.   The reimbursement which is intended to cover all of the expenses amount-

10.   Reg. § 1.162–17(b)(1).   12.   Reg. § 1.162–17(b)(3).

11.   Reg. § 1.162–17(b)(2).   13.   Reg. § 1.162–5(a).

ed to $2,500. The deductions *for* and *from* adjusted gross income are computed as follows:

Travel (100%)	$2,500	
Transportation (100%)	500	
Other ($\frac{750}{3750} \times 2,500$)	500	
Deductible *for* AGI	$3,500	
Less: Reimbursements	2,500	
Net deductible *for* AGI		$1,000
Total other	750	
Less: deducted *for* AGI	500	
Deductible *from* AGI	$ 250	250
Total Deductible		$1,250

Another approach to solving the same problem is to determine the ratio of reimbursements to expenses and, again, use a pro-rata basis. Given the same facts as above, the deductions *for* and *from* AGI can be obtained as follows:

Example 6.

$$\frac{\text{Total Reimbursements}}{\text{Total Expenses}} = \frac{\$2500}{\$3750} = \frac{2}{3}$$

	Travel	Transportation	Other	Total
Expense	$2,500	$ 500	$ 750	$3,750
Reimbursed (⅔)	1,667	333	500	2,500
Unreimbursed	$ 833	$ 167	$ 250	$1,250

Travel and transportation are deductible *for* AGI and the other expenses are deductible *from* AGI.

Travel	$ 833	
Transportation	167	
Deductible *for* AGI		$1,000
Other: Deductible *from* AGI		$ 250

As can be seen, the same result is obtained: If the employee itemized his deductions, he is entitled to a $1,000 net deduction *for* AGI and $250 *from* AGI. If the standard deduction were used, only a $1,000 deduction for *AGI* is allowed.

TRANSPORTATION EXPENSES

QUALIFIED EXPENDITURES

An employee is permitted a deduction *for* adjusted gross income for transportation expenses paid in connection with services performed as an employee.[14] Transportation expense includes only the cost of transporting the employee from one place to another in the course of employment where the employee is not "away from home" in a travel status.[15] Such costs include taxi fares, automobile expenses, tolls, parking, etc.

Commuting from home to one's place of employment is a personal nondeductible expense and the fact that one employee drives 30 miles to work and another employee walks 6 blocks is of no significance.[16]

> **Example 7.** G is employed by the X Corporation. He drives 22 miles each way to work. One day he had to drive to a customer's office from work. It was 7 miles each way. He can take a deduction for 14 miles of business travel. The remainng 44 miles is a nondeductible commuting expense.

One exception to the disallowance of commuting expenses is where an employee has to use an automobile to transport heavy tools to work and who otherwise would not drive to work. A deduction is allowed only for the "additional costs" incurred to transport work implements. "Additional costs" are those exceeding the cost of commuting by the same mode of transportation without the tools (i. e., the rental of a trailer but *not* the expenses of operating the automobile).[17] The Supreme Court has held that a deduction is permitted only if the taxpayer can show that he would not have used his automobile were it not necessary to transport tools or equipment.[18]

Another exception is where an employee has a second job. The expenses of getting from one job to another are deductible.[19] If the employee goes home between jobs, the deduction is limited to the lesser of (1) the cost of the transportation (or mileage) between the two jobs or (2) the actual expenditure.

---

14. § 62(2)(C).

15. Reg. § 1.62–1(g).

16. *Tauferner v. U. S.,* 69–1 USTC ¶ 9241, 23 AFTR2d 69–1025, 407 F.2d 243 (CA–10, 1969).

17. Rev.Rul. 75–380, 1975–2 C.B. 59.

18. *D. W. Fausner v. Comm.,* 73–2 USTC ¶ 9515, 32 AFTR2d 73–5202, 93 S.Ct. 2820 (USSC, 1973).

19. "Travel, Entertainment and Gift Expenses," *IRS Publication 463,* p. 6 (Oct.1974).

Example 8. In the current year T holds two jobs; a full-time job with B Corporation and a part-time job with C Corporation. During the 250 days that he worked (adjusted for weekends, vacation and holidays) T customarily left home at 7:30 A.M. and drove 30 miles to the B Corporation plant where he worked until 5:00 P.M. After dinner at a nearby cafe, he drove 20 miles to C Corporation and worked from 7:00–11:00 P.M. The distance from the second job to T's home is 40 miles. Only 20 miles (the distance between jobs) is allowed as a deduction.

A final exception to the disallowance of commuting expenses is for temporary or minor assignments beyond the general area of the tax home. Thus, a bank manager who must spend an occasional day at a remote branch office in the suburbs can deduct transportation expenses (or mileage) as an employee expense. The important distinction between commuting (personal) expenses and employee transportation (deductible) expenses is the temporary nature of the assignment. If an employee is permanently reassigned to a new location, the assignment is deemed to be for an indefinite period and the expenses are nondeductible commuting expenses. Furthermore, if an employee customarily works on several temporary assignments in a localized area, that localized area becomes the "regular place of employment", and transportation from home to these locations becomes a personal, nondeductible commuting expense.

Example 9. V works for a firm in downtown Denver. He commutes to work. He occasionally works in a customer's office. On one such occasion he drove directly to the customer's office (a round-trip distance from his home of 40 miles). He did not go into his office, which is a 52-mile round-trip distance. None of his mileage is deductible.

Example 10. Assume in the previous example that V drove to his office (16 miles) and then drove home via the customer's office on business, which was a total distance (office-to customer-to home) of 26 miles. The employee can deduct the cost of 10 miles (the additional distance from work to customer).

COMPUTATION OF AUTOMOBILE EXPENSES

Basically, a taxpayer has two choices in computing automobile expenses. The actual operating cost may be used which includes depreciation, gas, oil, repairs, licenses, insurance, etc. Records must be kept which show the amount the automobile was used for personal travel and business travel. Only the percentage (based upon the ratio of business miles to total miles) which is allocable to business transportation and travel, is allowed as a deduction.

The second alternative is to use the automatic mileage method. For the first 15,000 business miles, the deduction is based upon 15 cents per mile. Ten cents per mile is allowed for any miles in excess of 15,000.[20] Parking fees, tolls and the investment credit are allowed in addition to the automatic mileage method.

Generally, a taxpayer may elect either method for any particular year. However, the following restrictions apply:

(1) If two or more vehicles are in use (for business purposes) at the same time, a taxpayer may not use the automatic mileage method;

(2) If the taxpayer changes from the automatic mileage method to the actual operating cost method, the cost basis of the automobile must be reduced by the amount of straight-line depreciation that would have been allowed had the automatic mileage method not been used;

(3) A taxpayer cannot switch to the automatic mileage method if additional first-year depreciation or accelerated depreciation has previously been taken; and

(4) If an automobile has been fully depreciated under the straight-line method, the standard mileage rate of 10 cents per mile is used for all miles thereafter.[21]

Example 11. W uses her automobile 60% for business and 40% for pleasure. During 19X5 she drove a total of 40,000 miles. She had purchased the automobile for $8,000 on January 1, 19X2 and depreciated it on the straight line method over three years. She can use the automatic mileage method but, because the automobile has been fully depreciated, she is limited to 10 cents per mile or $2,400 (.10 x 40,000 x 60%).

Any reimbursement for auto expenses must be reported on the tax return (i. e., to reduce the deduction) if the automatic mileage method is used. Where an employee receives a reimbursement for transportation expenses from his employer, it may still be possible to claim a deduction if there is an excess of actual expenses over the reimbursed amounts. Also, if the standard mileage rate (15 cents) exceeds the reimbursed rate, e. g. 10 cents, the taxpayer is entitled to a deduction for the difference where the optional method is elected. Frequently, taxpayers discover that the actual automobile expenses, e. g. for depreciation, gas, oil, repairs, etc., exceed the amount of expense calculated under the standard mileage rate prescribed by the IRS.

20. Rev.Proc. 74–23, 1974–2 C.B. 476.   **21.** Rev.Proc. 75–3, 1975–1 C.B. 643.

TRAVEL EXPENSES

DEFINITION OF TRAVEL EXPENSES

A deduction *for* adjusted gross income is allowed for travel expenses related to a trade or business or employment.[22] Travel expenses are more broadly defined in the Code than transportation expenses. Travel expenses also include meals and lodging (that are not lavish or extravagant under the circumstances) while *away from home* in the pursuit of a trade or business (including that of an employee), in addition to transportation expenses. Transportation expenses are deductible even though the taxpayer is not "away from home" whereas a deduction for travel expenses is available only if the taxpayer is away from his tax home. Travel expenses also include reasonable laundry and incidental expenses.[23] Entertainment expenses are not a traveling expense even if incurred while traveling. They are treated as an "other employee expense" and (unless fully reimbursed) are an itemized deduction.

AWAY FROM HOME REQUIREMENT

The crucial test of the deductibility of travel expense is whether the employee is "away from home overnight". "Overnight" need not be a 24-hour period nor from dusk to dawn but it must be a period substantially longer than an ordinary day's work and require rest, sleep or relief-from-work period.[24] Thus a one-day or intracity business (employee) trip is not travel and meals and lodging are not deductible.

The employee must be away from home for a temporary period. If the taxpayer-employee is reassigned to a new post for an indefinite period of time, that new post becomes his "tax home". Temporary means that the assignment's termination is expected within a reasonably short period of time. The position of the IRS is that "tax home" is the business location, post or station of the taxpayer. Thus, the IRS position is that travel expenses are not deductible if a taxpayer is reassigned and does not move his place of residence to the new location if the reassignment is for an indefinite period. The IRS "rule of thumb" is that reassignments for one year or more are indefinite.[25] The courts are in conflict regarding what constitutes a person's "home" for tax purposes. Some courts have held that the test is whether it is reasonable to expect the taxpayer to move to his new

---

22. §§ 62(2)(B) and 162(a)(2).

23. Reg. § 1.162(a)(1).

24. *U. S. v. Correll,* 68–1 USTC ¶ 9101, 20 AFTR2d 5845, 88 S.Ct. 445

(USSC, 1968); Rev.Rul. 63–239, 1963–2 C.B. 87.

25. Rev.Rul. 60–189, 1960–1 C.B. 60.

job location [26] while other courts including the Tax Court have accepted the IRS' view.[27] As a result of this uncertainty, the IRS has established criteria which it will attempt to apply in making the determination of a person's "tax home".[28]

The rationale for the "away from home" requirement is that an employee who has a duplication of living expenses due to a work assignment should be able to deduct those duplicated expenses. Where there is no duplication of expenses (i. e., an employee establishes a new home as the result of a work assignment), those living expenses are of a personal nature and are, therefore, non-deductible.

> **Example 12.** H is employed as a long haul truck driver. He stores his clothes, etc., at his parents' home and stops by their home for periodic visits and vacations. The rest of the time he is on the road, sleeping in his truck and at truck stops and motels. His meals, lodging, laundry and incidental expenses are not deductible because he has no tax home to be away from.[29]

> **Example 13.** Assume that H is employed as a short distance hauler. His wife and children live in Chicago and he makes trips of both long and short duration but quite often makes one-day trips in the surrounding area. His meals on a one-day trip are not deductible. If he makes a 10-day trip to Florida, he is "away from home" and his meals are deductible.

COMBINED BUSINESS AND PLEASURE TRAVEL

To be deductible, travel expenses need not be incurred in the performance of specific job functions. For example, travel expenses incurred in attending a professional convention are deductible by an employee, if attendance is connected with services as an employee. Thus, an employee of a CPA firm could deduct travel expenses incurred in attending the annual American Institute of Cerified Public Accountants' meeting. Unfortunately, this deduction area has been abused in the past by persons who wanted a tax deduction for what was essentially a personal vacation. As a result, several rules have been enacted for combined business-pleasure trips. If the business-pleasure trip is within the United States (i. e., the trip is from one point in the U. S. to another point in the U. S.), the transportation expenses are deductible only if the trip is *primarily* business.[30] If the trip is primarily for pleasure, no travel expenses there and back can

---

26. *Emil J. Michaels,* 53 T.C. 28, (1969); *Comm. v. Flowers,* 46–1 USTC ¶ 9127, 34 AFTR 301, 66 S.Ct. 250 (USSC, 1946).

27. *Rosenspan v. U. S.,* 71–1 USTC ¶ 9241, 27 AFTR2d 71–707, 438 F.2d 905 (CA–2, 1971).

28. Rev.Rul. 73–529, 1973–2 C.B. 37.

29. *Moses Mitnick,* 13 T.C. 1 (1949).

30. Reg. § 1.162–2(b)(1).

be taken as a deduction. Even if the trip is primarily for pleasure (or other personal reasons), the expenses incurred at the destination are deductible provided those expenses are properly allocable to business.

Example 14. J traveled from Seattle to New York on a combined business-pleasure trip. She spent 5 days conducting business and 3 days sightseeing and seeing shows. Her plane and taxi fare amounted to $260. Her meals, lodging and incidental expenses amounted to $80 per day. Since the trip was primarily business (5 days versus 3 days) the transportation is deductible. Only $400 of the other expenses (5 days) are deductible.

Example 15. In the previous example, what would the answer be if she conducted business for 2 days and vacationed the remaining 6 days? The trip is then primarily personal and no transportation expenses are deductible. However, the $80 per day for two days can be deducted.

If an employee taxpayer is accompanied by one or more family members, the incremental costs paid for the family's travel cannot be deducted unless the family members' presence has a bona fide business purpose. Incidental services performed by family members does not constitute a bona fide business purpose.[31]

If the trip is outside the United States, special rules apply.[32] If the taxpayer is away from home for seven days or less or if less than 25% of the time was for personal purposes, no allocation of transportation expenses need be made. No allocation is required if the taxpayer had no substantial control over arranging the trip and the desire for a vacation was not a major factor in taking the trip. If the trip was primarily for pleasure, none of the transportation charges are deductible. In all other cases, all travel expenses must be allocated between business and personal expenses.

Example 16. K took a trip from New York to Japan primarily for business purposes. He was away from home from June 10 through June 19. He spent 3 days vacationing and seven days conducting business (including two travel days which are counted as business days). His air fare was $1,900 and his meals and lodging amounted to $85 per day. He could deduct only 70% of his transportation expenses and $85/day for 7 days since K was away from home for more than seven days and more than 25 percent of the time was devoted to personal purposes.

FOREIGN CONVENTION EXPENSES

For years after 1976, deductions for attendance at business or professional conventions in foreign countries have been restricted.

---

31. Reg. § 1.162–2(c).   **32.** § 274(c); Reg. § 1.274–4.

Generally, an individual may not attend more than 2 foreign conventions during the taxable year.[33] If an employee attends foreign conventions and is reimbursed by his employer the employer is permitted a deduction only to the extent that the employee would be permitted to deduct such amounts under § 274(h).[34]

The following additional restrictions and reporting requirements have been imposed: [35]

1. Deductible transportation cost cannot exceed the cost of coach or economy air fare;

2. Transportation costs are deductible in full only if at least one half of the days are devoted to business. Otherwise it is necessary to allocate transportation expenses based upon the number of business and nonbusiness days;

3. No deduction for subsistence (i. e., meals and lodging, etc.) is permitted unless the taxpayer attends at least $\frac{2}{3}$ of the scheduled business activities and at least 6 hours of business activity are scheduled during the day;

4. Deductions for subsistence are limited to the per diem rate for U. S. civil servants; and

5. The taxpayer is required to submit detailed written documentation with the tax return including a written statement from the convention sponsor.

MOVING EXPENSES

GENERAL REQUIREMENTS

The expense an individual incurs in moving permanently from one job to another has been allowed as a deduction since 1964. Under the 1964 law only the direct costs of moving were deductible (i. e., cost of moving the household goods and traveling expenses of the household). The Tax Reform Act of 1969 recognized that employees incur indirect expenses when moving from one job location to another (e. g. house hunting trips and temporary living costs) and provided for the deductibility of certain indirect moving expenses (subject to limitations).

Moving expenses are now deductible *for* adjusted gross income.[36] Reimbursements from employers are required to be included in gross income under § 82. To be eligible for a moving expense deduction, a

33. § 274(h)(1).

34. § 274(h)(6)(D).

35. §§ 274(h)(2)–(7).

36. §§ 62(8) and 217(a).

taxpayer must meet two basic tests: the distance and time require-ments.[37]

DISTANCE TEST

The distance test requires that the taxpayer's new job must be at least 35 miles farther from the old residence than the old residence was from the old place of work. This is to eliminate a moving deduc-tion for taxpayers who buy a new home in the same general area or accept a new job in the same general area. If a new job doesn't neces-sitate moving or if the move is for personal reasons (e. g. a better neighborhood), the taxpayer is not permitted a tax deduction.

> **Example 17.** J was permanently transferred from his old job to a new location. Given the diagram below, he has met the distance requirements for a moving expense deduction since the distance from his old home to his new job (80 miles) exceeds the distance from his old home to his old job (30 miles) by more than 35 miles. If the employee were not previously employed, the new job must be at least 35 miles from the former residence. In this instance, the new job was 80 miles and the distance re-quirements would be met if the employee were not previously employed.

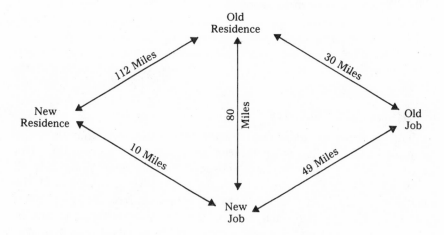

TIME REQUIREMENTS

In the 12-month period following the move, the employee must be employed (on a full-time basis) at the new location for 39 weeks. If the taxpayer is a self-employed individual, an additional require-ment must be met: The taxpayer must work (either self-employed or

37. § 217(c); for years prior to 1977, the distance requirement was 50 miles.

as an employee of another) in the new location for 78 weeks during the next two years. (The first 39 weeks must be in the first 12 months). The time requirement is suspended if the taxpayer dies, becomes disabled, or is discharged or transferred by the new employer through no fault of the employee.[38]

Because of the 39-week rule, it is obvious that an employee might not be able to meet the 39-week requirement by the calendar year-end. For this reason, there are two alternatives allowed: The taxpayer can take the deduction in the year the expenses were incurred even though the 39-week test has not been met. If the taxpayer later fails to meet the test, an amount equal to the deduction must be included in the income of the first year that the test cannot be met (i. e., the following year). The second alternative is to wait until the test is met and then file an amended tax return for the prior year.

WHEN DEDUCTIBLE

The general rule is that expenses of a cash basis taxpayer are deductible only in the year of payment. However, if a reimbursement is received from the employer, an election may be made to deduct the moving expenses in the year subsequent to the move under the following circumstances: [39]

1. The moving expenses are incurred and paid in 19X1 and the reimbursement is received in 19X2.

2. The moving expenses are incurred in 19X1 and are paid in 19X2 (on or before the due date including extensions for filing the 19X1 return) and the reimbursement is received in 19X1.

The election to deduct moving expenses in the year the reimbursement is received is made by claiming the deduction on the return, amended return or claim for refund for the taxable year the reimbursement is received.[40]

The moving expense deduction is allowed regardless of whether the employee is transferred by the existing employer, employed by a new employer, moves to a new area and obtains employment then, or if one switches from self-employed status to employee status or vice versa.

CLASSIFICATION OF MOVING EXPENSES

There are five classes of moving expenses and each has different limitations and qualifications. So called "direct" moving expenses include:

---

38. Reg. § 1.217–2(d)(1).   **40.** *Ibid.*

39. Reg. § 1.217–2(a)(2).

1. Expense of moving household and personal belongings.[41] This class includes fees paid to a moving company for packing, storing and moving possessions and the rental of a truck if the taxpayer "moves himself". There is no limit upon these "direct" expenses except reasonableness. Included is the cost of moving household pets. However, certain items are not deductible as moving expenses including expenses of refitting rugs or draperies, disconnecting utilities, losses on the disposal of club memberships, etc.[42]

2. Traveling to the new residence. This includes the cost of transportation and of meals and lodging en route of the taxpayer and the members of the taxpayer's household, but does not include the cost of moving servants or others who are not members of the household.[43] The taxpayer can elect to take actual auto expenses (no depreciation is allowed) or mileage. Moving expense mileage is limited to 7 cents per mile.[44] These expenses are also unlimited except for reasonableness (i. e., if one moves from Texas to Florida via Maine and takes six weeks to do so, the transportation, meals and lodging must be allocated between personal and moving expenses).

Indirect moving expenses include the following:

1. House-hunting trips.[45] Expenses of traveling (including meals and lodging) to the new place of employment to look for a place to live are deductible only if the job has been secured in advance of the house-hunting trip. The dollar limitation is explained below.

2. Temporary living expenses.[46] Meals and lodging expenses incurred while living in temporary quarters in the general area of the new job while waiting to move into a new residence are deductible within limits (see below). However, these living expenses are limited to a 30 day consecutive period commencing after employment is secured.

3. Certain residential buying and selling expenses.[47] These expenses are those that would normally offset against the selling price on the sale of a home and those expenses incurred in buying a new home. Examples are commissions, escrow fees, legal expenses, "points" paid to secure a mortgage, transfer taxes and advertising. "Fixing-up" expenses are not deductible. Also deductible are costs involved in settling

---

41. § 217(b)(1)(A).

42. Reg. § 1.217–1(b)(3).

43. Reg. § 1.217–1(b)(4); § 217(b)(1) (B).

44. Rev.Proc. 74–25, 1974–2 C.B. 477.

45. § 217(b)(1)(C); Reg. § 1.217–2(b)(5).

46. § 217(b)(1)(D); Reg. § 1.217–2(b)(6).

47. § 217(b)(1)(E); Reg. § 1.217–2(b)(7).

an old lease and/or acquiring a new lease. Damage deposits, prepaid rent, and the like are not deductible.

Any buying and selling expenses taken as a moving expense deduction cannot be added to the basis of the new home or subtracted from the amount realized on the sale of an old home. This restriction is to avoid the double benefit of taking the costs both places. Generally, since the taxpayer can defer the gain on the sale of a personal residence, the election to take the maximum amount as a moving expense deduction will be preferable. The dollar limits are discussed below.

The indirect moving expenses are limited to a total of $3,000. Furthermore, house-hunting and temporary living expenses may not in the aggregate exceed $1,500.[48] Again, direct moving expenses are unlimited. Generally, these dollar limitations apply equally, regardless of filing status. However, if both spouses change jobs and file separately, the limitations are $1,500 and $750 unless only one spouse makes a job change (the spouse who did not make a job change gets -0- and the other one gets the full amount) or if both change jobs, do not live together and work at job sites at least 35 miles apart.[49] In the latter case, whether they file jointly or separately, each spouse gets $3,000 and $1,500 as limits.

Example 18. T, an employee of X Corporation, is hired by Y Corporation for a better position with a substantial increase in salary. T is hired in February 19X1 and is to report for work in March 19X1. The new job requires a move from Los Angeles to New York City.

Pursuant to the move, T incurs the following expenses:

February 19X1 house-hunting trip for T	$ 600
Temporary living expenses in New York City incurred for T and family from March 10–30, 19X1 while awaiting the renovation of new apartment	$1,000
Penalty for breaking lease on Los Angeles apartment	$2,400
Charge for packing and moving household goods	$4,200
Travel expense during move (March 5–10)	$ 600

---

48. § 217(b)(3); for years prior to 1977, the ceiling limitations were $2,500 and $1,000.

49. Reg. § 1.217–2(b)(9)(v).

Assuming no reimbursement of any of these expenses by T's new employer, she can deduct the following amount:

Moving household goods		$4,200
Travel expense		600
House-hunting trip	$ 600	
Temporary living expense	1,000	
	$1,600	
Limited to		$1,500
Lease penalty		2,400
		$3,900
Limited to		3,000
Allowed		$7,800

A statement should be attached to the tax return showing the detailed calculations of the ceiling limitations, reimbursements, change in job locations, etc. Form 3903 may be used for this purpose. For years prior to 1977, the ceiling limitations were $1,000 and $2,500.

EDUCATION EXPENSES

GENERAL REQUIREMENTS

An employee may deduct expenses incurred for education as ordinary and necessary business expenses providing such items were incurred either (1) to maintain or improve existing skills required in the present job or (2) to meet the express requirements of the employer or the requirements imposed by law which are required to retain his employment status.

Exceptions. The expenses are *not* deductible under any condition if the education either (1) is required to meet the minimum educational standards for qualification in the taxpayer's existing job or (2) qualifies the taxpayer for a new trade or business.[50] Thus, fees incurred for professional qualification exams (the bar exam, for example) and fees for review courses (such as a CPA review course) are not deductible.[51] If the education incidentally results in a promotion or raise, the deduction can still be taken so long as the education maintained and improved existing skills and did not qualify a person for a new trade or business. In addition, a change in duties is not always fatal to the deduction if the new duties involve the same gener-

---

50. Reg. § 1.162–5(b)(2) and (3).

51. Reg. § 1.212–1(f); Rev.Rul. 69–292, 1969–1 C.B. 84.

al work.[52] For example, the IRS has ruled that a practicing dentist's educational expenses incurred to become an orthodontist are deductible.[53]

REQUIREMENTS IMPOSED BY LAW OR BY THE EMPLOYER FOR RETENTION OF EMPLOYMENT

Teachers most often qualify under the provision that the educational expenses are deductible if they are required by the employer or that the requirements are imposed by law. Many states require a minimum of a bachelor's degree and a specified number of courses in following years to keep an existing teaching job. Also, some public school systems have imposed a master's degree requirement and have required teachers to make satisfactory progress toward a master's degree in order to keep their existing position. On the other hand, a teacher with a master's degree who is teaching at a college where the minimum degree for a permanent post is a doctorate is not permitted to deduct the expenses of obtaining a Ph.D. because the teacher is obtaining the minimum education required for that position.[54]

MAINTAINING OR IMPROVING EXISTING SKILLS

The "maintaining or improving existing skills" requirement in the Code has been difficult to interpret by taxpayers and the courts. For example, a business executive may be permitted to deduct the costs of obtaining an M.B.A. degree on the grounds that the advanced management education is undertaken to maintain and improve existing management skills. However, if the business executive incurred the expenses to obtain a law degree, the expenses would not be deductible because they resulted in training for a new trade or business. For example, the Regulations deny a deduction for a self-employed accountant for expenses relative to night law school.[55] In addition, several courts have disallowed deductions to IRS agents for the cost of obtaining a law degree since the degree was not required as a condition of retained employment on the grounds that the education qualified the agent for a new profession.[56] Clearly, the executive would be eligible to deduct the costs of specialized non degree management courses which were taken for continuing education and/or to maintain or improve existing skills.

52. Reg. § 1.162–5(b)(3).

53. Rev.Rul. 74–78, 1974–1 C.B. 44.

54. Reg. § 1.162–5(b)(2)(iii) Example (2); *Kenneth C. Davis*, 65 T.C. 1014 (1976).

55. Reg. § 1.162–5(b)(3)(d)(ii) Example (1).

56. *J. L. Weiler*, 54 T.C. 398 (1970).

CLASSIFICATION OF SPECIFIC ITEMS

Education expenses include books, tuition, typing, and transportation (i. e., from the office to night school) and travel (meals and lodging while away from home at summer school, for example). Transportation and travel are deductible *for* adjusted gross income (whether or not reimbursed) and all other educational expenses are deductions *from* adjusted gross income (unless such expenses are reimbursed by the employer or incurred by a self-employed individual or an "outside salesman").

> **Example 19.** T holds a Bachelor of Education degree. T is a teacher of secondary education in the school system at Corpus Christi, Texas. Last year the school board changed its minimum education requirement for new teachers by prescribing five years of college training instead of four. Under a grandfather clause, teachers who have only four years of college (such as T) would continue to qualify if they show satisfactory progress toward a graduate degree. Pursuant to this new requirement, T enrolls at the University of Houston and takes three graduate courses. T's unreimbursed expenses for this purpose are as follows:

Books and tuition	$ 250
Meals and lodging while in travel status (June–August)	1,150
Laundry while in travel status	220
Transportation	600

> T can deduct the meals and lodging, laundry and transportation as a deduction *for* adjusted gross income as a travel expense. The books and tuition are deductible *from* adjusted gross income if T itemizes his deductions.

ENTERTAINMENT EXPENSES

In 1962 Congress enacted § 274 of the Code to place restrictions upon the deductibility of entertainment expenses due to alleged abuses by business executives and other employees. The law now contains strict recordkeeping requirements and provides restrictive tests for the deduction of certain types of entertainment expenses.

CLASSIFICATION OF EXPENSES

Entertainment expenses may be categorized as follows: those *directly related* to business and those *associated with* business.[57] "Directly related" generally means that an actual business meeting or discussion was conducted as contrasted with the goodwill type (associated with) entertainment.[58] To obtain a deduction for directly related

---

57. § 274(a)(1)(A).   **58.** Reg. § 1.274–2(c).

entertainment, it is not necessary to show that actual benefit resulted from the expenditure as long as there was a "reasonable" expectation of benefit. To qualify as "directly related" the expense should be incurred in a "clear business setting", e. g. if there was little possibility of engaging in the active conduct of a trade or business due to the nature of the social facility, it may be difficult to qualify the expenditure as "directly related".[59]

"Associated with" means that there must be a business purpose for incurring the expense such as obtaining new business or continuing existing business.[60] These expenditures qualify only if the expenses are incurred immediately before or after a bona fide business discussion.[61]

RESTRICTIONS UPON DEDUCTIBILITY

Business Meals. § 274(e) provides for several exceptions to qualify entertainment expenses which would otherwise not be deductible. The most frequently encountered exception applies to the cost of meals or beverages served in surroundings which are conducive to a business discussion (so called "quiet business" rule).[62] Under this rule there is no requirement that business actually be discussed providing that the taxpayer can show a business relationship for the entertainment and a reasonable expectation of business benefit as opposed to social or personal purpose. This so called "quiet business" rule also extends to the furnishing of meals or beverages at business programs, conventions, etc.; e. g. a dental equipment supplier may purchase meals or buy drinks for dentists at a convention.[63]

Entertainment Facilities. To obtain a deduction for the cost of an entertainment facility (e. g. a yacht or country club membership fees and dues), an "all or nothing" test is imposed. Unless it can be shown that over 50 percent of the facility use was for business purposes, no deduction is permitted for the cost of the facility; e. g. depreciation and operating costs for the yacht or membership dues to the country club.[64] In the computation of the more than 50 percent qualification, the amount of time spent "directly related" and "associated with" business is included in this determination. For this purpose, quiet business meals qualify as "directly related" entertainment.[65] The determination of whether a facility is used primarily for business (50 percent test) is made on a daily use basis.[66]

59. Reg. § 1.274–2(c)(4) & (7).

60. Reg. § 1.274–2(d)(2).

61. Reg. § 1.274–2(d)(3).

62. Reg. § 1.274–2(f)(2)(i).

63. Reg. § 1.274–2(f)(2)(d)(i)(d).

64. Reg. § 1.274–2(e)(4)(iii).

65. Rev.Rul. 63–144, 1963–2 C.B. 129.

66. Supra, *note* 64.

If the club is used for both business and personal use in one day, the day is counted as a "business day".

Once the determination is made that the facility is used primarily for business, the deduction for the cost of the facility is calculated by including only the time the facility was used for "directly related" business entertainment including "quiet business" meals.

Example 20. T is the sales manager of an insurance agency and, as such is expected to incur entertainment expenditures in connection with the sale of insurance to existing and potential clients. None of these expenses are reimbursed by his employer. During the year he paid the following amounts for joining and using the St. Louis Country Club:

Membership fee (refundable upon termination of membership)	$2,000
Annual dues	1,200
Meals and other charges related to business use (including "associated with.")	900
Meals and other charges related to personal use	400

The club was used 30 days for purposes "directly related" to business; 70 days for entertainment "associated with" business; 20 days for quiet business meals; 80 days for personal use; and not used at all during the rest of the year.

Since the facility was used for business more than 50% of the time (120 days out of 200), a portion of the annual dues can be deducted. That part is 50/200 or 25% × $1,200 or $300. None of the membership fee is deductible since it is refundable and all of the business charges (including the "associated with" expenses) are deductible.

Therefore, the taxpayer can deduct $1,200 if he itemizes his deductions ($300 of the dues and $900 "directly related" and "associated with" meals).

Recordkeeping Requirements. Prior to 1962 the courts frequently permitted a deduction for entertainment expenses under the so called Cohan rule whereby a portion of the taxpayer's expenses were permitted where the exact amount could not be determined due to incomplete records.[67]

§ 274(d) now provides that no deduction is permitted unless adequate substantiation is maintained including:

1. The amount of the expense;

2. The time and place of the expense;

67. *Cohan v. Comm.,* 2 USTC ¶ 489, 8 AFTR 10552, 39 F.2d 540 (CA–2, 1930); In Rev.Rul. 75–169, 1975–1 C. B. 59, the IRS held that due to the passage of 274(d) no deduction will be allowed on the basis of the Cohan rule or unsupported testimony.

3.   The business purpose and

4.   The business relationship.

If an employee furnishes an adequate accounting to his employer, it is not necessary to report the expenses and employer reimbursements on the tax return if the reimbursement is equal to the expenses. The employee is only required to state on the return that the reimbursements did not exceed the allowable expenses.[68] In all other cases, it is necessary to submit a statement with the return, i. e., where the reimbursements exceed the allowable expenses the excess must be included in income or where the expenses exceed the reimbursement and the taxpayer deducts such excess amounts on the return.[69] In all cases involving a shareholder-employee relationship, e. g. where the employee owns more than 10% of the employer corporation's stock, the employee's expenses must be submitted with the tax return.[70]

Business Gifts. Business gifts are deductible only to the extent that each gift does not exceed $25 per person per year, directly or indirectly.[71] An exception is made for gifts costing $4 or less (i. e., pens with the employee's or company's name on them) or promotional materials. Such items are *not* treated as business gifts (subject to the $25 limitation). In addition, incidental costs such as customary engraving on jewelry, nominal giftwrapping or charges for mailing and delivery are not included in the cost of the gift for purposes of applying the $25 per gift limitation.[72] A gift is made "indirectly" if made to a person's spouse or other family member or to a corporation or partnership on behalf of the individual. All such gifts must be added together in applying the $25 limit. Excluded from the $25 limit are gifts or awards to employees for length of service, etc., that are under $100.[73]

It is necessary to maintain records substantiating the gifts. These substantiation requirements are similar to the rules for deducting entertainment expenses.

If the taxpayer is an "outside salesman" or if the expenses are reimbursed by an employer, employee gifts are deductible *for* adjusted gross income; otherwise, the deduction is *from* adjusted gross income and can be taken only if the taxpayer itemizes his deductions.

---

68. Reg. §§ 1.162–17(b)(1) and 1.274–5(e)(2).

69. Reg. § 1.274–5(e)(2)(iii); Rev.Rul. 73–191, 1973–1 C.B. 151.

70. Reg. § 1.274–5(e)(5)(ii).

71. § 274(b)(1).

72. Reg. § 1.274–3(c).

73. § 274(b)(1)(C).

Example 21. T, an outside salesman, makes the following gifts during the year (none of which are reimbursed):

Dr. Lykes (a client)	$20
Mr. Lykes (a non-client and husband of Dr. Lykes)	10
Mr. Pierre (a client)	30
Mr. Allen (T's supervisor)	15
Miss Lowndes (T's secretary)	26 (includes a $1 charge for gift-wrapping)

The gifts to Dr. and Mr. Lykes must be combined and are limited to $25. The gift to Mr. Pierre is likewise limited to $25. The $15 to Mr. Allen is not deductible since a gift by an employee to his supervisor does not qualify as a "business" gift. Such gifts are personal nondeductible expenditures. The $26 to Miss Lowndes is not limited to $25 due to the nominal gift-wrapping charge. T must maintain adequate records to substantiate the business relationships and amounts of gifts. Since T is an "outside salesman" all these gifts are deductible *for* adjusted gross income.

OTHER EMPLOYEE EXPENSES

OFFICE IN THE HOME

The Tax Reform Act of 1976 placed substantial restrictions upon the deductibility of employment and business related expenses attributable to the use of a residence (e. g. den or office) for business purposes. No deduction is now permitted unless a portion of the residence is *exclusively used on a regular basis* (1) as the taxpayer's principal place of business or (2) as a place of business which is used by patients, clients, or customers.[74] Employees must meet an additional test; the use must be for the convenience of the employer as opposed to being merely "appropriate and helpful".[75] Prior to this change in the law, some courts had permitted a deduction for "office in home" expenses despite the fact that the office was not required if it was merely "appropriate and helpful" to the performance of the employee's duties.[76]

The *exclusive* use requirement means that a specific part of the home must now be used *solely* for business purposes. Formerly, it was acceptable to allocate a portion of the total expenditures between business (office in home) and personal use based upon hours of

74. § 280A(c)(1).

75. *Ibid.*

76. *Stephin A. Bodzin v. Comm.,* 60 T.C. 820, *rev'd* 75-1 USTC ¶ 9190, 35 AFTR2d 75-618, 509 F.2d 69 (CA-4, 1975).

usage.[77] Since the "office in home" must now be used exclusively for business, a deduction, if permitted, will require an allocation of total expenses of operating the home between business and personal use based upon floor space or number of rooms.

Even if the taxpayer meets the above requirements, the allowable business expenses may not exceed the gross income from the business activity reduced by an allocable portion of expense deductions which would otherwise qualify as personal type itemized deductions, e. g. mortgage interest and real estate taxes.[78]

Example 22. Sam Smith is a self-employed CPA who maintains an office in his home which is devoted exclusively to client work. Clients regularly visit his "office in home". The gross income from his practice was $2,000 during 19X1. The portion of mortgage interest and real estate taxes allocated to business use amounted to $1,500; an *allocable* portion of maintenance expenses, utilities, maid service and depreciation on the house was $1,000.

Gross income from self-employment	$2,000	
Less: Allocable portion of itemized deduction items – interest and taxes	(1,500)	– deductible as itemized deductions.

His other business expenses of $1,000 are, therefore, limited to $500 which is the excess of gross income of $2,000 over the allocable portion of Smith's itemized deductions of $1,500.

Example 23. Jean Jones is an accountant for the XYZ Corporation who maintains an office in her home. She uses the office primarily for reading professional journals. Her family also uses the office for personal reasons. She occasionally brings work home from her company and uses the office at home on weekends and during the evenings. Her outside consulting activities are limited to the preparation of a few tax returns from which she received $1,000 gross income during 19X1.

Mortgage interest and real estate taxes allocable to the office amounted to $1,500 and an allocable portion of other household expenses including utilities, depreciation, etc., was $1,000.

The $1,500 mortgage interest and real estate taxes are deductible *from* AGI as itemized deductions. None of the other expenses are deductible since the office in home is not used exclusively

---

77. *George W. Gino,* 60 T.C. 304 (1973); Rev.Rul. 62–180, 1962–2 C.B. 52.

78. § 280A(c)(4).

and on a regular basis by Jones as her principal place of business. In addition, an employee must show that the use is for the convenience of her employer. It appears that the office is merely "helpful and appropriate" in the performance of her duties as an employee which is not sufficient to permit a deduction.

MISCELLANEOUS EMPLOYEE EXPENSES

Other employee expenses which are deductible include special clothing and its upkeep; [79] union dues; [80] professional expenses such as dues and attendance of professional meetings; [81] and employment agency fees for seeking employment in the same trade or business after 4–21–75 (whether or not a new job is secured). [82] These deductions are *for* adjusted gross income only if the employee is an "outside salesman," if the expenses are travel or transportation, or if they are reimbursed. In all other cases, they are deductions *from* adjusted gross income.

Other employee expenses which are *not* deductible include regular clothes, commuting expenses and any other expenditures of a personal nature.

TAX PLANNING CONSIDERATIONS

EDUCATION EXPENSES

Education expenses are treated as nondeductible personal items if an individual is *not* employed (unless such individual is engaged in a trade or business activity, e. g. a self-employed CPA. Thus an individual who terminates his employment status for the purpose of obtaining further education, is not permitted to deduct the education expenses. Therefore, if the requirements for deducting education expenses are otherwise met, such persons should be advised to seek an approved temporary leave of absence so as to preserve their employment status.

MOVING EXPENSES

Commissions on the sale of a personal residence may either be treated as indirect moving expenses subject to the overall ceiling limitations or they may be deducted from the selling price of the resi-

79. Rev.Rul. 70–474, 1970–2 C.B. 34.

80. Rev.Rul. 72–463, 1972–2 C.B. 93.

81. Reg. § 1.162–6.

82. Rev.Rul. 75–120, 1975–1 C.B. 55. However, such expenses are not deductible according to the IRS if an individual is seeking employment in a new trade or business.

dence in arriving at the amount realized. It is generally preferable to deduct the commissions as moving expenses since a deduction from the selling price of the house merely reduces the capital gain on the sale (or increases a nondeductible loss). In addition, such capital gains may be postponed if a new residence is acquired within the prescribed time period and certain other requirements of the Code are met. Postponement of gain rules for the sale of a personal residence are discussed in Chapter 13. Consideration should be given to the fact that sale related expenses which are not used as moving expenses (due to the ceiling limitations) may be deducted from the selling price of the residence.

Since reimbursements of moving expenses are required to be included in gross income and certain moving expenses may not be deductible due to the ceiling limitations, an employee may be required to pay additional income tax due to the move. Therefore, some employers reimburse their employees for these additional taxes. The additional taxes are estimated and included in the employee's reimbursement.

ENTERTAINMENT

Proper documentation of expenditures is essential due to the strict recordkeeping requirements and the restrictive tests which must be met. For example, credit card receipts as the sole source of documentation may be inadequate to substantiate the business purpose and business relationship. Taxpayers should be advised to maintain detailed records of amounts, time, place, business purpose and business relationships.

"Associated with" or goodwill type entertainment is not deductible unless a business discussion is conducted immediately before or after the entertainment and there is a business purpose for such entertainment. Taxpayers should be advised to arrange for a business discussion before or after such entertainment and to provide documentation of the business purpose (e. g. to obtain new business from a prospective customer).

Since an "all or nothing" 50 percent test is imposed for the deductibility of entertainment facilities, e. g. country club dues, it may be necessary to accelerate business use or cut down on personal use of a club facility. The 50 percent test is made on a daily use basis. Therefore, detailed records should be maintained to substantiate business versus personal use.

PROBLEM MATERIALS

Questions for Class Discussion

1. What criteria are used to determine whether an employee-employer relationship exists?

2. What difference does it make if an individual's expenses are classified as employment related versus expenses from self-employment?

3. One employee commutes one block to work whereas another employee travels 60 miles to his place of employment. Does the distance traveled have any effect upon the deductibility of these transportation expenses?

4. Distinguish between the terms *transportation* expense and *travel* expense.

5. Is an employee permitted to deduct commuting expenses where an automobile is required to transport heavy tools to work? Under what conditions have the courts permitted a deduction?

6. What alternative methods may be used to calculate automobile expenses?

7. If an employee receives a reimbursement of 15 cents per mile for job related automobile expenses, can he deduct any excess expense amounts on his tax return?

8. Where the automatic mileage method is used for deducting automobile expenses, what restrictions exist where the automobile was previously depreciated under the actual cost method?

9. Employee Jones incurred travel expenses while away from home on company business. These expenses were not reimbursed by his employer. Can Jones deduct the travel expenses? If so, *for* adjusted gross or *from* adjusted gross income (itemized deductions)?

10. What requirements must be met for an employee to deduct "office in home" expenses?

11. If an employee takes a combined business-pleasure trip, what portion of the expenses are deductible?

12. Why did Congress provide special treatment for "outside salesmen"?

13. If an employee performs service or delivery functions, e. g., television repairman or milkman, does the "outside salesman" classification apply?

14. Why did Congress change the tax law regarding moving expenses in 1964 and 1976?

15. Are moving expenses deductible *for* or *from* adjusted gross income?

16. Distinguish between those items which are treated as direct moving expenses with indirect moving expenses. Why is it important to classify such items properly?

17. What is the reason for imposing time and distance requirements in the determination of whether moving expenses are deductible?

18. Why is a taxpayer permitted a deduction for AGI for reimbursed expenses which would be treated as itemized deductions if no reimbursement was received?

19. What tax return reporting procedures must be followed by an employee under the following circumstances:

    a. Expenses and reimbursements are equal and an adequate accounting is made to the employer.

    b. Reimbursements exceed expenses and an adequate accounting is made to the employer.

    c. Expenses exceed reimbursements and no accounting is made to the employer.

20. Why is it sometimes necessary to make an allocation of expenses where reimbursements cover all employee expenses?

21. What difference does it make if a taxpayer is improving existing skills or acquiring new ones for the purpose of the educational deduction and under what general tax principle does the justification for this lie?

22. Why are educational travel and transportation expenses deductions for AGI and all other unreimbursed expenses deductions *from* AGI?

23. Discuss whether each of the following employees could deduct education expenses. Why or why not?

    1. A, a CPA who attended night school in order to take computer courses so she could be a better auditor.

    2. B, a CPA who is a tax specialist attended night law school so he could gain greater expertise in the tax area.

    3. C, a computer programmer who attended night school in order to become a computer analyst for her present employer.

    4. D, an elementary school teacher who took courses in Art Appreciation during the summer because he had never had any art training and art is taught in his school. It was not a requirement of the employer.

    5. E, a marketing manager who took a Dale Carnegie course.

    6. F, a homemaker who took a Dale Carnegie course.

    7. G, a retiring Army officer, who went back to school to pick up a few business courses in order to prepare for some civilian job.

8.   What if G (above) took the courses after he had obtained a civilian business position?

24.   Discuss the difference between "directly related" and "associated with" entertainment.

25.   What requirements must be met in order to deduct the cost (or a portion of the cost) of an entertainment facility? Why were these restrictive tests imposed?

26.   To what extent may a taxpayer make business gifts to a business associate?; to an employee?; to a superior?

27.   Why is it necessary to maintain detailed records for entertainment expenses?

28.   Why does the law now place restrictions upon deductions for attendance at foreign business or professional conventions? What criteria must be met to qualify for deductibility?

Problems

1.   A taxpayer has two jobs. He drives 20 miles to his first job. From the first job to the second is 16 miles. During the year he worked 200 days at both jobs. On 150 days, he drove from job #1 to job #2; on the remaining 50 days, he drove home (20 miles) and then to the second job (24 miles). How much can he deduct?

2.   The taxpayer's job requires her to carry tools and equipment to work every day. If she did not have to take these tools to work, she would commute by bus at a cost of $1 per day. It costs her $2.50 per day to drive. How much can she deduct?

3.   A taxpayer has asked you to determine whether he should use the automatic mileage method or the actual operating cost method in computing his deduction for transportation. He is an outside salesman and uses two cars: one, a Volvo, is used 40% for business and the other, a Lincoln, is used 80% for business. What would your answer be and what factors would you take into consideration?

4.   A taxpayer incurred the following expenses on a business trip: (It was 100% business plus she was away from home overnight).

Airfare	$982
Taxi	20
Meals	60
Room	105
Entertainment	37
Laundry	15

None of the expenses are reimbursed by her employer. How much can she deduct and is it *for* or *from* AGI.

5. In (4) above assume she had taken her husband along. His airfare was $491 of the total; they shared the taxi to the hotel (which would have cost $15 for 1 person); half the meals were eaten by him; and they shared a double room (a single room would have cost $90). All of the laundry was hers as was the entertainment. What can she deduct on her return and where (*for* or *from* AGI)?

6. The taxpayer took a trip to Hawaii (from Kansas City) primarily for business. He spent 5 days conducting business and 3 days vacationing. His airline ticket cost $884 and meals and lodging amounted to $93 per day. How much can he deduct on his income tax return? Is it a deduction *for* or *from* AGI?

7. The taxpayer was permanently transferred from Houston to New York City. He incurred the following expenses:

House-hunting trip	$ 900
Temporary living expenses for 20 days	800
Travel expense during move	900
Moving company's charges	3,800
Broker's fee on old home sale	3,000
	$9,400

How much can the taxpayer deduct assuming there are no reimbursements?

8. In (7) above, assume the taxpayer was reimbursed $9,400 by his employer. How is this handled on the tax return?

9. A taxpayer had the following job related expenses during the year: (She made an adequate accounting to her employer.)

Auto expense	$ 500
Airline fares	1,300
Meals, lodging and incidentals while	
away from home	1,200
Dues and subscriptions	500
Telephone and Entertainment	1,000

(a) Compute her deductions *for* and *from* AGI, assuming she received a $3,000 reimbursement from her employer which was intended to cover a pro-rata share of all expenses.

(b) If she had received $4,800 from her employer, how would it be handled on her return?

10. The taxpayer belongs to a private club which he uses for both business and personal purposes. Assuming none of his expenses are reimbursed, how much can he deduct on his tax return?

Annual Dues	$3,000
Business Meals "Directly related"	380
Business Meals "Associated with"	260
Business Meals "quiet business meals"	300
Personal meals and charges	1,000

(a) Days directly related to business	75
Days associated with business	20
Days quiet business meals	25
Days for personal use	130
(b) Days directly related to business	50
Days associated with business	50
Days for quiet business meals	50
Days for personal use	100

11. A college professor accepted a position with the GAO in Washington, D.C. The assignment was designated as temporary and was for a fifteen-month period. The professor left his wife and children in Cleveland and rented an apartment in Washington during the period of employment. He incurred the following expenses none of which were reimbursed by his employer:

1. Air fare—weekend trips to and from Washington and Cleveland to visit his family—$6,000

2. Rent—Washington apartment—$3,000

3. Meals, laundry, etc., in Washington—$2,000

4. Entertainment of fellow employees and his boss in the GAO—$1,000

Which, if any, of these expenses are deductible by the college professor? *For* adjusted gross or *from* adjusted gross income?

12. John Jones is a salesman for the XYZ Company. He solicits orders from commercial businesses within the general vicinity of the company offices which is also his tax home. When business is slow, he promotes the company's residential line by making house-to-house calls within the general area. The company provides a desk for Mr. Jones which he occasionally uses to write up an order. On Friday of each week he goes to the Company office to pick up his mail.

Mr. Jones incurred the following expenses during 19X1 none of which are reimbursed:

1. Automobile, e. g., depreciation, gas, oil, etc.—$3,000

2. Luncheons for clients—$2,500

Jones maintains that he "never" eats lunch unless he entertains a client.

a. Is Mr. Jones classified as an "outside salesman"?

b. Is Jones entitled to a tax deduction for these expenses? If so, *for* adjusted gross or *from* adjusted gross income?

13. John Smith is a tax specialist for a large CPA firm. During the year he enrolled in the following course of study for his program of continuing education and incurred the following expenses:

1. Law school courses in taxation—enrolled as a non-degree special student (tuition)—$1,500 plus transportation expenses of $150.

2. Special courses offered by the Texas Society of CPA's for continuing education (tuition)—$1,000, plus transportation expenses of $200.

3. CPA review exam and CPA License fee—$800 plus transportation expenses of $100.

a. Which, if any, of these expenses are deductible by Mr. Smith? *For* adjusted gross or *from* adjusted gross income?

b. What would your answer be if Mr. Jones took course work on a Ph.D. in accounting with the eventual expectation of becoming a college professor?

14. Joe Phillips is an engineer and full-time employee of the XYZ Company. He also is a self-employed consulting engineer for several other companies and earned approximately $12,000 from the outside consulting practice. Joe maintained an "office in home" in which he spent approximately two hours per night during the week days and eight hours per day on weekends working on his outside consulting practice. The office is not used exclusively for business and is not maintained for the convenience of his consulting clients. The XYZ Company does not require Joe to maintain an office in his home. However, the office in his home is "helpful" and appropriate to his employment with XYZ since he frequently brings work home from the company. Approximately 10% of the total time spent in his "office in home" is devoted to company business. Joe estimates based upon a floor space allocation basis that his total "office in home" expenses amounted to $4,000 (which includes a pro-rata allocation of real estate taxes and mortgage interest of $1,000) in 19X1.

a. Is Phillips entitled to a deduction for his "office in home" relative to the time spent on his consulting activities? If so, how would this expense be reported on his tax return?

b. Is Phillips entitled to a deduction for his "office in home" relative to the portion of time devoted to company business? If so, *for* adjusted gross or *from* adjusted gross income?

c. Is Phillips entitled to deduct the $1,000 of real estate tax and interest as itemized deductions or as business expenses?

15. In January 1977, X was transferred by his company from Cleveland, Ohio to Houston, Texas. He incurred the following expenses in connection with the transfer all of which were reimbursed by his employer:

1. House-hunting trips with his wife in February and March, 1977—Traveling expenses of $1,500.

2. X rented an apartment in Houston for the month of May, 1977 until the new home was ready for occupancy. Rental expenses were $1,400. He also incurred meals at restaurants in Houston during this period amounting to $900.

3. X paid the following expenses relative to the sale of his former home in Cleveland; real estate commissions $3,000, fixing-up expenses $2,000.

4. The trip from Cleveland to Houston was 1300 miles. Mr. and Mrs. X drove both family automobiles to their new location. Meals and lodging enroute amounted to $400. In addition, Mr. X transported his great dane by airplane since the dog was not amenable to automobile travel. The travel cost for the dog was $300.

5. The cost of the moving van was $3,000.

    a. Calculate the amount of direct moving expense.

    b. Calculate the amount of indirect moving expenses.

    c. If the reimbursements from the employer exceed the amount of allowable expense, how is this excess reported on X's income tax return?

Research Problems

1. The taxpayer is a mechanic employed by a bridge building company. His job is to repair the bridges when breakdowns occur. He does most of his work in the Portland, Oregon area.

    One day he is told he will have to go to Seattle, Washington, to repair a bridge. He drove the distance to Seattle (200 miles) because he needed to use some special tools that were quite heavy. His wife can't bear to be without him so he didn't spend the night in Seattle but left early and came home late. While in Seattle, he ate three meals at a total cost of $50. On the way home, he became tired and took a twenty minute nap at a rest stop.

    You are his friend and he is asking you what is the maximum amount that can be deducted for this trip.

2. The Ultra Modern National Bank devoted considerable effort to maintaining the goodwill of the key people, e. g., lawyers,

customers, politicians, etc., in the local community. One of their efforts was to invite such individuals to the bank president's home for gala celebrations (cocktail parties, dinners, etc.). During such occasions the bank officials were instructed to mingle with the invited guests and to engage in business discussions when warranted by the occasion. The officers maintained detailed records of the business conversations with the guests and the Bank feels that it is entitled to deduct the full cost of the entertainment expenses as "associated with" entertainment.

Are these expenses deductible under § 274?

Chapter 9

DEDUCTIONS AND LOSSES, CERTAIN ITEMIZED DEDUCTIONS

GENERAL CLASSIFICATION OF EXPENSES

Under § 262, personal expenditures are specifically disallowed as deductions in arriving at taxable income. Personal expenses may be contrasted with business expenses which are incurred in the production or expectation of profit. Business expenditures are adjustments to gross income in arriving at adjusted gross income and are placed on Schedule C of Form 1040. Certain non-business expenses are also deductible in arriving at adjusted gross income, e. g. (1) expenses attributable to rents and royalties and (2) forfeited interest on a time-savings deposit.

This chapter is principally concerned with expenses which are essentially personal in nature but which are deductible due to specific legislative sanction, e. g. contributions, medical expenses and state and local taxes. If the Code does not specifically state that a personal type expense is deductible, no deduction is permitted. Allowable personal type expenses are deductible *from* AGI in arriving at taxable income if a taxpayer does not use the standard deduction in lieu of itemizing his deductions. At this point, it may be helpful to review

234

the computation of the tax formula for individuals which appears in Table 1 of Chapter 4.

In certain instances, it is unclear whether an item is deductible under a specific section of the Code or if the item is personal and nondeductible. For example, the following expenditures have been held to be personal nondeductible expenses: the construction of a bomb shelter;[1] the cost of a chauffeur to drive a taxpayer to and from his place of business;[2] the expenses of an executive's vacation, although incurred for reconditioning and health restoration.[3]

MEDICAL EXPENDITURES

GENERAL REQUIREMENTS

§ 213 allows as a deduction those expenses incurred during the year for medical expenses for the care of the taxpayer, his spouse, and dependents not compensated for by insurance. However, medical expenses are deductible only to the extent that the total expenses exceed 3 percent of the taxpayer's adjusted gross income. The rationale for allowing a medical deduction solely for amounts in excess of such limits is based upon social welfare considerations. Since 3% of adjusted gross income is considered to be a normal yearly expenditure, only amounts in excess of 3% are permitted.

The term "medical care" includes expenditures incurred for the "diagnosis, cure, mitigation, treatment, or prevention of disease".[4] The term also includes expenditures incurred for "affecting any structure or function of the body".[5] A taxpayer cannot deduct medical expenses that have both therapeutic benefits and personal enjoyment, unless the expenditure is necessary and is the only method of treating the illness. Thus, the IRS has held that the cost of a swimming pool, even though installed upon advice of a physician was not a medical expense but rather a non-deductible home improvement.[6] However, a Federal District Court has held that the cost of a specially designed swimming pool was deductible since the pool was installed on the advice of a physician for hydrotherapeutic treatment of the taxpayer's wife who was suffering from an attack of paralytic poliomyelitis.[7]

1. *IRS News Release,* I.R.No.372, March 27, 1961.

2. *W. E. Buck,* 47 T.C. 113 (1966).

3. Rev.Rul. 57–130, 1957–1 C.B. 108.

4. Reg. § 1.213–1(e).

5. § 213(e)(1)(A).

6. Rev.Rul. 54–57, 1954–1 C.B. 67.

7. *Mason v. U. S.,* 57–2 USTC ¶ 10012, 52 AFTR 1593, Riach v. Frank, 302 F.2d 374 (D.Ct.Haw., 1957).

The deductibility of nursing home expenses depends upon the medical condition of the patient and the nature of the services received.[8] If an individual enters a home for the aged for personal or family considerations and not because he or she requires medical or nursing attention, medical deductions are allowed only for the costs which are attributable to the medical and nursing care, i. e., meals and lodging are not considered a cost of medical care.[9]

> **Example 1.** X is totally disabled and has a chronic heart ailment. His children have decided to place X in a nursing home which is equipped to provide medical and nursing care facilities. Total nursing home expenses amount to $10,000 per year. Of this amount, $3,000 are directly attributable to medical and nursing care. Since X is in need of significant medical and nursing care and is placed into the facility primarily for this purpose, all $10,000 of the nursing home costs are deductible. Only $3,000 of the expenses would be deductible if X were placed in the home primarily for personal or family considerations.

CAPITAL EXPENDITURES FOR MEDICAL PURPOSES

Normally, capital expenditures are adjustments to basis and are not deductible since the Code makes no provision for depreciation relative to capital improvements for medical expenses. However, a capital expenditure for a permanent improvement and expenditures made for its operation or maintenance may both qualify as medical expenses. For example, a capital improvement which otherwise qualifies as a medical expenditure, is deductible to the exent that the expenditure exceeds the increase in value of the related property.[10] It should also be noted that the appraisal costs would also be deductible under § 212 since such amounts are expenses incurred in the determination of the taxpayer's tax liability.

> **Example 2.** The taxpayer is advised by his physician to install an elevator in his residence so that the taxpayer's wife, who is affected with heart disease, will not be required to climb stairs. If the cost of installing the elevator is $1,000 and the increase in the value of the residence is determined to be only $700, $300 is deductible as a medical expense. Additional utility costs to operate the elevator should also be deductible as medical expenses.

TRANSPORTATION EXPENSES

Expenditures for a taxi, airplane, train, etc., to and from a point of treatment are deductible as medical expenses. However, the

8.   Reg. § 1.213–1(3)(1)(v).   10.   Reg. § 1.213–1(e)(1)(iii).

9.   Reg. § 1.213–1(3)(1)(v)(b).

amount allowable as a deduction for "transportation primarily for and essential to medical care" does not include meals and lodging while away from home receiving medical treatment.[11] Note, however, that some courts have allowed a medical deduction for the cost of meals and lodging incurred "in transit" to reach the place of medical treatment if it was necessary to travel to another location to receive treatment.[12]

Beginning after 1974, the IRS allows a standard mileage rate of seven cents a mile incurred in using an automobile in traveling for medical treatment.[13]

AMOUNTS PAID FOR MEDICAL PREMIUMS

One-half of the amount paid for medical care insurance for the taxpayer, spouse, or dependent is not subject to the 3 percent limitation for total medical expenses. Such amounts are fully deductible up to $150 per year. Premiums paid in excess of $150 (if any) are included with the other medical expenses and are subject to the overall 3 percent limitation rules.

If amounts are paid under an insurance contract to cover loss of life, limb, sight, etc., no amount can be deducted unless the coverage for medical care is separately stated in the contract.

Example 3. H and W filed a joint return for the calendar year 19X7. Their adjusted gross income was $10,000. H and W incurred and paid a total of $350 for health insurance premiums. Such premiums are specifically for medical care coverage. H and W incurred other medical expenses of $400 which were not compensated for by insurance. The allowable deduction under § 213 for medical expenses paid in 19X7 is $450, computed as follows: [14]

(1) Lesser of $175 ($350 insurance premiums × ½) or $150 .... $150

(2) Payments for medical care (including $350 of insurance premiums and $400 of other medical expenses) $750

(3) Less insurance premiums not subject to the 3 percent limitation .... (150)

(4) Medical expenses to be taken into account under 3 percent limitation $600

(5) Less 3 percent of $10,000 (adjusted gross income) .... (300)

(6) Excess allowable as a deduction for 19X7 (excess of line 4 over line 5) 300

(7) Allowable medical expense deduction for 19X7 (line 1 plus line 6) $450

11. Reg. § 1.213–1(e)(1)(iv).

12. *Montgomery v. Comm.*, 70–2 USTC ¶ 9466, 26 AFTR2d 70–5001, 428 F.2d 243 (CA–6, 1970); Reg. § 1.213–1(e)(1)(iv) denies a deduction if the location of the treatment center is purely for personal reasons.

13. Rev.Proc. 74–24, 1974–2 C.B. 477.

14. Reg. § 1.213–1(a)(5)(ii).

Example 4. Assume the same facts as in the previous example except that H and W incurred and paid only $200 for health insurance premiums and other medical expenses amount to $20.

(1) Deductible health insurance premiums not subject to
3 percent limitation—$200 × ½ $100

(2) Payments for medical care subject to 3 percent
limitation:

    Insurance premiums not deductible above $100

    Other medical expenses   20

                                        $120

(3) Less 3 percent of AGI ($10,000 × 3 percent)   (300)

(4) Deductions allowable under the 3 percent limits .... –0–

(5) Allowable medical expense deductions $100

EXPENDITURES FOR MEDICINE AND DRUGS

§ 213(b) permits a deduction for expenses incurred with respect to medicine and drugs to the extent such amounts are in excess of 1 percent of AGI. The term "medicine and drugs" only includes those drugs that are "legally procured" and are purchased either with or without a prescription. However, expenditures for personal items are not deductible, e. g. toothpaste, shaving lotion, shaving and face creams, deodorants and hand lotions.[15] Amounts paid for vitamins, iron supplements and similar items for the general health of the taxpayer are deductible if recommended by a doctor.[16] Also, the cost of birth control pills, if prescribed by a physician, is considered expended for "medical care" and is deductible as a medicine.[17]

If the total amount paid for medicine and drugs exceeds 1 percent of adjusted gross income, the excess is added to other medical expenses for the purpose of computing the medical expense deduction.

Example 5. The taxpayer, a single individual with no dependents, had adjusted gross income of $6,000 for the calendar year 19X7. During 19X7, he paid a doctor $300 for medical services, a hospial $100 for hospital care, and also spent $100 for medicine and drugs. These payments were not compensated for by insur-

15. Reg. § 1.213–1(e)(2).

16. *Your Federal Income Tax*, IRS
Publication, 1977 Edition, p. 76.

17. Rev.Rul. 73–200, 1973–1 C.B. 140.

ance. The deduction allowable under § 213 for the calendar year 19X7 is $260, computed as follows: [18]

Payments for medical care in 19X7:		
Doctor		$300
Hospital		100
Medicine and Drugs	$100	
Less 1 percent of $6,000 (AGI)	(60)	40
Total medical expenses taken into account		$440
Less 3 percent of $6,000 (AGI)		(180)
Allowable deduction for 19X7		$260

REIMBURSEMENT FOR MEDICAL EXPENSES PAID IN PRIOR YEARS

When a taxpayer receives an insurance reimbursement for medical expenses taken in a previous year, the reimbursement must be included in gross income in the year of receipt. Taxpayers are not permitted to include anticipated reimbursements in the computation of the medical expenses for the year such expenses are incurred. Reimbursements in the following year are included in gross income only to the extent that the expenses were deductible in the prior year.[19] If the taxpayer had used the standard deduction in the year of the deduction in lieu of itemizing, any reimbursement received in a subsequent year will not be included in gross income since the deduction did not reduce the taxpayer's taxable income for the prior year,[20] i. e., the taxpayer received no tax benefit from the deduction.

The following rules apply to reimbursements for medical expenses: [21]

1. If the amount of the reimbursement is equal to or less than the amount which was deducted in a prior year, the entire amount is includible in gross income; or

2. If the amount of the reimbursement is greater than the amount which is deducted, the portion of the reimbursement received which is equal to the deduction taken shall be included in gross income.

Example 6. Taxpayer X has adjusted gross income of $20,000 for 19X7. He was injured in a car accident and paid $1,200 for hospitalization expenses and $800 for doctor bills. He also incurred medical expenses for his wife and child of $600. In 19X8 X was reimbursed $800 by his insurance company for his car ac-

18.   Reg. § 1.213–1(b)(1)(i).   **20.**   Reg. § 1.213–1(g)(2).

19.   Reg. § 1.213–1(g)(1).   **21.**   Reg. § 1.213–1(g)(3).

cident. His deduction for medical expenses in 19X7 would be computed as follows:

Hospitalization	$1,200
Doctor's bills	800
Medical expenses for dependents	600
Total	$2,600
Less: 3 percent of $20,000	600
Medical Expense deduction (assuming X itemizes his deductions)	$2,000

If medical care reimbursement occurred in 19X7, the medical expense deduction would have been only $1,200. Since the reimbursement was made in a subsequent year, the $800 would be included in gross income for 19X8. If X used the standard deduction in 19X7, the $800 reimbursement would *not* be included in 19X8 gross income due to the absence of tax benefit in 19X7.

TAXES

The general rule for deducting taxes under § 164 is that state and local taxes paid or accrued by a taxpayer are deductible for Federal income tax purposes. The Committee Reports indicate that the rationale for permitting a deduction for state and local taxes was to relieve taxpayers from the burden of multiple taxes upon the same source of revenue. Further, the Committee Reports state that if there were no provision for the deductibility of *all* non-Federal taxes, state and local governments might be forced to impose additional taxes to generate operating revenues.[22]

DEDUCTIBILITY AS A TAX

One must make a distinction between a "tax" and a "fee" since fees are not deductible unless incurred as an ordinary and necessary business expense under § 162 or as an expense in the production of income under § 212.

The IRS has defined a tax as follows:

A tax is an enforced contribution exacted pursuant to legislative authority in the exercise of taxing power, and imposed and collected for the purpose of raising revenue to be used for public or governmental purposes, and not as payment for some special

---

22. H.R.Rep.No.749, 88th Cong., 1st Sess., 1964–1 C.B. 171.

privilege granted or service rendered. Taxes are, therefore, distinguished from various other contributions and charges imposed for particular purposes under particular powers or functions of the government. In view of such distinctions, the question whether a particular contribution or charge is to be regarded as a tax depends upon its real nature.[23]

Thus, in accordance with the above definition, fees for dog licenses, automobile inspection, automobile titles and registration, hunting and fishing licenses, bridge and highway tolls, drivers' licenses, parking meter deposits, postage, etc., are not considered to be currently deductible unless incurred as a business expense under § 162 or for the production of income under § 212.[24]

As amended by the Revenue Act of 1964, § 164 lists the following taxes to be deductible whether paid or accrued during the taxable year:

1. State, local and foreign real property taxes;

2. State and local personal propery taxes;

3. State, local and foreign income taxes;

4. State and local general sales taxes; and

5. State and local gasoline, diesel fuel and other motor fuels taxes.[25]

Those taxes which cannot be deducted are: [26]

1. Federal income taxes, including social security and railroad retirement taxes paid by the employee;

2. Estate, inheritance, legacy, succession, and gift taxes;

3. Foreign income taxes, if the taxpayer claims a foreign tax credit; and

4. Taxes on real property, to the extent that such taxes are to be apportioned and treated as imposed on another taxpayer.

PROPERTY TAXES, ASSESSMENTS AND APPORTIONMENT OF TAXES

Property Taxes. State, local and foreign taxes on real and personal property are generally deductible only by the person against whom the tax is *imposed*. Cash basis taxpayers may deduct these taxes in the year of actual payment and accrual basis taxpayers may deduct them in the year which fixes the right to deductibility.

Personal property taxes must be ad valorem; that is, assessed in relation to the value of the property.[27] Therefore, a motor vehicle

---

23. Rev.Rul. 57–345, 1957–2 C.B. 132 and Rev.Rul. 70–622, 1970–2 C.B. 41.

24. Rev.Rul. 57–345, 1957–2 C.B. 132 and Rev.Rul. 70–622, 1970–2 C.B. 41.

25. § 164(a) and Reg. § 1.164–1.

26. Reg. §. 1.164–2(a)–(e); § 164(c)(2).

27. Reg. § 1.164–3(c).

tax based upon weight, model year, and horsepower is not an ad valorem tax. However, a tax based upon value and other criteria may qualify in part.

> **Example 7.** State X imposes a motor vehicle registration tax on 4 percent of the value of the vehicle plus 40 cents per hundredweight. A, a resident of the State, owns a car having a value of $4,000 and weighing 3,000 pounds. A pays an annual registration fee of $172. Of this amount, $160 (4 percent of $4,000) would be deductible as a personal property tax. The remaining $12, based upon the weight of the car, would not be deductible.

Assessments for Local Benefits. As a general rule, real property taxes do not include taxes assessed for local benefits since such assessments tend to increase the value of the property, e. g. special assessments for streets, sidewalks, curbing, and other like improvements.[28] A taxpayer cannot deduct the cost of a new sidewalk (relative to a personal residence) even though the construction was required by the city and the sidewalk may have provided an incidental benefit to the public welfare.[29] Such assessments are added to the adjusted cost basis of the taxpayer's property.

Assessments against local benefits are deductible as a tax if they are made for the purpose of maintenance or repair or for the purpose of meeting interest charges with respect to such benefits. In such cases, the burden is on the taxpayer to show the allocation of the amounts assessed for the different purposes. If the allocation cannot be made, none of the amount paid is deductible.[30]

Apportionment of Taxes on Real Property Between Seller and Purchaser. In the year of sale, the real estate taxes for the entire year are apportioned between the buyer and seller on the basis of the number of days the propery was held by each.[31] This apportionment is required without regard to whether the tax is paid by the buyer or the seller, or is prorated pursuant to the purchase agreement. The rationale for apportioning the taxes between the buyer and seller is based upon administrative convenience for the IRS in determining who is entitled to deduct the real estate taxes in the year of sale. In making the apportionment, the assessment date and the lien date are disregarded.

> **Example 8.** The real property tax year in County R is April 1 to March 31. A, the owner on April 1, 19X6, of real property located in County R sells the real property to B on June 30, 19X6. B owns the real property from June 30, 19X6 through March 31, 19X7. The real property tax for the real property tax year

28. Reg. §§ 1.164–2(g) and 1.164–4(a).

29. *Erie H. Rose,* 31 TCM 142, T.C. Memo. 1972–39; Reg. § 1.164–4(a).

30. Reg. § 1.164–4(b)(1).

31. § 164(d).

April 1 through March 31, 19X7 is $365. For purposes of §
164(a), $90 (90/365 x $365, April 1 to June 29 of 19X6) of the
real property tax is treated as imposed upon A, the seller, and
$275 (275/365 x $365, June 30 to March 31 of the following year)
of such real property tax is treated as imposed upon B, the
purchaser.[32]

If the actual real estate taxes are not prorated between the buyer and seller as part of the purchase agreement, adjustments are required in the determination of the amount realized to the seller and
the adjusted cost basis of the property to the buyer.[33] If the buyer
pays the entire amount of the tax, he has, in effect, paid the seller's
portion of the real estate tax and has, therefore, paid more for the
property than the actual selling price. Thus, the amount of real estate tax which is apportioned to the seller (for tax purposes) is added
to the buyer's adjusted cost basis. The seller must increase the
amount realized on the sale by the same amount.

Example 9. Assume that real estate is sold on June 30, 19X6 for
$50,000 and that the *buyer* B pays the real estate taxes of $1,000
for the calendar year. $500 of the real estate taxes are appor-
tioned to and are deductible by the seller S and $500 of the taxes
are deductible by B. The buyer B has, in effect, paid S's real estate taxes of $500 and has, therefore, paid $50,500 for the property. B's basis is increased to $50,500 and the amount realized
to S from the sale is increased to $50,500.

The opposite result occurs if the seller (rather than the buyer)
pays the real estate taxes. In this case the seller reduces the amount
realized from the sale by the amount which has been apportioned to
the buyer. In such case, the buyer is required to reduce his adjusted
cost basis by a corresponding amount.

Example 10. Assume that the seller S pays the real estate taxes
of $1,000 for the calendar year and that the property is sold for
$50,000 on June 30, 19X6. If $500 of the taxes are apportioned
to and are, therefore, deductible by the buyer B, the buyer has,
in effect, paid only $49,500 for the property. The amount real-
ized by the seller is reduced by $500 and the buyer reduces his
cost basis in the property to $49,500.

INCOME TAXES

State, local, or foreign income taxes are not deductible *for* adjusted gross income unless the taxes are incurred in a trade or business or for the production of income. Personal use type taxes are de-

32. Reg. § 1.164–6(b)(3) Ex. (1).

33. §§ 1001–1(b)(2) and 1012; Reg. §§
1.1001–1(b) and 1.1012–1(b).

ductible only *from* AGI as itemized deductions.[34]   It is the position of the IRS that state income taxes imposed upon an individual are deductible only as itemized deductions even if the taxpayer's sole source of income is from business, rents, or royalties.[35]

Cash basis taxpayers are entitled to deduct state income taxes withheld by the employer in the year such amounts are withheld.[36] In addition, estimated state income tax payments are deductible in the year the payment is made by cash basis taxpayers even if the payments relate to a prior or subsequent year.[37]   If the taxpayer overpays his state income taxes due to excessive withholdings and/or estimated tax payments, the refund which is received must be included in gross income of the following year to the extent that the deduction provided a tax benefit in the prior year.[38]

Example 11.   X is a cash basis taxpayer who had $800 state income tax withheld during 19X7.   In addition, he made quarterly estimated payments amounting to $400 in 19X7.   These payments and withholdings of $1,200 were deducted on his 19X7 return which was filed in April, 19X8.   However, if his actual liability for the 19X7 state income tax was only $1,000, the $200 refund received in 19X8 would be included in 19X8 gross income on his Federal income tax return.

GENERAL SALES AND GASOLINE TAXES

State and local sales and gasoline taxes are deductible by the consumer providing the tax is separately stated and imposed upon the consumer, e. g. the tax is added to the sales price and collected or charged as a separate item.[39]   Whether a state or local tax is imposed upon the retailer or consumer depends upon local and state law.   In most instances, state and local sales and gasoline taxes are deemed to be passed on to the consumer and are, therefore, deductible.[40]

The requirement that the amount of tax must be separately stated will be deemed complied with where it clearly appears that at the time of sale to the consumer, the tax was added to the sales price and collected or charged as a separate item.   It is not necessary that the

34.   Rev.Rul. 70–40, 1970–1 C.B. 50; *Tanner v. Comm.,* 66–2 USTC ¶ 9537, 18 AFTR2d 5125, 363 F.2d 36 (CA–4, 1966).

35.   *Supra,* note 16 at p. 81.

36.   Rev.Rul. 56–124, 1956–1 C.B. 97.

37.   *Lillian B. Glassell,* 12 T.C. 232 (1949); *Estate of Aaron Lowenstein,*

First National Bank of Mobile, Executor, 12 T.C. 694 (1949); Rev.Rul. 71–190, 1971–1 C.B. 70.

38.   *Supra,* note 16 at p. 81.

39.   Reg. § 1.164–5.

40.   772 CCH–Std.Fed.Tax Rep. ¶ 1458.

consumer be furnished with a sales slip, bill, invoice, or other statement on which the tax is separately stated.[41]

To aid the taxpayer, the IRS issues optional state sales and gasoline tax tables. These tables are reprinted in Appendix A–3 and A–4. It should be noted that these tables can be used only if the deductions are being itemized on Schedule A of Form 1040.

The state sales tax tables are based upon the taxpayer's adjusted gross income plus other nontaxable items such as tax exempt interest, social security benefits, etc. The table does not include sales taxes on major purchases such as automobiles, boats, airplanes and materials for a new home (if the tax is separately stated on the invoice).[42] In addition, the tables do not make any provision for county and local sales taxes. Thus, sales tax on major purchase items and county and local sales taxes must be added to the amount which is derived from the sales tax table.

> **Example 12.** X has a wife and 2 dependent children and was a resident of Ohio during 19X1. His adjusted gross income is $28,000. X received $2,000 of income which was nontaxable during the year, i. e., tax exempt interest and one-half of his net long-term capital gains which were deducted in arriving at adjusted gross income. He had no major purchases during the year. County and local sales taxes are levied at a rate of 2 percent. His sales tax deduction using the optional sales tax tables is computed as follows:
>
> | | | | |
> |---|---|---|---|
> | 1. | Adjusted gross income | $28,000 | |
> | | Add: Nontaxable income | 2,000 | |
> | 2. | Base for tax table | $30,000 | |
> | 3. | Tax on $20,000 per table | | $165 |
> | | Add: 2 percent for each $1,000 of income over $20,000 (2 percent × 10 = 20%) | | |
> | 4. | Sales tax on amounts over $20,000 (20% × $165) | | 33 |
> | 5. | Total deduction per table | | 198 |
> | 6. | Add: County and local sales taxes | | |
> | | $\dfrac{2 \text{ percent}}{4 \text{ percent}} \left(\dfrac{\text{Local and County rate}}{\text{Ohio Rate}}\right) \times \$198$ | | 99 |
> | 7. | Total sales tax deduction | | $297 |

State gasoline tax tables may be used in lieu of keeping actual records of gasoline purchases. If the taxpayer's automobile has only 4 cylinders and the tax table is used, only one-half of the table amount may be deducted.

If the taxpayer's records indicate that more taxes were paid than the amount shown in the tables, the larger amount may be deducted. However, a taxpayer has the burden of proving that he is entitled to

---

41. *Supra*, note 39.   **42.** *Supra*, note 16 at p. 82.

the amount claimed as a sales tax deduction since there is judicial authority for the position that where there is no evidence to indicate that the amount allowed by the IRS is incorrect, the allowance stated in the optional tables will be approved.[43]

INTEREST

A deduction for interest has been allowed since the enactment of the income tax law in 1913. Despite its long history of congressional acceptance, the interest deduction continues to be one of the most controversial areas in the current tax law.

The controversy centers around the propriety of deducting interest charges for the purchase of consumer goods and services and interest on borrowings which are used to acquire investments, i. e., investment interest. Currently, various limitations are imposed upon the deductibility of prepaid interest and upon the deduction of interest on funds which are used to acquire investment property. In addition, no deduction is permitted for interest on debt incurred to purchase or carry tax-exempt securities.

ALLOWED AND DISALLOWED ITEMS

Interest has been defined by the Supreme Court as compensation for the use or forbearance of money.[44] The general rule permits a deduction for all interest paid or accrued within the taxable year on indebtedness.[45] This general rule is modified by other Code provisions which disallow or restrict certain interest deductions.[46] Generally, a deduction is allowed for the following:

1. Mortgage interest;
2. Loan origination fees—"points" if you are a buyer;
3. Mortgage prepayment penalty;
4. Finance charges separately stated;
5. Bank credit card plan interest;
6. Note discount interest; and
7. Penalty for late payment of utility bills.

43. *Bradford v. Comm.*, 65–1 USTC ¶ 9401, 15 AFTR2d 1106, Harry A. Koch Co. v. Vinal, 228 F.Supp. 782 (CA–2, 1965).

44. *Old Colony Railroad Co. v. Comm.*, 3 USTC ¶ 880, 10 AFTR 786, 52 S.Ct. 211 (USSC, 1936).

45. § 163(a).

46. §§ 163(b) and (d), 264 through 267 and 483.

Generally, a deduction is not allowed for:

1. "Points" if you are a seller;
2. Service charges;
3. Credit investigation fees;
4. Loan placement fees paid by a seller of property;
5. Non-redeemable ground rents;
6. Interest relative to tax exempt income;
7. Interest paid to carry "single premium" life insurance; and
8. Premium paid on the purchase of a convertible bond arising from the conversion feature.

RESTRICTIONS UPON DEDUCTIBILITY AND TIMING CONSIDERATIONS

Taxpayer's Obligation. To be deductible, the related debt must represent a bona fide obligation for which the taxpayer, himself, is liable.[47] Thus, a taxpayer is not allowed a deduction for interest paid on behalf of someone else. Both parties must intend that the loan be repaid. Intent of the parties can be crucial especially between related parties such as a shareholder and his closely held corporation. Thus, a stockholder may not deduct interest paid by his corporation on his behalf.[48] Likewise, a husband can not deduct interest paid on his wife's property if they file separate returns.[49] There is nothing to prevent the deduction of interest paid to a related party as long as the payment actually took place and meets the usual requirement for deduction as stated above. There is a special rule, however, for related taxpayers when the debtor uses the accrual basis and the related creditor is on the cash basis.[50] In such instance, interest which has been accrued but not paid at the end of the debtor's tax year, must be paid within 2½ months. Otherwise, no interest deduction is permitted to the accrual basis debtor even if such amounts are paid following the expiration of the 2½ month period.

> **Example 13.** Corporation X is on the accrual method and is on the calendar year for tax purposes. X has accrued but not paid $300 in interest on a valid debt to its major shareholder Y (a cash basis taxpayer) who qualifies as a related party under § 267 (b). X pays the $300 interest to Y on April 1 of the following year. Since the payment is not made within 2½ months, no deduction is permitted to X in the year the interest is accrued or

47. *Arcade Realty Co.,* 35 T.C. 256 (1960).

48. *Continental Trust Co.,* 7 B.T.A. 539 (1927).

49. *Colston v. Burnet,* 3 USTC ¶ 947, 11 AFTR 606, 59 F.2d 867 (CA–D.C., 1932).

50. § 267(a)(2).

in the following year of payment. Y must include the $300 interest in income when it is received even though no deduction is permitted to the corporation.

Time of Deduction. As a general rule, interest must be paid to be deductible unless the taxpayer uses the accrual method of accounting. Under the accrual method, interest is deductible ratably over the life of the loan.[51]

Example 14. Taxpayer X borrows $1,000 on November 1, 19X6, payable in 90 days @ 6% interest. On February 1, 19X7 X pays off the note and interest amounting to $1,015. The accrued portion ($\frac{2}{3}$ x $15 or $10) of the interest is deductible by X in 19X6 only if he is an accrual basis taxpayer. Otherwise, the entire amount of interest ($15) is deductible in 19X7.

Prepaid Interest. The Tax Reform Act of 1976 effectively imposes accrual method requirements upon cash basis taxpayers relative to interest prepayments which extend beyond the end of the taxable year.[52] Such payments must be capitalized and allocated to the subsequent periods to which the interest payments relate. These restrictions do not apply to "points" (loan origination fees) paid by the purchaser of a principal residence if the charging of points is customary and do not exceed a normal rate.[53]

These changes were intended to prevent cash basis taxpayers from "manufacturing" tax deductions prior to the end of the year by entering into "prepayment of interest" agreements.

The position of the IRS since 1968 has been that prepayments of interest for more than 12 months following the end of the taxable year must be prorated whereas prepayments for periods of less than 12 months may require proration if their effect is a material distortion of income.[54] The tax law now requires the capitalization of all interest prepayments which extend beyond the end of the taxable year even if such prepayments do not extend for more than 12 months.

CLASSIFICATION OF INTEREST EXPENSE

Whether interest is deductible *for* adjusted gross income or as an itemized deduction depends upon whether the indebtedness has a business, investment, or personal purpose. If the indebtedness is incurred for use in a business or for the production of rent or royalty income, the interest is deductible *for* adjusted gross income.[55] However, if the indebtedness was for personal use, the deduction must be

---

51. Reg. § 1.461–1(a)(2) and *Chas. Schaefer and Son, Inc.,* 20 T.C. 558 (1953).

52. § 461(g).

53. § 461(g)(2).

54. Rev.Rul. 68–643, 1968–2 C.B. 76.

55. § 62(1) and (5).

reported as an itemized deduction on Schedule A of Form 1040. Schedule A deductions are allowed only if the taxpayer does not use the standard deduction. See Appendix B–2 Form 1040. Business expenses appear on Schedule C of Form 1040.

The courts have established the precedent that the use to which the borrowed funds are put, not the security behind the obligation, governs whether the debt is business or non-business.[56]

Example 15. If T mortgages his home to raise money for his business, the interest is deductible as a business expense. However, if the funds were used to purchase security investments, the interest expense would be deductible only if T elected to itemize his deductions on Schedule A of Form 1040.

DISALLOWANCE POSSIBILITIES

Tax Exempt Securities. § 265 provides that no deduction is allowed for interest on debt incurred to purchase or carry tax-exempt securities. A major problem has been for the courts to determine what is meant by the words "to purchase or carry." See Chapter 6 for a detailed discussion of these complex issues.

Interest on Investment Indebtedness. A frequent practice of high income taxpayers has been to borrow funds which are then used to acquire low income producing assets, e. g. vacant land held for appreciation or low dividend payment growth stocks. The deduction of interest expense with little or no offsetting amount of ordinary income coupled with an eventual sale of the assets at favorable long-term capital gain rates would result in substantial tax benefits. Congress, therefore, has placed limitations upon the deductibility of interest when funds are borrowed for the purpose of purchasing or continuing to hold investment property.[57] The limitations do not apply to corporate taxpayers and to interest expense which is incurred for business use. After 1975, interest that can be deducted is limited to the following:

A. $10,000 * plus

B.   The amount of net investment income (if any).
   * An additional deduction of up to $15,000 may be allowed in certain instances where a taxpayer borrows funds to acquire stock in a corporation which he controls or the taxpayer acquires a partnership interest.[58]

Amounts which are disallowed may be carried forward and treated as investment interest of the succeeding year.[59] Investment in-

---

56. *Wharton v. U. S.*, 53–2 USTC ¶ 9597, 44 AFTR 512, 207 F.2d 526 (CA–5, 1953).

57. § 163(d).

58. § 163(d)(7).

59. § 163(d)(2).

come is defined as the gross income from interest, dividends, rents, royalties, net short-term capital gains attributed to the property held for investment, and ordinary income from the recapture of depreciation under § 1245 and § 1250.[60] Investment expenses are deducted from investment income in arriving at net investment income.[61]

> **Example 16.** T had net investment income of $15,000 and paid $60,000 of investment interest. His deduction is $25,000 in the current year, calculated as follows:

Floor	$10,000
plus	
Net investment income	15,000
Current year deduction	$25,000

T would be allowed a carry forward of $35,000.

The above rules generally apply to taxable years beginning after December 31, 1975. However, if the interest is attributable to property acquired during prior years, the deductions are based upon prior law and it becomes necessary to fragment the computation into pre 1976 and post 1976 elements.[62] Under pre 1976 law, the investment interest limitations were calculated as follows:

Interest deduction limitation =

1. $25,000 plus

2. Net investment income plus

3. The excess of net long-term capital gain over net short-term capital loss from the disposition of investments, plus

4. One-half of the investment interest less the sum of 1, 2, and 3 above.

Amounts disallowed in any year are carried forward to 1976 and subsequent years.

INTEREST PAID FOR SERVICES

It is common practice in the mortgage loan business to charge a fee for finding, placing, or processing a mortgage loan. Such fees are often called "points" and are expressed as a percentage of the loan amount. In periods of tight money it may be necessary to pay "points" in order to obtain the necessary financing. To qualify as deductible interest, the "points" must be considered compensation to a lender solely for the use or forbearance of money.[63] The "points"

---

60. § 163(d)(3)(B).

61. § 163(d)(3)(C).

62. Act § 209(b) Tax Reform Act of 1976.

63. Rev.Rul. 69–188, 1969–1 C.B. 54; amplified by Rev.Rul. 69–582, 1969–2 C.B. 29; Rev.Rul. 69–189, 1969–1 C.B. 55.

can not be a form of service charge or payment for specific services to qualify as deductible interest.[64] If the "points" are paid by the seller, they are not deductible because the debt with respect to which they are paid is not the debt of the taxpayer.[65] "Points" paid by the seller are treated as a reduction of the selling price of the property. If the "points" are paid by the buyer and are for the use of forbearance of money, the "points" are immediately deductible providing they are not prepaid interest which would be capitalized subject to amortization.[66]

The 1968 Federal Truth in Lending Act, which required disclosure of finance charges as an annual percentage, simplified the determination of whether a charge is interest or a fee for servicing the account. The IRS has now ruled that the following charges are deductible as interest: [67] charges on gasoline credit cards, revolving charges on department store purchases, and bank credit card charges.

CHARITABLE CONTRIBUTIONS

RATIONALE FOR DEDUCTIBILITY

Under § 170, individuals and corporations can deduct contributions made to qualified organizations with certain limitations (as described below). The policy consideration for permitting this type of deduction is that contributions to qualified charitable organizations serve certain social welfare needs and, therefore, relieve the government from the cost of providing these needed services to the community.

CRITERIA FOR A "GIFT"

§ 170(c) defines the phrase "charitable contribution" as a gift made to a qualified organization. The major elements needed to qualify a contribution as a gift are donative intent and absence of consideration. Consequently, the taxpayer has the burden of establishing that the transfer was made from motives of "disinterested generosity" as established by the courts.[68] As one can imagine, this test is quite subjective and has led to problems of interpretation. For example, a taxpayer engaged in a trade or business may attempt to qualify an expenditure as an ordinary and necessary business expense

---

64. Rev.Rul. 67–297, 1967–2 C.B. 87.

65. *Robert T. Hunt*, 24 TCM 915, T.C. Memo. 1965–172.

66. § 461(g)(2).

67. Rev.Rul. 73–136, 1973–1 C.B. 68; Rev.Rul. 72–315, 1972–1 C.B. 49 and Rev.Rul. 71–98, 1971–1 C.B. 57.

68. *Comm. v. Duberstein*, 60–2 USTC ¶ 9515, 5 AFTR2d 1626, 80 S.Ct. 1190 (USSC, 1960).

under § 162 rather than a charitable contribution since contributions are subject to certain ceiling limitations. For example, in one case, a travel agent regularly transacted a large portion of his business with clients who were exempt as charitable organizations under § 170.[69] At the end of each year payments were made to these organizations, the amounts of which depended upon the volume and profitability of the business relationship. The Tax Court held that these payments were not charitable contributions, and, therefore, the charitable contribution limitations did not apply.

QUALIFIED ORGANIZATIONS

For a contribution to be deductible, it must be made to the following organizations: [70]

1. A State or possession of the United States, or any subdivisions thereof;

2. A corporation, trust, or community chest, fund or foundation that is situated in the United States and is organized and operated exclusively for religious, charitable, scientific, literary, or educational purpose or for the prevention of cruelty to children or animals;

3. A veterans' organization;

4. A fraternal organization operating under the lodge system;

5. A cemetery company.

The IRS publishes a list of all organizations, *Cumulative List of Organizations* which have applied for and received tax exempt status under § 501 of the Code. This publication is updated frequently, and may be helpful to identify whether a gift has been made to a qualifying charitable organization.

Gifts made to needy individuals are not deductible. Therefore, a deduction will not be permitted if a gift is received by a donee in an individual capacity rather than as a representative of the qualifying organization.

Example 17. A dies and by will bequeaths a sum of money to B for the saying of Masses for the dead. B is a member of a religious order that requires as a prerequisite to membership the taking of a vow of poverty. In this instance, the amount of the bequest is not deductible from A's gross estate as a transfer to a public charity for religious use since the bequest is deemed to have passed initially to B and then to the order (under the vow of poverty agreement).[71]

69. *Sarah Marquis,* 49 T.C. 695 (1968).   **71.** Rev.Rul. 68–459, 1968–2 C.B. 411.

70. § 170(c).

TIME OF PAYMENT

The Code permits a contribution deduction solely in the year the payment is made. This requirement extends to both cash and accrual basis individuals.[72] An accrual basis corporation, however, is permitted a deduction if the payment is made within 2½ months following the close of the taxable year if the Board of Directors authorizes such payment prior to the end of the taxable year.[73]

A contribution is ordinarily deemed to have been made upon the delivery of the property to the donee. For example, if a gift of securities (properly endorsed) is made to a qualified charitable organization, the gift is considered complete on the day of delivery or mailing. However, if the donor delivers the certificate to his bank, broker or to the issuing corporation, the gift is considered completed on the date that the stock is transferred on the books of the corporation.[74]

VALUATION PROBLEMS

Property donated to a charity is generally valued at fair market value at the time the gift is made. The Code and Regulations give very little guidance on how to measure fair market value except to say that, "The fair market value is the price at which the property would change hands between a willing buyer and a willing seller, neither being under any compulsion to buy or sell and both having reasonable knowledge of relevant facts." [75] The IRS has established guidelines [76] for appraising contributed property and many established charities offer appraisal services to donors. Contributed property that has a value of $200 or more must be fully described and a statement of how the property was valued must be attached with the taxpayer's return.[77]

LIMITATIONS ON CHARITABLE DEDUCTIONS

In General. Charitable contributions are subject to certain overall ceiling limitations, i. e., contributions for individuals are limited to 50 percent of the taxpayer's adjusted gross income and in some cases a 30 percent ceiling limitation is imposed for contributions of capital gain property. Certain contributions of individuals are subject to an overall 20 percent limitation, i. e., contributions to private foundations. Corporations are subject to an overall limitation of 5 percent of taxable income computed without regard for the contributions made and certain other adjustments.[78]

72. § 170(a)(1).

73. § 170(a)(2).

74. Reg. § 1.170–1(b).

75. Reg. § 1.170–1(c)(1).

76. Rev.Proc. 66–49, 1966–2 C.B. 1257.

77. Reg. § 1.170A–1(a)(2)(ii).

78. § 170(b)(2).

In addition, the contribution of certain types of property, e. g. inventory, may result in a deduction of less than the fair market value of such property.

Ordinary Income Property. Ordinary income property is any property which if sold would have resulted in the recognition of ordinary income.[79] The term includes inventory for sale in the taxpayer's trade or business, a work of art created by the donor, a manuscript prepared by the donor, and a capital asset held by the donor for less than the required holding period for receiving long-term capital gain treatment. Also included is property that results in the recognition of ordinary income due to the recapture of depreciation. If ordinary income property is contributed, the deduction is equal to the fair market value of the property less the amount of ordinary income which would have been reported if the property were sold, i. e., in most instances the deduction is limited to the cost basis of the property to the donor.[80]

> **Example 18.** Taxpayer X owned stock in Energy Conservation Corporation which he donated to a local University on May 1, 19X7. He had purchased the stock for $2,500 on April 3, 19X7 and the stock had a value of $3,600 when he made the donation. Since the property has not been held for a sufficient period to meet the long-term capital gain requirements, a $1,100 short-term capital gain would have been recognized if the property were sold. Since short-term capital gains are treated as ordinary income property, X's charitable contribution deduction is limited to the extent of its adjusted cost basis of $2,500.

A special exception was added by the Tax Reform Act of 1976 which permits a corporation to contribute inventory (ordinary income property) to a public charity or private operating foundation (50% charities) and receive a deduction equal to the following: [81]

1. The adjusted cost basis of the property, plus

2. One-half of the difference between the fair market value and adjusted basis of the property.

3. In no event may the deduction exceed twice the adjusted cost basis of the property.

To qualify for this special rule, the inventory must be used by the charity in its exempt purpose for the care of children or the ill or needy.

The limitations upon ordinary income property were intended to prevent taxpayers from obtaining undue advantage from the contribution of substantially appreciated ordinary income type property, e.

---

79. Reg. § 1.170A–4(b)(1).   **81.** Act § 2135 adding § 170(e)(3).

80. § 170(e)(1).

g. a taxpayer (in a 50 percent bracket) who contributed inventory with a fair market value of $100 and cost of $40 would receive a tax benefit of 50% x $100 or $50 and have a net profit in effect of $10 if these limitations did not apply.

Capital Gain Property. Capital gain property is any property that would have resulted in the recognition of long-term capital gain if the property had been sold by the donor.[82] If capital gain property is contributed to a private foundation as defined in § 509(a), the taxpayer must reduce the contribution by 50% of the long-term capital gain which would have been recognized if the property had been sold at its fair market value.[83] This reduction was imposed in the law since a taxpayer receives the benefit of not being taxed on the appreciated portion of the contributed property at long-term capital gain rates, e. g. ½ of the long-term capital gain would have been subject to tax at ordinary rates if the property were sold rather than contributed to the private foundation. It should be noted, however, that contributions of capital gain property to public charities are not generally reduced by 50 percent of the capital gain element.

> **Example 19.** Taxpayer X purchases stock for $800 on January 1, 19X5, and donates it to a *private foundation* on June 21, 19X7 when it was worth $2,000. X's charitable contribution is $1,400 ($2,000 minus ½ of $1,200.)

> **Example 20.** Assume the same facts as in the previous example except that X contributed the stock to a public charity, e. g. the YMCA, his church or to a University. X's charitable contribution would be $2,000 since these limitations apply only to private foundations.

Special rules apply to capital gain property which is *tangible personal* property. If *tangible personal* property is contributed to a public charity such as a museum, church, university, etc., the charitable deduction is reduced by one-half of the long-term capital gain *if* the property is put to an "unrelated use." A taxpayer, in this instance, has the burden of proof to (1) establish that the property is not in fact being put to an unrelated use by the donee; (2) at the time of the contribution it was reasonable to anticipate that the property would not be put to an unrelated use. In the case of a contribution of personal property to a museum, if the work of art is the kind of art normally retained by the museum, it will be reasonable for a donor to anticipate that the work of art will not be put to an unrelated use (even if the object is later sold or exchanged).[84]

> **Example 21.** Taxpayer X contributes a Picasso, for which he had paid $20,000 to a local museum. It had a value of $30,000 at

82. Reg. § 1.170A–4(b)(2).   **84.** Reg. § 1.170A–4(b)(3)(ii)(b).

83. § 170(e)(1)(B)(ii).

the time of the donation. The painting was displayed by the museum for a period of two years and subsequently sold for $50,000. The charitable contribution is not reduced by one-half of the unrealized appreciation ($\frac{1}{2} \times$ ($30,000 − $20,000)) since the painting was put to a related use even though it was later sold by the museum.

Contribution of Services. No deduction is allowed under § 170 for a contribution of one's services to a qualified charitable organization. However, unreimbursed expenses related to the services rendered, may be deductible. For example, the cost of a uniform (without general utility) which is required to be worn while performing services may be deductible. Deductions are also permitted for transportation expenditures and reasonable expenses for meals and lodging while away from home incurred in performing the donated services.[85]

50 percent Ceiling Limitation. Contributions made to public charities may not exceed 50 percent of an individual's adjusted gross income for the year.[86] Excess contributions are carried over to the next five years.[87] The 50% ceiling on contributions applies to the following types of public charities: [88]

1. a church or a convention or association of churches,
2. an educational organization which maintains a regular faculty and curriculum,
3. a hospital or medical school,
4. an organization supported by the government which holds property or investments for the benefit of a college or University,
5. a governmental unit which is Federal, state or local,
6. an organization normally receiving a substantial part of its support from the public or a governmental unit, and
7. certain types of private foundations.

20 percent Ceiling. Contributions to most types of private foundations are generally limited to 20 percent of adjusted gross income. However, if substantial contributions are also made to public (50 percent) charities, the limitation to private charities may be less than 20 percent.

The deduction for contributions in these cases is the lesser of: [89]

20 percent of the taxpayer's contribution base (generally adjusted gross income) or 50% x AGI less the amount of charitable

---

85. Reg. § 1.170A–1(g).   88. § 170(b)(1)(A).

86. § 170(b).   89. § 170(b)(1)(B).

87. § 170(d)(1).

contributions qualifying for the 50 percent deduction ceiling. The excess, if any, cannot be carried over.

Example 22. Taxpayer X has adjusted gross income of $15,000. He contributes $5,000 to a local University, which is a 50% charity, and $4,000 to the XYZ Foundation for the Deaf, which is a private foundation. X's contribution deduction is $7,500 which is the sum of $5,000 to the University and $2,500 of the $4,000 to the XYZ Foundation. Lesser of (1) 20% × $15,000 = $3,000 or (2) 50% × $15,000 − $5,000 = $2,500 is allowed.

30 percent Ceiling. To prevent possible abuse when a taxpayer contributes appreciated property, specific rules apply to limit the deduction. For example, if capital gain property does not come under the 20 percent limitation for contributions to a private foundation, it is subject to a 30 percent limitation based upon the taxpayer's adjusted gross income.[90] Consequently, any capital or § 1231 asset that would result in a long-term capital gain if sold, is subject to the 30 percent limitation. When applying the limitation rules, contributions that come under the 30 percent limit are the last to be considered.[91]

Example 23. Taxpayer X has adjusted gross income for the taxable year of $20,000. X contributes $6,000, in cash, to a local University and stock with a cost basis of $3,000 and fair market value of $7,000 which has been held for two years. Since the appreciated stock is a capital asset which has been donated to a public charity, it is subject to the 30 percent limitation of $6,000 (30 percent of $20,000). Since this contribution plus the cash contribution exceed 50 percent of adjusted gross income ($10,-000), the actual deduction must be limited to $10,000 or $6,000 cash plus $4,000 in appreciated stock. The $3,000 unused capital gain property contribution can be carried over under the 30 percent rule during subsequent years.

Under the law, a taxpayer may elect to reduce his deduction for donated capital gain property by one-half of the difference between its fair market value and the adjusted cost basis.[92] In effect, under this election a taxpayer may receive a larger deduction in the year the contributions are made due to the higher ceiling, i. e., 50 percent in lieu of 30 percent. However, if the property is substantially appreciated, the election will result in a scaling down of the contributions which might otherwise be carried forward to subsequent years.

Excess Contributions Carryover. Excess contributions to public charities subject to the 50 percent limitation may be carried forward for five years.[93] Excess contributions under the 30 percent ceiling are also carried forward but are subject to the 30 percent ceiling limita-

---

90. § 170(b)(1)(D).

91. § 170(b)(1)(D)(i).

92. § 170(b)(1)(D)(iii).

93. § 170(d)(1).

tion in the carryforward years. In the carryover year, the contributions made during such year are first applied before any carryover amounts are deducted.[94]

> **Example 24.** Taxpayer X, in 19X1, contributes $20,000 cash to a public charity while his adjusted gross income for 19X1 is $30,000. Since X's contribution ceiling is $15,000 (50% of $30,000), she may carry forward $5,000 to 19X2, 19X3, 19X4, 19X5, and 19X6.

> **Example 25.** Assume the same facts as in the prior example except for the following:

	19X1	19X2	19X3	19X4
Adjusted gross income	$30,000	$25,000	$35,000	$40,000
Contributions subject to the 50 percent limitations	20,000	20,000	10,000	10,000
Deductible contributions:				
Current year	15,000	12,500	10,000	10,000
Carryovers from:				
19X1			5,000	
19X2			2,500	5,000
Unused Carryovers from:				
19X1	5,000		—	—
19X2		7,500	5,000	—
Total deduction	$15,000	$12,500	$17,500	$15,000

FILING REQUIREMENTS

The deduction for contributions is made as an itemized deduction on Schedule A of Form 1040. Cash contributions which are supported by receipts, cancelled checks, etc., are listed separately on Schedule A. If the taxpayer makes a gift of property in excess of $200, the Regulations require that the taxpayer state the name of each organization to which a contribution was made; the amount and the date. In addition, it is necessary to provide a description of the property; the manner of acquisition; the fair market value of the property at the time of the gift; the basis of the property and the terms of any agreement relating to the contribution.[95]

94. § 170(d)(1)(A).   95. Reg. § 1.170A–1(a)(2).

TAX PLANNING CONSIDERATIONS

EFFECTIVE UTILIZATION OF ITEMIZED DEDUCTIONS

Since an individual may use the standard deduction in one year and itemize his or her deductions in another year, it is frequently possible to obtain maximum benefit by shifting itemized deductions from one year to another. For example, if a taxpayer's itemized deductions and the amount of standard deduction are approximately the same for a 2 year period, the taxpayer should use the standard deduction in one year and shift itemized deductions (to the extent permitted by law) to the other year. The individual could, for example, prepay a church pledge for a particular year or avoid paying end of the year medical expenses so that the deduction is received in the following year.

It may be preferable to delay payment of a medical reimbursment claim if an individual anticipates that his effective tax rate will be higher in the current year than in the subsequent year. Even though the reimbursement must be included in the gross income of the subsequent year, the effective rate of tax on such income will be less than the tax benefit received from excluding the reimbursement in the current year's calculation of the medical expense deduction.

NEED FOR DOCUMENTATION

Medical Expenses. To assure a deduction for the entire cost of a nursing home for aged parents, it is helpful if the transfer of the individual to the home is for medical reasons which are prescribed by a doctor.

In addition, the nursing home facilities should be adequate to provide the necessary medical and nursing care. To assure a deduction for all of the nursing care expenses it is necessary to show that the individual was placed in the home due to required medical or nursing care rather than for personal or family considerations.

Sales Taxes. In a year of major purchases such as in a year of remodeling, refurbishing or building a new house, individuals should keep track of actual sales tax payments since such amount may be in excess of the amount obtained under the optional tax table. If a new home or addition is planned, it is possible to receive a sales tax deduction for the building materials if the tax is separately stated and is billed to the taxpayer.

Contributions. The taxpayer should obtain and retain appraisals for property which is donated to charitable organizations.

UTILIZING CHARITABLE CONTRIBUTIONS

If an individual is approaching the ceiling limitations upon charitable contributions for a particular year, the limitations may be avoided by spreading a deduction over several years. For example, a taxpayer may give a fractional interest in real estate, i. e., ⅒ interest in land per year over 10 years.

PROBLEM MATERIALS

Questions for Class Discussion

1. In Rev.Rul. 72–593, 1972–2 C.B. 18 the IRS concluded that the costs of acupuncture treatment are deductible as a medical expense. What criteria does the IRS look at to judge the legitimacy of a new form of medical treatment as a medical expense deduction?

2. Discuss the general rules for deducting medical care insurance premiums.

3. If a taxpayer incurred medical expenses of $500 and deducted such amounts in 19X1, how would a $300 insurance reimbursement be treated if such amounts were received in 19X2? Received in 19X1? What if the taxpayer elected the standard deduction in 19X1 and received the $300 reimbursement in 19X2?

4. Discuss the difference between a tax and a fee.

5. What is an *ad valorem* tax? Why should a distinction be made between an *ad valorem* tax based upon value and one based upon other factors such as weight, year, model, etc.?

6. Why is it necessary to make an apportionment of real estate taxes between the buyer and seller in the year of sale? What affect does the apportionment have upon the adjusted basis of the property to the buyer if the seller pays the real estate taxes?

7. If a taxpayer overpays his state income tax due to excessive withholdings and/or estimated tax payments, how is the refund check treated when received in the subsequent year? Are the excess amounts paid deductible in the current year?

8. What difference does it make whether a state or local sales or gasoline tax is passed on to the consumer or not?

9. If a taxpayer's records indicate that he has paid state sales taxes in excess of the amount allowed per the tax tables, is such excess amount deductible? Do the IRS tax tables include major purchase items such as automobiles or appliances, etc.? Is it necessary to make adjustments for local and county sales taxes? Why?

10. Which of the following is generally deductible as interest:

    1. Bank credit card interest;

    2. Service charges;

    3. "Points" for the seller of property;

    4. Finance charges separately stated;

    5. Late payment fees on the payment of utility bills.

11. Discuss the special problems that arise for the deductibility of interest on a debt that arose between related parties. How does § 267 of the Code relate to this problem?

12. What is meant by the phrase "material distortion of income" as it relates to the deductibility of prepaid interest? Is there a problem of distortion of income when a purchaser of a home deducts mortgage points?

13. Why does the tax consequence differ when the use to which borrowed funds is put for a debt is business or non-business? Does it matter whether the taxpayer uses borrowed funds in his capacity as a shareholder or as a sole proprietor where the funds are used in the respective businesses?

14. Why has Congress imposed limitations upon the deductibility of interest when funds are borrowed for the purpose of purchasing or continuing to hold investment property? Why are corporate taxpayers exempt from these limitations?

15. Why did the Federal Truth in Lending Act simplify the determination of whether an item is interest or a service fee?

16. Why is it necessary for a charitable organization to receive tax exempt status under § 501 of the Code?

17. What is "ordinary income" property? If inventory with an adjusted cost basis of $60 and fair market value of $100 is contributed to a public charity, how much is deductible? (Assume that the inventory is not used by the charity for the care of children, the ill or needy.)

18. What is "capital gain property"? What tax treatment is required if capital gain property is contributed to a private foundation? To a public charity? What difference does it make if the contribution is tangible personal property and the property is put to an unrelated use by the donee?

19. Why did Congress establish different ceiling limitations for charitable contributions? Do you think that Congress has accomplished its objectives? Why?

20. Do you think that the tax cost to the U. S. Treasury of allowing charitable contribution deductions is justified because they relieve the government of providing these charitable services to the

community? Do you think that Congress supports established religions by allowing this tax deduction?

21. Mr. Accountant normally charges fifty dollars an hour when preparing financial statements for his clients. If Mr. Accountant performs accounting services for the University of Houston without charge, then why can he not deduct the value of his donated services on his tax return?

22. Compare the deductibility of contributions made to private foundations versus contributions to public charities, e. g., percentage limitations and carryover rules.

23. Discuss the filing requirements for contributions of property in excess of $200; cash contributions supported by receipts, etc.

Problems

1. H and W, who have a dependent child, made a joint return for the calendar year 19X6. H became 65 years of age on September 15, 19X6. The adjusted gross income of H and W for 19X6 is $10,000. During the year, H and W paid the following amounts for medical care: (1) $1,000 for doctors and hospital expenses and $180 for medicine and drugs for themselves; and (2) $500 for doctors and hospital expenses and $140 for medicine and drugs for their dependent child. These payments were not compensated for by insurance or otherwise. Determine the deduction allowable under § 213 for medical expenses paid in 19X6.

2. During 19X2 T paid the following medical expenses:

	Medical	Drugs
For T	$800	$100
For T's wife	300	200
For M	200	50
For C	100	50

M is T's mother who is supported equally by T and his three brothers. For 19X2 T has agreed to allow one of his brothers to claim her as a dependency exemption. C is T's uncle who otherwise qualifies as T's dependent except that C had gross income of $750 during 19X2. Of the $800 of T's own medical expenses, $200 was incurred in late 19X1 but paid in early 19X2. The $300 listed for T's wife can be explained as follows: in late December 19X2 T prepaid a surgeon $300 for a gall bladder operation to be performed in June 19X3. The surgeon regarded the procedure as irregular but T was insistent about the prepayment. If T and his wife file a joint return for 19X2 (which reflects AGI of $20,000) and choose to itemize their deductions, how much tax benefit will these expenses provide?

3. H and W, who have a dependent child, C, were both under 65 years of age at the close of the calendar year 19X4, and made a joint return for that calendar year. During the year 19X4, H's mother, M, attained the age of 65, and was a dependent of H. The adjusted gross income of H and W in 19X4 was $12,000. During 19X4 H and W paid the following amounts for medical care: (1) $600 for doctors and hospital expenses and $120 for medicine and drugs for themselves; (2) $350 for doctors and hospital expenses and $60 for medicine and drugs for C; and (3) $400 for doctors and hospital expenses and $100 for medicine and drugs for M. These payments were not compensated for by insurance or otherwise. How much is allowed as a deduction for medical expenses for the taxable year 19X4?

4. During 19X1 Y had AGI of $20,000 and medical expenses of $900 (only $300 of which were deducted because of the 3% limitation). In 19X2 Y is reimbursed for $400 of these expenses. Has taxable income resulted to Y?

5. T uses the cash method and lives in a state that imposes an income tax (including withholding from wages). On April 14, 19X2 he files his state return for 19X1 paying an additional $400 in income taxes. During 19X2 his withholdings for state income tax purposes amount to $2,200. On April 13, 19X3 he files his state return for 19X2 claiming a refund of $100. The refund is received by T on August 3, 19X3.

   a. If T itemizes his deductions how much may he claim as a deduction for state income taxes on his Federal return for calendar year 19X2 (filed in April 19X3)?

   b. How will the refund of $100 received in 19X3 be treated for Federal income tax purposes?

6. S, an individual, sells his personal residence on February 3, 19X5 for $80,000 (adjusted basis of $60,000). The real estate taxes for each year become due and payable on July 1—the tax year of the taxing authority begins on January 1 and all unpaid taxes become a lien on the property as of October 1. P, the purchaser of S's residence, paid the taxes of $2,190 for calendar year 19X5 on July 1, 19X5. Both S and P use the cash method of accounting and 19X5 is not a leap year.

   a. Discuss the tax effect of the 19X5 property taxes to S (the seller).

   b. To P (the purchaser).

7. T lives in a state that imposes an annual motor vehicle registration tax of 1% of value plus 50 cents per hundred weight. In the current year he paid $60 for this tax based on a value of $4,000 and a weight of 4,000 pounds as to his personal automobile. How much, if any, of the $60 is deductible?

8. On July 1, 19X2, T borrows $12,000 at 6% for one year, interest discounted in advance. Under the loan agreement T receives the net proceeds of $11,280 and repays $12,000 on July 1, 19X3. T uses the calendar year for tax purposes.

   a. If T is a cash basis taxpayer, discuss the tax treatment of the interest deduction.

   b. Discuss the treatment of the interest deduction if T is an accrual basis taxpayer.

9. Assume the same facts as in problem 8 except that T is required to repay the loan in twelve monthly payments of $1,000 starting with August 1, 19X2. Assuming the repayment takes place as scheduled and T uses the cash basis of accounting, how much of an interest deduction is allowable for 19X2 and 19X3?

10. X, a cash basis individual, entered into a "prepayment of interest" agreement in December, 1977. He prepaid $8,000 of interest on a loan for the 9 month period from 1/1/78 to 9/30/78.

   How much, if any, of the interest is deductible in 1977? 1978?

11. Determine the amount of the charitable deduction allowed in each of the following situations:

   a. Donation of X Corporation stock (a publicly traded corporation) to taxpayer's church. The stock cost the taxpayer $1,000 four months ago and has a fair market value of $1,500 on the date of the donation.

   b. Donation of a painting to the Salvation Army. The painting cost the taxpayer $3,000 five years ago and has a fair market value of $4,000 on the date of the donation.

   c. Taxpayer allows the local branch of the American Red Cross to use his building rent-free for half of the current year. The building normally rents for $300 per month.

   d. Taxpayer purchases for $100 each two tickets to a benefit performance put on by the Houston Grand Opera Association, Inc., in order to raise funds for the coming season. Tickets for this type of performance normally sell for $10 each. Taxpayer dislikes opera and did not attend the benefit performance.

12. A is an individual using the cash receipts and disbursements method of accounting. On January 1, 19X0, A contributed to a charitable organization real estate having a fair market value of $10,000. In connection with the contribution the charitable organization assumed an indebtedness of $8,000 which A had incurred. A has prepaid two years' interest on that indebtedness (for 19X0 and 19X1) amounting to $960, and has taken an interest deduction of $960 for such amount. Determine the amount of contribution deduction for 19X0.

13. In 19X1, B, a farmer using the cash method of accounting and the calendar year as the taxable year, contributed to a church a quantity of grain which he had raised having a fair market value of $600. In 19X0, B paid expenses of $450 in raising the grain which he properly deducted for such year. Determine B's contribution deduction for 19X1.

14. X, an individual taxpayer, had the following items of income and expense in 1977:

1.	Dividend income	$15,000
2.	Interest income	5,000
3.	Investment interest	70,000

   a. Calculate the amount of interest deduction for 1977.

   b. How are any excess or nondeductible amounts treated?

15. X, an individual with adjusted gross income of $50,000 in 19X3 contributed 100 shares of IBM stock to a local college. The adjusted basis of the IBM stock to X was $200 per share whereas its fair market value was $300 per share on the date of the gift. The stock was acquired in 19X1 and contributed by X to the college in 19X3.

   a. Calculate the amount of the contribution which qualifies for the charitable contribution deduction.

   b. How are any excess amounts, if any, treated?

16. X, an individual, had adjusted gross income of $20,000. He contributed $8,000 to a public charity during 19X1 and $6,000 to a private foundation.

   a. Calculate the total contribution for 19X1.

   b. How are any excess amounts treated?

17. Upon the advice of his physician T, a heart patient, installs an elevator in his personal residence at a cost of $6,000. The elevator has an estimated useful life of 15 years and no salvage value. A next door neighbor who is in the real estate business charges T $30 for an appraisal in which he estimates the value of the residence was $40,000 before the improvement and $44,000 after. The reason for the increase in value is that T lives in a region where many older people retire and, therefore, would find the elevator an attractive feature in buying a house. As a result of the operation of the elevator, T noticed an increase of $40 in his utility bills for the current year.

Disregarding percentage limitations, which of the above expenditures qualify as a medical deduction?

18. During the year T pays the following expenses in connection with his dependent father:

Room and lodging to Green Acres Rest Home	$4,800
Drugs (patent medicines)	200
Operation to correct hernia (paid to the attending physician and the hospital)	800

   a. Under what conditions would the payments to Green Acres Rest Home qualify as medical care?

   b. In the event such payments to Green Acres Rest Home do not qualify, what about the deductibility of the other payments?

19. X is married, has two dependent children and files a joint return with his spouse. X's adjusted gross income was $25,000 during 19X1 and he also had $1,000 of tax exempt interest and $2,000 of net long-term capital gains ($\frac{1}{2}$ of which was excluded from AGI). X acquired a new automobile during the year and he paid $500 state, county and local sales tax on the purchase. X is a resident of Ohio. County and local sales taxes amount to a total of 2 percent of consumer purchases.

   a. Calculate X's sales tax deductions using the table in Appendix A–3.

   b. If X's actual payments of sales tax were greater than the amount determined in part A, which amount should be deducted?

Research Problem

The First Bank of Houston (taxpayer) created a tax exempt one hundred percent owned subsidiary known as the First Bank of Houston Foundation. The Foundation was tax exempt under Section 501 (c)(3) of the Code and its operations consisted of maintaining the Playhouse in the Park, a summer playhouse-in-the-round in Houston, in such a manner that admission prices were kept low and any profits were remitted to the City of Houston. Any losses are absorbed by the Foundation which is, in turn, subsidized by the taxpayer.

The Bank now claims that it entered into the above arrangements as a means of capturing business in the community and the payments to subsidize the Foundation were not gratuitous and, consequently, should be allowed as an ordinary and necessary business expense under Section 162 of the Code. To support this position the taxpayer shows that its efforts in operating the Foundation have been publicized in the local newspapers and on television. Also, since tickets to the plays can only be purchased at the bank or its branches, the ticket outlets generated more customer traffic and thus more opportunity to obtain new customers.

The question to be answered is whether the payments by taxpayer to the Foundation are Section 162 business expenses or are they Section 170 charitable contributions? May the payments be disallowed under Sections 267 and 269 of the Code?

Partial list of research aids:

Revenue Ruling 69–90, 1969–1 C.B. 63.

Revenue Ruling 73–113, 1973–1, C.B. 65.

Singer Company v. U. S., 449 F.2d 413 (Ct.Cls., 1971).

Chapter 10

STANDARD DEDUCTION, PERSONAL AND DEPENDENCY EXEMPTIONS AND DETERMINATION OF TAX

TAX FORMULA FOR INDIVIDUALS

Before discussing the computation of an individual's tax liability, it is necessary to understand how the standard deduction (also referred to as zero bracket amount) affects the tax formula. The Code has authorized the IRS to establish newly revised tables which will be used by middle and lower income bracket taxpayers.[1] For taxpayers who are eligible to use these tax tables, the computation of the tax is now based upon "tax table income." In effect, the computation of

---

1. Act § 101(b) amending § 3, Tax Reduction and Simplification Act of 1977. Prior to 1977, tax tables were used by individuals having taxable income of less than $20,000. The Committee Reports indicate that * * * "It is intended that the Service publish tax tables in the ranges of approximately $20,000 and 3 or fewer exemptions for single persons and $40,000 and 9 or fewer exemptions for joint returns." S.Rep. No.95–66, 95th Cong., 1st Sess. 51, 1977.

the standard deduction, personal exemptions and the general tax credit are built into the tax tables.

Table 1

TAX FORMULA FOR INDIVIDUALS USING
THE TAX TABLES

	Income (broadly conceived)		$20,000
−	Exclusions, e. g. tax exempt interest		(1,000)
=	Gross Income		19,000
−	Deductions *for* adjusted gross income		(2,000)
=	Adjusted gross income		17,000
−	Excess itemized deductions:		
	Total itemized deductions	$4,200	
	Minus: Standard deduction (zero bracket amount)	(3,200)	(1,000)
=	Tax table income		$16,000

The tax tables are reproduced in Appendix A–2.

Individuals who are ineligible to use the tax tables, compute their tax based upon one of the tax rate schedules (reproduced in Appendix A–1). The rate schedules are based on taxable income. For such individuals it is, therefore, necessary to subtract excess itemized deductions and personal exemptions *from* adjusted gross income to arrive at taxable income. It is also necessary to make separate computations for tax credits (including the general tax credit) since these computations are not included in the rate schedules.

Table 2

TAX FORMULA FOR INDIVIDUALS USING
THE RATE SCHEDULES

	Income (broadly conceived)		$60,000
−	Exclusions, e. g. tax exempt interest		(2,000)
=	Gross Income		58,000
−	Deductions *for* adjusted gross income		(3,000)
=	Adjusted gross income		55,000
−	Excess itemized deductions:		
	Total itemized deductions	$8,200	
	Minus: Standard deduction (zero bracket amount)	(3,200)	(5,000)
−	Personal and dependency exemptions (4 × $750)		(3,000)
=	Taxable income		$47,000

The rules for computing the standard deduction and the personal and dependency exemptions are covered more fully in the remainder of this chapter which also discusses the tax rate schedules, tax tables, and special methods for computing the tax. Tax credits are covered in Chapter 11.

STANDARD DEDUCTION

UNDERLYING RATIONALE

The need to simplify the tax law for low to moderate income level taxpayers has been a principal reason for the enactment of the standard deduction. These provisions permit taxpayers to use the standard deduction in lieu of itemizing their deductions. The standard deduction is of principal benefit to moderate and low income level taxpayers since the amount of the deduction (e. g. $3,200 for married individuals filing a joint return) is usually less than the total itemized deductions which means that such individuals need not report their itemized deductions.[2] Thus, the need to audit such returns by the IRS is substantially reduced since the opportunities for error or misstatement of taxable income are lessened.

HISTORICAL CHANGES IN THE STANDARD DEDUCTION RULES

Prior to 1977, the standard deduction was based upon a fixed percentage of adjusted gross income with specified ceiling limitations upon the amount which could be deducted, e. g. the computation was 16 percent of AGI with a ceiling of $2,800 for married taxpayers filing a joint return in 1976. In 1964, a minimum standard deduction was enacted to provide relief for poverty level taxpayers. This minimum standard deduction was transformed by the Tax Reform Act of 1969 into a "low-income allowance" which was of primary benefit to low income individuals.

The Tax Reduction and Simplification Act of 1977 replaced the low income allowance and the percentage standard deduction with a "flat" standard deduction of $3,200 for married individuals filing jointly and for surviving spouses, $2,200 for single taxpayers, and $1,600 for married individuals filing separately.[3] It should be noted that the term "standard deduction" has been replaced by the term "zero bracket amount" although it is expected that the standard de-

2. S.Rep.No.95–66, 95th Cong., 1st Sess. 50, 1977. The Committee Reports indicate that the changes in the standard deduction rules in 1977 will decrease the percentage of taxpayers who itemize their deductions from 31 percent to 23 percent.

3. Act § 101(a), (b) and (d) amending §§ 1 and 3 and repealing §§ 141, 142, 144 and 145.

duction terminology will continue to be used.[4] Table 3 includes a comparison of the standard deduction rules for the years 1974–1977.

Table 3

STANDARD DEDUCTION AND LOW INCOME
ALLOWANCE PROVISIONS *

Percentage Standard Deduction	1974	1975	1976	1977
Single taxpayer:				
Ceiling (flat amount in 1977)	$2,000	$2,300	$2,400	$2,200
Percent of adjusted gross income	15	16	16	N.A.
Married—filing jointly:				
Ceiling (flat amount in 1977)	2,000	2,600	2,800	3,200
Percent of adjusted gross income	15	16	16	N.A.
Married—filing separately:				
Ceiling (flat amount in 1977)	1,000	1,300	1,400	1,600
Percent of adjusted gross income	15	16	16	N.A.
Low-income allowance:				
Single taxpayer	1,300	1,600	1,700	N.A.
Married—filing jointly	1,300	1,900	2,100	N.A.
Married—filing separately	650	950	1,050	N.A.

* For years prior to 1977 the standard deduction was defined as the larger of the "percentage standard deduction" or the "low income allowance."

COMPUTATION OF THE STANDARD DEDUCTION

Since the standard deduction is now built into the tax rate schedules and the tax tables, an individual may deduct only those itemized deductions which are in excess of the amount of the standard deduction.

Example 1. H and W are married taxpayers who file a joint return and use the rate schedules. They have itemized deductions of $8,000 and 4 personal and dependency exemptions. Assuming adjusted gross income of $50,000, their taxable income is computed as follows:

Adjusted gross income		$50,000
Less (1) Excess itemized deductions:		
Total itemized deductions	$8,000	
Minus: Standard deduction (zero		
bracket amount)	(3,200)	(4,800)
(2) Personal and dependency exemp-		
tions (4 × $750)		(3,000)
Taxable income		$42,200

---

4. *Supra*, note 2.

Example 2. Assume the same facts as in the prior example except that their total itemized deductions are only $3,000.

Adjusted gross income		$50,000
Less (1) Excess itemized deductions:		
Total itemized deductions	$3,000	
Minus: Standard deduction (zero bracket amount)	(3,200)	–0–
(2) Personal and dependency exemptions (4 × $750)		(3,000)
Taxable income		$47,000

Example 3. H and W are married taxpayers who file a joint return and use the tax table. They have itemized deductions of $4,000 and 4 personal and dependency exemptions. Assuming adjusted gross income of $20,000, their tax table income is computed as follows:

Adjusted gross income		$20,000
Less Excess itemized deductions:		
Total itemized deductions	$4,000	
Minus: Standard deduction (zero bracket amount)	(3,200)	(800)
Tax table amount		$19,200

Example 4. Assume the same facts as in the prior example except that their total itemized deductions are only $3,000.

Adjusted gross income		$20,000
Less Excess itemized deductions:		
Total itemized deductions	$3,000	
Minus: Standard deduction (zero bracket amount)	(3,200)	–0–
Tax table income		$20,000

LIMITATIONS AND EXCEPTIONS

Special computations are required for the following individuals:[5]

1. A married individual filing a separate return where either spouse itemizes deductions;

2. A nonresident alien;

3. A U.S. citizen who is entitled to exemption under § 931 for income from U.S. possessions; and

---

5. Act § 102(a) amending § 63(b)(1).

4. A dependent child who is either under 19 or a full-time student where the parent is entitled to a dependency exemption for the child and the child had unearned income, e. g. dividends or interest.

Example 5. X is a full-time college student who is supported by his parents. X made $1800 from a part-time job and has dividend income of $700 after the $100 dividends exclusion has been subtracted. His itemized deductions amounted to $600. His tax table income would be computed as follows:

Adjusted gross income		$2,500
Less Excess itemized deductions:		
Total itemized deductions	$ 600	
Minus: Standard deduction (zero bracket amount)	(2,200)	–0–
Plus unused zero bracket amount:		
Standard deduction (zero bracket amount)	$2,200	
Minus: Earned income (wages)	(1,800)	400 *
Tax table income		$2,900

* The excess of the standard deduction of $2,200 over the amount of earned income of $1,800 or $400 must be added to adjusted gross income since the law permits a standard deduction for such individuals only to the extent of earned income. X's standard deduction is, in effect, $1,800 since $2,200 was built into the tax table.

Example 6. H and W are married individuals who file separate returns. H files a separate return and itemizes his deductions. W's adjusted gross income is $15,000 and she has itemized deductions of $1,400. W's tax table income would be adjusted as follows:

Adjusted gross income		$15,000
Less Excess itemized deductions:		
Total itemized deductions	$1,400	
Minus: Standard deduction (zero bracket amount)	(1,600)	–0–
Plus unused zero bracket amount		
Standard deduction (zero bracket amount)	$1,600	
Minus: Total itemized deductions	(1,400)	200 *
Tax table income		$15,200

* The $200 must be added back to adjusted gross income since a $1,600 standard deduction is, in effect, built into the tax table and W is entitled to only $1,400 of itemized deductions. W is required to itemize her deductions since H itemized his deductions and they filed separate returns.

TAX PLANNING POSSIBILITIES FOR THE CASH BASIS TAXPAYER

In situations where the total itemized deductions are approximately equal to the standard deduction it is possible by a proper timing of payments for cash basis taxpayers to obtain a deduction for excess itemized deductions in one year and claim the standard deduction in another. For example, an individual may prepay church pledges in one year and therefore increase contributions for the entire year. It may also be possible to pay real estate taxes or city and state income tax estimated payments prior to the end of the year. In this instance the taxpayer would claim the standard deduction in the following year.

PERSONAL AND DEPENDENCY EXEMPTIONS

UNDERLYING RATIONALE

Personal and dependency exemptions provide some measure of equity to our Federal income tax system by providing relief for taxpayers with large families. Other social welfare considerations are reflected in the additional exemptions which are allowed for blindness, old age, and for dependent children who are under 19 or are full-time students.

PERSONAL EXEMPTIONS FOR THE TAXPAYER AND HIS SPOUSE

The Code provides a $750 personal exemption for the taxpayer and an additional $750 exemption for the spouse if a joint return is filed.[6] However, in the unusual situation where separate returns are filed, a married taxpayer can not claim a $750 exemption for his spouse unless the spouse has no gross income and is not claimed as a dependent of another taxpayer.

Determination of Marital Status. The determination of whether an individual is married is generally made at the end of the taxable year except for situations where one spouse dies. If two former spouses enter into a legal separation under a decree of divorce or separate maintenance prior to the end of the year, they are considered to be unmarried at the end of the taxable year.

Example 7. The Effect of Death or Divorce Upon Marital Status:

	Marital Status for 19X1
1. W who is the wife of H who dies on January 3, 19X1	They are considered to be married for purposes of filing the 19X1 return.
2. W and H entered into a divorce decree which is effective on December 31, 19X1	They are considered to be unmarried for purposes of filing the 19X1 return.

6. § 151(b).

In addition to the regular $750 exemptions for a taxpayer and his spouse, additional $750 exemptions are permitted if either has attained the age of 65 prior to the end of the year and/or if either is blind.[7]

Example 8. Additional Exemptions for Blindness and Age:

	Regular Exemption	Additional Exemption
Facts:		
1. H and W are married and file a joint return.		
2. H is 66 years old and W is 62.		
3. W is not totally blind but has a doctor's certified statement that her visual acuity does not exceed 20/200 in her better eye with corrective lenses. She is, however, considered to be blind for purposes of the personal exemption.[8]		
1. H	$ 750	
2. H's age		$ 750
3. W	750	
4. W's blindness	———	750
		$1,500
	$1,500	1,500
Total personal exemptions		$3,000

Note that the personal exemptions for blindness and old age are applicable only to the taxpayer and his spouse and not to dependents of the taxpayer, e. g. a taxpayer who supports his aged parent cannot claim more than one dependency exemption for the parent.

DEPENDENCY EXEMPTIONS

To qualify as a dependent, the following 5 tests must be met:

1. Support;

2. Relationship or member of the household;

3. Gross income;

4. Joint return; and

5. Citizenship or residency.

Support Requirements. Over one-half of the support of a dependent must generally be furnished by the taxpayer. Support includes food, shelter, clothing, medical and dental care, and education.[9] In computing whether more than one-half of the support was furnished, amounts such as FICA payments are included.[10] However, a

---

7. § 151(d).

8. § 151(d)(3).

9. Reg. § 1.152–1(a)(2).

10. Reg. § 1.152–1(a)(2)(ii).

scholarship received by a student is not included for purposes of computing whether the taxpayer furnished more than one-half of the child's support.[11]

Example 9. H contributed $2,500 consisting of food, clothing, and medical care toward the support of his son, S, who earned $1,500 from a part-time job and received a $2,000 scholarship to attend a local university.

Assuming that the other dependency tests are met, H may claim S as a dependent since he has contributed more than one-half of S's support. The $2,000 scholarship is not included as support.

Example 10. S contributed $1,000 to his father's support during the year. His father received $800 social security benefits and $400 of dividend income. All of these amounts were used for his support during the year.

Since the $800 social security payments are includible in the determination of whether the support test has been met, S can not claim his father as a dependent since he has not contributed more than one-half of the total support.

Relationship or Member of the Household. The dependent must either be a relative of the taxpayer or a member of the taxpayer's household.[12] The Code contains a detailed listing of the various blood and marriage relationships which are permitted and should be referred to as specific questions arise. Note, however, that the relationship test is met if the dependent is a relative of either spouse and that a relationship, once established by marriage, continues regardless of subsequent changes in marital status.

The following rules are also prescribed in the Code:

1. A legally adopted child is treated as a natural child.[13]
2. A foster child qualifies if the child has his principal place of abode in the taxpayer's household.[14]

Dependent's Gross Income. The dependent's gross income must be less than $750 unless the dependent is a child under 19 or is a full-time student.[15]

Joint Return Filed by a Married Dependent. If a dependent is married, the supporting taxpayer (e. g. the father of a married child) is not permitted a dependency exemption if the married individual files a joint return with his or her spouse.[16]

---

11. Reg. § 1.152–1(c).

12. § 152(a).

13. § 152(b)(2).

14. *Ibid.*

15. § 151(e).

16. § 151(e)(2).

Citizenship or Residency Requirements. A dependent must generally be a U.S. citizen or resident of the U.S., or country which is contiguous to the U.S.[17]

EXCEPTIONS AND SPECIAL RULES

Support of Minor Children or Full-Time Students. A parent who provides over one-half of the support of a child who is under 19 at the end of the year or who is a full-time student may claim a $750 dependency exemption. In addition, the child is entitled to a personal exemption. A child is defined as a son, stepson, daughter, stepdaughter, adopted son or daughter and may include a foster child.[18] If the child qualifies for the exemption as a student, he or she must be a full-time student for at least 5 months at an educational institution.[19] The exception for dependent children who are under 19 or full-time students was intended to permit a child or college student to earn money from part-time or summer jobs, etc. without being penalized by virtue of the loss of the dependency exemption.

Multiple Support Agreements. A second exception, which is known as a "multiple-support agreement," permits one of a group of taxpayers who furnish more than one-half of the support of a dependent to claim a dependency exemption in situations where no one person provides more than 50 percent of the support.[20] Any individual who contributed more than 10 percent of the support is entitled to claim the exemption if each person in the group who contributed more than 10 percent files a written consent. This provision frequently enables the children of aged dependent parents to claim an exemption in situations where none of the children meets the 50 percent support test.

Special Rules for Children of Divorced or Separated Parents. Special rules have been established to help resolve disputes and uncertainty relative to dependent children of divorced or separated parents.[21] The general rule is that the parent having custody of the child for the greater portion of the year is entitled to the $750 dependency exemption. However, the noncustodial parent may be entitled to the dependency exemption under the following situations:

1. The noncustodial parent contributed more than $600 support for each child claimed as a dependent and the divorce or separate maintenance decree or a written agreement between the parents provides that the noncustodial parent is to receive the dependency exemption, or

17.   § 152(b)(3).

18.   Reg. § 1.151–3(a).

19.   Reg. § 1.151–3(b) and (c).

20.   § 152(c).

21.   § 152(e); Reg. § 1.152–4.

2. The noncustodial parent provides more than $1,200 child support for each child and the custodial parent can not establish that he (or she) provided more than one-half of the support.[22]   In such cases each parent is entitled to receive an itemized statement of the expenditures which were made by the other parent.

Example 11.   H and W enter into a divorce decree in 1976.   In 1977 their two children are in the custody of W.   H contributed $700 of child support for each child.   Absent any written agreement relative to the receipt of the dependency exemptions, W should be entitled to the exemptions.

Example 12.   Assume the same facts as in Example 11 except that H contributed $3,000 of child support for each child.   Unless W can establish that she provided more than one-half of the support, H should be entitled to the two dependency exemptions.

Example 13.   Assume the same facts as in Example 11 except that H contributed $3,000 of child support for each child and the divorce decree provides that H is entitled to the exemptions.   H should be entitled to the two dependency exemptions since his contribution exceeded the $600 minimum.

Note that it may be desirable to provide in the decree that the noncustodial parent is entitled to the dependency exemptions if the noncustodial parent is in a higher tax bracket since the relative benefits from the dependency exemptions are therefore increased.

DETERMINATION OF TAX AND FILING REQUIREMENTS

TAX TABLES

Tax rate schedules are required to be used by upper-middle and upper income taxpayers whereas the tax tables are used by middle and lower income level taxpayers.   In 1976, the tax tables were used by individuals whose taxable income was $20,000 or less.   The Tax Reduction and Simplification Act of 1977 has authorized the IRS to establish new tax tables which are based upon "tax table" income rather than taxable income.   It is anticipated that approximately 96 percent of all taxpayers will use the tax tables rather than the tax rate schedules.[23]   The rate schedules and tax tables appear in Appendix A–1 and A–2.   Single taxpayers and heads of households use

22.   Act § 2139 amending § 152(e)(2) (B)(1).   This rule is effective for years after 1976.

23.   *Supra*, note 1.

the tax tables if their tax table income is $20,000 or less. Married taxpayers filing jointly use the tax tables if their tax table income is $40,000 or less.

In the tax tables, separate columns are provided for single tax-payers, married taxpayers filing jointly, head of household and married taxpayers filing separately. It is no longer necessary to deduct and compute the standard deduction, the personal and dependency exemptions or the general tax credit (discussed in Chapter 11) since these amounts are automatically built into the tax tables. If an individual itemizes his deductions, it will be necessary to deduct the total itemized deductions in excess of the standard deduction (zero bracket amount).

INELIGIBLE INDIVIDUALS OR TAX ENTITIES

The tax tables may not be used by the following taxpayers: [24]

1. An estate or trust (estates and trusts use the same rate schedule which applies to married individuals filing separately);

2. An individual who claims the exclusion for foreign earned income (see Chapter 5);

3. An individual who claims the alternative capital gains tax (see Chapter 14);

4. An individual who uses income averaging (discussed subsequently in this chapter);

5. An individual electing the maximum tax on earned income provisions (discussed subsequently in this chapter);

6. An individual who files a short period return (see Chapter 16); and

7. Upper middle and upper income level taxpayers.

TAX RATE SCHEDULES

Rate Schedules for Married Individuals. The joint return (Rate Schedule Y Code § 1(a)) was originally enacted to establish equity for married taxpayers in common law states since in community property states married taxpayers are able to split their income. Therefore, under the joint return table the progressive rates are constructed upon the assumption that income is earned equally by the two spouses. If married individuals elect to file separate returns both must use a separate table (§ 1(d)) which is applied to married taxpayers filing separately and to estates and trusts. It is generally advantageous for married individuals to file a joint return since the combined amount of tax is lower. However, special circumstances (e. g. significant medical expenses incurred by one spouse subject to 3 percent limita-

24. Act § 101(b) amending § 3(b).

tions) may warrant the use of the separate return election. Note also that the Code places numerous limitations upon deductions, credits, etc. where married individuals file separately. The joint return rates also apply for two years following the death of one spouse providing the surviving spouse maintains a household for a dependent child.[25]

Rate Schedules for Unmarried Individuals. Unmarried individuals who maintain a household for dependents are entitled to use head of household rates—Schedule Z.[26] The head of household rates are approximately halfway between (in terms of progression) the joint return rate schedule and the rate schedule for individual taxpayers. The unmarried taxpayer must maintain a household which is the domicile of a relative as defined in § 152(a).[27] Over one-half of the cost of maintaining the household must be furnished by said individual. Generally, a relative need not qualify as a dependent of the taxpayer unless he or she is married. Head of household status is also available if a non-related dependent resides in the household.[28] Head of household status may also be claimed where the taxpayer maintains a home for his parent or parents who also qualify as dependents.[29]

In 1971, Congress liberalized the rate schedule for single taxpayers (Schedule X) so that the tax paid by a single individual will not exceed 120 percent of the comparable rates for married individuals. Generally, it is advantageous from a tax standpoint to enter into marriage. However, where the former single individuals' incomes are approximately equal, the opposite result may occur.

Example 14. Computation of Tax for Married Individuals:

		Tax Liability	
		Prior to marriage	Married filing jointly
H's taxable income	$24,000	$ 5,914	
W's taxable income	24,000	5,914	
Total	$48,000	$11,828	$14,460

It is questionable whether Congress considered this result which was created by the liberalization of the rate tables for single individuals. This so-called marriage tax has been partially rectified by the 1977 changes in the standard deduction. The standard deduction for single taxpayers is now a flat $2,200 whereas in 1976 the ceiling limitation was $2,400 for such individuals. The standard deduction for

---

25. § 2(a).

26. § 2(b).

27. § 2(b)(1)(A)(i).

28. § 2(b)(1)(A)(ii).

29. § 2(b)(1)(B).

married individuals filing jointly, however, was increased to a flat $3,200 from a ceiling of $2,800 in 1976.

FILING REQUIREMENTS

Any individual must file a tax return if certain minimum amounts of gross income have been earned. A self-employed individual with net earnings from a business or profession of $400 or more must file a tax return regardless of the amount of his gross income. The filing requirements for 1977 are as follows: [30]

Single (legally separated; divorced; or married, and living apart from spouse, with dependent child) and under 65	$2,950
Single (legally separated; divorced; or married, and living apart from spouse, with dependent child) and 65 or over	$3,950
Single, can be claimed as a dependent on parent's return, and have taxable dividends, interest, or other unearned income	$ 750
Qualified surviving spouse [widow(er) with dependent child] under 65	$3,950
Married couple filing jointly, living together at the end of the year (or at date of death of spouse), both under 65	$4,700
Married couple filing jointly, living together at the end of the year (or at date of death of spouse), one spouse 65 or over	$5,450
Married couple filing jointly, living together at the end of the year (or at date of death of spouse), both 65 or over	$5,580
Married individual filing a separate return	$ 750

If an individual's gross income is below the required amounts above and he or she does not, therefore, owe any tax, it may be necessary to file a return to obtain a tax refund on amounts which have been withheld. A return is also necessary to obtain the benefits of the earned income credit which accrue to taxpayers with little or no tax liability. Chapter 11 discusses the earned credit.

SPECIAL METHODS FOR COMPUTING THE TAX

INCOME AVERAGING

Due to progressive tax rates, an individual may suffer hardship where his income fluctuates significantly from one year to another. Therefore, the 5-year income averaging provisions were enacted in

---

30. Act § 104 amending § 6012(a).

1964 and subsequently liberalized in 1969 to provide relief for these situations.

Eligibility Determined. To qualify for income averaging the adjusted taxable income in the computation year must be at least $3,000 greater than 120 percent of the average base period income.[31] Therefore, taxpayers should make the following calculation to determine if they are eligible to use income averaging:

Example 15. Income Averaging—Eligibility Determination:

Adjusted taxable income for 1977 $43,200

Less: Average base period income: *

	Taxable Income for Year	+	Zero Bracket Amount for Computation Year	=	Adjusted Taxable Income
1976	$20,000	+	$3,200	=	$23,200
1975	20,000	+	3,200	=	23,200
1974	20,000	+	3,200	=	23,200
1973	20,000	+	3,200	=	23,200
					$92,800

Average base period income:

$$92,800 \div 4 \times 120\% =$$ (27,840)

Averageable income $15,360

Averageable income of $15,360 > $3,000 so the taxpayer is eligible to use income averaging.

* Since the Tax Deduction and Simplication Act of 1977 changed the definition of taxable income for individuals, it is necessary to make adjustments to taxable income during the base period years prior to 1977. The 1977 Act therefore provides that taxable income for each year prior to 1977 is to be increased by the standard deduction (zero bracket amount) in effect for the computation year.[32] The above computation assumes the taxpayer is married and filed a joint return.

Computation of Tax. Example 16 illustrates the computation of income averaging under the 5-year averaging rules.

31.   §§ 1301 and 1302(a).   32.   *Supra*, note 1 at p. 58.

Example 16.　Income Averaging—Computation of Tax:

Tax liability under regular computation ($43,200 taxable income using joint return rates)	=	$12,140

Tax liability under income averaging:

Step 1.	Tax on 120% of average base period income + 20% of averagable income (120% × $23,200 = 27,840 + 20% × $15,360 = $30,012). Tax on $30,012	$ 6,672
Step 2.	Tax on 120% of average base period income ($23,200 × 120% = $27,840) Tax on $27,840	$ 5,890
Step 3.	Computation of tax—Tax determined under Step 1 plus 4 times (Step 1 less Step 2 tax) $6,672 + 4($6,672 − $5,890)	= $ 9,800

Savings due to income averaging $12,140 − $9,800	=	$ 2,340

The computation of income averaging is made on Schedule G of Form 1040. Since this schedule is not distributed by the IRS in its mailing of returns to taxpayers, many taxpayers do not realize that the averaging benefits are available. The election may be made or changed at any time prior to the running of the statute of limitations.[33] Further, the Tax Court has held that an election may be made even though the statute of limitations has run for the computation year.[34]

Adjustments to Taxable Income. It may be necessary to make certain additional adjustments to taxable income for the base year and the computation year, e. g. taxable income for the computation year is not reduced by exclusions for earned income from foreign countries.[35]

Special Eligibility Rules. Special rules have been provided to prevent young people from using income averaging during their initial working years. Under these restrictions a taxpayer must generally have furnished one-half or more of his support during the base years.[36] These eligibility rules are extremely complex. Therefore, reference should be made to the Code, Regulations and instructions to Schedule G. It should be noted that the benefits of the alternative tax on long-term capital gains and the 50 percent maximum tax are not available if income averaging is elected.[37]

33.　§ 1304(a).

34.　*Louis R. Hosking,* 62 T.C. 635, 1974.

35.　§ 1304(b)(1).

36.　§ 1303.

37.　§ 1304(b)(3) and (4).

MAXIMUM TAX ON EARNED INCOME

The Code places a 50 percent ceiling tax rate on personal service income, e. g. wages, salaries, professional fees, pensions, deferred compensation and other forms of compensation for personal services.[38]

If an individual is engaged in a noncorporate trade or business in which capital is a material producing factor, up to 30% of the net profits may be deemed to be personal service income.[39] Even though substantial amounts of capital may be required in the operations of a professional practice, e. g. doctor, lawyer, C.P.A., etc., the 30 percent limitations do not apply.[40] For 1977 and later years, personal service income includes most forms of deferred compensation, e. g. pensions earned in prior years and deferred from tax until the current period.[41]

Computation of Maximum Tax. The computation of the maximum tax requires several steps as illustrated in the following examples.

Example 17. Computation of Personal Service Net Income:

Personal service income, salaries, wages, pensions, etc.	$200,000
Less: Allocable portion of deductions to arrive at adjusted gross income, e. g. unreimbursed employee expenses or business expenses	(30,000)
Personal Service Net Income	$170,000

Example 18. Computation of Personal Service Taxable Income: [42]

$$\frac{\text{Personal Service Net Income } \$170,000}{\text{Adjusted gross income * } \$200,000} \times \text{Taxable income of } \$130,000 = \$110,500$$

Less: Tax preferences for the Year **	(20,000)
Personal Service Taxable Income	$ 90,500)

* Includes $30,000 of investment income + $170,000 of net personal service income. The effect of this computation is to allocate a portion of the itemized deductions to the personal service income, e. g., adjusted gross income of $200,000 − $70,000 of excess itemized and personal exemptions = $130,000 taxable income. The ratio cannot exceed 100 percent.

** The effect of these requirements is to scale down the benefits of the maximum tax to the extent a taxpayer has tax preferences for the year.

38. § 1348(a).	**41.** § 1348(b)(1).
39. Reg. § 1.1348–3(a)(3).	**42.** § 1348(b)(2).
40. Reg. § 1.1348–3(a)(3)(ii).	

Example 19. Computation of the Tax Liability (Joint return rate Schedule Y):

Step 1.	Tax on personal service taxable income up to the 50 percent bracket (joint return tax on $55,200). Note that if personal service taxable income is less than $55,200 on a joint return, the benefits from the maximum tax are not available	$18,060

Step 2.	Tax on personal service taxable income over $55,200: $90,500 total personal service taxable income less tax on personal service income up to $55,200 ($90,500 – 55,200 × 50%)	=	$17,650

Step 3.	Tax on non-earned income, e. g. investment income: Regular tax on taxable income of $130,000	=	$61,932
	Less: Tax at regular rates on personal service taxable income of $90,500		(37,574)
	Tax on non-earned income portion		$24,358

Total Tax:

Tax on personal service income Step 1 plus Step 2	$35,710
Tax on non-earned income	24,358
Total tax liability	$60,068

Savings from using maximum tax ($61,932 – $60,068)	=	$ 1,864

Tax Planning Considerations. Note that non-personal service income may be subject to tax at rates in excess of 50 percent. It may therefore be possible to reduce non-earned income through investments in tax shelters. However, such investments may produce additional amounts of tax preferences which may result in reduced benefits from the maximum tax provisions.

The maximum tax provisions are not available for taxpayers using income averaging.[43] Therefore, it is necessary to weigh the relative benefits from income averaging and the maximum tax and elect the provision which produces the lowest tax. Form 4726 is used to compute the tax under the maximum tax provisions.

MINIMUM TAX ON TAX PREFERENCES

In 1969, a 10 percent minimum tax was enacted by Congress to effect a more equitable distribution of the tax burden among taxpayers. Treasury Department studies had indicated that some wealthy taxpayers were not paying taxes on significant amounts of economic income. The minimum tax provisions were applied, however, to individuals, estates, trusts and corporations.

43. § 1348(a).

The minimum tax is a special form of tax which is imposed upon certain taxpayers in addition to the regular Federal income tax. In 1976, the minimum tax rules were substantially revised so as to encompass a greater number of taxpayers, e. g. the rate was increased to 15 percent; the list of tax preference items was expanded, and the specific exemption was reduced from $30,000 to the greater of $10,000 or one-half of the taxpayer's regular tax liability.

COMPUTATION OF MINIMUM TAX

Example 20. Computation of the Minimum Tax for Individuals.

Sum of tax preference items (described below)		$80,000
Less: Specific exemption: Greater of (1)	$10,000	
or (2) ½ of the taxpayers regular Federal income tax liability (e. g. $12,140 tax on taxable income of $43,200 × ½) = $ 6,070		(10,000)[44]
		70,000
		× 15%
Minimum tax liability		$10,500

Tax Preferences. Tax preference items appear in § 57.[45] The following items of preference are frequently incurred.

1. One-half of the amount of the excess of long-term net capital gains over short-term net capital losses;

2. Accelerated depreciation (i. e., the excess claimed over the straight-line method) on real property and personal property subject to a net lease;

3. Excess of itemized deductions (other than medical expenses and casualty losses) over 60 percent but not more than 100 percent of adjusted gross income;

4. Intangible drilling cost deductions in excess of the amounts which would have been deductible if such costs were (1) capitalized subject to amortization over 10 years or (2) if such costs were deducted using cost depletion (whichever method is more favorable).[46]

An individual's tax preference items are reduced by the greater of $10,000 or ½ of his regular income tax for the year. The regular income tax is computed by subtracting various tax credit items from the income tax before credits.[47] If a taxpayer has a net operating

44. Act § 301 amending § 56(a).

45. Items 3 and 4 were added in 1976; §§ 57(a)(1), 57(a)(11), 57(b) and 57(d).

46. For taxable years beginning after December 31, 1976 and before January 1, 1978 an individual's tax prefer-
ence is only to the extent the excess intangible drilling costs exceed the net income from the oil and gas properties for the year. Act § 38 amending § 57(a)(11).

47. § 56(c).

loss which can be carried forward, any minimum tax which would otherwise be payable for the year is deferred until the loss carryover benefits are utilized during the succeeding years.[48]

Applicability to Corporations. The minimum tax is also applicable to corporate taxpayers. The 15 percent rate also applies to corporations. However, corporations are entitled to an exemption equal to the greater of (1) $10,000 or (2) the full amount of the regular tax.[49]

Reporting. The minimum tax computation is made on Form 4625 which is attached to the return. Most taxpayers are still not subject to the minimum tax provisions due to the large exemptions which offset the amounts of tax preference items, e. g. the greater of $10,000 or ½ of the taxpayer's regular tax reduces tax preference items to zero for many taxpayers.

ESTIMATED TAX PAYMENTS AND SELF–EMPLOYMENT TAX

DECLARATION OF ESTIMATED TAX BY INDIVIDUALS

Any individual who reasonably expects his gross income to exceed the following amounts must file a declaration of estimated tax (Form 1040–ES): [50]

1. $20,000 for single, head of households, surviving spouses or married individuals entitled to file a joint return;

2. $10,000 for married individuals entitled to file a joint declaration where both spouses have wages; and

3. $5,000 for married individuals not entitled to file a joint declaration.

Regardless of the above amounts of income, a declaration of estimated tax is required if more than $500 is from sources other than wages, e. g. dividends and interest. The declaration is not required, however, if the estimated tax can reasonably be expected to be less than $100. Therefore, it is possible for an employee to avoid these filing requirements by requesting his employer to increase the amounts of Federal income tax withheld.

Filing Requirements. Declarations of estimated tax are due when an individual first meets these filing requirements. Payments are made in quarterly installments beginning on April 15 for calendar

48. § 56(b).

49. *Supra*, note 47.

50. § 6015.

year taxpayers. An amended estimate is required if the taxpayer discovers that his original estimate was inaccurate and the newly determined tax amount (less amounts previously paid) is spread equally over the remaining installments. A 7 percent (9 percent for periods from July 1, 75 to January 31, 76 and 6 percent for periods prior to July 1, 75) nondeductible penalty is imposed on the amount of underpayment of estimated tax.

Exceptions. Several exceptions have been provided in the Code in recognition of the inherent difficulty associated with the estimation of income. Therefore, the following exceptions are provided which will prevent the imposition of the penalty: [51]

1. Installment payments (including amounts withheld) are equal or exceed the amount of the tax liability on the prior year's return;

2. Installment payments (including amounts withheld) are equal or exceed the prior year's tax liability using current year's rates;

3. Installment payments (including amounts withheld) are equal to or exceed 80 percent of the tax due for the current year based upon the annualization of current year's income; and

4. Such payments are equal to or exceed 90 percent of the tax computed by applying current year rates to actual taxable income and self-employment income.

To avoid the underpayment penalty it is advisable to base the estimated payments upon one of the exceptions, e. g. estimated tax payments should be based upon an amount which is equal to the prior year's tax liability. If a possible underpayment of estimated tax is indicated, Form 2210 should be filed to compute the penalty due or to justify qualification under one or more of these exceptions.

SELF–EMPLOYMENT TAX

The tax on self-employment income (7.9 percent up to $16,500 in 1977) is levied in order to provide social security benefits for self-employed individuals. Individuals with net earnings from self-employment of $400 or more are subject to the self-employment tax.[52] If an individual also receives wages subject to FICA tax, the $16,500 ceiling amount upon which the self-employment tax is computed is reduced. Thus, no self-employment tax is due (Form 1040–SE) if a self-employed individual receives wages of $16,500.

Net earnings from self-employment includes gross income from a trade or business less allowable trade or business deductions and the distributive share of any partnership income or loss derived from a trade or business activity.

---

51. § 6654(d).   **52.** § 6017.

PROBLEM MATERIALS

Questions for Class Discussion

1. Why does the tax law provide tax tables for middle and lower income level individuals and tax rate schedules for higher income individuals?

2. What is the difference between the terms "tax table income" and "taxable income"?

3. How do the standard deduction provisions help to simplify the Federal income tax law?

4. How is it possible for certain individuals to save income tax by arranging their affairs so as to use the standard deduction in one year and itemize their deductions in another year? (Assume that income earned and itemized deductions incurred are relatively stable during such years.)

5. Has the elimination of the low income allowance in 1977 created additional tax burdens for poverty level individuals? Why?

6. Why is it necessary for dependent children (who are under 19 or are full-time students) to add back any "unused zero bracket amounts" to their adjusted gross income in the computation of tax table income?

7. What is the underlying rationale for permitting personal and dependency exemptions?

8. What tests must be met to qualify as a dependent of another person?

9. What is the difference between a personal exemption and a dependency exemption?

10. Why are FICA payments included as support while scholarships are specifically excluded?

11. Is a dependent child, who is a full-time student or under 19 years of age, permitted a $750 personal exemption for himself even though the supporting parent claims a dependency exemption for the child?

12. Would the answer to the prior question be the same if the child were 19 years old and not attending school on a full-time basis?

13. What is a "multiple-support agreement"? When is it necessary to file such an agreement with the IRS?

14. Why was it necessary to provide special rules relating to the claim of dependency exemptions for children of divorced or separated spouses?

15. Why is it frequently desirable to provide in the divorce or separate maintenance decree that the noncustodial spouse is entitled to the dependency exemptions for dependent children?

16. Under what conditions are individuals ineligible to use the tax tables? Will such individuals pay a greater amount of Federal income tax because they must use the tax rate schedules?

17. What rate schedules are used by estates and trusts?

18. Are head of household rates preferable to the rates for single taxpayers?

19. How was the "so called" marriage tax partially rectified by the 1977 changes in the computation of the standard deduction?

20. Will married individuals always use the joint return rate schedules? Why?

21. Is it possible to itemize one's deductions if an individual uses the tax tables?

22. When is it desirable to file a tax return even though the filing of such return is not required?

23. If the maximum tax provisions are elected, is it possible to elect income averaging?

24. How does the incurrence of tax preference items affect the computation of the maximum tax?

25. Why was the minimum tax imposed by Congress? Are most taxpayers required to pay additional amounts of tax due to the minimum tax provisions? Why?

26. Discuss the requirements for filing a declaration of estimated tax for individuals.

27. How is it possible to avoid the imposition of a penalty upon the underpayment of estimated taxes?

28. If an individual is employed and receives wages of $25,000 which are subject to FICA tax, is he or she subject to self-employment tax on net earnings from self-employment? Why?

Problems

1. In each of the following cases determine the number of personal and dependency exemptions T may claim. Note that each case is different and assume any dependency test not mentioned has been met. Unless otherwise specified T is not married and is not entitled to a personal exemption for old age or blindness.

   Case 1. T provides 80 percent of the support of an uncle who does not live with him. The uncle has gross receipts of $800 from rent property. Expenses attributable to this income amount to $80 and are paid by the uncle.

   Case 2. T provides 80 percent of the support of his nephew (age 17) who lives with him. During the year the nephew has taxable income of $800 and is a full-time student.

Case 3. Assume the same facts as in Case 2 except that the $800 was paid to the nephew as a scholarship.

Case 4. T provides over 50% of the support of his son, S, and his son's wife, D. S is a full-time student at a university. During 19X1 D earned $1,100 on which income taxes were withheld. On January 31, 19X2 S and D file a joint return for tax year 19X1.

Case 5. During 19X1 T gave his father, F (age 68), cash of $1,000 and a used automobile (cost of $2,000). F's total expenditures for food, lodging, and clothing for 19X1 amount to $3,000 ($1,000 received from T and $2,000 withdrawn from F's savings account). F meets the tax test for blindness although he possesses an unrestricted driver's license. F comes to a tragic end on June 3, 19X1 while making a left turn off of a bridge.

Case 6. T and his two brothers each provide 15 percent of the support of their mother. The mother derives the remainder of her support from a Social Security benefit of $950.

2. Determine the correct number of personal and dependency exemptions in each of the following situations:

   a. T, age 66 and blind, is a widower who maintains a home for his unmarried daughter who is 24 years old. The daughter earned $3,000 and attends college on a part-time basis. T provides more than 50 percent of her support.

   b. T, a bachelor age 45, provides more than 50 percent of the support of his father, age 70. The father had gross income of $1,600 from a part-time job.

   c. T, age 45, is married and has 2 dependent foster children who live with and are totally supported by T. One of the foster children, age 14, had $800 of gross income. T and his spouse file a joint return.

   d. T, age 67, is married and has a married daughter, age 24. The daughter attended college on a full-time basis and was supported by T. She filed a joint return with her spouse and T filed a joint return with his spouse, age 62.

3. Which of the following individuals are required to file a tax return for 1977?

   a. T is married and files a joint return with his spouse. Their combined amount of gross income was $5,200.

   b. T is a dependent child under age 19 who earned $1,000 wages from a part-time job and had $600 of dividend income.

   c. T is single and is 67 years old. His gross income from wages was $3,000.

d. T is a self-employed single individual with gross income of $12,000 from an unincorporated business. Business expenses amounted to $11,000.

Should any of these individuals file a return even if such filing is not required? Why?

4. X, Y, and Z contribute to the support of their father, age 72 who is blind. The father lives with each of the children for approximately 4 months during the year. The father's total living costs amounted to $3,000 and consisted of the following:

1.	Pension from a qualified plan	$1,000
2.	Social security payments	400
3.	Support from X	600
4.	Support from Y	800
5.	Support from Z	200
		$3,000

a. Which if any of these individuals may claim the father as a dependent (assume no multiple support agreement is filed)?

b. If X, Y, and Z file a multiple support agreement, which of these individuals are entitled to the dependency exemption?

5. Compute the number of personal and dependency exemptions under the following situations:

a. T, a single individual, provides 60 percent of the support of his mother—age 69. She earned $700 gross income from dividends and received $1,500 in social security benefits.

b. T, a married individual filing a joint return, provides 100 percent of the support of his son age 21 who is a full-time college student. The son earned $2,000 during the year from part-time employment.

c. T, who is divorced and single, provides $2,000 child support for a child who is living with his mother. The divorce decree provides that the noncustodial parent is to receive the dependency exemption.

6. In each of the following situations can T use Rate Schedule Z (head-of-household) in 19X3?

a. T's wife died in 19X2. He maintained a household for his two dependent children during 19X3. Over one-half of the cost of the household was provided by T.

b. T is unmarried and lives in an apartment. He supported his aged parents who live in a separate home. J maintains over one-half of the cost of maintaining the parent's home. He also claimed the parents as dependents since he provided more than one-half of their support during the year.

c.   T is unmarried and maintains a household (over one-half of the cost) for his eighteen year old married daughter and her husband. The daughter filed a joint return with her husband.

7.   Compute T's tax table income under the following circumstances:

a.   T is married and files a joint return with his spouse. They have two dependent children. T and his spouse had adjusted gross income of $20,000 and $3,600 of itemized deductions.

b.   T is unmarried and has no dependents. He had adjusted gross income of $18,000 and itemized deductions of $2,700.

c.   T is a full-time college student who is supported by his parents. He made $2,000 from a part-time job and had interest income of $600. T's itemized deductions amounted to $500.

8.   Compute T's taxable income under the following circumstances:

a.   T is married and files separately. T has two dependent children. T's adjusted gross income was $60,000 and he had itemized deductions of $7,000. T's spouse also itemizes her deductions.

b.   Assume the same facts as part (a) except that his itemized deductions are only $2,000.

c.   Assume the same facts as part (a) except that T and his spouse file a joint return.

9.   T is a cash basis, calender year, taxpayer. For each of years 19X1 and 19X2 he expects AGI of $20,000 and the following itemized deductions:

Church pledge	$1,000
Interest on home mortgage	1,600
Other (sales taxes, etc.)	600

Assuming the flat standard deduction for each year is $3,200, discuss the tax consequences of the following alternatives:

Alternative #1—In 19X1 T prepays his church pledge ($1,000) and interest on home mortgage ($1,600) for 19X2.

Alternative # 2—In 19X2 T pays his church pledge ($2,000) for 19X1 and 19X2.

Alternative #3—T does nothing different (i. e., deductions from adjusted gross income for each year are $3,200).

10.   Indicate in each of the following situations the Tax Rate Schedule T should use for calendar year 19X2: (Assume that T is not eligible to use the tax table).

a.   ——T, the mother and sole support of her three minor children, has been abandoned by her husband who left for parts unknown in late 19X1.

b.   ——T is a widower whose wife died in 19X0. T furnishes all of the support of his household which includes two dependent children.

c.   ——T furnishes all of the support of his parents who live in their own home in a different city. T's parents qualify as his dependents. T is not married.

d.   ——T's household includes an unmarried stepchild age 18, who has a gross income of $6,000 during the year. T furnishes all of the maintenance of the household. T is not married.

11. T has the following amounts of income, deductions, and tax preferences for 1978:

   1. Wages—$150,000
   2. Interest and Dividend income—$100,000
   3. Excess itemized deductions and personal exemptions—$40,000
   4. Tax preference items—$60,000
   5. Taxable income for 1978—$210,000.

Compute the amount of tax using the regular and maximum tax provisions using the joint return rate schedule.

12. T has the following amounts of income, deductions, and tax preference items for 1978:

1. Net earnings from a law practice	$90,000
2. Interest and dividend income	20,000
3. Excess itemized deductions and personal exemptions	16,000
4. Tax preference items	40,000
5. Taxable income for 1978	94,000

T's average base period income (after adjustments are made for the zero bracket amount) was $30,000. T files a joint return with his spouse.

a. Calculate whether T is eligible to use income averaging for 1978.

b. Compute the amount of T's personal service taxable income for purposes of the maximum tax.

c. Should T elect to use income averaging or the maximum tax?

13. T anticipates the following amounts of income, deductions, and tax preference items for 1978:

1. Net income from an unincorporated business (capital is significant)	$150,000
2. Interest and dividend income	40,000
3. Salary	60,000
4. Excess itemized deductions and personal exemptions	30,000
5. Tax preference items	40,000
6. Unreimbursed employee expenses	10,000
7. Taxable income for 1978	210,000

T's average base period income (after adjustments) was $250,-000. T files a joint return with his spouse.

a. Calculate the amount of T's tax using the maximum tax provisions.

b. Is T eligible to use income averaging? Why?

c. Suppose that T's broker advises him to purchase tax sheltered investments and that such investments will increase his itemized deductions by $30,000 in 1978 and will increase his tax preferences by $20,000. What impact would the additional investment have upon T's tax liability for 1978?

14. T has the following items on his tax return for 1978:

1. Long-term net capital gains	$100,000
2. Accelerated depreciation on real estate investments (straight-line depreciation would have been $60,000)	80,000
3. Itemized deductions (other than medical expenses and casualty losses)	90,000
4. Adjusted gross income	120,000
5. Tax liability (regular method)	20,000

a. Calculate the amount of T's tax preferences for 1978.

b. Calculate T's minimum tax for 1978.

15. For the calendar year 1977 T has taxable income of $50,000. His taxable income for the four preceding years is as follows:

1973	$12,000
1974	15,000
1975	18,000
1976	20,000

IM–118

Assume T otherwise meets the requirements set forth in §§ 1301–1305 and uses Rate Schedule X.

1. What is T's tax liability for 1977 using income averaging? Use Schedule G of Form 1040.

2. Without income averaging?

16. T's calendar year tax liability for 19X1 (as reported on his return filed on April 15, 19X2) was $36,000. T paid $10,000 in estimated tax for 19X1 (four equal installments on the prescribed dates). Assume 19X2 is not leap year. See Form 2210.

1. Compute T's additional charge, if any, for underpayment of estimated taxes.

2. Would any such charge be deductible by T?

17. During 1977, T, the owner of a store, had the following income and expenses:

Gross profit on sales	$30,000
Income from part-time job (subject to Social Security)	4,000
Business expenses (related to store)	15,000
Fire loss on store building	1,200
Dividend income (unadjusted for any exclusion)	300
Long-term capital gain on the sale of GMC stock investment	2,000

Compute T's self-employment tax for 1977 by using Schedule SE of Form 1040.

Research Problem

Ruth Jones was divorced during 1976. She has custody over the two minor children and contributed more than one-half of their support during 1977. The divorce decree provides that her husband John is required to pay $300 per month child support and is entitled to the dependency exemptions for income tax purposes. John paid the child support payments for the first six months of 1977. However, John became unemployed and is now a hopeless alcoholic. He was, therefore, unable to pay any child support payments during the last six months of 1977. Ruth has little hope of receiving any future payments or a recovery of the unpaid amounts.

a. Is Ruth entitled to claim the children as dependents in 1977?

b. Is Ruth entitled to claim the children in 1978 and future years if the divorce decree is not modified and John does not make any child support payments?

Chapter 11

TAX CREDITS

TAX POLICY
CONSIDERATIONS

Tax credits have become increasingly popular during the 1960's and 1970's. Congress has enacted various tax credit measures to stimulate the economy or to provide equity for various types of tax-payers.

INVESTMENT TAX CREDIT

The investment tax credit was initially enacted in 1962 and has been a significant fiscal policy tool for controlling the economy. The logic for providing a tax credit upon the purchase of certain types of business property is that businesses will be encouraged to expand. The resulting expansion stimulates the economy and generates additional employment. The investment credit has been suspended and reenacted several times in response to varying economic conditions and political pressures. In 1971, the rationale for its restoration was to create jobs and the Act was entitled the "Job Development Investment Credit".

FOREIGN TAX CREDIT

Both individuals and corporations are eligible to claim a credit for certain taxes paid to foreign countries. The foreign tax credit is intended to alleviate the problem of double taxation for foreign income taxes paid by U.S. citizens or domestic corporations since the foreign income is also subject to U.S. Federal Income Tax.

TAX CREDIT FOR THE ELDERLY

Elderly individuals may be entitled to a 15 percent tax credit. Retirement income credit provisions were originally enacted in 1954 principally to provide tax relief for certain elderly taxpayers who were not receiving substantial tax-free social security benefits. In 1976, these provisions were substantially modified.

WORK INCENTIVE PROGRAM CREDIT

The Revenue Act of 1971 created a 20 percent tax credit for wages paid to certain employees hired under the Federal Work Incentive Program. The credit has also been extended to Federal recipients of the Aid to Dependent Children Program. The purpose of this credit is to foster training and employment for unemployed and welfare recipients.

GENERAL TAX CREDIT

In 1975, a general tax credit was enacted to allegedly increase the buying power of low-income taxpayers who were hurt by rampant inflation during this period.

EARNED INCOME CREDIT

Congress enacted a 10 percent credit on earned income in 1975 for low income workers who maintain a household for dependent children. This credit may be characterized as a form of negative income tax since the credit is refundable to the taxpayer if he or she has no tax liability. Its rationale was to offset substantial increases in FICA taxes which had been enacted during this period.

FEDERAL GASOLINE AND OIL TAX CREDIT

Certain taxpayers are eligible to receive a credit of 2 cents per gallon for gasoline purchased for nonhighway use, e. g., gasoline for a motor boat, power lawn mower, etc. This provision was intended as an equity measure since a portion of the Federal gasoline tax is earmarked for the construction and maintenance of our Federal highways.

CREDIT FOR CONTRIBUTIONS TO CANDIDATES FOR POLITICAL OFFICES

Individuals may claim a limited tax credit for certain political contributions. This credit was enacted in 1971 to broaden the base of citizen participation in political campaigns.

TAX CREDIT FOR NEW HOUSING

In 1975, Congress attempted to stimulate the construction of new housing by providing a 5 percent tax credit with a ceiling limitation of $2,000 to individuals who acquired a new principal residence. This credit is no longer applicable.

CREDIT FOR CHILD AND DEPENDENT CARE EXPENSES

For taxable years after 1975, a tax credit replaces a former tax deduction for qualified child and dependent care expenses. These provisions reflect the social desirability of encouraging taxpayers to provide care for their children while they work. The credit also provides some measure of relief for "working wives" who have assumed an increasing role in the workforce during recent years.

JOBS TAX CREDIT

The Tax Reduction and Simplification Act of 1977 provides employers with a tax credit based upon wages paid to new employees. Its intent is to reduce overall unemployment in the U.S. economy.

CREDIT VERSUS A DEDUCTION

A tax credit should not be confused with an income tax deduction. Certain deductions for individuals are permitted as a deduction from gross income in arriving at adjusted gross income, e. g., business expenses or certain unreimbursed employee expenses. Additionally, individuals are permitted to deduct nonbusiness personal and investment related expenses *from* adjusted gross income. A tax credit is generally worth substantially more to a taxpayer since the credit is directly offset against the tax liability whereas a deduction merely reduces taxable income.

Example 1. Comparative Benefits of a Credit Versus a Deduction:

Facts:

1. A taxpayer has paid a 10 percent Japanese withholding tax in the amount of $30.00 on royalties for books published in that country.

2. This type of item qualifies as either a business deduction or tax credit.

3. The taxpayer's marginal (effective) tax rate is 50 percent.

Use of a tax as a

a.	Business deduction	$30.00
	tax rate	50 per cent
Resulting reduction in tax		$15.00
b.	Value of direct tax credit	$30.00

The remainder of this chapter is devoted to a detailed coverage of the various types of tax credits.

SPECIFIC TAX CREDIT PROVISIONS

INVESTMENT TAX CREDIT

Problems of Tax Compliance. The investment credit provisions have been suspended and reinstated several times since the original passage of these provisions in 1962. Changes have also been made in the definition of what constitutes "qualified investment credit property". In addition, the effective rates and unused credit carryforward rules have been modified.

These changes in the tax law have created a "nightmare" for tax practitioners. Both suspension and reenactment of the investment credit have necessitated the adoption of special transitional rules relative to qualification and to the carryback and carryover of unused credits. Further complications have been created by modifications as to what constitutes qualified investment credit property and changes in the carryback and carryover rules. As a result of these changes the Code contains numerous provisions relative to specific suspension and reenactment years and other transitional rules.

Current Provisions. A 10 percent credit is generally permitted for qualified investment in investment credit property which is acquired and placed into service or is constructed during the period beginning on January 22, 75 and ending on December 31, 80. The Tax Reduction Act of 1975 raised the rate from 7 percent to 10 percent for this period and the 10 percent rate has been extended through

Act.[1] Due to the change in rates from 7 to 10 percent, the former rate may still apply to certain types of qualified property.[2]

Special Rules and Exceptions. Special rules are provided for public utilities. In general, such companies are permitted a 10 percent credit (formerly 4 percent) and the maximum ceiling limitations (subject to being phased out beginning in 1977) are increased to $25,000 of the tax liability plus 100 percent (formerly 50 percent) of the tax liability in excess of $25,000.[3] Utilities were granted special treatment due to their recent economic difficulties and the need for raising significant amounts of new capital to provide for replacement and capital expansion requirements.

For all taxpayers, an 11 percent credit may be claimed in lieu of the regular 10 percent rate if the extra amount is contributed to an employee stock ownership plan.[4] For years beginning in 1977, an additional credit of ½ of one percent is permitted if additional amounts of employer securities are transferred to the plan and an equal amount is contributed by employees.[5] If additional amounts are contributed, however, certain requirements must be met in order to prevent recapture of such amounts.

A taxpayer may now elect to claim the investment credit for progress payments for property that takes two or more years to construct if the property has a useful life of at least seven years.[6] Previously, the credit was not available until the property was placed into service. Special transitional rules are provided if this election is made.[7]

Qualifying Property. Qualifying property for 1971 and subsequent years (§ 38 property) includes the following types of property which is placed into service during the year:[8]

1. Tangible personal property which is depreciable and has a useful life of at least 3 years.

2. Other tangible depreciable property (excluding buildings and their structural components) with a useful life of at least 3 years if used in manufacturing, production, or extraction, or of furnishing transportation or certain public utility services.[9]

---

1. § 46(a)(1); Act § 802 amending § 46(a); Tax Reform Act of 1976.

2. § 46(a)(1)(D); Act § 802(a)(2)(C) and (D) amending § 46(a)(2).

3. § 46(a)(6).

4. Act § 301(d) amending § 46(a); Tax Reduction Act of 1975.

5. Act § 803(d) amending § 46(a); Tax Reform Act of 1976.

6. § 46(d)(1).

7. § 46(d)(7).

8. § 48(a).

9. This category also includes certain research and bulk storage facilities.

3.   New elevators and escalators.

4.   Coin-operated vending and washing machines and dryers.

5.   Livestock (excluding horses).

The credit is also available for:

1.   Assets accessory to a business, e. g. grocery store counters, printing presses, individual air-conditioning units.

2.   Assets of a mechanical nature even though located outside of a building, e. g. gasoline pumps.

The investment credit is *not* permitted for the following types of property:

1.   Intangible property, e. g. patents, copyrights, etc.;

2.   Buildings and their structural components (including central air-conditioning, plumbing and wiring units) ;

3.   Property (other than coin-operated vending and washing machines and dryers) used primarily for nontransient lodging (such as the operation of an apartment building) ;

4.   Certain property used outside of the U.S.;

5.   Foreign-produced property whenever the temporary import surcharge is in effect (as determined by the President of the U.S.) ;

6.   Property such as rehabilitation expenditures for low-income housing, pollution-control facilities, etc., where a special 5-year amortization provision is elected. For pollution control equipment placed in service after 1976, the investment credit is available for the portion being amortized under the 5-year provision; [10] and

7.   Certain property leased by noncorporate lessors.

§ 1.48–1 of the Regulations contains detailed rules and examples of eligible and excluded property and should be referred to for resolving specific questions.

Investment Credit Limitations. The full amount of the investment credit is allowed (subject to certain limitations) for the acquisition of qualified property which has a useful life of 7 years or longer. The taxpayer is required to use the same useful life for investment credit purposes which is used for computing depreciation.[11]   For property which has a useful life of less than 7 years, the following percentages are applied which reduce the amount of "qualified investment":

---

10. Act § 2112(a) amending § 48(a)(8).   **11.**   § 46(c)(2).

Example 2. Computation of Qualified Investment Credit Property:

Business Qualified Property	Useful Life	Adjusted Cost Basis	Percent	Qualified Investment	Range Specified By Law
Office Equipment	7	$10,000	100	$10,000	7 years or more
Factory Machinery	6	30,000	66⅔	20,000	5 or more but less than 7
Automobiles	3	18,000	33⅓	6,000	3 or more but less than 5

$36,000 × 10 percent =

$3,600 credit subject to ceiling limitations

Under prior law the comparable useful life ranges were 4–6 years, 6–8 years and 8 years or longer.

Qualified investment property is the aggregate of new § 38 property which is placed into service during the year.[12] Used § 38 property is includible in the above calculation but the maximum amount of cost (before reduction by the applicable percentages) is limited to $100,000.[13] The cost basis of § 38 property is determined under the general rules for determining the basis of property. If § 38 property is acquired in a like-kind exchange, the cost basis of the newly acquired property is equal to the adjusted basis of the property exchanged plus any cash paid.[14] Special apportionment and limitation rules are provided for married individuals filing separately, controlled corporate groups and partnerships.[15] Form 3468 is used to compute the allowable credit.

Example 3. T acquired *used* machinery for use in his business. The cost of such property was $200,000 and a useful life of 8 years was assigned to the equipment. Only $100,000 of the machinery qualifies as investment credit property due to the $100,000 limitations on used property.

Example 4. T traded in an automobile used in his business for a new business automobile which had a fair market value of $7,000 and paid the dealer $4,000. The basis of the automobile exchanged was $1,000. Since the transaction qualifies as a like-kind exchange, (see Chapter 13 on Nontaxable Exchanges) the basis of the new automobile is equal to the basis of the old automobile of $1,000 plus $4,000 boot given or $5,000. The cost for investment credit purposes is also $5,000.

12. Regs. § 1.46–3(a)(1).

13. § 48(c)(2).

14. Regs. § 1.46–3(c)(1).

15. *Supra*, note 13.

Ceiling Limitations. The maximum allowable investment credit in any taxable year is 100 percent of the first $25,000 tax liability plus 50 percent of the tax liability in excess of $25,000.[16] The limitation is imposed on the amount of the tax liability computed in the regular manner but without regard to any minimum tax (§ 56) or other special taxes such as the accumulated earnings tax which have been imposed. This regular tax liability is reduced by certain tax credits for computing the limitation, e. g. foreign tax credits. Controlled corporate groups are required to apportion the basic $25,000 limitation and the basic limitation for married taxpayers filing separately is $12,500 unless one of the spouses is not entitled to investment credit.

Example 5.   Computation of Unused Investment Credit:

Qualified investment $600,000 × 10 percent =	$60,000
Tax liability (without regard for special taxes) =	50,000
Total credit allowed $25,000 + 50 percent × $25,000 =	37,500
Unused investment credit	$22,500

Treatment of Unused Investment Credits. Unused credits are initially carried back 3 years (to the earliest year in the sequence) and are applied to reduce any amounts in excess of the ceiling during these years. Thus, the taxpayer may receive a refund of tax from the benefits of such carryback. Any remaining unused credits are then carried forward for 7 years.[17] Carryovers from pre-1971 years are permitted a 10 year carryover and are used up before applying the regular credits for the carryover year.[18] For 1976 and later years, a FIFO method is applied to the carryovers, carrybacks and utilization of credits earned during a particular year.[19] The oldest credits are used first in determining the amount of investment credit.

Example 6.

1. Investment Credit carryovers:

pre 1971 years	$4,000
1975	6,000
1976	2,000

2. 1977 investment credit earned

10 percent × $400,000 qualified investment	40,000

3. Total credit allowed in 1977 — 50,000

Applied against:

pre 1971 carryovers	(4,000)
1975	(6,000)
1976	(2,000)

4. Remaining credit allowed — 38,000

Applied against:

1977 investment credit earned	(38,000)
1977 unused amount carried forward to 1978	$2,000

16.   § 46(a)(2) through (5).

17.   § 46(b).

18.   § 46(b)(1) through (3).

19.   Act § 802 amending § 46(a)(1).

The FIFO method should minimize the potential for a loss of investment credit benefit due to the expiration of credit carryovers since the earliest years are now used before the earned credit for the taxable year.

Recapture of Investment Credit. If investment credit property is prematurely disposed of or ceases to be qualified investment property, investment credit which was previously taken is recaptured in part or in full.[20] In effect the tax liability in the year of premature disposition is increased by the difference between the investment credit taken and the credit based upon the actual useful life. Recapture provisions were included in the law to prevent taxpayers from assigning an artificially long useful life to qualified investment credit property.

Example 7. Recapture of Investment Credit:

Machinery—Cost $10,000 assigned a seven year life
   in 1972 $10,000 × 7 percent = $700.00
The machinery is sold in 1977 after 6 years
   Recomputed credit   66⅔ percent × $10,000 × 7 percent   (466.67)
Recaptured amount—included in 1977 tax $233.33

Note: The recapture percentage is consistent with
      the amount of credit originally taken, e. g.
      7, 10 or 11 percent.

Recapture is generally triggered under the following circumstances.[21]

1. Disposition of property through sale, exchange or sale-and leaseback transactions;

2. Retirement or abandonment of property or conversion to personal use;

3. Gifts of § 38 property;

4. Transfers to partnerships and corporations unless certain conditions are met; and

5. Like-kind exchanges (certain exceptions are provided).

Exceptions are provided for in the Code to prevent inequities. The following transactions illustrate some situations where the recapture provisions are not applicable:

1. A transfer of property to an estate by reason of death.[22]

2. A transfer pursuant to certain tax-free reorganizations.[23]

3. A liquidiation of a subsidiary corporation where the assets are transferred to the parent without receiving a step-up in basis.[24]

---

20. § 47(a)(1).

21. Regs. § 1.47–2.

22. § 47(b)(1).

23. § 47(b)(2).

24. *Ibid.*

WORK INCENTIVE PROGRAM CREDIT

The Work Incentive Program Credit is equal to 20 percent of wages paid to certain employees hired under the Federal Work Incentive Program (WIN).[25] The credit has been extended to Federal recipients of the Aid to Dependent Children Program. The credit is based upon 20 percent of the WIN expenses paid or incurred during the first 12 months of employment.

The limitations and carryback-carryover provisions of the WIN tax credit are similar but not identical to the investment credit provisions, e. g. the overall limit in any one year is $50,000 of the tax liability plus 50 percent of the tax liability in excess of $50,000 (after deducting foreign tax and investment credits). Unused credits are carried back 3 years and forward 7 years.

The WIN credit may be recaptured if the employer terminates the employee during the first 180 days of employment. Specific exceptions are, however, provided for terminations due to reasonable cause.[26]

EARNED INCOME CREDIT

The earned income credit was originally enacted in 1975 and has been extended through 1978.[27] Since the credit is a form of negative income tax, i. e., a refundable credit for taxpayers who do not have a tax liability, a tax return must be filed (even though not required) to obtain the tax benefits of the credit.

The maximum credit is 10 percent of earned income up to $4,000 or a credit of $400.[28] The amount of credit is reduced if the taxpayer's earned or adjusted gross income is greater than $4,000 so that the credit is completely eliminated at $8,000.

Example 8. Earned Income Credit:

Salaries and wages (earned income)	$6,000
Interest and dividend income	1,000
Adjusted gross income	$7,000
Maximum credit 10 percent × $4,000 earned income	$ 400
Less: 10 percent × the greater of earned income or adjusted gross income (greater of $6,000 or $7,000) less $4,000 ($7,000 – $4,000 × 10 percent)	(300)
Earned income credit	$ 100

To be eligible for the credit an individual must maintain a household which is the principal abode of a dependent child who is under

25. §§ 40, 50A and 50B.

26. Regs. § 1.50A–3(a)(1)(ii).

27. Act § 103b amending § 209(b) of the Tax Reduction Act of 1975, as amended by § 401(c) of the Tax Reform Act of 1976.

28. § 43(a).

19 or is a student or a disabled adult child.[29] Married individuals must file a joint return in order to receive the benefits from the credit.[30]

TAX CREDIT FOR THE ELDERLY

As previously mentioned, retirement income credit provisions were originally enacted in 1954 to provide tax relief for certain elderly taxpayers who were not receiving substantial benefits from tax-free social security payments. In 1976, the retirement income credit provisions were substantially modified. Unfortunately, many elderly taxpayers receive social security benefits in excess of the ceiling limitations and continue to be ineligible to receive the credit. The newly revised eligibility requirements and the tax computation are highly complicated. Therefore, the Code now permits an individual to elect to have the IRS compute his tax and the amount of the tax credit.[31]

The general approach of § 37 is illustrated in Example 9.

Example 9. Tax Credit for the Elderly:

The credit is based upon an initial $2,500* (designated as a § 37 amount)

> Less: social security, railroad retirement and certain excluded pension benefits *and* one-half of the taxpayer's adjusted gross income in excess of $7,500.**

The remaining amount is multiplied by 15 percent to compute the credit.

* The amounts are $2,500 for a single individual and married individuals filing a joint return where only one spouse is 65 or older; $3,750 for married individuals filing jointly (both 65 or older) and $1,875 for married individuals filing separately.

** This amount is $10,000 for married taxpayers filing jointly and $5,000 for married individuals filing separately.

Special Rules. A multitude of special rules are provided by the Code including the following: [32]

> 1. The initial amount of the credit is $2,500. However, if both spouses who are 65 or older file a joint return, a credit of $3,750 is permitted on the combined retirement income of both spouses. To qualify for the credit, married taxpayers must generally file a joint return. However, if the married

---

29. § 43(c). See § 44A(f)(1) for the definition of head of household status and § 151(e)(1)(B) for the dependency rules.

30. § 43(d).

31. § 6014.

32. For 1976 only, retired individuals may compute the tax credit based upon the pre-1976 retirement income credit rules; Act § 403 of The Tax Reduction and Simplification Act of 1977.

individuals live apart, under certain conditions they may each claim a maximum credit of $1,875 under separate returns.

2. Special rules for determining the credit are provided for taxpayers who receive pensions from a Federal, state, or local government retirement system.[33]

3. The maximum amount of the credit is reduced by F.I.C.A. and Railroad Retirement benefits received and by pension amounts which are excludible from gross income.

4. All types of taxable income now qualify for the tax credit, e. g. salaries, wages and investment income whereas under prior law earned income was generally excluded.

5. The maximum credit taken may not exceed the taxpayer's tax liability after reduction by the general tax credit.

Example 10. H and his wife W are both over 65 and receive F.I.C.A. benefits of $2,000 in 19X1. On a joint return H and W reported adjusted gross income of $12,000.

Initial (§ 37 amount)		$3,750.00 [34]
Less:		
1. F.I.C.A.	$2,000	
2. ½ × the excess of adjusted gross income of $12,000 over $10,000	= 1,000	(3,000.00)
Balance subject to credit		$ 750.00
Tax credit allowed $750 × 15 percent		$ 112.50

FOREIGN TAX CREDIT

Both individual taxpayers and corporations may claim a foreign tax credit on income earned and subject to tax in a foreign country or U.S. possession.[35] As an alternative to the credit a taxpayer may claim a deduction under § 164 of the Code. In most instances the tax credit is advantageous since it is a direct offset against the tax liability.

The purpose of the foreign tax credit was to eliminate double taxation, e. g. income earned in a foreign country is subject to both U.S. and foreign taxes. However, the operation of the ceiling limitation formula may result in some form of double taxation or taxation at rates in excess of U.S. rates, e. g. where the foreign rate of tax is in excess of U.S. rates. In addition, recent changes in the law now place added restrictions upon the benefits of the credit.

Computation. For years ending after 1975, taxpayers are required to compute the foreign tax credit based upon an "overall"

---

33. § 37(e).   **35.** § 901(b).

34. § 37(b)(2).

1980 by the 1976 limitation.[36]   Formerly, a taxpayer could elect to compute the credit on a "per country" basis.   The "per country" method is still available for taxpayers with income from U.S. possessions.

Example 11.   Computation of the Foreign Tax Credit:

Facts: 1.   Corporation A has $10,000 income from Foreign country Y which imposes a 15 percent tax rate and $20,000 from country Z which imposes a 50 percent tax.

2.   Corporation A has taxable income of $70,000 from within the U. S.   U. S. tax before the credit is $34,500.

Overall Limitation:

$$\frac{\text{Foreign income}}{\text{Total U. S. taxable income}} \quad \frac{\$30,000}{\$100,000} * \times \$34,500 \text{ (U.S. Tax before}$$
$$\text{F.T.C.)} = \$10,350$$

Foreign taxes imposed $1,500 + $10,000 = $11,500

Total foreign tax credit $10,350

* For individual taxpayers taxable income is computed without deductions for personal exemptions.

U.S. citizens working overseas are generally permitted to exclude only $15,000 of foreign earned income from gross income on their U. S. tax return.   However, such individuals must exclude a portion of the foreign taxes in computing their foreign tax credit.[37]

Example 12.   X, a U.S. citizen employed in Country Y, earned $30,000 in 1977 and paid $6,000 in foreign taxes.   Since $15,000 of the $30,000 foreign income is excluded from U.S. tax, the foreign tax which may be taken into account in applying the credit limitation is only $3,000$\left(\dfrac{\$15,000}{\$30,000} \text{ x } \$6,000 \right)$.

If any individual has earned income which is excluded under § 911(c), the U.S. tax is computed by subjecting the foreign income to U.S. tax rates that would apply if none of the foreign earned income were excluded.[38]   This requirement results in a higher tax due to the progressive U.S. tax rates.

Unused foreign taxes may be carried back 2 years and then forward 5 years.   Special transitional rules are applied for carryovers from pre 1976 years for taxpayers who were using the per-country limitation method.[39]   Form 1116 is used to compute the limitation on the amount of foreign tax credit.

36.   Act § 1031(a) amending § 904.

37.   Act § 1011(a) and (b) amending § 911(a) and § 911(c)(1); the $15,000 exclusion applies to years beginning after 1976.

38.   Act § 1011(b)(2) amending § 911(c) and adding § 911(d).

39.   § 904(e)(2).

CREDIT FOR CHILD AND DEPENDENT CARE EXPENSES

For taxable years ending after 1975, a tax credit replaces a former tax deduction for qualified child and dependent care expenses.[40] The tax credit is now of substantial benefit for working spouses who have child care expenses which were formerly not deductible due to income limitations, e. g. under the former law if gross income exceeded $35,000, the employment related expenses were scaled down or eliminated. There are now no comparable income limitations applicable to the tax credit provisions. The credit also benefits individuals who do not itemize their deductions since the former deduction was *from* AGI.

Eligibility. An individual must maintain a household for any of the following: [41]

1. A dependent child under age 15; or

2. A dependent or spouse who is physically or mentally incapacitated.

Generally, married taxpayers must file a joint return to obtain the credit.[42] In the case of a divorced taxpayer, the child care credit belongs to the divorced parent who provides custody of the child (under age 15) for more than one-half of the year.[43]

Eligible Employment Related Expenses. Eligible expenses include amounts paid for household services and care of a qualifying individual which are incurred to enable the taxpayer to be employed.[44] Child care payments to relatives do not qualify unless the relative is not a dependent of the taxpayer and the amounts paid constitute wages for F.I.C.A. purposes.

Allowable Amounts. The credit is equal to 20 percent of employment related expenses up to $2,000 for one qualifying individual and $4,000 for two or more individuals.[45] Therefore, the maximum tax credit is 20 percent x $4,000 or $800.

Special tax rules are provided for individuals who have limited amounts of earned income, e. g. less than $2,000 or $4,000 and taxpayers with nonworking spouses who are disabled or are full-time students.[46] For example, if a nonworking spouse is physically or mentally disabled or is a full-time student, the spouse is deemed to have earned income of $166 per month or $333 per month if there are two or more qualifying individuals in the household.

Example 13. X and Y are married and file a joint return. They have two children under 15 and incurred $6,000 of child care ex-

40. Act § 504 repealing § 214 and adding § 44A.

41. § 44A(c).

42. § 44A(f)(2), (3) and (4).

43. § 44A(f)(5).

44. § 44A(c)(2).

45. § 44A(d).

46. § 44A(f)(7) and (8).

penses of a housekeeper during the year. X and Y were fully employed and each earned $10,000 during the year.

X and Y are entitled to a tax credit of 20 percent x $4,000 or $800 for the tax year.

Example 14. W has two children under 15 and worked full-time while her spouse H was attending college for 10 months during the year. W earned $10,000 and had $5,000 of child care expenses. H is deemed to be fully employed and to have earned $333 for each of 10 months or a total of $3,330.

H and W are therefore entitled to a tax credit of 20 percent x $3,330 or $666 for the year.

GENERAL TAX CREDIT

A general tax credit is permitted equal to the greater of (a) 2 percent of taxable income up to $9,000 (e. g. 2 percent x $9,000 = $180) or (b) $35 for each personal and dependency exemption.[47] The general tax credit, which was originally enacted in 1976, has been extended through 1978. If a taxpayer uses the tax tables, the general tax credit is not computed separately since the credit is automatically built into these tables.[48] In addition, a married taxpayer who files a separate return must use the $35 per exemption method in computing the credit.[49]

Example 15. T has a spouse, age 62, and 6 dependent children. T is 66 years old and is blind. T files a joint return with his spouse and claims 10 personal and dependency exemptions, i. e., T, age, blindness, spouse and 6 dependents. T and his spouse's combined taxable income is $50,000.

Their general tax credit is $35 x $10 or $350 since $350 is greater than 2 percent x $50,000 which is limited to a ceiling amount of $180.

POLITICAL CAMPAIGN CONTRIBUTIONS

Individuals may elect a tax credit amounting to one-half of certain political contributions. This credit is limited to $25 ($50 on a joint return). As an alternative the taxpayer may take a deduction (from AGI) for such contributions up to $100 ($200 on a joint return).[50] Contributions qualify for the credit or deduction if they are made to the following persons or organizations: [51]

1. A candidate for nomination to any Federal, state or local office;

47. § 42(a); for years prior to 1977 individuals were not permitted the $35 credit for blindness and old age exemptions; Act § 101(c) amending § 42(a) of the Tax Reduction and Simplification Act of 1977.

48. Act § 101(c) adding § 42(e); Tax Reduction and Simplification Act of 1977.

49. § 42(c).

50. § 41.

51. § 41(c).

2. A political campaign committee sponsoring such individual; and

3. A national, state, or local committee of a national political party.

Individuals who do not itemize their deductions will use the tax credit since the deduction is *from* AGI. However, the deduction is preferable for high income bracket taxpayers who itemize their deductions.

> **Example 16.** H and W are married and file a joint return. H made a $300 political contribution to a candidate for Federal office during the year. H and W's marginal tax rate is 50 percent. The allowable deduction is $200 since a joint return was filed. The allowable tax credit is $50. The benefit from the tax deduction is 50 percent x $200 or $100 (if H and W itemize their deductions) versus a $50 benefit from the tax credit.

CREDIT FOR NONHIGHWAY USES OF GASOLINE AND LUBRICATING OIL

Taxpayers may claim a tax credit for Federal excise taxes for the nonhighway use of gasoline, special fuels and lubricating oil.[52] The credit is 2 cents per gallon for gasoline and 6 cents per gallon for lubricating oil.[53] Nonhighway use includes farming activities, operating a motor boat, power lawn mower, etc.

JOBS TAX CREDIT

The tax law provides a jobs tax credit based upon 50 percent of the first $4,200 of wages paid to each new employee providing certain other requirements are met.[54] The credit is generally based on the total Federal Unemployment Act wages (levied on amounts up to $4,200 of an employee's wages) in excess of 102 percent of FUTA wages paid during the prior year.[55]

> **Example 17.** XYZ Company had 4 employees who were paid $7,000 each during 1976. In 1977, the company retained the four employees and added 2 new employees at $7,000 per year. The credit may not exceed to 50 percent x [$4,200 x 6 employees (1977 FUTA wages) less 102 percent x $4,200 x 4 employees (1976 FUTA wages)] or $25,200 − $17,136 x 50 percent = $4,032. Note a further limitation based upon total wages (explained below) may also apply.

---

52. § 39.

53. *Your Federal Income Tax,* IRS Publication, 1977 Edition, p. 161.

54. Act § 200 adding § 44B and § 51; Tax Reduction and Simplification Act of 1977.

55. Act § 202(b) adding § 51(a).

A further limitation was placed upon the jobs credit to prevent employers from artificially increasing the unemployment insurance wages by dividing full-time jobs into part-time or part-year jobs.[56] The amount of the allowable credit cannot exceed 50 percent x total wages (without regard to FUTA wages) over 105 percent of the total wages of the prior year.[57]

> **Example 18.** Assume the same facts as in the prior example. The allowable jobs tax credit cannot be greater than 50 percent x $7,000 x 6 employees less 105 percent x $6,300 x 4 employees or $42,000 − $29,400 x 50 percent = $6,300. In this example, the $6,300 second limitation does not apply since it is greater than the initial amount of the credit. The credit should, therefore, be $4,032.

A further limitation upon the jobs credit is that the maximum allowable credit is $100,000 per year for an employer.[58] The 1977 Act also provides an additional 10 percent tax credit for newly hired handicapped individuals who received vocational rehabilitation.[59] This additional credit, however, is limited to one-fifth of the 50 percent jobs credit which would have been allowed before applying the $100,000 limitation.

> **Example 19.** Assume the same facts as Example 17 except that one of the two new workers hired in 1977 was a handicapped individual who received vocational rehabilitation. The additional credit for the handicapped worker is 10 percent x $4,200 or $420. This amount cannot exceed one-fifth x $4,032 or $806.40.

Computation of the Jobs Credit. The actual FUTA wage limits have been increased to $6,000 for 1978 whereas the amount of tax credit is based upon $4,200. However, the IRS' 1978 FUTA forms are expected to include a line for wages over $4,200 as well as wages over $6,000.[60] Therefore, in computing the tax credit it should be helpful to refer to the FUTA forms for the necessary information relative to wages paid.

Loss of Wage Expense Deduction. The overall benefits from this credit are lessened by the requirement that the employer's deduction for wages paid must be reduced by the amount of the credit. Thus, the benefits are reduced by 48 percent for a corporation whose effective rate is 48 percent.

TAX PLANNING CONSIDERATIONS

INVESTMENT CREDIT

The optimal utilization of investment credits including unused carryovers should be considered by management in the formulation

---

56. S.Rep.No.95–66, 95th Cong., 1st Sess. 67, 1977.

57. Act § 202(b) adding § 51(c).

58. Act § 202(b) adding § 51(d).

59. Act § 202(b) adding § 51(e).

60. *Supra*, note 56 at p. 67.

of capital expenditure and project abandonment decisions. Companies who are frequently subject to the ceiling limitations should be particularly aware of the potential for losing part or all of the tax benefits from investment credit due to the expiration of loss carryovers. It should also be noted that if a company incurs net operating losses which are carried back to prior years, the previously allowed investment credits for such prior years may be scaled down or lost.

FOREIGN TAX CREDITS

Individuals who are intending to take a job assignment in a foreign country and companies who have international operations should consider the related income tax effect. Recent tax changes limit the amounts of foreign income which may be excluded from U.S. tax to $15,000 for years beginning in 1977. Also, the foreign tax credit for such individuals will now be scaled down since the foreign income which is exempt from U.S. tax is no longer used in the computation of the foreign tax credit. Companies should consider the adoption of an equitable reimbursement policy for employees who are given a foreign assignment. Otherwise, such individuals may be subject, in part, to the effects of double taxation.

CREDIT FOR CHILD AND DEPENDENT CARE EXPENSES

Upper-middle and upper income level taxpayers, who were formerly ineligible for a child care deduction due to the ceiling limitations, may now qualify for the tax credit. Thus, if a nonworking spouse is considering full-time employment or if the nonworking spouse is attending college on a full-time basis, the availability of the child-care credit should not be overlooked.

JOBS TAX CREDIT

Employers should evaluate their manpower needs relative to the jobs credit. To be eligible for the credit, an expanding workforce is required.

PROBLEM MATERIALS

Questions for Class Discussion

1. Discuss the underlying rationale for the enactment of the following tax credits:

   a. Investment credit;

   b. Foreign tax credit;

   c. Tax credit for the elderly;

   d. General tax credit;

    e.   Earned income credit;

    f.   Credit for child and dependent care expenses; and

    g.   Jobs credit.

2.   Which of the following is correct?

    a.   Investment credit is not available for the purchase of buildings used in a trade or business.

    b.   The useful life for investment credit property must be the same as that used for depreciation purposes.

    c.   Investment credit is allowed for a year in which the corporation incurs a net operating loss.

    d.   Unused investment credits are carried back 3 years and are generally carried forward for 7 years.

    e.   Conversion of qualified investment credit property to personal use may result in recapture of the credit in part or in full.

3.   Why has the investment credit been enacted, suspended and subsequently reenacted several times since 1962? What problems does this create for taxpayers and tax specialists?

4.   What general limitations are imposed upon the amount of investment credit which may be taken in any one year?

5.   The FIFO method is now applied to investment credit carryovers, carrybacks and the utilization of credits earned during a particular year. What effect does the FIFO method have on the utilization of investment credit carryovers?

6.   Why have special investment credit ceiling limitation and percentage rules been granted to public utilities?

7.   What limitations have been placed upon used investment credit property? Why did Congress impose such limitations?

8.   Is it possible to increase the useful life of eligible property so as to obtain maximum investment credit while using a shorter useful life for depreciation purposes?

9.   How is the investment credit computed if § 38 property is acquired in a like-kind exchange?

10.   If investment credit property is prematurely disposed of or ceases to be qualified property, how is the tax liability affected in the year of the premature disposition?

11.   What happens if a 3 year useful life is initially assigned to investment credit property, and the property is actually held for 7 years?

12.   What is a "general" tax credit? How is the credit computed if an individual uses the tax tables?

13.   Is a tax credit worth more than a tax deduction? Why?

14. Is the earned income credit a form of negative income tax? Why?

15. Which of the following is correct?

   a. Individuals who receive substantial social security payments are usually not eligible for the tax credit for the elderly since the FICA payments effectively eliminate the base upon which the credit is computed.

   b. A taxpayer may claim a foreign tax credit under § 901 or a deduction under § 164.

   c. If a U.S. citizen receives an exclusion of $15,000 of foreign earned income from his U.S. gross income, the foreign tax credit is also available for foreign taxes paid on such amounts.

   d. Taxpayers are now required to compute the foreign tax credit on a "per country" basis.

16. Discuss the requirements for obtaining a tax credit for child and dependent care expenses.

17. Do child care payments to relatives qualify for the child care credit?

18. Are political campaign contributions deductible as a deduction or as a tax credit?

19. Would a high income level individual generally receive greater benefit from a deduction or a credit? Would the same answer be true for political campaign contributions? Why?

20. Discuss the general requirements for obtaining a jobs credit. Will the credit be more beneficial to expanding or contracting businesses?

21. Is the tax credit for gasoline and lubricating oil available for an automobile acquired for personal use? Why?

Problems

1. In 19X1 XYZ Corporation made the following purchases:

	Useful Life	Cost Basis
a. New factory building	30	$600,000
b. Land for future building site	—	400,000
c. New auto and trucks used in business	4	100,000
d. Used equipment	6	80,000
e. Plant machinery (new)	8	300,000

XYZ Corporation's tax liability (before investment credit) was $30,000 during 19X1.

Compute the following:

    a.   Qualified investment in 19X1.

    b.   The credit allowed in 19X1.

2.   XYZ Corporation acquired the following new properties during 1977:

		Useful Life	Cost Basis
a.	Office equipment	8 years	$140,000
b.	Trucks	4 years	150,000
c.	Factory building	40 years	410,000
			$700,000

XYZ's tax liability for 1977 was $30,000 (before investment tax credits). XYZ has an unused investment tax credit of $18,000 from 1976 which is carried over to 1977.

    1.   Calculate the amount of allowable investment credit for 1977.

    2.   Calculate the amount of investment credit carryover to 1978 and identify the years to which the carryover relates.

3.   During the current year T sells for $10,000 some investment credit property acquired $4\frac{1}{2}$ years ago at a cost of $15,000. An investment credit of $1,050 was claimed (based on an estimated life of 10 years) in the year the property was acquired. At the time of its disposition the property has an adjusted basis of $12,000.

    1.   How much, if any, of the original credit must be recaptured?

    2.   Would your answer to (1) be any different if the property has an adjusted basis of $8,000 (instead of $12,000) at the time of its disposition?

    3.   Suppose the property was sold by the executor of T's estate four months after T's death.

4.   XYZ Corporation acquired used machinery for use in its business. Its cost was $200,000 and had a useful life of 6 years. XYZ also acquired a new machine by paying the vendor $4,000 and trading in an old machine which had an adjusted cost basis of $2,000. The new machine had a fair market value of $7,000 and a 7 year useful life. XYZ's tax liability in 19X1 (before being reduced by the investment credit) was $28,000.

    a.   Calculate the amount of qualified investment credit property.

    b.   Calculate the amount of investment tax credit allowed during 19X1.

    c.   How does the tax law treat any unused investment credit amounts during the year?

5. T is a CPA who uses his automobile totally for business purposes. On January 1, 1976 he acquired a new Lincoln for $10,-000 and used a 5-year life. T claimed investment credit on the car during 1976. On April 1, 1978 T acquired a new automobile for use in his business and kept the Lincoln for use as a second car for his wife.

   a. Calculate the amount of investment credit recapture, if any, during 1978.

   b. Would your answer be different if T traded in the Lincoln on the new car?

   c. Would your answer be different if T gave the car to his son?

6. T, a widower, lives in an apartment with 3 minor children whom he supports. T earned $7,000 wages during 19X1. He incurred $1,000 of unreimbursed employment related expenses and uses the standard deduction.

   a. Is T required to file a tax return? (See Chapter 10—Filing Requirements)

   b. Calculate the amount, if any, of T's earned income credit.

7. H and W are married taxpayers who live in an apartment. Both H and W are full-time students and have part-time jobs. Their combined gross income from these jobs was $6,000 during 19X1. H and W have no dependents; no deductions from AGI; no other sources of income, e. g. from investments; and they file a joint return.

   Calculate the amount, if any, of H and W's earned income credit.

8. H, age 67 and W, age 66 are married retirees who received the following sources of income and retirement benefits during 19X1:

a.	Fully taxable pension income from H's former employer	$ 9,000
b.	Dividends and interest (fully taxable)	2,000
c.	F.I.C.A. payments	6,000
		$17,000

   Assuming H and W file a joint return and have no deductions *for* AGI and do not itemize, are they eligible for the "Tax Credit for the Elderly"? If so, calculate the amount of the credit.

9. H, age 67 and W, age 66, are married retirees who received the following sources of income and retirement benefits during 19X1.

a.	Fully taxable pension from H's former employer	$3,000
b.	Dividends and interest (fully taxable)	8,000
c.	F.I.C.A. payments	1,500

Assuming H and W file a joint return and have no deductions *for* AGI and do not itemize, are they eligible for the "Tax Credit for the Elderly"? If so, calculate the amount of the credit.

10. During the current year T received wages of $1,400, taxable pension income of $2,000, interest income of $200, dividends from domestic corporations of $300, and F.I.C.A. benefits of $700.

    1. If T is 66 years old and is single, compute his tax credit for the elderly for the current year.

    2. If T and his spouse are both 66 years old and file a joint return, compute the tax credit for the elderly.

11. X, a U.S. citizen, had taxable income of $50,000 from sources within the U.S. and $10,000 foreign income from investments in France. X paid a tax of $2,000 to the French government. X files a joint return with his wife and they have 2 minor children. X and his spouse use the standard deduction and have no other items of income or deductions.

Compute the net tax payable if X elects to take the foreign tax credit.

12. XYZ Corporation is a U.S. corporation which has foreign operations (a division) in England. XYZ had U.S. taxable income of $200,000 which included $100,000 from the foreign division. XYZ paid foreign taxes of $60,000. XYZ's U.S. tax liability was $82,500 before deducting any foreign tax credit.

Compute the amount of XYZ Corporation's foreign tax credit.

13. H and W maintain a household for 2 minor children under age 15. H and W are employed on a full-time basis and had gross income of $60,000 during 1977. They incurred $2,000 unreimbursed employee expenses (automobile travel while attending job related meetings) and $7,000 of child care expenses. H and W file a joint return and have itemized deductions of $6,000.

    a. Calculate the amount, if any, of the credit for child care expenses.

    b. Calculate the amount, if any, of the credit if H and W had only one child.

14. H and W are married and have two dependent children under age 15. W works full time and earned $8,000 during 1977 while her husband attended college on a full-time basis for the entire year. They incurred child care expenses of $4,000 during the year; filed a joint return and used the standard deduction.

Calculate the amount, if any, of their child care credit for 1977.

15. During 19X1, X made a political campaign contribution of $400 to the next door neighbor who was running for a local political office in the community. X had adjusted gross income of $110,-

000; itemized deductions of $12,000 and personal and dependency exemptions of $3,000. X files a joint return with her spouse.

   a. If X claims a deduction for the contribution, calculate the allowable amount. Is the deduction *for* or *from* AGI?

   b. If X claims a tax credit for the contribution, calculate the amount of the credit.

   c. Should X claim a credit or a deduction?

16. Calculate the amount of the general tax credit under the following situations:

   a. H and W are married and file a joint return. They have 8 dependent children. Their combined taxable income was $12,000.

   b. H and W are married and file a joint return. H and W are both over 65 and W is legally blind. They have no dependency exemptions and their combined taxable income was $8,-000.

   c. D is an unmarried child who lives with and is supported by her father. D is attending college on a full-time basis and had gross income from wages of $1,000. Due to her personal exemption and standard deduction, D did not owe any tax.

17. XYZ Company had 4 employees who were paid $10,000 each during 1976. In 1977, the company added 3 new employees to their workforce and paid each of the seven employees $12,000 for the year. XYZ Company had taxable income of $70,000 in 1976 and $120,000 in 1977.

   a. Calculate the amount of the jobs tax credit for 1977.

   b. Calculate the amount of wage expense for 1977.

Research Problems

1. X acquired an automobile for $10,000 on January 1, 1976. During 1976 he used the automobile 50 percent for business and claimed investment credit based upon a 3 year life of $5,000 x 10 percent x $\frac{1}{3}$ or $167. In 1977 and 1978 he used the automobile only 20 percent for business and 80 percent for personal use.

   a. Is any amount of the original investment credit recaptured? If so, in what year?

   b. Would your answer be different if X continued to use the automobile for business purposes and increased its business use to 60 percent during 1979?

2. XYZ Company, a retailer, is planning to acquire a used department store for $1,200,000. The purchase price is allocated to the following items:

a.	Land	$200,000
b.	Building	400,000
c.	Components:	
	Central air conditioning	100,000
	Wiring	60,000
	Elevators	120,000
	Fixtures, lighting, etc.	80,000
	Movable partitions	40,000
	Carpeting	40,000
d.	Office furniture	60,000
e.	Storage sheds for inventory	100,000
		$1,200,000

What items, if any, will qualify for the investment credit?

Chapter 12

PROPERTY TRANSACTIONS—DETERMINATION OF GAIN OR LOSS AND BASIS CONSIDERATIONS

This chapter and the following three chapters are concerned with the income tax consequences of property transactions. The term "property transactions" includes the sale or other disposition of property. The questions to be considered with respect to the sale or other disposition of property are:

1. Is there a realized gain or loss?

2. If so, is the gain or loss recognized?

3. If the gain or loss is recognized, is it ordinary or capital?

Chapters 12 and 13 are concerned with the determination of realized and recognized gain or loss, while chapters 14 and 15 are concerned with determining whether a recognized gain or loss is ordinary or capital.

DETERMINATION OF GAIN OR LOSS

REALIZED GAIN OR LOSS

Realized gain or loss is the difference between the amount realized from the sale or other disposition of property and its adjusted basis on the date of disposition. If the amount realized exceeds the property's adjusted basis, the result is a realized gain. Conversely, if the property's adjusted basis exceeds the amount realized, the result is a realized loss.[1]

> **Example 1.** T sells X Corporation stock with an adjusted basis of $3,000 for $5,000. T's realized gain is $2,000. If T had sold the stock for $2,000 he would have had a $1,000 realized loss.

Sale or Other Disposition. The term "sale or other disposition" is defined broadly in the tax law, and includes virtually any disposition of property. Thus, transactions such as trade-ins, casualties, condemnations and bond retirements are treated as dispositions of property. The most common disposition of property arises from a sale or exchange. The key factor in determining whether a disposition has occurred is usually whether an identifiable event has occurred[2] as opposed to a mere fluctuation in the value of the property.[3]

> **Example 2.** T sells X Corporation stock which costs $3,000 for $5,000 on December 31, 19X6. This is a disposition and T realizes a $2,000 gain in 19X6.

> **Example 3.** T exchanges X Corporation stock which costs $3,000 for another taxpayer's stock in S Corporation worth $5,000 on December 31, 19X6. This is a disposition and T realizes a $2,000 gain in 19X6.

> **Example 4.** T does not dispose of the X Corporation stock and it has appreciated in value by $2,000 during 19X6. T has no realized gain since the mere fluctuation in value is not a disposition or identifiable event for tax purposes.

Amount Realized. The amount realized from a sale or other disposition of property is the sum of any money received plus the fair market value of other property received.[4] The amount realized also includes amounts representing real property taxes treated under § 164(d) as imposed on the taxpayer if they are to be paid by the buyer.[5] The reason for including these taxes in the amount realized is that their payment by the purchaser is in effect an additional amount paid to the seller of the property. That is, the seller is relieved of paying the taxes in addition to receiving money or other property.

The amount realized also includes any liability on the property disposed of, such as a mortgage debt, if the buyer assumes the mort-

1. § 1001(a) and Reg. § 1.1001–1(a).

2. Reg. § 1.1001–1(c)(1).

3. *Lynch v. Turrish*, 1 USTC ¶ 18, 3 AFTR 2986, 38 S.Ct. 537 (USSC, 1918).

4. § 1001(b) and Reg. § 1.1001–1(b).

5. § 1001(b)(2) and Reg. § 1.1001–1(b)(2); See Chapter 9 for a discussion of this subject.

gage or the property is sold subject to the mortgage.[6] A legal distinction exists between the direct assumption of a mortgage and taking property "subject to a mortgage." The original mortgagee is no longer secondarily liable if the mortgage is assumed. However, if property is taken subject to the mortgage, the original party holding the mortgage may be liable if, upon default, the proceeds from the sale of the property are insufficient to pay off the mortgage.

> **Example 5.** T sells property subject to a mortgage of $20,000 to U for $50,000 cash. T's amount realized from the sale is $70,000 whether or not the mortgage is assumed by U.

The fair market value of property received in a sale or other disposition has been defined by the courts as the price at which property will change hands between a willing seller and a willing buyer where neither is compelled to sell or buy.[7] Fair market value is determined by considering the relevant factors in each case.[8] An expert appraiser is often required to evaluate these factors in arriving at fair market value. In cases where the fair market value of the property received cannot be determined the value of the property given up may be used.[9]

Finally, the amount realized is reduced by selling expenses such as advertising, commissions and legal fees relating to the disposition. The amount realized is the net amount received directly or indirectly by the taxpayer from the disposition of property regardless of whether it is in the form of cash.

Adjusted Basis. The adjusted basis of the property disposed of is its original basis adjusted to the date of disposition.[10] Original basis is the cost or other basis of the property on the date it is acquired by the taxpayer. Capital additions or recoveries of capital increase or decrease the original basis so that on the date of disposition the adjusted basis reflects the unrecovered cost or other basis of the property.[11] Adjusted basis is determined as follows:

> Cost or Other Original Basis (Date of Acquisition)
> Add: Capital Additions
> Subtract: Capital Recoveries
> = Adjusted Basis (Date of Disposition)

---

6. *Crane v. Comm.*, 47–1 USTC ¶ 9217, 35 AFTR 776, 67 S.Ct. 1047 (USSC, 1947).

7. *Comm. v. Marshman*, 60–2 USTC ¶ 9484, 5 AFTR 2d 1528, 279 F.2d 27 (CA–6, 1960).

8. *O'Malley v. Ames*, 52–1 USTC ¶ 9361, 42 AFTR 19, 197 F.2d 256 (CA–8, 1952).

9. *U. S. v. Davis*, 62–2 USTC ¶ 9509, 9 AFTR 2d 1625, 82 S.Ct. 1190 (USSC, 1962).

10. § 1011(a) and Reg. § 1.1011–1.

11. § 1016(a) and Reg. § 1.1016–1.

Capital Additions. Capital additions include the cost of capital improvements and betterments made to the property by the taxpayer.[12] These expenditures are to be distinguished from expenditures for the ordinary repair and maintenance of the property which are not capitalized or added to the original basis. The latter expenditures are deductible on a current basis if they are related to business or income-producing property.[13] Amounts representing real property taxes treated under Code Section 164(d) as imposed on the seller, but paid or assumed by the buyer, are part of the cost of the property.[14] Any liability on property transferred to the taxpayer upon purchase is also included in the original basis of the property.[15]

Capital Recoveries. Examples of capital recoveries are:

(1) *Depreciation.* The original basis of depreciable property is reduced by the annual depreciation charges while the property is held by the taxpayer.[16] The amount of depreciation which is subtracted from the original basis is the greater of the allowed or allowable depreciation on an annual basis.[17] But, in practice the allowed and allowable depreciation amounts are usually the same.

Allowed depreciation is the amount actually deducted on the taxpayer's return.[18] Allowable depreciation is the amount the taxpayer should have deducted given the useful life and salvage value of the property and the method of depreciation used.[19] The application of the greater of allowed or allowable rule is illustrated as follows:

Example 6. T purchased depreciable property on January 2, 19X6 at a cost of $100,000. The property had a 10 year useful life and no salvage value. T used the straight-line method of depreciation and deducted the following amounts of depreciation for taxable years 19X6 through 19X8:

19X6	$10,000
19X7	10,000
19X8	None

---

12. § 1016(a)(1) and Reg. § 1.1016–2(a).

13. See the discussion of capital expenditures v. repairs in Chapter 6.

14. Reg. §§ 1.1001–1(b)(2) and 1.1012–1(b).

15. See Footnote 6.

16. § 1016(a)(2) and Reg. § 1.1016–3(a)(1)(i).

17. *Ibid.*

18. But only to the extent resulting in a reduction of the taxpayer's income taxes. § 1016(a)(2)(B) and Reg. § 1.1016–3(a)(1)(i).

19. Reg. § 1.1016–3(a)(1)(ii). If no depreciation deductions have been taken by the taxpayer, the amount allowable is determined by using the straight-line method of depreciation. Reg. § 1.1016–3(a)(2)(i).

T sold the property on January 2, 19X9 for $90,000. T reported a gain of $10,000 on the 19X9 tax return (amount realized of $90,000 less adjusted basis of $80,000). The proper gain is $20,000. The reason is that the adjustment for depreciation is $30,000, the greater of allowed or allowable on an annual basis. Thus, the adjusted basis is $70,000 when the property is sold, and the gain is $90,000 less $70,000 or $20,000.[20]

(2) *Certain Corporate Distributions.* A corporate distribution to a stockholder which is not taxable is treated as a return of capital, and reduces the basis of the shareholder's stock in the corporation.[21] For example, if a corporation distributes cash dividends to its shareholders and has no earnings and profits, such distributions are treated as a return of capital.

(3) *Amortizable Bond Premium.* The basis in a bond which is sold at a premium is reduced by the amortized portion of the bond premium.[22] This rule applies to both corporate bonds (where the amortization is allowed as a deduction) and tax-exempt bonds (where the amortization is not allowed as a deduction).[23] The reason the basis of corporate bonds is reduced is that the amortization deduction is a recovery of the cost or basis of the bonds. The basis of tax-exempt bonds is reduced even though the amortization is not allowed. No amortization deduction is permitted on tax-exempt bonds since the interest income is exempt from tax and the amortization of bond interest merely represents an adjustment of the effective amount of such income. The accounting treatment of bond premium amortization is the same as for tax purposes. The amortization results in a decrease in the bond investment account. The tax treatment is illustrated in the following example:

Example 7. T purchases S Corporation bonds with a face value of $100,000 for $110,000, thus paying a premium of $10,000. The annual interest rate is seven percent and the bonds mature ten years from the date of purchase. The annual interest income is $7,000 (seven percent of $100,000) and the annual amortization deduction is $1,000. Each year the basis of the bonds will be reduced by the $1,000 premium amortization. After T holds the bonds for one year their

---

20. The taxpayer could file an amended return and claim depreciation not taken for any taxable years within the statute of limitations, which is generally three years from the date the original return was filed. § 6511 (a) and Reg. § 301.6511(a)–1.

21. § 1016(a)(4) and Reg. § 1.1016–5(a).

22. § 1016(a)(5) and Reg. § 1.1016–5(b).

23. *Ibid.*

basis will be $109,000 (original basis of $110,000 less $1,000 first year premium amortization).

RECOGNIZED GAIN OR LOSS

Recognized gain is the amount of the realized gain that is included in the taxpayer's gross income.[24] A recognized loss, on the other hand, is the amount of a realized loss that is deductible (for tax purposes).[25] As a general rule, the entire amount of a realized gain or loss is recognized.[26]

NONRECOGNITION OF GAIN OR LOSS SITUATIONS

In certain cases a realized gain or loss is not recognized upon the disposition of the property.[27] One of the exceptions to the recognition of gain or loss rule involves nontaxable exchanges which are covered in Chapter 13.[28] A second exception applies to realized losses from the sale, exchange or condemnation of personal assets as opposed to business or income-producing property, and realized gain from the sale of a residence by taxpayers 65 years of age or older.[29] A third exception is the nonrecognition of realized losses from the sale or exchange of business or income-producing property (again business or income-producing as opposed to personal assets) between certain related parties.[30]

The sale of a residence by taxpayers 65 years of age and older is covered in Chapter 13 and the nonrecognition of realized losses from sales or exchanges between related parties is discussed in this chapter.

Sale, Exchange and Condemnation of Personal Assets. As indicated above a realized loss from the sale, exchange or condemnation of personal assets, e.g. a personal residence or an automobile which is not used for business or income producing purposes, is not recognized.

If the property is not held for business or income-producing purposes, a realized loss from the disposition of the property is not recognized for tax purposes. The law provides an exception to this rule for casualty or theft losses from personal use assets. In contrast, any gain realized from the sale or other dispositon of personal use assets is fully taxable. The following examples illustrate the tax consequences of the sale of personal type assets.

---

24. § 61(a)(3) and Reg. § 1.61–6(a).

25. § 165(a) and Reg. § 1.165–1(a).

26. § 1002 and Reg. § 1.1002–1(a).

27. Reg. § 1.1002–1(b).

28. Reg. § 1.1002–1(c).

29. Reg. §§ 1.165–1(e) and 1.262–1(b)(4); § 121(a).

30. § 267(a)(1).

Example 8. T sells an automobile, which is held exclusively for personal use, with an adjusted basis of $5,000 for $6,000. T has a $1,000 realized and recognized gain.

Example 9. T instead sells the autmobile in the prior example for $4,000. T has a $1,000 realized loss, but the loss is not recognized.

RECOVERY OF COST DOCTRINE

Doctrine Defined. The recovery of cost doctrine pervades all the tax rules relating to property transactions and is a very significant doctrine with respect to these transactions. The doctrine derives its roots from the very essence of the income tax law—a tax on income. Therefore, as a general rule, a taxpayer is entitled to recover the cost or other original basis of property acquired and is not taxed on that amount.

The cost or other original basis of depreciable property is recovered through annual depreciation deductions. Thus, the basis is reduced as the cost is recovered over the period the property is held. Therefore, when property is sold or otherwise disposed of, it is the adjusted basis (unrecovered cost or other basis) which is compared to the amount realized from the disposition in determining realized gain or loss.

Relationship of the Recovery of Cost Doctrine to the Concepts of Realization and Recognition. It follows by definition that if a disposition results in a realized gain, the taxpayer has recovered more than his adjusted basis (unrecovered cost or other basis) of the property. Conversely, if a disposition results in a realized loss, the taxpayer has recovered less than his adjusted basis (unrecovered cost or other basis).

If a realized gain is not recognized, the taxpayer has recovered more than his cost for tax purposes. Conversely, if a realized loss is not recognized, the taxpayer has recovered less than his cost for tax purposes.

The general rules for the relationship between the recovery of cost doctrine and the realized and recognized gain and loss concepts can be summarized as:

Rule 1. A realized gain that is never recognized, (e.g. a portion of the realized gain on the sale of a personal residence by taxpayers 65 years of age and older is excluded from tax), results in the permanent recovery of more than the taxpayer's cost or other basis for tax purposes.

Rule 2. A realized gain whose recognition is postponed (e.g. an exchange of like-kind property under § 1031 or a replacement of a personal residence under § 1034) results in the temporary recovery of more than the taxpayer's cost or other basis for tax purposes.

Rule 3.   A realized loss that is never recognized (e.g. a nondeductible loss from the sale of an automobile held for personal use) results in the permanent recovery of less than the taxpayer's cost or other basis for tax purposes.

Rule 4.   A realized loss whose recognition is postponed (e.g. a loss which is not recognized due to a sale of property between related parties) results in the temporary recovery of less than the taxpayer's cost or other basis for tax purposes.

These rules will be illustrated in discussions to follow in this and the next chapter.

BASIS CONSIDERATIONS

DETERMINATION OF COST BASIS

The basis of property is generally its cost.[31]   Cost is the amount paid for the property in cash or other property.[32]   This general rule follows logically from the recovery of cost doctrine.   That is, the cost or other basis of property is to be recovered tax-free by the taxpayer.

A bargain purchase of property is an exception to the general rule for determining basis.[33]   The basis of property acquired in a bargain purchase is its fair market value.[34]

Example 10.   T buys a machine from his or her employer for $10,000 on December 30, 19X6.   The fair market value of the machine is $15,000.   T must include the $5,000 difference between cost and the fair market value of the machine in gross income for taxable year 19X6.   The bargain element represents additional compensation to the employee.   T's basis for the machine is $15,000, the machine's fair market value.

Identification Problems.   Cost identification problems are frequently encountered in securities transactions.   For example, the Regulations require that the taxpayer must adequately identify the particular stock which has been sold.[35]   A problem arises when the taxpayer has purchased separate lots of stock on different dates or at different prices, and cannot adequately identify the lot from which a

---

31.   § 1012.

32.   Reg. § 1.1012–1(a).

33.   Reg. §§ 1.61–2(d)(2)(i) and 1.301–1(j).

34.   *Ibid.*

35.   Reg. § 1.1012–1(c)(1).

particular sale takes place.   In this case the stock is presumed to come from the first lot or lots purchased; i.e., a FIFO presumption.[36] When securities are left in the custody of a broker, it may be necessary to provide specific instructions and receive written confirmation as to which securities are being sold.

>   **Example 11.**   T purchases 100 shares of S Corporation stock on July 1, 19X6 for $5,000 ($50 a share), and another 100 shares of the same stock on July 1, 19X7 for $6,000 ($60 a share).   She sells 50 shares of the stock on January 2, 19X8.   The cost of the stock sold, assuming T cannot adequately identify the shares sold, is $50 a share or $2,500.   This is the cost she will compare to the amount realized in determining the gain or loss from the sale.

Allocation Problems.   When a taxpayer acquires multiple assets in a lump-sum purchase it is necessary to allocate the total cost among the individual assets.[37]   Allocation is necessary because some of the assets acquired may be depreciable and others not (e.g. buildings and land); a portion of the assets acquired may be sold, or some of the assets may be capital or § 1231 assets which receive special tax treatment upon subsequent sale or other disposition.

A lump-sum cost is allocated on the basis of the fair market values of the individual assets acquired.[38]

>   **Example 12.**   T purchases a building and land for $100,000.   The fair market value of the building is $60,000 and the fair market value of the land is $40,000.   Therefore, the basis of the building is $60,000 and the basis of the land is $40,000.

Allocation is also necessary in certain nonpurchase situations such as the receipt of nontaxable stock dividends and rights under § 305(a).   §§ 307(a) and 307(b), respectively, stipulate the rules for allocation in these cases.

In the case of nontaxable stock dividends the allocation depends on whether the dividend is common stock on common stock or preferred stock on common stock.   If the dividend is common on common, the cost of the original common shares is allocated to the new total shares owned.[39]

>   **Example 13.**   T owns 100 shares of S Corporation common stock for which he paid $1,000.   He receives a 100% common stock dividend giving him a new total of 200 shares.   The cost of each

---

36. *Ibid.*

37. Reg. § 1.61–6(a) and Harris v. Comm., 71–1 USTC ¶ 9259, 27 AFTR2d, 439 F.2d 704 (CA–9, 1971).

38. Reg. § 1.61–6(a), Example (2).

39. The holding period of the new shares includes the holding period of the old shares. § 1223(5) and Reg. § 1.1223–1(e).

share after the stock dividend is $5 ($1,000 divided by 200 shares).

If the dividend is preferred on common, the cost of the original common shares is allocated between the common and preferred shares on the basis of their relative fair market values at the date of distribution.

> **Example 14.** S owns 100 shares of X Corporation stock for which she paid $1,000. She receives a 100% preferred stock dividend giving her 100 shares of common and 100 shares of preferred. The fair market values on the date of distribution of the preferred stock dividend are $30 a share for common and $20 a share for preferred. The cost of S's common after the dividend is $600 or $60 a share ($30/$50 times $1,000), and the cost of the preferred is $400 or $40 a share ($20/$50 times $1,000).

In the case of nontaxable stock rights, the cost basis of the rights is zero unless the taxpayer elects or is required to allocate a portion of the cost of the stock to the rights. The result is that the rights will either have no basis or the cost of the stock on which the rights are received will be allocated between the stock and rights on the basis of their relative fair market values.[40] The holding period of nontaxable stock rights includes the holding period of the stock on which the rights were distributed.[41] If the rights are exercised, the holding period of the newly acquired stock begins with the date the rights are exercised.[41.1]

GIFT BASIS

When a taxpayer receives property as a gift there is, of course, no cost to the recipient. However, a basis is assigned to the property received depending upon the date of the gift, the basis of the property to the donor, and the fair market value of the property.[42] Since gifts are not taxable, the property must have a basis in order to prevent the gift from being taxed indirectly in a subsequent disposition of the property.

Gifts Prior to 1921. If the gift property was acquired prior to 1921, its basis for income tax purposes is its fair market value on the date of the gift.[43]

---

40. If the fair market value of the rights is fifteen percent or more of the fair market value of the stock the taxpayer must allocate, but if the value of the rights is less than fifteen percent of the value of the stock the taxpayer may elect to allocate. § 307(b).

41. § 1223(5) and Reg. § 1.1223–1(e).

41.1 Reg. § 1.1223–1(f).

42. § 102(a).

43. § 1015(c) and Reg. § 1.1015–3(a).

Present Gift Basis Rules. The present basis rules for gifts of property may be described as follows:

(1) If the donee subsequently disposes of gift property in a transaction which results in a gain, the basis to the donee is the same as the donor's adjusted basis.[44]

Example 15. T purchased stock in 19X6 for $10,000. He gave the stock to his son, S, in 19X7 when its fair market value was $15,000. Assuming no gift tax was paid on the transfer and the property is subsequently sold by S at a gain, S's basis would be $10,000 and S would have a realized gain of $5,000.

(2) If the donee subsequently disposes of gift property in a transaction which results in a loss, the basis to the donee is the lower of the donor's adjusted basis or fair market value on the date of the gift.[45]

Example 16. T purchases stock in 19X6 for $10,000. T gives the stock to his son, S, in 19X7 when its fair market value is $7,000. S sells the stock for $6,000. S's basis is $7,000 (fair market value is less than donor's adjusted basis of $10,000) and his loss from the sale is $1,000 ($7,000 basis less $6,000 amount realized).

Note that the loss rule prevents the donee from benefiting from the decline in value while the donor held the property. That is, in the prior example, S has a loss of $1,000 and not $4,000. The $3,000 difference represents the decline in value while T held the property. It is perhaps ironic, however, that the basis for gain rule results in the donee being subject to tax on appreciation while the donor held the property.

Adjustment for Gift Tax. The previous discussion ignores the fact that gift taxes paid by the donor which are attributable to the net unrealized appreciation on the gift, are added to the basis of the gift property to the donee.[46] For example, if the donor's basis is $10,000 and the fair market value is $40,000, ¾ of the gift tax paid is added to the basis of the property. However, the amount of gift taxes when added to the donor's adjusted basis cannot exceed the property's fair market value on the date of the gift.[47]

---

44. § 1015(a) and Reg. § 1.1015–1(a)(1). See Reg. § 1.1015–1(a)(3) for cases where the facts necessary to determine donor's adjusted basis are unknown.

45. *Ibid.*

46. Act § 2005(c) amending § 1015(d) and adding § 1015(d)(6). For gifts made prior to 1977, the full amount of the gift tax paid is added to the donor's basis up to the fair market value of the property.

47. § 1015(d)(1)(A) and Reg. § 1.1015–5(a)(1)(i).

Other Rules. Two other rules relating to gift property are:

(1) The holding period of property acquired by gift begins on the date the property was acquired by the donor if the donor's adjusted basis is the basis to the donee.[48] It starts on the date of the gift if fair market value is the basis to the donee.[49] The significance of the holding period for capital assets is discussed in Chapter 14.

(2) The basis for depreciation on depreciable gift property is always the same as the basis for gain.[50] Using the higher fair market value on the date of the gift would allow the donee to escape tax on the donor's appreciation through higher depreciation deductions.

Example 17. T receives depreciable gift property with a donor's basis of $10,000 and fair market value of $7,000. The basis for gain is $10,000 and for loss is $7,000 (assume no gift taxes paid). T will depreciate the property using a basis of $10,000. Assuming a 10-year life and the straight-line method of depreciation, depreciation will be $1,000 per year. Two years after the gift, T's gain basis will be $8,000 and his loss basis will be $5,000. Neither basis can be depreciated below zero so after 7 years T's loss basis will be zero and will remain zero from then on.

The following example summarizes the basis and holding period rules for gift property:

Example 18. T acquires 100 shares of X Corporation stock on December 30, 1976 for $40,000. On January 3, 1978, when the stock has a fair market value of $38,000, T gives it to U. There is no increase in basis for a portion of the gift tax paid since the property is not appreciated.

S's basis for determining loss is $38,000 (fair market value) since the fair market value is less than the donor's adjusted basis.

1. If S sells the stock for $45,000, he has a recognized gain of $5,000. The holding period for determining whether the capital gain is short-term or long-term begins on December 30, 1976; the date the property was acquired by the donor.

2. If S sells the stock for $36,000, he has a recognized loss of $2,000. The holding period for determining whether the capital loss is short-term or long-term begins on January 3, 1978; the date of the gift.

---

48. § 1223(2) and Reg. § 1.1223–1(b)

49. Rev.Rul. 59–86, 1959–1 C.B. 209.

50. §§ 1011 and 167(g) and Reg. §§ 1.-1011–1 and 1.167(g)–1.

3. If S sells the property for $39,000, there is no gain or loss since the amount realized is less than the gain basis of $40,000 and more than the loss basis of $38,000.

PROPERTY ACQUIRED FROM A DECEDENT

The basis of property acquired from an individual who dies after 1976 is generally its adjusted cost basis to the decedent at the date of death.[51] The following exceptions are provided:

1. The basis is increased by the Federal and State Estate taxes attributable to the post 1976 appreciation on the property; [52]

2. Up to $10,000 of personal or household effects of the decedent can be valued at fair market value; [53]

3. The carryover basis of all property may be increased to $60,000 but may not exceed the fair market value of the property; [54]

   This provision applies only to small estates.

4. For the purpose of computing depreciation and *gain* on a subsequent sale or other disposition of the property, the basis is increased to the fair market value on December 31, 1976.[55] This increase in basis for computing gain is referred to as the "fresh start" adjustment.

Example 19. In 1970 D acquired securities at a cost of $200,000. These securities have a quoted price of $400,000 on December 31, 1976 and $350,000 on July 10, 1981 (the date of D's Death).

If the securities are subsequently sold by D's heir, the basis for determining gain is $400,000 (value at December 31, 1976). The basis for determining loss is the carryover basis of the decedent or $200,000.

1. If the securities are sold for $500,000, D's heir has a gain of $100,000.

2. If the securities are sold for $150,000, D's heir has a loss of $50,000.

3. If the securities are sold for $375,000, D's heir has no gain or loss since the basis for gain is $400,000 and the basis for loss is $200,000.

For property other than marketable bonds and securities, the partial step-up in basis to December 31, 1976 is deemed to have occurred uniformly over the period of time the property was held by the decedent.

---

51. Act § 2005(a) amending § 1014(d) and adding § 1023.

52. § 1023(c).

53. § 1023(b)(3).

54. § 1023(d).

55. § 1023(h).

Example 20. X acquired land for $50,000 on January 1, 1973 which was valued in the estate at $100,000 on the date of X's death—December 31, 1980. The property was held for a total of eight years, four of which were prior to December 31, 1976.

The basis to the beneficiary for determining a subsequent gain (but not loss) on the sale of the land is:

$$\$50{,}000 + \frac{\text{4 years before December 31, 1976}}{\text{8 year total holding period}} \times \$50{,}000 \text{ (appreciation)}$$

$$= \$75{,}000.$$

Prior to the Tax Reform Act of 1976, inherited property received a stepped-up basis generally equal to the fair market value of the property on the date of death. Thus, unrealized appreciation on property owned by the decedent was not subject to income tax. The 1976 changes continue to exempt unrealized appreciation from the income tax law. However, beneficiaries will now receive only a partial step-up in basis for computing depreciation and for purposes of computing gain on a future sale or other disposition of the inherited property. The exceptions to this general carryover basis rule were intended to soften the impact of the change during the period of transition.

Survivor's Share of Community Property. The surviving spouse's share of community property is not includible in the estate and does not receive any adjustment in basis in the case of a decedent dying after 1976.[56] Formerly, both the decedent's share and the survivor's share of community property had as its basis the fair market value on the date of the decedent's death.

Example 21. H and W reside in a community property state. H and W own community property (200 shares of XYZ stock) which were acquired in 1970 for $100,000. On December 31, 1976 the value of the securities was $200,000. Assume that H dies in 1981 when the securities were valued at $300,000. One one-half of the XYZ stock is included in H's estate.

If W inherits H's share of the community property, the basis for determining gain is:

1. $50,000 (W's cost of ½ of the community property) plus $100,000 (½ x $200,000)—value of XYZ stock at December 31, 1976 or a total of $150,000 for the 200 shares of XYZ Stock.

2. The basis to W for determining loss is:
    $50,000 (W's original cost of ½ of the community property) plus $50,000 (H's carryover basis in ½ of the community property) or a total of $100,000.

56. Act § 2005(a)(1) amending § 1014(d).

In a common law state, only one-half of jointly-held property is includible in the estate if a completed gift was made upon the creation of the joint interest.[57] In such event, no adjustment of the cost basis is permitted for the excluded property interest.

Example 22. Assume the same facts as in the prior example except that the property is jointly held by H and W who reside in a common law state. Also assume that H made a gift of one-half of the property when the stock was acquired. Only one-half of the XYZ stock is included in H's estate and W's basis (for determining gain) in the excluded half is not adjusted upward for the increase in value to December 31, 1976.

If jointly held *real* property was not treated as a gift (i. e., an election may be made to treat the creation of a joint tenancy in real property as a gift), the entire amount of the property is included in the estate unless it can be proved that the survivor contributed to the original purchase price.[58]

Example 23. If in the prior example, all of the property is included in H's estate because no gift was made upon the creation of the joint tenancy, W's basis for determining gain or loss is as follows:

1. Basis for gain—$200,000 (fair market value at December 31, 1976).

2. Basis for loss—$100,000 (H's cost basis which becomes the carryover basis to W).

The executor of an estate is now required to furnish both the IRS and the beneficiaries with information relative to the carryover basis of the estate property.[59]

Holding Period. If property is inherited from decedents who died prior to 1977, the holding period to the estate or the heir is deemed to be long-term regardless of the actual period held.[60] However, for property received from decedents who have died after December 31, 1976, the basis of property received is subject to the carryover basis rules under § 1023 and § 1014 basis rules do not apply.[61] Therefore, the date basis for such property should be governed by the date the property is received. Note, however that the "Technical Corrections Act of 1977," which is currently under consideration by Congress, includes an amendment which, if enacted, will correct the unintended results produced under the 1976 Act. If enacted, inherited property will be deemed to be long-term regardless of

---

57. Act § 2002(c) amending § 2040.

58. *Ibid.*

59. Act § 2005(d) amending § 6039.

60. Act § 1402(b) amending § 1223(11).

61. § 1014(d).

the holding period. The taxation of capital gains and losses is discussed in Chapter 14.

DISALLOWED LOSSES

Related Taxpayers.   § 267 provides that realized losses from sales or exchanges of property, directly or indirectly, between certain related parties are not recognized.[62] The Code indicates several types of related party transactions, but the most common involve (1) members of a family and (2) those between an individual and a corporation in which the individual owns, directly or indirectly, more than 50 percent in value of the corporation's outstanding stock.[63] Members of a family include the taxpayer's parents and grandparents, children and grandchildren, spouse, and brothers and sisters.[64] In determining whether a taxpayer owns more than 50% of a corporation's stock, stock owned directly or indirectly by the members of the family and by partners in a partnership is considered to be owned by the taxpayer.[65] Also, the taxpayer is considered to own a proportionate share of stock owned by a corporation in which he or she is a stockholder.[66] The following example illustrates the application of the constructive ownership rules:

> **Example 24.**   H owns 75% of Wesley Corporation's stock. H's wife, W, owns the remaining 25%. Wesley Corporation owns 80% of Patricia Corporation's stock. W's father owns no stock.
>
> 1.   H is considered to own 100% of Wesley Corporation's stock (75% plus W's 25%). W is considered to own 100% of Wesley Corporation's stock (25% plus H's 75%).
>
> 2.   W's father is considered to own 25% of Wesley Corporation's stock (W's 25%). W's father is *not* considered to own H's 75% because they are not related parties for purposes of § 267.
>
> 3.   H and W are both considered to own 80% of Patricia Corporation's stock, and W's father (F) is considered to own 20%:[67]

	Actual	Constructive
H	None	75% × 80% plus 25% × 80% = 80%
W	None	25% × 80% plus 75% × 80% = 80%
F	None	25% × 80% = 20%

If income-producing or business property is transferred to a related taxpayer and results in a disallowed loss, the basis of such property to the recipient is its adjusted cost basis to the transferor.

---

62.   § 267(a)(1).

63.   §§ 267(b)(1) and (b)(2).

64.   § 267(c)(4).

65.   §§ 267(c)(2) and (c)(3).

66.   § 267(c)(1).

67.   Reg. § 1.267(c)–1(a)(2).

However, if a subsequent sale or other disposition of the property results in a recognized gain, the amount of gain is reduced by the loss which was previously disallowed.[68] This right of offset is not applicable if the original sale involved the sale of a personal use asset, e. g. the sale of a personal residence between related taxpayers.

Example 25. F sells business property (adjusted basis of $50,-000) to his daughter, D, for its fair market value of $40,000.

1. F's realized loss of $10,000 is not recognized.

2. How much gain will D recognize if she sells the property for $52,000? D recognizes a $2,000 gain. Her realized gain is $12,000 ($52,000 less her basis of $40,000 (cost)), but she can offset F's $10,000 loss against the gain.

3. How much gain will D recognize if she sells the property for $48,000? D recognizes no gain or loss. Her realized gain is $8,000 ($48,000 less her basis of $40,000), but she can offset $8,000 of F's $10,000 loss against the gain. Note that F's loss can only offset D's gain. It cannot create a loss for D.

4. How much loss will D recognize if she sells the property for $38,000? D recognizes a $2,000 loss, the same as her realized loss ($38,000 less $40,000). F's loss does not increase D's loss. F's loss can only be offset against a gain. Since D had no gain, F's loss cannot be used, and therefore, is never recognized. Of course, it is assumed in this example that the property is business or income-producing to D. If not, D's $2,000 loss would be personal and not recognized.

Wash Sale. § 1091 provides that in certain cases a realized loss from the sale or exchange of stock or securities is not recognized. The wash sale provisions do not apply to gains. Specifically, if a taxpayer sells or exchanges stock or securities and within thirty days before or after the date of such sale or exchange acquires (or enters into a contract or option so to acquire) "substantially identical" stock or securities, then any loss realized from the sale or exchange is not recognized.[69] The term "acquire" means acquire by purchase or in a taxable exchange and includes an option to purchase substantially identical securities.[70] Substantially identical means the same in all important particulars. Bonds and preferred stock of a corporation are normally not considered substantially identical to the common stock of the same corporation, but if they are convertible into common stock they may be under certain circumstances.[71] Attempts to avoid the application of § 1091 by having a related taxpayer repurchase the securities have been unsuccessful.[72]

---

68. § 267(d) and Reg. § 1.267(d)–1(a).

69. § 1091(a) and Reg. § 1.1091–1(a).

70. Reg. § 1.1091–1(f).

71. Rev.Rul. 56–406, 1956–2 C.B. 523.

72. *McWilliams v. Comm.*, 47–1 USTC ¶ 9289, 35 AFTR 1184, 67 S.Ct. 1477 (USSC, 1947).

The reason for disallowing the recognition of the loss is that the taxpayer is considered to be in substantially the same economic position after the sale and repurchase as before the sale and repurchase. This rule does not apply to taxpayers engaged in the business of buying and selling securities.[73] The average investor, however, is not allowed to create losses through wash sales in order to offset his income for tax purposes.

Basis Rule. Realized loss not recognized is added to the basis of the substantially identical stock or securities whose acquisition resulted in the non-recognition.[74] In other words, the basis of the replacement stock or securities is increased by the amount of the unrecognized loss.[75] If the loss was not added to the basis of the newly acquired stock or securities, the taxpayer would never recover the entire basis of the old stock or securities. By adding the unrecognized loss to the basis of the newly acquired stock or securities the taxpayer is able to recover the cost of the new stock or securities plus the unrecovered cost or other basis of the old stock or securities. In other words, the taxpayer will have a greater loss or lesser gain from the subsequent disposition of the new stock or securities to the extent of the unrecognized loss from the wash sale.

Since the basis of the new stock or securities includes the unrecovered portion of the old stock or securities basis, the holding period of the new stock or securities begins on the date the old stock or securities were acquired.[76] The following examples illustrate the application of the wash sale rules:

Example 26. T owns 100 shares of Aristotle Corporation stock (adjusted basis of $20,000), 50 shares of which she sells for $8,000. Ten days later she purchases 50 shares of the same stock for $7,000. T's realized loss of $2,000 ($8,000 less $10,000 adjusted basis of 50 shares) is not recognized because it resulted from a wash sale. Her basis in the newly acquired stock is $9,000 ($7,000 purchase price plus $2,000 unrecognized loss from the wash sale).

In those cases where the taxpayer acquires less than the number of shares sold in a wash sale, the loss from the sale is prorated between recognized and unrecognized loss (§ 1091) on the basis of the ratio of the number of shares acquired to the number of shares sold.[77]

Example 27. In the prior example, if T had purchased 25 new shares only $1,000 of the loss would be disallowed, and the

73. Reg. § 1.1091–1(a).

74. § 1091(d).

75. Reg. § 1.1091–2(a).

76. § 1223(4) and Reg. § 1.1223–1(d).

77. § 1091(b) and Reg. § 1.1091–1(c).

basis of the new shares would be $8,000 ($7,000 purchase price plus $1,000 unrecognized loss from the wash sale).

Year-End Tax Planning Implications. Taxpayers are frequently advised to sell depreciated securities prior to the year-end to establish deductible capital losses for the current tax year. If a taxpayer has previously recognized short-term capital gains during the year, it may be desirable to offset such short-term gains with long or short-term capital losses through the sale of depreciated securities at year-end. To accomplish this result, an investor may sell a security and immediately replace it with a similar (although not substantially identical) security without violating the wash sale provisions, e. g. a sale of Bethlehem Steel common stock and a purchase of U.S. Steel common stock is not a wash sale. Also, a sale of one monthly issue of a municipal bond fund with the purchase of another monthly issue is permitted.

CONVERSION OF PROPERTY FROM PERSONAL TO BUSINESS OR INCOME-PRODUCING USE

As discussed previously, losses from the sale of personal use assets are not recognized for tax purposes, but losses from the sale of business and income-producing assets are deductible. What is to prevent a taxpayer from converting a personal asset which has declined in value to business use, and then selling it and recognizing a business loss? The law prevents this by requiring that the original basis for loss on personal assets converted to business or income-producing use is the lower of the property's adjusted basis or fair market value on the date of conversion.[78] Thus, if a taxpayer whose personal residence had an adjusted basis of $100,000 converted it to rental use when it was worth $60,000, it would have a basis of $60,000 for purposes of determining a loss from its subsequent sale. The $40,000 decline in value is a personal loss and can never be recognized for tax purposes. The gain basis for converted property is simply its adjusted basis on the date of conversion. The law is not concerned with gains on converted property because gains are recognized regardless of whether property is business, income-producing or personal.

The basis for loss is also the basis for depreciating the converted property.[79] The reason for this is to prevent the taxpayer from recovering a personal loss indirectly through depreciation of the higher original basis. Finally, after the property is converted both its loss and gain bases are adjusted for depreciation deductions from the date of conversion to the date of disposition in determining realized gain or loss. These rules only apply where a conversion from personal to business or income-producing use has actually occurred. For example, if a taxpayer owned a summer home and made no real effort to

78. Reg. § 1.165–9(b)(2).　　　　　　**79.** Reg. § 1.167(g)–1.

rent it during the other months of the year when he and his family did not occupy it, the home would be a personal asset and not converted to rental use. A conversion to rental use would require a real effort to rent or the actual renting of the property.

The following two examples illustrate the application of these rules:

Example 28. At a time when her personal residence (adjusted basis of $40,000) is worth $50,000, T converts one-half of it to rental property. At this point the estimated useful life of the residence is 20 years and there is no estimated salvage value. After renting the converted portion for five years, T sells the property for $44,000. Assume all amounts relate only to the building—the land has been accounted for separately. T has a $2,000 realized gain from the sale of the personal portion of the residence and a $7,000 realized gain from the rental portion. These gains are computed as follows:

	Personal	Rental
Original basis for gain and loss— adjusted basis on date of conversion (Fair market value is *greater* than the adjusted basis)	$20,000	$20,000
Depreciation—five years	None	$ 5,000
Adjusted basis—date of sale	$20,000	$15,000
Amount realized	22,000	22,000
Realized gain	$ 2,000	$ 7,000

As discussed in Chapter 13, T may be able to defer recognition of part or all of the $2,000 gain from the sale of the personal portion of the residence under § 1034. The $7,000 gain from the business portion is recognized.

Example 29. Assume the same facts as the prior example except the fair market value on the date of conversion is $30,000 and the sales proceeds are $16,000. T has a $12,000 realized loss from the sale of the personal portion of the residence and a $3,250 realized loss from the rental portion. These losses are computed as follows:

	Personal	Rental
Original basis for loss—fair market value on date of conversion (Fair market value is *less* than the adjusted basis)		$15,000
Depreciation—five years	None	3,750
Adjusted basis—date of sale	$20,000	$11,250
Amount realized	8,000	8,000
Realized loss	$12,000	$ 3,250

The $12,000 loss from the sale of the personal portion of the residence is not recognized. The $3,250 loss from the business portion is recognized.

PROBLEM MATERIALS

Questions for Class Discussion

1. Upon the sale or other disposition of property, what three questions should be considered for income tax purposes?

2. When will a property transaction result in a *realized* gain? A *realized* loss?

3. What is the key factor in determining whether a disposition of property has occurred?

4. What is included in the amount realized from a sale or other disposition of property?

5. What is the definition of fair market value?

6. If the buyer of property assumes the seller's mortgage, why is the amount of the mortgage included in the amount realized by the seller?

7. Explain the relationship of depreciation to adjusted basis and implementation of the recovery of cost doctrine.

8. Why is the amortization of bond premium considered a capital recovery?

9. Define recognized gain and recognized loss.

10. List the three exceptions to the recognized gain (loss) rule on property transactions.

11. Why are gains from the sale or exchange of personal assets recognized whereas losses are never recognized?

12. Discuss why the recovery of cost doctrine is central to all income tax provisions relating to property transactions.

13. When, as a general rule, does a taxpayer recover more than his cost? Less than his cost? Give some examples.

14. In a bargain purchase, how is the basis of the property determined and why is this method used?

15. Outline the general rules for determining the basis of stocks which are sold where the owner holds more than one lot of the previously owned stock.

16. How is cost allocated for lump-sum purchases?

17. Indicate three reasons an allocation of cost is necessary where there is a lump-sum purchase of assets.

18. Discuss the differences in tax treatment when stock rights are allocated a cost basis and when stock rights have no cost basis. When do each of the above situations occur?

19. Why must gifts of property be given a basis to the donee?

20. What is the basis for gifts prior to 1921? Why did Congress change the basis rules for gifts made after 1920?

21. What are the rules for determining the basis for property gifts made after 1920?

22. How is it possible to have no gain or loss recognized upon the sale of stock which was previously received as a gift?

23. How do gift taxes paid by the donor affect the income tax rules for gift property?

24. Outline the rules concerning depreciation and holding period for gift property. Why are these rules important?

25. Discuss the basis rules for inherited property. What affect will the 1976 tax reform changes have upon the recognition of gain upon subsequent sale of inherited property?

26. Discuss the differences in tax treatment between property sold prior to death and property which is inherited. Why is this important?

27. What is the holding period for inherited property. What tax consequences does this rule cause?

28. What are related party transactions and why are they important?

29. When is it possible to offset an unrecognized loss against a realized gain? Are there any exceptions? Explain.

30. What is a wash sale? Why isn't a realized loss recognized on a wash sale? How is the recovery of cost doctrine maintained?

31. What is the basis for property which is converted from personal use to business or income-producing use when there is a loss? When there is a gain? Why is there a difference? How does conversion affect depreciation and why?

32. Define the following terms:
    realized
    recognized
    adjusted basis
    capital recoveries
    capital additions
    recovery of cost doctrine

33. Discuss the similarities and differences in the tax rules for gift property and inherited property.

34. Give some examples where tax planning can be implemented relative to property transactions.

Problems

1. B sells real estate for a contract price of $50,000. Real property taxes of $1,000 for the real property tax year in which the sale occurred were previously paid by the seller. $750 of the taxes are treated under Section 164(d) as imposed upon the purchaser and he reimburses the seller in that amount in addition to the contract price.

    (a) What is the amount realized by B?

    (b) What is the purchaser's cost?

    (c) What would your answers be to (a) and (b) if the purchaser made no payment other than the contract price of $50,000?

2. S bought a rental house at the beginning of 19X0 for $16,000. Early in 19X1 he had a swimming pool built in the backyard for $5,000. Depreciation on the house is $400 a year and on the pool is $200 a year. At the beginning of 19X5 he sells the house and pool for $50,000 cash.

    (a) What is his realized gain (loss)?

    (b) If an original mortgage is still outstanding in the amount of $5,000, and the buyer assumes the mortgage, what is the realized gain (loss)?

    (c) If the buyer takes the property subject to the mortgage, what is S's realized gain (loss)?

3. J paid $108,000 for bonds with a face value of $100,000 at the beginning of 19X0. The bonds mature in ten years and pay five percent interest per year.

    (a) If J sells them for $102,000 at the beginning of 19X4, does he have a realized gain (loss)? How much?

    (b) If he trades them at the beginning of 19X6 for stock worth $105,000, does he have a realized gain (loss)? If so, how much?

4. Which of the following would definitely *not* result in a recognized gain (loss)?

    (a) S's personal residence is in the path of a new super-rapid-transit system and is condemned by the city. He receives $60,000 for the house (the adjusted basis is $80,000).

    (b) Assume the same conditions as in Part (a), except the adjusted basis is $40,000.

    (c) O sells his personal residence, which has an adjusted basis of $30,000, for $60,000.

    (d) D sells his lakeside cabin (adjusted basis $15,000) for $10,000.

5. An asset was purchased January 1, 19X0, at a cost of $10,000. The useful life of the asset is 10 years. It has no salvage value. Depreciation was deducted and allowed for 19X0 through 19X4 as follows:

19X0	$ 500
19X1	—
19X2	$1,000
19X3	$1,000
19X4	$1,000

What is the adjusted basis of the asset as of December 31, 19X4?

6. In 19X0 T purchased real property for $80,000 to be used as a factory. In addition to the purchase price T paid commissions of $2,000 and title search and legal fees of $600. The total cost of $82,600 was allocated $10,325 to the land and $72,275 to the building. Immediately, T expended $20,000 in remodeling the building. T was allowed depreciation totaling $12,000 for the years 19X0 through 19X4. In 19X3 T suffered a casualty loss to the building of $5,000 as a result of a fire not covered by insurance, and this loss was claimed as a deduction. The fire damage was not repaired. What is the adjusted basis of the property as of January 1, 19X5?

7. T acquired a building four years ago for $70,000 which was used in his business. T made certain permanent improvements at a cost of $20,000. Depreciation, computed under the straight-line method, has been claimed in the amount of $10,000. T sold the building for $100,000 cash, plus other property having a fair market value of $20,000. The buyer assumed the accrued real estate taxes of $3,000 and a mortgage of $17,000. The selling expenses were $4,000. What is T's realized gain or loss from the sale?

8. W buys an automobile from her employer for $4,000. The fair fair market value of the automobile is $10,000. Assuming that the excess amount of $6,000 represents compensation for services rendered;

(a) What is W's basis for the automobile?

(b) Why?

9. T makes the following purchases and sales of stock:

Date	No. of Shares	Company	Price	Transaction
1–1–X0	100	CL	$ 25	Purchase
6–1–X0	50	ATT	100	Purchase
11–1–X0	20	CL	20	Purchase
12–1–X0	60	CL	20	Sale
3–1–X1	40	ATT	125	Purchase
8–1–X1	30	ATT	110	Sale
1–1–X2	50	CL	30	Sale
2–1–X2	25	ATT	140	Sale

(a) What is the realized gain (loss) on each type of stock as of:

(1) 7–1–X0 (Assume that T is unable to identify the particular lots which are sold with the original purchase).

(2) 12–31–X0

(3) 12–31–X1

(4) 7–1–X2

10. S sells his truck, tools, and contract with USA, Inc. to T for $16,500. His truck has a fair market value of $4,000; his tools, $2,000; and the contract, $5,000. What is the cost basis for each of the three items to T?

11. S owns an active portfolio of stocks. During the year he received the following dividends:

(1) Fifty shares of common stock in Unsafeway on 200 common stock shares he already owns. He paid $20 a share for the original 200 shares.

(2) Ten shares of preferred stock in Xelax on 100 common stock shares for which he paid $2,500. The fair market value of the preferred stock on the date of distribution was $20 and the fair market value of the common stock was $30.

What is the basis per share for each of the common stocks and the preferred stocks?

12. P received various gifts over the years. He has decided to dispose of the following gifts:

(1) In 1919 he received a Rolls Royce worth $15,000. The donor's basis for the auto was $12,000. He sells the auto for $18,000 in 1976.

(2) In 1935 he received stock in W Company. The donor's adjusted basis was $300. The fair market value on the date of the gift was $500. P sells it for $1,000 in 1976.

(3) In 1940 he received land worth $10,000. The donor's adjusted basis was $8,000. He sells the land for $2,000 in 1976.

(4) In 1949 he received land worth $8,000. The donor's adjusted basis was $10,000. He sells it for $7,000 in 1976.

What is the realized gain (loss) from each of the above transactions? Assume that no gift tax was paid in each of the gift transactions.

13. B receives a car from T as a gift. T paid $18,000 for the car. He had used it for business purposes and deducted $3,000 depreciation up to the time he gave the car to B. The fair market value of the car is $10,000.

(a) Assuming B uses the car for business purposes, what is her depreciation basis?

(b) If the estimated useful life is three years (from the date of the gift) what is her depreciation deduction for each year? Use the straight-line method and ignore salvage value.

(c) If she sells the car one year after receiving it, what is her gain (loss) if she received $4,000?

(d) If she sells the car two years after receiving it, what is her gain (loss) if she receives $6,000?

14. K receives a gift of income-producing property which has an adjusted basis of $100,000 on the date of gift. The fair market value of the property on the date of gift is $90,000. Gift tax amounting to $2,000 was paid by the donor. K later sells the property for $95,000. Determine her recognized gain or loss.

15. T was given a residence in 19X5. At the time of the gift, it had a fair market value of $20,000 and its adjusted basis to the donor was $10,000. The donor paid a total tax of $500 on the gift. What is T's basis for gain? For loss? For depreciation if T rents out the residence?

16. T dies on 12/31/80 leaving the following estate to his wife W:

	FMV 12/31/76	FMV 12/31/80	Adjusted Cost Basis to T
1. Personal residence*	?	$100,000	$ 50,000
2. Marketable stocks	$ 30,000	50,000	20,000
3. Land**	?	50,000	40,000

* The house was owned solely by T and was acquired on 1/1/73.

** The land was acquired from T's separate funds but was held jointly with the right of survivorship to W. T and W lived in a common law state and T did not elect to pay gift tax upon the original transfer to the joint tenancy. The land was acquired on 1/1/69.

(a) What amounts are used for estate tax purposes assuming that the date of death is used as the valuation date?

(b) What is the basis of the properties to W if she disposes of the properties on 6/14/81 for the following amounts: (Assume that no estate tax is attributable to the appreciation on the properties)?

       1. Residence $120,000 (adjusted sales price)
       2. Stocks $ 40,000
       3. Land $ 20,000

(c) Calculate the gain or loss on the above sales in 1981. Are the gains or losses long or short term? (Assume that none of the gain or loss is postponed or excluded on the sale of the personal residence.)

17. K bought the Camalot Hotel for $600,000 on 1/1/77. In January, 1983, he died and left the hotel to P. K deducted $35,000 depreciation on the hotel prior to his death. The fair market value in January, 1983 was $650,000.

(a) What is the basis of the property to P?

(b) If the land is worth $200,000, what is P's depreciation basis?

18. Which of the following are related party transactions?

(a) W sells her yacht to her sister's son.

(b) W sells office equipment to San Antonio Alamo Corporation. Her husband, H, owns 12% of the shares; her son, B, owns 6%; her grandfather owns 20% and her cousin owns 15%.

(c) W sells a vacant lot to K Corporation. Her son owns 5%; her husband owns 10%; her father, 25%; and her partner owns 40%.

(d) W buys a car from Y & F Corporation. She owns 10%; her son owns 5%; her daughter owns 5%; her partner owns 20%; and XYZ Corporation owns 60% (W owns 30% of XYZ Corporation).

(e) W buys a house from her husband's father.

19. J owns four pieces of land in different parts of Alaska. Land A has an adjusted basis of $25,000; Land B, $30,000; Land C, $35,000; and Land D, $40,000. J sells Land A to his father-in-law for $20,000. He sells Land B to his sister for $35,000. Land C is sold to his partner for $25,000, and Land D is sold to his mother for $30,000.

(a) What is the recognized gain (loss) from the sale of each of the pieces of land?

(b) If J's father-in-law sells his land for $50,000, what is his recognized gain (loss)?

(c) If J's sister sells her land for $30,000, what is her recognized gain (loss)?

(d) If J's partner sells his land for $30,000, what is his recognized gain (loss)?

(e) If J's mother sells her land for $35,000, what is her recognized gain (loss)?

20. On June 15, 19X7, all of the stock of the T Corporation was owned in equal proportions by J and her partner, E. As a general rule, would losses be deductible from sales or exchanges of property made on June 15, 19X7, between:

(a) J and the T Corporation?

(b) E and the T Corporation?

21. H sells to his wife, W, for $500, corporation stock with an adjusted basis for determining loss to him of $800.

    (a) Is the loss allowable as a deduction to H?

    (b) What is W's realized gain or loss if she later sells the stock for $1,000? Her recognized gain or loss?

    (c) When does the holding period of the stock commence for W?

22. H sells to his wife, W, for $5,500, farmland with an adjusted basis for determining loss to him of $8,000.

    (a) Is the loss allowable as a deduction to H?

    (b) If W exchanges the farmland, held for investment purposes, with J, an unrelated individual, for two city lots, also held for investment purposes, what is W's basis for the city lots?

    (c) If W sells the lots for $10,000, what is her realized gain or loss? Her recognized gain or loss?

23. T sells stock with a cost basis of $10,000 to his brother for $7,600. Later the brother sells the same stock for $10,500.

    (a) What is T's recognized gain or loss?

    (b) What is the brother's recognized gain or loss when he sells the stock?

24. On December 15, 19X5 J decides to revise some of his stock holdings.

Date	Company	No. of Shares	Transaction	Price	Cost
12–10–X5	Ford	80	Buy	$25/share	
12–15–X5	IBM	100	Sale	20/share	$25/share
	Kodak	50	Sale	25/share	20/share
	PanAm	75	Sale	5/share	10/share
	Ford	80	Sale	20/share	30/share
	WYZ	200	Sale	8/share	5/share
	ITT	60	Sale	10/share	15/share
1– 4–X6	Kodak	80	Buy	20/share	
1– 8–X6	ABC	100	Buy	7/share	
1–25–X6	IBM	75	Buy	30/share	
1–14–X6	United	30	Buy	4/share	

    (a) What is the recognized gain (loss) for each of the stocks sold on December 15?

    (b) Explain why the gain (loss) is recognized or not for each sale.

25. A, on December 1, 19X4, purchased 100 shares of M Corporation common stock for $10,000 and, on December 15, 19X4, purchased 100 additional shares for $9,000. On January 3, 19X5, she sold the 100 shares purchased on December 1, 19X4, for $9,000. Is the loss allowable as a deduction?

26. A, on September 21, 19X4, purchased 100 shares of M Corporation common stock for $5,000. On December 21, 19X4, A purchased 50 additional shares for $2,750 and, on December 27,

19X4, purchased 25 additional shares for $1,125. On January 3, 19X5, he sold the 100 shares purchased on September 21, 19X4, for $4,000.

(a) What is A's realized gain or loss on January 3, 19X5?

(b) What is his recognized gain or loss?

(c) What is the basis of A's remaining shares after the sale on January 3?

27. V retires from the Shepherd School of Music. He decides to convert one-fourth of his home into a shop where he can sell music and violins, and give lessons. He bought the home ten years earlier for $34,000. The fair market value of the home is $80,000 on the date of conversion (the adjusted basis is $44,000). From 19X2 through 19X6, V lives and works in the home. He sells it in January 19X7. The home had an estimated useful life of twenty years on the date of conversion. V used the straight-line method. Disregard salvage value.

(a) How much gain (loss) is recognized if V sells the property for $44,000 in 19X7?

(b) If he sells the property for $32,000?

(c) If he sells the property for $50,000?

28. Residential property is purchased by G in 19X0 for use as his personal residence at a cost of $25,000, of which $15,000 is allocable to the building. G uses the property as his personal residence until January 1, 19X6, at which time its fair market value is $22,000, of which $12,000 is allocable to the building. G rents the property from January 1, 19X6 until January 1, 19X9 at which time it is sold for $16,000. On January 1, 19X6, the building has an estimated useful life of 20 years. Depreciation is computed on the straight-line method. Disregard salvage value.

(a) What is G's realized gain or loss from the sale?

(b) G's recognized gain or loss?

29. Residential property is purchased by M in 19X0 for use as his personal residence at a cost of $23,000, of which $10,000 is allocable to the building. M uses the property as his personal residence until January 1, 19X5, at which time its fair market value is $20,000, of which $12,000 is allocable to the building. M rents the property from January 1, 19X5 until January 1, 19X9, at which time it is sold for $17,000. On January 1, 19X5, the building has an estimated useful life of 20 years. Depreciation is computed on the straight-line method. Disregard salvage value.

(a) What is M's realized gain or loss?

(b) What is M's recognized gain or loss?

Research Problems

1. On January 1, 19X5, X, a major shareholder in Corporation H, purchased land from the company for $200,000. The fair market value of the land is $1,000,000, and its basis in the hands of the corporation is $250,000.

   (a) What are the possible tax consequences to X?

   (b) What is the basis of the land to X?

   (c) What is the tax consequence to Corporation H?

2. W is advised by his broker to sell some of his investments at a loss prior to year-end so as to offset $15,000 of short-term capital gains which were recognized earlier in the year. W has unrealized losses from the following securities:

   (1) Municipal bond investment fund—17th series ($5,000)

   (2) U.S. Steel common stock—($8,000)

Since W feels that both investments are desirable and wants to maintain an equivalent position in each, the following alternatives have been suggested:

   (1) Sell the municipal bond funds and immediately acquire an equivalent amount of the 18th monthly series of a similar bond fund.

   (2) Sell U.S. Steel and immediately acquire a call option to buy an equivalent number of shares.

Will either of these two proposals result in a wash sale under § 1091?

Chapter 13

PROPERTY TRANSACTIONS—
NONTAXABLE EXCHANGES

In a nontaxable exchange, realized gains or losses are not recognized.[1] However, the nonrecognition is usually temporary because the recognition of gain or loss is merely postponed until the property received in the nontaxable exchange is subsequently disposed of in a taxable exchange.

The tax law recognizes that nontaxable exchanges result in a change in the taxpayer's relative economic position in form, but not in substance. The new property received in the exchange is viewed as substantially a continuation of the old investment.[2] In other words, the taxpayer has merely replaced existing property with new property, and is in substantially the same relative economic position after the transaction as before the transaction. Certain exceptions should be noted. For example, the nonrecognition provisions do not apply to realized losses from the sale of personal use assets since such losses are not deductible. Also, nonrecognition applies only to gains and not to losses from involuntary conversions even if the property involved is business or income-producing.

In cases where the taxpayer receives cash or other nonqualifying property, gain is recognized from the exchange. The reason for this

1. Reg. § 1.61–6(b).   2. Reg. § 1.1002–1(c).

is that the taxpayer has changed or improved his relative economic position and has the wherewithal to pay income tax on the gain to the extent of the cash or other property received. The following material in this chapter deals with situations where realized gains or losses are not immediately recognized.

LIKE KIND EXCHANGES

The Code provides that "no gain or loss shall be recognized if property held for productive use in trade or business or for investment * * * is exchanged solely for property of a like kind to be held either for productive use in trade or business or for investment." [3]

Like-kind exchanges include business for business, business for investment, investment for business, or investment for investment property.[4] Property held for personal use, inventory and securities do not qualify under the like-kind exchange provisions.[5] Finally, this provision is *not* elective. If the exchange qualifies as like-kind, the nonrecognition rule is mandatory.

LIKE–KIND PROPERTY

"The words 'like-kind' have reference to the nature or character of the property and not to its grade or quality. One kind or class of property may not * * * be exchanged for property of a different kind or class." [6]

Thus, under this broad definition of what constitutes a like-kind exchange, real estate can only be exchanged for other real estate and personal property can only be exchanged for other personal property. For example, a machine exchanged for an office building is not a like-kind exchange. Real estate includes principally rental buildings, office and store buildings, manufacturing plants, warehouses and land. It is immaterial whether real estate is improved or unimproved.[7] Thus, unimproved land can be exchanged for an apartment house. Personal property includes principally machines, equipment, trucks and automobiles. Of course, if the property exchanged, (real estate or personal property) is held for personal use, it will not qualify as a like-kind exchange under § 1031.

---

3. § 1031(a).

4. § 1031(a) and Reg. § 1.1031(a)–1(a).

5. *Ibid.*

6. Reg. § 1.1031(a)–1(b).

7. *Ibid.*

MUST BE AN EXCHANGE

The transaction must actually involve a direct exchange of property to qualify as a like-kind exchange. Thus, the sale of old property and the purchase of new property, even though like-kind, is generally not an exchange. However, if the two transactions are mutually dependent the Internal Revenue Service may treat the two interdependent transactions as a like-kind exchange. For example, if the taxpayer sells an old business machine to a dealer and purchases a new one from the same dealer, a like-kind exchange would result.[8]

The taxpayer might want to avoid the nontaxable exchange treatment when a gain is realized in order to obtain a higher basis for depreciation (basis of the new property received in a like-kind exchange is discussed below) or when a loss is realized in order to recognize the loss for tax purposes. To the extent that such gains would, if recognized, receive favorable capital gains treatment, it may be preferable to avoid the nonrecognition of gain provisions by not entering into a direct exchange transaction, i. e., the sale of property to one individual followed by a purchase of similar property from another individual. However, in many instances it is not possible to recognize favorable capital gains upon the sale of depreciable property since part or all of the gain is recaptured as ordinary income due to the depreciation recapture provisions.[9] However, if the gain is not recognized and thus postponed, the recapture potential carries over to the new property received in the like-kind exchange.[10]

BOOT

Realized losses are not recognized on like-kind exchanges even where boot is received.[11] However, realized gains are recognized to the extent of boot received.[12] Boot is cash or property other than like-kind property. The term "boot" is derived from the expression "something to boot"—received or given in addition to the principal items exchanged. Cash or other property given (boot given) in a like-kind exchange has no effect on the recognition of realized gains or losses.

To summarize, if the taxpayer has a realized gain from a like-kind exchange and receives boot, then the realized gain is recognized to the extent of the boot received. The recognized gain cannot exceed the realized gain regardless of the amount of boot received.

---

8. Rev.Rul. 61–119, 1961–1 C.B. 395.

9. §§ 1245 and 1250.

10. §§ 1245(a)(2) and 1250(b)(3) and Reg. §§ 1.1245–2(a)(4) and 1.1250–2(d)(1).

11. § 1031(c) and Reg. § 1.1031(c)–1.

12. § 1031(b) and Reg. § 1.1031(b)–1(a).

BASIS OF PROPERTY RECEIVED

The basis of the property received in a like-kind exchange depends upon whether it is like-kind or not. If it is not like-kind, its basis is fair market value.[13] If it is like-kind property then its basis must be adjusted to reflect any postponed gain or loss.

Therefore, the basis of like-kind property received in the exchange is its fair market value less postponed gain or plus postponed loss.

If there is a postponed loss (a realized loss which is not recognized because the exchange is like-kind) then by not recognizing the loss from the exchange the taxpayer has recovered less than the cost or other basis of the old property exchanged, in an amount equal to the loss. If there is a postponed gain, then by not recognizing the gain from the exchange the taxpayer has recovered more than the cost or other basis of the old property exchanged, in an amount equal to the gain.

> **Example 1.** T exchanges a building (used in his business) with an adjusted basis of $30,000 and fair market value of $38,000 for land with a fair market value of $38,000 which will be held as an investment. The exchange qualifies as like-kind (e. g. an exchange of business real property for investment real property). Thus, the basis of the land is its fair market value of $38,000 less $8,000 postponed gain on the building or $30,000. If the land is later sold for its fair market value of $38,000, the $8,000 postponed gain will be recognized.

> **Example 2.** Assume the same facts as in the prior example except that the building has an adjusted basis of $48,000 and fair market value of only $38,000. The basis in the newly acquired land is $48,000 (its fair market value of $38,000 plus $10,000 of loss which is not recognized on the building). If the land is later sold for its fair market value of $38,000, the $10,000 postponed loss will be recognized.

The Code provides an alternative approach for determining the basis of like-kind property received: [14]

> Adjusted basis of property given up
> Plus any boot given
> Plus any gain recognized
> Minus any boot received
> = Basis of like-kind property received

The Code approach is logical in terms of the recovery of cost doctrine. That is, the old unrecovered cost or other basis is increased by additional cost (boot given) or decreased by cost recovered (boot

13. § 1031(d) and Reg. § 1.1031(d)–1(c).　**14.** § 1031(d) and Reg. §§ 1.1031(d)–1(a) and (b).

received). Finally, any gain recognized is included in the basis of the new property because the taxpayer has been taxed on that amount and is now entitled to recover it tax-free.

The holding period of the new like-kind property carries over from the acquisition of the old property exchanged.[15] The reason for this rule is derived from the basic concept of the new property as a continuation of the old investment.

The following comprehensive example illustrates the like-kind exchange rules:

Example 3. T exchanged the following old machines for new machines in nine independent like-kind exchanges:

Exchange	Adjusted basis of old machine	Fair market value of new machine	Boot given	Boot received
1	$4,000	$9,000	$ 0	$ 0
2	4,000	9,000	3,000	0
3	4,000	9,000	6,000	0
4	4,000	9,000	8,000	0
5	4,000	9,000	0	3,000
6	4,000	3,500	0	300
7	3,500	4,000	200	0
8	9,000	4,000	0	0
9	9,500	9,000	0	500

T's realized and recognized gains and losses and the bases of the new properties are:

Exchange	Realized Gain (Loss)	Recognized Gain Loss	Adj. Basis Old	+	Boot Given	+	Gain Recognized	−	Boot Received	=	Basis New
1	$5,000	$ 0	$4,000	+	$ 0	+	$ 0	−	$ 0	=	$ 4,000*
2	2,000	0	4,000	+	3,000	+	0	−	0	=	7,000
3	(1,000)	(0)	4,000	+	6,000	+	0	−	0	=	10,000**
4	(3,000)	(0)	4,000	+	8,000	+	0	−	0	=	12,000
5	8,000	3,000	4,000	+	0	+	3,000	−	3,000	=	4,000
6	(200)	(0)	4,000	+	0	+	0	−	300	=	3,700
7	300	0	3,500	+	200	+	0	−	0	=	3,700
8	(5,000)	(0)	9,000	+	0	+	0	−	0	=	9,000
9	0	0	9,500	+	0	+	0	−	500	=	9,000

* Basis may be determined for gain situations under the alternative method by subtracting the gain not recognized from the fair market value of the new property, i. e.,
$9,000 – $5,000 = $4,000 for exchange 1.
$9,000 – $2,000 = $7,000 for exchange 2.

** For loss situations, basis may be determined by adding the loss not recognized to the fair market value of the new property, i. e.,
$9,000 + $1,000 = $10,000 for exchange 3.
$9,000 + $3,000 = $12,000 for exchange 4.

15. § 1223(1) and Reg. § 1.1223–1(a).

Example 4 illustrates the like-kind exchange rules for both parties involved in the exchange:

Example 4. X and Y exchange real estate investments. X gives up property with an adjusted basis of $250,000 (fair market value $400,000) which is subject to a mortgage of $75,000 (assumed by Y). In return for this property X receives from Y property with a fair market value of $300,000 (adjusted basis $200,000) and cash of $25,000.

1. X's realized gain is $150,000. X gave up property with an adjusted basis of $250,000 and received $400,000 from the exchange ($300,000 fair market value of like-kind property plus $100,000 boot received (the mortgage assumed by Y is treated as boot received by X)).[16]

2. X's recognized gain is $100,000. The gain is recognized to the extent of boot received.

3. X's basis in the real estate received from Y is $250,000. This basis can be computed either by subtracting the postponed gain ($50,000) from the fair market value of the real estate received ($300,000); or by adding the recognized gain ($100,000) to the basis of the real estate given up ($250,000), and subtracting the boot received ($100,000).

4. Y's realized gain is $100,000. Y gave up property with an adjusted basis of $200,000 plus boot of $100,000 ($75,000 mortgage assumed plus $25,000 cash) or a total of $300,000 and received $400,000 from the exchange (fair market value of like-kind property received).

5. Y has no recognized gain because he did not receive any boot. The entire gain of $100,000 is postponed.

6. Y's basis in the real estate received from X is $300,000. This basis can be computed either by subtracting the postponed gain ($100,000) from the fair market value of the real estate received ($400,000), or by adding the boot given ($75,000 mortgage assumed by Y plus $25,000 cash or $100,000) to the basis of the real estate given up ($200,000).

Example (2) of Reg. § 1.1031(d)–2 illustrates a special situation where both the buyer and seller transfer liabilities which are assumed or are taken subject to the property by the other party.

Example from the Regulations:

1. D transfers an apartment house with an adjusted basis of $100,000 and a fair market value of $220,000 to E.

2. D's old apartment is subject to a mortgage of $80,000.

---

16. Reg. § 1.1031(d)–2.

3.   D receives $40,000 cash.

4.   D receives an apartment house from E with a fair market value of $250,000 which is subject to a mortgage of $150,000.

D's realized and recognized gain:

Received:	
Value of property received	$250,000
Cash received	40,000
Mortgage on property transferred to E	80,000
Total consideration received	$370,000
Less:	
Adjusted basis of property transferred	$100,000
Liabilities to which new property is subject	150,000
	$250,000
Gain realized	$120,000

Gain recognized: In computing boot received, D is permitted to offset the $80,000 mortgage on the property transferred against the $150,000 mortgage to which the new property is subject. Boot received and gain recognized under § 1031(b) is, therefore, $40,000; the amount of cash received.

INVOLUNTARY CONVERSIONS

GENERAL SCHEME

§ 1033(a) provides that a taxpayer who suffers an involuntary conversion of his or her property may postpone recognition of gain realized from the conversion. The objective of this provision is to provide some relief to the taxpayer who has suffered undue hardship from having property involuntarily converted. Another reason for the provision is that the taxpayer does not have the wherewithal to pay tax on any gain realized from the conversion to the extent he or she reinvests the amount realized from the conversion in replacement property. The rules for nonrecognition of gain are:

(1) If the amount realized exceeds the amount reinvested in replacement property, realized gain is recognized to the extent of the excess.[17]

(2) If the amount reinvested in replacement property equals or exceeds the amount realized, realized gain is not recognized.[18]

The following two examples illustrate the application of these rules:

17. § 1033(a)(3)(A) and Reg. § 1.-1033(a)–2(c)(1). This excess amount is analogous to boot under § 1031.

18. § 1033(a)(3)(A) and Reg. § 1.-1033(a)–2(c)(1).

Example 5. T's property with an adjusted basis of $20,000 is condemned by the State. T is awarded $50,000 as compensation for the involuntarily converted property. T's realized gain is $30,000 ($50,000 amount realized less $20,000 adjusted basis). T reinvests $40,000 in replacement property. The recognized gain under § 1033 is $10,000 (excess of $50,000 amount realized over $40,000 reinvested—Rule (1) above). The remaining $20,000 of realized gain is postponed if T so elects.

Example 6. Assume the same facts as in the prior example except that T reinvests $60,000 in replacement property. Since T reinvested an amount at least equal to the condemnation award, T's entire realized gain of $30,000 is not recognized (Rule (2) above) and is postponed if T so elects.

INVOLUNTARY CONVERSION DEFINED

An involuntary conversion is the result of the destruction (completely or partially), theft, seizure, or requisition or condemnation, or the sale or exchange under threat or imminence of requisition or condemnation of the taxpayer's property.[19] The threat or imminence of condemnation requires that the taxpayer obtain confirmation from a representative of the governmental body or public official involved that there has been a decision to acquire the property for public use, and that the taxpayer must also have reasonable grounds to believe the property will be taken.[20]

COMPUTING THE AMOUNT REALIZED

The amount realized from the condemnation of property usually includes only the amount received as compensation for the property.[21] Any amount received which is designated as severance damages by both the government and the taxpayer is not included in the amount realized.[22] Severance awards usually occur when only a portion of the entire property is condemned, e. g., to build a highway. Severance damages are awarded because the value of the taxpayer's remaining property has declined as a result of the condemnation. Such damages reduce the basis of the property. However, if (1) severance damages are used to restore the usability of the remaining property,[23] or (2) if the usefulness of the remaining property is destroyed by the condemnation and it is sold and replaced at a cost exceeding the sum of the condemnation award, severance damages and sales proceeds;[24] the nonrecognition provision of § 1033 applies to the severance damages.

19. § 1033(a) and Reg. §§ 1.1033(a)–1(a) and 1.1033(a)–2(a).

20. Rev.Rul. 63–221, 1963–2 C.B. 332.

21. *Pioneer Real Estate Co.*, 47 B.T.A. 886 (1942), *acq.* 1943 C.B. 18.

22. Rev.Rul. 59–173, 1959–1 C.B. 201.

23. Rev.Rul. 271, 1953–2 C.B. 36.

24. Rev.Rul. 73–35, 1973–1 C.B. 367.

SPECIAL PROVISIONS

There are some special provisions relating to events considered to be involuntary conversions; such as livestock destroyed by or on account of disease or sold or exchanged because of disease or solely on account of drought, but most involuntary conversions are casualties or condemnations.[25]

REPLACEMENT PROPERTY

The requirements for replacement property are generally more restrictive than those for like-kind property under § 1031. The basic requirement is that the replacement property be "similar or related in service or use" to the involuntarily converted property.[26]

Until 1964, the IRS maintained the position that "similar or related in service or use" meant that replacement property must be functionally the same as the involuntarily converted property (the *functional use test*). In 1964, however, the IRS changed its position with respect to owner-investors (such as lessors) as opposed to owner-users to conform with several appellate court decisions.[27] The test for owner-investors is the taxpayer use test and requires only that the properties be similar in the relationship of the services or uses which they have to the owner-investor.[28]

Taxpayer Use Test. This test would be met if an investor replaced a manufacturing plant with a wholesale grocery warehouse where both properties were held for the production of rental income.[29] A rental residence replaced by a personal residence does not meet this test.[30]

Functional Use Test. This test requires that the taxpayer's use of the replacement property and the involuntarily converted property must be the same. The rental residence replaced by a personal residence does not meet this test either. The manufacturing plant replaced by a wholesale grocery warehouse, both rented or not, does not meet this test, but as indicated above, the IRS applies the taxpayer use test to owner-investors. However, the functional use test still applies to owner-users, i. e., a manufacturer whose manufacturing plant is destroyed by fire is required to replace the plant with another facility of similar functional use.

25. §§ 1033(e) and (f) and Reg. §§ 1.-1033(e)–1(a) and 1.1033(f)–1(a).

AFTR2d 5359, 306 F.2d 207 (CA–8, 1962).

26. § 1033(a) and Reg. § 1.1033(a)–1.

28. Rev.Rul. 64–237, 1964–2 C.B. 319.

27. *Liant Record, Inc. v. Comm.*, 62–1 USTC ¶ 9494, 9 AFTR2d 1557, 303 F.2d 326 (CA–2, 1962); *Loco Realty Co. v. Comm.*, 62–2 USTC ¶ 9657, 10

29. *Loco Realty Co. v. Comm.*, cited in note 27.

30. Rev.Rul. 70–466, 1970–2 C.B. 165.

Special Rule. Business or investment condemned real property need only be replaced by like-kind property (the § 1031 rule).[31] Therefore, the above tests do not apply.

Example 7.

Type of property and user	Like-kind test	Taxpayer use test	Functional use test
1. Land used by a manufacturing company is condemned by a local government authority	✕		
2. Apartment and land held by an investor is sold due to the threat or imminence of condemnation	✕		
3. An investor's rented wholesale grocery warehouse is destroyed by fire. Therefore, the warehouse may be replaced by other rental properties, e. g. an apartment		✕	
4. A manufacturing plant was destroyed by fire. Therefore, replacement property must consist of another manufacturing plant which is functionally the same as the property converted			✕

TIME LIMITATION

The taxpayer has until two years (three years for condemnations of real property used in a trade or business) after the close of the taxable year in which any gain is realized from the involuntary conversion to replace the property.[32] This rule affords as much as three years (or possibly four years in the case of condemnation of business real property) to replace if the conversion took place on the first day of the taxable year.[33] The rule was changed from one year to two years and the replacement period was extended to three years for real property condemnations to permit adequate time to acquire replacement property.[34]

NONRECOGNITION OF GAIN

Nonrecognition of gain can be either mandatory or elective depending upon whether the conversion is direct or into money.

---

31. § 1033(g) and Reg. § 1.1033(g)–1(a).

32. § 1033(a)(3)(B) and Reg. § 1.1033(a)–2(c)(3).

33. The taxpayer can apply for an extension of this time period anytime prior to its expiration. Reg. § 1.1033(a)–2(c)(3). Also, if the taxpayer shows reasonable cause the period for filing the application for extension can be extended for a reasonable time.

34. Reg. § 1.1033(a)–2(c)(3).

Direct Conversion. If the conversion is directly into replacement property as opposed to money, nonrecognition of realized gain is mandatory, and the basis of the replacement property is the same as the adjusted basis of the converted property.[35] Direct conversion is rare in practice and usually involves condemnation when it does occur. The following example illustrates the application of the rules for direct conversions:

> **Example 8.** T's property with an adjusted basis of $20,000 is condemned by the State. T receives property with a fair market value of $50,000 as compensation for the property. T's realized gain of $30,000 is not recognized and the basis of the replacement property is $20,000 (adjusted basis of the condemned property *or* $50,000 fair market value of the new property less $30,000 postponed gain).

Conversion into Money. If the conversion is into money then "at the election of the taxpayer the gain shall be recognized only to the extent that the amount realized upon such conversion * * * exceeds the cost of such other property or such stock." [36] This is the usual case and nonrecognition (postponement) is elective.

A special rule allows the taxpayer to purchase an 80% or more interest in the stock of a corporation owning property which qualifies as replacement property in lieu of purchasing the replacement property directly.[37] This rule does not apply however, to condemnations of real property held for business or investment use where the like-kind reinvestment rules are applicable.[38]

The basis of the replacement property is its cost less postponed gain.[39] The holding period of the replacement property where the election to postpone gain is made includes the holding period of the converted property.[40]

§ 1033 applies only to gains, and not to losses. Losses from involuntary conversions are recognized if the property is held for business or income-producing purposes. Personal casualty losses are recognized, but condemnation losses related to personal use assets, e. g., a personal residence, are not recognized *or* postponed.

> **Example 9.** T's residence with an adjusted basis of $50,000 is condemned by the State. T receives $20,000 from the State. T's realized loss of $30,000 is not recognized and not postponed regardless of how much T reinvests in replacement property because losses from the condemnation of personal use property are

---

35. §§ 1033(a)(1) and 1033(c) and Reg. § 1.1033(a)–2(b).

36. § 1033(a)(3)(A) and Reg. § 1.1033(a)–2(c)(1).

37. *Ibid.*

38. § 1033(g)(2)(A) and Reg. § 1.1033(g)–1(b).

39. § 1033(c).

40. § 1223(1)(A) and Reg. § 1.1223–1(a).

never recognized. If the property was business or income-producing, the loss would be recognized. If the personal loss was a casualty loss, i. e., a loss from fire, storm, theft, etc., it would be recognized subject to the limitations of § 165(c)(3) and Reg. § 1.-165–7.

Examples 10 and 11 illustrate the application of the involuntary conversion rules:

Example 10. T's building (used in his trade or business activity) with an adjusted basis of $50,000 is destroyed by fire in 19X6. In 19X6 T receives insurance for the loss in the amount of $100,000. T invests $75,000 in a new building.

1. T has until December 31, 19X8 to make the new investment and qualify for the nonrecognition of gain election under § 1033(a)(3)(A).

2. T's realized gain is $50,000 ($100,000 insurance proceeds less $50,000 adjusted basis of old building).

3. Assuming the replacement property qualifies under § 1033(a)(3), T's recognized gain is $25,000. He reinvested $25,000 less than the insurance proceeds, and, therefore, his realized gain is recognized to that extent.

4. T's basis in the new building is $50,000, its cost of $75,000 less the postponed gain of $25,000 (realized gain of $50,000 less recognized gain of $25,000).

5. The answers (1–4) would be the same even if T is a real estate dealer and the building destroyed by fire was part of his inventory. § 1033 does not generally exclude inventory as § 1031 does.[41]

Example 11. Assume the same facts as in the prior example except that T receives only $45,000 (instead of $100,000) insurance proceeds. T would have a realized and recognized loss of $5,000, and the basis of the new building would be its cost of $75,000. Of course, if the building destroyed was held for personal purposes the recognized loss would be subject to the limitations of § 165(c)(3) and Reg. § 1.165–7. That is, the loss would be limited to the decline in fair market value of the property and the amount of the loss would be reduced by $100.

41. The exception is that the real property in § 1033(g) cannot be inventory. 1033(g)(1) and Reg. § 1.-1033(g)–1(a).

INVOLUNTARY CONVERSION OF A PERSONAL RESIDENCE

The tax consequences of the involuntary conversion of a personal residence depend on whether the conversion is a casualty or condemnation, and whether the result is a realized loss or gain.

Loss Situations. If the conversion is a condemnation, the loss realized is not recognized. Loss from the condemnation of a personal asset is never recognized.

If the conversion is a casualty, i. e., a loss from fire, storm, etc., the loss is recognized, subject to the personal casualty loss limitations.

Gain Situations. If the conversion is a condemnation, the gain may be postponed under either § 1033 or 1034. That is, the taxpayer may elect to treat the condemnation as a sale under the deferral of gain rules relating to the sale of a personal residence under § 1034.[42] As a practical matter this election has little if any significance today because in most cases the involuntary conversion deferral of gain provisions (§ 1033) afford at least as much time to replace the old residence as § 1034.

If the conversion is a casualty, the gain can only be postponed under the involuntary conversion provisions of § 1033.

REPORTING CONSIDERATIONS

If the taxpayer elects to postpone gain, either because he has replaced or intends to replace the converted property within the prescribed time period, supporting details should be included in a statement attached to the return for the taxable year in which gain is realized. If the property has not been replaced before filing the return for the taxable year in which gain is realized, the taxpayer should attach a supporting statement to the return for the taxable year in which the property is replaced.

If the property is either not replaced within the prescribed period or is replaced at a cost less than anticipated, an amended return must be filed for the taxable year in which the election was made. If no election is made in the return for the taxable year in which gain is realized, an election may still be made within the prescribed time period by filing a claim for credit or refund.[43]

SALE OF A RESIDENCE — § 1034

A realized loss from the sale of a personal residence is not recognized.[44] A realized gain is, however, subject to taxation. There

---

42. § 1034(i)(2) and Reg. §§ 1.1033(b)–1 and 1.1034–1(h)(2)(i).

43. Reg. § 1.1033(a)–2(c)(2).

44. Reg. §§ 1.165–9(a) and 1.262–1(b)(4).

are, however, two provisions in the tax law whereby all or part of a realized gain is either postponed or excluded from taxation. The first of these, § 1034, is discussed below. The second, § 121, is discussed later in this chapter.

§ 1034 provides for the mandatory nonrecognition of gain from the sale or exchange of a personal residence.[45] Both the old and new residences must be the taxpayer's principal residence.[46] A houseboat or house trailer qualify if used by the taxpayer as his or her principal residence.[47]

The reason for not recognizing gain from the sale or exchange of a residence which is replaced by a new residence within the prescribed time period (discussed below) is basically that the new residence is substantially a continuation of the investment in the old residence. Also, if the proceeds from the sale are reinvested, the taxpayer does not have the wherewithal to pay tax on the gain. Beyond these fundamental concepts, Congress, in enacting § 1034, was concerned with the hardship of involuntary moves and the socially desirable objective of encouraging the mobility of labor.

REPLACEMENT PERIOD

The period within which the old residence must be replaced depends on whether the new residence is purchased or constructed. If the new residence is purchased, the purchase must take place within 18 months before or after the date the old residence is sold.[48] Also, the taxpayer must physically occupy and use the new residence as his principal residence within the same time period.[49] If the new residence is constructed or reconstructed, the construction or reconstruction must begin either before or within 18 months after the date the old residence is sold.[50] The taxpayer must physically occupy and use the new residence as his principal residence within two years after the date the old residence is sold.[51]

The running of the time periods specified above is suspended during any time the taxpayer or spouse is on extended active duty (over 90 days or for an indefinite period) with the Armed Forces of the United States after the date the old residence is sold.[52] This suspension is limited to four years after the date the old residence is sold.[53]

45. § 1034(a) and Reg. § 1.1034–1(a).

46. § 1034(a) and Reg. §§ 1.1034–1(b)(1) and (2).

47. Reg. § 1.1034–1(c)(3)(i).

48. § 1034(a).

49. Rev.Rul. 69–434, 1969–2 C.B. 163 and § 1034(a).

50. §§ 1034(c)(2) and (5).

51. § 1034(c)(5) and Rev.Rul. 69–434, 1969–2 C.B. 163.

52. § 1034(h) and Reg. § 1.1034–1(g)(1).

53. Ibid.

PRINCIPAL RESIDENCE

As indicated above, both the old and new residences must be the taxpayer's principal residence. If the old residence ceases to be the taxpayer's principal residence prior to its sale or the new residence ceases to be the taxpayer's principal residence before he occupies it, the nonrecognition provision does not apply. For example, if the taxpayer abandons the old residence prior to its sale it no longer qualifies as his principal residence.[54] Or if the old residence is converted to other than personal use (e. g. rental) prior to its sale, the nonrecognition provision, of course, does not apply. If it is only partially converted to business use, gain from the sale of the personal portion still qualifies.[55]

However, temporarily renting out the old residence prior to its sale does not necessarily terminate its status as the taxpayer's principal residence.[56] Neither does temporarily renting out the new residence before the taxpayer occupies it.[57]

NONRECOGNITION OF GAIN REQUIREMENTS

Realized gain from the sale of the old residence is not recognized if the taxpayer reinvests an amount at least equal to the adjusted sales price of the old residence.[58] Realized gain is recognized to the extent the taxpayer does not reinvest the adjusted sales price in a new residence. Therefore, the amount not reinvested is treated similarly to the situation where boot is received in a like-kind exchange. Adjusted sales price is the amount realized from the sale of the old residence less fixing-up expenses.[59]

Fixing-up expenses are expenses incurred by the taxpayer to assist in the sale of the old residence.[60] They are personal in nature and not deductible by the taxpayer. They are distinguished from selling expenses which are deducted from the selling price to determine the amount realized from the sale.[61] Selling expenses include items such as advertising the property for sale, real estate broker commissions, legal fees in connection with the sale and loan placement fees paid by the taxpayer as a condition to the arrangement of financing for the buyer.[62] To the extent that selling expenses are deducted as moving expenses, they are not allowed as deductions in the computation of the amount realized.[63] Fixing up expenses include items such as ordinary repairs, painting and wallpapering.

54. *Richard T. Houlette*, 48 T.C. 350 (1967) and *Stolk v. Comm.*, 64–1 USTC ¶ 9228, 13 AFTR2d 535, 326 F. 2d 760 (CA–2, 1964).

55. Reg. § 1.1034–1(c)(3)(ii).

56. *Robert W. Aagaard*, 56 T.C. 191 (1971), *acq.* 1971–2 C.B. 1; *Robert G. Clapham*, 63 T.C. 505 (1975), and Rev.Rul. 59–72, 1959–1 C.B. 203.

57. Reg. § 1.1034–1(c)(3)(i).

58. § 1034(a) and Reg. § 1.1034–1(a).

59. § 1034(b)(1) and Reg. § 1.1034–1(b)(3).

60. § 1034(b)(2) and Reg. § 1.1034–1(b)(6).

61. Reg. § 1.1034–1(b)(4)(i) and Rev. Rul. 54–380, 1954–2 C.B. 155.

62. Reg. § 1.1034–1(b)(4)(i) and Rev. Rul. 68–650, 1968–2 C.B. 78.

63. § 217(b)(2).

Fixing-up expenses must: (1) be incurred for work performed during the 90-day period ending on the date of sale, (2) be paid within 30 days after the date of sale. and (3) not be capital expenditures.[64]

Fixing-up expenses are subtracted from the amount realized in arriving at adjusted sales price. Realized gain is not recognized and is postponed to the extent the adjusted sales price is reinvested in a new residence. Therefore, the greater the fixing-up expenses, the less the adjusted sales price, and the less that needs to be reinvested in a new residence in order to postpone the realized gain from the sale of the old residence.

However, fixing-up expenses are not considered in determining realized gain. They are considered only in determining how much realized gain is to be postponed. In addition, fixing-up expenses have no direct effect on the basis of the new residence. Indirectly, through their effect on postponed gain they can bring about a greater or lesser basis of the new residence. The effects of fixing-up expenses on the computation of gain realized and recognized and basis of the new residence is illustrated in Chart 1 and in Example 12.

BASIS OF THE NEW RESIDENCE

The basis of the new residence is its cost less unrecognized (postponed) gain.[65] If there is any postponed gain, the holding period of the new residence includes the holding period of the old residence.[66]

Chart 1 summarizes the sale of residence concepts. Example 12 illustrates these concepts and the application of the nonrecognition provision:

OPERATION OF SECTION 1034

Step 1. Sales price – Selling expenses = Amount realized
      ($40,000 – $2,000 = $38,000)

Step 2. Amount realized – Adjusted basis of old residence = Gain realized
      ($38,000 – $30,000 = $8,000)

Step 3. Amount realized – Fixing-up expenses = Adjusted sales price (amount
      ($38,000 – $1,000 = $37,000) which must be reinvested to avoid any recognized gain)

Step 4. Adjusted sales price – Cost of new residence = Excess of adjusted sales
      ($37,000 – $30,000 = $7,000) price over cost

Step 5. Recognized gain = lesser of realized gain or excess determined in Step 3
      ($7,000 = lesser of $8,000 or $7,000)

Step 6. Gain not recognized (postponed) = Gain realized – Gain recognized
      ($1,000 = $8,000 – $7,000)

Step 7. Basis of new residence = Cost of new residence – Gain not recognized
      ($29,000 = $30,000 – $1,000)

Note: If no fixing-up expenses were incurred, the gain recognized would have been $8,000 instead of $7,000 and the adjusted basis of the new residence would have been $30,000.

64. § 1034(b)(2) and Reg. § 1.1034-1(b)(6).

65. § 1034(e) and Reg. §§ 1.1034–1(e) and 1.1016–5(d).

66. § 1223(7) and Reg. § 1.1223–1(g).

Example 12. T sells her personal residence (adjusted basis of $36,000) for $44,000. She receives only $41,400 after payment of a brokerage fee of $2,600. Ten days before the sale T incurred and paid for qualified fixing-up expenses of $1,400. Two months later T acquires a new residence. Determine the gain, if any, T must recognize and the basis of the new residence under each of the following circumstances:

1. The residence acquired two months after the sale of the old residence cost $60,000. The cost of the new residence has no effect on determining the realized gain from the sale of the old residence. The realized gain is $5,400 ($41,400 amount realized less $36,000 adjusted basis of old residence). None of the gain is recognized because T reinvested at least $40,000 (the adjusted sales price) in the new residence. The $5,400 gain is postponed and the basis of the new residence is $54,600 ($60,000 cost less $5,400 unrecognized gain).

2. The new residence cost $38,000. $2,000 of the realized gain of $5,400 is recognized because T reinvested $2,000 less than the adjusted sales price of $40,000. The remaining gain of $3,400 is not recognized and is postponed. The basis of the new residence is $34,600 ($38,000 cost less $3,400 postponed gain).

3. The new residence cost $32,000. All of the realized gain of $5,400 is recognized because T reinvested $8,000 less than the adjusted sales price of $40,000. Since the amount not reinvested exceeds the realized gain, the entire gain is recognized and Code Section 1034 does not apply. The basis of the new residence is simply its cost of $32,000 because there is no postponed gain.

REPORTING PROCEDURES

The taxpayer is required to report the details of the sale in the tax return for the taxable year in which gain is realized even if all of the gain is postponed. If a new residence is acquired and occupied before filing, a statement should be attached to the return showing the purchase date, its cost, and date of occupancy. Form 2119 may be used to show the details of the sale and replacement, and should be retained by the taxpayer as support for the basis of the new residence. If a replacement residence has not been purchased when the return is filed, the taxpayer should submit the details of the purchase when it is purchased. If the old residence is not replaced within the prescribed time period, or if some recognized gain results, the taxpayer must file an amended return for the year in which the sale took place.

In any case, it is necessary to report the sale for the statute of limitations to begin running. If the taxpayer has an unreported recognized gain, either because he did not purchase a new residence or because he is otherwise not entitled to postpone the gain, the statute of limitations does not expire until three years after the date he notifies the Internal Revenue Service in writing of (1) the cost of the new residence which he claims results in nonrecognition of gain, (2) his intention not to purchase a new residence, or (3) his failure to purchase a new residence within the prescribed period.[67]

SALE OF A RESIDENCE — § 121

In 1964, Congress enacted a special provision for taxpayers age 65 or older who sell or exchange their principal residence. This provision allows the taxpayer to elect to exclude all or part of a realized gain from the sale or exchange.[68] The excluded amount is a function of a formula discussed below. The election can only be made once.[69] The provision is contrasted with § 1034 where nonrecognition is mandatory and may occur many times during a taxpayer's lifetime. Also, § 121 does not require the taxpayer to purchase a new residence. The excluded gain is never recognized whereas the unrecognized gain under § 1034 is postponed by subtracting it from the cost of a new residence.

This provision is the only case in the tax law where a realized gain from the disposition of property is not recognized and not postponed. In other words, the provision allows the taxpayer a permanent recovery of more than the cost or other basis of his residence tax-free.

The reason for § 121 is simply Congress's desire to relieve older citizens of the large capital gains tax they might incur from the sale of their residence. Ceiling amount limitations (currently $35,000) were built into the exemption provisions to restrict the benefit of § 121 to taxpayers who presumably have a greater need for increased tax-free dollars. Older citizens who sell higher priced residences receive less relative benefit from the provision.

REQUIREMENTS

The taxpayer must be at least 65 before the date of the sale and have owned and used the residence as a principal residence for at least five years during the eight-year period ending on the date of sale.[70] Short temporary absences, e. g., vacations, count as periods of use.[71] If the residence is owned jointly by husband and wife, only

67. § 1034(j) and Reg. § 1.1034–1(i)(1).   **70.** § 121(a) and Reg. § 1.121–1(a).

68. § 121(a) and Reg. § 1.121–1(a).   **71.** Reg. § 1.121–1(a)(2).

69. § 121(b)(2) and Reg. § 1.121–2(b).

one of the spouses is required to meet these requirements if a joint return is filed for the taxable year in which the sale took place.[72]

RELATIONSHIP TO OTHER PROVISIONS

The taxpayer can treat an involuntary conversion of his principal residence as a sale for purposes of § 121(a).[73] Any gain not excluded under § 121 is then subject to postponement under § 1033 or 1034 (condemnation only) assuming the requirements of those provisions are met.[74]

Any gain not excluded under § 121 from the sale of a residence is subject to postponement under § 1034 assuming the requirements of that provision are met.[75]

MAKING AND REVOKING THE ELECTION

The election not to recognize gain under § 121 may be made or revoked at any time before the statute of limitations runs out.[76] Therefore, the taxpayer generally has until the later of (1) three years from the due date of the return for the year the gain is realized or (2) two years from the date the tax is paid, to make or revoke the election. Making the election is accomplished by attaching a signed statement (showing all the details of the sale) to the return for the taxable year in which the sale took place.[77] Form 2119 may be used for this purpose. Revocation is accomplished by filing a signed statement (showing the taxpayer's name, social security number and taxable year for which the election was made) indicating such revocation.[78]

COMPUTATION PROCEDURE

The amount of realized gain which the taxpayer may elect to exclude is computed as follows: [79]

$$\frac{\$35,000^*}{\text{Adjusted Sales Price}} \times \text{Realized Gain}$$

* For years prior to 1977 the excluded amount was $20,000.

It is interesting to note that in this case fixing-up expenses increase the amount of the excluded gain since the adjusted sales price is the denominator in the above formula and fixing-up expenses re-

72. § 121(d)(1) and Reg. § 1.121–5(a).

73. § 121(d)(4) and Reg. § 1.121–5(d).

74. §§ 121(d)(7) and 1034(i) and Reg. §§ 1.121–5(g) and 1.1034–1(h).

75. § 121(d)(7) and Reg. § 1.121–5(g).

76. § 121(c) and Reg. § 1.121–4(a).

77. Reg. § 1.121–4(b).

78. Reg. § 1.121–4(c).

79. § 121(b)(1) and Reg. § 1.121–2(a).

duce the adjusted sales price. Since the gain is never recognized it results in a permanent recovery of more than the taxpayer's cost or other basis tax-free. The following example illustrates the application of this provision:

Example 13. Assume the same facts as in example 12, except T does not acquire a new residence and meets the requirements of § 121. T may elect not to recognize $4,725 of the $5,400 realized gain.

$$\frac{\$35,000}{\$40,000} \times \$5,400 = \$4,725$$

The following comprehensive example illustrates the application of both the § 121 and § 1034 provisions:

Example 14. T sells his personal residence (adjusted basis of $32,000) for $80,000, of which he receives only $70,400 after the payment of selling expenses. Ten days before the sale T incurred and paid for qualified fixing-up expenses of $6,400.

1. T's realized gain is $38,400 ($70,400 amount realized less $32,000 adjusted basis of residence). If he is less than 65 years old and does not acquire a new residence within the prescribed time period, T has a recognized gain of $38,400.

2. If T acquires a new residence within the prescribed period at a cost of $40,000, he has a recognized gain of $24,000 ($64,000 adjusted sales price of old residence less $40,000 cost of new residence). The postponed gain is the difference between the realized gain of $38,400 and the recognized gain of $24,000, or $14,400. The basis of the new residence is $40,000 cost less the $14,400 postponed gain, or $25,600.

3. Assume T is 65, does not acquire a new residence and elects to exclude a portion of the gain under § 121. T's recognized gain is $17,400. This is the difference between the realized gain of $38,400 and $21,000 not recognized under § 121 ($35,000/$64,000 × $38,400).

4. Assume T is 65, acquires a new residence for $40,000 within the prescribed time period, *and* elects under § 121. T's recognized gain is $3,000, computed as follows:

$$\frac{\$35,000}{\$64,000} \times \$38,400 = \underline{\$21,000} \text{ excluded portion of gain}$$

Adjusted sales price	$64,000
Less tax-free gain	(21,000) *
	$43,000
Less cost of new residence	40,000
Recognized gain	$ 3,000

The basis of the new residence in this case is $25,600 ($40,000 cost of new residence less $14,400 postponed gain). The postponed gain is the difference between the realized gain of $38,400 and $24,000 ($21,000 tax-free gain plus $3,000 recognized gain).

* The taxpayer is not required to reinvest an amount equal to the tax-free gain ($21,000). If T were required to reinvest such amount, the requirement would negate the benefits of § 121.

OTHER NONRECOGNITION PROVISIONS

Several additional nonrecognition provisions which are not as common as those already discussed in this chapter are discussed briefly in the remainder of the chapter.

EXCHANGE OF STOCK FOR PROPERTY—§ 1032

Under this section, no gain or loss is recognized to a corporation on the receipt of money or other property in exchange for its stock (including treasury stock).[80] In other words, no gain or loss is recognized by a corporation when it deals in its own stock. This provision is consistent with the accounting treatment of such transactions.

CERTAIN EXCHANGES OF INSURANCE POLICIES—§ 1035

Under this section, no gain or loss is recognized from the exchange of certain insurance contracts or policies.[81] The rules relating to exchanges not solely in kind and the basis of the property acquired are the same as under § 1031.[82] Exchanges qualifying for nonrecognition include (1) the exchange of life insurance contracts, (2) the exchange of a life insurance contract for an endowment or annuity contract, (3) the exchange of an endowment contract for another en-

80. § 1032(a) and Reg. § 1.1032–1(a).   **82.** § 1035(c) and Reg. § 1.1035–1.

81. § 1035(a) and Reg. § 1.1035–1.

dowment contract which provides for regular payments beginning at a date not later than the date payments would have begun under the contract exchanged, (4) the exchange of an endowment contract for an annuity contract, or (5) the exchange of annuity contracts.

EXCHANGE OF STOCK FOR STOCK OF THE SAME CORPORATION —§ 1036

Under this section, no gain or loss is recognized from the exchange of common stock solely for common stock in the same corporation, or from the exchange of preferred stock for preferred stock in the same corporation.[83] Exchanges between individual stockholders as well as between a stockholder and the corporation are included.[84] The rules relating to exchanges not solely in kind and the basis of the property acquired are the same as under § 1031.[85] An example of a nonrecognition exchange is where common stock with different rights, such as voting for nonvoting, is exchanged. Gain or loss from the exchange of common for preferred or preferred for common are recognized even though the stock exchanged is in the same corporation.

CERTAIN EXCHANGES OF U. S. OBLIGATIONS—§ 1037

Under this section, no gain or loss is recognized from certain exchanges of United States obligations. Specifically, the exchanges involve the surrender of so-called Liberty Bonds to the government solely in exchange for other Liberty Bonds.[86] The rules relating to exchanges not solely in kind and the basis of the property acquired are the same as under § 1031.[87]

CERTAIN REACQUISITIONS OF REAL PROPERTY—§ 1038

Under this section, no loss is recognized from the repossession of real property which is sold on an installment basis.[88] Gain is recognized to a limited extent.[89]

Chapter 13 has covered certain cases where realized gains or losses are not recognized; i. e., nontaxable exchanges. Chapters 14 and 15 are concerned with the nature of recognized gains and losses. That is, if a gain or loss is recognized, is it an ordinary or capital gain or loss? Chapter 14 discusses the tax consequences of capital gains and losses as opposed to ordinary gains and losses.

---

83. § 1036(a) and Reg. § 1.1036–1(a).

84. Reg. § 1.1036–1(a).

85. § 1036(b) and Reg. § 1.1036–1(b).

86. § 1037(a) and Reg. § 1.1037–1.

87. § 1037(c) and Reg. § 1.1037–1(a)(2).

88. § 1038(a) and Reg. § 1.1038–1(a).

89. § 1038(b) and Reg. § 1.1038–1.

TAX PLANNING
CONSIDERATIONS

LIKE–KIND EXCHANGES

Since the application of the like-kind provisions are not elective, in certain instances it may be preferable to avoid falling under § 1031. If the like-kind provisions do not apply, the end result may be the recognition of long-term capital gain and a higher basis for the newly acquired asset. The immediate recognition of gain may be preferable in certain situations, e. g. if the taxpayer has unused net operating loss carryovers.

> **Example 15.** X sells a machine (used in his business) for $4,000 which has an adjusted basis of $3,000. X also acquires a new business machine for $9,000. If § 1031 applies, the $1,000 gain is not recognized and the basis of the new machine is reduced by $1,000. If § 1031 does not apply, a $1,000 gain is recognized and may receive favorable long-term capital gain treatment to the extent that the gain is not recognized as ordinary income due to the depreciation recapture provisions. In addition, the basis for depreciation on the new machine is $9,000 rather than $8,000 since there is no amount of unrecognized gain.

SALE OF A PERSONAL RESIDENCE

If a taxpayer does not wish to acquire a new personal residence, he may be subject to substantial capital gain tax and minimum tax. The significance of this tax effect has been increased in recent years due to rapid inflation in housing and the liberalization of the minimum tax provisions. Older individuals who may be contemplating a move from their home to an apartment, should consider the following possibilities for minimizing or deferring taxes:

1. Wait until age 65 to sell the residence and elect under § 121 to exclude up to $35,000 of the realized gain.

2. Sell the personal residence under an installment contract to spread the gain over several years and to thereby avoid or minimize the payment of minimum tax.

3. Sell the personal residence and purchase a condominium instead of renting an apartment thereby permitting further deferral of the cumulative unrecognized gain.

Taxpayers should maintain records of both the purchase and sale of personal residences since the sale of one residence results in an adjustment of the basis of the new residence if the deferral provisions of § 1034 apply. Form 2119 should be filed with the tax return and retained as support for the basis of the new residence. Detailed cost records should be retained for an indefinite period.

PROBLEM MATERIALS

Questions for Class Discussion

1. In general, what is a nontaxable exchange? Are nontaxable exchanges ever taxed? If so, how?

2. Is it necessary to have a direct exchange of like-kind property to qualify under the provisions of § 1031?

3. Will an exchange of real estate for personal property qualify as a like-kind exchange?

4. Why would a taxpayer want to avoid like-kind exchange treatment?

5. What is boot and how does it affect a like-kind exchange where boot is received by the taxpayer? Where boot is given?

6. What adjustment is made to the basis of property received in a like-kind exchange when boot is received? When it is given?

7. Discuss the relationship between the recovery of cost doctrine and the rules for basis of property received and recognition of gain (loss) in like-kind exchanges.

8. Is a postponed gain from a like-kind exchange ever recognized?

9. How is the basis of property received in a like-kind exchange determined in the Code?

10. What is the holding period of property received in a like-kind exchange? Why?

11. How are each of the following determined for like-kind exchanges:

      realized gain?
      realized loss?
      recognized gain?
      recognized loss?
      postponed gain?
      postponed loss?
      basis of property received?

12. Why was § 1033 enacted?

13. What are the rules for determining nonrecognition of gain from an involuntary conversion?

14. What constitutes an involuntary conversion?

15. What are severance damages and when are they included in determining nonrecognition of gain from an involuntary conversion?

16. What happens when severance damages are not included in the amount realized?

17. Explain the differences between the two tests for replacement property in involuntary conversions.

18. When do the functional and taxpayer use tests not apply to replacement property in an involuntary conversion?

19. How long does a taxpayer have to replace involuntarily converted property and still qualify for nonrecognition of gain under § 1033?

20. When is nonrecognition of gain from an involuntary conversion elective?

21. Does § 1033 cover losses? How are the following losses treated for income tax purposes:

    a. Business property losses from involuntary conversion?
    b. Income producing property losses from involuntary conversion?
    c. Personal casualty losses?
    d. Personal condemnation losses?

22. Why are personal condemnation losses neither recognized *nor* postponed?

23. When a residence is involuntarily converted and a loss results what is the tax treatment in the following cases:
    a. The conversion is a casualty?
    b. The conversion is a condemnation?

24. When a residence is involuntarily converted and a gain results, under what conditions can either §§ 1033 or 1034 be applied to postpone recognition of the gain? How is § 1034 applied? Is there any significant difference between applying § 1033 as opposed to 1034?

25. How are corrections made when a taxpayer elected to postpone gain and then does not reinvest within the time limits or does not reinvest a sufficient amount? How is postponement accomplished if reinvestment is made but postponement was not elected in the return for the taxable year in which gain was realized?

26. What does § 1034 cover? Is it elective?

27. Why are losses not covered by § 1034?

28. Discuss the justification for nonrecognition of gain on the sale or exchange of a principal residence.

29. Discuss *all* of the requirements for replacement period of both purchased and constructed residences. Are there any exceptions?

30. What is meant by principal residence in the sale or exchange of a residence?

31. What is adjusted sales price? What are fixing-up expenses? Selling expenses?

32. How are the following determined on the sale or exchange of a residence:
    a. Realized gain?
    b. Recognized gain?
    c. Postponed gain?
    d. Basis of new residence?

33. Discuss fixing-up expenses in relation to:
    a. Postponed gain
    b. Realized gain
    c. Basis of new residence

34. What is the basis of the new residence if there is a realized loss?

35. What are the requirements for the statute of limitations to begin running on the sale or exchange of a residence?

36. What does § 121 cover? Is it elective?

37. Why was § 121 enacted?

38. How many times can § 121 treatment be elected by a taxpayer? If the taxpayer is filing a joint return with his or her spouse, do both taxpayers have to meet the age requirement?

39. Can § 121 apply to anything other than a sale or exchange of a residence? Does the old residence have to be replaced?

40. How does the statute of limitations apply to § 121?

41. How is the amount of gain not recognized under § 121 determined?

42. Can any other provision or provisions be applied to any remaining gain which is not excluded under § 121?

43. How do fixing-up expenses affect the application of § 121?

44. Who benefits most from § 121?

Problems

1. Which of the following are like-kind exchanges?
   (a) Grocery store for a drug store (both used for business)
   (b) Bookstore (used for business) for land (held for investment)
   (c) Land held for investment for securities
   (d) Apartment building (held for investment) for land (held for investment)
   (e) Rental house for farm equipment (used in business)
   (f) Truck (used in business) for a boat used for personal recreation
   (g) Rental house for land (held for investment)
   (h) Truck (used in business) for inventory

2. What is the basis of the new property for each of the following?

   (a) Stock (adjusted basis $5,000) for drug store (used in business) (fair market value $10,000)

   (b) Rental house (adjusted basis $8,000) for land held for investment (fair market value $9,000)

   (c) Grocery store (adjusted basis $10,000) for drug store (fair market value $8,000) both held for business use

   (d) Bookstore (adjusted basis $6,000) for farm equipment (fair market value $4,000) both held for business use

   (e) Apartment building held for investment (adjusted basis $20,000) for land held for investment (fair market value $20,000)

3. T buys a rental house for $30,000 with a thirty year life (ignore land) in January 19X1. He exchanges the house at the beginning of 19X5 for rental real estate to be used in a business which has a fair market value of $28,000. The newly acquired rental property is depreciated at the rate of $1,000 a year. At the beginning of 19X7 T sells the rental property for $25,000. What is the realized, recognized, and postponed gain (loss), and the new basis for each of these transactions?

4. T received a boat (used in business) with a six year useful life and a fair market value of $6,000 in a like-kind exchange in January, 19X2. He has a postponed loss of $1,500. At the beginning of 19X5 he exchanges it for another boat to be used in his business with a three year useful life and a fair market value of $3,000. After two years he sells the second boat for $1,000. What is the realized, recognized, and postponed gain (loss), and the new basis for each transaction? Assume straight-line depreciation and no salvage value for both boats.

5. Determine the basis of the new asset for each of the following like-kind exchanges:

	Adjusted Basis of Old Asset	Boot Given	Fair Market Value of New Asset	Boot Received
(a)	$ 8,000	0	$10,000	0
(b)	10,000	0	9,000	0
(c)	4,000	2,000	5,000	0
(d)	5,000	500	4,500	0
(e)	3,000	7,000	8,000	0
(f)	10,000	0	11,000	1,000
(g)	7,000	0	4,000	4,000
(h)	5,000	0	4,000	3,000

6. What is the realized, recognized, and postponed gain (loss), and the new basis for each of the following:

	Adjusted Basis of Old Asset	Boot Given	Fair Market Value of New Asset	Boot Received
(a)	$ 3,000	0	$ 5,000	0
(b)	8,000	1,000	10,000	0
(c)	9,000	2,000	10,000	0
(d)	4,000	5,000	9,000	0
(e)	6,000	2,000	7,000	0
(f)	1,000	0	500	600
(g)	5,000	0	4,000	0
(h)	8,000	0	7,000	500
(i)	10,000	0	8,000	3,000
(j)	2,000	0	1,000	1,000
(k)	11,000	0	12,000	500
(l)	8,000	0	10,000	2,000
(m)	500	0	800	400
(n)	1,000	200	900	0
(o)	1,000	100	800	0
(p)	600	200	400	0

7. For both T and M determine the realized, recognized, and postponed gain (loss), and the new basis for each of the following independent transactions:

(a) T gives up an apartment building with an adjusted basis of $200,000 and a fair market value of $600,000. The apartment building carries a $250,000 mortgage which is assumed by M. M gives up a drugstore building which was used in business with an adjusted basis of $250,000 and a fair market value of $350,000.

(b) T gives up business equipment with an adjusted basis of $8,000 and a fair market value of $6,000. He also gives M $1,000. M gives up business equipment with an adjusted basis of $4,500 and a fair market value of $7,000.

(c) T gives up a car (used in business) with an adjusted basis of $3,000 and a fair market value of $2,500. M gives up a business machine with an adjusted basis of $1,000 and a fair market value of $1,500. M also gives T $1,000.

8. K exchanges real estate held for investment which she purchased for $5,000, for other real estate (to be used in her business), which has a fair market value of $6,000, and $2,000 in cash.

(a) What is K's realized gain or loss?

(b) Her recognized gain or loss?

(c) The basis of the newly acquired real estate?

9. W transfers real estate held for investment which he purchased for $10,000 in exchange for other real estate (to be held for investment) which has a fair market value of $9,000, an auto-

mobile (to be held for personal use) which has a fair market value of $2,000, and $1,500 in cash.

(a) What is W's realized gain or loss?

(b) His recognized gain or loss?

(c) The basis of the newly acquired real estate?

10. F exchanges real estate held for investment plus stock for real estate to be held for investment. The real estate transferred has an adjusted basis of $10,000 and a fair market value of $11,-000. The stock transferred has an adjusted basis of $4,000 and a fair market value of $2,000. The real estate acquired has a fair market value of $13,000.

(a) What is F's realized gain or loss?

(b) His recognized gain or loss?

(c) The basis of the newly acquired real estate?

11. R owns an apartment house which has an adjusted basis of $500,-000, but which is subject to a mortgage of $150,000. On September 1, 19x4 he transfers the apartment house to I, receiving in exchange therefor $50,000 in cash and another apartment house with a fair market value on that date of $600,000. The transfer to I is made subject to the $150,000 mortgage.

(a) What is R's realized gain or loss?

(b) His recognized gain or loss?

(c) The basis of the newly acquired apartment house?

12. W owns an apartment house (held for investment). On December 1, 19X5 the apartment house has an adjusted basis of $100,000 and a fair market value of $220,000, but is subject to a mortgage of $80,000. J also owns an apartment house. On December 1, 19X5 the apartment house owned by J has an adjusted basis of $175,000 and a fair market value of $250,000, and is subject to a mortgage of $150,000. On December 1, 19X5 W transfers his apartment house to J receiving in exchange therefor $40,000 in cash and the apartment house owned by J. Each apartment house is transferred subject to the mortgage on it.

(a) What is W's realized gain or loss?

(b) W's recognized gain or loss?

(c) The basis of W's newly acquired apartment house?

13. D trades an old cab used in his business for a new one. The new cab costs $3,800. He is allowed $1,000 for the old cab which has an adjusted basis of $1,500, and pays $2,800 cash. What is D's recognized gain or loss? If D had sold the old cab to a third party for $1,000 and then purchased a new cab, what would have been his recognized gain or loss?

14. Real estate held for investment, with an adjusted basis of $5,000 is exchanged for other real estate (to be held for investment), a truck, and $1,000 cash. At the time of the exchange, the fair market value of the other real estate is $2,500 and the fair market value of the truck is $1,800.

    (a) What is the recognized gain or loss?

    (b) What is the basis of the properties received?

15. T exchanged a boat, used in business, having an adjusted basis of $8,000, for another boat to be used in the business, land to be held for investment, and $500 cash. The fair market values of the boat and the land received are $5,000 and $1,500, respectively.

    (a) What is the recognized gain or loss?

    (b) What is the basis of the properties received?

16. T exchanged real estate held for investment, having an adjusted basis of $8,000, for other real estate to be held for investment. The real estate received has a fair market value of $10,000, and T also received $1,000 in cash.

    (a) What is T's *realized* gain or loss?

    (b) What is T's *recognized* gain or loss?

    (c) What is the basis of the real estate received?

17. Suppose, in Problem 16, that the property transferred is subject to a $3,000 mortgage.

    (a) What is T's realized gain or loss?

    (b) What is T's recognized gain or loss?

    (c) What is the basis of the real estate received?

18. If a truck having an adjusted basis of $3,000 (original cost $4,500 minus $750 depreciation for each of 2 years) is exchanged solely for another truck having a fair market value of $4,500, what is the basis of the truck received?

19. If a truck having an adjusted basis of $3,000 is traded in on another truck having a fair market value of $4,500, and additional cash of $1,000 is paid for the new truck, what is the basis of the truck received?

20. A truck having an adjusted basis of $3,000 is exchanged for a new, smaller truck having a fair market value of $2,200 plus $1,000 cash.

    (a) What is the recognized gain or loss?

    (b) What is the basis of the new truck?

21. Do the following qualify for involuntary conversion treatment?

    (a) An earthquake destroys the taxpayer's residence.

    (b) Sale of a home because a neighbor converted his residence to a nightclub.

(c) Purchase of an apartment building to replace a rental house by an investor. The rental house was destroyed by fire.

(d) Purchase of a bookstore as a replacement for a grocery store (used in business) which was destroyed by fire.

(e) Purchase of a delivery truck to replace a shrimp boat (used in business) which was wrecked in a storm.

22. What is the *maximum* postponed gain (loss) for the following involuntary conversions:

Property	Type of Conversion	Amount Realized	Adjusted Basis	Amount Reinvested
(a) Residence (personal)	casualty	$ 16,000	$ 18,000	$ 17,000
(b) Residence (personal)	casualty	20,000	18,000	19,000
(c) Apartments (investment)	condemned	150,000	100,000	200,000
(d) Apartments (investment)	casualty	100,000	120,000	200,000
(e) Vacant lot (investment)	condemned	120,000	80,000	120,000
(f) Residence (personal)	condemned	18,000	20,000	26,000
(g) Grocery store (business)	casualty	200,000	150,000	175,000
(h) Bookstore (business)	condemned	80,000	60,000	50,000

23. A's vessel (held for business use) which has an adjusted basis of $100,000 is destroyed in 19X0 and A receives in 19X1 insurance in the amount of $200,000. He invests $150,000 in a new business vessel.

(a) What is A's realized gain or loss?

(b) His recognized gain or loss?

(c) The basis of the new vessel?

24. A taxpayer realizes $22,000 from the involuntary conversion of a barn (used in farming) in 19X5; the adjusted basis of the barn was $10,000, and he spent in the same year $20,000 for a new barn.

(a) What is the taxpayer's realized gain or loss?

(b) His recognized gain or loss?

(c) The basis of the new barn?

If the replacement of the converted barn had been made by the purchase of two smaller barns which, together, were similar or related in service or use to the converted barn and which cost $8,000 and $12,000, what would be the basis of each new barn?

25. The State has condemned for public use certain undeveloped real estate which was used as a parking lot for customers. The adjusted basis of this property is $5,000. The State offered and the taxpayer accepted, a similar tract of land having a fair market value of $7,500.

(a) What is the *realized* gain or loss?

(b) What is the *recognized* gain or loss?

(c) What is the basis of the new property?

26. A building which is used in business, having an adjusted basis of $9,000, was totally destroyed by fire. During that year the taxpayer received $11,000 from the insurance company and immediately spent $9,500 to replace the destroyed building.

    (a) What is the realized gain or loss?

    (b) How much gain, if any, can the taxpayer elect to postpone?

    (c) Assume the taxpayer elects to postpone the maximum, what is the basis of the new building?

    (d) How much gain, if any, could the taxpayer elect to postpone if only $8,500 had been used to replace the destroyed building?

    (e) Assume the taxpayer elects to postpone the maximum, what would be the basis of the new building if only $8,500 was used to replace the old building?

27. T owned business property that was condemned by the State. The property had an adjusted basis of $26,000, and $31,000 was received from the State. T bought new property of similar functional use for $29,000 and elected to not recognize gain.

    (a) What is T's realized gain?

    (b) What is T's recognized gain?

    (c) What is the basis of the new property?

28. Which of the following are selling expenses, fixing-up expenses or neither?

    (a) Advertising the residence for sale

    (b) Paint outside of residence

    (c) Legal fees to clear title to residence

    (d) Repair leaky faucets of residence

    (e) New roof

    (f) Wallpaper inside rooms

    (g) New fence and patio

    (h) Loan placement fees

29. What is the realized, recognized, and postponed gain (loss), the new basis, and the adjusted sales price for each of the following? Assume that none of the taxpayers are 65 years of age or older.

    (a) D sells his residence for $85,000. The adjusted basis was $60,000. The selling expenses were $2,000. The fixing-up expenses were $3,000. D reinvested $80,000 in a new personal residence.

    (b) D sells his residence for $70,000. It had an adjusted basis of $65,000. The selling expenses were $6,000. He reinvested $80,000.

(c) L sells his residence for $90,000. The adjusted basis was $55,000. The selling expenses were $5,000. The fixing-up expenses were $3,000. He did not reinvest in a new residence.

(d) D sells his residence for $50,000 and his mortgage was assumed by the buyer. The adjusted basis was $40,000; the mortgage, $25,000. The selling expenses were $2,000 and the fixing-up expenses were $1,000. He reinvested $60,000.

(e) D sells his residence for $65,000. It had an adjusted basis of $35,000. The selling expenses were $2,000. The fixing-up expenses were $1,000. He reinvested $40,000.

30. L sold his residence which he had owned and occupied for 20 years. The adjusted basis is $18,000 and the selling price was $25,000. The selling expenses were $2,000 and the fixing-up expenses were $4,000. He reinvested $30,000 in a new residence. L is over sixty-five years of age. What is the realized, recognized, and postponed gain (loss), the new basis, and the adjusted sales price?

31. A taxpayer, age 42, decides to sell his residence, which has a basis of $17,500. To make it more attractive to buyers, he paints the outside at a cost of $300 in April, 19X4. He pays for the painting when the work is finished. In May, 19X4, he sells the house for $20,000. Brokers' commissions and other selling expenses are $1,000. In October, 19X4, the taxpayer buys a new residence for $18,000.

(a) What is the taxpayer's realized gain or loss?

(b) The recognized gain or loss?

(c) The adjusted basis of the new residence?

32. The facts are the same as in Problem 31, except that the cost of purchasing the new residence is $17,000.

(a) What is the taxpayer's realized gain or loss?

(b) The recognized gain or loss?

(c) The adjusted basis of the new residence?

33. On January 1, 19X4, the taxpayer, age 58, buys a new residence for $10,000. On March 1, 19X4, he sells for an adjusted sales price of $15,000 his old residence, which has an adjusted basis to him of $5,000 (no fixing-up expenses are involved, so that $15,000 is the "amount realized" as well as the "adjusted sales price"). Between April 1 and April 15 a new wing is constructed on the new house at a cost of $5,000. Between May 1 and May 15 a garage is constructed at a cost of $2,000.

(a) What is the taxpayer's realized gain or loss?

(b) The recognized gain or loss?

(c) The adjusted basis of the new residence?

34. Taxpayer Calvin, age 82, a college professor, purchased and moved into a house on January 1, 19X0. He used the house as his principal residence continuously to February 1, 19X4, on which date he went abroad for a 1-year sabbatical leave. During a portion of the period of leave the property was unoccupied and it was leased during the balance of the period. On March 1, 19X5, 1 month after returning from such leave, he sold the house. May Calvin make an election under § 121(a)?

Research Problems

1. A owned and used his house as a principal residence since 1946. However, 10 percent of the house was used for business purposes as an office. On January 1, 1978, at which time A is over 65, he retired and moved to Florida. A rented his former residence for six months before its sale since no qualified buyer could be found. A purchased a new residence in Florida at a price which exceeded the adjusted sales price of the former residence.

    (a) May A make an election under § 121(a)?

    (b) Are the nonrecognition of gain provisions of § 1034 available to A?

    (c) What is the treatment accorded to the portion of the former residence which was used for business? Rental property?

2. On 12/31/19X1 T sold his personal residence in Houston for $60,-000. Selling expenses amounted to $4,000 of which $2,500 was deducted as moving expenses. The Houston home originally cost T $45,000 although he used 10% of the home for business use and took depreciation of $2,000 on this portion.

    T acquired a new residence in Alaska on 4/1/19X1 for $45,000. The home was badly in need of repair. Comparable houses in the neighborhood were selling for $60,000. Since T's wife wanted to completely remodel and redecorate to her tastes, T purchased the $45,000 house instead of one of the $60,000 models.

    During the remainder of 19X1 T spent the following amounts for remodeling and redecorating:

1.	Carpeting	$ 3,000
2.	Addition to family room	5,000
3.	Remodel kitchen and bathrooms	2,000
4.	Custom drapes	2,000
5.	New fence	1,000
6.	New roof	3,000
7.	Wallpaper, paint and repairs	4,000
	Total expenditures	$20,000

    In filing of his tax return, T claims that the new residence cost $45,000 plus $20,000 of expenditures which should be capitalized or $65,000. Therefore, T deferred the entire amount of gain realized on the home in Houston.

T calculated the realized and recognized gain as follows:

Selling price	$60,000
Less: Selling expenses	(4,000)
Adjusted sales price	56,000
Less: Adjusted basis	43,000
	$13,000
Cost of new residence (The bank appraisal after the remodeling was $62,000)	$65,000
Adjusted sales price	56,000
Gain recognized	–0–

A revenue agent now contends that the business portion of the former residence does not qualify for nonrecognition of gain under Section 1034. Further, that the $20,000 of expenditures should not have been capitalized. Therefore, the full amount of the realized gain should have been recognized in 19X1.

(a) Are the selling expenses deductible in arriving at the adjusted sales price?

(b) Was T entitled to capitalize the $20,000 of expenditures on the new residence?

(c) Is § 1034 nonrecognition of gain applicable to the business portion of the former residence?

Your task is to advise T and to assist in the negotiations with the IRS agent.

3. W has been a real estate developer for ten years. In 19X3, he acquired a large tract of land and built houses thereon. The total cost of the properties was $140,000 and W received a $90,000 mortgage to finance the project. One year later W exchanged the development for a similar development which had a fair market value of $350,000 and was subject to a $150,000 mortgage; he also received $30,000 in cash. The new development was held by B, who assumed W's mortgage of $90,000.

(a) Compute the amount realized, the gain or loss realized and recognized, and the basis of the new property in the above transaction. What is the character of any gain recognized?

(b) If T were not a real estate dealer, but rather this was an investment, what would be the realized and recognized gain and the basis of the new property, assuming that $6,000 depreciation had been taken on the properties computed on the straight-line basis? What is the character of any gain recognized?

(c) What would your answer to (b) be if the property received was instead subject to a $40,000 mortgage and $30,000 cash was again received?

(d) Would your answer to Parts (b) or (c) be different if T received vacant land only in the exchange and accelerated depreciation had been claimed on the buildings located in the development?

Chapter 14

PROPERTY TRANSACTIONS— CAPITAL GAINS AND LOSSES

GENERAL CONSIDERATIONS

RATIONALE FOR FAVORABLE CAPITAL GAIN TREATMENT

This chapter is concerned with the nature of a recognized gain or loss. That is, given that a gain or loss is recognized, is it capital or ordinary? The preferable capital gain provisions are intended to encourage the formation of private capital investment and to encourage risk-taking by investors. In addition, preferential capital gain treatment is, in part, a recognition that appreciation in value over a long period of time should not be taxed in full in the year of realization. Favorable capital gain rates, in effect, offset the adverse "bunching effect" due to the requirement to recognize all of the gain in one year.

GENERAL SCHEME OF TAXATION

Long-term capital gains of noncorporate taxpayers are subject to either a 50 percent capital gains deduction or an alternative tax rate of 25 percent on the first $50,000 of such gains. Ordinary gains (including short-term capital gains) are taxable in full and subject to the taxpayer's regular tax rates. This preferential treatment given long-term capital gains is discussed in detail later in the chapter.

An ordinary loss is generally preferable to capital loss treatment since ordinary losses are deductible in full, while the deductibility of capital losses is subject to certain limitations. The sum of an individual taxpayer's long-term and short-term capital losses for a taxable year is limited to a maximum $1,000 deduction in 1976, $2,000 in 1977 and $3,000 in 1978 and subsequent years. However, both long-term and short-term capital losses are offset dollar for dollar against capital gains before this limitation comes into effect.

Short-term capital losses are preferable to long-term capital losses because the latter are only deductible fifty cents on the dollar (after offsetting capital gains). This result is similar to the fifty percent long-term capital gains deduction which results in these gains only being taxed at regular rates on fifty cents for each dollar of gain. The capital loss rules are discussed in detail later in this chapter.

A capital gain or loss arises from the recognition of gain or loss from the sale or exchange of a capital asset. In addition, a long-term capital gain or loss results only when a capital asset has been held for more than six months. The holding period has been extended to "more than nine months" in 1977 and "more than one year" for 1978 and subsequent years.[1] If the capital asset has been held for less than the required period, the resulting capital gain or loss is short-term.[2]

WHAT IS A CAPITAL ASSET

DEFINITION OF A CAPITAL ASSET

§ 1221 defines a capital asset as property held by the taxpayer (whether or not connected with his trade or business), but not including:

1. Stock in trade, inventory, or property held primarily for sale to customers in the ordinary course of a trade or business. The Supreme Court, in *Malat v. Riddell,* defined primarily as meaning "of first importance" or "principally."[3]

2. Depreciable property or real estate used in a trade or business.

3. Certain copyrights, literary, musical, or artistic compositions, letters or memorandums or similar property.

1. §§ 1222(3) and (4) and Reg. § 1.-1222-1(a); Act § 1402 amending § 1222.

2. §§ 1222(1) and (2) and Reg. § 1.-1222-1(a); Act § 1402 amending § 1222.

3. *Malat v. Riddell,* 66–1 USTC ¶ 9317, 17 AFTR2d 604, 86 S.Ct. 1030 (USSC, 1966).

4. Accounts or notes receivable acquired in the ordinary course of trade or business for services rendered or from the sale of inventory.

5. Certain short-term governmental obligations issued at a discount.

6. Certain U. S. Government publications.[4]

The Code indirectly defines a capital asset by describing those items which are not capital assets. Therefore, by definition all other assets held by the taxpayer are capital assets. The principal assets excluded from the definition of a capital asset are inventory and business fixed assets (buildings, land, machinery and equipment). Therefore, gains or losses from dispositions of these assets result in ordinary gain or loss as opposed to capital gain or loss. Business fixed assets may, however, qualify for long-term capital gains treatment under § 1231 (discussed in Chapter 15).

The principal capital assets held by an individual taxpayer include personal (as opposed to business) assets, such as a personal residence or automobile; and assets held for investment purposes, e. g. land and corporate stock. Of course, losses from the sale or exchange of a taxpayer's personal assets (as opposed to business or investment assets) are not recognized, and therefore their classification as capital assets is irrelevant for capital loss purposes.

EFFECT OF JUDICIAL ACTION

Court decisions are especially important in the capital gain and loss area because the Code definition of a capital asset is very broad and the Code does not specifically define what constitutes a sale or exchange.

Example 1. T Corporation, a large manufacturer of products made from corn, engaged in future operations (i. e., contracts calling for delivery in the future) in corn to order to protect itself from a price rise and a short supply (its storage facilities were adequate for its production requirements for only a short period). As it turned out, some of the futures were not needed and were sold at a gain.

This example is based on a landmark Supreme Court case, *Corn Products Refining Co.*[5] The question was whether the corn futures were inventory or investment property. § 1221(1) indicates that inventory is not a capital asset. If the corn futures were considered inventory the gain from their sale would be ordinary as opposed to capital. The Court held that the sales

4. Act § 2132 amending § 1221.

5. *Corn Products Refining Co. v. Comm.*, 55–2 USTC ¶ 9746, 47 AFTR 1789, 76 S.Ct. 20 (USSC, 1955).

were an integral part of the company's business and the futures were not held for investment. Therefore, the gain was ordinary.

The above case points out the need to look beyond the broad definition of a capital asset in the Code. The crux of determining whether an asset is capital or not is usually whether it is held for investment as opposed to business purposes. Congress did not intend to exempt profits from the ordinary operations of a business from ordinary income treatment.

STATUTORY EXPANSIONS

The following are situations where Congress has felt it necessary to expand the general definition of a capital asset in § 1221.

Dealers in Securities. As a general rule, securities held by a dealer are considered to be inventory and are not, therefore, subject to capital gain or loss treatment. A dealer in securities is a merchant, e. g. a brokerage firm that regularly engages in the purchase and resale of securities to customers. If a dealer clearly identifies certain securities as held for investment purposes within thirty days after their acquisition, and they are not held at any time after such identification primarily for sale to customers in the ordinary course of business, gain from their sale will be capital gain.[6] Losses will also be capital if at any time the securities have been clearly identified by the dealer as held for investment.[7]

Real Property Subdivided for Sale. Substantial development activities relative to real property may result in the owner being considered a dealer for tax purposes. Thus, income from the sale of real estate property lots is treated as the sale of inventory (ordinary income) if the owner is considered to be a dealer. § 1237 provides relief for investors in real estate who engage in limited development activities by allowing capital gain treatment if certain requirements are met:

1. The taxpayer cannot be a corporation.[8]

2. The taxpayer cannot be a real estate dealer.[9]

3. No substantial improvements can be made to the lots sold.[10] Substantial generally means more than a ten percent increase in the value of a lot.[11] Shopping centers and other commercial or residential buildings are considered substantial, while filling, draining, levelling and clearing operations are not.[12]

6. § 1236(a) and Reg. § 1.1236–1(a).

7. § 1236(b) and Reg. § 1.1236–1(b).

8. § 1237(a) and Reg. § 1.1237–1(a)(1).

9. § 1237(a)(1) and Reg. § 1.1237–1(a)(1).

10. § 1237(a)(2) and Reg. § 1.1237–1(a)(5).

11. Reg. § 1.1237–1(c)(3)(ii).

12. Reg. § 1.1237–1(c)(4).

4. The taxpayer must hold the lots sold for at least five years, except for inherited property.[13] The substantial improvements test is less stringent if the property is held at least ten years.[14]

If the above requirements are met, the taxpayer will only have ordinary income, starting in the taxable year he sells the sixth lot, to the extent of 5 percent of the selling price.[15] All gain is capital gain until the taxable year in which the taxpayer sells the sixth lot.[16] Contiguous lots sold to a single buyer in a single sale count as only one lot.[17] All selling expenses offset the 5 percent ordinary income portion first, which increases the relative amount of capital gain.[18]

This provision does not apply to losses.[19] A loss from the sale of subdivided real property is ordinary unless the property qualifies as a capital asset under § 1221. A gain which does not qualify under § 1237 may qualify as capital under §§ 1221 or 1231 if the requirements of those sections are satisfied. The following example illustrates the application of § 1237:

Example 2. T owns a large tract of land and subdivides it for sale. Assume T meets all the requirements of § 1237 and sells the first ten lots in 19X6 for $10,000 each. T's basis of each lot sold is $3,000 and he incurred total selling expenses of $4,000 on the sale. T's gain is computed as follows:

Selling price (10 × $10,000)		$100,000
Basis (10 × $3,000)		30,000
Excess over basis		70,000
Five percent of selling price	$5,000	
Selling expenses	(4,000)	
Amount of ordinary income		$ 1,000
Five percent of selling price	$5,000	
Excess of expenses over five		
percent of selling price	–0–	(5,000)
Capital gain		65,000
Total gain ($70,000 – $4,000 selling expenses)		$66,000

Lump-Sum Distributions. § 402(a)(2) provides that lump-sum distributions from qualified pension and profit-sharing plans are treated as long-term capital gain to the extent that the distribution exceeds the taxpayer's contributions to the plan.[20] However, the

13. § 1237(a)(3) and Reg. §§ 1.1237–1(d)(1) and (2).

14. § 1237(b)(3) and Reg. § 1.1237–1(c)(5)(i)(a).

15. § 1237(b)(1) and Reg. § 1.1237–1(a)(5).

16. Reg. § 1.1237–1(e)(2).

17. *Ibid.*

18. § 1237(b)(2) and Reg. § 1.1237–1(e)(2)(ii).

19. Reg. § 1.1237–1(a)(4)(i).

20. §§ 402(a)(2) and 402(e)(4)(D).

amount treated as capital gain is limited to the portion of the excess which is attributable to participation in the plan prior to January 1, 1974.[21] The amount attributable to participation after December 31, 1973 is ordinary income. A lump-sum distribution is defined generally as a distribution of the employee's entire balance within one taxable year following any of the following: death or disability of the employee, age $59\frac{1}{2}$, or separation from service with the employer.[22] The amount treated as ordinary income is subject to a special elective 10-year forward averaging device which can somewhat lighten the burden of this amount not receiving capital gain treatment.[23] An employee may now elect to treat all of the gain as ordinary income rather than a portion as long-term capital gain.[24] In some instances this election is preferable due to the imposition of the minimum tax on the long-term capital gain portion and due to the favorable averaging treatment for the ordinary income amount. The following example illustrates the application of the lump-sum distribution rules. These rules are discussed in greater detail in Chapter 17.

> **Example 3.** In December, 1975 T receives a $46,000 lump-sum distribution from a qualified pension plan when he retires from employment with H Corporation. T had contributed $6,000 to the plan and H Corporation had contributed the rest, of which $8,000 was deemed to have been contributed in plan years after 1973. The computation of the capital gain element is made under the following formula:

$$\frac{\text{Years of participation before 1974}}{\text{Total years of participation}} \quad \text{e. g.} \quad \frac{1966\text{--}1973}{1966\text{--}1975}$$

or $\frac{8}{10} \times \$40,000$ (taxable portion) $= \$32,000$ long-term capital gain.

T has a $32,000 capital gain and $8,000 ordinary income from the distribution. The capital gain is long-term. The $8,000 is subject to the special ten-year averaging device. T's long-term capital gain is computed as follows:

Distribution	$46,000	
Less: T's contribution	6,000	recovery of cost
	$40,000	
Less: Corporation's contribution after 1973	(8,000)	ordinary income
Long-term capital gain	$32,000	

Nonbusiness Bad Debts. As discussed in Chapter 7, nonbusiness bad debts are treated as short-term capital losses in the taxable year in which they become completely worthless regardless of how long

---

21. § 402(a)(2).

22. § 402(e)(4)(A).

23. § 402(e)(1).

24. Act § 1512 adding 402(e)(4)(L).

the debt has been outstanding.[25]   This is an excellent example of statutory expansion in the capital gain and loss area.   Whether the property involved is a capital asset or not, whether a sale or exchange has taken place, and determining the holding period are not problems because the Code automatically provides that nonbusiness bad debts are short-term capital losses in all cases.

SALE OR EXCHANGE

Recognition of capital gain or loss requires a sale or exchange of a capital asset.   § 1222 uses the term "sale or exchange" but does not define the term.   Generally, a sale involves the receipt of money or the assumption of liabilities for property and an exchange involves the transfer of property for other property.   Thus, an involuntary conversion is not a sale or exchange.   In several areas the determination of whether a sale or exchange has taken place has been clarified by the enactment of Code sections which specifically provide for sale or exchange treatment as discussed below.

WORTHLESS SECURITIES

§ 165(g)(1) provides that "if any security which is a capital asset becomes worthless during the taxable year, the loss resulting therefrom shall   *   *   *   be treated as a loss from the sale or exchange, on the last day of the taxable year, of a capital asset."

The reason for this provision is to solve the problems of determining (1) whether a sale or exchange has taken place, and (2) the date of the loss.   The transaction is treated as being analogous to a sale or exchange of the security for nothing.   Therefore, an amount equal to the entire adjusted basis of the security is a capital loss.   It should be noted that under certain circumstances the worthless stock of a subsidiary corporation may be treated as an ordinary loss by the parent company.[26]

A loss from worthless securities, which would otherwise be short-term, may be converted to long-term because the holding period is extended to the last day of the taxable year regardless of when the security actually became worthless.   This provision does not, however, solve the problem of determining in what year the loss took place.   The year of worthlessness is discussed in Chapter 7, but a common example is the year in which a corporation enters bankruptcy proceedings.   The following example illustrates the application of this provision:

25.   § 166(d)(1)(B) and Reg. § 1.166–   **26**.   § 165(g)(3).
    5(a)(2).

Example 4. T purchases stock in P Corporation on December 1, 19X5 for $10,000. On August 1, 19X6, the corporation files a petition in a bankruptcy proceeding. In accordance with § 165(g)(1), T has a $10,000 long-term capital loss for taxable year 19X6. The stock is considered to be sold or exchanged on December 31, 19X6, which results in a holding period of more than one year.

SPECIAL RULE—RETIREMENT OF CORPORATE OBLIGATIONS

Under the general rule, the collection of a debt obligation does not constitute a sale or exchange. Therefore, any gain or loss upon the collection of a note or other obligation cannot be capital gain or loss since there must be a sale or exchange. § 1232 provides an exception for corporate and certain government obligations. The retirement of corporate and certain government obligations is considered to be an exchange and is, therefore, usually subject to capital gain or loss treatment.

Example 5. T acquires XYZ Corporation bonds at $980 in the open market. If the bonds are held to maturity, the $20 difference between the maturity value of $1,000 and the taxpayer's cost of $980 is treated as a capital gain. If the obligation were issued by an individual instead of a corporation, the gain would be ordinary income rather than capital gain since there was not sale or exchange.

Special rules apply to corporate and certain government obligations which were issued at a discount after May 27, 1969. Gain upon the retirement or the sale of such discount obligations is generally treated as long-term capital gain if the obligation is a capital asset to the holder and has been held for the required long-term holding period (more than 12 months in 1977 and subsequent years).[27]

If at the time of original issue there was an intention to call the obligations prior to maturity, the gain will be ordinary income to the extent of original issue discount not already included in the gross income of any holder. Original issue discount is required to be included in ordinary income through the amortization of the discount on a ratable basis over the life of the bond.[28] Original issue discount is defined as the difference between the issue price and the redemption price at maturity of the obligations.[29] The basis of the obligations is increased by the amounts included in ordinary income in order to prevent the taxpayer from being taxed twice when the obligations are disposed of.[30]

27. § 1232(a)(2)(A) and Reg. § 1.1232-3(a)(1)(i).

28. § 1232(a)(3) and Reg. § 1.1232-3A(a)(1).

29. § 1232(b)(1).

30. § 1232(a)(3)(E) and Reg. §§ 1.-1232-3A(c) and 1.1016-5(s).

West's Fed. Tax: Individuals—14

Example 6. T purchases ten $1,000 bonds from X Corporation for $9,600. The bonds mature in ten years. T will amortize the $400 discount over the period he holds the bonds. If he holds the bonds until maturity T will report $40 ordinary income each year, and because the basis of the bonds is increased annually by the amount of amortization he will have no gain when the bonds are redeemed at maturity.

Special rules apply to original issue discount corporate and government obligations which are issued prior to May 28, 1969 since holders of such securities are not required to include the amortized discount in income. The sale or exchange of such securities generally results in capital gain treatment. However, all or a portion of the original issue discount may be treated as ordinary income.[31]

§ 1232 does not apply to corporate obligations which are purchased in the open market at a discount if the bonds were not subject to original issue discount. Further, most new bond issues do not carry original issue discount since the interest rate is set so that the market price upon issue approximates the original issue price. In addition, a bond discount is not considered to be original issue discount if the discount is less than one-fourth of one percent of the redemption price at maturity multiplied by the number of years to maturity.[32]

Example 7. X Corporation issues 20-year bonds at 96 percent of the maturity price. There is no original issue discount since the issue price is in excess of 95 percent of the maturity price ¼% x 20 years = 5%.

Therefore, in most instances an investor is not required to amortize corporate bond discount over the life of the issue. If the bonds are held to maturity, the difference between the amount received and the taxpayer's cost basis is granted capital gain treatment.

OPTIONS

As a general rule, the sale or exchange of an option to buy or sell property results in capital gain or loss if the property, subject to the option, is or would be a capital asset in the hands of the option holder.[33]

Loss from Failure to Exercise Options. If an option holder fails to exercise the option, the lapse of the option is considered a sale or

---

31. § 1232(a)(2)(B) and Reg. § 1.1232–3(a)(3).

32. § 1232(b)(1) and Reg. § 1.1232–3(b)(1)(ii).

33. § 1234(a) and Reg. § 1.1234–1(a)(1).

exchange on the option expiration date.[34] The loss is a capital loss if the property, subject to the option, is or would be a capital asset in the hands of the option holder.[35]

The grantor of an option currently receives short-term capital gain or loss treatment upon the closing of the option transaction for options which are granted after September 1, 1976.[36] Formerly, the grantor of an option recognized ordinary income or loss on the option transaction.[37] For example, an individual investor who owns certain stock may write a call option which entitles the purchaser of the option to acquire the stock at a certain price. The writer of the call receives a premium, e. g. 10 percent for writing the option. If the price of the stock does not increase during the option period, the option will expire. The premium received is now treated as short-term capital gain instead of ordinary income upon the expiration of the option.

The provisions of § 1234 do not apply to securities dealers who hold securities for sale to customers (inventory).[38]

Exercise by Grantee. If the option is exercised, the amount paid for the option is added to the selling price of the property subject to the option. This increases the gain to the grantor from the sale of the property. The gain is capital or ordinary depending on the nature of the property sold. The grantee, of course, adds the cost of the option to the basis of the property; it is part of the grantee's cost of the property. The grantor (writer of a call option granted after September 1, 1976) recognizes short-term capital gain or loss upon the closing of the transaction.

> **Example 8.** X purchases 100 shares of Y Company stock for $5,000 on September 1, 1974. On January 1, 1977 he writes a call option on the stock which gives the option holder the right to buy the stock for $6,000 during the following six month period. X receives a call premium of $500 for writing the call.
>
> 1. If the call is exercised by the option holder on August 1, 1977, X has $500 short-term capital gain from the call premium and $1,000 long-term capital gain from the sale of the stock.
>
> 2. Assume that X decides to sell his stock prior to exercise for $6,000 and enters into a closing transaction by purchasing a a call on 100 shares of Y Company stock for $5,000. Since the Y stock is selling for $6,000, X must pay a call premium of $1,000. He recognizes a $500 short-term capital loss ($1,000 call premium paid — $500 call premium received)

34. § 1234(b) and Reg. § 1.1234–1(b).

35. § 1234(a) and Reg. § 1.1234–1(a).

36. Act § 2136 amending § 1234.

37. Reg. § 1.1234–1(b) and Rev.Rul. 57–40, 1957–1 C.B. 266.

38. Act § 2136 amending § 1234.

on the closing transaction. On the actual sale of the Y
Company stock, X has a long-term capital gain of $1,000
($6,000 selling price − $5,000 cost).

3. Assume that the original option expired unexercised. X has
a $500 short-term capital gain equal to the call premium re-
ceived for writing the option. This gain is not recognized
until the option expires.

PATENTS

Rationale for Capital Gain Treatment. The justification for §
1235 (which usually results in long-term capital gain) is primarily to
encourage technological progress. This is perhaps ironic if the provision is contrasted with the treatment of authors, composers and art-
ists. The latter do not qualify for capital gain treatment in any case
because the results of their efforts are not capital assets, and they do
not qualify under § 1231 either. Presumably, Congress does not desire to encourage cultural progress, at least through the tax law.
The following example illustrates the application of § 1235:

Example 9. T, a druggist, invents a pill-counting machine which
he patents. In consideration of a lump sum payment of $200,000
plus $10 per machine sold, T assigns the patent to Drug Products,
Inc. Assuming T has transferred all substantial rights, the question of whether the transfer is a sale or exchange of a capital
asset is not relevant. T automatically has a long-term capital
gain from both the lump sum payment and the $10 per machine
royalty.

Statutory Requirements. The key issues relating to the transfer
of patent rights are (1) whether the patent is a capital asset, (2)
whether the transfer is a sale or exchange, and (3) whether all substantial rights to the patent or an undivided interest therein are
transferred. § 1235 was enacted primarily to solve the problems of
whether the transfer is a sale or exchange of a capital asset. This
section provides that:

"a transfer * * * of property consisting of all substantial
rights to a patent, or an undivided interest therein which includes
a part of all such rights, by any holder shall be considered the
sale or exchange of a capital asset held for more than 6 months,
[9 months in 1977 and one year in 1978 and thereafter], regardless of whether or not payments in consideration of such transfer
are (1) payable periodically over a period generally coterminous
with the transferee's use of the patent, or (2) contingent on the
productivity, use, or disposition of the property transferred." [39]

39. § 1235(a) and Reg. § 1.1235–1(a).

The crux of this provision is that if the transfer meets the requirements of § 1235 any gain or loss is automatically a long-term capital gain or loss regardless of whether the patent is a capital asset or not, whether the transfer is a sale or exchange, and how long the patent was held by the transferor.

Substantial Rights. To receive favorable capital gain treatment under § 1235, "all substantial rights" to the patent must be transferred. The position of the IRS is that the transfer of patent rights which are limited geographically within the country of issuance or rights which are limited in duration to a period less than the remaining life of the patent do not constitute the transfer of "all substantial rights." [40] Three appellate courts have upheld the IRS' position. [41]

Holder Defined. § 1235 applies to the creator or inventor, and anyone who purchases the patent rights from the creator, except for the creator's employer and certain related parties. [42] Also, a transfer by a holder to a related party does not qualify. [43]

If the transfer does not qualify under § 1235, the taxpayer must look elsewhere for long-term capital gain treatment. That is, the transfer would have to be the sale or exchange of a capital or § 1231 asset held for the required long-term holding period. [44]

FRANCHISES

Prior to the enactment of § 1253 in 1969, there was a great deal of controversy in the courts as to the proper tax treatment relative to transfers of franchises. The key issue was whether the transfer was a sale or exchange as opposed to a license. § 1253(a) generally solves this problem by providing that "a transfer of a franchise, trademark, or trade name shall not be treated as a sale or exchange of a capital asset if the transferor retains any significant power, right, or continuing interest with respect to the subject matter of the franchise, trademark, or trade name."

A franchise is defined as an agreement which gives the transferee the right to distribute, sell, or provide goods, services, or facilities, within a specified area. [45] A transfer includes the granting of a franchise, the transfer of a franchise by a grantee to a third party, or the renewal of a franchise. [46]

---

40. Reg. § 1.1235–2(b)(1).

41. *Mros v. Comm.*, 74–1 USTC ¶ 9350, 33 AFTR2d 74–996, 493 F.2d 813 (CA–9, 1974); *Fawick v. Comm.*, 71–1 USTC ¶ 9147, 27 AFTR2d 71–381, 436 F.2d 655 (CA–6, 1971); *Estate of Klein v. Comm.*, 75–1 USTC ¶ 9127, 35 AFTR2d 75–457, 507 F.2d 617 (CA–7, 1975).

42. § 1235(b) and Reg. § 1.1235–2(d)(1).

43. Reg. § 1.1235–1(a).

44. Reg. § 1.1235–1(b); Act § 1402(b)(1)(v) amending § 1235(a).

45. § 1253(b)(1).

46. § 1253(b)(3).

Significant Power, Right, or Continuing Interest. Significant powers, rights, or continuing interests include control over assignment, quality of products and services, sale or advertising of other products or services, and the right to require substantially all supplies and equipment be purchased from the transferor. Also included are the right to terminate the franchise at will and the right to substantial contingent payments.[47] It is apparent that most modern franchising operations involve some or all of these powers, rights, or continuing interests.

Transferee Deduction. § 1253 is unique in that it covers the tax consequences to both the transferor and the transferee. § 1253(d) indicates the tax treatment of amounts paid by the transferee. Contingent payments are deductible as business expenses.[48] Other payments are either deductible currently or over a longer period of time depending on the nature of the payment and the tax treatment afforded the transferor on the payments.[49] The transferee's tax treatment is consistent with the transferor, e. g. if the payment is ordinary income to the transferor of the patent, it is an ordinary deduction to the payor (transferee).

Sports Franchises. § 1253 does not apply to professional sports franchises.[50] However, the Tax Reform Act of 1976 has imposed certain restrictions upon the allocation of the costs of acquiring a sports franchise to the cost basis of players contracts.[51] In addition, if a sports franchise is sold, gain from the sale of the players contracts is now subject to depreciation recapture as ordinary income under § 1245.[52]

LEASE CANCELLATION PAYMENTS

The tax treatment of payments received in the consideration of a lease cancellation depends on whether the recipient is the lessor or the lessee, and whether the lease is a capital asset or not.

Lessee Treatment. Payments received by a lessee in consideration of a lease cancellation are capital gains if the lease is a capital or § 1231 asset.[53] For example, payment received by a tenant for cancellation of the lease on a residential apartment held for investment would be a capital gain.

Lessor Treatment. Payments received by a lessor in consideration of a lease cancellation are always ordinary income because they are considered to be in lieu of rental payments.[54]

47. § 1253(b)(2).

48. § 1253(d)(1).

49. § 1253(d)(2); See Prop.Reg. § 1.-1253–1(c).

50. § 1253(e).

51. Act § 212(a) adding § 1056.

52. Act § 212(b) amending § 1245(a).

53. § 1241 and Reg. § 1.1241–1(a).

54. *Hort v. Comm.,* 41–1 USTC ¶ 9354, 25 AFTR 1207, 61 S.Ct. 757 (USSC, 1941).

HOLDING PERIOD

The required holding period for long term capital gain or loss is "more than six months" for years prior to 1977, "more than nine months" for 1977 and "more than one year" for 1978 and subsequent years.[55] Conversely, gains or losses from the sale or exchange of capital assets held for less than the required period are short-term capital gains or losses.[56] In computing the holding period, exclude the date of acquisition and include the date of disposition; and then count by months.[57] The following example illustrates the computation of the holding period:

> **Example 10.** T purchases a capital asset on March 15, 19X6 and sells it on September 22, 19X6. T's holding period is six months and seven days (six months from March 16 through September 15 plus seven days from September 16 through September 22).

A capital asset acquired on the last day of any month must not be disposed of until the second day of the tenth succeeding month to be held for more than nine months.[58]

> **Example 11.** T purchases a capital asset on January 31, 1977 and sells it on November 8, 1977. T's holding period is nine months and seven days (the asset is considered to be held nine months on November 1, 1977.

REVIEW OF VARIOUS HOLDING PERIOD RULES

§ 1223 provides detailed rules for determining holding period. The application of these rules depends upon the type of asset and how it was acquired.

Tax-free Exchanges. The holding period of property received in a nontaxable exchange includes the holding period of the former asset if the property which has been exchanged is a capital or § 1231 asset.[59] In certain nontaxable transactions involving a substituted basis, the holding period of the former property is "tacked on" to the holding period of the newly acquired property.

> **Example 12.** X exchanges a business truck for another truck in a like-kind exchange under § 1031. The date basis of the former truck "tacks on" to the holding period of the new truck.

---

55. §§ 1222(3) and (4) and Reg. § 1.-1222–1(a); Act § 1402 amending § 1222.

56. §§ 1222(1) and (2) and Reg. § 1.-1222–1(a); Act § 1402 amending § 1222.

57. Rev.Rul. 66–5, 1966–1 C.B. 91.

58. Rev.Rul. 66–7, 1966–1 C.B. 188.

59. § 1223(1).

Example 13. X sells his former personal residence and acquires a new residence. If the transaction qualifies under § 1034 for nonrecognition of gain on the sale of a residence, the holding period of the new residence includes the holding period of the former residence.[60]

Certain Nontaxable Transactions Involving a Carryover of Basis. The holding period of a former owner of property is "tacked on" to the present owner's holding period if the transaction is nontaxable and the basis of the property to the former owner carries over to the new owner.

Example 14. X transfers land to a controlled corporation in exchange for its common stock. If the transaction is nontaxable under § 351 (discussed more fully in Chapter 18), the corporation's holding period for the land includes the period the land was held by X.

Example 15. X acquires 100 shares of ABC corporation stock for $1,000 on December 31, 1975. The shares are transferred by gift to Y on December 31, 1976 when the stock is worth $2,000. Y's holding period begins with the date the stock was acquired by X since the donor's basis of $1,000 becomes the basis for determining gain or loss on a subsequent sale by Y.

Example 16. Assume the same facts as in the prior example except that the fair market value of the ABC shares is only $800 on the date of the gift. The holding period begins on the date of the gift if Y sells the ABC stock for a loss since the value of the shares at the date of the gift is used in the determination of basis.[61] If the shares are sold for $500 on April 1, 1977, Y has a $300 recognized capital loss and the holding period is from December 31, 1976 to April 1, 1977.

SPECIAL RULES FOR SHORT SALES

The holding period of property sold short is determined under special rules provided in § 1233. A short sale occurs where a taxpayer sells borrowed property and repays the lender with substantially identical property either held on the date of the sale or purchased after the sale. Short sales usually involve corporate stock. The seller's objective is to make a profit in anticipation of a decline in the price of the stock. If the price declines, the seller of a short sale recognizes a profit equal to the difference between the price he sold the borrowed stock for and the price paid for the replacement stock.

§ 1233(a) provides that "gain or loss from the short sale of property shall be considered as gain or loss from the sale or exchange of a capital asset to the extent that the property * * * used to close

---

60. § 1223(7).   **61.** § 1223(2) and Reg. § 1.1223–1(b).

the short sale constitutes a capital asset in the hands of the taxpayer." No gain or loss is recognized until the short sale is closed.[62]

The general rule is that the holding period of the property sold short is determined by the length of time the seller held the property used to repay the lender when closing the short sale.[63]

If substantially identical property has been held for less than the required long-term holding period (e. g. nine months or less in 1977) on the date of the short sale, the gain or loss is short-term.[64] If substantially identical property is acquired after the date of the short sale and on or before the closing date, the gain or loss is also short-term.[65] If, however, substantially identical property has been held for the required long-term holding period on the date of the short sale, a gain on closing is long-term if the substantially identical property is used to close the sale and a loss on closing is long-term regardless of whether the substantially identical property is used to close the sale.[66]

The purpose of these special rules is to prevent the taxpayer from engaging in short sales in order to convert short-term capital gains to long-term capital gains or convert long-term capital losses to short-term capital losses. The discussion of capital gains and losses later in this chapter points out the advantage of long-term capital gains and short-term capital losses over short-term capital gains and long-term capital losses. The following examples illustrate the application of the special rules for short sales:

> **Example 17.** T purchases five shares of XYZ Corporation common stock on January 2, 19X6 for $100. On April 14, 19X6 she engages in a short sale of five shares of the same stock for $150. On August 15 she closes the short sale by repaying the borrowed stock with the five shares purchased on January 2. T has a $50 short-term capital gain from the short sale because she held substantially identical shares for less than the required long-term holding period on the date of the short sale.

> **Example 18.** Assume the same facts as in the prior example, except that T closes the short sale on August 29 by repaying the borrowed stock with five shares purchased on August 29 for $200. Assume further that T sells the five shares purchased on January 2 for $200 on August 30. T has a $50 short-term capital loss from the short sale because substantially identical shares were acquired after the short sale and on or before closing the sale. T has a $100 short-term capital gain from the sale on Au-

---

62. Reg. § 1.1233–1(a)(1).

63. Reg. § 1.1233–1(a)(3).

64. § 1233(b) and Reg. §§ 1.1233–1(c)(1) and (2).

65. *Ibid.*

66. § 1233(d) and Reg. § 1.1233–1(c)(4).

gust 30 because she held substantially identical shares for less than the required long-term holding period when she sold short. The holding period for the shares sold on August 30, therefore, begins on the closing date, August 29.[67]

Example 19. T purchases five shares of XYZ Corporation common stock on January 2, 19X5 for $100 and five more shares of the same stock on April 14, 19X6 for $200. On August 15, 19X6 she sells short five shares of the same stock for $150. On September 30 she repays the borrowed stock with the five shares purchased on April 14, and sells the five shares purchased on January 2, 19X5 for $200. T has a $50 long-term capital loss from the short sale because she held substantially identical shares for more than one year on the date of the short sale. T has a $100 long-term capital gain from the sale of the shares purchased on January 2, 19X5.

TAX TREATMENT OF CAPITAL GAINS AND LOSSES OF NONCORPORATE TAXPAYERS

TREATMENT OF CAPITAL GAINS

Computation of Net Capital Gain. The first step is to net all long-term capital gains and losses and all short-term capital gains and losses. The result is the taxpayer's net long-term capital gain or loss and the taxpayer's net short-term capital gain or loss.[68] The following examples illustrate this computation:

Example 20. T has the following capital gains and losses for taxable year 19X6:

LTCG $15,000 LTCL ($10,000) STCG $15,000 STCL ($5,000)

T's net long-term capital gain is $5,000 and the net short-term capital gain is $10,000.

The second step is to compute the taxpayer's net capital gain or loss. In the prior example T has a net capital gain of $15,000, the total of the net long-term and net short-term capital gains.[69]

Treatment of Net Capital Gain. The following rules summarize the tax treatment of a net capital gain:

Rule 1. If the net capital gain is entirely long-term, the noncorporate taxpayer has two options; (1) a capital gains

---

67. § 1233(b)(2) and Reg. § 1.1233–1(c)(2).

68. §§ 1222(5), (6), (7) and (8).

69. § 1222(9).

deduction equal to fifty percent of the net gain or (2) an alternative tax of twenty-five percent on the net gain up to $50,000. Net long-term capital gains in excess of $50,000 are includible in gross income in full and are subject to the long-term capital gain deduction discussed below.

Rule 2.   If the net capital gain is all short-term, there is no capital gains deduction or alternative tax. The net gain is taxed as ordinary income at the regular tax rates.

Of course, if the net capital gain is part long-term and part short-term, Rule 1 applies to the long-term part and Rule 2 applies to the short-term part. The following examples illustrate the three possibilities; net capital gain—all long-term, net capital gain—all short-term, and net capital gain—part long-term and part short-term:

Example 21.   Assume T has a net long-term capital gain of $10,000 and a net short-term capital loss of $5,000. T's net capital gain is $5,000 and it is all long-term (Rule 1 applies).

Example 22.   Assume T has a net long-term capital loss of $5,000 and a net short-term capital gain of $10,000. T's net capital gain is $5,000 and it is all short-term (Rule 2 applies).

Example 23.   In Example 20, T has a net capital gain of $15,000 ($5,000 long-term and $10,000 short-term). Rule 1 applies to the $5,000 long-term part and Rule 2 applies to the $10,000 short-term part.

Long-term Capital Gains Deduction.   As discussed above (Rule 1), if the taxpayer's capital gains and losses for the taxable year result in a net capital gain which is long-term (all or part of the net capital gain) the long-term net capital gain is subject to two special provisions. These provisions are the capital gains deduction and the alternative tax. The capital gains deduction is equal to fifty percent of the long-term net capital gain.[70] In Example 21, assuming T uses the deduction as opposed to the alternative tax, the result is: Net capital gain of $5,000 less the fifty percent deduction of $2,500 = taxable amount of $2,500. T's tax on the $2,500 depends on his or her filing status (Married, single, etc.) and his or her tax bracket.

In Example 22, the result is: The capital gains deduction does not apply and the taxable amount is $5,000. In Example 23, the result is: Net capital gain of $15,000 less the fifty percent deduction of $2,500 (fifty percent of the $5,000 long-term part) = taxable amount of $12,500.

Alternative Tax.   The noncorporate taxpayer may, in lieu of the capital gains deduction, apply a twenty-five percent alternative tax

---

70.   § 1202 and Reg. § 1.1202–1(a).

rate to a maximum of $50,000 long-term net capital gains.[71] The maximum is $25,000 each for married persons filing separate returns.[72] Amounts above $50,000 are taxed at a maximum rate of thirty-five percent because the highest individual tax rate is seventy percent and the taxpayer applies the fifty percent capital gains deduction on these amounts. The alternative tax will apply for taxpayers whose marginal tax rate on the long-term capital gain is in excess of fifty percent, i. e., the effective rate under the capital gains deduction for the first $50,000 of long-term net gain for a taxpayer in a 60 percent bracket would be thirty percent. The alternative tax places a ceiling tax of 25 percent on the first $50,000 of long-term net capital gain.[73] The following examples illustrate the application of the alternative tax rate:

> **Example 24.** T has a net capital gain of $15,000 ($5,000 long-term and $10,000 short-term) for taxable year 19X6. If the alternative method is used, $5,000 is taxed at twenty-five percent and $10,000 is taxed at T's regular tax rates.

> **Example 25.** T has a net capital gain of $5,000 (all long-term) for taxable year 19X6. If the alternative tax applies, $5,000 is taxed at twenty-five percent.

> **Example 26.** T has a net capital gain of $5,000 (all short-term) for taxable year 19X6. The alternative tax does not apply and $5,000 is taxed at T's regular tax rates.

> **Example 27.** T has a net capital gain of $70,000 ($60,000 long-term and $10,000 short-term) for taxable year 19X6. Under the alternative tax method, $50,000 is taxed at twenty-five percent, and $10,000 long-term gain less $5,000 (fifty percent deduction) plus $10,000 short-term gain is taxed at T's regular tax rates.

Tax Preference Item. Fifty percent of a taxpayer's long term part of a net capital gain is treated as a tax preference item for purposes of the 15 percent minimum tax discussed in Chapter 10, regardless of whether the taxpayer uses the capital gains deduction or applies the alternative tax rate with respect to the long-term part of the net capital gain.[74] The minimum tax provisions also apply to corporate taxpayers.

TREATMENT OF CAPITAL LOSSES

Computation of Net Capital Loss. The computation of a taxpayer's net capital loss involves the same netting process used for com-

---

71. §§ 1201(b) and (d) and Reg. §§ 1.-1201–1(b) and (f).

72. § 1201(d)(3) and Reg. § 1.1201–1(f)(1)(iii).

73. § 1201(c) and Reg. § 1.1201–1(e).

74. § 57(a)(9)(A).

puting net capital gain. A net capital loss results if the taxpayer's capital losses exceed his capital gains for the taxable year.[75] Again it is necessary to differentiate between long-term and short-term capital losses. Both long-term and short-term capital losses offset either long-term or short-term capital gains, but losses remaining after such offset are treated differently depending on whether they are long-term or short-term.[76] The following examples illustrate the computation of a taxpayer's net capital loss:

> **Example 28.** T has the following capital gains and losses for taxable year 19X6:
>
> LTCG $1,000 LTCL ($2,800) STCG $1,000 STCL ($500)
>
> T's net capital loss is $1,300 (NLTCL of $1,800 less NSTCG of $500) and it is all long-term.

> **Example 29.** T has the following capital gains and losses for taxable year 19X6:
>
> LTCG $1,000 LTCL ($500) STCG $1,000 STCL ($2,800)
>
> T's net capital loss is $1,300 (NSTCL of $1,800 less NLTCG of $500) and it is all short-term.

> **Example 30.** T has the following capital gains and losses for taxable year 19X6:
>
> LTCG $500 LTCL ($1,200) STCG $500 STCL ($1,200)
>
> T's net capital loss is $1,400 (NLTCL of $700 plus NSTCL of $700) and it is part long-term ($700) and part short-term ($700).

Treatment of Net Capital Loss. The general rule is that a net capital loss is deductible from gross income up to an amount equal to the lower of the taxpayer's ordinary taxable income (taxable income before deducting any net capital loss and personal exemptions) or $1,000.[77] For 1977 the deductible amount has been increased to $2,000 and for 1978 and subsequent years it is $3,000. As a practical matter the taxpayer's ordinary taxable income will usually exceed these dollar limitations and subsequent discussion assumes that it does. Married persons filing separate returns are limited to one half of the allowable amounts each for taxable years after December 31, 1969.[78]

---

75. § 1222(10) defines a net capital loss as the net loss after the deduction from ordinary taxable income discussed later in this chapter. But this definition confuses the discussion of the treatment of capital losses, and, therefore, net capital loss is defined for practical purposes as the net loss before the deduction from ordinary taxable income.

76. § 1211(b)(1) and Reg. § 1.1211–1(b)(1).

77. §§ 1211(b)(1) and (3) and Reg. §§ 1.1211–1(b)(2) and (6).

78. § 1211(b)(2) and Reg. § 1.1211–1(b)(7)(i).

Special Limitation for Long-term Capital Loss After 1969. Prior to 1970 both long-term and short-term net capital losses offset ordinary taxable income dollar for dollar up to $1,000. Since long-term net capital gains are subject to the fifty percent capital gains deduction, Congress changed the law effective January 1, 1970 to give a similar effect to long-term net capital losses. The new rule is that the taxpayer permanently loses a dollar of long-term net capital loss for every dollar of such loss deducted from ordinary taxable income.[79] The following examples illustrate the application of the provisions for deducting net capital losses:

> **Example 31.** T has a net capital loss, all long-term, of $1,300. Prior to 1970 $1,000 could be deducted in the taxable year and $300 was carried over to the following taxable year (carryovers are discussed below). Under the new rule, if T incurs the long-term capital loss in taxable years after 1969, $650 is deductible and T permanently loses the remaining $650 as a deduction. It is not carried over to the following year.

> **Example 32.** T has a net capital loss either before or after 1969, all short-term, of $1,300. T deducts $1,000 in the taxable year and carries over the remaining $300 to the following taxable year. Therefore, it is generally preferable to recognize short-term rather than long-term capital losses. In 1977 and subsequent years, T could deduct the entire amount ($1,300) since the dollar limitations have been increased to $2,000 and $3,000 respectively.

> **Example 33.** T has a net capital loss of $3,000 in 1977. $1,500 is long-term and $1,500 is short-term. Short-term losses are always deducted first.[80] Since the total amount which is deductible in 1977 is limited to $2,000 ($3,000 for 1978 and subsequent years), T deducts the $1,500 of net short-term loss and $500 of net long-term loss in 1977. The $500 deduction effectively uses up $1,000 of the net long-term loss. Therefore, only $500 of long-term net loss is carried forward to 1978 as a long-term capital loss.

Carryovers. The taxpayer carries unused capital losses, short-term or long-term over indefinitely (except for amounts of long-term capital loss permanently lost).[81] Unused capital losses are carried over according to their original nature.[82] That is, if a short-term capital loss is carried over to the following year it is treated the same as a short-term capital loss occurring in that year.[83] Accordingly, it would first be used to offset short-term capital gains occurring in the

---

79. § 1211(b)(1)(C)(ii) and Reg. § 1.-1211–1(b)(2)(iii).

80. Reg. § 1.1211–1(b)(4)(i).

81. § 1212(b) and Reg. § 1.1212–1(b).

82. § 1212(b)(1).

83. Reg. § 1.1212–1(b)(1).

following year. The following examples illustrate the capital loss carryover provisions:

Example 34. In *1969*, T incurred a LTCL of $3,000 and a STCL of $1,000. In 1970 T has no capital gains or losses.

1. T's net capital loss for taxable year 1969 is $4,000. T deducts $1,000 (short-term) in 1969 and carries over $3,000 (long-term) to 1970.

2. T deducts $1,000 (long-term) in 1970 and carries over $2,000 (long-term) to 1971.

There is no permanent loss of long-term loss in the year the loss occurred if the loss occurred prior to 1970. The transitional rules for the carryover of pre-1970 capital losses are now rarely applicable. Due to the complexity of these transitional rules, a tax advisor should consult the Regulations where such rules are applicable.[84]

The treatment of a corporation's net capital gain or loss differs from the rules for individuals. Briefly, the differences are:

1. No fifty percent capital gains deduction.[85]

2. Alternative tax rate is thirty percent.[86]

3. Capital losses only offset capital gains; no deduction is permitted against ordinary taxable income, e. g., $2,000 in 1977 and $3,000 in 1978.[87]

4. Five year carryover and three year carryback of net capital loss (back first).[88] Carryovers and carrybacks always short-term regardless of original nature.[89]

These corporate rules are discussed in greater detail in Chapter 18.

Reporting. Capital gains and losses are reported on Schedule D of Form 1040 while other gains and losses are reported on Form 4797, "Suplemental Schedule of Gains and Losses."

TAX PLANNING
CONSIDERATIONS

MAXIMIZING BENEFITS

Due to the favorable tax rates applicable to long-term capital gains, consideration should always be given to the relative tax bene-

---

84. Reg. §§ 1.1212–1(b)(4) and 1.1211–1(b)(8), Example (9).

85. § 1202.

86. § 1201(a)(2).

87. § 1211(a).

88. § 1212(a)(1).

89. *Ibid.*

fits which accrue from holding a capital asset for the required long-term capital gain holding period. Since net short-term capital gains are includible in income in full, consideration should be given prior to the end of the year to the sale of capital assets at a loss to offset any short-term gains which have been recognized during the year.

Ordinary losses are generally preferable to capital losses due to the limitations which are imposed upon the deductibility of capital losses (e. g. $2,000 limitation on net capital losses in 1977 and $3,000 in 1978) and the requirement that capital losses must be used to off-set capital gains. The taxpayer may be able to convert what would otherwise have been capital loss to ordinary loss. For example, business as opposed to nonbusiness bad debts, losses from the sale or exchange of small business investment company stock and losses from the sale or exchange of small business stock all result in ordinary losses.[90] These provisions are discussed in Chapter 7. Finally, if the taxpayer has to have a capital loss it is preferable to have a short-term capital loss.

Although capital losses can be carried over indefinitely, indefinite becomes definite when a taxpayer dies. Any loss carryovers not used by then are permanently lost; that is, no tax benefit can be derived from the carryovers subsequent to death.[91] Therefore, the potential benefit of carrying over capital losses diminishes when dealing with older taxpayers.

SPREADING GAINS

If possible, it is usually beneficial to spread gains over more than one taxable year. In some cases this can be accomplished by electing the installment sales method of accounting. The bunching of long-term capital gains in one taxable year can be detrimental if they exceed $50,000 (alternative tax limit) or the minimum tax applies. Since the 15 percent minimum tax is generally applicable only when the taxpayer's tax preferences exceed the greater of $10,000 or ½ of his federal income tax liability for the year, it is possible to spread the long-term capital gains over several years and, therefore, avoid payment of any minimum tax.

YEAR–END PLANNING

Some general rules for timing the recognition of capital gains and losses near the end of a taxable year are:

1. If the taxpayer already has LTCL, recognize STCG.
2. If the taxpayer already has STCG, recognize LTCL.
3. If the taxpayer already has STCL, recognize STCG. Do not recognize LTCG because then the fifty percent capital gains

---

90. §§ 166(d), 1242 and 1244.   **91.** Rev.Rul. 74–175, 1974–1 C.B. 52.

deduction or alternative tax benefits are eliminated on the gain which is offset against the loss.

STOCK SALES

The following rules apply in determining the date of a stock sale:

1. If the taxpayer is on the accrual basis the date the sale is executed is the date of the sale.[92] The execution date is the date the broker completes the transaction on the stock exchange.

2. If the taxpayer is on the cash basis and the sale results in a gain, the date the sale is settled is the date of the sale.[93] The settlement date is the date the cash or other property is paid for the stock.

3. If the taxpayer is on the cash basis and the sale results in a loss, the date the sale is executed is the date of the sale.[94]

These rules are of particular importance in the determination of how long stock must be held to receive long-term treatment. In addition, year-end sales at a gain will not be recognized in the current year if the settlement date for the sale falls in the following year.

PROBLEM MATERIALS

Questions for Class Discussion

1. What type of preferential treatment is afforded long-term capital gains? What is the justification for this treatment?

2. Is there any reason a taxpayer would prefer to recognize a loss as a capital loss rather than as an ordinary loss?

3. What are the two ingredients necessary for the recognition of a capital gain or loss?

4. Define a long-term capital gain or loss.

5. What broad class of assets are not capital assets?

6. What types of assets can result in capital gains?

7. Can the sale of personal use assets result in capital losses?

8. Under what circumstances are copyrights capital assets?

9. Under what circumstances might an investment not be considered a capital asset?

10. What does "statutory expansion" mean with regard to § 1221?

11. Can a dealer in securities have investments (as opposed to inventory) in securities? Explain.

---

92. Rev.Rul. 70–344, 1970–2 C.B. 50.   **94.** Rev.Rul. 70–344, 1970–2 C.B. 50.

93. Rev.Rul. 72–381, 1972–2 C.B. 233.

12. Goods held primarily for sale are not capital assets. There is one exception to this rule. What is it? Why do you think this exception was enacted? To whom is it available?

13. Under what circumstances does § 1237 apply?

14. What expenses serve to increase the relative amount of capital gain under § 1237? How does this work?

15. Under what circumstances is the distribution of an employee's balance of a profit-sharing or pension plan a lump-sum distribution? What is the significance of such a distribution for tax purposes?

16. When is the worthlessness of a security which is a capital asset recognized? Does this always result in a capital loss?

17. Differentiate between the treatment of corporate obligations issued at a discount before May 28, 1969, and those issued after May 27, 1969.

18. True or false: Options are capital assets. Why or why not?

19. Suppose an option is a capital asset, is failure to exercise it considered a sale or exchange of a capital asset in all cases?

20. If an individual pays a $100 premium to acquire an option to buy stock, how does the call premium effect the basis of the stock if the option is exercised?

20.1 If an individual writes an option on a stock after 9/1/76, what treatment is accorded if (1) the option lapses unexercised or (2) the option is exercised?

21. When does the transfer of a patent result in long-term capital gain? Short-term capital gain? Ordinary income?

22. What three elements are generally required for capital gain (loss) treatment on a patent? (Do not consider statutory expansion.)

23. Define by example "substantial rights" (in connection with patents). Are these always substantial?

24. To whom is § 1235 treatment available?

25. What is a franchise? In practice does the transfer of a franchise usually result in capital gain (loss) treatment? Why or why not?

26. What is unique about § 1253? Describe the unusual provision.

27. When are lease cancellation payments capital in nature?

28. How is the required holding period computed for purposes of determining if capital gain (loss) is eligible for long-term treatment?

29. Define a short sale. Why does a seller enter into a short sale?

30. What is the general rule used to determine the holding period of property sold short? What is an exception to this rule and why was it enacted?

31. Comment on: "The maximum tax rate that can be applied to long-term net capital gains is twenty-five percent (25%)."

32. True or false: The portion of a taxpayer's capital gain which is not taxed (fifty percent of the long-term net capital gain) is the amount that is a tax preference item. Why?

33. True or false: When the taxpayer has a long-term net capital loss in 1978 or subsequent years, a maximum of $3,000 can be deducted from gross income in any one year. However, the long-term net capital loss must be at least $6,000 to receive a $3,000 deduction.

34. Differentiate between the capital loss carryover rules for unused capital losses of individuals and corporations.

35. Do the unused capital losses of individuals retain their same character upon the carryover to succeeding years? Explain.

36. What are the major differences in the treatment afforded capital gains of a corporation as opposed to those of an individual?

37. What can you plan to do to maximize the benefits of a long-term capital loss? Of a short-term capital loss? Why?

Problems

1. T gives M a copyright on his book, *How to Buy and Sell Cottages at a Profit* which had a basis of $18,000 to T. After one year, M sold the copyright to Y Corporation for $25,000.

   What was M's recognized gain upon the sale of the copyright? What was the nature of M's gain?

2. B inherits an old plantation worth $28,000 in 19X5. Being a city dweller with no use for country land, B is determined to sell the plantation. He parcels it out into twenty lots of seven acres each, numbering the lots one through twenty, adjacent numbers representing adjacent lots. In 19X5 he sells lots numbered one, three, seven, and nine, as they are for $3,500 each. The selling expenses are $250 on each lot. In 19X6 he sells lots numbered four and five to R and lot number two to S. The sale to R is for $7,000 with expenses of $300. The sale to S is for $3,500 with expenses of $250.

   (a) What gain is realized on each lot? What is the recognized gain on each lot? What is the nature of the gain?

   (b) In 19X7 B decides to install roads to and water facilities on the remaining lots which have now been in the family for ninety years.

The cost of this is roughly $1,500 per lot. However, the value of the lots is now $5,000. B neither expenses the improvement costs nor adjusts his basis to reflect these improvements. Late in 19X7, lots numbered six and eight are sold, and in 19X8, lot number ten is sold. All lots are sold for $5,800 each with selling expenses of $350 each. What is the realized and recognized gain? What is the nature of the gain?

(c) Having saved much of his earlier gains, B decides to simply enjoy his land with his family and friends. He ceases sales for seven years and then finds himself short of cash so he sells lots numbered eleven and twelve to his friend A for $12,500. There are no selling expenses. What is the realized and recognized gain? What is the nature of the gain?

3. A meets all the conditions of § 1237 in subdividing and selling a single tract. In 19X6 he sells 4 lots to B, C, D and E. In the same year F buys 3 adjacent lots. What is A's gain, and what is its nature?

4. Assume the taxpayer meets all the conditions of § 1237 and the selling price of the sixth lot of a tract is $10,000, the basis of the lot in the hands of the taxpayer is $5,500, and the expenses of sale are $750.

(a) What is the taxpayer's realized gain?

(b) What is the taxpayer's recognized gain and its nature?

5. JP had been employed by M International for twelve years. In January, 1976 he left M to assume the presidency of V Enterprises. During his association with M, JP had contributed $12,000 to a qualified pension plan. M matched each $1.00 JP put in with $3.00. In the fall of 1976, JP received full distribution of $60,000 from the pension plan.

(a) What was JP's total income from the plan? How much of it was ordinary income? How much of it was capital gain?

(b) Suppose JP had not received the lump-sum amount until the fall of 1977. Would your answers to part (a) change? How and why?

6. A, a farmer, purchased securities of the XYZ Corporation on April 7, 19X5, for $500. On August 8, 19X5 the XYZ Corporation filed for bankruptcy.

(a) What is A's realized and recognized loss? What is the nature of the loss?

(b) If A were a dealer in securities, would your answer to part (a) change? How and why?

7. On January 1, 19X0 (after May 27, 1969), A, a calendar-year taxpayer, purchases at original issue for cash of $7,600, M Corpora-

tion's 10-year, 5 percent bond which has a stated redemption price at maturity of $10,000. On January 1, 19X2, A sells the bond to B for $9,040. A has previously included $480 of the original issue discount in gross income and increased his basis in the bond by that amount to $8,080. At the time of original issue there was no intention to call the bond before maturity. What is A's gain, and what is its nature?

8. Assume the same facts as in problem 7, except that at the time of original issue there was an intention to call the bond before maturity. Now what is A's gain, and what is its nature?

9. In August of 19X0 (after May 27, 1969), C bought seven ten-year $1,000 bonds of the L Corporation for $6,650. In August, 19X4, L Corporation redeemed four of C's bonds for $980 each. C held the remaining three bonds to maturity in August of 19X10.

   (a) Indicate the amount of income and its nature which C will realize and recognize from 19X0 to 19X10. (Assume he is a fiscal year taxpayer whose year commenced at the time the bonds were purchased.)

   (b) Suppose L Corporation bonds are fifteen-year bonds issued before May 28, 1969 for $6,510. Does this change your answer to part (a)? How and why?

10. A taxpayer is considering buying a new house for his residence and acquires an option to buy a certain house at a fixed price. Although the property goes up in value, the taxpayer decides he does not want the house for his residence and sells the option for more than he paid for it. What is the nature of the taxpayer's gain?

11. Assume the same facts as in Problem 10, except that the property goes down in value and the taxpayer decides not to purchase the house. He sells the option at a loss. What is the nature of the taxpayer's loss?

12. A dealer in industrial property acquires an option to buy an industrial site and fails to exercise the option. What is the nature of the dealer's loss?

13. H Inc. owns a patent on mining equipment which a Consortum would like to use for eight months to build their own equipment in that design. H agrees to this in return for $1,000 each month that the Consortum uses the patent. They are to have exclusive right to make, use, and sell such equipment in a designated sales region. H has a basis of $3,000 in the patent which because of rapid development in the field has an uncertain life.

   (a) Has a sale or exchange occurred? Explain. How much income and what kind will H recognize? When is the income recognized?

(b) Suppose the Consortum tried to buy the patent directly from G, its creator, who by the way, owns twenty-eight percent of the Consortum. Assuming the same price and basis, how does your answer change?

(c) Suppose H were in the business of buying and selling patents. How does your answer in part (a) change?

14. H is an exclusive distributor for M Corp. of certain frozen food products which he distributes to frozen food freezer and locker customers. The terms of his distributorship do not make it necessary to have any substantial investment in inventory. H rents a loading platform for a nominal amount, but has no warehouse space. Orders for goods from customers are consolidated by H and forwarded to the producer from time to time. Upon receipt of these goods, H allocates them to the individual orders of customers and delivers them immediately by truck. Although it would require a fleet of fifteen or twenty trucks to carry out this operation, the distributor uses only one truck of his own and hires cartage companies to deliver the bulk of the merchandise to the customers. Would payments received upon the cancellation of the distributorship agreement be treated under § 1241 as though received upon the sale or exchange of the agreement?

15. Sonic Burger Number Seven would like to sell the franchise that it has from Sonic Burger, Inc., to J who is in the process of purchasing Number Seven's location and equipment. Under the terms of the franchise, it may be sold only with the approval of Sonic Burger, Inc. Number Seven purchased the ten-year franchise two years ago for $10,000. The current basis is $8,000. They will sell it for $12,000.

What type of income does Number Seven realize and recognize? How does J treat his payment(s) if they are contingent on Sonic Burger, Inc. remaining in business?

16. BBQ Corporation, a nationwide franchisor of BBQ sparerib drive-ins, transfers to M the right to establish BBQ drive-ins in State X, including the right to franchise others to establish BBQ drive-ins in State X. BBQ Corporation also transfers to S the right to establish BBQ drive-ins in State Y. M then establishes 25 BBQ drive-ins in State X and franchises ten other persons to establish BBQ drive-ins in State X. Which of these transfers qualify for purposes of § 1253?

17. A buys 100 shares of XYZ stock at $10 per share on February 1, 19X5, sells short 100 shares of XYZ stock at $16 per share on July 1, 19X5, and closes the short sale on August 2, 19X5, by delivering the 100 shares of XYZ stock purchased on February 1, 19X5, to the lender of the stock used to effect the short sale.

What is the amount and the nature of A's gain or loss upon the the closing of the short sale?

18. B buys 100 shares of XYZ stock at $10 per share on February 1, 19X4, sells short 100 shares of XYZ stock at $16 per share on July 1, 19X5, closes the short sale on August 1, 19X5, with 100 shares of XYZ stock purchased on that date at $18 per share, and on August 2, 19X5, sells at $18 per share the 100 shares of XYZ stock purchased on February 1, 19X4.

   (a) What is the amount and nature of B's gain or loss upon the closing of the short sale?

   (b) What is the amount and nature of B's gain or loss upon the sale of the stock on August 2, 19X5?

19. J sells short 100 shares of XYZ stock at $16 per share on February 1, 19X5. He buys 250 shares of XYZ stock on March 1, 19X5, at $10 per share and holds the latter stock until April 2, 19X6, at which time, 100 shares of the 250 shares of XYZ stock are delivered to close the short sale made on February 1, 19X5.

   (a) What is the amount and the nature of J's gain or loss upon the closing of the short sale?

   (b) When does the holding period start for the remaining 150 shares?

20. H and W, husband and wife, who file a joint return for the calendar year 19X1, have taxable income (exclusive of capital gains and losses) of $80,000. In 19X1 they realize long-term capital gain of $30,000 on the installment method under § 453. From securities transactions in 19X1, they have long-term capital gains of $60,000 and a short-term capital loss of $10,000. Compute their tax.

21. You are single and your taxable income (after deducting your itemized deductions and personal exemption) is $44,000. This includes a capital-gain deduction of $2,000. The 50% maximum tax on earned income does not apply.

   (a) Compute your regular tax.

   (b) Compute your alternative tax.

22. A, an unmarried individual with no dependents, has the following transactions in 1977:

Taxable income exclusive of capital gains and losses	$13,300
Long-term capital gain	400
Long-term capital loss	(600)
Short-term capital gain	900
Short-term capital loss	(1,400)

What is A's net capital gain or loss? How is it treated?

23. C, an unmarried individual with no dependents, has the following transactions in 1980:

Taxable income exclusive of capital gains and losses	$13,300
Long-term capital loss	(6,000)
Long-term capital gain	3,000
Short-term capital gain	3,000
Short-term capital loss (carried to 1980 from 1979)	(3,000)

What is C's net capital gain or loss? How is it treated?

24. D, an unmarried individual with no dependents, has the following transactions in 1980:

Taxable income exclusive of capital gains and losses	$13,300
Long-term capital gain	5,000
Long-term capital loss	(7,000)
Long-term capital loss carried to 1980 from 1979	(500)
Short-term capital gain	1,100
Short-term capital loss	(1,400)

What is D's net capital gain or loss? How is it treated?

25. E, an unmarried individual with no dependents, has the following transactions in 1980:

Taxable income exclusive of capital gains and losses	$13,300
Long-term capital loss	(2,000)
Long-term capital loss carried to 1980 from 1979	(500)
Short-term capital gain	2,600
Short-term capital loss carried to 1980 from 1979	(3,000)

What is E's net capital gain or loss? How is it treated?

26. For the taxable year 1977, F, an unmarried individual, has a long-term capital loss of $2,000, and no other capital gains or losses. What is F's net capital loss? How is it treated?

27. For the taxable year 1977, G, an unmarried individual, has a $500 short-term capital gain, a $700 short-term capital loss, a $1,000 long-term capital gain, and a $1,700 long-term capital loss. What is G's net capital gain or loss? How is it treated?

28. For 19X0, H, a married individual filing a separate return, has a long-term capital loss of $3,500 and a short-term capital gain of $3,000. He also has a pre-1970 short-term capital loss of $2,000 which is carried to 19X0. Discuss the tax treatment of these items.

29. M owned a boat which is held for personal use, the "Flying Queen," which he purchased in 19X2 for $10,000. M wants a bigger boat so he sold the "Flying Queen" in 19X7 for $20,000.

(a) How much gain does M include in his tax computations for 19X7? How is it treated?

(b) What if M is in a fifty-five percent (55%) tax bracket, how does he treat the gain on the "Flying Queen?"

(c) Suppose M had really cleaned up in the stock market that year and had $54,000 in long-term capital gains in addition to the gain on the "Flying Queen." Describe the tax treatment of all his gains assuming once again that M is in the fifty-five percent (55%) income tax bracket.

(d) In each of the above parts, assuming M's total gain is that indicated in each part, what tax preference items does M have?

30. M had poor luck in the stock market in 1976 and showed a net long-term capital loss of $2,000. In 1977 he sold five shares of XYZ stock for $700 each. He had purchased the stock in August of the same year for $550 each. He also had a profit of $800 on the sale of his life-time residence.

(a) What is the gain (loss) which M realized? What is its nature?

(b) How much is recognized? Is there any difference between the amount recognized and the total taxed? What and why?

(c) Any considerations that M should remember for 1978?

31. E lost $6,000 in 1969 extricating himself from a land deal he had bought into in the sixties. The loss was so disillusioning for E that it was not until 1977 that he had the courage to try investing again. Having considerable gross income, he bought ten shares of XYZ Corp. in January 1977 for $900 each. In August 1977 he sold three shares for $1,500 each.

(a) What type of gain (loss) does he recognize and realize? What effect does this have on his taxable income, assuming the $6,000 loss from 1969 is carried forward to 1977? What considerations should E remember for future years?

(b) In 1978 E sold his remaining shares of XYZ Corp. for $1,-550 each. What type of gain (loss) does he realize and recognize? What effect does this have on his taxable income? What considerations should E remember for future years?

32. W had $9,000 taxable income in 1977. He also had $500 in short-term capital gains, $800 in short-term capital losses, $500 in long-term capital gains, and $4,700 in long-term capital losses.

(a) How much loss is deductible from taxable income? How much is actually deducted? Are there any considerations for 1978?

(b) How does your response change if the loss occurred before 1970?

33. You had capital gains and losses for the year 1977 as follows:

	Short-term	Long-term
Gains	$700	$ 400
Losses	(800)	(2,000)

(a) Compute your net capital gain or loss.

(b) How will your net capital gain or loss be treated?

34. In 1977 you realize short-term capital losses of $400 and long-term capital losses of $2,300.

(a) How much of your net capital loss is deductible in 1977?

(b) How much is carried over to 1978?

35. You are single and your taxable income (after deducting your itemized deductions and personal exemption) is $150,000. This includes $38,000 of ordinary income and $112,000 net capital gain ($224,000 long-term capital gain less $112,000 capital gain deduction).

(a) What is your regular tax?

(b) What is your alternative tax?

36. In addition to taxable income of $100,000 per year (without regard to capital gains and losses), B incurred the following capital gains and losses:

	1975	1976	1977	1978
LTCG(L)	($2,500)	($4,000)	$___	$3,000
STCG(L)	($3,500)	($2,000)	$___	$2,000

(a) What is the maximum deduction B may claim in each year?

(b) What are the amounts and character of the carryovers to 1976, 1977, 1978, and 1979?

(c) What difference does it make if a carryover is long- or short-term?

(d) What is the source of losses deemed used for the deduction in each year?

(e) Could he carry back the losses?

(f) How long can he carry forward unused capital losses, in general?

(g) Answer Parts (a) through (f) for B's wholly-owned corporation, B, Inc., which incurred identical losses.

Research Problems

1. X inherited 500 shares of IBM stock during 1977 with a basis of $300 each. Since the stock pays a low dividend relative to its market value, X's broker advises him to write call options on the

IBM stock. X can write a 6-month option which entitles the holder to acquire the stock at $330. X receives a call premium of $30 × 500 shares or $15,000 in 1977.

(a) What are the tax consequences to X upon the receipt of the $15,000 call premium in 1977?

(b) If the option is exercised during 1978, what are the tax consequences to X?

(c) If the option is not exercised, what are the tax consequences to X?

2.   Y sold a tract of land which he acquired several years ago as an investment. The adjusted basis of the land was $40,000 and its selling price was $100,000. The buyer was a major corporation who paid $60,000 cash and a corporate note for $40,000 (payable in equal installments over 10 years and bearing interest at 7%). X's bank offered to buy the note for $36,000.

(a) How will X report the land sale in the year the transaction is consummated? Upon the subsequent collections on the note assuming X does not sell the note to the bank?

(b) Is gain from the sale capital gain or ordinary income?

3.   Y received a lump-sum distribution from a noncontributory qualified profitsharing plan amounting to $100,000 in 1977. The distribution consisted solely of common stock of the employer corporation which had a cost basis of $40,000 to the profitsharing trust.

(a) How should Y report the lump-sum distribution in 1977?

(b) What is the basis of the employer stock to Y?

Chapter 15

PROPERTY TRANSACTIONS— SECTION 1231 AND RECAPTURE PROVISIONS

A long-term capital gain was defined in Chapter 14 as the recognized gain from the sale or exchange of a capital asset where certain holding period requirements are met. The required holding periods are "more than nine months" for 1977 and "more than twelve months" in 1978 and subsequent years. This chapter is concerned with:

(1) § 1231 which applies to the sale or exchange of business properties and certain involuntary conversions; and

(2) recapture provisions which provide that certain gains which

(a) might otherwise qualify for long-term capital gain treatment or

(b) would not otherwise be recognized, receive ordinary income treatment.

SECTION 1231 ASSETS

RELATIONSHIP TO § 1221

§ 1221(2) provides that depreciable or real property used in a trade or business is not a capital asset.[1] Thus, recognized gains from

---

1. § 1221(2) and Reg. § 1.1221–1(b).

the disposition of such types of property (principally machinery and equipment, buildings and land) would be ordinary income as opposed to capital gain. § 1231, however, provides that in certain cases long-term capital gain treatment applies to sales, exchanges and involuntary conversions of these business assets. § 1231 also applies in certain cases to involuntary conversions of capital assets. The latter would not otherwise qualify for long-term capital gain treatment under § 1222 because an involuntary conversion is not a sale or exchange.

JUSTIFICATION FOR FAVORABLE CAPITAL GAIN TREATMENT

Congress enacted the predecessor to § 1231 in 1942 to ease the burden of taxation for sales or other dispositions of business assets. At this time, such gains were treated as ordinary income. Congress also wanted to encourage transfers which would be more beneficial to the war effort. Involuntary conversions were included primarily because taxpayers whose property was requisitioned by the Government for the war effort were usually not able to postpone gain under the predecessor to § 1033, due to the unavailability of either replacement funds or property.

PROPERTY INCLUDED

§ 1231 property includes:

(1) Depreciable or real property used in a trade or business (principally, machinery and equipment, buildings and land).[2]

Inventory and property described in § 1221(3), such as copyrights and literary compositions are not § 1231 property.[3]

(2) Timber, coal, or domestic iron ore to which § 631 applies.[4]

(3) Livestock, regardless of age, held for draft, breeding, dairy, or sporting purposes. Poultry is not included.[5]

(4) Unharvested crop on land used in a trade or business.[6]

Timber. A taxpayer can elect to treat the cutting of timber held for sale or for use in a trade or business as a sale or exchange.[7] If the taxpayer makes this election, the transaction qualifies under § 1231. The taxpayer must have owned the timber or a contract to cut it, for more than nine months prior to the date the cutting takes place. The required holding period is more than one year for 1978 and subsequent years. The recognized § 1231 gain or loss is determined at

---

2. § 1231(b)(1) and Reg. § 1.1231–1(a). **5.** § 1231(b)(3).

3. § 1231(b)(1) and Reg. § 1.1231–1(a). **6.** § 1231(b)(4).

4. § 1231(b)(2). **7.** § 631(a) and Reg. § 1.631–1.

the time the timber is cut and is equal to the difference between the timber's fair market value as of the first day of the taxable year and its adjusted basis for depletion. If a taxpayer sells the timber for more or less than its fair market value as of the first day of the taxable year in which it is cut, the difference is ordinary income or loss.

This provision was enacted to provide preferential treatment relative to the natural growth value of timber, whose maturation is a relatively long-term process. Congress also believed this favorable treatment would encourage reforestation of timber lands. § 631 also provides that if a taxpayer disposes of timber, held for the required long-term holding period, under a royalty contract (where the taxpayer retains an economic interest in the property), the disposal is treated as a sale of the timber.[7.1] Therefore, any gain or loss qualifies under § 1231.

Coal or Domestic Iron Ore. If a taxpayer disposes of coal or domestic iron ore, held for the required long-term capital gain holding period under a royalty contract (where the taxpayer retains an economic interest in the property), the disposal is treated as a sale of the coal or domestic iron ore.[8] Therefore, any gain or loss qualifies under § 1231.

The provisions including timber, coal and domestic iron ore royalties under § 1231 were enacted primarily to encourage the development and preservation of natural resources in the United States and to enable domestic producers to compete more favorably with foreign producers.

Livestock. Cattle and horses must be held for at least 24 months, and other livestock for at least 12 months to qualify under § 1231.[9] The primary reason for enacting this provision was the considerable amount of litigation over the character of livestock. That is, whether it was held primarily for sale to customers (ordinary income) or for use in a trade or business (§ 1231 property).

Unharvested Crops. An unharvested crop on land used in a trade or business, where the land has been held for the required long-term capital gain holding period, qualifies under § 1231 if the crop and land are disposed of at the same time to the same person.[10] The cost of producing the crop must be capitalized (not expensed) or § 1231 does not apply.[11] This provision was enacted because taxpayers were previously able to recover the costs of producing crops

---

7.1 § 631(b) and Reg. § 1.631–2.

8. § 631(c) and Reg. § 1.631–3.

9. § 1231(b)(3) and Reg. § 1.1231–2(a)(1). Cattle and horses acquired prior to 1970 only had to be held for at least 12 months. All livestock ac-

quired prior to 1970 and held for sporting purposes does not qualify under § 1231. Reg. § 1.1231–2(a)(2).

10. § 1231(b)(4) and Reg. § 1.1231–1(c)(5).

11. § 268 and Reg. § 1.268–1.

through current deductions and were usually allowed long-term capital gain treatment when the crops were disposed of.

EXCLUDED PROPERTY

§ 1231 property does not include:

(1) Property held for less than the required long-term capital gain holding period, i. e., nine months in 1977.[12] Since the benefit of § 1231 is long-term capital gain treatment, the holding period must correspond with the same holding periods which apply to capital assets. Of course, livestock must be held either 12 or 24 months or more. Unharvested crops do not have to be held for the required long-term holding period, but the land must be held for the required period, i. e., "more than nine months" in 1977 and "more than one year" in 1978.

(2) Property where casualty losses exceed casualty gains for the taxable year.[13] If a taxpayer has a net casualty loss, the individual casualty gains and losses are treated as ordinary gains and losses.[14] If the netting of casualty gains and losses results in a net gain, the net gain is merged with the § 1231 gains and losses.

(3) Inventory and property held primarily for sale to customers.[15]

(4) § 1221(3) property; copyrights, literary compositions, etc.[16]

GENERAL PROCEDURE FOR § 1231 COMPUTATION

Step 1. Net all gains and losses from casualties and thefts. The losses from personal casualties are deducted after reduction by the $100 floor. Casualty gains result where insurance proceeds exceed the adjusted basis of the property.

A. If the casualty gains exceed the casualty losses, add the excess to the other § 1231 gains for the taxable year.[17]

B. If the casualty losses exceed the casualty gains, exclude all losses and gains from further § 1231 computation.[18] If this is the case, all casualty gains are ordinary income and all cas-

---

12. § 1231(a) and Reg. § 1.1231–1(a).

13. § 1231(a) and Reg. § 1.1231–1(e)(3).

14. Reg. §§ 1.1231–1(e)(3) and 1.1231–1(g) Example 2.

15. § 1231(b)(1)(A) and (B) and Reg. § 1.1231–1(a).

16. § 1231(b)(1)(C).

17. § 1231(a) and Reg. § 1.1231–1(e)(1).

18. § 1231(a) and Reg. § 1.1231–1(e)(3).

ualty losses are either deductible *from* adjusted gross income (personal casualty losses) or deductible *for* adjusted gross income (business casualty losses).

Step 2. After adding any net casualty gain from Step 1 A to the other § 1231 gains, net all § 1231 gains and losses.

A. If the gains exceed losses, the excess is a long-term capital gain.[19]

B. If the losses exceed gains, all gains are ordinary income and all losses are deductible *from* adjusted gross income (personal casualty losses) or *for* adjusted gross income (all business losses).[20]

If the taxpayer is in a position to recognize § 1231 gains in one year and § 1231 losses in another year, the losses will not have to be offset against the gains. The result is that all the gains in one year are long-term capital gains and all the losses in the other year are ordinary losses deductible in full against ordinary income. The following chart summarizes the § 1231 computational procedure.

Chart I

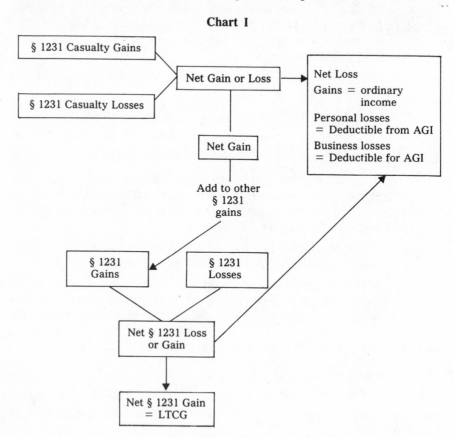

19. § 1231(a).   20. *Ibid.*

The following examples express the application of the § 1231 computation procedure:

Example 1. During the current Year T had the following recognized gains and losses:

Capital Gains and Losses

Long-term capital gain	$3,000
Long-term capital loss	(400)
Short-term capital gain	1,000
Short-term capital loss	(200)

Casualties

Theft of diamond ring (owned four months)	$ (800)
Fire damage to personal residence (owned ten years)	(400)
Gain from insurance recovery on accidental destruction of business truck (owned two years)	200

§ 1231 Gains and Losses from Depreciable Business Assets
Held Over Nine Months in 1977 or One Year in 1978

Asset A	$ 300
Asset B	1,100
Asset C	(500)

Gains and Losses from Depreciable Business Assets
Held Less than the Required Long-term Capital Gain Holding Period

Asset D	$ 200
Asset E	(300)

Disregarding the recapture of depreciation possibility (discussed later in this chapter) the tax treatment of the above gains and losses is as follows:

1. The theft of the diamond ring is not a § 1231 transaction because it was not held for the required long-term holding period.

2. The casualty loss of $400 exceeds the casualty gain of $200. Therefore, both the loss and gain are excluded from § 1231 treatment. The $400 loss is deductible from adjusted gross income (personal loss) and the $200 gain is ordinary income.

3. The gains from § 1231 transactions (Assets A–C) exceed the losses by $900 ($1,400 less $500). This excess is a long-term capital gain and is added to T's other long-term capital gains.

4. T's net long-term capital gain is $3,500 ($3,000 plus $900 from § 1231 less the long-term capital loss of $400). T's net short-term capital gain is $800 ($1,000 less $200). The result is a net capital gain of $4,300. The long-term portion ($3,500) is subject to either the 50% capital gains deduction or the 25% alternative tax, depending upon which provision results in the lowest tax liability for T. The $800 short-term portion is ordinary income and subject to T's regular tax rates.

5. The gain and loss from Assets D and E (depreciable business assets held for less than the required holding period) are treated as ordinary gain and loss by T.

Example 2. Assume the same facts as in Example 1 except the loss from Asset C was $1,500 instead of $500:

1. The treatment of the casualty losses is the same as in Example 1.

2. The losses from § 1231 transactions now exceed the gains by $100 ($1,500 less $1,400). The result is that the gains from Assets A and B are ordinary income and the loss from Asset C is a deduction for adjusted gross income (business loss).

3. The net capital gain is $3,400 ($2,600 long-term plus $800 short-term). The $2,600 long-term portion is subject to either the 50% capital gains deduction or the 25% alternative tax. The $800 short-term portion is ordinary income.

Example 3. Assume the same facts as in Example 1 except that the casualty gain was $600 instead of $200:

1. The casualty gain of $600 exceeds the casualty loss of $400. Therefore, the $200 excess gain is added to the other § 1231 gains.

2. The gains from § 1231 transactions (Assets A–C and the net casualty gain) exceed the losses by $1,100 ($1,400 plus net casualty gain of $200 less $500). This excess is a long-term capital gain and is added to T's other long-term capital gains.

3. T's net long-term capital gain is $3,700 ($3,000 plus $1,100 from Section 1231 less the long-term capital loss of $400). T's net short-term capital gain is $800. The result is a net capital gain of $4,500. The long-term portion ($3,700) is subject to either the 50% capital gains deduction or the 25% alternative tax, depending upon which provision results in the lowest tax liability for T. The $800 short-term portion is ordinary income and subject to T's regular tax rates.

SECTION 1245 RECAPTURE

§ 1245 was enacted to prevent taxpayers from receiving the dual benefits of depreciation deductions which offset ordinary income and long-term capital gain treatment under § 1231 upon the disposition of the depreciated property.

§ 1245 provides, in general, that the portion of recognized gain from the sale or other disposition of § 1245 property which represents depreciation taken since January 1, 1962 (including additional first year depreciation under § 179), is recaptured as ordinary income.[21] This does not mean the depreciation deductions are lost. It only means that to the extent of depreciation taken, the gain does not qualify for long-term capital gain treatment under § 1231. If § 1245 property is disposed of in a transaction other than a sale, exchange or involuntary conversion, the maximum amount recaptured is the excess of the property's fair market value over its adjusted basis.[22]

§ 1245 PROPERTY

Generally, § 1245 property includes all depreciable personal (as opposed to real) property—principally, machinery and equipment.[23] Depreciation taken on livestock after 1969 is included.[24] Buildings and their structural components are not § 1245 property.[25] The following property is also § 1245 property:

(1) Amortizable personal property such as patents, copyrights and leaseholds of § 1245 property.[26] Professional baseball and football players contracts are § 1245 property.[27]

(2) Elevators and escalators.[28] However, only depreciation taken after June 30, 1963, is recaptured.[29]

(3) Certain depreciable tangible real property (other than buildings and their structural components) employed as an integral part of certain activities such as manufacturing and production.[30]

(4) Amortization taken on pollution control facilities, railroad grading and tunnel bores, on-the-job training and child care facilities.[31]

§ 1245 Potential. The following examples express the general application of § 1245:

Example 4. Assume § 1245 property with an estimated useful life of 12 years and no salvage value. Cost when acquired on

---

21. §§ 1245(a)(1) and (2) and Reg. §§ 1.1245–1(a), 1.1245–2(a)(2)(i) and 1.-1245–2(a)(3).

22. § 1245(a)(1) and Reg. § 1.1245–1(a).

23. § 1245(a)(3)(A) and Reg. §§ 1.-1245–3(a)(1) and 1.1245–3(b).

24. § 1245(a)(2)(C) and Reg. §§ 1.-1245–2(a)(2)(iii) and 1.1245–3(a)(4).

25. § 1245(a)(3)(B) and Reg. § 1.1245–3(c)(1).

26. § 1245(a)(3)(A) and Reg. §§ 1.-1245–3(a)(1)(i), 1.1245–3(a)(2) and 1.-1245–3(b)(2).

27. Act § 212(b) adding § 1245(a)(4). Previously, it was the IRS position that such amounts were subject to recapture. Rev.Rul. 67–380, 1967–2 C.B. 291 and Rev.Rul. 71–137, 1971–1 C.B. 104.

28. § 1245(a)(3)(C) and Reg. § 1.1245–3(a)(1)(iii).

29. § 1245(a)(2)(B) and Reg. § 1.1245–2(a)(2)(ii).

30. § 1245(a)(3)(B) and Reg. §§ 1.-1245–3(a)(1)(ii) and 1.1245–3(c)(1).

31. § 1245(a)(3)(D).

January 1, 1961 was $12,000. The asset is sold on January 1, 1971 for $13,000. Depreciation amounting to $10,000 has been deducted under the straight-line method.

1. The recognized gain from the sale is $11,000. This is the amount realized of $13,000 less the adjusted basis of $2,000 ($12,000 cost less $10,000 depreciation taken).

2. Depreciation taken since January 1, 1962, is $9,000. Therefore, $9,000 of the $11,000 recognized gain is ordinary income and the remaining $2,000 gain is § 1231 gain.

Example 5. Assume the same facts as in Example 4 except the asset is sold for $9,000 instead of $13,000.

1. The recognized gain from the sale is $7,000. This is the amount realized of $9,000 less adjusted basis of $2,000.

2. Depreciation taken since January 1, 1962 is $9,000. Therefore, since the $9,000 depreciation taken since January 1, 1962 exceeds the recognized gain of $7,000, the entire $7,000 recognized gain is ordinary income.

Example 6. Assume the same facts as in Example 4 except the asset is sold for $1,500 instead of $13,000.

1. The recognized loss from the sale is $500. This is the amount realized of $1,500 less adjusted basis of $2,000.

2. § 1245 does not apply because the recapture rules do not apply to losses. The entire $500 recognized loss is § 1231 loss.

Observations on § 1245.

1. In most instances the total depreciation taken since 1961 will exceed the recognized gain. Therefore, the disposition of § 1245 property usually results in ordinary income rather than capital gain under § 1231.

2. Recapture applies to the total amount of depreciation allowed or allowable regardless of the depreciation method used.

3. Recapture applies regardless of the holding period of the property. Of course, the entire recognized gain would be ordinary income if the property were held for less than the required long-term capital gain holding period because § 1231 would not apply.

4. § 1245 does not apply to losses.[32] Losses receive § 1231 treatment.

SECTION 1250 RECAPTURE

§ 1250 was enacted in 1964 for depreciable real property. The provision prevents taxpayers from receiving both the benefits of ac-

---

32. Reg. § 1.1245–1(d).

celerated depreciation deductions and subsequent long-term capital gain treatment upon the sale of the property.

§ 1250 recapture applies only to additional depreciation taken, and in certain cases is a function of how long the property has been held. Generally, § 1250 provides that the portion of recognized gain from the sale or other disposition of § 1250 property which represents additional depreciation (excess of accelerated depreciation over straight-line) taken since January 1, 1964 is recaptured as ordinary income.[33] If § 1250 property is disposed of in a transaction other than a sale, exchange or involuntary conversion, the maximum amount recaptured is the excess of the property's fair market value over its adjusted basis.[34]

Generally, § 1250 property is depreciable real property (principally, buildings and their structural components) that is not subject to § 1245.[35] Intangible real property such as leaseholds of § 1250 property is also included.[36]

§ 1250 POTENTIAL

The potential recapture is equal to the amount of additional depreciation taken since January 1, 1964. However, the lower of this amount or the gain is multiplied by a percentage to determine the amount of gain recaptured as ordinary income. Since the percentage differs depending on whether the additional depreciation was taken before 1970 or after 1969, pre-1970 and post-1969 recapture amounts must be determined separately. The following general rules apply:

1. Post-1969 additional depreciation is depreciation taken in excess of straight-line after December 31, 1969.[37]

2. Pre-1970 additional depreciation is depreciation taken in excess of straight-line prior to January 1, 1970 and since January 1, 1964.[38]

3. The post-1969 percentage is 100%.[39]

4. The pre-1970 percentage is 100% less one percentage point for each full month the property is held over 20 months.[40]

---

33. § 1250(a) and Reg. §§ 1.1250–1(a)(1) and 1.1250–1(b)(1).

34. §§ 1250(a)(1) and (2) and Reg. §§ 1.1250–1(a)(1) and (4) and 1.1250–1(b)(1) and (4).

35. § 1250(c) and Reg. § 1.1250–1(e).

36. Reg. § 1.1250–1(e)(3).

37. § 1250(b)(1) and Reg. § 1.1250–2(a)(1).

38. *Ibid.*

39. § 1250(a)(1)(C)(v) and Reg. § 1.-1250–1(d)(1)(i)(e); for residential rental housing the percentage is 100% less one percentage point for each full month the property is held over 100 months. See § 1250(a)(1)(C)(iii).

40. § 1250(a)(2)(B) and Reg. § 1.1250–1(d)(2).

Therefore, there is no pre-1970 recapture if the property is held for at least ten years.

5. Post-1969 additional depreciation is recaptured first (before pre-1970 additional depreciation).[41]

6. If the property is held for one year or less (usually not the case) all depreciation taken, even under the straight-line method, is additional depreciation.[42]

7. Special rules apply to dispositions of substantially improved § 1250 property. These rules are rather technical and the reader should consult the examples in the Regulations for illustrations of their application.[43]

It should be observed that the recapture rules under § 1250 are substantially less punitive than § 1245 recapture rules since only the additional amount of depreciation is subject to recapture. Straight-line depreciation (except for property held one year or less) is not recaptured. Also, for pre-1970 periods, the longer the property is held (the more inflation generally affects the gain) the lower the percentage applied in determining the recapture amount.

COMPUTING RECAPTURE

The following steps are taken in computing recapture under § 1250:

1. Determine the gain from the sale or other disposition of the property.

2. Determine post-1969 additional depreciation.

3. The lower of the gain in (1) or the post-1969 additional depreciation is ordinary income.

4. If any gain remains (total gain in (1) less recapture under (3)), determine the amount of pre-1970 additional depreciation.

5. Multiply the lower of the remaining gain (gain not recaptured in (3)) or pre-1970 additional depreciation by the applicable percentage for years prior to 1970. The result of this calculation is the recaptured ordinary income for pre-1970 additional depreciation.

6. If any gain remains (total gain in (1) less amounts recaptured as ordinary income under (3) and (5)), it is § 1231 gain.

41. § 1250(a)(2)(A) and Reg. § 1.1250–1(a)(1).

42. § 1250(b)(1) and Reg. § 1.1250–2(a)(1)(i).

43. § 1250(f) and Reg. § 1.1250–5.

The following example expresses the application of the § 1250 computational procedure:

Example 7. On January 3, 1967, T Corporation acquired a new building at a cost of $200,000 for use in its business. The building had an estimated useful life of 40 years and no estimated salvage value. Depreciation has been taken under the double declining balance method through December 31, 1972. Pertinent information as to this depreciation as well as additional depreciation is as follows:

Year	Undepreciated Balance as of Beginning of the Year	Depreciation Actually Taken for the Year	Straight-Line Depreciation	Additional Depreciation
1967	$200,000	$10,000	$5,000	$ 5,000
1968	190,000	9,500	5,000	4,000
1969	180,500	9,025	5,000	4,025
Total 1967–69				$13,525
1970	171,475	8,574	5,000	$ 3,574
1971	162,901	8,145	5,000	3,145
1972	154,756	7,738	5,000	2,738
Total 1970–72				$ 9,457

On January 2, 1973 the building is sold for $177,018. Compute the amounts of § 1250 ordinary income and § 1231 gain.

1. The recognized gain from the sale is $30,000. This is the difference between $177,018 amount realized and the $147,-018 adjusted basis ($200,000 cost less $52,982 depreciation taken).

2. The amount of post-1969 ordinary income is $9,457; the post-1969 additional depreciation of $9,457 is less than the recognized gain of $30,000.

3. The amount of pre-1970 ordinary income is $6,492. The pre-1970 additional depreciation of $13,525 is less than the remaining gain of $20,543 ($30,000 less $9,457). The pre-1970 percentage is 48% (100% less (72% less 20%)). The building was held for 72 months or 52 months over 20 months. 48% of $13,525 is $6,492.

4. Since only $15,949 ($9,457 post-1969 plus $6,492 pre-1970) is recaptured as ordinary income under § 1250 and the remaining $14,051 of the $30,000 gain is § 1231 gain and may receive favorable long-term capital gain treatment.

CONSIDERATIONS COMMON TO
§§1245 and 1250

EXCEPTIONS

Recapture under §§ 1245 and 1250 does not apply, except where indicated, to the following transactions:

1. *Gifts.*[44] However, the recapture potential carries over to the donee.[45]

Example 8. T gives his daughter, D, § 1245 property with an adjusted basis of $1,000. The amount of recapture potential is $700 (depreciation taken since January 1, 1962). D uses the property in her business and takes $100 depreciation before selling it for $1,900. D's recognized gain is $1,000 (amount realized of $1,900 less $900 adjusted basis). $800 of the gain is recaptured as ordinary income ($100 depreciation taken by D plus $700 recapture potential carried over from T) and the remaining $200 is § 1231 gain. Even if D used the property for personal purposes the $700 recapture potential would still be carried over.[46]

2. *Charitable Transfers.* The recapture potential reduces the amount of the charitable contributions deduction under § 170.[47]

Example 9. T donates § 1245 property with a fair market value of $10,000 and an adjusted basis of $7,000 to his church. Assume that the amount of recapture potential is $2,000, i. e., the amount of recapture if the property were sold. T's charitable contributions deduction (subject to the limitations discussed in Chapter 8) is $8,000 ($10,000 fair market value less $2,000 recapture potential).

3. *Certain Tax-Free Transactions.* These are transactions where the transferor's adjusted basis of the property carries over to the transferee.[48] The recapture potential, however, also carries over to the transferee.[49] Included in this category are transfers of property pursuant to (1) tax-free incorporations under § 351; (2) certain liquidations of subsidiary companies under § 332 and (3) tax-free reorganizations.

---

44. §§ 1245(b)(1) and 1250(d)(1) and Reg. §§ 1.1245–4(a)(1) and 1.1250–3(a)(1).

45. Reg. §§ 1.1245–2(a)(4), 1.1250–2(d)(3) and 1.1250–3(a)(3).

46. Reg. §§ 1.1245–3(a)(3) and 1.1250–1(e)(2).

47. § 170(e)(1)(A) and Reg. § 1.170–1(c)(3).

48. §§ 1245(b)(3) and 1250(d)(3) and Reg. §§ 1.1245–4(c) and 1.1250–3(c).

49. Reg. §§ 1.1245–2(a)(4), 1.1245–2(c)(2), 1.1250–2(d)(1) and (3) and 1.1250–3(c)(3).

Gains may be recognized in these transactions if boot is received. To the extent that gain is recognized, such gain is treated as ordinary income to the extent of the recapture potential or recognized gain, whichever is lower.[50]

Example 10. T transfers § 1245 property with a fair market value of $12,000 and an adjusted basis of $8,000 to a controlled corporation under Section 351. The amount of recapture potential is $3,000. T receives stock of the corporation with a fair market value of $11,000 and cash of $1,000. T's realized gain is $4,000 ($12,000 less $8,000). $1,000 gain is recognized because T received boot of $1,000. Since the amount of recapture potential ($3,000) exceeds the recognized gain ($1,000), the entire $1,000 recognized gain is ordinary income. The remaining recapture potential of $2,000 carries over to the corporation.

4. *Like-kind Exchanges (§ 1031) and Involuntary Conversions (§ 1033).* Gain is recognized to the extent of boot received under Section 1031, and gain is also recognized to the extent the proceeds from an involuntary conversion are not reinvested in similar property under § 1033. This recognized gain is subject to recapture as ordinary income under §§ 1245 and 1250. In addition, gain may be recaptured to the extent of any non § 1245 like-kind property which is received in the exchange.[51]

Example 11. T exchanges § 1245 property with an adjusted basis of $300 for § 1245 property with a fair market value of $6,000. The exchange qualifies as a like-kind exchange under § 1031(a). T also gives $5,000 cash (boot). T's realized gain is $700 (amount realized of $6,000 less $5,300 (adjusted basis of property plus boot given)). Assuming recapture potential is $4,500, no gain is recognized because no boot or non-Section 1245 like-kind property is received. The entire recapture potential of $4,500 carries over to the like-kind property received whose basis is $5,300.

OTHER APPLICATIONS

§§ 1245 and 1250 apply notwithstanding any other provisions in the Code.[52] That is, the recapture rules under these sections override all other sections. Special applications include:

1. *Installment Sales.* Recapture takes place as cash is received and gain is recognized. Recapture applies first. That is, all

---

50. §§ 1245(b)(3) and 1250(d)(3) and Reg. §§ 1.1245–4(c) and 1.1250–3(c).

51. §§ 1245(b)(4) and Reg. §§ 1.1245–4(d). Also, see § 1250(d)(4) and Reg. § 1.1250–3(d)(1) for recapture rules for real property.

52. §§ 1245(d) and 1250(i).

53. Reg. §§ 1.1245–6(d) and 1.1250–1(c)(6).

gain is ordinary income until recapture potential is fully applied.[53]

Example 12. T sells § 1245 property for $20,000, to be paid in ten annual installments of $2,000 each plus interest at 7%. T realizes a $6,000 gain from the sale, of which $4,000 is attributable to depreciation taken since January 1, 1962. If T elects the installment method the entire $600 gain in each of the payments for the first six years plus $400 of the gain in year seven is recaptured as ordinary income. The remaining $200 of gain in year seven and the entire $600 gain in each of the last three years is § 1231 gain.

2. *Property Dividends.* Even though gain is otherwise not recognized by a corporation if it distributes property as a dividend recapture under §§ 1245 and 1250 applies to the extent of the lower of the recapture potential or the excess of the property's fair market value over its adjusted basis.[54]

Example 13. XYZ Corporation distributes § 1245 property as a dividend to its stockholders. The amount of recapture potential is $300. The excess of the property's fair market value over its adjusted basis is $800. XYZ Corporation recognizes $300 ordinary income.

SPECIAL RECAPTURE PROVISIONS

GAIN FROM SALE OF DEPRECIABLE PROPERTY BETWEEN CERTAIN RELATED PARTIES

In general, § 1239 provides that in the case of a sale or exchange, directly or indirectly, of depreciable property (principally, machinery and equipment and buildings, but not land) between spouses or between an individual and his or her controlled corporation, any gain recognized is ordinary income.[55] Depreciable means subject to depreciation in the hands of the transferee.[56]

§ 1239 was enacted to prevent certain related parties from having the dual benefits of long-term capital gains treatment (transferor) and a stepped-up basis for depreciation (transferee). Recapture under §§ 1245 and 1250 is applied before applying recapture under § 1239.[57]

---

54. Reg. §§ 1.1245–1(c), 1.1245–6(b), 1.-1250–1(a)(4), 1.1250–1(b)(4) and 1.-1250–1(c)(2).

55. § 1239(a) and Reg. § 1.1239–1.

56. § 1239(b) and Reg. § 1.1239–1.

57. Reg. §§ 1.1245–6(f) and 1.1250–1(c)(4).

Control for purposes of § 1239 means ownership of 80 percent in value of the corporation's outstanding stock.[58] In determining the percentage of stock owned the taxpayer must include that owned by related taxpayers as determined under the constructive ownership rules of § 318.[59]

It should be noted that § 267(a)(1) disallows a loss on the sale of property between related taxpayers. Therefore, a sale of property between related parties may result in ordinary income (if the property is depreciable) or a nondeductible loss.

§ 1239 applies regardless of whether the transfer is from a stockholder to the corporation or from the corporation to a stockholder.[60] Ordinary income treatment also applies to transfers between two corporations controlled by the same stockholder.[61] Prior to recent changes in the law, the courts had held that § 1239 ordinary income treatment was not applicable to transfers between two controlled corporations.[62]

> **Example 14.** T sells a building to a corporation in which he owns more than 80% in value of its outstanding stock. T received $100,000 cash from the corporation and the adjusted basis of the building was $40,000. T's entire recognized gain of $60,000 is ordinary income. Recapture under § 1239 is not a function of depreciation taken on the property transferred. Since the transfer is subject to § 1239, the *entire* recognized gain is ordinary income. The basis of the building to the corporation is $100,000.

RESIDENTIAL RENTAL HOUSING

§ 1250 recapture applies to the sale or other disposition of residential rental housing. The rules are the same as for other § 1250 property except that only the post-1975 excess depreciation is recaptured in full.[63] The post-1969 through 1975 recapture percentage is 100 percent less one percentage point for each full month the property is held over 100 months.[64] Therefore, the excess depreciation for periods after 1975 is initially applied against the recognized gain and such amounts are recaptured in full as ordinary income. Any remaining gain is then tested under the percentage rules applicable to the post-1969–1975 period. If any of the recognized gain is not absorbed by the recapture rules pertaining to the post-1969 period, recapture is tested under the pre-1970 rules. Property qualifies as resi-

58. Act § 2129 amending § 1239.

59. Ibid.

60. Reg. § 1.1239–1.

61. Act § 2129 amending § 1239.

62. *10–42 Corporation,* 55 T.C. 593 (1971).

63. Act § 202(a) amending 1250(a).

64. § 1250(a)(1)(C)(iii) and Reg. § 1.1250–1(d)(i)(c).

dential rental housing only if at least 80 percent of gross rental income is rental income from dwelling units.[65]

REHABILITATION EXPENDITURES FOR LOW–INCOME RENTAL HOUSING

§ 1250 recapture applies to the sale or other disposition of Federally assisted housing projects and low-income housing with respect to which is eligible for rapid amortization of rehabilitation expenditures under § 167(k). The rules are generally the same as for residential rental housing except that post-1975 excess depreciation is not recaptured in full, i. e., the post-1969 percentage rules continue to apply.[66]

This preferential treatment afforded residential rental housing and low-income rental housing is the result of Congress's desire to stimulate the construction and reconstruction of residential rental property. The special rules for depreciating or amortizing these properties are discussed in Chapter 7.

FARM RECAPTURE PROVISIONS

The cash method of accounting can be and usually is used for farming operations. It should be noted that the Tax Reform Act of 1976 requires certain large corporations and partnerships who are engaged in farming, to use the accrual method of accounting and to capitalize preproductive period expenses.[67] Under the cash method the taxpayer is allowed the dual benefits of current deductions for the costs of raising livestock and producing crops, and long-term capital gain treatment under § 1231 upon the sale or other disposition of farm property. Many higher income nonfarmer taxpayers have engaged in farming activities as a hobby. Such activities are particularly attractive if a nonfarmer is permitted a deduction for farm losses as an offset against income from nonfarming sources, e. g. salaries or professional fees. Therefore, Congress enacted two farm recapture provisions in 1969 with an eye toward minimizing the use of farming investments by higher income taxpayers as shelters for their income from other sources. The objective of these provisions was to limit long-term capital gain treatment for such taxpayers upon the disposition of certain farm property.

§ *1251.* This provision required a cash basis taxpayer to establish an Excess Deductions Account (EDA) to the extent that the taxpayer incurred a net farm loss over $25,000 and his non-farm ad-

---

65. § 167(j)(2)(B) and Reg. § 1.167(j)–3(b)(1)(i).

66. Act § 202(a) amending 1250(a).

67. Act §§ 207a–c adding §§ 447 and 464 and amending § 278.

justed gross income exceeded $50,000.[68] In that year and all subsequent years where the taxpayer's net farm loss exceeded $25,000 and his non-farm adjusted gross income exceeded $50,000, the taxpayer was required to add the net farm loss over $25,000 to his EDA. Upon the sale or other disposition of certain farm recapture property, (e. g. farm machinery and equipment, livestock held for draft, breeding or sporting purposes and certain unharvested crops), any gain is recaptured as ordinary income to the extent of the balance in the EDA at the end of the year in which the sale or other disposition took place.[69] The balance of the gain, if any, qualifies under § 1231.[70] The Tax Reform Act of 1976 provides that no additions are made to the Excess Deductions Account for 1976 and subsequent years.[71] The recapture rules continue to apply, however, to amounts in the EDA account.[72]

Example 15. T incurs his first net farm loss, $105,000, in 1975. His non-farm adjusted gross income for 1975 is $135,000. T's gains from the sale and other disposition of farm recapture property total $50,000 for 1975.

1. T must establish an EDA in 1975 and add $80,000 to it. This is the excess of T's net farm loss over $25,000.

2. The balance in the EDA at the end of 1975 is greater than T's gains from the sale and other disposition of farm recapture property ($80,000 balance versus $50,000 gains). Therefore, T recognizes $50,000 ordinary income from the sale or other disposition of the farm recapture property.

3. Amounts recaptured under § 1251 reduce the EDA.[73] Therefore, T's EDA balance as of January 1, 1976 is $30,000. Recapture under § 1245 takes precedence over recapture under § 1251. Amounts recaptured under § 1245 are reflected as increases in net farm income or decreases in net farm losses.[74]

Example 16. T has an EDA balance of $10,000 on December 31, 1975. T recognizes a $5,000 gain from the sale of farm ma-

68. § 1251(b)(1) and (2)(A) and (B) and Reg. §§ 1.1251–1(a) and 1.1251–2(a) and (b)(1) and (2). The amounts for married persons filing separately are $12,500 instead of $25,000 and $25,000 instead of $50,000. These amounts apply only if the taxpayer's spouse has some non-farm adjusted gross income for the taxable year. § 1251(b)(2)(C) and Reg. § 1.1251–2(b)(4).

69. §§ 1251(c) and (e)(1); Reg. §§ 1.-1251–1(b) and 1.1251–3(a).

70. Reg. § 1.1251–1(e).

71. Act § 206(a) adding § 1251(b)(2) (E).

72. "Tax Reform Act of 1976—Law and Explanation," *CCH*, § 635.

73. § 1251(b)(3)(B) and Reg. § 1.1251–2(c)(1)(ii).

74. Reg. §§ 1.1251–1(b)(5) and 1.1251–3(b)(2).

chinery in 1977. Depreciation taken on the machinery since January 1, 1962, is $4,000.

1. $4,000 is recaptured as ordinary income under § 1245. The EDA is reduced from $10,000 to $6,000.

2. $1,000 is recaptured as ordinary income under § 1251. The EDA is reduced from $6,000 to $5,000.

§ *1252.* This section provides that if farm land held for nine years or less is disposed of in 1970 or later years, a percentage of the total deductions taken for post-1969 soil and water conservation expenditures (§ 175) and land clearing expenditures (§ 182) is recaptured as ordinary income if the disposition results in a gain.[75] That is, gain is recaptured as ordinary income to the extent of a percentage of these deductions. If the land is held five years or less the applicable percentage is 100%. The percentage declines by twenty percent for each year and land is held over five years (e. g. 60 percent for seven years or less and 20 percent for nine years or less). There is no recapture if the land is held more than nine years.[76] § 1252 applies notwithstanding any other provisions in the Code.[77] The exceptions and limitations under § 1252 are similar to those under § 1245.[78] The following example expresses the application of § 1252:

Example 17. T purchased farm land in 19X6 for $50,000. T sells the land six years later for $80,000. During the period T held the land he took $10,000 of deductions under §§ 175 and 182.

1. T's realized and recognized gain is $30,000 ($80,000 amount realized less $50,000 adjusted basis).

2. T held the land six years or less. Therefore, the applicable percentage is 80%. 80% of $10,000, or $8,000 is T's recapture potential under § 1252.

3. Since T's gain of $30,000 exceeds the recapture potential of $8,000, $8,000 is recaptured as ordinary income.

INTANGIBLE DRILLING COSTS

§ 263(c) provides that taxpayers may elect to expense or capitalize intangible drilling and development costs. In most instances, taxpayers have elected to expense IDC due to the opportunities for accelerating tax deductions.

Intangible drilling and development costs that are paid or incurred after December 31, 1975 are recaptured if such costs were

---

75. § 1252(a)(1) and Reg. § 1.1252–1(a)(1).

76. § 1252(a)(3) and Reg. §§ 1.1252–1(a)(3)(iv) and 1.1252–1(b).

77. § 1252(a)(1) and Reg. §§ 1.1252–1(a)(2) and 1.1252–1(d)(1) and (2).

78. § 1252(b) and Reg. § 1.1252–2.

expensed rather than capitalized. Upon the sale or other disposition of such oil or gas properties, the gain is treated as ordinary income to the extent of the lesser of the following: [79]

1. IDC expenses after 1975 less amounts which would have been deductible as cost depletion if the IDC had been capitalized; or

2. The excess of the amount realized from the sale, exchange, or involuntary conversion of the property (or fair market value if the property is otherwise disposed of) over the adjusted basis of the property.

Special rules are provided for determining recapture where a portion or an undivided interest in oil and gas property is sold or otherwise disposed of.[80]

Example 18. X acquired a working interest in certain oil and gas properties for $50,000 during 1977. He incurred $10,000 of intangible development and drilling costs, e. g. (labor, fuel, repairs and supplies used in the drilling, shooting and cleaning of wells, clearing of the grounds, construction of derricks, etc.). X elected to expense these costs in 1977. In January, 1978 the properties were sold for $60,000. (Disregard any depreciation on tangible depreciable properties).

1. The gain realized and recognized is $10,000 ($60,000 − $50,000)

2. The gain is recaptured as ordinary income to the extent of
   a. $10,000 IDC costs less amount which would have been deducted as cost depletion, e. g. $2,000 = $8,000 or
   b. $60,000 − $50,000 = $10,000. Therefore, $8,000 is recaptured.

TAX PLANNING CONSIDERATIONS

TIMING OF RECAPTURE

Since recapture is usually not triggered until the property is sold or disposed of, it may be possible to plan for recapture in low bracket or in loss years. If a taxpayer has net operating loss carryovers which are about to expire, the recognition of ordinary income from recapture may be advisable to absorb the loss carryforwards.

It may be also be desirable to spread the recaptured income amounts over a number of years. The spreading of such amounts may be accomplished through the use of an installment sale under § 453.

---

79. Act § 205 adding § 1254(a)(1).   **80.** § 1254(a)(2).

It is also possible to postpone recapture or to shift the burden of recapture to others. For example, recapture is avoided upon the disposition of a § 1231 asset if the taxpayer replaces the property by entering into a like-kind exchange. In this instance, recapture potential is merely carried over to the newly acquired property. Recapture can be shifted to others through the gratuitous transfer of § 1245 or § 1250 property to family members. A subsequent sale of such property by the donee will trigger recapture to the donee rather than the donor who may be in a higher tax bracket.

ECONOMIC CONSIDERATIONS

The advisability of using accelerated depreciation methods should not be diminished by the fact that such depreciation amounts may subsequently be recaptured. Assuming no significant change in tax rates, the time value of money usually dictates deducting as much depreciation as possible, i. e., a dollar of depreciation deduction today is usually worth more than a dollar of ordinary income in the future.

PROBLEM MATERIALS

Questions for Class Discussion

1. What type of transactions involving capital assets are included under Section 1231? Why wouldn't they qualify for long-term capital gain treatment without § 1231?

2. Why was § 1231 originally enacted? Why do you think it is still in the law today?

3. Why is timber, coal, and domestic iron ore entitled to preferential capital gain treatment under § 1231?

4. Can ordinary income be recognized from the sale of timber? How?

5. Is it possible to recognize both a gain and a loss on the sale of timber in one taxable year? How? What are the planning implications of your answer?

6. True or false: All livestock held for twelve months qualifies for § 1231 treatment. Why?

7. Why is there a specific provision concerning livestock in § 1231?

8. What circumstances must be met for an unharvested crop to receive preferential treatment under § 1231?

9. What is the effect of an asset's holding period on its ability to qualify for special treatment under § 1231? Why?

10. Under what circumstances is a casualty gain not afforded long-term capital gain treatment? Why?

11. Describe the treatment that results if a taxpayer has net § 1231 losses.

12. Why was § 1245 enacted? How does it achieve this objective?

13. Differentiate between the types of property covered by §§ 1245 and 1250.

14. Is a gain from the sale or exchange of a contract for the services of a professional athlete subject to depreciation recapture?

15. What is the potential recapture under § 1245? What factors limit it?

16. What is "additional depreciation"? Why is such a concept necessary?

17. What is the potential recapture under § 1250? What factors limit it?

18. Can straight-line depreciation be additional depreciation? If so, when? If not, why?

19. What are the two major differences in the computation of depreciation recapture under §§ 1245 and 1250? Why do these differences exist?

20. What happens to recapture potential when a gift is involved? What effect does the donee's use have on the recapture potential?

21. Does recapture apply when § 1245 property is donated to charity? Why?

22. Comment on: Death eliminates all recapture potential. Why or why not?

23. List the tax-free transactions which do not cause recapture to be recognized immediately but require it to be carried over to the transferee.

24. What provisions do the recapture rules override?

25. In what cases can recapture occur even though there is otherwise no recognition of gain? To what extent?

26. Would recapture provisions ever affect your decision to maximize depreciation deductions? Why or why not? (Consider all tax planning aspects.)

27. Why was § 1239 enacted? How does it accomplish its goals?

28. § 1239 applies to transactions between what parties?

29. How does § 1239 differ from §§ 1245 and 1250 in general?

30. How has residential real estate been granted special treatment under Section 1250? What changes have been made in 1976 and how will the changes affect subsequent sales of residential property?

31. What are the dual benefits available to cash method farmers? How have these benefits been restricted by recent changes in the tax law?

32. How does § 1251 attempt to minimize the use of farming investments as tax shelters?

33. Why did the Tax Reform Act of 1976 provide that farming taxpayers are no longer required to make additions to their EDA account for years after 1975?

34. Contrast the recapture treatment which is accorded to intangible drilling and development costs for 1976 and subsequent years with prior years treatment.

Problems

1. W purchased a contract to cut the timber on a sixty acre lot in North Carolina in February of 1976 for $18,000. On January 1, 1977, the timber has a fair market value of $34,000. Because of careless cutting in November when the fair market value is $35,000, the wood is sold on January 30, 1978 for only $32,000.

   (a) What gain (loss) is realized and recognized by W in each year of the contract? Identify the nature of the gain (loss). What assumption is necessary to do this?

   (b) Does your answer change if the timber is sold in December of 1977? Why?

   (c) What would happen if on January 1, 1977, the timber was worth only $15,000; was cut in November when worth $19,000; and sold in December for $20,000? What would be your answers to the questions in Part (a) under these circumstances?

2. The following unusual transactions were encountered by a taxpayer in 1977.

   1. Damage from the wreck of a pleasure boat held over one year due to hurricane ($23,000 loss) and insurance recovery ($20,000).

   2. Sale of cornland held three years with the unharvested crop ($30,000 gain).

   3. Sale of plow purchased on March 12th and sold October 9th ($500 gain). Ignore recapture.

   4. Fire in barn on August 7th, originally purchased May 10th ($5,000 loss).

   5. Recovery on theft of family heirloom ($7,000 gain).

   6. Sale of eight shares of N Corporation held over one year ($3,000 gain).

   7. Sale of tractor held six years ($50 loss).

   How is each transaction treated? What is the net § 1231 gain (loss)? What is the net capital gain (loss)?

3. A, an individual, files his income tax return on the calendar year basis. A's recognized gains and losses for 19X7 of the kind described in § 1231 are as follows:

	Gains	Losses
(a) Gain on sale of machinery used in the business and subject to an allowance for depreciation, held for more than one year	$4,000	
(b) Gain reported in 19X7 (under § 453) on installment sale in 19X6 of factory premises used in the business (including building and land, each held for more than one year	6,000	
(c) Gain reported in 19X7 (under § 453) on installment sale in 19X7 of land held for more than one year, used in the business as a storage lot for trucks	2,000	
(d) Gain on proceeds from requisition by government of boat, held for more than one year, used in the business and subject to an allowance for depreciation	500	
(e) Loss upon the destruction by fire of warehouse, held for more than one year and used in the business (excess of adjusted basis of warehouse compensation by insurance, etc.)		$3,000
(f) Loss upon theft of unregistered bearer bonds, held for more than one year		5,000
(g) Loss in storm of pleasure yacht, purchased in 19X0 for $1,800 and having a fair market value of $1,000 at the time of the storm		1,000

What are the tax consequences of these items to A?

4. W's yacht, used for pleasure and acquired for that use in 19X5 at a cost of $25,000, was requisitioned by the Government in 19X7 for $15,000. What are the tax consequences to W?

5. During the current tax year, T had the following gains and losses on property he held for more than one year:

1. Casualty loss (storm) to T's residence (excess of loss over insurance and $100 limitation)	$ (500)
2. Gain from insurance reimbursement for stolen diamond ring	800
3. Loss on sale of business real property	$(1,500)
4. Gain realized during year on installment sale of a factory used in T's business	1,000
5. Involuntary conversion (condemnation) loss on land used in T's business	(200)

IM–256

What is the nature of T's gains and losses?

6. XYZ, Inc. owns two drill presses. Press A was purchased for $10,000 on July 7, 19X3 and has an adjusted basis of $4,000.

Press B was purchased for $9,000 on July 7, 19X6, and has an adjusted basis of $7,000. XYZ sells the two assets on November 23, 19X6 for $4,500 and $7,900, respectively.

(a) What is the realized and recognized gain on each? What is the nature of the gain?

(b) Would your answer change if XYZ were in the business of selling drill presses? How and why?

7. E owns the patent to the bean counter employed by his sole proprietorship to count the coffee beans it grinds. He purchased the patent on January 1, 19X3, for $6,000 and is amortizing it over sixty months. The machine was constructed on June 1, 19X3, at a cost of $8,000 and is depreciated on the straight-line method. It has an estimated life of ten years and no salvage value. On June 1, 19X7, E sells the patent and the machine for $2,300 and $7,000, respectively.

(a) What gain or loss is recognized on the sales and what is the nature of the gain (loss)? How do you treat them?

(b) Does your answer change if the patent is sold for $500? How and why?

8. On January 1, 19X4, B purchased machinery for use in his manufacturing business. The property has a basis for depreciation of $3,300. After taking depreciation deductions of $1,300 (the amount allowable) B realizes (after selling expenses) $2,900 upon sale of the property on January 1, 19X9.

(a) What is B's realized gain or loss?

(b) What is B's recognized gain or loss?

(c) What is the nature of any recognized gain or loss?

9. On January 1, 19X0, T bought a machine for $6,000. He claimed $600 depreciation on it each year and sold it for $12,000 on July 1, 19X9.

(a) What is his recognized gain?

(b) What is the nature of any recognized gain?

10. In 1970 X Company acquired a building used in its business for $500,000. Depreciation expense amounting to $100,000 was taken using an accelerated method. In 1976 the building was sold for $700,000. At the time of the sale the additional depreciation in respect of the property attributable to periods after December 31, 1969, is $30,000. What is the amount of § 1250 ordinary income?

11. Depreciable real property with an adjusted basis of $20,000 is sold in 1976 for $29,000. Additional depreciation attributable to the property is $1,600, of which $1,000 is for tax years after 1969. The applicable percentage for additional depreciation before 1970 is 10% and the applicable percentage for additional depreciation

after 1969 is 100%. What is the maximum gain to be recaptured as ordinary income?

12. On July 1, 1976, F sells for $59,000 real property with an adjusted basis of $44,000 acquired on October 1, 1967. The property qualified as residential rental property for each tax year after 1969. For additional depreciation after 1969 of $3,500, the applicable percentage is 95%, that is, 100% minus 5% (105 months – 100 months). For additional depreciation before 1970 of $5,-000, the applicable percentage is 15%, that is, 100% minus 85% (105 months – 20 months). No additional depreciation was taken in 1976.

(a) What is the amount of gain treated as ordinary income?

(b) What is the nature of the remaining gain, if any?

(c) How would additional depreciation be treated for 1976 and subsequent periods?

13. M bought a warehouse in January, 1974, for $30,000. He took double-declining-balance depreciation assuming a twenty year life and no salvage value. In January, 1976 the warehouse was sold for $35,000. How much gain was realized? What are the various types recognized and how are they treated? What if M had taken straight-line depreciation?

14. An anonymous millionaire donated an office building to a charitable organization on December 31, 19X3. The millionaire had bought the office building on January 1, 19X1 for $100,000 and had taken double declining-balance depreciation on it using an estimated life of ten years with no salvage. At the time of the gift the property had a fair market value of $120,000. What are the tax effects to the millionaire in the year of the gift?

15. N transferred equipment used in his pecan shelling factory having recapture potential of $3,500 to a dealer for new equipment worth $4,000 and $500 of marketable securities. The transaction qualified as a like-kind exchange under Section 1031. N had an adjusted basis in the equipment of $3,000.

(a) What is N's realized and recognized gain (loss)? Does he have any other type of income? What is the nature of his gain (loss)?

(b) Answer the same questions assuming no marketable securities were received.

16. J contracts to sell an item of § 1245 property for $10,000 to be paid in 10 equal payments of $1,000 each, plus a sufficient amount of interest so that § 483 does not apply. The total gain recognized is $3,000 of which $2,000 is recaptured as ordinary income under § 1245 and the remainder is § 1231 gain. What amount of each installment payment is Section 1245 ordinary income and what amount is § 1231 gain?

17. On January 4, 19X4, T purchased office furniture for $1,500. On T's 19X4 return he claimed $300 additional first-year depreciation and $240 ordinary depreciation computed under the declining-balance method. On January 2, 19X5, a fire destroyed the furniture and T received $1,200 as a result of the insurance claim. However, it cost T $1,000 for the replacement furniture.

    (a) What is T's recognized loss or gain?

    (b) What is the nature of any recognized gain or loss?

18. S operates a hardware store as a sole proprietorship. During 1977 the following transactions occurred:

    1. A pickup truck owned by the proprietorship and used exclusively for merchandise deliveries was sold for $2,440 on January 13, 1977. The pickup truck was purchased on January 13, 1975 at a total cost of $4,000. The pickup truck was depreciated over a five-year life using the 200% declining-balance method. The adjusted basis on the date of sale was $1,-440.

    2. Unimproved land adjacent to the west side of the hardware store and used as a parking lot was condemned by the city on February 1, 1977. The condemnation proceeds were $20,000. The land was acquired in 1949, and the allocable basis of the land condemned was $15,000. Because S feels that the remaining land on the east side of the building will provide sufficient parking space, she intends to use the condemnation proceeds to finance the purchase of additional inventory.

    3. S's yacht, used exclusively for personal purposes, was stolen on May 1, 1977. The yacht was acquired in April of 1976 at a cost of $15,000. The fair market value immediately preceding the theft was $11,000. Unfortunately, S was only insured to the extent of 60% of the original cost; therefore, she received $9,000 in insurance proceeds on July 1.

    4. The proprietorship sold an old safe at an antique auction. The net proceeds of the sale were $3,700. The safe was purchased used twenty-two years ago at a cost of $6,000. The safe had been depreciated over a twenty-year life using the straight-line method. Straight-line depreciation taken after December 31, 1961 was $2,500. The adjusted basis at the date of sale was $1,000 (salvage value).

    5. On July 1, 1977, S sold an apartment house for $120,000. The rental property was purchased on July 1, 1973 at a cost of $100,000. The property was being depreciated over a 40-year useful life using the straight-line method. The adjusted basis on the date of sale was $90,000.

    6. The hardware store's entire stock of power tools was stolen on August 23, 1977. The total cost of these items was $3,000.

S's business insurance will not cover the loss because she forgot to pay the premium.

7. A calculator used by the proprietorship's bookkeeper was sold on September 1, 1977. The net sales proceeds were $116. The calculator was acquired on September 1, 1975 at a total cost of $500. It was being depreciated over a five-year useful life using the straight-line method.. The adjusted basis on the date of sale was $300.

8. On October 21, 19X4, S sold her 19X3 Cadillac for a total price of $5,500. The auto was used exclusively for personal purposes. The car was purchased on September 19, 19X2 at a total cost of $7,200.

   (a) What is the amount of the ordinary gain or loss without regard to §§ 1231, 1245, or 1250?

   (b) What is the amount of the gain subject to §§ 1245 and 1250?

   (c) What is the amount of the net § 1231 gain or loss?

   (d) What is the amount of the capital gain or loss?

19. E, Inc. owns several apartment complexes that are strictly residential rental housing. Since their purchase in January 1974, E has taken double-declining-balance depreciation on them. The L'amour Lane complex was bought for $80,000 and was expected to have a twenty-year life and no salvage. In January, 1977, E sold L'amour Lane for $150,000. Ignore land values.

   (a) What is the recognized gain? Describe its composition.

   (b) How does your answer change if the sale is to E's principal stockholder who holds eighty-two percent (82%) of the corporation?

20. In 1975, Dr. G, noted pathologist and agriculture buff, had a gross income of $75,000 from his medical practice but a loss of $29,000 from his farm. In 1976, Dr. G determined to modernize operations, sold an old tractor in which he had an adjusted basis of $1,500 for $4,000; a hopper in which he had an adjusted basis of $2,000 for $3,000; and two breeding bulls in which he had an adjusted basis of $200 each for a total of $1,000. In the past he had taken depreciation of $1,800, $500, and $1,000 on the assets, respectively. In 1976 he realized a loss on his farm from operations of $3,000.

   (a) What is Dr. G's EDA at the beginning of 1976?

   (b) What gain is realized on the sales? What gain is recognized? Describe how it is determined. What is the nature of the gain?

(c) What is his net farm income after an allowance is made for the above sales?

(d) What is his EDA at December 31, 1976?

21. T acquired a working interest in certain oil and gas properties during 1977 for $100,000. He also incurred intangible drilling and development costs of $40,000 during 1977 which he elected to write off on his 1977 tax return. If the IDC costs would have been capitalized, cost depletion of $4,000 would have been allowed in 1977. In January, 1978 T sells his interest in the oil and gas properties for $110,000.

   a. Calculate the amount of gain or loss realized and recognized in 1978. (Ignore any depreciation on the tangible depreciable property.)

   b. What amount, if any, is recognized as ordinary income?

Research Problems

1. Dr. S purchased a personal residence for $100,000 on January 1, 1975. 20% of the residence was converted to a business office and Dr. S claimed $1,950 total depreciation on the business portion for 1975 and 1976. (Straight-line depreciation would have been $1,000 for the two-year period.)

   On January 1, 1977 Dr. S sold his home for $120,000 and acquired another personal residence for $150,000.

   (a) Compute the amount of gain realized and recognized on the former residence. What is the nature of the gain?; i. e., ordinary income or capital gain.

   (b) If the requirements for non-recognition of gain on the sale of a personal residence are met (§ 1034), is it possible to defer the entire amount of the gain? Why?

2. On January 1, 19X4 J purchased a new Lincoln automobile for $12,000 which he used exclusively for business. J used straight-line depreciation with zero salvage value and a three-year life. In 19X7 the Lincoln was fully depreciated and J deducted $.15 per mile for business use during 19X7. In 19X8 J converted the auto to personal use and sold the car for $5,000 in 19X9.

   (a) Was J permitted to deduct $.15 per mile for business use during 19X7 after the auto had been fully depreciated?

   (b) How much gain is recognized and what is the nature of such gain

      (1) Upon the conversion of the car to personal use?

      (2) Upon its sale in 19X9?

      See Rev.Rul. 69–487, 1969–2 C.B. 165.

Chapter 16

ACCOUNTING PERIODS AND METHODS

An entire subchapter of the Code, Subchapter E, is devoted to "accounting periods," and "accounting methods." Over the long run, the accounting period used by a taxpayer will not affect the aggregate amount of reported taxable income. However, taxable income for any particular year may vary significantly due to the use of a particular accounting method or reporting period. Due to the progressive nature of tax rates, advantages can be obtained from the use of a particular method of accounting. In addition, through the choice of accounting methods or periods it is possible to postpone the recognition of taxable income and to therefore enjoy the benefits from such deferral of the related tax.

ACCOUNTING PERIODS

IN GENERAL

Our tax determination and collection system is founded on the concept of an annual reporting by the taxable entity of its income, deductions and credits. Most individual taxpayers use a calendar year since the Code and Regulations place restrictions upon the use of a fiscal year for taxpayers who do not keep books.[1] However, both corporate and noncorporate taxpayers may elect to use a fiscal

---

1. § 441(c) and Reg. § 1.441–1(b)(1)(ii).

year ending on the last day of any month (other than December), provided the books of the taxpayer are maintained on the basis of the same fiscal year.[2] Generally, a taxable year may not exceed 12 calendar months. However, if certain requirements are met, a taxpayer may elect to use an annual period which varies from 52 to 53 weeks.[3] In such case the year-end must always end on the same day of the week, e. g. the Tuesday falling closest to October 31 or the last Tuesday in October.

> **Example 1.** The taxpayer is in the business of selling farm supplies. His natural business year ends with the completion of harvesting, at the end of October. At the end of the fiscal year it is necessary to take an inventory and this is easiest to do on a Tuesday. Therefore, he could adopt a 52–53 week year ending on the Tuesday nearest October 31. If this method is selected, the year-end date may fall in the following month if it is closer to October 31. The year ending in 1976 will contain 53 weeks beginning on Wednesday, October 29, 1975, and ending on Tuesday, November 2, 1976. The year ending in 1977 will have 52 weeks beginning on Wednesday, November 3, 1976, and ending on Tuesday, November 1, 1977.

Partnerships are subject to additional restrictions to prevent partners from deferring partnership income by selecting a different year-end for the partnership, e. g. if the year for the partnership ended on January 31 and the partners used a calendar year, partnership profits for the first eleven months would not be reported by the partners until the following year. In brief, the law provides that the partnership tax year must generally be the same as the year used by its principal partners.[4]

MAKING THE ELECTION

A taxpayer elects to use a calendar or fiscal year by filing an initial tax return.[5] For all subsequent years, this same period must be used unless prior approval for change is obtained from the Commissioner.[6] Newly formed corporations often fail to make a valid election to use a fiscal year in the initial year. In such event, the corporation is required to report on a calendar year basis.

---

2. Reg. § 1.441–1(e)(2).

3. § 441(f).

4. § 706(b)(2); however, the Commissioner is authorized to allow the partner's and partnership's tax year to differ, if there is a good business purpose for the different years. See Rev.Proc. 72–51 for the procedure for a change in the partnership year.

5. Reg. § 1.441–1(b)(3).

6. Reg. § 1.441–1(b)(4).

CHANGES IN THE ACCOUNTING PERIOD

A taxpayer must obtain the consent of the Commissioner before changing his tax year.[7] This power to approve or not to approve a change is significant in that it permits the IRS to issue authoritative administrative guidelines which must be met by taxpayers who wish to change their accounting period. An application for permission to change tax years must be made on Form 1128, which must be filed on or before the fifteenth day of the second calendar month following the close of the short period.[8]

> **Example 2.** T Corporation has filed its return on a calendar year basis but would like to switch to fiscal year ending March 31, beginning in 19X2. The corporation must file Form 1128 by May 15, 19X2.

IRS Requirements. The Commissioner will not grant permission for the change unless the taxpayer can establish a "substantial business purpose" for the change.[9] One "substantial business purpose" is a request to change to a tax year that coincides with the natural business year.[10] Generally, the natural business year will end at or soon after the peak period of business. Thus, a ski lodge may end its year on March 31; a Miami Beach hotel on May 31; a department store on January 31; a soft drink bottler on September 30; and a college textbook publisher may end its year on June 30. If a business does not have a peak income period, it may not be able to establish a "natural business year" and may therefore be prevented from changing its tax year.

The IRS will usually establish certain conditions which the taxpayer must accept if the approval for change is to be granted. In particular, if there is a substantial reduction in taxable income in the year of change, the Commissioner will generally require the spreading of such benefits over a ten-year period beginning in the year following the change.

TAXABLE PERIODS OF LESS THAN ONE YEAR

A short year is a period of less than twelve calendar months. A taxpayer may have a short year for (1) the first tax reporting period, (2) the final income tax return, or (3) upon a change in the tax year.[11] A taxpayer is not required to annualize the taxable income for the short period for the purpose of computing the tax liability if the short period constitutes the first or final period, i. e., the computations are the same as for a return filed for a twelve month period.[12]

7. § 442.

8. Reg. § 1.442–1(b)(1).

9. *Ibid.*

10. Rev.Proc. 74–33, 1974–2 C.B. 489.

11. Reg. § 1.443–1(a).

12. Reg. § 1.443–1(a)(2).

REQUIREMENT TO ANNUALIZE TAXABLE INCOME

If the short period results from a change in the taxpayer's annual accounting period, the taxable income for such period must be annualized. Due to the progressive tax rate structure, taxpayers could reap substantial tax benefits during the short period if such annualization of income were not required. Once the taxable income is annualized, the tax must first be computed on the amount of annualized income. The annualized tax is then converted to a short period tax. The latter conversion is accomplished as follows:

$$\text{Tax on annualized income} \quad \times \quad \frac{\text{Number of months in the short period}}{12}$$

For individuals, annualizing requires some special adjustments: [13]

(1) Deductions must be itemized for the short period (the standard deduction is not allowed):

(2) Personal exemption deductions must be prorated.

Example 3. Mr. and Mrs. Brown obtained permission to change from a calendar year to a fiscal year ending September 30. For the short period, January 1 through September 30, 19X1, they had income and deductions as follows:

Gross income		$29,000
Deductions *for* adjusted gross income		(3,000)
Adjusted gross income		26,000
Excess Itemized Deductions:		
Total itemized deductions	$5,000	
Minus: standard deduction (referred to as the zero bracket amount)	(3,200)	(1,800)
Taxable income before exemptions		24,200
Exemptions ($4 \times \$750 \times \frac{9}{12}$)		(2,250)
Taxable income		$21,950

Annualized income:

($21,950 $\times \frac{12}{9}$)	$29,267

Tax on annualized income—$6,404

Short period tax, $6,404 $\times \frac{9}{12}$ = $ 4,803

MITIGATION OF THE ANNUAL ACCOUNTING PERIOD CONCEPT

There are several provisions in the Code designed to give the taxpayer relief from the seemingly harsh results that may be produced by the combined effects of an arbitrary accounting period and

13. Reg. § 1.443–1(b)(1)(iv) and (v).

a progressive rate structure. For example, favorable capital gain treatment has been provided, in part, to offset the unfavorable effects which may result from the "bunching" of income in one accounting period, i. e., the period in which the capital gains are realized. In addition, income averaging provisions are available for mitigating the adverse effects which result from other types of income being "bunched-up" in any one period.[14] Therefore, an individual receiving substantial amounts of taxable income in one year may be able to obtain the benefits from, in effect, spreading the income over the prior four years and the current year.

The net operating loss carry-back and carry-forward rules also mitigate the effects of a tax based upon one year's income. Under these provisions, a loss in one year can be carried back and offset against taxable income for the preceding three years. Unused net operating losses are then carried forward for seven years.[15] In addition, the Code provides special relief provisions for casualty losses pursuant to a disaster and for the reporting of insurance proceeds from destruction of crops.[16]

ACCOUNTING METHODS

PERMISSIBLE METHODS

§ 446 requires that taxable income be computed under the method of accounting regularly employed by the taxpayer in keeping its books, provided the method "clearly reflects" income. The Code recognizes as generally permissible methods:

(1) the cash receipts and disbursements method;

(2) the accrual method;

(3) a combination of (1) and (2), a hybrid method.

The Regulations refer to the above alternatives as "over-all methods" and add that the term "method of accounting" includes not only the overall "method of accounting" of the taxpayer but also the accounting treatment of any item.[17]

Any of the three methods of accounting may be used if the method is consistently employed and clearly reflects income. However, the taxpayer is required to use the accrual method for sales and cost of goods sold if inventories are an income-producing factor to the business.[18] Special methods are also permitted for installment sales, long-term construction contracts and for farmers.

A taxpayer who has more than one trade or business may use a different method of accounting for each trade or business activity.[19]

---

14. §§ 1301–1305.

15. § 172.

16. §§ 165(h) and 451(d).

17. Reg. § 1.446–1(a)(1).

18. Reg. § 1.446–1(a)(4)(i).

19. § 446(d).

Furthermore, a different method of accounting may be used to determine income from a trade or business than is used to compute non-business items of income and deductions.[20]   For example, an individual's income from an unincorporated business could be determined under the accrual method whereas the cash method could be used for all other types of income and deductions.

The Code grants the Commissioner broad powers to determine whether the taxpayer's accounting method clearly reflects income.[21] Thus, if the method employed does not clearly reflect income, the Commissioner has the power to prescribe the method to be used by the taxpayer.

> § 446(b) Exceptions—If no method of accounting has been regularly used by the taxpayer, or if the method used does not clearly reflect income, the computation of taxable income shall be made under such method as, in the opinion of the Secretary or his delegate, does clearly reflect income.

Under these broad powers, the Commissioner may require that a taxpayer involuntarily change to another method of accounting.   For example, the Regulations now require taxpayers to adopt the full absorption inventory costing method if they are not presently using this method.[22]

CASH RECEIPTS AND DISBURSEMENTS METHOD—"CASH BASIS"

Most individuals and many businesses use the cash basis to report income and deductions.   The popularity of this method can largely be attributed to its simplicity and flexibility.   Under the cash method, income is not recognized until the taxpayer receives (actually or constructively) cash or its equivalent.[23]   Deductions are generally permitted in the year of payment.[24]   Thus, year-end accounts receivable, payables, and accrued items of income and deductions are not included in the determination of taxable income.   The cash basis permits a taxpayer to postpone or accelerate the payment of expenses and in some cases to defer the collection of income.

Constructive Receipt of Income.   An item of gross income must be recognized by the taxpayer in the year it is actually or constructively received in the form of cash or its equivalent.   A "cash equivalent" is anything with a readily ascertainable market value.   Income is constructively received when it is credited to the taxpayer's account, "set apart for him, or otherwise made available so that he may draw upon it at any time, or so that he could have drawn upon it during the taxable year if notice of intention to withdraw had been given

20.   Reg. § 1.446–1(c)(1)(iv)(b).

21.   § 446(b).

22.   Reg. § 1.471–11.

23.   Reg. § 1.451–1(a).

24.   Reg. § 1.461–1(a)(1).

* * *" [25] Chapter 4 includes a more comprehensive discussion of the doctrine of constructive receipt.

Deductions. Generally, the cash basis taxpayer is permitted a deduction only in the year of actual payment.[26] The doctrine of constructive receipt has no corollary principle applicable to deductions, i. e., payment must actually be made before the deduction is allowed.[27]

> **Example 4.** Mr. A owned 100% of X Corporation's common stock and served as its president. Both Mr. A and X Corp., were cash basis taxpayers. In December, Mr. A declared a $5,000 bonus payable to himself. Mr. A's total compensation, including the $5,000 bonus, was reasonable in amount. The corporation had sufficient cash to pay Mr. A his bonus in December and there were no substantial limitations or restrictions upon the withdrawal of such funds.
>
> Mr. A was in constructive receipt of the income in December, but the cash basis corporation would not be entitled to a deduction in December since the bonus was not actually paid in that month.

Exceptions. Not all cash payments are deductible in the period in which the payment is made. If an expenditure is for "an asset having a useful life which extends substantially beyond the close of the taxable year," the cash basis taxpayer must account for the item in the same manner as an accrual basis taxpayer; [28] that is, the cost of the asset must be capitalized and its cost must be amortized or depreciated over its useful life. Also, if a taxpayer acquires an asset and part of the consideration paid is in the form of a note or mortgage, the total cost of the asset is used to compute the annual amortization or depreciation even though the taxpayer has not paid-off the note or mortgage.

Prepaid Expenses. Due to early court decisions, cash basis taxpayers have been required to capitalized prepayments for rent and insurance that cover more than one year. Prepaid interest must also be capitalized in the year paid and amortized over the life of the loan, [29] except in the case of points paid in connection with the purchase or improvement of a personal residence.[30]

Taxpayers have also attempted to deduct prepaid cattle feed costs in the year paid as a form of tax shelter. This type of shelter results in a shifting of deductions into an earlier year since the cattle investor's income is not recognized until the following year when the

25. Reg. § 1.451–2(a).

26. *Supra*, note 24.

27. *Vander Poel, Francis & Co., Inc.*, 8 T.C. 407 (1947).

28. *Supra*, note 24.

29. Act § 208 adding § 461(g).

30. *Ibid.* This section applies to interest paid after December 31, 1975.

cattle are sold. The IRS' position is that such costs should be capitalized if the full deduction in the year of payment "distorts" income or if the payment is, in fact, a deposit.[31] Some courts have permitted a current deduction in the year of payment where the terms of the prepaid feed agreement required the taxpayer to accept a specific quantity at a fixed price or to substitute specific quantities at a maximum price.[32] The Tax Reform Act of 1976 has imposed restrictions upon farming syndicates who are now required to deduct expenses for feed, fertilizers, etc., when these items are used rather than when they are paid.[33]

It should be recognized that there is a lack of consistency in the treatment of prepaid income and deductions. The recipient of prepaid income (as discussed in Chapter 4) must generally recognize income in the year of receipt, regardless of the taxpayer's method of accounting; but the taxpayer making a prepayment may be required to capitalize such amounts.

> **Example 5.** Mr. A, an accrual basis taxpayer, rented a restaurant building for a 24-month period for $5,000 which was prepaid on the date the lease was signed. Mr. C, the tenant, was a cash basis taxpayer.
>
> Mr. A must include the entire $5,000 as rental income in the year received even though he is an accrual basis taxpayer and the $5,000 is not yet earned. Mr. C must capitalize the $5,000 of prepaid rent and amortize the cost over 24 months even though he is a cash basis taxpayer.

ACCRUAL METHOD

The Regulations provide that "under the accrual method of accounting, income is includible in gross income when (1) all the events have occurred which fix the right to receive such income and (2) the amount thereof can be determined with reasonable accuracy."[34]

> **Example 6.** Ms. A, a calendar year taxpayer who uses the accrual basis of accounting was to receive a bonus equal to six percent of B Corporation's net income for its fiscal year ending each June 30th. For the fiscal year ended June 30, 19X1, B Corporation had net income of $240,000 and for the six months ended December 31, 19X1, the corporation's net income was $150,000.
>
> Ms. A will report $14,400 (.06 × $240,000) for 19X1 because her rights to the amount became fixed when B Corporation's year closed. However, Ms. A would not accrue income based on the

---

31. TIR–1261 (11/6/73).

32. *Mann v. Comm.*, 73–2 USTC ¶ 9618, 32 AFTR2d 73–5667, 483 F.2d 673 (CA–8, 1973).

33. Act § 213(d) amending § 704(b).

34. Reg. § 1.451–1(a).

corporation's profits for the last six months of 19X1 since her right to the income does not accrue until the close of the corporation's tax year.

The Globe Corporation case provides a good example of the application of the tests for accrual of income and a bad example of how to conduct business.[35] In 1945 Globe entered into a contract to perform services for the government. According to the agreement, the price was to be negotiated after completion of the work. Globe completed the work in 1945 and the final price agreement was not reached until 1946. The Tax Court held that the amount of income could not be "determined with reasonable accuracy" until 1946, and accordingly the income was not recognized until then.

In a situation where the accrual basis taxpayer's right to income is being contested, and the income has not yet been collected, generally no income is recognized until the dispute has been settled.[36] Prior to the settlement not "all of the events have occurred which fix the right to receive the income."

> **Example 7.** The accrual basis taxpayer, a painter, painted a customer's house in 19X1. The mutually-agreed charge was to be $1,200. However, the customer refused to pay because he thought the contractor's performance under the agreement was unacceptable (the painting was sloppy). Finally in 19X2, the painter and the customer settled the dispute, and the customer agreed to pay $1,000.

> The painter had no income in 19X1 since the work had not been accepted and, therefore, he was not entitled to the income. In 19X2, the accrual basis painter must recognize the $1,000 as income whether or not it is actually collected in that year.

Just as in the case of revenues, § 1.461–1(a) of the Regulations provides an "all events" test to determine the year in which a deduction is to be allowed:

> * * * an expense is deductible for the year in which all the events have occurred which determine the fact of the liability and the amount thereof can be determined with reasonable accuracy.

Reserves for Estimated Expenses. In financial accounting, reserves or allowances for estimated expenses are frequently provided to attain a proper matching of costs and revenues for an accounting period. Allowances for estimated expenses are often accrued for bad debts, sales returns, warranty service costs, collection expenses, and maintenance expense. However, except in the case of bad debts, reserves for expenses are seldom permitted for tax purposes. The Code

---

35. *Globe Co. v. Comm.,* 20 T.C. 299 (1953).

36. *Burnet v. Sanford & Brooks Co.,* 2 USTC ¶ 636, 9 AFTR 603, 51 S.Ct. 150 (USSC, 1931).

specifically provides for the use of the reserve method in accounting for bad debts.[37] However, the courts have not generally permitted the use of other types of reserves for estimated expenses since the all events test (definite liability that can be reasonably estimated) cannot be satisfied at the time the addition is made to the reserve.[38]

Hybrid Method. A hybrid method of accounting involves the use of more than one method. For example, a taxpayer who uses the accrual basis to report sales and cost of goods sold, but uses the cash basis to report other items of income and expense, is employing a hybrid method. The Code permits the use of a hybrid method providing the taxpayer's income is "clearly reflected." [39] A taxpayer who uses the accrual method for business expenses must also use the accrual method for business income.[40] In addition, a cash method for income items may not be used if the taxpayer's expenses are accounted for under an accrual basis.

It may be preferable for a business, which is required to report sales and cost of sales on the accrual method, to report other items of income and expense under the cash method since the cash method permits greater flexibility relative to the timing of income and expense recognition.

CHANGE OF METHOD

The taxpayer, in effect, makes an election to use a particular accounting method when he files an initial tax return and uses a particular method.[41] If a subsequent change in method is desired, the taxpayer must obtain the permission of the Commissioner.[42]

As previously mentioned, the term "accounting method" encompasses not only the overall accounting method used by the taxpayer, i. e., the cash or accrual method, but also the treatment of any material item of income or deduction.[43] Thus, a change in the method of deducting property taxes on a cash basis to an accrual basis, which results in a deduction for taxes in a different year, would constitute a change in an accounting method. Other examples of accounting method changes include changes involving the method or basis used in the valuation of inventories and a change from the direct charge-off method to the allowance method for deducting bad debts.

---

37. § 166.

38. *Little & Ives Co.*, TCM 372, T.C. Memo. 1966–68; *Atlas Mixed Mortar Co.*, 23 B.T.A. 245 (1931); *National Bread Wrapping Machine Co.*, 30 T.C. 550 (1958); *Pacific Grape Products*, 17 T.C. 1097 (1952); *Bell Electric Co.*, 45 T.C. 158 (1965).

39. § 446(c).

40. Reg. § 1.446–1(c)(1)(iv)(a).

41. Reg. § 1.446–1(e)(1).

42. § 446(e).

43. Reg. § 1.446–1(a)(1).

Correction of an Error. A change in accounting method should be distinguished from the correction of an error. An error can be corrected (by filing amended returns) by the taxpayer without special permission and the Commissioner can simply adjust the taxpayer's liability if an error is discovered upon audit of the return. Some examples of errors are incorrect postings; errors in the calculation of the tax liability, tax credits, etc.; deductions of business expense items that are actually personal; and omissions of income and deductions.[44] Furthermore, the Regulations provide that a change in treatment resulting from a change in underlying facts does not constitute a change in the taxpayer's method of accounting. For example, a change in the useful life of depreciable property results from a change in the underlying facts and is not, therefore, an accounting method change.

Change from an Erroneous Method. If a taxpayer is employing an "erroneous method" of accounting, permission must be obtained from the Commissioner to change to a correct method. An erroneous method is not treated as a mechanical error which can be corrected by merely filing an amended tax return. For example, the failure to include manufacturing overhead in the computation of inventory is an erroneous method of accounting which can be changed only upon obtaining the consent of the Commissioner.

Procedure for Obtaining the Commissioner's Consent. Generally, a taxpayer must file a request for changing his accounting method (on Form 3115) within the first 180 days after the beginning of the taxable year of the desired change.[45] The deadline may be extended to within the first nine months of the year of change, if the taxpayer can show good cause for the delay in filing the request, but the Commissioner has virtually total discretion to accept or reject the proposed change.[46] In any event, the permission for change will not be granted unless the taxpayer agrees to certain terms or adjustments which are prescribed by the IRS; [47] i. e., a ten-year spread of the tax benefits resulting from the change in the taxpayer's method.

Net Adjustments Due to Change in Accounting Method. In the year of change in an accounting method, certain adjustments may be required to items of income and expense to prevent a distortion of taxable income resulting from the change.

Example 8. The Z Corporation switched from the cash to the accrual basis for reporting sales and cost of goods sold in 19X3.

---

44. Reg. § 1.446–1(e)(2)(ii)(b).   **46.** Rev.Proc. 72–52, 1972–2 C.B. 833.

45. Reg. § 1.446–1(e)(3).   **47.** *Supra,* note 45.

The corporation's accrual basis gross profit for the year was computed as follows:

Sales		$100,000
Beginning inventory	$15,000	
Purchases	60,000	
Less, ending inventory	(10,000)	
Cost of goods sold		(65,000)
Gross profit		$ 35,000

At the end of the previous year, Z corporation had accounts receivable of $25,000 and accounts payable for merchandise of $34,000.

The accounts receivable from the previous year, in the amount of $25,000 were never included in gross income since the taxpayer was on the cash basis and did not recognize the uncollected receivables. In the current year the $25,000 was not included in the accrual basis sales since the sales were made in a prior year. Therefore, a $25,000 adjustment to income would be required to prevent the omission of the receivables from income.

The corollary of failure to recognize prior year's receivables is the failure to recognize prior year's accounts payable. The beginning of the year's accounts payable were not included in current or prior year's purchases. Thus, a deduction for the $34,000 was not taken in either year and is therefore included as an adjustment to income for the period of change.

An adjustment is also required to reflect the $15,000 beginning inventory which was previously deducted (due to the use of a cash method of accounting) by the taxpayer in the previous year. In this instance the cost of goods sold during the year of change was reduced by the beginning inventory; thus resulting in a double deduction.

Continuing the above example, the net adjustment due to the change in accounting method would be computed as follows:

Beginning inventory (deducted in prior and current year)	$15,000
Beginning accounts receivable (omitted from income)	25,000
Beginning accounts payable (omitted from deductions)	(34,000)
Net increase in taxable income	$ 6,000

Disposition of Positive Net Adjustment of More Than $3,000. The general rule is that all adjustments arising from a change in accounting method are recognized in the year of the change.[48] However, due to the adverse effects which might result from the "bunch-

---

48.   § 481(a).

ing" of income arising from the inclusion of net positive adjustments in the year of change, § 481(b) prescribes an averaging computational technique for alleviating this hardship. Where the net adjustment is positive (an increase in income) and exceeds $3,000, the Code provides for two possible methods of computing the tax on the additional income:

(1) If the taxpayer used the former method of accounting in the two preceding years, the tax is computed by adding one-third of the adjustment to the taxable income for the year of the change and one-third to each of the two preceding years' income. The resulting additional tax for the two preceding years is then added to the current year's tax liability.[49]

(2) If the taxpayer can compute taxable income for one or more taxable years consecutively preceding the taxable year of the change, the adjustment may be made to those prior years and the current year.[50]

However, the final tax liability cannot be greater than the tax computed by including the entire adjustment in the taxable income for the year of change.

Net Adjustments Which Reduce Taxable Income. The Regulations provide that net adjustments which reduce taxable income are taken into account during the year of change.[51] However, such treatment is seldom permitted if the net decreasing adjustments are substantial. The Commissioner has discretionary authority to require that the taxpayer spread the adjustment over a period of 10 years beginning with the year of change, i. e., 1/10 of the total adjustment is applied to each year's taxable income.[52]

Involuntary Changes. Where the Commissioner requires a taxpayer to change its method of accounting in order to "clearly reflect" income, any positive adjustment that is attributable to years prior to 1954 is permanently excluded from income.[53] This rule was put into the Code to facilitate the transition from the 1939 Code to the 1954 Code and applies solely to involuntary changes initiated by the IRS.

Since a taxpayer can only enjoy the benefits from the exclusion of pre-1954 adjustments if the Commissioner initiates the change, it is important to determine whether the IRS or the taxpayer has initiated the change. In some cases taxpayers have lost the tax benefits of the 1954 adjustments when changes were merely suggested by the

49. § 481(b)(1).

50. § 481(b)(2).

51. Reg. § 1.481–1(c)(4).

52. See Rev.Proc. 70–27, 1970–2 C.B. 509, as clarified in Rev.Proc. 75–18, 1975–1 C.B. 687.

53. § 481(b)(4).

IRS agent.[54] The agent's mere suggestion that the change be made, rather than actually requiring it, was not considered the initiation of a change in method. Where the agent informed the taxpayer that the law required a change in method, the courts have deemed this to be an involuntary change.[55]

When the issue arises, a taxpayer who is required to change its method (or merely strongly urged) by the IRS should be cognizant of the possible consequences. In many cases, the IRS will refrain from causing the taxpayer to make a change from an erroneous method because of the potential reduction in taxes due to the existence of pre-1954 items.

Changes in Depreciation. § 167(e)(1) permits a change from the declining balance method to the straight-line method without consent of the Commissioner. To make any other change in depreciation methods the taxpayer must file a request for change in accounting method on Form 3115 within the first 180 days of the tax year of the change. Currently, the Commissioner grants automatic approval of the change if certain conditions set forth in Revenue Procedure 74–11 are satisfied.[56]

When the taxpayer changes depreciation methods, subsequent computations of depreciation are made by using the new method. The unrecovered cost is merely depreciated over the remaining useful life of the asset. Thus the depreciation deduction is not recomputed for prior years.

Example 9. In 19X2 the taxpayer acquired new depreciable tangible personal property for $15,000. The asset had a five year life and no estimated salvage value. The taxpayer depreciated the asset by the sum-of-the-year's digits method in 19X1 and 19X2, and in 19X3 obtained permission to switch to the straight-line method. The depreciation for 19X3 and subsequent years will be computed as follows:

Cost	$15,000
Less, prior depreciation	
19X1 $5/15 \times 15,000 =$	(5,000)
19X2 $4/15 \times 15,000 =$	(4,000)
Undepreciated cost	$ 6,000
Remaining useful life	÷ 3 years
Annual deduction, 19X3	$2,000

54. *Irving Falk v. Comm.,* 37 T.C. 1078 (1962).

55. *U. S. v. Linder,* 62–2 USTC ¶ 9694, 10 AFTR2d 5462, 307 F.2d 262 (CA–10, 1962).

56. Rev.Proc. 74–11, 1974–1 C.B. 420.

SPECIAL ACCOUNTING
METHODS

Generally, accrual basis taxpayers recognize income when goods are sold and shipped to the customer. Cash basis taxpayers generally recognize income from a sale upon the collection of cash from the customer. The tax law provides special accounting methods, however, for unusual situations, e. g., for long-term contracts where the contract requires more than 12 months to complete. In addition, the installment method (which is a variation of the cash method) is available to taxpayers providing certain conditions are met. These special methods were enacted, in part, to provide equity based upon the wherewithal to pay concept since the taxpayer does not have the cash to pay the tax at the time of sale.

LONG–TERM CONTRACTS

The Regulations define a "long-term contract" as follows: (1) a building, installation, construction or manufacturing contract which is not completed within the taxable year entered into, and (2) is either (a) a contract involving the manufacture of unique items not normally carried in finished goods inventory or (b) a contract which normally requires more than 12 months to complete.[57]

> **Example 10.** Ajax Architectural and Engineering, Inc., a calendar year taxpayer, entered into two contracts during the year. One contract was to construct a special building foundation. Work was to begin in October 19X1 and was to be completed by June 19X2. The position of the IRS is that the contract is not long-term even though it straddles two years, since it takes less than twelve months to complete. It should be noted that these Regulations have been successfully challenged by taxpayers in a number of cases cited above.
>
> The second contract was for architectural services to be performed on a new building over a two-year period. These services will not qualify for long-term contract treatment because the taxpayer will not "build, install, or construct."

The taxpayer may elect to use either (1) the completed contract, (2) percentage of completion method, (3) cash, (4) accrual or a (5) hybrid method in the year the costs are incurred for such long-term contracts. Once the election is made, the taxpayer must apply the

---

57. Reg. § 1.451–3(b). But in *L. A. Wells Construction Co. v. Comm.*, 43–1 USTC ¶ 9311, 30 AFTR 1177, 134 F.2d 623 (CA–6, 1943); the taxpayer was allowed to use the completed contract method even though the project took less than 12 months to complete. See also *Daley v. U. S.*, 57–1 USTC ¶ 9602, 51 AFTR 117, 243 F.2d 466 (CA–9, 1957).

same method to all subsequent long-term contracts unless permission is obtained for a change in accounting method.[58]

Completed Contract Method. Under the completed contract method, no revenue from the contract is recognized until the contract is completed and accepted.[59] However, a taxpayer may not delay completion of a contract for the principal purpose of deferring tax.[60] Nevertheless, it may be possible for a taxpayer to select the year in which income is recognized by either accelerating or decelerating nearly completed projects prior to the end of the tax year. Some courts have, in effect, applied a de minimus rule holding that a contract is complete upon its substantial completion, i. e., minor amounts of work to be completed or defects to be corrected do not postpone the recognition of income if the contract has been accepted.[61] Other courts have applied a literal interpretation to the Regulations and have required total completion and acceptance of the contract.[62] In some instances the original contract price may be disputed or the buyer may desire additional work to be done on a long-term contract. If the disputed amount is substantial, i. e., it is not possible to determine whether a profit or loss will ultimately be realized on the contract, the Regulations provide that no amount of income or loss is recognized until the dispute is resolved.[63] In all other cases, the profit or loss (reduced by the amount in dispute) is recognized in the current period upon completion of the contract. However, if additional work is to be performed with respect to the disputed contract, the difference between the amount in dispute and the actual cost of the additional work will be recognized in the year such work is completed rather than in the year in which the dispute is resolved.[64]

All costs allocable to the contract are accumulated in a contract in progress account (an inventory account) until the revenue is recognized, at which time the costs are offset against the income from the contract. Construction costs such as direct labor and materials must be allocated to individual contracts.[65] In addition, certain indirect costs must be allocated to the extent incident to and necessary for the performance of the long-term contract.[66] Such costs include repairs,

58. Reg. § 1.453–3(f).

59. Reg. § 1.451–3(b)(2).

60. Ibid.

61. *Ehret-Day Co.,* 2 T.C. 25 (1943) acq., 1943 C.B. 7; *Nathan Wohlfeld,* 17 TCM 677, T.C.Memo. 1958–128; *Charles G. Smith,* 66 T.C. 213 (1976).

62. *Thompson-King-Tate v. U. S.,* 62–1 USTC ¶ 9116, 8 AFTR2d 5920, 296 F.

2d 290 (CA–6, 1961); *E. E. Black Limited v. Alsup,* 54–1 USTC ¶ 9340, 45 AFTR 1345, 211 F.2d 879 (CA–9, 1954).

63. Reg. § 1.451–3(d)(2)(ii).

64. Reg. § 1.451–3(d)(2)(iii)–(v).

65. Reg. § 1.451–3(d)(5)(i).

66. Reg. § 1.451–3(d)(5)(ii).

maintenance, utilities, rent, depreciation, etc. Certain of the following costs are not required to be allocated to the long-term contracts and may be written off immediately: selling, advertising, distribution, interest, general and administrative, research, depreciation on idle equipment, pension costs, etc.

Frequently the contractor will receive payment at various stages of completion. For example, when the contract is fifty percent complete, the contractor may receive fifty percent of the contract price less a retainage. The taxation of these payments is generally governed by Regulation 1.451-5 "advanced payments for goods and long-term contracts," which is discussed in Chapter 4. Generally, contractors are permitted to defer the advance payments until they are recognized as income under the taxpayer's accounting method.

Percentage of Completion Method. Under the percentage of completion method, a portion of the gross contract price is included in income during each period. The accrued amount represents the percentage of the contract which is completed during the year multiplied by the gross contract price. All of the expenditures made on the contract during the year (after adjustment for variations between the beginning and ending inventories of materials and supplies) are deductible as an offset against the accrued revenue.[67]

The Regulations provide that the determination of the percentage of completion may be determined by either of the following methods:

(1) By comparing the costs incurred with the estimated total costs, or

(2) By comparing the work performed with the estimated total work to be performed.[68]

If the estimate is based upon a comparison of work performed, certificates of architects or engineers or other appropriate documentation must be available for inspection upon audit by the IRS.[69]

Comparison of the Completed Contract and Percentage of Completion Methods. To illustrate the two methods, assume a contractor agrees to construct a building for $125,000. In the initial year of construction, costs of $80,000 are incurred and the architect estimates

---

67. Reg. § 1.451–3(c)(3).

68. Reg. § 1.451–3(c)(2).

69. Reg. § 1.451–3(c)(2)(ii).

the job is 80 percent complete. In the second year the contract is completed at an additional cost of $25,000.

PERCENTAGE OF COMPLETION METHOD

	Year 1	Year 2
Revenue (.80 × $125,000 in year 1)	$100,000	$ 25,000
Costs incurred on the contract	(80,000)	(25,000)
Gross profit	$ 20,000	$ –0–

COMPLETED CONTRACT METHOD

	Year 1	Year 2
Revenue	–0–	$125,000
Costs incurred on the contract	===	(105,000)
Gross profit	–0–	$ 20,000

As illustrated above, an advantage to using the completed contract method is that the income is deferred which means that the contractor has the use of funds which would otherwise be payable to the government as income taxes during periods prior to completion. Of course, the completed contract method can result in a bunching of income in one year. However, if the contractor is incorporated and regularly reports taxable income of more than $50,000, the 48% rate will always apply. Therefore, the deferral can be accomplished with no increase in total tax. If the taxpayer is an individual, income averaging may afford some relief from the bunched income problem. In addition, the completed contract method may minimize disputes with the IRS since there is no need to make yearly estimates of the percentage of completion. Other considerations relative to the use of a desired method involve "ability to pay" tax considerations. Under the percentage of completion method, unless advance payments are substantial, cash may not be available during periods prior to the completion of the contract, when the tax is due.

INSTALLMENT METHOD

The general rule for computing the gain or loss from the sale of property is that the entire amount of gain or loss is recognized upon the sale or other disposition of the property.

Example 11. A sold property to B for $20,000 cash plus B's note which had a market value and face amount of $80,000. A's basis in the property was $40,000. Gain or loss computed under the cash or accrual basis would be as follows:

Amount realized:	
Cash down payment	$ 20,000
Notes receivable	80,000
	$100,000
Basis in the property	(40,000)
Realized gain	$ 60,000

In the prior example, under the general rule for recognizing gain or loss, A would be required to pay a substantial amount of tax on the gain in the year of sale even though only $20,000 cash was received. Congress enacted the installment sale provisions to prevent this sort of hardship by allowing the taxpayer to elect to spread the gain from certain sales over the collection periods.

The installment sales method is a very important tax planning tool. In addition to its obvious tax deferral possibilities, the installment method can be used to avoid a bunching of income, and in the case of a sale of a capital asset, the installment method may sufficiently spread the capital gain exclusion so as to avoid any minimum tax on tax preferences.

Who Can Use the Installment Method. The election is available for reporting gains (but not losses) from the following types of transactions: [70]

(1) sales of inventories by a dealer in personal property who regularly sells on the installment plan;

(2) casual sales of personal property (other than inventories) where the selling price exceeds $1,000 and the buyer's payments in the year of sale do not exceed 30 percent of the selling price; and

(3) the sale or disposition of real property where the buyer's payments in the year of sale do not exceed 30 percent of the selling price.

Regardless of the type of property sold, the installment method may be used only in situations where the selling price is determinable, e. g., a selling price which is contingent upon a percentage of business profits or sales is not determinable.

Dealers in Personal Property. In order to qualify as a dealer in personal property, the taxpayer must "regularly" sell personal property on the installment plan. [71] "Regularly" would seem to imply a high ratio of installment sales to total sales. However, the Tax Court has interpreted the "regularly sells" requirement to merely mean that

---

70. §§ 453(a) and (b).   **71.** § 453(a)(1).

the taxpayer holds himself out to the public as selling on the installment plan.[72]   In this case, despite the fact that the taxpayer made
only one sale on the installment plan during the year and made only
11 such sales during a 13-year period, The Tax Court ruled the "regularly sells" requirement was satisfied.

The election may be used to report income from revolving charge
accounts as well as traditional installment contracts providing that
the plans contemplate that the sale will be paid for in two or more
payments.[73]   More than one payment is required to qualify for the installment sale treatment.[74]

Making the Election.   A dealer in personal property can elect to
use the installment method in the first year sales are made on an installment plan, by computing the income in accordance with the installment method and attaching a statement to the tax return that
the method is being adopted.[75]   Once the election is made, it applies
to all subsequent installment sales unless the taxpayer receives permission to change to the accrual method.   However, the election can
be retroactively revoked by filing a notice of revocation within three
years from the last date prescribed for the filing of the return for the
year of the original election.[76]

Example 12.   In 19X1 the taxpayer, an individual, initially began to sell goods on the installment basis.   The installment method was used in the 19X1 through 19X3 tax returns.   In March
19X4, the taxpayer decided to revoke the election.   The revocation must be made for 19X1, 19X2, and 19X3.   Therefore, the
taxpayer must prepare amended returns for those years recomputing gross profit by the accrual method.

In some cases, the taxpayer does not elect the installment method in the first year in which sales are made on an installment basis.
In such instances, the taxpayer is required to compute taxable income
as if the installment method had been used for all of the prior years.
This requirement results in the inclusion of gross profit from collections on prior year's sales which were previously included in taxable
income resulting in a double tax on such amounts.[77]   This double inclusion of income is offset by an adjustment procedure which is provided for in the Regulations.[78]   In many instances, however, the adjustment or tax credit is insufficient to fully offset the adverse effects
of the double inclusion in income.

72. *Davenport Machine & Foundry Co.*, 18 T.C. 38 (1952).

73. Reg. § 1.453–2(d).

74. Reg. § 1.453–2(b)(1).

75. Reg. § 1.453–8(a).

76. Reg. § 1.453–8(d).

77. Reg. § 1.453–7.

78. Reg. § 1.453–7(b).

Therefore, if an installment election is deemed to be desirable, it may be preferable to sell all of the outstanding installment obligations existing at the beginning of the year of change in the year preceding the change. The sale eliminates the inclusion of the gross profit from prior year's installment sales which were previously taxed under the accrual method since none of these accounts are collected in the current year.

Computing the Realized Gross Profit. The gross profit percentages may be computed for each sale and the percentage can then be applied to each collection. In most instances, however, all of the installment sales for a particular year are grouped and one gross-profit percentage for the year is computed.[79] A dealer in personal property is required to add carrying charges or interest (determined at the time of the sale) to the cash selling price of the property.[80]

Example 13. A home appliance dealer had installment sales, cost of goods sold, and gross profit computed by the accrual method as follows:

	Installment Sales Including Carrying Charges and Interest	Cost of Goods Sold	Gross Profit	Gross Profit %
19X1	$100,000	$ 60,000	$40,000	40%
19X2	120,000	90,000	30,000	25%
19X3	150,000	105,000	45,000	30%

In computing the gross profit under the installment method on the 19X3 return, the dealer must take into account collections on current and previous year's installment sales as follows:

Year of Sale	19X3 Collections		Gross Profit %	Gross Profit on Collections
19X1	$20,000	×	40%	$ 8,000
19X2	50,000	×	25%	12,500
19X3	60,000	×	30%	18,000
Total 19X3 realized gross profit				$38,500

Bad Debts and Repossessions. When the installment method is used and accounts become uncollectible, the vendor receives a bad debt deduction for the unrecovered cost of the merchandise.[81] The deferred gross profit which is included in the receivable cannot be deducted since it has never been included in gross income.

Example 14. During the current year the dealer in the above example had to write-off as uncollectible $10,000 of installment

---

79. Reg. § 1.453–2(c).

80. Reg. § 1.453–2(c)(2)(i).

81. Reg. § 1.453–1(d).

receivables from sales made in 19X2, when the gross profit rate was 25 percent. The bad debt deduction is the balance of the account less the profit included in the receivable, $10,000 — .25 × $10,000 = $7,500.

If the dealer repossesses the merchandise, its value at the time of repossession must be used to reduce the loss (and expenses of repossession which are added to the loss). Assuming in the above example, the merchandise was repossessed when it had a value of $1,500, the dealer incurred $100 costs of repossession and later sold the merchandise for $2,000, a $6,100 loss on repossession would be reported, ($7,500 + $100 — $1,500). The dealer would also report a $500 gain on the subsequent sale of the property since the repossessed goods are included in inventory at their fair market value ($2,000 selling price less $1,500 cost = $500 gain).

Sales of Real Property and Casual Sales of Personal Property. As previously mentioned, the installment method may be used to report gains from: (1) casual sales of personal property (other than inventories) where the selling price is greater than $1,000 and the buyer's payments in the year of sale do not exceed 30 percent of the selling price; and (2) sales of real estate where the buyer's payments in the year of sale do not exceed 30 percent of the selling price.

The Election. The installment sale election must be made for each sale and is made by attaching a statement to a timely filed return showing the gross profit computations by the installment method.[82] If the taxpayer fails to make a timely election (unless the failure to elect was intentional) the election can usually be made on an amended or delinquent return.[83]

The 30% Limitation on Collections in the Year of Sale. Since payments in excess of 30 percent of the selling price in the year of sale will invalidate an installment method election, the computations of "selling price" and "payments in the year of sale" are very important. Selling price is the total consideration received by the seller. It includes: cash, notes or mortgages of the buyer, the fair market value of all other property received by the seller and any liabilities of the seller that are assumed by the buyer. If the buyer takes the property subject to a mortgage (rather than personally assuming the mortgage), the amount of the mortgage is also included in the selling price.[84] Selling expenses do not reduce the selling price.[85] The gen-

82. Reg. § 1.453–8(b).

83. Rev.Rul. 65–297, 1965–2 C.B. 152; The Supreme Court in *Pacific National Co. v. Welch*, 38–1 USTC ¶ 9286, 20 AFTR 1248, 58 S.Ct. 857 (USSC, 1938), held that a taxpayer who reported the sale by the deferred payment method on his original return can not file an amended return and use the installment method.

84. Reg. § 1.453–4(c).

85. *Ibid.*

eral rule is that payments to the seller do not include the buyer's note or mortgages assumed by the purchaser. However, if the buyer gives a demand note to the seller, the fair market value of such note is considered to be the equivalent of cash and is, therefore, treated as a payment in the year of sale.[86]

> **Example 15.** A sells a building to B for $100,000 who gives A a demand note of $75,000 and $25,000 cash. The sale does not qualify for the installment method since the $75,000 note is included as a payment. Thus, payments in the year of sale are $100,000 or 100% of the selling price.

If the buyer assumes certain of the seller's obligations (other than notes or mortgages on the property), e. g., accrued property taxes and interest, such amounts are not treated as payments made to the seller.[87] However, if the purchaser merely pays off the seller's notes, mortgage or other debt upon the closing of the sale rather than assuming such obligations, these amounts are treated as payments.[88]

If the mortgage which is assumed by the buyer exceeds the seller's basis in the property, such excess is treated as a payment to the seller in the year of sale.[89]

> **Example 16.** Mr. A's cost basis on certain real estate is $10,000 and its fair market value is $100,000. A wants to sell the property and recognize the gain over an extended period by using the installment method. He also wants to receive a substantial amount of cash from the property for use in other investments. Therefore, he places an $80,000 mortgage on the property and sells the property to B who assumes the mortgage. $70,000, which represents the amount in excess of basis, is treated as a payment in the year of sale and the installment method is not available.

It should be possible to place a mortgage on property immediately prior to the installment sale without invalidating the installment sale election if the mortgage does not exceed the adjusted basis of the property.[90]

Computing the Gain for the Period: The gain on each sale reported in a year is computed by the following formula:

$$\frac{\text{Total gain}}{\text{Contract price}} \times \text{Collections} = \text{recognized gain}$$

86. § 453(b)(3).

87. Rev.Rul. 73–555, 1973–2 C.B. 159.

88. *Sterling v. Ham,* 3 USTC ¶ 1080, 12 AFTR 728, 3 F.Supp. 386 (D.Ct. Me., 1933).

89. Reg. § 1.453–4(c).

90. *Albert W. Turner,* 33 TCM 1167, T.C.Memo. 1974–264.

The computation of the total gain for a taxpayer who is not a dealer in real property is selling price reduced by selling expenses less the adjusted cost basis of the property. For a dealer in real property, selling expenses are treated as a business expense and are, therefore, deducted (in full) in the year of sale, rather than being used to offset the selling price.[91]

The contract price is generally the total amount (excluding interest payments) the seller will ultimately collect from the purchaser. Therefore, the contract price is usually computed by subtracting any existing mortgage or notes which are assumed by the buyer. If the mortgage or notes which are assumed by the buyer exceed the adjusted basis of the property, such excess amount is treated as a payment and must be added back to the selling price to arrive at the contract price.[92]

The character of the gain depends upon the type of asset sold. Where the gain includes some ordinary income under §§ 1245 and 1250, as well as § 1231 gain, the Regulations require that all ordinary income be recognized before the § 1231 gain is reported.[93]

Below are some examples of the recognized profit computations for "dealers" and "non-dealers."

Example 17 (non-dealer).

Sales price		
Cash down payment	$ 1,000	
Seller's mortgage assumed	3,000	
Notes payable to the seller	13,000	$17,000
Selling expenses		(500)
Seller's basis		(10,000)
Total gain		$ 6,500

Contract price = $17,000 − $3,000 = $14,000, assuming the $1,000 is the only payment in the year of sale, the gain in that year is computed as follows:

$$\frac{\text{Total Gain}}{\text{Contract price}} \times \$1,000 = \frac{\$ 6,500}{\$14,000} \times \$1,000 = \underline{\$464} \text{ (gain recognized in year of sale)}$$

Example 18 (non-dealer). Assumed mortgage in excess of basis.

Same as above except the seller's basis in the property is only $2,000. The total gain is, therefore, $14,500. Collections in the year of sale = $1,000 + (3,000 − 2,000) = $2,000.

Contract price = $17,000 − $3,000 + (3,000 − 2,000) = $15,000.

$$\frac{\text{Total gain}}{\text{Contract price}} \frac{\$14,500}{\$15,000} \times \$2,000 = \underline{\$1,933} \text{ (gain recognized in year of sale)}$$

---

91. Reg. § 1.453–1(b)(1).

92. *Supra,* note 89.

93. Reg. §§ 1.1245–6(d) and 1.1250–1(b)(6).

In the subsequent years, as the seller collects the $13,000 notes he will report the balance of the gain $14,500 × $13,000 = $12,567.

$$\frac{\$14,500 \times \$13,000}{\$15,000} = \$12,567.$$

It should be noted that the total payments in the year of sale of $1,000 cash plus $1,000, which represents the excess of the assumed mortgage over the adjusted basis of the property, or $2,000 were less than 30% of the selling price and did not, therefore, invalidate the installment method election.

Example 19. Same as the prior example except the seller is a "dealer." The total gain is $15,000 since the selling expense is deducted as a business expense.

$\dfrac{\text{Total gain}}{\text{Contract price}}\ \dfrac{\$15,000}{\$15,000} \times \$2,000 = \$2,000$	
Less selling expense	(500)
Gain recognized in year of sale	$1,500

As the $13,000 in notes is collected, income will be reported as follows:

$$\frac{\text{Total gain}}{\text{Contract price}}\ \frac{\$15,000}{\$15,000} \times \$13,000 = \$13,000$$

Imputed Interest. § 483 provides that if a deferred payment contract for the sale of property with a selling price of at least $3,000 does not contain a reasonable interest rate, a reasonable rate is imputed. Currently, under the Regulations if a contract entered into on or after July 24, 1975 does not provide a simple interest rate of at least 6%, a rate of 7% compounded semiannually is imputed.[94] The imputing of interest effectively reduces the selling price of the property and treats a portion of the payments received as interest income. § 483 thus prevents sellers of capital assets from increasing the effective selling price to reflect the equivalent of interest on a deferred contract thereby converting ordinary (interest) income into long-term capital gain.

If an installment contract does not provide for interest at 6%, the imputed interest effectively reduces the selling price and thereby increases the percentage relationship of the payment in the year of sale to the total selling price. The adjustment may cause an inadvertent invalidation of the installment method election if the down payment in the year of sale exceeds 30% of the selling price. For example, if property is sold for $100,000 with a $30,000 down payment and a $70,000 noninterest bearing 5-year note is taken by the seller, the downward adjustment of the selling price to reflect imput-

94. Reg. § 1.483–1(g)(2), Table IV.

ed interest at 7 percent will cause the down payment to exceed the 30 percent limitation.

DISPOSITION OF INSTALLMENT OBLIGATIONS

§ 453(d) prevents taxpayers from avoiding the recognition of deferred gross profit on installment obligations through various means such as the sales of installment notes or the distribution of such notes to shareholders. This section of the Code requires the taxpayer to, in effect, pay the tax on the portion of gross profits which was previously deferred. § 453(d)(1) provides as follows:

> If an installment is satisfied at other than its face value or distributed, transmitted, sold, or otherwise disposed of, gain or loss shall result to the extent of the difference between the basis of the obligation and
>
> (A) the amount realized, in the case of satisfaction at other than face value or a sale or exchange, or
>
> (B) the fair market value of the obligation at the time of distribution, transmission, or disposition, in the case of the distribution, transmission, or disposition otherwise than by sale or exchange.

The Regulations provide examples for the computation of gain which is recognized upon the sale or other disposition of installment obligations.[95] Certain exceptions to the recognition of gain provisions are provided for transfers of installment obligations pursuant to tax free incorporations under § 351; contributions of capital to a partnership; certain corporate liquidations and transfers due to the taxpayer's death.[96] In such instances, the deferred profit is merely shifted to the transferee who is responsible for the payment of tax upon the subsequent collections of the installment obligations.

DEFERRED–PAYMENT SALES

A cash basis taxpayer who sells real property under a deferred payment plan but cannot qualify for the installment method (e. g., collections in the year of sale exceed 30 percent of the selling price, or if the taxpayer simply does not elect to use the installment method), is governed by the general rule for reporting income. Gain or loss in the year of sale is recognized and is measured by the difference between (1) the amount realized—"the sum of any money received plus the fair market value of the property (other than money) received"—and (2) the basis in the property sold.[97]

---

95. Reg. § 1.453–9(a)(3), Examples 1 and 2.

96. §§ 453(d)(4) and (5); Reg. § 1.453–9(c).

97. § 1001.

The purchaser's notes or mortgages are treated as other property received by the cash basis seller. Thus, if the market value of the purchaser's obligation is less than its face amount, the seller must recognize additional income when the obligation is collected.

Example 20. D sold real property to E for $40,000 cash plus E's notes payable with a face amount of $80,000 and a market value of $70,000. D's basis in the property was $60,000 and the notes were collected in a year subsequent to the year of sale. The sale does not qualify for installment sales treatment since the collections in the year of sale were more than 30 percent of the selling price. D's gain recognized in the year of sale is computed as follows:

Amount realized	
Cash down payment	$ 40,000
Market value of notes	70,000
	$110,000
Basis in the property	(60,000)
Gain realized and recognized	$ 50,000

Upon collection of the note, D will recognize an additional $10,000 gain. This $10,000 gain is treated as ordinary income, regardless of the type of property sold, because the collection is not deemed to be a sale or exchange.[98] As discussed in Chapter 14, "a sale or exchange" is a requisite for capital gain treatment. It should be noted that if the issuer is a corporation and the provisions of § 1232 are otherwise satisfied, capital gain treatment may be accorded upon the subsequent collection of the obligations.[99]

In rare cases where the obligations do not have a fair market value, gain is not recognized until the collections are received (open transaction doctrine.) [100] In such instances, the initial collections are treated as a return of capital to the extent of the basis in the obligations. Further collections are capital gain if the property sold was a capital asset.[101] The position of the IRS is that only in rare and extraordinary cases does property have no fair market value.[102] Thus, it is usually difficult for the taxpayer to sustain the contention that the transaction is "open" based upon the argument that the obligation received does not have a fair market value.

In the case of an accrual basis taxpayer, the courts have held that the amount realized and recognized in the year of sale is generally measured by the face amount rather than the fair market value

98. *Pat O'Brien*, 25 T.C. 376 (1955).

99. § 1232(a)(2).

100. Reg. § 1.453–6(a)(2).

101. *Westover v. Smith*, 49–1 USTC ¶ 9189, 37 AFTR 1001, 173 F.2d 90 (CA–9, 1949).

102. Reg. § 1.453–6(a)(2).

of the purchaser's obligations.[103]   Thus, in the prior example, if D were an accrual basis taxpayer, the $60,000 gain would be recognized in the year of the sale.

For sales of personal property under a deferred payment plan not qualifiying under § 453, the courts have required taxpayers to include the full amount of the gain in the year of the sale based upon the face amount of the purchaser's obligation without regard to fair market value.[104]

INVENTORIES

The tax accounting and financial accounting for inventories are much the same:

(1) The use of inventories is necessary to "clearly reflect" the income of any business engaged in the production and sale or purchase and sale of goods.[105]

(2) The inventories should include all finished goods, goods in process, and raw materials and supplies which will become part of the product (including containers).[106]

(3) Inventory rules must give effect to the "best" accounting practice of a particular trade or business and the taxpayer's method should be consistently followed from year to year.[107]

(4) All items included in inventory should be valued at either

(a) cost or (b) the lower of cost or market value.[108]

(5) The following are not acceptable methods or practices in valuing inventories: [109]

(a) deducting a reserve for anticipated price changes;

(b) using a constant price or nominal value for a so-called normal quantity of materials or goods in stock (e. g., the base stock method);

(c) including stock in transit in inventory, the title to which is not vested in the taxpayer;

(d) direct costing, i. e., excluding fixed indirect production costs from inventory;

(e) prime costing, i. e., excluding all indirect production costs from inventory.

DETERMINING INVENTORY COST

For merchandise purchased, cost is the invoice price less trade discounts, plus freight and other handling costs.[110]   Cash discounts ap-

103. *Spring City Foundry Co. v. Comm.,* 4 USTC ¶ 1276, 13 AFTR 1164, 54 S.Ct. 644 (USSC, 1934).

104. *George L. Castner Co. Inc.,* 30 T. C. 1061 (1958).

105. Reg. § 1.471–1.

106. *Ibid.*

107. Reg. § 1.471–2(b).

108. Reg. § 1.471–2(c).

109. Reg. § 1.471–2(f).

110. Reg. § 1.471–3(b).

proximating a fair interest charge can be deducted or capitalized at the taxpayer's option providing the method used is consistently applied.[111]

The cost of goods produced or manufactured by the taxpayer must be determined by using the full absorption method of inventory costing.[112] Under this method, production costs (e. g., direct materials and labor) must be included in computing the cost of the inventory. In addition, all indirect production costs must be included in inventory except for the following: [113]

(A) So called "Category 2 costs" need not be included in inventory, e. g., advertising, selling, administrative, distribution, interest, etc.

(B) So called "Category 3 costs" may be either included or excluded depending upon the taxpayer's treatment of such costs for financial reporting purposes, i. e., property and payroll taxes, depreciation, certain employee benefits, etc.

Category 3 costs may be excluded from inventory only if the treatment of a particular item is consistent with generally accepted accounting principles. Furthermore, the Commissioner has ruled that the determination of whether the treatment of the item is consistent with generally accepted accounting principles should be decided without regard to the materiality of the item, or the consistency of its treatment.[114]

> **Example 21.** The taxpayer is in a manufacturing business which has consistently expensed real property tax on the factory in the year of accrual. The company accountant recognizes that the property tax should be included in manufacturing overhead (and thus, included in the cost of the inventory); however, the item is not material so the accountant does not require that the financial statements be adjusted.
>
> In order to comply with the Commissioner's regulations, the property tax must be added to the cost of goods sold and ending inventory, rather than deducted currently.

A taxpayer may use the "standard cost" method to value inventory. However, if indirect production cost variances are significant, a pro-rata portion of the variance must be reallocated to the ending inventories.[115]

Lower of Cost or Market. Except for those taxpayers who use the LIFO method, inventories may be valued at the lower of (1) cost

111. *Ibid.*

112. Reg. § 1.471–11(a).

113. Reg. § 1.471–11(c)(2).

114. TIR 1365, April 17, 1975; modified by Rev.Proc. 75–40, 1975–2 C.B. 571.

115. Reg. § 1.471–11(d)(3).

or (2) replacement cost, "market." [116] Those taxpayers using LIFO must value inventory at cost. However, the write-down of damaged or shop-worn merchandise and goods which are otherwise unsalable at normal prices is not considered to be an application of the lower of cost or market method. Such items should be valued at bona fide selling price less direct cost of disposal.[117]

In applying this method, each item included in the inventory must be valued at the lower of its cost or market value.[118]

Example 22. The taxpayer's ending inventory is valued below:

Item	Cost	Market	Lower of Cost or Market
A	$5,000	$ 4,000	$4,000
B	3,000	2,000	2,000
C	1,500	6,000	1,500
	$9,500	$12,000	$7,500

Under the lower of cost or market method, the taxpayer's inventory would be valued at $7,500 rather than $9,500.

Determining Cost—Specific Identification, FIFO, and LIFO. In some cases it is feasible to determine the cost of the particular item sold. For example, an automobile dealer can easily determine the specific cost of each automobile which has been sold. However, in most businesses it is necessary to resort to a flow of goods assumption such as "first in, first out" (FIFO), "last in, first out" (LIFO) or an average cost method. A taxpayer may use any of these methods provided the method selected is consistently applied from year to year.

During a period of rising prices, LIFO will generally produce a lower ending inventory valuation and therefore results in a greater cost of goods sold than would be obtained under the FIFO method. The effects upon the computation of cost of goods sold using LIFO and FIFO are illustrated in the following example:

Example 23. On January 1, 19X1 the taxpayer opened a retail store to sell refrigerators. At least 10 refrigerators must be carried in inventory to satisfy customer demands. The initial investment in the 10 refrigerators is $5,000. During the period 10 refrigerators were sold at $750 each and were replaced at a cost

116. Reg. § 1.472–4.

117. Reg. § 1.471–2(c).

118. Reg. § 1.471–4(c).

of $6,000 ($600 each). Gross profit under the LIFO and FIFO methods is computed below:

		FIFO		LIFO
Sales (10 × $750)		$7,500		$7,500
Beginning inventory	$ 5,000		$ 5,000	
Purchases	6,000		6,000	
	11,000		11,000	
Ending inventory:				
10 × 600	(6,000)			
10 × 500	——		(5,000)	——
Cost of goods sold		(5,000)		(6,000)
Net income		$2,500		$1,500

THE LIFO ELECTION

A taxpayer may adopt LIFO by merely using the method in the tax return for the year of the change.[119] The application for the change to LIFO is made on Form 970 and filed with the return for the first year LIFO is used. Thus, a taxpayer does not have to request approval for changes within the first 180 days of the tax year. Once the election is made, it cannot be revoked. However, a prospective change from LIFO to any other inventory method can be made if consent by the Commissioner is obtained.[120] Currently, the Commissioner will grant automatic approval if the request is timely filed and the taxpayer agrees to a ten year spread of any positive adjustment.[121]

The beginning inventory valuation for the first year LIFO is used is computed by the costing method employed in the preceding year. Thus, the beginning LIFO inventory is generally the same as the closing inventory for the preceding year. However, since lower of cost or market cannot be used in conjunction with LIFO, previous write-downs to market for items included in the beginning inventory must be restored to income. This upward adjustment in the beginning inventory results in the recognition of additional taxable income for the year of change.[122]

Example 24. In 19X1 the taxpayer used the lower of cost or market and FIFO inventory method. The FIFO cost of its ending inventory was $25,000 and its market value was $20,000. Therefore, the ending inventory for 19X1 was $20,000.

The taxpayer switched to LIFO in 19X2 and must write-up the beginning inventory to $25,000 and must recognize $5,000 addi-

119. Reg. § 1.472–3(a).   121. Rev.Proc. 72–24, 1972–1 C.B. 749.

120. Reg. § 1.472–6.   122. Reg. § 1.472–2(c).

tional income for 19X1. Thus, the LIFO election may be inadvisable in a tax year following substantial write-downs.

TAX PLANNING
CONSIDERATIONS

ACCOUNTING METHODS

The selection of an accounting method is also important since the use of a particular method may offer substantial tax planning opportunities. For example, the use of the cash basis of accounting provides greater opportunities for shifting items of income and expense from one year to another.

Income from long-term construction contracts may be reported by either the percentage of completion or completed contract method. Under the percentage of completion method, income is recognized based upon the percentage of completion of a project in any one year whereas no income is recognized under the completed contract method until the contract is completed. The use of percentage completion may result in the avoidance of the bunching of taxable income in a single year. However, the completed contract method postpones the recognition of income until the contract is complete and may, therefore, offer important cash flow advantages.

One of the most useful tax planning tools is the installment sales provision. The election of this method enables the taxpayer to both defer income and avoid the bunching of income. The installment method may also be used to avoid the minimum tax on tax preference items. Since $\frac{1}{2}$ of a taxpayer's net long-term capital gain is a tax preference item, an installment method election can spread the gain over a period of years thereby avoiding the minimum tax.

However, there are some pitfalls to be avoided before the full benefits of the installment method can be realized. Transactions must be structured so that the thirty percent limitation on payments in the year of sale will not be violated. The subtle effects of liabilities in excess of the seller's basis and the imputed interest on the thirty percent limit must be considered. A competent tax planner should also be aware of the tax consequences of repossession and dispositions of installment obligations. In the case of a dealer in personal property, the installment method should generally be elected in the first year the taxpayer begins to regularly sell on the installment basis to avoid the double-taxation (with only partial relief) that results from a change to the installment method.

INVENTORIES

The LIFO inventory method offers significant tax deferral opportunities during periods of inflation. However, if LIFO is used for income tax, it must also be used for financial reports to shareholders, creditors and others. Therefore, the adverse effects upon earnings per share implications should also be considered if a change to LIFO is under consideration. In addition, the mechanics for changing to and using LIFO are relatively complex and may result in additional record keeping and conversion costs.

PROBLEM MATERIALS

Questions for Class Discussion

1. What types of taxpayers are eligible to use a fiscal year?

2. When should a business be on a 52–53 week basis?

3. (a) When would a fiscal year be preferable to a calendar year?

   (b) How is a fiscal year elected?

4. In which of the following situations must a taxpayer annualize his income?

   (a) the first tax year;

   (b) for an individual in the year he or she marries;

   (c) for the final return; or

   (d) in the year of a change in the tax year.

5. What is the tax procedure for changing a tax year?

6. Is the taxpayer required to use the same method of accounting for all items of income and deductions?

7. Compare the cash basis and accrual basis of accounting as applied to:

   (a) fixed assets;

   (b) prepaid rental income;

   (c) prepaid interest expense;

   (d) a note received for services performed where the market value and face amount of the note differ;

   (e) the deduction for a contested item.

8. What is the general rule as to when income is to be recognized under the accrual basis of accounting?

9. What is the general rule as to when a deduction will be recognized under the accrual basis of accounting?

10. (a) When are reserves for estimated expenses allowed for tax purposes?

    (b) What is the role of the matching concept in tax accounting?

11. A taxpayer has consistently used the accrual basis to report income and deductions for several years. During the year he bought some rental property and would like to report the income from the property by the cash method. Would the use of the cash basis to report the rental income constitute a change in accounting method?

12. What is the procedure for obtaining consent to change a method of accounting?

13. Which of the following require the permission of the Commissioner?

    (a) A change from the cash to the accrual basis for deducting property tax expenses.

    (b) The correction of a prior year's return when the double-declining balance method was incorrectly used to compute the amortization of a patent.

    (c) A change from direct costing to the full absorption method of valuing inventories.

    (d) A change from FIFO to LIFO inventory method.

    (e) A change from cost to the lower of cost or market method of valuing inventories.

    (f) A write-down of damaged merchandise to net realizable value, where the taxpayer has consistently used cost to value the inventories.

    (g) The use of lower of cost or market in conjunction with the LIFO inventory method.

    (h) A change from LIFO to FIFO inventory method.

    (i) A change from FIFO to LIFO for valuing raw materials only.

14. Compare the disposition of positive and negative adjustments due to a change in accounting method.

15. What difference does it make whether the taxpayer or the Commissioner initiates the change in accounting method?

16. (a) The taxpayer began work on a contract in June 19X1 and completed the contract in April 19X2. Can the percentage completion method be used to report the income from the contract?

    (b) If the taxpayer in (a) uses the accrual basis to report income, assuming no advance payments are received, when will the income be recognized?

17. What are the tax advantages of using the completed contract method?

18. What are the differences in requirements a department store must meet to report its sales on the installment basis as com-

pared to an individual who sold an investment in some common stock?

19. In 19X1 the taxpayer sold some real estate and received an installment note. The sale met all of the requirements for electing the installment method, but the taxpayer did not know that the installment method could be used. Thus, the entire gain was reported in the year of sale. In 19X2 you discover that the taxpayer could have used the installment method. Is there anything you can do?

20. How does the buyer's assumption of the seller's liabilities in an installment sale affect:

    (a) selling price;

    (b) contract price;

    (c) buyer's payments in the year of sale?

21. How can the imputed interest provisions affect the computation of the thirty percent limitations on collections in the year of sale?

22. What are the tax effects of a gift of installment obligations?

23. What alternatives are available to a taxpayer for deferring gain if the sale cannot qualify for the installment method?

24. What options are available for the treatment of cash discounts received on the purchase of merchandise?

25. For financial reporting purposes, the taxpayer has consistently expensed all payroll taxes on manufacturing salaries and wages rather than including them in inventories and cost of goods sold. Although the accountant recognized the treatment of the taxes was not theoretically correct, he continued to use the incorrect method because its effect on income was not material. Can the IRS require the taxpayer to change its method of accounting for the payroll taxes?

26. What is "cost" and how is "lower of cost or market" computed for purposes of valuing inventories?

27. If the taxpayer uses standard cost to value inventories what must be done with variances between standard and actual cost?

28. Discuss the problems that could result from footnote disclosures of net income computed by the FIFO method when the taxpayer uses the LIFO method to report its taxable income.

29. Contrast the procedures for changing to the LIFO inventory method with the general requirements for making a change in an accounting method.

Problems

1. The RJ Construction Company reports its income by the completed contract method. At the end of year 1 the company com-

pleted a contract to construct a building at a total cost of $980,-000. The contract price was $1,200,000. However, the customer refused to accept the work and would not pay anything on the contract because he claimed the roof did not meet specifications. RJ's engineers estimated it would cost $140,000 to bring the roof up to the customer's standards. In year 2, the dispute was settled in the customer's favor; the roof was improved at a cost of $170,000; the customer accepted the building and paid the $1,200,000.

    a. What would be the effects of the above on RJ's taxable income for

      Year 1?

      Year 2?

    b. Same as above except RJ had $1,100,000 accumulated cost under the contract at the end of year 1.

2. MT receives appliances from the manufacturer on consignment and collects a 5 percent commission on any sales it makes during the year. MT is an accrual basis taxpayer and made total sales during the year of $750,000. However, the manufacturer is usually a few weeks behind in recording MT's sales and at the end of the year recorded only $600,000 in sales by MT.

    MT argues that he should only report income for the year of .05 × $600,000 = $30,000, since that was all he had a right to receive for the year. He had no right to the commissions on the other $150,000 sales until the manufacturer reported them, in the following year. What is MT's correct taxable income for the year? (Explain.)

3. A is an accrual basis taxpayer. Gross income for the year was $90,000, which included $5,000 for services provided a customer who paid with a note whose market value was only $3,000, due to the poor financial condition of the customer. A's accounts receivable of $40,000 includes approximately $800 in discounts that will be given for early payments.

    A's total expenses per books are $50,000. This included $3,500 in office supplies purchased from a supplier, but have not been paid for as of year-end. A discovered that the supplier had billed him twice for the same $500 order, but the supplier contends that Mr. A ordered and received two identical orders. Also included in total expenses per books was $5,000 in addition to the reserve for service under product warranties. An analysis of that account is presented below:

Reserves

Costs incurred $7,000	15,000 beginning balance 5,000 additions
	<u>13,000</u> balance

Compute A's correct accrual basis taxable income.

4.　In 19X2 the taxpayer was required to switch from the cash to the accrual basis of accounting for sales and cost of goods sold. Taxable income for 19X2 computed under the cash basis was $62,000. There were no pre-1954 adjustments.

	Beginning of the year	End of the year
Accounts receivable	$ 6,000	$ 7,000
Accounts payable	15,000	12,000
Inventory	6,200	5,500

Compute the following:

(a) The adjustment due to the change in accounting method.

(b) The accrual basis taxable income for 19X2, assuming the taxpayer agreed to spread the adjustment due to the change over ten years.

5.　C is a cash basis taxpayer who had adjusted gross income of $40,000 before considering the effect of the following payments made on December 31, 19X1, in connection with business activities.

(a) January 19X2 rent—$1,000

(b) January 19X2 through June 19X3 property insurance— $2,700

(c) A refundable deposit for telephone extensions—$300

(d) 19X2 professional dues and subscriptions—$480

(e) January through June 19X2 interest on a real estate mortgage—$3,200

(f) Payment on a lawyer's bill for services rendered in 19X0, net of a $500 refundable deposit made in 19X0—$1,500.

Compute C's adjusted gross income.

6.　D sold his controlling interest in the stock of D, Inc. to E under the following terms:

Down payment—Cash	$ 15,000
8% installment notes, $30,000 per year for 5 years	150,000

Payments on the note were to begin in the year following the sale. D was also to receive additional contingent consideration equal to 5 percent of the net profit or would be required to refund 5 percent of any losses, for the five years following the year of the sale. D's basis in the stock was $80,000.

Can D use the installment method to report his gain?

7. GB Appliances, Inc., is an appliance dealer and reports its sales on the installment method. GB groups its sales by years for purposes of computing its realized gross profit for each year. Its collections in the year 19X4 and other relevant information are presented below:

Year of Sale	Current Year Collections	Gross Profit %	Receivables 12–31–X4	Accounts Written-off	Value of Repossessions
19X1	$ 10,000	45	$ 5,000	$ 3,000	$ 600
19X2	25,000	40	8,000	4,000	2,000
19X3	70,000	35	40,000	5,000	4,000
19X4	120,000	38	150,000	500	450
	$225,000		$203,000	$12,500	$7,050

(a) Compute GB's realized gross profit for the year.

(b) Compute GB's loss from repossessions.

(c) In 19X4, GB pledged $100,000 of its 19X4 installment obligations to the bank for $80,000. The bank was to apply collections on the receivables against the loan but the bank had no recourse against GB if the total collections did not equal $80,000. What are the possible tax consequences of pledging the receivables?

8. Mr. P sold an apartment house to T during the current year, 19X2; the closing statement for the sale is presented below:

Total sales price	$120,000
P's mortgage assumed by T	70,000
T's binder (deposit paid in 19X1)	1,000
T's 9% installment notes given to P	25,000
Cash paid to the seller	$ 24,000

During 19X2 P collected $5,000 principal on the installment notes and $1,125 interest. P's basis in the property was $80,000 and there was $5,000 ordinary income recapture potential under Section 1250.

(a) Compute the following:

(1) Contract price

(2) Payments in the year of sale

(3) Recognized gain in the year of sale and its character.

(b) Assume P's basis in the property was $80,000 and in 19X3 he gave the installment notes with a principal amount of $20,000 to his son. What would be the effect of the gift on P's taxable income in 19X3?

(c) Same as (a) except P's basis in the property was $62,000.

9. L sold land to M for $50,000 plus 10 percent installment notes with a face amount of $60,000 and a market value of $50,000, due in two years. L's basis in the land was $60,000 and the land was a capital asset in his hands.

   (a) Compute L's recognized gain in the year of sale, assuming L is

      (1) a cash basis taxpayer;

      (2) an accrual basis taxpayer.

   (b) Assuming L is a cash basis taxpayer, what is his income and its character upon collection of M's note?

10. In 19X2 the taxpayer changed from the use of lower of cost or market FIFO method to the LIFO method. The ending inventory for 19X2 was computed as follows:

Item	FIFO Cost	Replacement Cost	Lower of Cost or Market
A	$10,000	$18,000	$10,000
B	25,000	20,000	20,000
			$30,000

C, damaged and valued at net realizable
  value (LIFO = $15,000)

			11,000
			$41,000

   (a) What is the correct beginning inventory in 19X2 under the LIFO method?

   (b) What immediate tax consequences (if any) would result from the switch to LIFO?

Research Problems

1. Your client sold an apartment building that he had owned for several years. The adjusted basis for the property was $80,000 and the selling price was computed as follows:

Cash down payment	$ 20,000
Assumption of the seller's mortgage	90,000
Buyer's 9% installment notes	40,000
	$150,000

Your client paid a $7,500 real estate commission on the sale. In a surprise move, the buyer paid $20,000 on the principle of the installment notes in the year of the sale. An IRS agent has computed the payments in the year of sale as follows:

Cash down payment	$20,000
Payments on notes	20,000
Excess of seller's mortgage over its basis (90,000 – 80,000)	10,000
	$50,000

Since the $50,000 exceeds 30 percent of the selling price, the agent says the installment method can't be used.

Your client argues that the actual investment was $80,000 plus the $7,500 in selling expenses and, therefore, argues that only $2,500 ($90,000 − $87,500) should be included in the payments in the year of sale. Can you find any support for your client's contention?

2. Your client inherited some raw land several years ago. The basis in the property is $20,000. It has appreciated substantially and the client has a $50,000 mortgage on it. A buyer has proposed to acquire the property by paying $30,000 cash and 9% installment notes for $80,000, but the buyer would not assume the seller's mortgage. Under the agreement the buyer's payments on the installment notes would first be committed to liquidating the mortgage on the property. What would be the effects of this arrangement on your client's ability to qualify for installment sales treatment?

Chapter 17

DEFERRED COMPENSATION

This chapter discusses various types of deferred compensation arrangements which are available to employees and self-employed individuals. The tax law encourages employers to offer deferred compensation plans for their employees to promote social welfare as a supplement to the Federal social security retirement system. For example, contributions to a qualified pension, profit-sharing or stock bonus plan are immediately deductible by the employer. Employees are generally not taxed until the pension funds are made available to them, e. g., during their retirement years when the former employees are usually in a lower tax bracket. In addition, the income which is earned on the contributions to the plan is not subject to tax until such amounts are made available to the employees.

The following is a sample of various deferred compensation arrangements which are being offered to employees:

1. Qualified profit-sharing plans;
2. Qualified pension plans;
3. Employee stock ownership plans;
4. Stock option plans;
5. Nonqualified deferred compensation plans; and
6. Restricted property plans.

In addition to the various types of deferred compensation, employees may receive other valuable fringe benefits such as group-term life insurance, medical reimbursement plans, company-paid automobiles, and interest-free loans, etc.

The tax law has also been liberalized to provide increased pension benefits for self-employed individuals under what is known as HR 10 or Keogh plans. In addition, individuals who are not covered by a qualified or government retirement plan, may now establish an Individual Retirement Account (IRA). These types of deferred compensation arrangements are also discussed in this chapter.

QUALIFIED PENSION, PROFIT-SHARING AND STOCK BONUS PLANS

The Federal government has encouraged private pension and profit-sharing plans to keep older people from becoming "wards of the state." Therefore, the Federal tax law provides substantial tax benefits for plans that meet certain requirements. The major requirement of qualification is that a plan may not discriminate in favor of employees who are officers, stockholders or highly compensated.

TYPES OF PLANS

There are three types of qualified plans: pension, profit-sharing, and stock bonus plans.

Pension Plans. A pension plan is a deferred compensation arrangement which provides for systematic payments of definitely determinable retirement benefits to employees who meet the requirements set forth in the plan. Benefits are measured generally by, and based upon, such factors as years of service and employee compensation. A pension plan may provide for payments due to a disability and may provide for payments of incidental death benefits through insurance (but not lay off benefits, benefits for sickness, accident, hospitalization, or medical expenses).[1] Employer contributions under a qualified pension plan must *not* depend upon profits, but must be sufficient to provide definitely determinable benefits on some actuarial basis.

A pension plan must expressly provide that forfeitures must be used to reduce the employer's contributions under the plan.[2] This requirement may be contrasted with the treatment of forfeitures pursuant to a profit-sharing or stock bonus plan where the plan may provide that forfeitures are reallocated to increase benefits for the remaining participants.

There are basically two types of qualified pension plans—a defined contribution plan and a defined benefit plan.

1. Reg. § 1.401–1(b)(1)(i).   2. Reg. § 1.401–7(a).

A *defined contribution pension plan* (or money purchase plan) requires a separate account for each participant in which benefits are based solely on (1) the amount contributed and (2) income from the fund which accrues to the participant's account.[3]   In essence, such a plan defines the amount the employer is required to contribute, such as a flat dollar amount, a special formula, or a certain percentage of compensation.   Thus, actuarial calculations are not required in order to determine the employer's annual contribution.   Upon retirement, the employee's pension is dependent upon the value of his individual account.   It is possible, although not required, for a plan to require or permit employee contributions to the pension fund.

A *defined benefit plan* provides a formula which defines the benefits employees are to receive.[4]   Under such a plan an employer must make annual contributions based upon actuarial computations which will be sufficient to pay the vested retirement benefits.   Separate accounts are not maintained for each participant.   A defined benefit plan provides some sense of security for employees since the benefits are expressed in fixed dollar amounts.   Under this type of plan, the benefits may be stated as a fixed amount, e. g., 30 percent of the employee's salary for the last five years prior to retirement.

Example 1.   The qualified pension plan of the XYZ Company calls for both the employer and employee to contribute 5% of the employee's compensation to the pension trust annually. Since the rate of contribution of the employer is fixed, this pension plan is a defined contribution plan.   If the plan called for contributions sufficient to provide retirement benefits equal to 30 percent of the employee's last five years' salary, it would be a defined benefit plan.

Profit-sharing Plans.   A profit-sharing plan is a deferred compensation arrangement established and maintained by an employer to provide for employee participation in the company's profits.   Contributions are paid from the profits of the employer to a trustee and are commingled in a single trust fund.   In a profit-sharing plan separate accounts are maintained for each participant.   The plan must provide a definite predetermined formula for allocating the contributions made to the trustee among the participants and for distributing the accumulated funds after a fixed number of years, the attainment of a stated age, or upon the prior occurrence of certain events such as illness, layoff, retirement, etc.   Any amounts allocated to the account of a participant may be used to provide incidental life, accident, or health insurance.[5]   A company is not required to contribute a definite predetermined amount to the plan, but substantial and recurring contributions must be made in order to meet the permanency requirement.[6]   Forfeitures arising under this plan do not have to be

3. § 414(i).   **5.** Reg. § 1.401–1(b)(1)(ii).

4. § 414(j).   **6.** Reg. § 1.401–1(b)(2).

used to reduce the employer's contribution, and may be used to increase the individual accounts of the remaining participants as long as such increases do not result in prohibited discrimination.[7] Since the primary emphasis of a profit-sharing plan is not necessarily on retirement income, lump-sum pay-outs may be the normal method of distributing benefits to employees.

Stock Bonus Plans. A stock bonus plan is a form of deferred compensation established and maintained by an employer to provide contributions of the employer's stock to the plan. However, there is no requirement that such contributions be dependent upon profits. This plan is subject to the same requirements as a profit-sharing plan for purposes of allocating and distributing the stock among the employees.[8] Any benefits of the plan are distributable in the form of stock of the employer company, except that distributable fractional shares may be paid in cash.[9]

An Employee Stock Ownership Trust (ESOT) is a stock bonus trust that qualifies as a tax-exempt employee trust under § 401(a). Technically an ESOT is a defined contribution plan which is a qualified stock bonus plan or a stock bonus and a money purchase plan both of which are qualified under § 401(a). An ESOT must be designed to invest primarily in qualifying employer securities.[10] Since the corporation can contribute stock rather than cash, there is no cash flow drain. In addition, the tax savings accruing under the plan may have a favorable impact upon working capital for the company. This plan provides flexibility since contributions may vary from year to year and, in fact, may be omitted in any one year.[11]

Although the ESOT has been in the law since 1954, recent law changes have provided further incentive for adoption, especially for small corporations. A corporation can elect an eleven or in certain instances an eleven and one-half percent investment credit instead of the usual ten percent investment credit if it establishes an ESOT for employees.[12] A company can fund the ESOT by acquiring outstanding shares of the company stock from its shareholders who receive favorable capital gain treatment upon the sale of their stock. Employees are not subject to tax until they receive a distribution of the stock from the trust. In addition, any unrealized appreciation relative to the employer securities is not taxed to the employee until he sells the stock.[13]

Example 2. The ESOT of T Company borrows $100,000 from Farmers' Bank & Trust. The loan is secured by the stock inter-

---

7. Reg. § 1.401–4(a)(1)(iii).

8. Reg. § 1.401–1(b)(1)(iii).

9. Rev.Rul. 71–256, 1971–1 C.B. 118; Rev.Rul. 62–195, 1962–2 C.B. 125.

10. § 4975(e)(7).

11. Reg. § 1.401–1(b)(2).

12. § 46(a)(1)(B).

13. § 402(e)(4)(D)(ii).

est and is guaranteed by the company. The ESOT buys 20% of stock from T for $100,000 and the shares are then allocated among the employees' retirement accounts. The shareholder obtains capital gain treatment on the sale. T Company makes deductible contributions to the ESOT, which, in turn, pays off the loan.

QUALIFICATION REQUIREMENTS

Exclusive Benefit Requirement. A pension, profit-sharing or stock bonus trust must be created by an employer for the exclusive benefit of employees or their beneficiaries.[14]

> **Example 3.** The pension trust agreement of P Company provides the trust with complete power to invest funds without regard to whether investments may be new, speculative, hazardous, adventurous, or productive of income. Such a plan is not designed for the exclusive benefit of the employees and would not qualify under § 401(a).[15]

Under a "prudent man" concept, the IRS specifies four investment requirements for meeting this exclusive benefit requirement: [16]

1. The cost of the investment must not exceed fair market value at the time of purchase.

2. A fair return commensurate with prevailing rates must be provided.

3. Sufficient liquidity must be maintained in order to permit distributions in accordance with the terms of the qualified plan.

4. The safeguards and diversity that a prudent investor would adhere to must be present.

Nondiscrimination Rules. In order to qualify, the contributions or benefits under a plan must not discriminate in favor of employees who are officers, stockholders, or highly compensated.[17] A plan is not deemed to exhibit this forbidden discrimination "merely because the contributions or benefits of or on behalf of the employees under the plan bear a uniform relationship to the total compensation, or the basic or regular rate of compensation of such employees. * * * " [18] Thus, a pension plan which provides for the allocation of the employer contributions based upon a flat 3% of each employee's compensation, would not be discriminating despite the fact

---

14. § 401(a).

15. Rev.Rul. 73–532, 1973–2 C.B. 128.

16. Rev.Rul. 65–178, 1965–2 C.B. 94;
Rev.Rul. 73–380, 1973–2 C.B. 124.

17. § 401(a)(4).

18. § 401(a)(5).

that highly paid employees receive proportionately greater benefits. Furthermore, in determining whether the plan is nondiscriminatory, employer FICA contributions for covered employees may be taken into account.[19]

Coverage Requirements. Since a qualified plan must be primarily for the benefit of employees and must be nondiscrimatory, the plan must cover a reasonable percentage of the company employees. The Code provides mathematical tests which may be met in order to satisfy the coverage requirements, e. g., 70% and 80% tests.[20] To meet these tests a plan must cover at least: (1) 70 percent of all employees or (2) 80 percent of all eligible employees as long as at least 70 percent of the employees are eligible for participation. In determining "all employees," part-time and employees who have not satisfied the minimum participation requirements as to age and years of service are not counted. Where these tests are not met, a plan can still qualify if the plan does not discriminate in favor of officers, shareholders or highly-compensated employees. It is possible to qualify a plan which covers "salaried only" employees if it can be shown that the plan covers a varied cross section of employees.[21]

Vesting Requirements. An employee's right to his accrued benefits derived from his own contributions must be nonforfeitable from the date of contribution.[22] The accrued benefits derived from employer contributions must be nonforfeitable in accordance with one of three alternative minimum vesting schedules—10-year rule, 5-to-15 year rule, or the Rule of 45.[23]

Under the ten-year rule, an employee with at least 10 years of service must have a nonforfeitable right to 100% of his accrued benefits derived from employer contributions.[24] Generally, a "year of service" means a 12-month period during which a participant has completed at least 1,000 hours of service.[25]

The 5-to-15 year vesting rule requires an employee who has at least 5 years of service to have a nonforfeitable right at least equal to

---

19. Rev.Rul. 70–580, 1970–2 C.B. 90.   **22.** § 411(a)(1).

20. § 410(b)(1).   **23.** § 411(a)(2).

21. Rev.Rul. 66–12, 1966–1 C.B. 72,   **24.** § 411(a)(2)(A).
clarified by Rev.Rul. 68–244, 1968–1
C.B. 158.   **25.** § 411(a)(5)(A).

a percentage of the accrued benefits derived from employer contributions determined under the following table: [26]

Table 1

Years of Service	Nonforfeitable Percentage
5	25%
6	30%
7	35%
8	40%
9	45%
10	50%
11	60%
12	70%
13	80%
14	90%
15 or more	100%

Under the Rule of 45, an employee who has at least five years of service and whose age and service together equal 45, must have at least a nonforfeitable interest in his accrued benefits derived from employer contributions to the extent of the amount determined under the following table: [27]

Table 2

If Years of Service Equal of Exceed	And Sum of Age and Service Equals or Exceeds	Then the Minimum Nonforfeitable Percentage Must Be
5	45	50%
6	47	60%
7	49	70%
8	51	80%
9	53	90%
10	55	100%

Notwithstanding the above general rule, no plan shall be treated as satisfying the Rule of 45 vesting requirements unless any participant who has completed ten years of service has a nonforfeitable right to at least 50 percent of his accrued benefits derived from employer contributions and to not less than an additional 10 percent for each additional year of service.[28] The Rule of 45 is generally more favorable to older employees.

A major exception permits service prior to reaching age 22 to be disregarded when using the 10-year rule and the 5-to-15 year rule. This exception does not apply when a plan is following the Rule of 45.[29] For example, under the Rule of 45 an employee hired at the age 18 would have to be 50% vested at the age of 28.

26. § 411(a)(2)(B).

27. § 411(a)(2)(C)(i).

28. § 411(a)(2)(C)(ii).

29. § 411(a)(4)(A).

Example 4. R was fired at age 33 after 10 years of noteworthy service because of a downturn in the economy. His employer's pension plan provides for vesting under the Rule of 45. Although under the Rule of 45, R is zero vested, a person with 10 years of service must be 50% vested.

Example 5. C resigns at age 30 to enter the employment of a competitor of his employer. He has 10 years of service with his current employer. Under the 10-year rule, he has only 8 years of service since the time before age 22 can be disregarded. Therefore, zero of C's interest under the qualified plan is vested under the ten year rule. Under the 5-to-15 year rule, 40% is vested since the years before age 22 may be disregarded. Therefore, if the company plan is qualified under the 5-15 year rule, C must be entitled to retirement benefits under the plan. Under the Rule of 45, the two years of service prior to age 22 cannot be disregarded and the employee would, therefore, be 50% vested.

TAX CONSEQUENCES TO THE EMPLOYEE AND EMPLOYER

In General. Employer contributions to qualified plans are not subject to taxation until such amounts are made available or distributed to employees.[30] This tax benefit to the employee amounts to a substantial tax deferral and may be viewed as an interest-free loan from the government to the trust fund. Another advantage of a qualified plan is the fact that any income earned by the trust is not taxable to the trust. Employees are, in effect, taxed on such earnings when they receive the retirement benefits.[31]

The taxation of amounts received by employees is generally subject to the annuity rules in § 72. Employee contributions have previously been subject to tax and are, therefore, included in the employee's "investment in contract."

A special "3-year rule" applies in situations where the employee contributions are nominal relative to the total value of the pension benefits. Under this special rule, if the former employee's pension amounts received during the first 3 years exceed the total employee contributions to the plan, all such distributions are excludable from income until the basis is recovered.[32] Thereafter, all distributions are fully taxable to the employee. In deciding whether this 3-year rule is applicable, no reduction is made for the value of any refund feature.

Example 6. E had contributed $9,000 to a qualified plan when he retired at age 65. He is to receive $300 per month for the remainder of his life. Since the payments to be received by E dur-

30. § 402(a)(1).   **32.** § 72(d)(1).

31. § 501(a).

ing the first three years ($10,800) exceed his total investment ($9,000), the first 30 payments are tax-free ($9,000 ÷ $300), and all subsequent payments are taxable. None of the payments are taxable until the $9,000 investment is recovered.

If the employee does not recover his own contributions within three years, the amount excludable is calculated by using the annuity formula: [33]

$$\frac{\text{Investment in Contract}}{\text{Annual Return Times Multiple}}^{34} \text{ times Yearly return} = \text{Excluded Amount}$$

Any difference between the "annual return" and the "excluded amount" is taxable.[35] A taxpayer does not have his choice as to which of the methods applies—the 3-year rule or the annuity rule.

Example 7. T is to receive $300 per month for the rest of his life upon retirement at age 65 from his employer's qualified pension plan. T contributed $12,000 to the plan himself. He retires on January 1 and the expected return multiple in Table 1 of Reg. § 1.72–9 for a 65-year old male is 15.0. Since T will not receive his investment back within a 3-year period, the exclusion ratio rules apply:

$$\frac{\$12,000}{\$3,600 \times 15.0} \times \$3,600 = \$800.00 \text{ per year or } \$66.67 \text{ per month}$$

Thus, $66.67 of each $300 distribution is excluded from income, with $233.33 being taxable as ordinary income.[36]

Lump-sum Distributions from Qualified Plans. Prior to 1969, employees received favorable long-term capital gain treatment for lump-sum distributions from qualified plans. This favorable capital gain treatment has been restricted by legislation which was enacted in 1969 and 1974. Under the current rules, the taxable amount is allocated between a capital gain portion and an ordinary income portion (which may be subject to a special 10-year averaging treatment).[37] That portion attributable to the employee's service after 1973 is included as ordinary income when received or taxed under the 10-year averaging provision. An employee must be a plan participant for at least five years to take advantage of this 10-year averaging option.

An employee may elect to treat all of the distribution as ordinary income subject to the 10-year averaging provision.[37.1] In some

---

33. § 72(b).

34. The multiple is the life expectancy of the employee determined by using the actuarial tables in Reg. § 1.72–9.

35. § 72(b).

36. §§ 72(a) and 402(a)(1).

37. § 402(e)(1)(c).

37.1 Act § 1512 adding 402(e)(4)(L).

instances ordinary income treatment is preferable to long-term capital gain due to the minimum tax on the capital gain and the favorable averaging treatment.

To determine the tax on a lump-sum distribution, it is necessary to compute the taxable portion of the lump-sum distribution by subtracting employee contributions and the net unrealized appreciation in the value of any distributed securities of the employer corporation. The taxable amount is then reduced by a "minimum distribution allowance" to arrive at the amount which is eligible for the 10-year income averaging provisions.[38] The portion of the lump-sum distribution which is treated as a long-term capital gain is equal to the following:

$$\text{Taxable amount} \times \frac{\text{Years of service prior to 1974}}{\text{Total years of service}}.$$

Example 8. T, age 65 and married, retires in 1984 and receives a lump-sum distribution of $100,000 from his company's profit-sharing plan. This plan includes $5,000 of his own contributions and $10,000 of unrealized appreciation of his employer's common stock. The distributee has been a participant in the plan for 20 years.

1. Taxable portion of the lump-sum distribution
   ($100,000 – $5,000 employee contribution –
   $10,000 unrealized appreciation of employer
   securities) $85,000
2. Less: Minimum distribution allowance:
   A. ½ of the taxable amount up to $20,000 = $10,000
   B. Less: 20% of the taxable amount in
       excess of $20,000:
       20% × ($85,000 – $20,000)   = (13,000)
       Minimum distribution allowance   0
       Taxable amount subject to averaging $85,000
3. Computation of tax under 10 year averaging:
   A. 10 times the tax on ¹⁄₁₀ of $85,000 $14,900
   B. $14,900 × $\frac{11}{20}$ $\frac{\text{service after 1973}}{\text{total service years}}$ = $8,195—

       (ordinary income tax due on ordinary income portion)
4. Long-term capital gain portion
   A. $85,000 × $\frac{9}{20}$ $\frac{\text{service before 1974}}{\text{total service years}}$ = $38,250

Thus, T's capital gain on the distribution is $38,250. Furthermore, his capital gain on the unrealized appreciation in his employer's common stock is not taxable *until he sells* the stock. In essence, the cost basis of the securities to the trust becomes the tax basis to the employee.[39] If T keeps the securities until he

38. § 402(e)(1)(D).   39. § 402(e)(4)(J).

dies, there may be some income tax saving on this gain if his heirs obtain a limited step-up in basis. This problem illustrates a major advantage of an ESOT.

LIMITATIONS ON CONTRIBUTIONS TO AND BENEFITS FROM QUALIFIED PLANS

Defined Contribution Plans. Under a defined contribution plan (i. e., money pension plans, profit-sharing plans, stock bonus plans), the amount of the annual addition to an employee's account cannot be greater than the smaller of $25,000 or 25 percent of the employee's compensation.[40] The Code, however, provides that the dollar limitations may be increased through cost-of-living adjustments.[41]

Example 9. An employee's compensation was $120,000 during the plan year of a money pension plan. The maximum annual addition to the participant's account is limited to $25,000.

Under a defined benefit plan the benefit payable to an employee is limited to the smaller of $75,000 or 100 percent of the employee's average compensation for his highest 3 years of employment.[42]

There are two methods for determining the maximum deduction by a corporation for contributions to pension plans. First, an aggregate cost method allows an actuarially determined deduction based upon a level amount or a level percentage of compensation over the remaining future service of covered participants. Second, the employer is permitted to deduct the so-called normal cost plus no more than 10 percent of the past service costs.

Example 10. During 19X6 the Y Corporation contributes $17,-500 to its qualified pension plan. Normal cost for this year is $7,200 and the amount necessary to pay retirement benefits on behalf of employee services before 19X6 was $82,000 (past service costs). The corporation's maximum deduction would be $15,400, made up of the $7,200 normal cost and 10% of the past service costs—$8,200. The corporation would have a $2,100 contribution carryover.

Example 11. Assume in Example 10 above, Y, Inc. has normal cost in 19X7 of $7,200 and contributes $10,000 to the pension trust. Here the corporation could deduct $12,100, composed of this year's contribution ($10,000) plus the $2,100 contribution carryover.

---

40. § 415(c)(1).

41. § 415(d).

42. §§ 415(b)(1) and (3); six possible adjustments may have to be made to this maximum amount. §§ 415(b)(2) (B) and (C), (b)(4) and (5), and (d) (1)(A) and (2)(A).

The employer contribution is deductible in the tax year such amounts are paid to the pension trust. However, both cash basis and accrual basis employers may defer the payment of contributions with respect to any fiscal year until the date fixed for filing the taxpayer's federal income tax return for such year (including extensions thereof).[43] In effect, the corporation is allowed a deduction to the extent it is compelled to make such contributions to satisfy the funding requirement. If an amount is contributed in any tax year which is in excess of the allowable amount, such excess may be carried forward and deducted in succeeding tax years to the extent such carryover plus that year's contribution does not exceed the deductible limitation for such succeeding year.[44]

Profit-sharing and Stock Bonus Plan Limitations. The maximum deduction permitted each year with respect to contributions to profit-sharing and stock bonus plans is 15 percent of the compensation paid or accrued with respect to plan participants.[45] Any nondeductible excess, a so-called contribution carryover, may be carried forward indefinitely and deducted in the subsequent years, with a maximum deduction in any succeeding year amounting to 15 percent of all compensation paid or accrued during such taxable year. An employer can circumvent this 15 percent limitation by establishing a money purchase pension plan as a supplement to the profit-sharing or stock bonus plan. Where there are two or more plans, a maximum deduction of 25 percent of the compensation paid is allowable.[46]

Credit Carryovers. Under the 15 percent limitation rule for profit-sharing or stock bonus plans, if the contributions are less than the allowable amount (15 percent) the difference is defined as a "credit carryover." During subsequent years the employer may contribute amounts in excess of the 15 percent limitation to the extent of any "credit carryovers." However, the credit carryover to any one year cannot exceed 10 percent of the compensation paid (i. e., 15 percent is allowed for the current contribution plus 10 percent for the credit carry-over contribution). In essence, the maximum deduction is the smaller of (a) 15 percent times Compensation + Unused credit carryover, or (b) 25 percent times Compensation.

Example 12. In 19X6 E Corporation had a payroll of $200,000 and made a $24,000 contribution to a qualified profit-sharing plan. Since the corporation could have contributed $30,000 (15% × $200,000), the corporation has a $6,000 ($30,000 − $24,000) *credit* carryover. During 19X7 the payroll was $240,000 and the plan contribution was $52,000. The corporation could deduct a total of $42,000, made up of this year's de-

43.   § 404(a)(1) and (6).   45.   § 404(a)(3)(A).

44.   § 404(a)(1)(D).   46.   § 404(a)(7).

ductible amount of $36,000 ($240,000 × .15) plus 19X6's $6,000 credit carryover. Furthermore, in 19X7 the corporation has a $10,000 *contribution* carryover ($52,000 − $42,000). During 19X8 the payroll was $300,000 and the plan contribution was $30,-000. Thus, for 19X8 the corporation could deduct $40,000, made up of this year's contribution of $30,000 plus last year's $10,000 contribution carryover. (This $40,000 figure does not exceed 15% of $300,000). Note the difference between a "credit carryover" and a "contribution carryover."

RETIREMENT PLANS FOR SELF EMPLOYED INDIVIDUALS

Since 1962 self-employed individuals and their employees have been eligible to receive qualified retirement benefits under what is known as HR 10 or Keogh plans. Due to contribution limitations and other restrictions, these HR 10 plans (or Keogh plans) were previously less attractive when compared with corporate plans. But with the new $7,500 maximum contribution limitation an HR 10 plan can provide a self-employed person with an adequate retirement base as indicated by Table 3. These amounts assume $7,500 is contributed each year, funds earn 7¾% annual interest compounded daily, and a 50% tax bracket:

Table 3

HR 10 PLAN ACCUMULATIONS

Years	Total Contributions	Earnings	Total Accumulation After Contributions Cease	Tax Savings
1	$ 7,500	$ 604.30	$ 8,104.30	$ 3,750.00
10	75,000	42,723.45	117,723.45	37,500.00
20	150,000	223,231.88	373,231.88	75,000.00

COVERAGE REQUIREMENTS

Where an owner-employee [47] participates in a HR 10 plan, the plan must actually cover all employees who have at least 3 years of service.[48] In addition, an employee's rights to contributions made on his behalf must be 100 percent vested when the contributions are made.[49] The term "employee" does not include part-time employees.[50]

---

47. *An owner-employee* is a self-employed individual who is the sole owner of a proprietorship or, in the case of a partner, owns more than 10% of the profit or capital interest of the partnership. Not all self-employed individuals are owner-employees. The distinction may be sig-

nificant since greater restrictions are placed upon owner-employees.

48. § 401(d)(3)(A).

49. § 401(d)(2)(A).

50. § 401(d)(3).

The fact that an owner-employee must cover at his expense all employees whose employment satisfies certain requirements may make the HR 10 plan expensive. Therefore, in some situations an owner-employee may wish to consider an individual retirement account (discussed subsequently) in lieu of an HR 10 plan.

CONTRIBUTION LIMITATIONS

Contributions made on behalf of owner-employees are limited to the smaller of $7,500 or 15 percent of earned income.[51] Earned income includes the net profits from a self-employed person's business where personal services are a material income producing factor.[52] Where a self-employed individual has earned income of less than $5,000, he may generally contribute the lesser of $750 or 100 percent of earned income.[53] However, if the self-employed individual has adjusted gross income of more than $15,000, his contribution is generally limited to 15 percent of earned income or $7,500.[54]

> **Example 13.** A 20% partner has earned income of $30,000 in 19X6. The maximum deductible contribution for his benefit would be $4,500 (15% × $30,000). If however, his earned income is $70,000, the participant is limited to $7,500 since 15 percent of $70,000 is $10,500 and exceeds $7,500.

For anti-discrimination purposes, the 15 percent limitation on the owner-employee contribution is computed on the first $100,000 of earned income.[55] Thus, where a self-employed individual has more than $100,000 of earned income, he will have to contribute at a rate of at least 7½ percent on behalf of his employees in order to obtain the full $7,500 deduction.

> **Example 14.** A self-employed accountant has a money purchase plan with a contribution rate of 5% of compensation. His salary is $140,000 and his only employee has a salary of $20,000. The accountant's contribution would be limited to $5,000 (5% × $100,000) on behalf of himself. In order to obtain the $7,500 maximum, the contribution rate must be increased to 7½% for both his and his employee's contribution.

Under certain circumstances an owner-employee may make additional nondeductible voluntary contributions of an amount equal to

---

51. § 404(e). For years before 1974, the limitation is the smaller of $2,500 or 10% of earned income.

52. § 401(c)(2).

53. § 404(e)(4).

54. Act § 1502 amending § 415(c). For years after 1975, the law also permits an owner-employee to make contributions in excess of the 25% compensation limitation if the plan is funded with level premium annuity, endowment, or life insurance contracts and certain other requirements are met. Act § 1511 amending § 415 (c)(7).

55. § 401(a)(17).

the lesser of $2,500 or 10 percent of earned income.[56] In essence, the total of the amount which may be contributed by or for an owner-employee in any tax year is the smaller of (a) $10,000 ($7,500 + $2,500) or (b) 25 percent of earned income (15% + 10%). Beginning after 1975 § 4972 imposes a 6 percent annual nondeductible excise tax on the amount of excess contributions, e. g., in excess of the regular allowed amounts plus additional voluntary contributions, (determined at the close of each year) for all self-employed persons.

> **Example 15.** An owner-employee would like to contribute the maximum to a HR 10 plan which includes some employees who are not owner-employees. If he has earned income of $25,000, he would be limited to a total contribution of $6,250 [$3,750 + $2,500]. Whereas, if earned income was $100,000, he would be limited to a total contribution of $10,000 [$7,500 + $2,500].

Under certain conditions, after 1975 the 25 percent limitation on contributions on behalf of an owner-employee is removed.

HR 10 PLAN VERSUS CORPORATE PENSION PLAN

In many situations a corporate pension plan is more favorable than a self-employed retirement plan. Some comparisons are summarized as follows:

1. A self-employed plan is subject to the smaller of $7,500 or 15 percent of earned income limitation, whereas employer contributions to corporate plans are subject to different limitations, e. g., the smaller of $25,000 or 25 percent of the employee's compensation for defined contribution plans.

2. Self-employed plans must provide for fully vested benefits from inception whereas there are three alternative vesting schedules for corporate plans. Under a corporate profit-sharing plan forfeitures may be reallocated to the remaining participants. All accounts under a self-employed plan are 100 percent vested immediately so the owners do not receive any allocated forfeitures.

3. The Tax Reform Act of 1976 provides that self-employed retirement benefits under HR 10 and IRA plans are excludible from the decedent's gross estate if the payments are made to the beneficiaries other than in lump-sum form.[56.1] This Federal estate tax treatment now corresponds to the benefits relative to employer contributions to qualified pension and profit-sharing plans which are generally exempt from Federal estate tax under § 2039(c).

4. Similar treatment is accorded to lump-sum distributions. Both corporate participants and self-employed persons are

56. § 4972(c).   **56.1** Act § 2009(c) adding § 2039(e).

entitled to report such portion of a qualifying lump-sum distribution pertaining to pre-1974 plan participation as a long-term capital gain and a special 10-year averaging provision is available for the ordinary income portion of the lump-sum distribution.

INDIVIDUAL RETIREMENT ACCOUNTS (IRA)

GENERAL RULES

Individuals who are not covered by a qualified or governmental retirement plan may obtain a limited deduction for cash paid by or on behalf of an individual to an individual retirement account.[57]   The IRA benefit provisions were enacted into law in 1974 to provide equity for individuals who were not otherwise eligible to participate in our private retirement system.   An individual need not itemize his deductions to obtain the benefits from this tax deduction since the deduction is *for* adjusted gross income.   The deduction is limited to the smaller of $1,500 or 15 percent of the individual's taxable compensation from personal services.[58]   In essence, an individual can set aside up to $1,500, take a tax deduction for such amount, and avoid any tax on the earnings on the funds set aside until received at retirement.   The IRA will generally be established as a domestic trust or custodial account, with a bank being the trustee or custodian.

Table 4 below indicates that over a period of 20 years a total of $74,646.38 will accumulate in an IRA with a tax savings of $9,000. These figures assume $1,500 is contributed each year, the funds earn $7\frac{3}{4}$ percent annual interest income compounded annually (i. e., certificates of deposit), and the participant is in the 30 percent tax bracket.

Table 4

IRA ACCUMULATION

Years	Total Contributions	Earnings	Total Accumulation After Contributions Cease	Tax Savings
1	$ 1,500	$ 120.86	$ 1,620.86	$ 450.00
10	15,000	8,544.69	23,544.69	4,500.00
20	30,000	44,646.38	74,646.38	9,000.00

Example 16.   K Company contributes $800 to an IRA in 19X5 on behalf of F, one of its employees.   His earned taxable income is $12,000.   K Company may deduct the $800 contribution on its tax return under § 162.   F would show $800 of compensation but would be allowed a $800 deduction *for* adjusted gross income.

57.   § 219(a).   **58.**   § 219(b).

Example 17. Assume the same facts in Example 16 except that F also contributes $700 to the same IRA (or another IRA). Since F is allowed to deduct the smaller of $1,500 or 15% of his compensation ($1,800), he would be allowed to contribute $700 to the IRA and deduct a total of $1,500.

If both spouses work, each individual may establish a separate IRA providing neither spouse is covered by a qualified or government retirement plan. However, where only one spouse is employed, for taxable years beginning after 1976 an IRA can be established for the nonemployed spouse providing the employed spouse is also eligible to establish an IRA. The maximum total deduction for the individual and his spouse is the lesser of: [58.1]

1. 15 percent of the compensation income of the working spouse;

2. $1,750; or

3. Twice the amount contributed to the IRA for the individual or for his spouse or for which the lesser amount was paid for the taxable year.

Example 17a. Mr. X is eligible to establish an IRA. He received $30,000 compensation in 1977. He may contribute a total of $1,750 consisting of $875 for himself and $875 for his nonemployed spouse. The $1750 aggregate limitation applies since $15\% \times \$30,000$ is in excess of this amount. If Mr. X only contributed $800 for his spouse, his contribution would be limited to $800 or a total of $1,600.

PENALTY TAXES FOR EXCESS CONTRIBUTIONS

A cumulative nondeductible 6 percent excise penalty tax is imposed on the smaller of (1) any excess contributions or (2) the market value of the plan assets determined at the end of each tax year.[59] Excess contributions are any contributions which exceed the maximum limitation and contributions made during or after the tax year in which the individual reaches age $70\frac{1}{2}$.[60] A taxpayer is, of course, not allowed a deduction for excess contributions. This excess contribution is taxable annually until returned to the taxpayer or reduced by the under-utilization of the maximum contribution limitation in a subsequent year. For taxable years beginning after 1976, the 6 percent penalty tax can be avoided if the excess amounts are returned prior to the due date for filing the tax return providing certain other conditions are met.[60.1]

Example 18. A, age 55, creates an individual retirement plan in 1976 and contributes $1,800 of cash to his plan. Mr. Anderson

58.1 § 220(b)(1).   **60.** § 4973(b).

59. § 4973(a)(1).   **60.1** §§ 408(d)(4) and 4973(b)(2).

has earned income of $22,000. He is allowed a $1,500 deduction for adjusted gross income for 1976. Assuming the market value of the plan assets is at least $300, there is a nondeductible 6% excise penalty tax of $18.00 ($300 × 6%). This $300 may be subject to an additional penalty tax in future years if not returned by A or reduced by under-utilization of the $1,500 maximum contribution limitation.

TAXATION OF BENEFITS

A participant has a zero basis in his contributions to an IRA since they are not taxed currently.[61] Once retirement payments are received, such payments are ordinary income and are not subject to the special averaging rules for lump-sum distributions. However, a taxpayer can use the regular averaging rules under § 1301. IRA accounts are subject to the gift and estate taxes under §§ 2517 and 2039(c). Payments made to a participant before he reaches the age 59½ are subject to a nondeductible 10 percent penalty tax on such actual or constructive payments.[62]

NONQUALIFIED DEFERRED COMPENSATION PLANS

UNDERLYING RATIONALE FOR TAX TREATMENT

Nonqualified deferred compensation plans (NQDC) may be appropriate in certain situations as a compensation tool. Nonqualified plans are frequently used to provide incentives and/or supplemental retirement benefits for key executives.

The doctrine of constructive receipt is an important concept relating to the taxability of nonqualified deferred compensation.[63] In essence, if a taxpayer irrevocably earns income but may elect to receive it now or at a later date, the income is constructively received and the income is immediately taxed. Income is not constructively received, however, if the taxpayer's control over the amounts earned is subject to substantial limitations or restrictions.[64]

Still another concept is the economic benefit theory. Although a taxpayer does not have a present right to income, it will be taxable if he holds a right in the form of a negotiable promissory note. Notes and other evidences of indebtedness received in payment for services constitute income to the extent of their fair market value at the time of the transfer.[65]

---

61. § 408(d)(1).

62. § 408(f).

63. Reg. § 1.451–2.

64. *Ibid.*

65. Reg. § 1.61–2(d)(4).

Example 19. R Corporation and B, a cash basis employee, enter into an employment agreement which provides an annual salary of $120,000 to B. Of this amount $100,000 is to be paid in current monthly installments and $20,000 is to be paid in 10 annual installments beginning on B's retirement or death. A separate account for B is maintained by the corporation. Under § 451(a) and Reg. § 1.451–2(a) the $20,000 would not be considered constructively received and would be deferred. Compensation of $100,000 would be immediately taxable to B and deductible to R Corporation. The other $20,000 would be taxable and deductible when paid in future years. Thus, compensation can be deferred even if the employer is willing to pay currently.

TAX TREATMENT TO THE EMPLOYER AND EMPLOYEE

The tax treatment of a NQDC plan depends upon whether it is funded or nonfunded and whether it is forfeitable or nonforfeitable. In an unfunded NQDC plan the employee relies upon the company's mere promise to make the compensation payment in the future. A Revenue Ruling indicates that an unfunded unsecured promise to pay, not represented by a negotiable note is effective to defer the recognition of the income.[66] Thus, the employee is taxed later when the compensation is actually paid or made available to him.[67] Similarly, the employer is allowed a deduction when the employee recognizes income.

An escrow account can be set up by the employer to accumulate deferred payments on behalf of the employee. These funds may be invested by the escrow agent for the benefit of the employee.[68] By avoiding income recognition until the employee receives the benefits from the escrow custodial account, there is a postponement of tax to the employee. It is usually desirable not to transfer securities to the escrow agent since the IRS might attempt to treat such transfers as property transferred in connection with the performance of services under § 83. Such a treatment would force the transaction to have a substantial risk of forfeiture and nontransferability (or else the compensation income would be taxable immediately).[69] An escrow arrangement can be well suited for a professional athlete or entertainer whose income is earned in a few peak years.

Example 20. H, a professional athlete, receives a bonus for signing an employment contract. A NQDC plan is established to defer the income beyond his few peak years. The bonus is transferred to an escrow agent who invests the bonus in securities,

---

66. Rev.Rul. 60–145, 1960–1 C.B. 182; Rev.Rul. 60–85, 1960–1 C.B. 181.

67. Reg. § 1.451–2(a); *U. S. v. Basye,* 73–1 USTC ¶ 9250, 31 AFTR 2d 73–802, 93 S.Ct. 1080 (USSC, 1973).

68. Rev.Rul. 55–525, 1955–2 C.B. 543.

69. Prop.Reg. § 1.83–1(a).

etc., which acts as an excellent hedge against inflation. The bonus is deferred for 10 years, and becomes payable gradually from years eleven through fifteen. The bonus is deferred and taxable when H begins to receive the payments.

It is also possible to provide for NQDC through an internally funded revocable trust or through an externally funded nonexempt trust.[70] The detailed requirements relative to such arrangements are beyond the scope of this book. Generally, however, funded nonqualified deferred compensation plans must be forfeitable in order to keep the compensation payments from being taxable immediately. In most instances, employees prefer to have some assurance that they will ultimately receive benefits from the nonqualified deferred compensation, i. e., that the plan provides for nonforfeitable benefits. In such instances, the plan will have to be unfunded to prevent immediate taxation to the employee. Notice that most funded NQDC plans are subject to many of the provisions which apply to qualified plans.

When to Use a NQDC Arrangement. As a general rule nonqualified deferred compensation plans (NQDC) are more appropriate for executives in a financially secure company. Due to the need for currently disposable income, such plans are usually not appropriate for young employees.

A NQDC plan can reduce an employee's overall tax payments by deferring the taxation of income to later years (possibly when the employee is in a lower tax bracket). In effect, these plans may produce a form of income averaging. Further NQDC plans may discriminate in favor of stockholders, officers, specific highly compensated key employees, or a single individual.

Certain disadvantages should be noted. Nonqualified plans are usually required to be unfunded which means that an employee is not assured that funds will be ultimately available to pay the benefits. Also, the employer's tax deduction is postponed until the employee is taxed upon such amounts.

RESTRICTED PROPERTY PLAN

GENERAL PROVISIONS

A restricted property plan is an arrangement whereby an employer transfers property (e. g., stock of the employer corporation) to an employee at no cost or at a bargain price. § 83 was enacted in 1969 to provide rules for the taxation of such arrangements which previously were governed by judicial and administrative interpretations, i. e., court cases and revenue rulings.

---

70. See Rev.Rul. 67–289, 1967–2 C.B. 163; Prop.Reg. § 1.83–1(a).

As a general rule, if an employee performs services and receives property (e. g., stock), the fair market value (FMV) of such stock in excess of any amount paid by the employee is includible in gross income of the employee at the earlier of (1) the time the stock is no longer subject to a substantial risk of forfeiture (SRF), or (2) the moment the employee has the right to transfer the property free of the SRF. The FMV of the stock is determined without regard to any restriction, except a restriction which by its terms will never lapse.[71] Since the amount of the compensation is determined at the date that the restrictions lapse or when the property is transferrable, the opportunity to generate capital gains on the stock during a period when the ordinary income element is being deferred is denied.

> **Example 21.** On October 1, 19X5 W Corporation sells to J an employee, 100 shares of W Corporation stock for $10.00 per share. At the time of the sale, the fair market value of the stock was $100.00 per share. Under the terms of the sale, each share of stock is nontransferable and subject to a substantial risk of forfeiture (which will not lapse until October 1, 19X9). Evidence of these restrictions is stamped on the face of the stock certificates. On October 1, 19X9 the fair market value of the stock is $250 per share. Since the stock is nontransferable and is subject to a SRF, J does not include any compensation in gross income during 19X5 (assuming no special election is made). Instead, during 19X9 J must include $24,000 of compensation in gross income (100 shares $\times$ $250 less $10 per share). If for some reason the SRF occurs, e. g., the plan requires J to surrender the stock to the corporation if he voluntarily terminates his employment with the company prior to 19X9, and J never gets the stock certificates, he would be allowed a capital loss of $1,000 (the extent of his investment). Any amount of appreciation beyond the employee's contribution and the taxable compensation is treated as capital gain. In determining whether the gain is long-term or short-term, the holding period includes only the period beginning at the first time his rights in such property are transferable or are not subject to a substantial risk of forfeiture (whichever occurs first).[72]

SUBSTANTIAL RISK OF FORFEITURE (SRF)

A substantial risk of forfeiture exists if a "person's rights to full enjoyment of such property are conditioned upon the future performance, or the refraining from the performance, of substantial services by an individual." [73] The Proposed Regulations include several examples of restricted property arrangements.[74] For example, if an em-

---

71. § 83(a)(1).

72. § 83(f).

73. § 83(c)(1).

74. Prop.Reg. § 1.83–3(c)(2).

ployee must give back his stock (receiving only his original cost, if any) should he fail to complete a substantial period of service, for any reason, his property is subject to a substantial risk of forfeiture. Other SRF's include the situations where an employer can compel an employee to return the stock or there is a substantial covenant not to compete.[75] Any SRF should be stated on the face of the stock certificates. Assuming that there does not exist a substantial risk of forfeiture, the stock received is valued at its fair market value, ignoring any restrictions, except of one instance dealing with closely-held stock.

> **Example 22.** On September 1, 19X1 the K Corporation transfers in connection with the performance of services to H, an employee, 1,000 shares of K Corporation stock for $9.00 per share. Under the terms of the transfer, H is subject to a binding commitment to resell the stock to K Corporation at $9.00 per share if he leaves the employment of K Corporation for any reason prior to the expiration of a 10 year period from the date of such transfer. Since the employee must perform substantial services to K Corporation, H's rights in the stock are subject to a substantial risk of forfeiture.[76]

Special Election Available. An employee may elect within 30 days after the receipt of restricted property to recognize immediately as ordinary income the excess of the FMV over the amount paid for the property. Thus, any appreciation in the value of the property after receipt is taxed as capital gain instead of ordinary income. But no deduction is allowed to the employee for taxes paid on the original amount included in income if the property is subsequently forfeited.[77] Furthermore, the employer must pay back any compensation deduction taken in the earlier year.[78] The employee may take a capital loss for any amounts which were actually paid for the stock.[79]

Any increase in value between the time the property is received and the time it becomes either nonforfeitable or transferable is taxed as ordinary income (if no special election is made by the executive). However, if the executive elects to be taxed immediately on the difference between his cost and FMV on date of issue, any future appreciation is treated as capital gain. In determining whether the gain is long-term or short-term, § 83(b)(1)(B) indicates that § 83(a) does *not* apply. Thus, the holding period for determining whether a gain is long or short-term starts when the employee is taxed on the ordinary income.[80]

75. Prop.Reg. § 1.83–3(c)(2) Ex. 4; But see Prop.Reg. § 1.83–3(c)(1).

76. Prop.Reg. § 1.83–3(c)(2), Ex. 1.

77. § 83(b)(1)(B).

78. Prop.Reg. § 1.83–6(c).

79. Prop.Reg. § 1.83–2(a)(1) and (2).

80. § 1223(6).

Example 23. On July 1, 1971 F Company sold 100 shares of its preferred stock, worth $15.00 per share, to D, an employee for $5.00 per share. The sale is subject to D's agreement to resell the preferred shares to the Company for $5.00 per share if he terminates employment in the following ten years. Assume that the stock has a value of $25 per share on July 1, 1981 and D sells the stock for $30 per share on October 10, 1981. He makes the special election to include the original spread between the value in 1971 of $15.00 and the amount paid of $5.00 in income for 1971. D must recognize $1,000 of compensation income in 1971 at which time his holding period in his stock begins ($15.00 − $5.00 = $10 × 100 shares). His tax basis in the stock is $1,500 ($1,000 + $500). When he sells the preferred stock in 1981, he will recognize a $1,500 long-term capital gain ($30 × 100 shares − $1,500).

This special provision is usually not elected since it results in an immediate recognition of income and adverse tax consequences result from a subsequent forfeiture. However, the special election may be attractive in the following situations:

1. The bargain element is relatively small.

2. Substantial appreciation is expected in the future.

3. There is a high probability that the restrictions will be met.

EMPLOYER DEDUCTION

The employer is allowed a tax deduction for the same amount and at the same time the employee is required to include the compensation in income. In the no-election situation, this deduction is limited to the fair market value of the restricted property (without regard to the restrictions), at the time the restrictions lapse, reduced by the amount originally paid for the stock by the employee.[81] Where the employee elects to be taxed immediately, the corporate deduction is also accelerated and deductible in like amount. In those cases where income recognition has been deferred, employers can receive a very sizable deduction if the property has appreciated.

Example 24. The F Corporation sells to G, an employee, 10 shares of F common stock for $100 per share on March 14, 1971. The common stock is subject to a SRF and is nontransferable— both lapse on March 14, 1981. At the time of the discount sale the fair market value of the common stock (without considering the restrictions) is $1,000 per share. On March 14, 1981 the restrictions lapse and the FMV of the stock is $2,000 per share. No special election is made by the employee. In 1981 G realizes ordinary compensation income of $19,000 (10 shares of F stock times $2,000 per share less $100 per share paid by G).

---

81.   Prop.Reg. § 1.83–6(a).

Likewise, F Corporation is allowed a $19,000 compensation deduction in 1981.

Example 25. In Example 24 above, assume that the employee makes the election under Sec. 83(b). Since the employee is taxed on $9,000 in 1971, the corporation is allowed to deduct a like amount in 1971, with no deduction available in 1981.

STOCK OPTIONS

IN GENERAL

There are various equity-type stock option programs available for an employer's compensation package. Some authorities believe that there is a need for some form of "equity kicker" in order to attract new management, to convert key officers into "partners" by giving them a share of the business, and to retain services of executives who might otherwise leave.[82] An "option" gives an individual the right to purchase a stated number of shares of stock from a corporation at a certain price within a specified period of time. The optionee must be under no obligation to purchase the stock, and the option may be revocable by the corporation. The option must be in writing and its terms must be clearly expressed.[83]

QUALIFIED STOCK OPTION PLANS

Qualified stock option plans were provided under § 422 for executives prior to the Tax Reform Act of 1976. However, favorable tax treatment for such options is now generally available only for qualified options which are granted before May 21, 1976.[84] These qualified stock options (granted prior to May 21, 1976) must meet the following key statutory requirements: [85]

1. The option price must be equal to or greater than the fair market value at the date of grant.

2. The employee generally may not own greater than 5 percent of the stock of the employer corporation.

3. The option must be exercised within 5 years from the date of grant. Qualified options must be exercised before May 21, 1981. Otherwise, the qualified option is treated as a nonqualified option under § 83.[85.1]

4. The option may not be exercised if a prior (higher priced) qualified stock option is outstanding.

82. See S.Rep.No.2375, 81st Congress, 2nd Sess., p. 59 (1950).

83. Reg. §§ 1.421–1(a)(1) and 1.421–7(a)(1).

84. Act § 603(a) amending 422(b).

85. § 422(b)(1)–(7); § 422(b).

85.1 Act § 603(b) adding § 422(c)(7).

5. The qualified option must be non-transferable except at death.

6. The stock must be held at least 3 years following the date of exercise to receive favorable qualified stock option treatment.

7. The employee must remain employed by the company within 3 months prior to the exercise of the qualified option.

If the requirements of a qualified stock option under § 422 are met, the employee receives favorable capital gain treatment upon the disposition of the option stock. If any of these requirements are not met, the qualified option is treated as nonqualified. While no taxable income is recognized upon the exercise of such options, the grantee may be subject to minimum tax since the spread between the option price and the fair market value of the stock at the date of exercise is a tax preference item.[86]

Example 26. E Corporation granted a qualified stock option for 100 shares of its stock to employee R on March 18, 1976. The option price was $100 and the fair market value was $100 on the date of grant. R exercised the option on April 1, 1977 when the market value of the stock was $200 per share. He sold the stock on April 6, 1980 for $300 per share.

1. No ordinary income is recognized by R on the date of grant or the exercise date since the option is qualified under § 422. E Corporation receives no corresponding tax deduction.[87]

2. R has a tax preference item of $200 − $100 × 100 shares or $10,000 on the exercise date (April 1, 1977).

3. R has a long-term capital gain upon the sale of the stock in 1980 of $300 − $100 × 100 shares or $20,000 since the 3 year holding period and other requirements have been met.

Example 27. Suppose R is no longer employed by the Company when he exercises the options. R must recognize ordinary income to the extent of the spread, assuming there is no substantial risk of forfeiture. Thus, R would recognize $10,000 of ordinary income on the exercise date ($200 − $100 × 100 shares).

Frequently an individual may not hold the stock for the required 3-year period. In such a case, a "disqualifying disposition" occurs and different tax rules apply. The individual must recognize ordinary income to the extent of "the spread" in the tax year in which such disposition occurs. In this "messed-up" qualified stock option situation, the corporation is also allowed a deduction under § 162 to the same extent.[88] Any appreciation beyond the spread is LTCG, if the long-term capital gain holding period requirements are met.

86. § 57(a)(6).

87. § 421(a)(2).

88. Reg. § 1.421–8(b)(1).

The spread between the fair market value and the option price on the exercise date is a tax preference item, and one-half of the LTCG would be a tax preference item. Any ordinary income recognized by the individual qualifies as earned income for purposes of the 50 percent maximum tax.[89]

§ 423 also provides qualified stock options for employee stock purchase plans. Generally, such plans must be nondiscriminatory, i. e., cover a broad cross-section of all employees; the option price must be at least 85 percent of the fair market value at the date of grant and the shares must be held for 2 years from the date of grant and for 6 months from the date of exercise.

NONQUALIFIED STOCK OPTIONS

The Commissioner has prescribed rules for the treatment of nonqualified stock options.[90] If the nonqualified stock option has a readily ascertainable fair market value, e. g., the stock is traded on an established market, the value of the option must be included in the employee's income at the date of grant.[91] Thereafter, capital gain or loss is recognized only upon the disposal of the optioned stock.

Example 28. On February 1, 19X1 S is granted a nonqualified stock option to purchase 100 shares of stock from his employer at $10 per share. On this date the stock is selling for $12 per share on an established market. J exercised the option on March 30, 19X2 when the stock was worth $20 per share. On June 5, 19X2 J sold the optioned stock for $22 per share.

1. J must report ordinary income of $200 ($12 − $10 × 100 shares) on the date of grant (February 1, 19X1) since the stock has a readily ascertainable market value.

2. Upon the sale of the stock J reports a long-term capital gain of $1,000 ($22 − $12 × 100 shares).

3. The employer receives a tax deduction at the date of grant (February 1, 19X1) equal to $200 which is the amount of income reported by the employee.

If a nonqualified stock option does not have a readily ascertainable fair market value, an employee does not recognize taxable income at the grant date, but, as a general rule, will report as ordinary income, in the year of exercise, the difference between the fair market value of the stock at the exercise date and option price.[92] The amount paid by the executive for the stock, plus the amount he reports as ordinary income, becomes his basis; any appreciation above such basis is taxed as a long-term capital gain upon disposition (as-

---

89. Reg. § 1.1348–3(b)–3 iii (a), Ex. 10.

90. Reg. §§ 1.421–6(c), (d) and (e); Prop.Reg. § 1.83–7.

91. Reg. § 1.421–6(c)(1); Prop.Reg. 1.-83–7(a)(1).

92. Prop.Reg. § 1.83–7(a)(2); Reg. § 1.-421–6(d).

suming the stock is held more than the required long-term holding period after exercise).

The corporation receives a corresponding tax deduction at the same time and to the extent that income is recognized by the employee.[93]

> **Example 29.** On February 3, 19X1, S is granted a nonqualified stock option for 100 shares of common stock at $10 per share. On the grant date there was no readily ascertainable fair market value for the stock. He exercises the options on January 3, 19X2 when the stock was selling for $15 per share. He sells one-half of the shares on April 15, 19X2 and the other half on September 17, 19X3. The sale price on both dates was $21 per share. S would recognize no income on the grant date (February 3, 19X1) but would recognize $500 of ordinary income on the exercise date (January 3, 19X2), calculated as $1500 less $1000. He would recognize a short-term capital gain of $300 on the sale of the first half and a $300 long-term capital gain on the sale of the second batch of stock ($\frac{1}{2} \times \$2100 - \$1500$). No tax preference item would be recognized on the "spread," but there would be a $150 tax preference item on the LTCG.

Major advantages of nonqualified stock options are summarized as follows:

1. A tax deduction is available to the corporation, without a cash outlay.

2. The executive receives capital gains treatment on any appreciation in the stock starting at exercise date or at the date of grant if the option has a readily ascertainable fair market value.

3. Options can be issued at more flexible terms than under qualified option plans (e. g., longer exercise period and discount on exercise price).

A major disadvantage is that the executive must recognize ordinary taxable income upon exercise of the option or at the date of grant if the option has a readily ascertainable market value without receiving cash to pay the tax.

TAX PLANNING CONSIDERATIONS

QUALIFIED PLANS

Qualified plans provide maximum tax benefits for employers since the company receives an immediate tax deduction for contributions to such plans and the income which is earned on the contributions is not taxable to the employer. The employer contributions and

93. Reg. § 1.421–6(f).

the fund earnings are not taxed to the employees until such amounts are made available to them.

Qualified plans are most appropriate where it is desirable to provide benefits for a broad cross-section of employees. In some closely-held corporations, the primary objective is to provide benefits for the officer-shareholder group and other highly paid personnel. The nondiscrimination requirements which must be met in a qualified plan may prevent such companies from attaining these objectives. Thus, a nonqualified arrangement may be needed as a supplement or used in lieu of the qualified plan.

NONQUALIFIED DEFERRED COMPENSATION PLANS

Nonqualified deferred compensation arrangements such as restricted property plans may be useful to attract executive talent and/or to provide substantial retirement benefits for executives. Such plans may discriminate in favor of officers and other highly paid employees. The employer, however, does not receive a tax deduction until the employee is required to include the deferred compensation in income (upon the lapse of the restrictions).

The principal advantage of a nonqualified deferred compensation plan is that the employee may defer the recognition of taxable income to future periods when his income tax bracket may be lower, e. g., during retirement years. The time value benefits from the deferral of income should also be considered.

STOCK OPTIONS

Nonqualified stock option plans have assumed increasing importance due to the 1976 tax changes which have eliminated the qualified stock option. Stock option plans are used more frequently by publicly traded companies than closely held private companies. This is due to the problems of determining the stock value of a company which is not publicly held.

In a publicly-traded company (where the stock has a readily ascertainable fair market value), the value of the option is included in the employee's income at the date of grant. If the stock increases in value, the employee receives favorable capital gain treatment if the stock is later disposed of (subsequent to exercise). This treatment may be contrasted with a non-public company where the stock does not have a readily ascertainable fair market value. In such case, the employee is taxed at ordinary income rates upon the value of the option at the exercise date rather than the date of grant.

SELF–EMPLOYED RETIREMENT PLANS AND IRA'S

If a self-employed individual is considering the incorporation of his business or professional practice, the retirement benefits which are available under both corporate and noncorporate forms of organization should be compared. In many instances, the corporate benefits will be more favorable than a self-employed retirement plan although the self-employed benefits have been liberalized by recent tax changes in the law.

HR 10 plans and IRA's both provide significant penalties for making excess contributions. Also, the contributions to an HR 10 or IRA plan are effectively "locked in" since the tax law imposes a 10 percent nondeductible penalty upon funds which are withdrawn prior to reaching age 59½.

PROBLEM MATERIALS

Questions for Class Discussion

1. Compare and contrast defined contribution and defined benefit pension plans.

2. Compare and contrast qualified pension and profit-sharing plans.

3. Would the incentive element for employees be stronger under a profit-sharing plan or a pension plan? Explain.

4. What are the differences between a defined contribution plan and a defined benefit plan?

5. What are the tax and financial advantages accruing to a company which adopts an Employee Stock Ownership Trust (ESOT) for employees?

6. Explain any advantages associated with the distribution of appreciated employer securities from a qualified plan.

7. Is it possible to provide greater vested benefits for highly paid employees and still meet the nondiscrimination requirements under a qualified pension plan? Explain.

8. If a plan does not meet the mathematical 70% and 80% coverage tests, is the plan automatically ineligible to be qualified under the law?

9. What is vesting and how will these requirements help employees who do not remain with one employer during their working years?

10. What is the "3-year rule" and how does this provision affect the taxation of pension payments to employees? Would this rule apply to noncontributory pension or profit-sharing plans?

11. How are lump-sum distributions from qualified plans taxed to the recipients, i. e., capital gain versus ordinary income? Is income averaging available to an employee who receives a lump-sum distribution?

12. What ceiling limitations have been placed upon employer contributions (relative to individual employees) to defined contribution and defined benefit plans?

13. Discuss the rules which prescribe the maximum deduction which can be taken by an employer for a profit-sharing or stock bonus plan. How do these ceiling requirements compare with the limitations upon qualified pension plan contributions?

14. Discuss the difference between a "credit-carryover" and a "contribution carryover" with respect to a profit-sharing plan. Can both of these occur in one year?

15. The Stanback Corporation is anticipating establishing a profit-sharing plan that will cover all 90 employees. Under the plan, the interest of the participants will vest at the rate of 5% per year. Would the IRS approve this plan? Discuss.

16. Discuss the differences between a Keogh Pension plan and an Individual Retirement Account (IRA).

17. Why is the postponement of tax on earnings from fund accumulations in qualified pension, profit-sharing, Keogh or IRA plans of particular advantage to participants of such plans?

18. Compare the tax advantages which are available to corporate employees covered under a qualified plan with self-employed retirement plan benefits.

19. Discuss the dilemma of an employee with respect to a nonqualified deferred compensation (NQDC) plan and the following items: funded and nonfunded; forfeitable and nonforfeitable.

20. Explain the differences in tax treatment of an employer and employee with respect to the general rule (i. e., no-election) and the special election under § 83(b) when dealing with a restricted property plan. Explain the gambling aspect of this tax provision.

21. What is a "substantial risk of forfeiture?" Why is it necessary to impose this restriction upon the transfer of restricted property?

22. Explain what is meant by the phrase "ascertainable fair market value." What is the significance of the phrase?

23. Discuss the advantages of a nonqualified stock option plan versus a qualified stock option plan.

24. Would you, a 30-year old executive of Govenberg, Inc. making $100,000, prefer an extra $20,000 bonus *or* the option to purchase $20,000 worth of securities from your employer under a nonqualified stock option plan for $5,000?

25. What factors should the employer and employee consider in determining whether the employee should receive capital gain compensation or ordinary income compensation? Be sure to relate to timing of income.

Problems

1. The L Company's pension plan provides that any full-time employee is eligible to participate if he has at least one year's service and is at least 25 years of age. R, the personnel director, provides you with the following information:

Eligible employees	1350
Ineligible employees because of age	300
Ineligible employees because of length of service	175
Employees with less than 1000 hours	175
Ineligible employees because of salary level	200

(a) Calculate the minimum coverage test for this corporation. § 410(b)(1).

(b) Is there any hope for this company if the minimum coverage test is failed?

2. R is permanently fired when he is 42 years old and has 10 years of service. Determine R's vested portion of his interest in a qualified pension plan under the three alternatives (A) 10-year rule, (B) 5-to-15 year rule, and (C) Rule of 45. Assume the employer established the rules to pay as little as possible.

3. Same facts as in 2 above, except that R is 32 years old and has 10 years of noteworthy service to his employer.

4. M is to receive $300 per month for the remainder of his life upon retirement at age 65 from his employer's qualified pension plan. M contributes $10,000 to the plan himself. He retires on January 1 and his expected return multiple is 15.0. Compute the amount of taxable income to M for each of the first three years and thereafter.

5. In 4 above, assume the pension trust will pay him only $80 per month. What amount, if any, is taxable each year to M?

6. R is a participant in a qualified pension plan. A pension of $500 per month is payable to R for life. Assume R's multiple is 15.0 and R's contribution is $22,500.

(a) Calculate the taxable amount, if any, during the first 12 months of R's retirement.

(b) Suppose R's contributions to the plan were $17,000 rather than $22,500. What amount in (a) above would be taxable during the first 12 months?

7. When K retires, he receives a lump-sum distribution of $50,000 from a noncontributory qualified pension plan. His active period of participation was from January 1, 1968 through December 31, 1975. If K files a joint return with his wife and he elects to use the 10-year averaging provision, (a) calculate his separate tax on this distribution and (b) the capital gain portion.

8. F receives a $130,000 lump-sum distribution from a contributory pension plan, which includes employer common stock with net

unrealized appreciation of $10,000. F contributed $20,000 to the qualified plan during which he was an active participant from December 10, 1971 to February 10, 1975.

(a) Calculate the total taxable amount.

(b) Calculate the separate tax assuming F elects to use the 10-year averaging provision.

(c) Calculate the capital gain portion. (Treat part of a calendar month as one month.)

9. R has been an active participant in a defined benefit plan for 17 years. His last five years of salary was $20,000, $30,000, $40,000, $50,000 and $60,000, respectively.

(a) Calculate R's maximum allowable benefits from this qualified plan.

(b) Assume that his average compensation for his high three years is $82,000. Calculate R's maximum allowable benefits.

(c) Would your answer change if his average compensation for his high three years is $9,600? How?

10. B is a participant in a profit-sharing plan. The corporation makes the maximum annual addition to his account during 19X1. His salary is $100,000.

(a) What is the maximum annual addition to B's account for 19X1?

(b) What is the maximum deduction allowable by the corporation for the contribution to the profit-sharing plan?

(c) In (b) above, calculate the maximum "credit-carryover" for 19X2.

(d) In 19X2 B's salary is again $100,000, but the corporation contributes only $14,000 to his account. Calculate the deductible amount for the corporation in 19X2.

(e) As a tax expert, what would you advise this corporation with respect to this situation?

11. You are given the following facts with respect to a profit-sharing plan. Fill in the blanks in the accompanying schedule.

Year	Total Compensation	Employer Contributions
19X1	$100,000	$ 2,000
19X2	110,000	30,000
19X3	90,000	8,000

| | (a) | (b) | (c) |
| | | Unused Credit | Contribution |
Year	Deduction	Carryover	Carryover
19X1	_____	_____	_____
19X2	_____	_____	_____
19X3	_____	_____	_____

12. G is a partner covered by a HR 10 plan. For the tax year 19X1 his earned income is $70,000.
    Calculate his maximum total contributions to the plan assuming he is an owner-employee.

13. C is an owner-employee of a HR 10 plan created by his partnership.

    (a) During 19X1 $5,000 is contributed to the HR 10 Plan for C. What amount is deductible if his earned income is $26,-500?

    (b) Again in 19X2, $8,000 is contributed on his behalf to the Keogh plan. If his earned income is $21,000, what deduction, if any, is allowed if C elects the standard deduction?

    (c) The partnership had a bad year in 19X3 and only $600 was contributed on his behalf to the HR 10 plan. He earns only $500 during 19X3. Calculate his allowable deduction.

    (d) In 19X4 when his earned income was $20,000, his partnership contributed $6,000 on his behalf to the Keogh plan. If C makes $600 of voluntary contributions, calculate any penalty tax for excess contributions.

14. On September 1, 1977, D, an author, and Vanity, Inc., a publisher, executed an agreement under which the author granted to the publisher the exclusive right to print, publish and sell a book. This agreement provides that the publisher will (a) pay the author specified royalties based upon the actual cash received from the sale of the published work, (b) render semi-annual statements of the sales, and (c) at the time of rendering each statement make settlement for the amount due. On the same day another agreement was signed by the same parties, mutually agreeing that, in consideration of, and notwithstanding any contrary provisions contained in the first contract, the publisher would not pay the author more than $100,000 accruing in any one calendar year. Under this second contract amounts in excess of $100,000 accruing in any one calendar year are to be carried over by the publisher into succeeding accounting periods; and the publisher shall not be required either to pay interest to the taxpayer on any such excess sums or to segregate any such sums in any manner. Is this second agreement an effective deferral and why? When would the publisher obtain a deduction?

15. G Company provides bonuses each year to its key executives. The specific employees to receive bonuses and the amount of bonus for each recipient is determined on December 1 of each year. Each employee eligible for consideration for a bonus may decide on or before November 15 of each year to postpone receipt of his bonus for such year, if any, until his re-

tirement or death. An employee electing to postpone receipt of a bonus is further allowed to designate at any time before his retirement the time and manner of the post-retirement payments and to designate the persons to receive any amount payable after his death. Since most employees elect to defer their bonuses, separate accounts are not maintained for each employee. When would these bonuses be taxed to the executives and deductible by G Company?

16. On February 20, 19X1, G, an executive of R Corporation, purchased 100 shares of R Corp. stock (selling at $20 a share) for $10. A condition of the transaction was that G must resell the stock to R Corp. at his cost if he leaves his employer voluntarily (assume a SRF) within 5 years of receiving the stock.

(a) Assuming no election is made, what amount is, if any, taxable to G in 19X1?

(b) Five years later the stock is selling for $50 a share and G is still employed by the same firm. What amount of ordinary income, if any, is taxable to G?

(c) What amount, if any, is deductible by R Corp. as compensation income five years later?

(d) Assume G made the special election in 19X1, what amount would be taxable to G in 19X1?

(e) In "d" above, what amount would be deductible by R Corp. five years later?

(f) Assume six years later G sold all the stock for $65 per share under the election in "d", what total capital gain is included in G's gross income?

(g) In "d" above what loss is available to G if he voluntarily resigns before the 5 year period and he does not sell the stock back to the corporation?

(h) In the year G resigns, what amount, if any, would be taxable to R Corporation?

17. R Corporation sold 100 of its common shares, worth $15.00 per share, to its employee B, for $5 per share on July 1, 19X1, subject to B's agreement to resell the shares to the corporation for $5 per share if his employment was terminated in the following four years. The shares had a value of $25 per share on July 7, 19X5. B sold the shares for $30 per share on September 15, 19X5. No special election is made. Circle correct answers; there may be more than one correct answer.

(a) B will be taxed on what amount, if any, on July 1, 19X1?

    1. ordinary income of $1500

    2. short-term capital gain of $1500

    3. long-term capital gain of $1000

     4.   tax-exempt income of $1500

     5.   none of the above

(b) B will be taxed on what amount, if any, on July 1, 19X5?

     1. $2500 ordinary income

     2. $2500 LTCG

     3. $2000 ordinary income

     4. $2000 LTCG

     5.   none of the above

(c) B will be taxed on what amount, if any, on September 15, 19X5?

     1. $2000 LTCG

     2. $2000 STCG

     3. $ 500 LTCG

     4. $ 500 STCG

     5.   none of the above

(d) R Corp. will obtain what deduction, if any?

     1. $ 500 ordinary deduction on September 15, 19X5

     2. $2000 ordinary deduction on July 1, 19X5

     3. $2500 ordinary deduction on September 15, 19X5

     4. $ 500 ordinary deduction on July 1, 19X5

     5. $1500 ordinary deduction on July 1, 19X5

(e) Assume the same facts, except that B makes a § 83(b) election. B will be taxed on what amount, if any?

     1. $1000 ordinary income on July 1, 19X1

     2. $1000 ordinary income on July 1, 19X5

     3. $2000 ordinary income on July 1, 19X5

     4. $2000 LTCG on September 15, 19X5

     5.   none of the above

(f) R Corp. in (e) will obtain what deduction?

     1. $1000 ordinary deduction on July 1, 19X1

     2. $1000 ordinary deduction on July 1, 19X5

     3. $2000 ordinary deduction on July 1, 19X1

     4. $2000 ordinary deduction on July 1, 19X5

     5.   none of the above

(g) Suppose B under (e) was fired from his employment on January 3, 19X5 and starts another company.

     1.   B may take a $1000 deduction on his 19X5 tax return

     2.   B may apply for a refund on the $1000 on his 19X1 tax return

3. R Corp. must pay back the $1000 deduction and B gets no refund on the $1000

4. B does obtain a $500 loss on the amount he paid for the stock initially when he sells it back to the corporation (i. e., he gets his money back)

5. none of the above

18. R exercises 100 qualified stock options of the XYZ Company at the option price of $100 per share when the fair market value is $120. He sells the 100 shares of common stock 3½ years later for $125.

(a) Calculate the total LTCG on this sale.

(b) Calculate total tax preference items for these 100 shares of common stock.

(c) Assume R holds the stock seven months and sells them for $125 per share. Calculate any ordinary income on the sale.

(d) In (c) above, XYZ Corp. can deduct what amount?

(e) Suppose R holds the stock for two years, and sells them for $115 per share. Calculate any capital gain on this transaction.

(f) In (a) above, assume the options are nonqualified options with a non-ascertainable FMV on the grant date. Calculate any total LTCG in the year of sale.

(g) In (f) above, assume that each option has an ascertainable FMV of $110 on the grant date and no SRF. Calculate any total LTCG on the sale date.

19. On November 19, 19X1, J is granted a qualified option to purchase 100 shares of S Company (on such date the stock is selling for $8 per share and the option price is $9 per share). J exercises the option on November 21, 19X3 when the stock is selling for $10 per share. Four months later he sells the shares for $9.-50 per share.

(a) What amount is taxable to J in 19X1?

(b) What amount is taxable to J in 19X3, assuming he is fully taxed on any tax preference items?

(c) What amount of ordinary income, if any, is taxable to J in 19X4?

(d) What amount of capital gain is taxable to J in 19X4?

(e) What amount, if any, is deductible by S Company in 19X4?

(f) What tax preference item would J recognize in 19X4 from this transaction?

Research Problems

1. F Corp. transferred to C, an employee, a new $35,000 home in 19X1 in which his interest is nontransferable and is subject to a substantial risk of forfeiture for a 5-year period. However, F Corp. allows C to live in the house rent-free. The fair rental value of the house per year is $3700. At the beginning of the fifth year C pays F Corp. $30,000 (which was the agreed price under the restricted property agreement) for the house which is then valued at $45,000. Discuss the tax treatment for both parties in each of the years.

2. The following information is provided by G with respect to a non-qualified stock option program granted to him by ABC Corp. which is an actively traded public corporation.

	Per Share
FMV on the date of grant, March 1, 19X1	$ 100.00
Option price on the date of grant, March 1, 19X1 (no substantial risk of forfeitute)	90.00
FMV on date of exercise July 1, 19X3	97.00
Selling price on August 1, 19X4	110.00
Number of shares acquired and sold	100

IM–207

(a) G asks you to calculate the effect on his 19X4 taxable income. You must show statutory authority for your answers in all of these questions.

(b) Would your answer change if there was a substantial covenant not to compete in the contract? If the employee cannot sell the stock for three years? In your answer include a discussion of whether the SRF definition is exclusive.

Chapter 18

CORPORATIONS

The purpose of this chapter is to present a general introduction to the Federal income tax provisions which are applicable to corporations. Corporate tax provisions are extremely complex. *West's Federal Taxation: Corporations, Partnerships, Estates, and Trusts* includes detailed coverage of these corporate tax provisions.

WHAT IS A CORPORATION?

Initially, a company must comply with the specific requirements for corporate status under state law, e. g., it is necessary to draft and file articles of incorporation with the state regulatory agency, be granted a charter, and issue stock to shareholders.

COMPLIANCE WITH STATE LAW

Compliance with state law, although important, is not the only requirement which must be met to qualify for corporate tax status. For example, a corporation qualifying under state law may be disregarded as a taxable entity if it is a mere "sham" lacking in economic substance. The key consideration is the degree of business activity conducted at the corporate level.

Example 1. C and D are joint owners of a tract of unimproved real estate that they wish to protect from future creditors. Consequently, C and D form R Corporation to which they transfer the land in return for all of the latter's stock. The corporation merely holds title to the land and conducts no other activities. In all respects, R Corporation meets the legal requirements of a corporation under applicable state law. R Corporation probably would not be recognized as a separate entity under the facts set forth in this example.[1]

Example 2. Assume the same facts as in Example 1.

In addition to holding title to the land, R Corporation leases the property, collects rents, and pays the property taxes thereon. R Corporation probably would be treated as a corporation for Federal income tax purposes due to the scope of its activities.

In some instances, the IRS has attempted to disregard (or "collapse") a corporation in order to make its income taxable directly to the shareholders.[2] In other cases, the IRS has asserted that the corporation is a separate taxable entity so as to assess tax at the corporate level and to tax corporate shareholder distributions as dividend income.[3]

ASSOCIATION APPROACH

An organization not qualifying as a regular corporation under state law may, nevertheless, be taxed as a corporation under the association approach. The designation given to an entity under state law is not controlling. For example, a partnership of physicians has been treated as an association (and therefore taxed under the corporate rules) even though state law prohibited the practice of medicine in the corporate form.[4]

Whether or not an entity will be considered an association for Federal income tax purposes depends upon the number of corporate characteristics it possesses. According to court decisions and the Regulations, corporate characteristics include: [5]

1. Associates;

2. An objective to carry on a business and divide the gains therefrom;

3. Continuity of life;

4. Centralized management;

---

1. See: *Paymer v. Comm.*, 45–2 USTC ¶ 9353, 33 AFTR 1536, 150 F.2d 334 (CA–2, 1945).

2. *Patterson v. Comm.*, 25 TCM 1230, T.C.Memo. 1966–239, *aff'd* in 68–2 USTC ¶ 9471, 22 AFTR2d 5810 (CA–2, 1968).

3. *Rafferty Farms Inc. v. U. S.*, 75–1 USTC ¶ 9271, 35 AFTR2d 75–811, 511

F.2d 1234 (CA–8, 1975); *Collins v. U. S.*, 75–2 ¶ 9553, 36 AFTR2d 75–5175, 514 F.2d 1282 (CA–5, 1975).

4. *U. S. v. Kintner*, 54–2 USTC ¶ 9626, 47 AFTR 995, 216 F.2d 418 (CA–5, 1975).

5. Reg. § 301.7701–2(a).

5. Limited liability; and

6. Free transferability of interests.

The Regulations state that an unincorporated organization shall not be classified as an association unless it possesses more corporate than noncorporate characteristics. In making this determination, the characteristics common to both corporate and noncorporate business organizations shall be disregarded.[6]

Example 3. Both corporations and partnerships generally have associates (i. e., shareholders and partners) and an objective to carry on a business and divide the gains. Therefore, if a partnership has 3 of the last 4 of the above attributes, it will be treated as an association (taxable as a corporation). The XYZ Partnership agreement provides for the following: (1) the partnership terminates with the withdrawal of a partner; (2) all of the partners have authority to participate in the management of the partnership; (3) all of the partners are individually liable for the debts of the partnership; and (4) a partner may not freely transfer his interest in the partnership to another. Since none of the above corporate attributes (items 3–6) are present, XYZ is not taxable as an association.

INCOME TAX CONSIDERATIONS

INDIVIDUALS AND CORPORATIONS COMPARED—AN OVERVIEW

Business operations may be conducted as a sole proprietorship, partnership or in corporate form.

1. Sole proprietorships are not separate taxable entities. The owner of the business will, therefore, report all business transactions on his or her individual income tax return.

2. Partnerships are not subject to the income tax. Under the conduit concept, the various tax attributes of the partnership's operations flow through to the individual partners to be reported on their personal income tax returns. Partnerships are discussed in *West's Federal Taxation: Corporations, Partnerships, Estates, and Trusts.*

3. The regular corporate form of doing business carries with it the imposition of the corporate income tax. The corporation is recognized as a separate tax-paying entity. Thus, income is taxed to the corporation as earned and taxed again to the shareholders as dividends when distributed.

4. A regular corporation may elect to be taxed as a Subchapter S corporation. Such special treatment is similar (although not identical) to the partnership rules. Income tax is gener-

6. Reg. § 301.7701–2(a)(3).

ally avoided at the corporate level and shareholders are taxed currently upon the undistributed taxable income of the Subchapter S corporation.

Similarities Between Corporate and Individual Tax Rules.   The gross income of a corporation is determined in much the same manner as it is determined for individuals.   Both individuals and corporations are entitled to exclusions from gross income, such as interest on municipal bonds.   The tax rules for gains and losses from property transactions are also treated similarly.   For example, whether a gain or loss is capital or ordinary depends upon the nature and use of the asset rather than the type of taxpayer.   Upon the sale or other taxable disposition of depreciable property, the recapture rules (e. g., §§ 1245 and 1250) generally make no distinctions between corporate and noncorporate taxpayers.

The business deductions of corporations also parallel those available to individuals.   Therefore, corporate deductions are allowed for all ordinary and necessary expenses paid or incurred in carrying on a trade or business under the general rule of § 162(a).   Corporations may also deduct interest (§ 163), certain taxes (§ 164), losses (§ 165), bad debts (§ 166), depreciation (§ 167), charitable contributions subject to corporate limitation rules (§ 170), net operating losses (§ 172), research and experimental expenditures (§ 174), and other less common deductions.

Many of the tax credits available to individuals also can be claimed by corporations.   The most important of these credits include the investment tax credit (§ 38) and the foreign tax credit (§ 33).

Corporations generally have the same choices of accounting periods and methods as do individuals.   Like an individual, a corporation may choose a calendar year or a fiscal year for reporting purposes.   Corporations who maintain inventory for sale to customers are required to use the accrual method of accounting for determining sales and cost of goods sold.

Dissimilarities.   Corporations and individuals are subject to different tax rate structures.   The corporate tax rates reflect a stairstep pattern of progression whereas individual rates reflect a continual pattern of progession.   Corporate tax rates are discussed in a later section of this chapter.

All allowable corporate deductions are treated as business deductions.   Thus, the determination of adjusted gross income, so essential in the case of individuals, has no relevance to corporations.   As such, corporations need not be concerned with itemized deductions.   The standard deduction and personal and dependency exemptions are not available to corporations.

SPECIFIC PROVISIONS COMPARED

Corporate and individual tax rules differ in the following areas:

1. Capital gain and losses; carryback and carryover provisions;

2. Charitable contribution ceiling limitations;

3. Net operating loss adjustments; and

4. Special deductions for corporations, e. g., the 85 percent or 100 percent dividends received deduction.

Capital Gains. Individuals are permitted to include net long-term capital gains in gross income with an offsetting 50 percent long-term capital gain deduction. As an alternative to this treatment, an individual may elect the alternative tax computation (25 percent for the first $50,000 of net long-term capital gains).

For corporate taxpayers, the 50 percent long-term capital gain deduction is not available. Second, the alternative tax rate is 30 percent instead of 25 percent.[7]

Example 4. T Corporation has the following capital transactions during the current year: a long-term net capital gain of $10,000 and a short-term net capital gain of $4,000. T Corporation may include the $10,000 of long-term capital gain in gross income. Under the alternative tax computation, $3,000 (i. e., 30 percent x $10,000) is added to T Corporation's regular tax liability. In either case, the short-term net capital gain of $4,000 must be included in gross income.

Capital Losses. As previously discussed in Chapter 14, noncorporate taxpayers can deduct up to $2,000 in 1977 and $3,000 in 1978 and thereafter of such net capital losses against ordinary income. However, if the net capital loss is long-term, it requires $2 of loss to generate $1 of deduction. Noncorporate taxpayers are permitted to carry any remaining capital losses forward to future years until absorbed by capital gains or by the $3,000 (subject to the changes noted above) deduction.

Unlike individuals, corporate taxpayers are not permitted to claim any net capital losses as a deduction against ordinary income.[8] Capital losses may only be used as an offset against capital gains. Corporations may, however, carryback net capital losses to the 3 preceding years, applying them initially to the earliest year. Carryforwards are allowed for a period of 5 years from the year of the loss.[9] When carried back or forward, a long-term capital loss becomes a short-term capital loss.

Example 5. T Corporation incurs a long-term net capital loss of $5,000 for 19X4. None of the capital loss may be deducted in

7. § 1201(a).   9. § 1212(a).

8. § 1211(a).

19X4. T Corporation may, however, carry the loss back to years 19X1, 19X2, and 19X3 (in this order) and offset any net capital gains recognized in these years. If the carryback does not exhaust the loss, it may be carried forward to 19X5, 19X6, 19X7, 19X8, and 19X9 (in this order). Such capital loss carrybacks or carryovers are treated as short-term capital losses.

Charitable Contributions. Generally, a charitable contribution deduction will only be allowed for the year in which the payment is made. However, an important exception is made in the case of accrual basis corporations. The deduction may be claimed in the year preceding payment if the contribution has been authorized by the Board of Directors by the end of that year and is, in fact, paid on or before the 15th day of the third month of the next year.[10]

Example 6. On December 28, 19X5, the Board of Directors of the XYZ Company authorizes a $5,000 donation to a qualified charity. XYZ is an accrual basis corporation with a calendar year. The donation is paid on March 14, 19X6. XYZ Company may claim the $5,000 donation as a deduction for 19X5. As an alternative, XYZ Company may claim the deduction in 19X6 (the year of payment).

Like individuals, corporations are not permitted an unlimited charitable contribution deduction. For any one year a corporate taxpayer is limited to 5 percent of taxable income, computed without regard to the charitable contribution deduction, any net operating loss carryback or capital loss carryback, and the dividends received deduction.[11] Any contributions in excess of the 5 percent limitation may be carried forward to the five succeeding tax years. Any carryforward must be added to subsequent contributions and will be subject to the 5 percent limitation. In applying this limitation, however, the most recent contributions must be deducted first.[12]

Example 7. During 19X4, T Corporation (a calendar year taxpayer) had the following income and expenses:

Income from operations	$140,000
Expenses from operations	110,000
Dividends received	10,000
Charitable contributions made in 19X4	5,000

For the purposes of the 5 percent limitation only, T Corporation's taxable income is $40,000 ($140,000 − $110,000 + $10,000). Consequently, the allowable charitable deduction for 19X4 is $2,000 (5 percent × $40,000). The $3,000 unused portion of the contribution may be carried forward to 19X5, 19X6, 19X7, 19X8 and 19X9 (in that order) until exhausted.

10. § 170(a)(2).   12. § 170(d)(2).

11. § 170(b)(2).

Example 8. Assume the same facts as in the prior example. In 19X5, T Corporation has taxable income (after adjustments) of $50,000 and makes a charitable contribution of $2,000. The maximum deduction allowed for 19X5 would be $2,500 (5 percent × $50,000). The first $2,000 of the allowed deduction must be allocated to the 19X5 contributions, and the $500 excess is carried over from 19X4. The remaining $2,500 of the 19X4 contribution may be carried over to 19X6, etc.

Special rules for property contributions, ordinary income property, long-term capital gain property, etc. apply to both corporate and noncorporate taxpayers. These special rules were discussed in Chapter 9.

Net Operating Losses. The computation of a net operating loss and the complex carryback and carryover rules for individuals was discussed in Chapter 7. Corporations are not subject to the complex adjustments required for individuals, e. g., a corporation has no adjustments for nonbusiness deductions or capital gains and losses.

For corporations, the net operating loss is computed by adding back the dividends received deduction (discussed below) to the amount of the loss.[13] Corporate net operating losses may be carried back 3 years and forward 5 (7 for taxable years ending after December 31, 1975, or taxpayers may elect to forego the carryback period) to offset taxable income for those years.

Example 9. In 19X5, XYZ Corporation has gross income of $200,000 and deductions of $300,000, excluding the dividends received deduction. XYZ Corporation received taxable dividends of $100,000 from A Corporation, a domestic corporation which is not a member of a controlled group of corporations with XYZ. XYZ Corporation has a net operating loss of $185,000, computed as follows:

Gross income (including dividends)		$200,000
Less:		
Business deductions	$300,000	
Dividends received deduction	85,000	(385,000)
(85 percent × $100,000)		
Taxable income (loss)		($185,000)

Example 10. Assume the same facts as in the prior example and that XYZ Corporation had taxable income of $40,000 in 19X2. The net operating loss of $185,000 is carried back to 19X2 (unless XYZ elects not to carryback the loss to such year). The carryover to 19X3 is $145,000, computed as follows:

Taxable income for 19X2	$ 40,000
Less: Net Operating Loss Carryback from 19X5	(185,000)
Carryover of unabsorbed 19X5 loss	($145,000)

13. § 172(d)(6).

Accounting Period Changes. Chapter 16 discussed the specific requirements which must be met for an individual to change his or her accounting period. Certain special rules have been established for corporate taxpayers.

Generally, a taxpayer must obtain permission from the IRS to change from one accounting period to another. However, a corporation (other than a Subchapter S corporation) may change its accounting period without prior approval if all of the following conditions are met: [14]

(1) The corporation has not changed its tax year within the past ten calendar years (or for the entire period of existence if less than 10 years);

(2) The corporation did not have a net operating loss for the short period year of change;

(3) The taxable income for the short period (e. g., the three months ending March 31 in the year of change from the calendar year to a fiscal year ended March 31) computed upon an annualized basis, is at least 80 percent of the taxable income for the full taxable year immediately preceding the short period;

(4) The corporation does not attempt to elect Subchapter S treatment for the first full tax year following the short period; and

(5) The corporation files a statement with the District Director by the due date for the tax return for the short period, explaining that the corporation has changed its tax year.

If a corporate or noncorporate taxpayer incurs a net operating loss in the short period, the IRS will ordinarily approve a request for a change in accounting period under the following circumstances: [15]

1. If the net operating loss cannot be carried back to prior years;

2. If the amount of the net operating loss is not substantial relative to the taxpayer's taxable income during prior years;

3. If the short period is at least nine months and the net operating loss during the full 12-month period is at least equal to the loss for the nine-month period.

If any of these requirements cannot be met, a change in accounting period may, nevertheless, be approved if the taxpayer agrees to take the tax benefits of the net operating loss for the short period as an adjustment to the tax liability over the 10 years following the short period.

These administrative requirements of the IRS have been imposed to prevent taxpayers from creating tax benefits which would not otherwise be available.

14. Reg. § 1.442–1(c).   15. Rev.Proc. 66–6, 1966–1 C.B. 615.

Taxable income must be annualized (for a corporation as well as for noncorporate taxpayers) if the change in accounting period results in a short taxable year.[16] An exception to this requirement occurs when the short period constitutes the first or final period for the taxpayer. In such instances, annualization is not required.

Example 11. The SY Corporation changed from a calendar year to a fiscal year ending March 31. For the short period in the year of the change, January 1, 19X1 to March 31, 19X1, the corporation had taxable income of $30,000. Its annualized income for the year of change was $30,000 × 12/3 = $120,000.

Once the taxable income is annualized, the tax must first be computed on the amount of annualized income. The annualized tax is then converted to a short period tax. The latter conversion is accomplished as follows:

$$\text{Tax on annualized income} \times \frac{\text{Number of months in the short period}}{12}$$

Example 12. The tax on SY Corporation's annualized income for the short period is:

$$
\begin{array}{rcl}
\$ 25,000 \times .20 & = & \$ 5,000 \\
\$ 25,000 \times .22 & = & 5,500 \\
\underline{\$ 70,000} \times .48 & = & \underline{33,600} \\
\$120,000 & & \$44,100
\end{array}
$$

Tax for the three months,
January through March 19X1 = $44,100 × 3/12 = $11,025

Annualization prevents a taxpayer from obtaining the benefits of a lower effective tax rate during the short period. In the above example, if SY were not required to annualize its income, $25,000 of the $30,000 earned during the short period would have been taxed at 20 percent and the remainder at 22 percent whereas the effective average annualized rate is 36.7 percent ($11,025 ÷ $30,000).

DEDUCTIONS AVAILABLE ONLY TO CORPORATIONS

Dividends Received Deduction. A corporation is allowed a deduction equal to (a) 85 percent of the amount of dividends received from a domestic corporation, or (b) 100 percent of the amount of dividends received from a corporation which is a member of a controlled group with the recipient corporation.[17]

The purpose of the 85 percent dividends received deduction is to prevent triple taxation. Absent the deduction, income paid to a corporation in the form of a dividend would be subject to taxation for a second time (once to the distributing corporation) with no corresponding deduction to the distributing corporation. A third level of

16. Reg. § 1.443–1(a).   17. § 243(a).

tax would be assessed when the recipient corporation paid the income to its shareholders. Since the dividends received deduction is usually only 85 percent, only partial relief is provided under the law.

In unusual situations the dividend deduction may be limited to 85 percent of the taxable income of a corporation computed without regard to the net operating loss, the dividend received deduction, and any capital loss carryback to the current tax year. However, this limitation does not apply if the corporation has a net operating loss for the current taxable year.[18]

Example 13. In the current year, T Corporation has the following income and expenses:

Gross income from operations	$400,000
Expenses from operations	340,000
Dividends received from domestic corporations	200,000

The dividends received deduction is $170,000 (85 percent × $200,000) unless 85 percent of taxable income is less. Because taxable income (for this purpose) is $260,000 ($400,000 − $340,000 + $200,000), and 85 percent of $260,000 is $221,000, the full $170,000 will be allowed.

Example 14. Assume the same facts as in Example 13 except that T Corporation's gross income from operations is $320,000 (instead of $400,000). The usual dividend received deduction of $170,000 (85 percent × $200,000) is not limited to 85 percent of the taxable income. Since 85 percent of $180,000 ($320,000 − $340,000 + $200,000) is $153,000, this amount is the dividends received deduction (i. e., $153,000 is less than $170,000). Nor can the full $170,000 be claimed because it generates or adds to a net operating loss. Taxable income of $180,000 less $170,000 does not result in a net operating loss.

Example 15. Assume the same facts as in Example 13 except that T Corporation's gross income from operations is $300,000 (instead of $400,000). The usual dividend received deduction of $170,000 can now be claimed under the net operating loss exception. Taxable income of $160,000 ($300,000 − $340,000 + $200,000) less $170,000 generates a net operating loss of $10,000.

In summary, Example 13 reflects the general rule that the dividends received deduction is 85 percent of the qualifying dividends. Example 14 presents the exception whereby the deduction may be limited to 85 percent of taxable income. Example 15 indicates the situation in which the taxable income exception will not apply because allowance of the full deduction generates or adds to a net operating loss.

---

18. § 246(b)(1) and (2).

Deduction of Organizational Expenditures. Under § 248, a corporation may elect to amortize organizational expenses over a period of 60 months or more. If the election is not made on a timely basis, such expenditures cannot be deducted until the corporation ceases to conduct business and liquidates. The election is made in a statement attached to the corporation's return for its first taxable year.

Organizational expenditures include: [19]

1. Legal services incident to organization (e. g., drafting the corporate charter, by-laws, minutes or organizational meetings, terms, or original stock certificates);

2. Necessary accounting services;

3. Expenses of temporary directors and of organizational meetings of directors and stockholders; and

4. Fees paid to the state of incorporation.

Expenditures that do not qualify include those connected with issuing or selling shares of stock or other securities (e. g., commissions, professional fees, and printing costs) or with the transfer of assets to a corporation.[20] Such expenditures are generally added to the capital account and are not subject to amortization.

Example 16. T Corporation, an accrual basis taxpayer, was formed and began operations on May 1, 19X5. The following expenses were incurred during its first year of operations (May 1–December 31, 19X5):

Expenses of temporary directors and of organizational meetings	$500
Fee paid to the state of incorporation	100
Accounting services incident to organization	200
Legal services for drafting the corporate charter and by-laws	400
Expenses incident to the printing and sale of stock certificates	300

Assume T Corporation makes a timely election under § 248 to amortize qualifying organizational expenses over a period of 60 months. The monthly amortization would be $20 [($500 + $100 + $200 + $400) ÷ 60 months], and $160 ($20 × 8 months) would be deductible for tax year 19X5. Note that the $300 of expenses incident to the printing and sale of stock certificates do not qualify for the election.

DETERMINATION OF TAX LIABILITY

Corporate Income Tax Rates. Unlike the income tax rates applicable to noncorporate taxpayers, the corporate rates are only mildly

---

19. Reg. § 1.248–1(b)(2).   **20.** Reg. § 1.248–1(b)(3).

progressive and reflect a stair-step pattern of progression. The tax for corporations is imposed upon taxable income and includes the following: [21]

Normal Tax:
1. 20 percent of the first $25,000 of taxable income.
2. 22 percent on taxable income over $25,000.

Surtax:
1. 26 percent of taxable income in excess of $50,000.

Example 17. T Corporation has taxable income of $100,000 in 1977. Its income tax liability would be computed as follows:

Taxable Income		$100,000
Surtax exemption		(50,000)
Balance subject to the surtax		$50,000
Normal Tax:		
(20 percent of the first $25,000)	$ 5,000	
(22 percent of the remaining $75,000)	16,500	$21,500
Surtax (26 percent × $50,000)		13,000
Total Tax		$34,500

The effective corporate tax rates are 20 percent on the first $25,000 of taxable income, 22 percent on taxable income from $25,000 to $50,000 and 48 percent on taxable income in excess of $50,000.

Minimum Tax. Corporations are also subject to the 15 percent (10 percent before January 1, 1976) minimum tax on tax preferences. The minimum tax rules for noncorporate taxpayers were discussed in Chapter 10. Certain differences should be noted. For corporations, tax preferences are reduced by the greater of $10,000 or the regular tax liability. (For other taxpayers, the reduction is the greater of $10,000 or one-half of the regular tax liability).

A further difference involves the computation of the tax preference for capital gains. (For noncorporate taxpayers, one-half of the long-term net capital gain is a tax preference). For corporations, it is the excess of long-term net capital gain over short-term net capital loss multiplied by 18/48.[22]

Example 18. XYZ Corporation has a regular tax liability of $30,000 for 1978. The corporation has long-term net capital

21. § 11(b).   22. § 57(a)(9)(B).

gains of $96,000 and no other tax preferences. Its tax preference items and minimum tax are computed as follows:

Tax Preferences and Computation of Minimum Tax:

    (Normal tax + Surtax – Alternative tax rate)

        22 percent + 26 percent – 30 percent = 18 percent

            (Normal tax + Surtax)

              22 percent + 26 percent   =   48 percent

    $\frac{18}{48}$ × $96,000   = $36,000

    Less: Greater of $10,000 or the regular
            tax liability of $30,000   (30,000)

                                            6,000

    Times applicable minimum tax rate   × 15 percent

= Minimum tax liability $900

A corporation must file Form 4626 if it has any tax preferences for a taxable year regardless of whether it is liable for the minimum tax.

Filing Requirements. The corporate income tax return is filed on Form 1120. Corporations electing under Subchapter S file Form 1120 S. The return must be filed on or before the 15th day of the third month following the close of the corporation's tax year. A corporation may pay the tax upon filing, or it may elect to pay the unpaid amount in two equal installments, the first upon filing the return and the remaining one-half on or before the 15th day of the sixth month following the close of the corporation's taxable year.[23] Corporations can receive an automatic extension of 3 months for filing the corporate return by filing Form 7004 by the due date of the return.[24]

A corporation must make payments of estimated tax if its tax liability can reasonably be expected to exceed $40. These payments are made in four installments due on or before the 15th day of the fourth month, the sixth month, the ninth month, and the twelfth month of the taxable year.[25]

RECONCILIATION OF TAXABLE INCOME AND ACCOUNTING INCOME

Taxable income and financial net income are seldom the same amount. For example, a difference may arise if the corporation uses accelerated depreciation for tax purposes and straight-line depreciation for financial purposes.

Many items of income for accounting purposes, such as proceeds from a life insurance policy on the death of a corporate officer and interest on municipal bonds, may not be taxable income. Some ex-

---

23. Reg. § 1.6152–1(a).   **25.** Reg. § 1.6154.

24. § 6081.

pense items for financial purposes, such as expenses to produce tax exempt income, estimated warranty reserves, a net capital loss, and Federal income taxes, may not be deductible for tax purposes.

Schedule M–1 on the last page of Form 1120 is used to reconcile financial net income (net income after Federal income taxes) with taxable income (as computed on the corporate tax return before the deduction for a net operating loss and for the dividend received deduction).

Example 19.

Schedule M–1

Net Income per Books	$ 87,200	Interest on Municipal Bonds	$ 5,000	
Federal Income Tax	12,700			
Net Capital Loss	2,000	Life Insurance Proceeds on Death of President	50,000	$55,000
Expenses Not Deducted on Return				
Interest to Purchase Tax Exempt Securities $ 500		Excess of Depreciation Deducted on Return Over Book Depreciation		10,000
Insurance Premiums on Life Insurance Policy on Life of President, Proceeds Payable to Corporation 2,600	3,100	Total		$65,000
		Taxable Income [before net operating loss deduction and dividends received deduction ($105,000 – $65,000)]		
	$105,000			$40,000

FORMING THE CORPORATION

CAPITAL CONTRIBUTIONS

The receipt of money or property in exchange for capital stock produces neither gain nor loss to the recipient corporation.[26] Gross income of a corporation also does not include shareholders' contributions of money or property to the capital of the corporation.[27]

Contributions by nonshareholders, such as land contributed to a corporation by a civic group or a contribution by a municipality to induce the corporation to locate in a particular community, are also excluded from the gross income of a corporation.[28] The basis of such property (capital transfers by nonshareholders) to the corporation is zero.

Example 20. A city donates land to X Corporation as an inducement for X to locate in the city. The receipt of the land does not represent taxable income. However, its basis to the corporation is zero.

26. § 1032.

27. § 118.

28. *Edwards v. Cuba Railroad Co.,* 1 USTC ¶ 139, 5 AFTR 5398, 45 S.Ct. 614 (USSC, 1925).

Thin Capitalization Problem. The advantages of capitalizing a corporation with debt may be substantial. Interest on debt is deductible by the corporation whereas dividend payments are not. Further, the shareholders are not taxed on loan repayments unless they exceed basis. If a company is capitalized solely with common stock, subsequent repayments of such capital contributions are likely to be treated as dividends to the shareholders.

In certain instances, the IRS will contend that debt is really an equity interest and will deny the shareholders the tax advantages of debt financing. If the debt instrument has too many features of stock it may be treated as a form of stock, and principal and interest payments will be considered dividends.[29]

Though the form of the instrument will not assure debt treatment, the failure to observe certain formalities in the creation of the debt may lead to an assumption that the purported debt is, in fact, a form of stock. The debt should be in proper legal form, should bear a legitimate rate of interest, should have a definite maturity date, and should be repaid on a timely basis. Payments should not be contingent upon earnings. Further, the debt should not be subordinated to other liabilities, and proportionate holdings of stock and debt should be avoided.

A debt to equity ratio of 3:1 or 4:1 was considered safe in the past. In some cases higher ratios have been permitted. Nonetheless, a ratio in excess of 4:1 would be highly risky. To be safe, the ratio should probably be no higher than 2:1.[30]

TRANSFERS TO CONTROLLED CORPORATIONS

Absent special provisions in the Code, a transfer of property to a corporation in exchange for its stock would be a sale or exchange of property and would constitute a taxable transaction. § 351 provides for the nonrecognition of gain or loss upon such transfers of property if the transferors are in control of the corporation immediately after the transfer. Gain or loss is merely postponed in a manner similar to the like-kind exchange provisions previously discussed in Chapter 13. The following requirements must be met to qualify under § 351:

1. The transferors must be in control of the corporation immediately after the exchange. Control is defined as ownership

---

29. § 385 was added to the Internal Revenue Code in 1969. This section lists several factors which will be used to determine whether a debtor-creditor relationship or a shareholder-corporation relationship exists. Treasury Regulations, which are forthcoming for § 385, should provide further guidelines.

30. In *Biritz Construction Co. v. Comm.*, 68–1 USTC ¶ 9118, 20 AFTR2d 5891, 387 F.2d 451 (CA–8, 1967), the Court stated that a 2:1 ratio " * * * is not so inordinately high as to denote 'thin capitalization.' "

of at least 80 percent of the total combined voting power of all classes of stock entitled to vote and at least 80 percent of the total number of shares of all other classes of stock.[31]

2. Gain (but not loss) is recognized to the extent that the transferors receive property other than stock and securities, e. g., cash or short-term notes.[32] Such nonqualifying property is defined as "boot" under the tax law.

Basis Considerations and Computation of Gain. The nonrecognition of gain or loss is accompanied by a carryover of basis. § 358(a) provides that the basis of stock or securities received in a § 351 transfer is the same as the basis the taxpayers had in the property transferred, increased by any gain recognized on the exchange and decreased by boot received. § 362(a) provides that the basis of properties received by the corporation is the basis in the hands of the transferor increased by the amount of any gain recognized to the transferor shareholder.

Example 21. A and B, individuals, form X Corporation. A transfers property with an adjusted basis of $30,000, fair market value of $60,000, for 50 percent of the stock. B transfers property with an adjusted basis of $40,000, fair market value of $60,000, for the remaining 50 percent of the stock. Gain is not recognized on the transfer because it qualifies under § 351. The basis of the stock to A is $30,000, while the basis of the stock to B is $40,000. X Corporation has a basis of $30,000 in the property transferred by A and a basis of $40,000 in the property transferred by B.

Example 22. C and D form Y Corporation with the following investment: C transfers property (basis of $30,000 and fair market value of $70,000) while D transfers cash of $60,000. Each receives 50 shares of the Y Corporation stock but C also receives $10,000 in cash. Assume each share of the Y Corporation stock is worth $1,200. Although C's realized gain is $40,000 [i. e., $60,000 (the value of 50 shares of Y Corporation stock) + $10,000 (cash received) − $30,000 (basis of the property transferred)], only $10,000 (the amount of the boot) is recognized. C's basis in the Y Corporation stock becomes $30,000 [i. e., $30,000 (basis of the property transferred) + $10,000 (gain recognized by C) − $10,000 (cash received)]. Y Corporation's ba-

---

31. § 368(c).

32. The courts have required that the definition of a "security" be limited to long-term obligations and exclude short-term notes. See: *Turner v. Comm.*, 62–1 USTC ¶ 9488, 9 AFTR2d 1528, 303 F.2d 94 (CA–4, 1962). The required length of maturity to qualify as a security is questionable. Some courts would draw a line at 5 years; others at 10 years. See: *Camp Wolters Enterprises, Inc. v. Comm.*, 22 T.C. 737 (1955), *aff'd* in 56–1 USTC ¶ 9314, 49 AFTR 283, 230 F.2d 555 (CA–5, 1956).

sis in the property transferred by C is $40,000 [$30,000 (basis of the property to C) + $10,000 (gain recognized to C)]. D neither realizes nor recognizes gain or loss and will have a basis in the Y Corporation stock of $60,000.

Example 23. Assume the same facts as in Example 22 except that C's basis in the property transferred is $68,000 (instead of $30,000). Because recognized gain cannot exceed realized gain, the transfer generates only $2,000 of gain to C. The basis of the Y Corporation stock to C becomes $60,000 [i. e., $68,000 (basis of property transferred) + $2,000 (gain recognized) − $10,000 (cash received)]. Y Corporation's basis in the property received from C is $70,000 [i. e., $68,000 (basis of the property to C) + $2,000 (gain recognized by C)].

OPERATING THE CORPORATION

DIVIDEND DISTRIBUTIONS

Corporate distributions of cash or property to shareholders are treated as ordinary dividend income to the extent the corporation has accumulated or current earnings and profits (E & P).[33] In determining the source of the distribution, a dividend is deemed to have been made initially from current E & P.[34]

Example 24. As of January 1, 19X1, Y Corporation has a deficit in accumulated E & P of $30,000. For tax year 19X1 it has current E & P of $10,000. In 19X1 the corporation distributed $5,000 to its shareholders. The $5,000 distribution will be treated as a taxable dividend since it is deemed to have been made from current E & P. This will be the case even though Y Corporation will still have a deficit in its accumulated E & P at the end of 19X1.

Concept of Earnings and Profits. The term "earnings and profits" is not defined in the Code although § 312 does include certain transactions that affect E & P. While E & P possesses certain similarities to the financial accounting concept of retained earnings, numerous differences may arise. For example, a stock dividend is treated for financial accounting purposes as a capitalization of retained earnings, but it does not decrease E & P for tax purposes. Generally, current earnings and profits for a taxable year is taxable income plus or minus certain adjustments, e. g., additions are made for (1) tax-exempt income and (2) the excess of accelerated depreciation over the amount which would have been allowed under the straight line method. Federal income taxes are subtracted from tax-

33. § 316.   **34.** Reg. § 1.316–2(a).

able income in arriving at the current E & P. A detailed discussion of the concept of E & P is beyond the scope of this chapter.[35]

Property Dividends. A distribution of property to a non-corporate shareholder is measured by the fair market value of the property on the date of distribution.[36] The non-corporate shareholder's basis in the property received is also its fair market value.[37]

Example 25. P Corporation has E & P of $60,000. It distributes land with a fair market value of $50,000 (adjusted basis of $30,000) to its sole shareholder, T (an individual). T has a taxable dividend of $50,000 and a basis in the land of $50,000.

Special rules apply to property distributions received by corporate shareholders. The amount distributed is the lesser of (a) the fair market value of the property or (b) the adjusted basis of the property in the hands of the distributing corporation increased by the amount of gain recognized (if any) to the distributing corporation.[38] The basis of the property received by the corporate shareholder is also computed under these special rules.[39]

Example 26. 10 percent of X Corporation is owned by Y Corporation. X Corporation has ample E & P to cover any distributions made during the year. X Corporation distributed land with an adjusted basis of $5,000 and a fair market value of $3,000 to Y Corporation. Y Corporation has a taxable dividend of $3,000, and its basis in the land becomes $3,000.

The special rules for property distributions to corporate shareholders are due to the 85 percent dividends received deduction which is available to corporate shareholders. The rule prevents a corporate shareholder from obtaining a step-up in basis in appreciated property at a cost of only a 15 percent inclusion in income.

STOCK REDEMPTIONS

If a shareholder's stock is redeemed by the corporation, one of two possible outcomes will occur:

1. The redemption may qualify as a sale or exchange under § 302. In such case, capital gain or loss treatment usually applies to the redeeming shareholders; or

2. The redemption will be treated as a dividend under § 301 providing the distributing corporation has earnings and profits.

35. See: *West's Federal Taxation: Corporations, Partnerships, Estates, and Trusts,* pp. 124–129 for a detailed discussion of the concept of earnings and profits.

36. § 301(b)(1)(A).

37. § 301(d)(1).

38. § 301(b)(1)(B).

39. § 301(d)(2).

Certain redemptions of corporate stock represent a bona-fide contraction of a shareholder's interest in the company and should, therefore, be treated as a sale or exchange of the shareholder's stock. However, absent specific rules in this area, it would be possible to structure a redemption of stock as a dividend in disguise.

Example 27. X and Y each own 100 shares of the voting stock of XY Corporation which represents 100 percent of the voting stock. Instead of paying a cash dividend, XY Corporation redeems 10 shares of X's stock and 10 shares of Y's stock for a total of $20,000. Since X and Y each continue to own 50 percent of the Corporation after the distribution, the redemption would be treated as a dividend under § 301 rather than as a sale or exchange of the stock under § 302 if XY Corporation has current and accumulated earnings and profits of at least $20,000.

Requirements for Sale or Exchange Treatment. A redemption of stock qualifies as a redemption § 302 if *any* of the following requirements are met:

1.   The redemption is not essentially equivalent to a dividend; [40]

2.   The distribution is substantially disproportionate, i. e., the redeeming shareholder now owns less than 80 percent of his total former interest in the corporation and the shareholder owns less than 50 percent of the voting stock of the corporation; [41] or

3.   There is a complete termination of a shareholder's interest.[42]

In determining whether there has been a substantially disproportionate redemption, the family stock attribution rules under § 318 are applied.

Example 28. T, an individual, owns 30 percent of the stock in X Corporation, the other 70 percent being held by her children. For purposes of § 318, T is treated as owning 100 percent of the stock in X Corporation. She owns 30 percent directly and, because of the attribution rules, 70 percent indirectly.

Example 29. A, B, and C, unrelated individuals, own 30 shares, 30 shares, and 40 shares, respectively, in X Corporation. X Corporation has E & P of $200,000. The corporation redeems 20 shares of C's stock for $30,000. C paid $200 a share for the

---

40. § 302(b)(1); In most instances, taxpayers should no longer place significant emphasis upon this subsection since the Supreme Court has ruled that the existence of a business purpose and the absence of a tax avoidance scheme are insufficient to cause the redemption to be treated as a sale or exchange under § 302(b)(1). There must be a * * * "meaning-
ful reduction of the shareholder's proportionate interest in the corporation." *U. S. v. Davis*, 70–1 USTC ¶ 9289, 25 AFTR2d 70–827, 90 S.Ct. 1041 (USSC, 1970).

41. § 302(b)(2).

42. § 302(b)(3).

stock two years ago. After the redemption C has a 25 percent interest in the corporation [20 shares of a total of 80 shares (100 − 20)]. This represents less than 80 percent of his original ownership (40% × 80% = 32%) and less than 50 percent of the total voting power; consequently, the distribution qualifies as a stock redemption. C has a long-term capital gain of $26,000 [$30,000 − $4,000 (20 shares × $200)].

Example 30. Given the situation in Example 29, assume, in addition, that B and C are father and son. The redemption described previously would not qualify for capital gain treatment. C is deemed to own the stock of B so that, after the redemption, he would have 50 shares of a total of 80 shares, more than 50 percent ownership. He would also fail the 80 percent test. Before the redemption C is deemed a 70 percent owner (40 shares owned by him and 30 shares owned by B, his son). After the redemption he is deemed a 62.5 percent owner (20 shares owned directly by him and 30 shares owned by B from a total of 80 shares). C has a taxable dividend of $30,000.

LIQUIDATING THE CORPORATION

GENERAL RULE OF § 331

Under the general rule, gain or loss is recognized to the shareholders in a corporate liquidation. The amount of recognized gain or loss is measured by the difference between the fair market value of the assets received from the corporation and the adjusted basis of the stock surrendered. Capital gain or loss is recognized by the shareholders if their stock is a capital asset.

Example 31. X Corporation has as its only asset unimproved land (adjusted basis of $100,000 and fair market value of $150,000). T, an individual, owns all of the outstanding stock in X Corporation, such stock having an adjusted basis of $80,000. X Corporation distributes the land to T in complete cancellation of its outstanding stock.

Pursuant to the general rule of § 331, T must recognize capital gain of $70,000 [$150,000 (fair market value of the land) minus $80,000 (adjusted basis of the stock)].

EXCEPTIONS TO THE GENERAL RULE

Liquidation of a Subsidiary. § 332 is an exception to the general rule that the shareholder recognizes gain or loss on a corporate liquidation. If a parent corporation liquidates a subsidiary corporation in which it owns at least 80 percent of the voting stock, no gain or loss is recognized to the parent company.[43] The subsidiary must distribute all of its property in complete liquidation of all of its stock within the taxable year or within 3 years from the close of the tax year in which the first distribution occurred. Note that § 332 is applicable only if the subsidiary is solvent immediately prior to the liquidation.[44]

> **Example 32.** P Corporation owns 100 percent of the stock of S Corporation which P acquired for $100,000. The fair market value of S's net assets is $200,000. S is liquidated into P Corporation under § 332. The assets and liabilities are transferred to P Corporation in complete liquidation of S. No gain or loss is recognized to P Corporation.

One-Month Liquidation. § 333 is another exception to the general rule that a shareholder recognizes gain or loss upon a corporate liquidation. If shareholders elect and the liquidation is completed within one calendar month, § 333 postpones the recognition of gain on assets which have appreciated in the hands of the liquidating corporation.[45] However, the shareholder does have recognized gain (to the extent of realized gain) in an amount equal to the greater of (a) the stockholder's share of earnings and profits accumulated after February 28, 1913, or (b) amounts received by the shareholder consisting of money and/or stock or securities acquired by the corporation after 1953.[46]

For noncorporate shareholders, recognized gain is treated as dividend income to the extent of the shareholder's pro-rata share of the corporate earnings and profits. Any excess amount of recognized gain is treated as capital gain.

For noncorporate shareholders, gain (to the extent recognized) is all treated as capital gain.[47]

---

43. §§ 332(a) and 332(b)(1).

44. Reg. § 1.332–2(a) and (b).

45. Note that only "qualifying electing" shareholders are entitled to the benefits of § 333. A corporate shareholder owning 50 percent or more of the stock is ineligible. Also, the remaining shareholders are divided into two groups: (a) noncorporate and (b) corporate shareholders owning less than 50 percent of the stock. For each group, owners of at least 80 percent of the stock must elect under § 333 or the election is not available to any member of the group.

46. § 333(e).

47. § 333(f) and Reg. § 1.333–4(b). The reason corporate shareholders are forced into capital gain treatment is due to the 85 percent dividends received deduction which would otherwise be available if dividend treatment were prescribed. Capital gain treatment, therefore, leads to a harsher tax effect on a corporate shareholder.

Example 33. The independent cases appearing below illustrate the possible tax consequences to a shareholder under a § 333 liquidation:

Case	Type of Shareholder	E & P	Cash plus Post-1953 Securities	Shareholder's Realized Gain	Shareholder's Recognized Gain	
					Capital	Dividend
A	Corporation	$10,000	$10,000	$ 5,000	$ 5,000	$ 0
B	Corporation	10,000	20,000	40,000	20,000	0
C	Corporation	20,000	10,000	30,000	20,000	0
D	Individual	10,000	10,000	5,000	0	5,000
E	Individual	10,000	20,000	40,000	10,000	10,000
F	Individual	20,000	10,000	30,000	0	20,000

In Example 33, note that gain recognized for both corporate and noncorporate shareholders can never exceed realized gain (Cases A and D). Also, all recognized gain by a corporate shareholder must be capital gain (Cases A, B, and C). An individual has a capital gain only if his share of the cash plus post-1953 securities exceeds his share of the corporation's E & P (contrast Cases E and F).

A corporate shareholder owning 50 percent or more of the stock of a liquidating corporation cannot qualify under § 333. The remaining shareholders are divided into two groups: (a) noncorporate shareholders and (b) those corporate shareholders owning less than 50 percent of stock in the liquidating corporation. Owners of stock possessing at least 80 percent of the total combined voting power of all classes of stock owned by shareholders in one of the above-mentioned groups must elect the provisions of § 333. If the 80 percent requirement is not met, the one-month liquidation treatment is not available to any member of that group.

BASIS DETERMINATION—§ 334

General Rule. Where gain or loss is recognized upon the complete liquidation of a corporation, the basis of the property received by the shareholders is its fair market value.[48] For example, in Example 31 the basis of the land to shareholder T is $150,000 (fair market value) since gain was recognized.

One-Month Liquidation Basis Rules. Since gain is recognized only to a limited extent under § 333, the basis of the property received by the shareholders is the same as the basis of the shares redeemed, decreased by the amount of any money received and increased by gain recognized and liabilities assumed by the shareholders.[49] This amount is allocated to the various assets received on the basis of the relative fair market values of the properties.

Subsidiary Liquidation Basis Rules. The general rule is that the property received by the parent corporation in a complete liquidation of its subsidiary under § 332 has the same basis it had in the hands

---

48. § 334(a).   **49.** § 334(c).

of the subsidiary.[50] The parent's basis in stock of the liquidated subsidiary disappears.

Example 34. P, the parent corporation, has a basis of $20,000 in stock in S Corporation, a subsidiary in which it owns 85 percent of all classes of stock. P Corporation purchased the stock of S Corporation 10 years ago. In the current year, P Corporation liquidates S Corporation and acquires assets worth $50,000 with a tax basis to S Corporation of $40,000. P Corporation would have a basis of $40,000 in the assets, with a potential gain upon sale of $10,000. P Corporation's original $20,000 basis in S Corporation stock disappears.

An exception to the carryover of basis rules is provided in § 334(b)(2). Under this exception, the parent company receives a step-up in basis for the assets equal to the adjusted basis of the stock of the subsidiary. In effect, the initial acquisition of the subsidiary is treated as if the parent company had acquired the assets (rather than the stock) of the subsidiary.

The following requirements must be met:

1. The parent must "purchase" at least 80 percent of the total combined voting power of all classes of stock and at least 80 percent of all other classes of stock (except nonvoting preferred) within a 12 month period; and

2. The subsidiary must be liquidated within 2 years following the date of acquisition.

Example 35. P Corporation acquired 100 percent of the stock of S Corporation for $1,000,000 cash in a taxable purchase transaction on January 1, 19X1. On April 1, 19X1, S Corporation was liquidated into P under § 332. The adjusted basis of S Corporation's net assets is $800,000. Since P acquired at least 80 percent of the stock in a taxable purchase transaction and liquidated S within 2 years under § 332, P Corporation's basis in the net assets of S is determined under § 334(b)(2) and is $1,000,000 (the amount paid for the S stock). The transaction is treated as if P acquired the S Corporation's assets for $1,000,000 instead of acquiring S's stock for $1,000,000.

THE SUBCHAPTER S ELECTION

JUSTIFICATION FOR THE ELECTION

Since there may be numerous nontax reasons for operating a business in corporate form, the existence of income tax disadvantages (e. g., double taxation of corporate income and shareholder dividends)

---

50. § 334(b)(1) and Reg. § 1.334–1(b).

should not deter businessmen from using the corporate form. In the interest of preventing tax considerations from interfering with the exercise of sound business judgment, Congress enacted Subchapter S of the Code.

The requirements to be a "Small Business Corporation" under Subchapter S include the following: [51]

1. Is a domestic corporation;
2. Is not a member of an affiliated group;
3. Has no more than 10 shareholders initially; [52]
4. Has as its shareholders only individuals, estates, and certain trusts; and
5. Issues only one class of stock.[53]

Making the Election. The election is made by filing Form 2553, and all shareholders must make the election. Special rules apply to husbands and wives where stock is jointly held and to minors.[54]

The election must be filed during the month preceding or following the beginning of the corporation's tax year for which the election is to be effective.[55] If the election is not timely, it will be ineffective.

Loss of the Election. Revocation of the Subchapter S election may occur voluntarily, i. e., all of the shareholders file to revoke the election or involuntarily, in any of the following ways: [56]

1. A new shareholder fails to consent to the election for tax years before 1977. For a tax year beginning after December 31, 1976, a new shareholder must *affirmatively refuse* to consent to the Subchapter S election within 60 days from the date the stock is acquired. Otherwise, the election remains in effect;
2. The corporation ceases to qualify as a Small Business Corporation, e. g., the corporation adds additional shareholders so that it has more than 10 (or 15 as the case may be) shareholders and the requirements of § 1371(a) for qualification are, therefore, not met;

---

51. § 1371(a).

52. For tax years beginning after 1976, an electing corporation may have up to 15 shareholders for the first 5 years of existence if the additional stockholders acquire their interest through inheritance. After 5 years as a Subchapter S Corporation, the number of shareholders may be increased to 15.

53. Originally the IRS argued that debt reclassified as equity could create a second class of stock. Reg. §

1.1371–1(g). After numerous court defeats, the IRS has finally announced that it will no longer litigate this issue, pending a change in its Regulations. TIR 1248 (July 27, 1973). See, for example, *Portage Plastics Co., Inc. v. U. S.*, 73–1 USTC ¶ 9261, 31 AFTR2d 73–864, 486 F.2d 636 (CA–7, 1973).

54. Reg. § 1.1372–3(a).

55. § 1372(c)(1).

56. § 1372(e).

3. The corporation derives more than 80 percent of its gross receipts from foreign sources; and

4. The corporation's passive investment income is more than 20 percent of its gross receipts.

If all of the shareholders consent to a voluntary revocation of Subchapter S status, the election must be made within the first month of the taxable year for which it is to be effective. If made after such time, the election will be effective only for the following taxable year.

> **Example 36.** The shareholders of T Corporation, a calendar year Subchapter S Corporation, elect to revoke the election on January 5, 1977. Assuming the election is duly executed and timely filed, T Corporation will become a regular corporation for calendar year 1977. If, on the other hand, the election is not made until June, 1977, T Corporation will not become a regular corporation until calendar year 1978.

Note that a voluntary revocation is always prospective in its effect. In this sense it can be contrasted to an involuntary loss of the election and an affirmative refusal which are applied retroactively to the beginning of the year. Using Example 36 for illustration purposes, assume that in June, 1977, some of T Corporation's stock is acquired by a new party who files the required refusal to continue the election. In such a case, T Corporation would lose its Subchapter S election as of January 1, 1977.

OPERATIONAL RULES

The Subchapter S Corporation is a tax-reporting rather than a tax-paying entity. In this respect, the entity is taxed somewhat like a partnership.[57] Under the "conduit concept," the taxable income and/or losses of a Subchapter S Corporation flows through to its shareholders and is reported by them on their personal income tax returns.[58]

Stock ownership at the end of the year provides the basis for allocating taxable income among shareholders. In essence, any income is simply assigned to the stockholders of record on the last day of the corporate tax year in proportion to their stock ownership.

Taxable income of an electing corporation is computed in much the same manner as the taxable income of a regular corporation. Under § 1373(d) there are two exceptions: First, a net operating loss carryback or carryforward is not allowed. Such operating losses are passed through to the stockholders in the years they occur. Second,

57. Note that although the tax treatment of a Subchapter S corporation is similar to a partnership, a Subchapter S corporation is subject to special rules and restrictions.

58. § 1373(b).

certain special deductions, such as the 85 percent dividends received deduction, are disallowed.

Undistributed Taxable Income (UTI) and Previously Taxed Income (PTI). Undistributed taxable income generally represents taxable income less cash dividend payments made during the taxable year. Once constructively taxed to shareholders, such income may be distributed during the current year or within two and one-half months after year-end without additional tax consequences. At the end of the two and one-half month grace period, undistributed taxable income becomes previously taxed income (PTI).

> **Example 37.** X and Y are equal owners of T, a Subchapter S Corporation. T Corporation had taxable income and earnings and profits of $100,000 during 19X1 and paid $60,000 cash dividends during the year. In addition, a cash dividend of $30,000 was paid on February 5, 19X2. The undistributed taxable income (UTI for 19X1 is $100,000 − $60,000 or $40,000. X and Y must include their share of the UTI of $40,000 on their personal tax returns as a constructive dividend for 19X1. In addition, X and Y are subject to tax upon their share of the $60,000 of cash dividends paid during 19X1. The cash distribution of $30,000 is received without further tax incidents since it was paid within 2½ months and, therefore, is deemed to have come from the $40,000 UTI in 19X1. Previously taxed income (PTI) is increased by $10,000 (i. e., $100,000 − $60,000 − $30,000).

PTI is income that remains in the corporation (i. e., is not paid out) and has been taxed to the shareholders as a constructive dividend of UTI. UTI becomes PTI two and one-half months after the close of the corporation's tax year. Therefore, any later distribution of PTI, made to a shareholder who has reported UTI, is tax-free.

Assuming Subchapter S status is in effect, PTI cannot be distributed tax-free until current UTI is first distributed (i. e., the order works on the LIFO principle). Once the election is terminated, PTI can be distributed only after current and accumulated earnings and profits are first distributed.

> **Example 38.** At the beginning of its first election year (19X5), a Subchapter S corporation has accumulated earnings and profits of $200,000. During 19X5, the corporation has $100,000 of UTI (current earnings and profits being the same) which is not distributed during the current year or during the two and one-half month grace period in 19X6. This $100,000 is taxed to the shareholders of the corporation even though not distributed to them (i. e., it is a constructive dividend). After two and one-half months, the $100,000 of UTI becomes PTI. Assume that during 19X6 the corporation has $50,000 more of UTI. At this point, before any of the PTI of $100,000 can be reached by the share-

holders, the corporation must first distribute $50,000 (the UTI for 19X6).

Example 39. Assume the same facts as in Example 38 except that the Subchapter S election is involuntarily terminated during 19X6. In order to reach the $100,000 of PTI, both current and accumulated earnings and profits first must be distributed. Thus, the corporation must distribute $350,000 for the shareholders to recover all of their PTI.

Pass-through of Net Operating Losses. One major advantage of a Subchapter S election is the ability to pass-through any net operating loss (NOL) directly to the corporate shareholders. Whereas the UTI is allocated based upon the actual stock ownership at the end of the year, NOL's are allocated on a daily basis to all shareholders who owned stock during the year.[59]

A shareholder's stock basis is reduced to the extent of any pass-through of the net operating loss. However, NOL pass-through benefits to shareholders cannot exceed a shareholder's adjusted basis in the stock plus the basis of any loans made to the corporation.[60] Once a shareholder's adjusted stock basis has been eliminated by a NOL, any excess net operating loss is used to reduce the stockholder's basis for any loans made to the corporation. If a stockholder's share of the NOL exceeds his basis in both the stock and loans, the excess is not deductible in the current year and is not available as a carryback or carryover to another year. Once a shareholder has exhausted the basis for his loans to the corporation, income results to the shareholder when the loans are later repaid.[61]

Example 40. X's adjusted basis in his stock of the XYZ Corporation (a Subchapter S Corporation) is $40,000 and he has made loans of $10,000 to the corporation. In 19X1 his share of the NOL is $60,000.

X may deduct $50,000 on his personal return as an ordinary deduction. His basis in the stock is reduced to zero. His basis in the loan is also reduced to zero. The excess amount of the NOL ($60,000 − $40,000 − $10,000) of $10,000 is never deductible by X. If the loans are repaid in 19X2, X will recognize income of $10,000 since his basis in the loan is zero.

Pass-through of Other Corporate Attributes. While most types of income and deductions flow through directly to the Subchapter S shareholders, some items either lose their identity of character or do not directly flow through to shareholders. These items are said to

59. § 1374(c)(1).

60. § 1374(c)(2).

61. *George W. Wiebusch v. Comm.,* 59 T.C. 777 (1973), *aff'd* in 73–2 USTC ¶ 9797, 32 AFTR2d 73–6181, 487 F.2d 515 (CA–8, 1973).

have retained their corporate attributes. The following items are of particular importance to a Subchapter S Corporation:

1. Long-term net capital gains in excess of short-term net capital losses generally retain their character and flow directly through to individual shareholder returns after being netted at the corporate level. In unusual cases, § 1378 provides that long-term net capital gains are also taxed directly to the Subchapter S Corporation.[62]

2. Net capital losses in excess of capital gains do *not* flow through to shareholders. Such excess capital losses retain their corporate attributes and are generally treated under the normal corporate tax rules.

3. Dividend income is not subject to the 85 percent dividends received deduction permitted to regular corporations. Dividend income does not directly flow through to the Subchapter S shareholders as dividends. Such dividends are added to operating income and flow through as the shareholders' part of UTI which is not eligible for the $100 dividend exclusion.

4. Contributions do not flow through directly to shareholders but are deductible (subject to the corporate 5 percent limitations) in arriving at UTI.

5. Tax preference items in the corporation are generally passed through to the individual shareholders who own stock on the last day of the tax year.[63]

6. Likewise, any investment credit the corporation is allowed from the purchase of § 38 property passes through to the shareholders.[64]

TAX PLANNING CONSIDERATIONS

CORPORATE VERSUS NONCORPORATE FORMS OF BUSINESS ORGANIZATION

The decision to use the corporate form in conducting a trade or business must be weighed carefully. Besides the nontax considerations attendant to the corporate form (i. e., limited liability, continuity of life, free transferability of interest, centralized management), tax ramifications will play an important role in any such decision. Close attention should be paid to the following:

1. The corporate form means the imposition of the corporate income tax. Corporate-source income will be taxed twice—

---

62. See: *West's Federal Taxation: Corporations, Partnerships, Estates, and Trusts*, pp. 334–335.

63. § 58(d).

64. § 48(e).

once as earned by the corporation and again when distributed to the shareholders. Since dividends are not deductible, a strong incentive exists in a closely-held corporation to structure corporate distributions in a deductible form. Thus, profits may be bailed out by the shareholders in the form of salaries, interest, or rents. Such procedures lead to a multitude of problems, one of which, the reclassification of debt as equity, has been discussed. The problems of unreasonable salaries and rents were previously discussed in Chapter 6.

2. Corporate source income loses its identity as it passes through the corporation to the shareholders. Thus, items possessing preferential tax treatment (e. g., interest on municipal bonds, long-term capital gains) are not taxed as such to the shareholders.

3. As noted in this chapter, it may be difficult for shareholders to recover some or all of their investment in the corporation without an ordinary income result since most corporate distributions are treated as dividends to the extent of the corporation's earnings and profits. Structuring the capital of the corporation to include debt is a partial solution to this problem. Thus, the shareholder-creditor could recoup part of his or her investment through the tax-free repayment of principal. Too much debt, however, may lead to such debt being reclassified as equity.

4. Corporate losses cannot be passed through to the shareholders.

5. Long-term capital gains and losses generally receive more favorable tax treatment in the hands of noncorporate taxpayers.

6. The liquidation of a corporation may well generate tax consequences to both the corporation and its shareholders.

7. On the positive side, the corporate form may be advantageous for shareholders in high individual tax brackets. With a maximum corporate income tax rate of 48 percent, such shareholders would be motivated to avoid dividend distributions and retain profits within the corporation. If the earnings are reinvested primarily in operating assets, the corporation may safely retain such earnings without being subject to penalty taxes.

8. The corporate form does provide the shareholders with the opportunity to be treated as "employees" for tax purposes if they, in fact, render services to the corporation. Such status makes a number of attractive tax sheltered fringe benefits available, e. g., group-term life insurance, accident and health plans and qualified pension and profit-sharing plans (previ-

ously discussed in Chapter 17). These benefits are not available to partners and sole proprietors.

REGULAR CORPORATION VERSUS SUBCHAPTER S STATUS

Effective tax planning with Subchapter S begins with determining whether the election is appropriate. In this context, one should consider the following factors:

1. Are losses from the business anticipated? If so, the election may be highly attractive because these losses pass through to the shareholders.

2. What are the tax brackets of the shareholders? If the shareholders are in high individual income tax brackets, it may be desirable to avoid Subchapter S and have profits taxed to the corporation at a maximum rate of 48 percent. When the immediate pass through of UTI is avoided, profits of the corporation may later be bailed out by the shareholders at capital gain rates through stock redemptions, liquidating distributions, or sales of stock to others; received as dividend distributions, in low tax bracket years; or negated by the "fresh-start" step-up in basis at the death of the shareholder. On the other hand, if the shareholders are in low individual income tax brackets, the pass-through of corporate profits does not impact so forcefully, and avoidance of the corporate income tax becomes the paramount consideration. Under these circumstances, the Subchapter S election could be highly attractive. Bear in mind, however, that a Subchapter S corporation escapes the Federal corporate income tax but may not be immune from state and local taxes imposed on corporations.

PROBLEM MATERIAL

Questions for Class Discussion

1. Will a business be treated as a corporation for Federal income tax purposes if the state legal requirements for a corporation are met, even if the business does not possess corporate characteristics?

2. Why would the IRS in some instances assert that an entity is taxable as a corporation rather than being taxed as a noncorporate entity?

3. Why is it unnecessary for corporate taxpayers to distinguish between deductions *for* and *from* adjusted gross income?

4. What is the effective corporate tax rate on net long-term capital gains? Are corporations allowed a 50 percent dividends received deduction?

5. Contrast the corporate tax rules for deducting net capital losses with the rules for individuals. Are the corporate capital loss rules *more* or *less* favorable than the capital loss provisions for individuals? Why?

6. What requirements must be met to properly accrue a charitable contribution, the payment of which is made in the year following the year of the deduction?

7. How are corporate charitable contributions treated if such amounts are in excess of the maximum limitations?

8. Why are the corporate net operating loss adjustments substantially different than the NOL adjustments for individual taxpayers?

9. Why is the 85 percent dividends received deduction added back to increase a NOL for a corporation?

10. Why would a corporation elect not to carry back an NOL to a particular year?

11. Why is it sometimes necessary for a taxpayer to annualize his taxable income when there is a change in the accounting period?

12. What is the rationale for the dividends received deduction for corporate shareholders?

13. What happens if a corporation fails to elect to amortize organizational expenditures incurred during its first taxable year?

14. Distinguish between expenditures which qualify as organizational expenditures and those which do not qualify.

15. What is the effective tax rate on taxable income in excess of $50,000 for a corporation?

16. Compare the minimum tax provisions for corporate taxpayers with the minimum tax rules for individuals. Are the corporate rules *more* or *less* favorable?

17. Why is taxable income different from financial accounting income for many corporations?

18. What purpose does the Schedule M reconciliation on Form 1120 serve (a) for the taxpayer (b) for the IRS?

19. If a corporation receives land from a municipality to induce the company to relocate, is the corporation required to recognize taxable income? What is your answer if the land were received as a capital contribution from a shareholder?

20. Why is it usually advantageous to capitalize a corporation using debt? Is it possible that the debt will be reclassified as equity? Why?

21. What is the rationale for § 351? What is "boot"? Why is gain recognized to the extent of "boot" received?

22. If appreciated property is transferred to a corporation in a non-taxable exchange under § 351, is gain recognized to the corporation if the property is immediately sold by the corporation at its fair market value? Why?

23. Why are some corporate stock redemptions treated as dividend income under § 301?

24. Which of the following statements are *true* or *false:*

   a. Earnings and profits is a tax term which is the same as retained earnings for financial accounting purposes. _____

   b. If a noncorporate shareholder receives a distribution of property, the amount of the distribution is equal to the fair market value of the property. _____

   c. If a corporate shareholder receives a property distribution, the amount of such distribution is measured by its fair market value. _____

25. What effect do the family attribution rules have in determining whether there has been a substantially disproportionate redemption of a shareholder's interest?

26. If a parent company liquidates a subsidiary company and the requirements of § 332 are met, is gain or loss recognized to the parent company?

27. How is the basis of the assets of a subsidiary determined upon the transfer of such assets to the parent in a § 332 liquidation? How is it possible for the parent company to receive a step-up in basis for the subsidiary assets if certain requirements are met?

28. Discuss the requirements of a one-month liquidation. When would the one-month liquidation be preferable to a liquidation under the general rules of § 331?

29. How is the basis of assets received by shareholders in a one-month liquidation determined?

30. What are the requirements to be a "Small Business Corporation" under Subchapter S?

31. Is it necessary to be a "small" company to qualify under Subchapter S? Can a large public company qualify? Why?

32. What is the difference between a voluntary and an involuntary revocation of the Subchapter S election? Does it make a difference if the Subchapter S election is voluntarily or involuntarily revoked? Why?

33. Is a Subchapter S corporation subject to the Federal income tax?

34. Define the following tax terms:

   a. Undistributed taxable income (UTI)

   b. Previously taxed income (PTI)

35. If a Subchapter S Corporation incurs a net operating loss, how are such losses apportioned to the shareholders?

36. Are net operating losses of a Subchapter S Corporation deductible by the shareholders without limit? Why?

37. How are long-term net capital gains of a Subchapter S Corporation treated?

38. If a Subchapter S Corporation has dividend income from investments, how is the dividend income reported on the tax returns of the individual shareholders?

39. How are contributions made by a Subchapter S Corporation treated?

Problems

1. The XYZ partnership is engaged in commercial real estate management and investment activities. The partners decided to form the XYZ Corporation, since interest rates were increasing and under state law a corporate lender was exempt from the state usury laws. It was intended that the corporation would be used solely to hold title to the real estate properties and would engage in no other activities. The corporation would act as a nominee or agent for the partners in obtaining adequate financing from bank and other lending institutions.

    It is anticipated that the real estate business will incur losses of $100,000 each year for the next five years. X, Y, and Z's tax basis in the XYZ Corporation stock would be nominal since most of the capital would be obtained or contributed by the partnership from outside debt financing.

    a. What are the possible risks resulting from the creation of a "dummy" corporation?

    b. If profits were generated after 5 years and the corporation made distributions to shareholders, how might these distributions be treated?

    c. Should X, Y, and Z consider the corporate form of organization with a Subchapter S election?

2. XYZ Corporation incurred a $50,000 net operating loss in 1978. In 1975, XYZ had taxable income of $201,000 consisting of a $200,-000 long-term net capital gain and $1,000 of ordinary taxable income. The alternative tax method was elected for 1975. Taxable income for 1976 was $30,000 (all ordinary taxable income) and $10,000 for 1977 (all ordinary taxable income).

    a. Should XYZ Corporation elect to carry the 1978 NOL back to 1975? Why?

    b. Would your answer be different if substantial additional NOL's are anticipated for 1979 and future periods?

3. XYZ Corporation had taxable income of $100,000 in 1978 consisting of $60,000 ordinary taxable income and $40,000 long-term net capital gains.

   a. Compute XYZ's tax under the regular tax computation.

   b. Compute XYZ's tax by using the alternative tax computation.

   c. Which method should be used?

4. XYZ Corporation incurred short-term net capital gains of $30,-000 and long-term net capital losses of $90,000 during 19X6. Taxable income from other sources was $400,000. Prior years included the following:

19X2	Long-term net capital gains	$80,000
19X3	Short-term net capital gains	20,000
19X4	Long-term net capital gains	10,000
19X5	Long-term net capital gains	10,000

   a. How are the capital gains and losses treated on the 19X6 tax return?

   b. Compute the capital loss carryback to the carryback years.

   c. Compute the amount of capital loss carryforward, if any, and designate the years to which the loss may be carried.

5. During the current year, T Corporation has $1,000,000 gross income and $1,250,000 in allowable expenses from its business. In addition, it receives $300,000 in cash dividends from domestic corporations.

   a. Determine T Corporation's net operating loss.

   b. What would your answer be if T Corporation received dividends in the form of property instead of cash? Assume that the fair market value of such property is $300,000 and its adjusted cost basis to the distributing corporation is only $100,000.

6. During 19X2 T Corporation, a calendar year taxpayer, had the following income and expenses:

Income from operations	$140,000
Expenses from operations	110,000
Dividends from domestic corporations	10,000
NOL carryover from 19X1	3,000

   On May 1, 19X2 T Corporation made a contribution to a qualified charitable organization of $2,500 in cash (not included in any of the items listed above).

   a. Determine T Corporation's deduction for charitable contributions for 19X2.

   b. What happens to any portion of the contribution not deductible in 19X2?

7. XYZ Corporation (an accrual basis corporation) had taxable income of $100,000 during 19X5. Its policy was to make charitable contributions in an amount equal to the maximum allowable for any one year. Thus, no contributions were made during 19X5 since the company could not determine the amount of its 19X5 taxable income until March, 19X6. In December, 19X5 the Board of Directors authorized the accrual of a 19X5 contribution to be paid in 19X6 in an amount equal to the maximum allowable contribution under the tax law. Since XYZ Corporation was short of cash in the early part of 19X6, it signed a pledge card for $5,-000 (the maximum allowable amount) to a qualified charity and made the cash payment in June, 19X6.

   a. What amount, if any, is deductible in 19X5?

   b. What amount is deductible, if any, in 19X6 when the payment was actually made?

8. The T Corporation changed from a calendar year to a fiscal year ending June 30. Taxable income for the short period January 1, 19X1 to June 30, 19X1 was $40,000. Taxable income for the period January 1, 19X1 to December 31, 19X1 was $90,000. Compute T Corporation's tax for the short period.

9. T Corporation had the following income and expenses for 19X2:

Gross income from operations	$300,000
Expenses from operations	340,000
Qualified cash dividends from stock	200,000

   a. Determine T Corporation's dividends received deduction for 19X2.

   b. Suppose the expenses from operations amounted to only $320,000 (instead of $340,000). Determine T Corporation's dividends received deduction for 19X2.

10. T Corporation, an accrual basis taxpayer, was formed and began operations on May 1, 19X2. The following expenses were incurred during its first year of operations (May 1 to December 31, 19X2):

Expenses of temporary directors and of organizational meetings	$ 500
Fee paid to the state for incorporation	100
Accounting services incident to organization	200
Legal services for drafting the corporate charter and bylaws	400
Expenses incident to the printing and sale of stock certificates	300
	$1,500

Assume T Corporation makes an appropriate and timely election under § 248(c) and the Regulations.

    a.   What is the maximum organizational expense T may write-off for the calendar year 19X2?

    b.   What would be the result if a proper election had not been made?

11. XYZ Corporation had tax preferences of $60,000 from excess depreciation on real property. In addition, XYZ had net long-term capital gains of $48,000. Its taxable income was $200,000 during the year.

    a.   Calculate XYZ Corporation's tax preferences.

    b.   Calculate XYZ Corporation's regular and minimum tax liability for the current year.

12. For 19X1 T Corporation, an accrual basis calendar year taxpayer, had net income per books of $59,900 and the following special transactions:

Prepaid rent received in 19X1 (10,000 related to 19X2)	$15,000
Capital loss in excess of capital gains (no carry-back to prior years)	4,000
Interest on loan to carry tax-exempt bonds	3,500
Interest income on tax-exempt bonds	3,000
Accelerated depreciation in excess of straight-line	5,500
Federal income tax liability for 19X1	51,100

Using Schedule M–1 of Form 1120 in Appendix B compute T Corporation's taxable income for 19X1.

13. X and Y formed XY Corporation with the following investment: X transferred property with a fair market value of $50,000 and basis of $30,000 while Y transferred property with a fair market value of $50,000 and adjusted basis of $80,000. X received $50,000 of XY voting stock and Y received $40,000 of XY voting stock and a demand note for $10,000.

    a.   Do the transfers qualify under § 351?

    b.   How much gain or loss is recognized by X? by Y?

    c.   If Y received $10,000 cash instead of the note, would your answer be different?

    d.   Would either X or Y prefer that the transaction be completely taxable? Why?

14. T owns 90 shares of the stock of X Corporation. T's children own the remaining 10 shares. Since T needs cash for personal reasons and the family desires to retain control of the company, 50 of T's shares were redeemed by the corporation during the year for $50,000. X Corporation has earnings and profits of $150,000.

a. Is the redemption treated as a sale or exchange of T's stock? If not, what tax treatment is applicable?

b. Would your answer be different if X Corporation had no earnings and profits?

c. Would your answer be different if all of T's shares were redeemed?

15. X Corporation was liquidated under the general rules of § 331. The company distributed its only asset (land with a fair market value of $100,000 and adjusted cost basis of $40,000) to T, an individual who owned all of the X Corporation stock. T's basis in the stock of X was $40,000. X Corporation had earnings and profits of $10,000 which were accumulated since February 28, 1913.

a. What is the amount and character of gain or loss recognized by T upon the receipt of the land in exchange for his stock?

b. What is T's basis in the land?

c. Assume that a one-month plan of liquidation was elected; calculate the amount and character of T's gain or loss and T's basis in the land.

d. If T were a corporate shareholder and X was liquidated into T, what liquidation section would apply? How much gain or loss would be recognized by T, and what would be T's basis in the land?

16. T Corporation enters into a plan of complete liquidation under § 333—one-month liquidation rules. T Corporation is owned in equal shares by A, B, and C (who is a corporate shareholder). T Corporation has earnings and profits of $60,000 and distributes land with a fair market value of $90,000 (adjusted basis of $40,-000) in equal shares to A, B, and C. Cash and post-1953 securities with a fair market value of $30,000 are also distributed in equal shares to A, B, and C. A's basis in the T stock is $10,000; B's basis is $30,000 and C's basis is $20,000.

a. Are A, B, and/or C Corporation qualified electing shareholders?

b. Calculate the amount of gain recognized, if any, to A, B, and C Corporation.

c. Calculate the basis of the land received by A, B, and C Corporation.

17. On June 30, 19X5, D Corporation, a Subchapter S corporation with a December 31 taxable year end, makes a $100,000 cash distribution. Earnings and profits for 19X5 are $50,000 and pre-19X5 accumulated earnings are $35,000. The total amount of previously taxed income prior to 19X5 equals $10,000. T is the sole shareholder.

    a. Calculate the amount of UTI taxable to T.

    b. Calculate any nontaxable PTI.

    c. Assume that T's basis in her D corporation stock is $12,000 before any distribution of PTI. Calculate any amount taxable as ordinary income and subject to the dividend exclusion.

    d. Calculate any return of capital.

    e. Calculate any capital gain.

18. B owns 50 percent of the stock in a Subchapter S corporation. This corporation sustains a $12,000 net operating loss and a $2,000 capital loss during 19X4. Her adjusted basis in the stock is $2,000, but she has a loan outstanding to the corporation in the amount of $2,000. What amount, if any, is she entitled to deduct with respect to these losses on her Form 1040 in 19X4?

Research Problems

1. A cash basis partnership is incorporated. The newly formed corporation elects the cash method of accounting. The partnership transfers $30,000 of accounts receivable along with equipment, land, and cash. The corporation also agrees to pay accounts payable of the partnership in the amount of $40,000. The corporation files its return for its first year of operation and does not report the $30,000 received on accounts receivable of the partnership as income. It does deduct the $40,000 it paid on the partnership's accounts payable. The IRS disallows the deductions totaling $40,000 and increases the corporation's taxable income by $30,000 which represents the collection of partnership accounts receivable. What result?

2. A, a wealthy farmer, wants to take advantage of gift tax exclusions and gives some of his property to his children. He decided to incorporate his farm operation in order to donate the property to his children more easily in the form of shares of stock. He transfers his property to a newly formed corporation for 100 percent of the stock. He gives 30 percent of the stock to his children immediately upon receipt. The IRS asserts, upon audit, that A is taxed on the initial transfer of property to the corporation because he failed to gain control of 80 percent of the stock. What result?

Partial list of research aids:

    Fahs v. Florida Machine and Foundry Co., 48–2 USTC ¶ 9329, 36 AFTR 1151, 168 F.2d 957 (CA–5, 1948).

    John C. O'Connor, 16 TCM 213, T.C.Memo. 1957–50. Rev.Rul. 54–96, 1954–1 C.B. 111.

*

APPENDIX A
TAX RATE SCHEDULES AND TABLES

567

A-1 1977 INCOME TAX RATE SCHEDULES

If you cannot use one of the Tax Tables, figure your tax on the amount on Schedule TC, Part I, line 3, by using the appropriate Tax Rate Schedule on this page. Enter tax on Schedule TC, Part I, line 4.

Note: Your zero bracket amount has been built into these Tax Rate Schedules.

1977 Tax Rate Schedules

SCHEDULE X—Single Taxpayers Not Qualifying for Rates in Schedule Y or Z

Use this schedule if you checked **Box 1** on Form 1040—

If the amount on Schedule TC, Part I, line 3, is:

Enter on Schedule TC, Part I, line 4:

Not over $2,200..........-0-

Over—	But not over—		of the amount over—
$2,200	$2,700	14%	$2,200
$2,700	$3,200	$70+15%	$2,700
$3,200	$3,700	$145+16%	$3,200
$3,700	$4,200	$225+17%	$3,700
$4,200	$6,200	$310+19%	$4,200
$6,200	$8,200	$690+21%	$6,200
$8,200	$10,200	$1,110+24%	$8,200
$10,200	$12,200	$1,590+25%	$10,200
$12,200	$14,200	$2,090+27%	$12,200
$14,200	$16,200	$2,630+29%	$14,200
$16,200	$18,200	$3,210+31%	$16,200
$18,200	$20,200	$3,830+34%	$18,200
$20,200	$22,200	$4,510+36%	$20,200
$22,200	$24,200	$5,230+38%	$22,200
$24,200	$28,200	$5,990+40%	$24,200
$28,200	$34,200	$7,590+45%	$28,200
$34,200	$40,200	$10,290+50%	$34,200
$40,200	$46,200	$13,290+55%	$40,200
$46,200	$52,200	$16,590+60%	$46,200
$52,200	$62,200	$20,190+62%	$52,200
$62,200	$72,200	$26,390+64%	$62,200
$72,200	$82,200	$32,790+66%	$72,200
$82,200	$92,200	$39,390+68%	$82,200
$92,200	$102,200	$46,190+69%	$92,200
$102,200	....	$53,090+70%	$102,200

SCHEDULE Y—Married Taxpayers and Qualifying Widows and Widowers

If you are a married person living apart from your spouse, see page 7 of the instructions to see if you can be considered to be "unmarried" for purposes of using Schedule X or Z.

Married Filing Joint Returns and Qualifying Widows and Widowers

Use this schedule if you checked **Box 2 or Box 5** on Form 1040—

If the amount on Schedule TC, Part I, line 3, is:

Enter on Schedule TC, Part I, line 4:

Not over $3,200..........-0-

Over—	But not over—		of the amount over—
$3,200	$4,200	14%	$3,200
$4,200	$5,200	$140+15%	$4,200
$5,200	$6,200	$290+16%	$5,200
$6,200	$7,200	$450+17%	$6,200
$7,200	$11,200	$620+19%	$7,200
$11,200	$15,200	$1,380+22%	$11,200
$15,200	$19,200	$2,260+25%	$15,200
$19,200	$23,200	$3,260+28%	$19,200
$23,200	$27,200	$4,380+32%	$23,200
$27,200	$31,200	$5,660+36%	$27,200
$31,200	$35,200	$7,100+39%	$31,200
$35,200	$39,200	$8,660+42%	$35,200
$39,200	$43,200	$10,340+45%	$39,200
$43,200	$47,200	$12,140+48%	$43,200
$47,200	$55,200	$14,060+50%	$47,200
$55,200	$67,200	$18,060+53%	$55,200
$67,200	$79,200	$24,420+55%	$67,200
$79,200	$91,200	$31,020+58%	$79,200
$91,200	$103,200	$37,980+60%	$91,200
$103,200	$123,200	$45,180+62%	$103,200
$123,200	$143,200	$57,580+64%	$123,200
$143,200	$163,200	$70,380+66%	$143,200
$163,200	$183,200	$83,580+68%	$163,200
$183,200	$203,200	$97,180+69%	$183,200
$203,200	....	$110,980+70%	$203,200

Married Filing Separate Returns

Use this schedule if you checked **Box 3** on Form 1040—

If the amount on Schedule TC, Part I, line 3, is:

Enter on Schedule TC, Part I, line 4:

Not over $1,600..........-0-

Over—	But not over—		of the amount over—
$1,600	$2,100	14%	$1,600
$2,100	$2,600	$70+15%	$2,100
$2,600	$3,100	$145+16%	$2,600
$3,100	$3,600	$225+17%	$3,100
$3,600	$5,600	$310+19%	$3,600
$5,600	$7,600	$690+22%	$5,600
$7,600	$9,600	$1,130+25%	$7,600
$9,600	$11,600	$1,630+28%	$9,600
$11,600	$13,600	$2,190+32%	$11,600
$13,600	$15,600	$2,830+36%	$13,600
$15,600	$17,600	$3,550+39%	$15,600
$17,600	$19,600	$4,330+42%	$17,600
$19,600	$21,600	$5,170+45%	$19,600
$21,600	$23,600	$6,070+48%	$21,600
$23,600	$27,600	$7,030+50%	$23,600
$27,600	$33,600	$9,030+53%	$27,600
$33,600	$39,600	$12,210+55%	$33,600
$39,600	$45,600	$15,510+58%	$39,600
$45,600	$51,600	$18,990+60%	$45,600
$51,600	$61,600	$22,590+62%	$51,600
$61,600	$71,600	$28,790+64%	$61,600
$71,600	$81,600	$35,190+66%	$71,600
$81,600	$91,600	$41,790+68%	$81,600
$91,600	$101,600	$48,590+69%	$91,600
$101,600	....	$55,490+70%	$101,600

SCHEDULE Z—Unmarried or legally separated taxpayers Who Qualify as Heads of Household

Use this schedule if you checked **Box 4** on Form 1040—

If the amount on Schedule TC, Part I, line 3, is:

Enter on Schedule TC, Part I, line 4:

Not over $2,200..........-0-

Over—	But not over—		of the amount over—
$2,200	$3,200	14%	$2,200
$3,200	$4,200	$140+16%	$3,200
$4,200	$6,200	$300+18%	$4,200
$6,200	$8,200	$660+19%	$6,200
$8,200	$10,200	$1,040+22%	$8,200
$10,200	$12,200	$1,480+23%	$10,200
$12,200	$14,200	$1,940+25%	$12,200
$14,200	$16,200	$2,440+27%	$14,200
$16,200	$18,200	$2,980+28%	$16,200
$18,200	$20,200	$3,540+31%	$18,200
$20,200	$22,200	$4,160+32%	$20,200
$22,200	$24,200	$4,800+35%	$22,200
$24,200	$26,200	$5,500+36%	$24,200
$26,200	$28,200	$6,220+38%	$26,200
$28,200	$30,200	$6,980+41%	$28,200
$30,200	$34,200	$7,800+42%	$30,200
$34,200	$38,200	$9,480+45%	$34,200
$38,200	$40,200	$11,280+48%	$38,200
$40,200	$42,200	$12,240+51%	$40,200
$42,200	$46,200	$13,260+52%	$42,200
$46,200	$52,200	$15,340+55%	$46,200
$52,200	$54,200	$18,640+56%	$52,200
$54,200	$66,200	$19,760+58%	$54,200
$66,200	$72,200	$26,720+59%	$66,200
$72,200	$78,200	$30,260+61%	$72,200
$78,200	$82,200	$33,920+62%	$78,200
$82,200	$90,200	$36,400+63%	$82,200
$90,200	$102,200	$41,440+64%	$90,200
$102,200	$122,200	$49,120+66%	$102,200
$122,200	$142,200	$62,320+67%	$122,200
$142,200	$162,200	$75,720+68%	$142,200
$162,200	$182,200	$89,320+69%	$162,200
$182,200	....	$103,120+70%	$182,200

A–2 1977 INCOME TAX TABLES

1977 Tax Table A—SINGLE (Box 1)

(For single persons with tax table income of $20,000 or less who claim fewer than 4 exemptions)

To find your tax: Read down the left income column until you find your income as shown on line 34 of Form 1040. Read across to the column headed by the total number of exemptions claimed on line 7 of Form 1040. The amount shown at the point where the two lines meet is your tax. Enter on Form 1040, line 35.

The $2,200 zero bracket amount, your deduction for exemptions and the general tax credit have been taken into account in figuring the tax shown in this table. **Do not take a separate deduction for them.**

Caution: *If you can be claimed as a dependent on your parent's return* **AND** *you have unearned income (interest, dividends, etc.) of $750 or more* **AND** *your earned income is less than $2,200, you must first use Schedule TC (Form 1040), Part II.*

If line 34, Form 1040 is—		And the total number of exemptions claimed on line 7 is—		
Over	But not over	1	2	3
		Your tax is—		
If $3,200 or less your tax is 0				
3,200	3,250	4	0	0
3,250	3,300	11	0	0
3,300	3,350	18	0	0
3,350	3,400	25	0	0
3,400	3,450	32	0	0
3,450	3,500	39	0	0
3,500	3,550	46	0	0
3,550	3,600	54	0	0
3,600	3,650	61	0	0
3,650	3,700	69	0	0
3,700	3,750	76	0	0
3,750	3,800	84	0	0
3,800	3,850	91	0	0
3,850	3,900	99	0	0
3,900	3,950	106	0	0
3,950	4,000	114	0	0
4,000	4,050	122	0	0
4,050	4,100	130	0	0
4,100	4,150	138	0	0
4,150	4,200	146	0	0
4,200	4,250	154	4	0
4,250	4,300	162	11	0
4,300	4,350	170	19	0
4,350	4,400	178	26	0
4,400	4,450	186	34	0
4,450	4,500	194	41	0
4,500	4,550	203	49	0
4,550	4,600	211	56	0
4,600	4,650	220	64	0
4,650	4,700	228	71	0
4,700	4,750	236	79	0
4,750	4,800	244	87	0
4,800	4,850	251	95	0
4,850	4,900	259	103	0
4,900	4,950	266	111	0
4,950	5,000	274	119	0
5,000	5,050	283	127	0
5,050	5,100	291	135	0
5,100	5,150	300	143	0
5,150	5,200	308	151	0
5,200	5,250	317	159	6
5,250	5,300	325	168	14
5,300	5,350	334	176	21
5,350	5,400	342	185	29
5,400	5,450	351	193	36
5,450	5,500	359	202	44
5,500	5,550	368	210	52
5,550	5,600	376	219	60
5,600	5,650	385	227	68
5,650	5,700	393	236	76
5,700	5,750	402	245	84
5,750	5,800	410	254	92
5,800	5,850	419	264	100
5,850	5,900	427	273	108
5,900	5,950	436	283	116
5,950	6,000	444	292	124
6,000	6,050	453	302	133
6,050	6,100	461	311	141
6,100	6,150	470	321	150
6,150	6,200	478	330	158
6,200	6,250	487	340	167
6,250	6,300	495	349	175
6,300	6,350	504	359	184
6,350	6,400	512	368	192
6,400	6,450	521	378	201
6,450	6,500	529	387	210
6,500	6,550	538	397	219
6,550	6,600	546	406	229
6,600	6,650	555	416	238
6,650	6,700	563	425	248
6,700	6,750	572	435	257
6,750	6,800	580	444	267
6,800	6,850	589	454	276
6,850	6,900	597	463	286
6,900	6,950	606	473	295
6,950	7,000	615	482	305
7,000	7,050	624	492	314
7,050	7,100	634	501	324
7,100	7,150	643	511	333
7,150	7,200	653	520	343
7,200	7,250	662	529	352
7,250	7,300	672	538	362
7,300	7,350	681	546	371
7,350	7,400	691	555	381
7,400	7,450	700	563	390
7,450	7,500	710	572	400
7,500	7,550	719	580	409
7,550	7,600	729	589	419
7,600	7,650	738	597	428
7,650	7,700	748	606	438
7,700	7,750	757	615	447
7,750	7,800	767	624	457
7,800	7,850	776	634	466
7,850	7,900	786	643	476
7,900	7,950	795	653	485
7,950	8,000	805	662	495
8,000	8,050	814	672	504
8,050	8,100	824	681	514
8,100	8,150	833	691	523
8,150	8,200	843	700	533
8,200	8,250	852	710	542
8,250	8,300	862	719	552
8,300	8,350	871	729	561
8,350	8,400	881	738	571
8,400	8,450	890	748	580
8,450	8,500	900	757	590
8,500	8,550	909	767	601
8,550	8,600	919	776	611
8,600	8,650	928	786	622
8,650	8,700	938	795	632
8,700	8,750	947	805	643
8,750	8,800	957	814	653
8,800	8,850	966	824	664
8,850	8,900	976	833	674
8,900	8,950	985	843	685
8,950	9,000	996	852	695
9,000	9,050	1,007	862	706
9,050	9,100	1,018	871	716
9,100	9,150	1,029	881	727
9,150	9,200	1,040	890	737
9,200	9,250	1,051	900	748
9,250	9,300	1,062	909	758
9,300	9,350	1,073	919	769
9,350	9,400	1,084	928	779
9,400	9,450	1,095	938	790
9,450	9,500	1,106	947	800
9,500	9,550	1,117	957	811
9,550	9,600	1,128	966	821
9,600	9,650	1,139	976	832
9,650	9,700	1,150	985	842
9,700	9,750	1,161	996	852
9,750	9,800	1,172	1,007	862
9,800	9,850	1,183	1,018	871
9,850	9,900	1,194	1,029	881
9,900	9,950	1,205	1,040	890
9,950	10,000	1,216	1,051	900
10,000	10,050	1,227	1,062	909
10,050	10,100	1,238	1,073	919
10,100	10,150	1,249	1,084	928
10,150	10,200	1,260	1,095	938
10,200	10,250	1,271	1,106	947
10,250	10,300	1,282	1,117	957
10,300	10,350	1,293	1,128	966
10,350	10,400	1,304	1,139	976
10,400	10,450	1,315	1,150	985
10,450	10,500	1,326	1,161	996
10,500	10,550	1,337	1,172	1,007
10,550	10,600	1,348	1,183	1,018
10,600	10,650	1,359	1,194	1,029
10,650	10,700	1,370	1,205	1,040
10,700	10,750	1,381	1,216	1,051
10,750	10,800	1,392	1,227	1,062
10,800	10,850	1,403	1,238	1,073
10,850	10,900	1,414	1,249	1,084
10,900	10,950	1,425	1,260	1,095
10,950	11,000	1,436	1,271	1,106

Continued next column

Continued next column

Continued on next page

1977 Tax Table A—SINGLE (Box 1) (Continued)

(If your income or exemptions are not covered, use Schedule TC (Form 1040), Part I to figure your tax)

If line 34, Form 1040 is— Over	But not over	1	2	3	If line 34, Form 1040 is— Over	But not over	1	2	3	If line 34, Form 1040 is— Over	But not over	1	2	3
		Your tax is—					Your tax is—					Your tax is—		
11,000	11,050	1,447	1,282	1,117	14,000	14,050	2,200	1,998	1,804	17,000	17,050	3,053	2,834	2,617
11,050	11,100	1,459	1,293	1,128	14,050	14,100	2,214	2,011	1,816	17,050	17,100	3,069	2,849	2,631
11,100	11,150	1,470	1,304	1,139	14,100	14,150	2,227	2,025	1,829	17,100	17,150	3,084	2,863	2,646
11,150	11,200	1,482	1,315	1,150	14,150	14,200	2,241	2,038	1,841	17,150	17,200	3,100	2,878	2,660
11,200	11,250	1,493	1,326	1,161	14,200	14,250	2,254	2,052	1,854	17,200	17,250	3,115	2,892	2,675
11,250	11,300	1,505	1,337	1,172	14,250	14,300	2,268	2,065	1,866	17,250	17,300	3,131	2,907	2,689
11,300	11,350	1,516	1,348	1,183	14,300	14,350	2,281	2,079	1,879	17,300	17,350	3,146	2,921	2,704
11,350	11,400	1,528	1,359	1,194	14,350	14,400	2,295	2,092	1,891	17,350	17,400	3,162	2,936	2,718
11,400	11,450	1,539	1,370	1,205	14,400	14,450	2,308	2,106	1,904	17,400	17,450	3,177	2,950	2,733
11,450	11,500	1,551	1,381	1,216	14,450	14,500	2,322	2,119	1,917	17,450	17,500	3,193	2,965	2,747
11,500	11,550	1,562	1,392	1,227	14,500	14,550	2,335	2,133	1,930	17,500	17,550	3,208	2,979	2,762
11,550	11,600	1,574	1,403	1,238	14,550	14,600	2,349	2,146	1,944	17,550	17,600	3,224	2,994	2,776
11,600	11,650	1,585	1,414	1,249	14,600	14,650	2,362	2,160	1,957	17,600	17,650	3,239	3,008	2,791
11,650	11,700	1,597	1,425	1,260	14,650	14,700	2,376	2,173	1,971	17,650	17,700	3,255	3,023	2,805
11,700	11,750	1,608	1,436	1,271	14,700	14,750	2,389	2,187	1,984	17,700	17,750	3,270	3,038	2,820
11,750	11,800	1,620	1,447	1,282	14,750	14,800	2,403	2,200	1,998	17,750	17,800	3,286	3,053	2,834
11,800	11,850	1,631	1,459	1,293	14,800	14,850	2,416	2,214	2,011	17,800	17,850	3,301	3,069	2,849
11,850	11,900	1,643	1,470	1,304	14,850	14,900	2,430	2,227	2,025	17,850	17,900	3,317	3,084	2,863
11,900	11,950	1,654	1,482	1,315	14,900	14,950	2,443	2,241	2,038	17,900	17,950	3,332	3,100	2,878
11,950	12,000	1,666	1,493	1,326	14,950	15,000	2,457	2,254	2,052	17,950	18,000	3,348	3,115	2,892
12,000	12,050	1,679	1,505	1,337	15,000	15,050	2,472	2,268	2,065	18,000	18,050	3,363	3,131	2,907
12,050	12,100	1,691	1,516	1,348	15,050	15,100	2,486	2,281	2,079	18,050	18,100	3,379	3,146	2,921
12,100	12,150	1,704	1,528	1,359	15,100	15,150	2,501	2,295	2,092	18,100	18,150	3,394	3,162	2,936
12,150	12,200	1,716	1,539	1,370	15,150	15,200	2,515	2,308	2,106	18,150	18,200	3,410	3,177	2,950
12,200	12,250	1,729	1,551	1,381	15,200	15,250	2,530	2,322	2,119	18,200	18,250	3,425	3,193	2,965
12,250	12,300	1,741	1,562	1,392	15,250	15,300	2,544	2,335	2,133	18,250	18,300	3,441	3,208	2,979
12,300	12,350	1,754	1,574	1,403	15,300	15,350	2,559	2,349	2,146	18,300	18,350	3,456	3,224	2,994
12,350	12,400	1,766	1,585	1,414	15,350	15,400	2,573	2,362	2,160	18,350	18,400	3,472	3,239	3,008
12,400	12,450	1,779	1,597	1,425	15,400	15,450	2,588	2,376	2,173	18,400	18,450	3,487	3,255	3,023
12,450	12,500	1,791	1,608	1,436	15,450	15,500	2,602	2,389	2,187	18,450	18,500	3,503	3,270	3,038
12,500	12,550	1,804	1,620	1,447	15,500	15,550	2,617	2,403	2,200	18,500	18,550	3,518	3,286	3,053
12,550	12,600	1,816	1,631	1,459	15,550	15,600	2,631	2,416	2,214	18,550	18,600	3,534	3,301	3,069
12,600	12,650	1,829	1,643	1,470	15,600	15,650	2,646	2,430	2,227	18,600	18,650	3,549	3,317	3,084
12,650	12,700	1,841	1,654	1,482	15,650	15,700	2,660	2,443	2,241	18,650	18,700	3,565	3,332	3,100
12,700	12,750	1,854	1,666	1,493	15,700	15,750	2,675	2,457	2,254	18,700	18,750	3,580	3,348	3,115
12,750	12,800	1,866	1,679	1,505	15,750	15,800	2,689	2,472	2,268	18,750	18,800	3,596	3,363	3,131
12,800	12,850	1,879	1,691	1,516	15,800	15,850	2,704	2,486	2,281	18,800	18,850	3,611	3,379	3,146
12,850	12,900	1,891	1,704	1,528	15,850	15,900	2,718	2,501	2,295	18,850	18,900	3,627	3,394	3,162
12,900	12,950	1,904	1,716	1,539	15,900	15,950	2,733	2,515	2,308	18,900	18,950	3,642	3,410	3,177
12,950	13,000	1,917	1,729	1,551	15,950	16,000	2,747	2,530	2,322	18,950	19,000	3,659	3,425	3,193
13,000	13,050	1,930	1,741	1,562	16,000	16,050	2,762	2,544	2,335	19,000	19,050	3,676	3,441	3,208
13,050	13,100	1,944	1,754	1,574	16,050	16,100	2,776	2,559	2,349	19,050	19,100	3,693	3,456	3,224
13,100	13,150	1,957	1,766	1,585	16,100	16,150	2,791	2,573	2,362	19,100	19,150	3,710	3,472	3,239
13,150	13,200	1,971	1,779	1,597	16,150	16,200	2,805	2,588	2,376	19,150	19,200	3,727	3,487	3,255
13,200	13,250	1,984	1,791	1,608	16,200	16,250	2,820	2,602	2,389	19,200	19,250	3,744	3,503	3,270
13,250	13,300	1,998	1,804	1,620	16,250	16,300	2,834	2,617	2,403	19,250	19,300	3,761	3,518	3,286
13,300	13,350	2,011	1,816	1,631	16,300	16,350	2,849	2,631	2,416	19,300	19,350	3,778	3,534	3,301
13,350	13,400	2,025	1,829	1,643	16,350	16,400	2,863	2,646	2,430	19,350	19,400	3,795	3,549	3,317
13,400	13,450	2,038	1,841	1,654	16,400	16,450	2,878	2,660	2,443	19,400	19,450	3,812	3,565	3,332
13,450	13,500	2,052	1,854	1,666	16,450	16,500	2,892	2,675	2,457	19,450	19,500	3,829	3,580	3,348
13,500	13,550	2,065	1,866	1,679	16,500	16,550	2,907	2,689	2,472	19,500	19,550	3,846	3,596	3,363
13,550	13,600	2,079	1,879	1,691	16,550	16,600	2,921	2,704	2,486	19,550	19,600	3,863	3,611	3,379
13,600	13,650	2,092	1,891	1,704	16,600	16,650	2,936	2,718	2,501	19,600	19,650	3,880	3,627	3,394
13,650	13,700	2,106	1,904	1,716	16,650	16,700	2,950	2,733	2,515	19,650	19,700	3,897	3,642	3,410
13,700	13,750	2,119	1,917	1,729	16,700	16,750	2,965	2,747	2,530	19,700	19,750	3,914	3,659	3,425
13,750	13,800	2,133	1,930	1,741	16,750	16,800	2,979	2,762	2,544	19,750	19,800	3,931	3,676	3,441
13,800	13,850	2,146	1,944	1,754	16,800	16,850	2,994	2,776	2,559	19,800	19,850	3,948	3,693	3,456
13,850	13,900	2,160	1,957	1,766	16,850	16,900	3,008	2,791	2,573	19,850	19,900	3,965	3,710	3,472
13,900	13,950	2,173	1,971	1,779	16,900	16,950	3,023	2,805	2,588	19,900	19,950	3,982	3,727	3,487
13,950	14,000	2,187	1,984	1,791	16,950	17,000	3,038	2,820	2,602	19,950	20,000	3,999	3,744	3,503

Continued next column   Continued next column

1977 Tax Table B—MARRIED FILING JOINTLY (Box 2) and QUALIFYING WIDOW(ER)S (Box 5)

(For married persons filing joint returns or qualifying widow(er)s with tax table income of $40,000 or less who claim fewer than 10 exemptions)

To find your tax: Read down the left income column until you find your income as shown on line 34 of Form 1040. Read across to the column headed by the total number of exemptions claimed on line 7 of Form 1040. The amount shown at the point where the two lines meet is your tax. Enter on Form 1040, line 35.

The $3,200 zero bracket amount, your deduction for exemptions and the general tax credit have been taken into account in figuring the tax shown in this table. **Do not take a separate deduction for them.**

If line 34, Form 1040 is—		And the total number of exemptions claimed on line 7 is—								If line 34, Form 1040 is—		And the total number of exemptions claimed on line 7 is—							
Over	But not over	2	3	4	5	6	7	8	9	Over	But not over	2	3	4	5	6	7	8	9
		Your tax is—										Your tax is—							
If $5,200 or less your tax is 0										8,400	8,450	499	341	186	36	0	0	0	0
5,200	5,250	4	0	0	0	0	0	0	0	8,450	8,500	506	349	194	44	0	0	0	0
5,250	5,300	11	0	0	0	0	0	0	0	8,500	8,550	514	358	202	51	0	0	0	0
5,300	5,350	18	0	0	0	0	0	0	0	8,550	8,600	521	366	210	59	0	0	0	0
5,350	5,400	25	0	0	0	0	0	0	0	8,600	8,650	529	375	218	66	0	0	0	0
5,400	5,450	32	0	0	0	0	0	0	0	8,650	8,700	536	383	226	74	0	0	0	0
5,450	5,500	39	0	0	0	0	0	0	0	8,700	8,750	544	392	234	81	0	0	0	0
5,500	5,550	46	0	0	0	0	0	0	0	8,750	8,800	553	400	242	89	0	0	0	0
5,550	5,600	53	0	0	0	0	0	0	0	8,800	8,850	561	409	250	96	0	0	0	0
5,600	5,650	60	0	0	0	0	0	0	0	8,850	8,900	570	417	258	104	0	0	0	0
5,650	5,700	67	0	0	0	0	0	0	0	8,900	8,950	578	426	266	111	0	0	0	0
5,700	5,750	74	0	0	0	0	0	0	0	8,950	9,000	587	434	274	119	0	0	0	0
5,750	5,800	81	0	0	0	0	0	0	0	9,000	9,050	595	443	282	127	0	0	0	0
5,800	5,850	89	0	0	0	0	0	0	0	9,050	9,100	604	451	290	135	0	0	0	0
5,850	5,900	96	0	0	0	0	0	0	0	9,100	9,150	612	460	298	143	0	0	0	0
5,900	5,950	104	0	0	0	0	0	0	0	9,150	9,200	621	468	306	151	1	0	0	0
5,950	6,000	111	0	0	0	0	0	0	0	9,200	9,250	629	477	314	159	9	0	0	0
6,000	6,050	119	0	0	0	0	0	0	0	9,250	9,300	638	485	323	167	16	0	0	0
6,050	6,100	126	0	0	0	0	0	0	0	9,300	9,350	646	494	331	175	24	0	0	0
6,100	6,150	134	0	0	0	0	0	0	0	9,350	9,400	655	502	340	183	31	0	0	0
6,150	6,200	141	0	0	0	0	0	0	0	9,400	9,450	663	511	348	191	39	0	0	0
6,200	6,250	149	4	0	0	0	0	0	0	9,450	9,500	672	520	357	199	46	0	0	0
6,250	6,300	156	11	0	0	0	0	0	0	9,500	9,550	680	529	365	207	54	0	0	0
6,300	6,350	164	18	0	0	0	0	0	0	9,550	9,600	689	539	374	215	61	0	0	0
6,350	6,400	171	25	0	0	0	0	0	0	9,600	9,650	697	548	382	223	69	0	0	0
6,400	6,450	179	32	0	0	0	0	0	0	9,650	9,700	706	558	391	231	76	0	0	0
6,450	6,500	186	39	0	0	0	0	0	0	9,700	9,750	714	567	399	239	84	0	0	0
6,500	6,550	194	46	0	0	0	0	0	0	9,750	9,800	723	577	408	247	92	0	0	0
6,550	6,600	201	54	0	0	0	0	0	0	9,800	9,850	731	586	416	255	100	0	0	0
6,600	6,650	209	61	0	0	0	0	0	0	9,850	9,900	740	596	425	263	108	0	0	0
6,650	6,700	216	69	0	0	0	0	0	0	9,900	9,950	748	605	433	271	116	0	0	0
6,700	6,750	224	76	0	0	0	0	0	0	9,950	10,000	757	615	442	279	124	0	0	0
6,750	6,800	232	84	0	0	0	0	0	0	10,000	10,050	765	624	450	288	132	0	0	0
6,800	6,850	240	91	0	0	0	0	0	0	10,050	10,100	774	634	459	296	140	0	0	0
6,850	6,900	248	99	0	0	0	0	0	0	10,100	10,150	782	643	467	305	148	0	0	0
6,900	6,950	256	106	0	0	0	0	0	0	10,150	10,200	791	653	476	313	156	4	0	0
6,950	7,000	264	114	0	0	0	0	0	0	10,200	10,250	799	662	485	322	164	11	0	0
7,000	7,050	272	121	0	0	0	0	0	0	10,250	10,300	808	672	494	330	172	19	0	0
7,050	7,100	280	129	0	0	0	0	0	0	10,300	10,350	816	681	504	339	180	26	0	0
7,100	7,150	288	136	0	0	0	0	0	0	10,350	10,400	825	691	513	347	188	34	0	0
7,150	7,200	296	144	0	0	0	0	0	0	10,400	10,450	833	700	523	356	196	41	0	0
7,200	7,250	304	151	4	0	0	0	0	0	10,450	10,500	842	710	532	364	204	49	0	0
7,250	7,300	312	159	11	0	0	0	0	0	10,500	10,550	850	719	542	373	212	57	0	0
7,300	7,350	320	166	19	0	0	0	0	0	10,550	10,600	859	729	551	381	220	65	0	0
7,350	7,400	328	174	26	0	0	0	0	0	10,600	10,650	867	738	561	390	228	73	0	0
7,400	7,450	336	181	34	0	0	0	0	0	10,650	10,700	876	748	570	398	236	81	0	0
7,450	7,500	344	189	41	0	0	0	0	0	10,700	10,750	884	757	580	407	244	89	0	0
7,500	7,550	352	197	49	0	0	0	0	0	10,750	10,800	893	765	589	415	253	97	0	0
7,550	7,600	360	205	56	0	0	0	0	0	10,800	10,850	901	774	599	424	261	105	0	0
7,600	7,650	368	213	64	0	0	0	0	0	10,850	10,900	910	782	608	432	270	113	0	0
7,650	7,700	376	221	71	0	0	0	0	0	10,900	10,950	918	791	618	441	278	121	0	0
7,700	7,750	384	229	79	0	0	0	0	0	10,950	11,000	927	799	627	450	287	129	0	0
7,750	7,800	393	237	86	0	0	0	0	0	11,000	11,050	935	808	637	459	295	137	0	0
7,800	7,850	401	245	94	0	0	0	0	0	11,050	11,100	944	816	646	469	304	145	0	0
7,850	7,900	410	253	101	0	0	0	0	0	11,100	11,150	952	825	656	478	312	153	0	0
7,900	7,950	418	261	109	0	0	0	0	0	11,150	11,200	961	833	665	488	321	161	6	0
7,950	8,000	427	269	116	0	0	0	0	0	11,200	11,250	969	842	675	497	329	169	14	0
8,000	8,050	435	277	124	0	0	0	0	0	11,250	11,300	978	850	684	507	338	177	22	0
8,050	8,100	444	285	131	0	0	0	0	0	11,300	11,350	986	859	694	516	346	185	30	0
8,100	8,150	452	293	139	0	0	0	0	0	11,350	11,400	995	867	703	526	355	193	38	0
8,150	8,200	461	301	146	0	0	0	0	0	11,400	11,450	1,003	876	713	535	363	201	46	0
8,200	8,250	469	309	154	6	0	0	0	0	11,450	11,500	1,012	884	722	545	372	209	54	0
8,250	8,300	476	317	162	14	0	0	0	0	11,500	11,550	1,020	893	732	554	380	218	62	0
8,300	8,350	484	325	170	21	0	0	0	0	11,550	11,600	1,029	901	741	564	389	226	70	0
8,350	8,400	491	333	178	29	0	0	0	0										

Continued next column   Continued on next page

1977 Tax Table B—MARRIED FILING JOINTLY (Box 2) and QUALIFYING WIDOW(ER)S (Box 5)
(Continued)

(If your income or exemptions are not covered, use Schedule TC (Form 1040), Part I to figure your tax)

If line 34, Form 1040 is— Over	But not over	And the total number of exemptions claimed on line 7 is— 2	3	4	5	6	7	8	9
		Your tax is—							
11,600	11,650	1,037	910	751	573	397	235	78	0
11,650	11,700	1,046	918	760	583	406	243	86	0
11,700	11,750	1,054	927	770	592	415	252	94	0
11,750	11,800	1,063	935	779	602	424	260	102	0
11,800	11,850	1,071	944	789	611	434	269	110	0
11,850	11,900	1,080	952	798	621	443	277	118	0
11,900	11,950	1,088	961	808	630	453	286	126	0
11,950	12,000	1,097	969	817	640	462	294	134	0
12,000	12,050	1,105	978	827	649	472	303	142	0
12,050	12,100	1,114	986	836	659	481	311	150	0
12,100	12,150	1,122	995	846	668	491	320	158	3
12,150	12,200	1,131	1,003	855	678	500	328	166	11
12,200	12,250	1,139	1,012	865	687	510	337	174	19
12,250	12,300	1,148	1,020	874	697	519	345	183	27
12,300	12,350	1,156	1,029	884	706	529	354	191	35
12,350	12,400	1,165	1,037	893	716	538	362	200	43
12,400	12,450	1,173	1,046	903	725	548	371	208	51
12,450	12,500	1,182	1,054	912	735	557	380	217	59
12,500	12,550	1,190	1,063	922	744	567	389	225	67
12,550	12,600	1,199	1,071	931	754	576	399	234	75
12,600	12,650	1,207	1,080	941	763	586	408	242	83
12,650	12,700	1,216	1,088	950	773	595	418	251	91
12,700	12,750	1,225	1,097	960	782	605	427	259	99
12,750	12,800	1,235	1,105	969	792	614	437	268	107
12,800	12,850	1,245	1,114	979	801	624	446	276	115
12,850	12,900	1,255	1,122	988	811	633	456	285	123
12,900	12,950	1,265	1,131	998	820	643	465	293	131
12,950	13,000	1,275	1,139	1,007	830	652	475	302	139
13,000	13,050	1,285	1,148	1,017	839	662	484	310	148
13,050	13,100	1,295	1,156	1,026	849	671	494	319	156
13,100	13,150	1,305	1,165	1,036	858	681	503	327	165
13,150	13,200	1,315	1,173	1,045	868	690	513	336	173
13,200	13,250	1,325	1,182	1,054	877	700	522	345	182
13,250	13,300	1,335	1,190	1,063	887	709	532	354	190
13,300	13,350	1,345	1,199	1,071	896	719	541	364	199
13,350	13,400	1,355	1,207	1,080	906	728	551	373	207
13,400	13,450	1,365	1,216	1,088	915	738	560	383	216
13,450	13,500	1,375	1,225	1,097	925	747	570	392	224
13,500	13,550	1,385	1,235	1,105	934	757	579	402	233
13,550	13,600	1,395	1,245	1,114	944	766	589	411	241
13,600	13,650	1,405	1,255	1,122	953	776	598	421	250
13,650	13,700	1,415	1,265	1,131	963	785	608	430	258
13,700	13,750	1,426	1,275	1,139	972	795	617	440	267
13,750	13,800	1,437	1,285	1,148	982	804	627	449	275
13,800	13,850	1,448	1,295	1,156	991	814	636	459	284
13,850	13,900	1,459	1,305	1,165	1,001	823	646	468	292
13,900	13,950	1,470	1,315	1,173	1,010	833	655	478	301
13,950	14,000	1,481	1,325	1,182	1,020	842	665	487	310
14,000	14,050	1,492	1,335	1,190	1,029	852	674	497	319
14,050	14,100	1,503	1,345	1,199	1,039	861	684	506	329
14,100	14,150	1,514	1,355	1,207	1,048	871	693	516	338
14,150	14,200	1,525	1,365	1,216	1,058	880	703	525	348
14,200	14,250	1,536	1,375	1,225	1,067	890	712	535	357
14,250	14,300	1,547	1,385	1,235	1,077	899	722	544	367
14,300	14,350	1,558	1,395	1,245	1,086	909	731	554	376
14,350	14,400	1,569	1,405	1,255	1,096	918	741	563	386
14,400	14,450	1,580	1,415	1,265	1,105	928	750	573	395
14,450	14,500	1,591	1,426	1,275	1,115	937	760	582	405
14,500	14,550	1,602	1,437	1,285	1,124	947	769	592	414
14,550	14,600	1,613	1,448	1,295	1,134	956	779	601	424
14,600	14,650	1,624	1,459	1,305	1,143	966	788	611	433
14,650	14,700	1,635	1,470	1,315	1,153	975	798	620	443
14,700	14,750	1,646	1,481	1,325	1,162	985	807	630	452
14,750	14,800	1,657	1,492	1,335	1,172	994	817	639	462
14,800	14,850	1,668	1,503	1,345	1,181	1,004	826	649	471
14,850	14,900	1,679	1,514	1,355	1,191	1,013	836	658	481
14,900	14,950	1,690	1,525	1,365	1,200	1,023	845	668	490
14,950	15,000	1,701	1,536	1,375	1,211	1,032	855	677	500
15,000	15,050	1,712	1,547	1,385	1,222	1,042	864	687	509
15,050	15,100	1,723	1,558	1,395	1,233	1,051	874	696	519
15,100	15,150	1,734	1,569	1,405	1,244	1,061	883	706	528
15,150	15,200	1,745	1,580	1,415	1,255	1,070	893	715	538

Continued next column

If line 34, Form 1040 is— Over	But not over	And the total number of exemptions claimed on line 7 is— 2	3	4	5	6	7	8	9
		Your tax is—							
15,200	15,250	1,756	1,591	1,426	1,266	1,080	902	725	547
15,250	15,300	1,767	1,602	1,437	1,277	1,089	912	734	557
15,300	15,350	1,778	1,613	1,448	1,288	1,099	921	744	566
15,350	15,400	1,789	1,624	1,459	1,299	1,108	931	753	576
15,400	15,450	1,800	1,635	1,470	1,310	1,118	940	763	585
15,450	15,500	1,811	1,646	1,481	1,321	1,127	950	772	595
15,500	15,550	1,822	1,657	1,492	1,332	1,137	959	782	604
15,550	15,600	1,833	1,668	1,503	1,343	1,146	969	791	614
15,600	15,650	1,844	1,679	1,514	1,354	1,156	978	801	623
15,650	15,700	1,855	1,690	1,525	1,365	1,165	988	810	633
15,700	15,750	1,866	1,701	1,536	1,375	1,176	997	820	642
15,750	15,800	1,877	1,712	1,547	1,385	1,187	1,007	829	652
15,800	15,850	1,888	1,723	1,558	1,395	1,198	1,016	839	661
15,850	15,900	1,899	1,734	1,569	1,405	1,209	1,026	848	671
15,900	15,950	1,910	1,745	1,580	1,415	1,220	1,035	858	680
15,950	16,000	1,921	1,756	1,591	1,426	1,231	1,045	867	690
16,000	16,050	1,932	1,767	1,602	1,437	1,242	1,054	877	699
16,050	16,100	1,943	1,778	1,613	1,448	1,253	1,064	886	709
16,100	16,150	1,954	1,789	1,624	1,459	1,264	1,073	896	718
16,150	16,200	1,965	1,800	1,635	1,470	1,275	1,083	905	728
16,200	16,250	1,976	1,811	1,646	1,481	1,286	1,092	915	737
16,250	16,300	1,987	1,822	1,657	1,492	1,297	1,102	924	747
16,300	16,350	1,998	1,833	1,668	1,503	1,308	1,111	934	756
16,350	16,400	2,009	1,844	1,679	1,514	1,319	1,121	943	766
16,400	16,450	2,020	1,855	1,690	1,525	1,330	1,130	953	775
16,450	16,500	2,031	1,866	1,701	1,536	1,341	1,141	962	785
16,500	16,550	2,042	1,877	1,712	1,547	1,352	1,152	972	794
16,550	16,600	2,053	1,888	1,723	1,558	1,363	1,163	981	804
16,600	16,650	2,064	1,899	1,734	1,569	1,374	1,174	991	813
16,650	16,700	2,075	1,910	1,745	1,580	1,385	1,185	1,000	823
16,700	16,750	2,086	1,921	1,756	1,591	1,396	1,196	1,010	832
16,750	16,800	2,099	1,932	1,767	1,602	1,407	1,207	1,019	842
16,800	16,850	2,111	1,943	1,778	1,613	1,418	1,218	1,029	851
16,850	16,900	2,124	1,954	1,789	1,624	1,429	1,229	1,038	861
16,900	16,950	2,136	1,965	1,800	1,635	1,440	1,240	1,048	870
16,950	17,000	2,149	1,976	1,811	1,646	1,451	1,251	1,057	880
17,000	17,050	2,161	1,987	1,822	1,657	1,462	1,262	1,067	889
17,050	17,100	2,174	1,998	1,833	1,668	1,473	1,273	1,076	899
17,100	17,150	2,186	2,009	1,844	1,679	1,484	1,284	1,086	908
17,150	17,200	2,199	2,020	1,855	1,690	1,495	1,295	1,095	918
17,200	17,250	2,211	2,031	1,866	1,701	1,506	1,306	1,106	927
17,250	17,300	2,224	2,042	1,877	1,712	1,517	1,317	1,117	937
17,300	17,350	2,236	2,053	1,888	1,723	1,528	1,328	1,128	946
17,350	17,400	2,249	2,064	1,899	1,734	1,539	1,339	1,139	956
17,400	17,450	2,261	2,075	1,910	1,745	1,550	1,350	1,150	965
17,450	17,500	2,274	2,086	1,921	1,756	1,561	1,361	1,161	975
17,500	17,550	2,286	2,099	1,932	1,767	1,572	1,372	1,172	984
17,550	17,600	2,299	2,111	1,943	1,778	1,583	1,383	1,183	994
17,600	17,650	2,311	2,124	1,954	1,789	1,594	1,394	1,194	1,003
17,650	17,700	2,324	2,136	1,965	1,800	1,605	1,405	1,205	1,013
17,700	17,750	2,336	2,149	1,976	1,811	1,616	1,416	1,216	1,022
17,750	17,800	2,349	2,161	1,987	1,822	1,627	1,427	1,227	1,032
17,800	17,850	2,361	2,174	1,998	1,833	1,638	1,438	1,238	1,041
17,850	17,900	2,374	2,186	2,009	1,844	1,649	1,449	1,249	1,051
17,900	17,950	2,386	2,199	2,020	1,855	1,660	1,460	1,260	1,060
17,950	18,000	2,399	2,211	2,031	1,866	1,671	1,471	1,271	1,071
18,000	18,050	2,411	2,224	2,042	1,877	1,682	1,482	1,282	1,082
18,050	18,100	2,424	2,236	2,053	1,888	1,693	1,493	1,293	1,093
18,100	18,150	2,436	2,249	2,064	1,899	1,704	1,504	1,304	1,104
18,150	18,200	2,449	2,261	2,075	1,910	1,715	1,515	1,315	1,115
18,200	18,250	2,461	2,274	2,086	1,921	1,726	1,526	1,326	1,126
18,250	18,300	2,474	2,286	2,099	1,932	1,737	1,537	1,337	1,137
18,300	18,350	2,486	2,299	2,111	1,943	1,748	1,548	1,348	1,148
18,350	18,400	2,499	2,311	2,124	1,954	1,759	1,559	1,359	1,159
18,400	18,450	2,511	2,324	2,136	1,965	1,770	1,570	1,370	1,170
18,450	18,500	2,524	2,336	2,149	1,976	1,781	1,581	1,381	1,181
18,500	18,550	2,536	2,349	2,161	1,987	1,792	1,592	1,392	1,192
18,550	18,600	2,549	2,361	2,174	1,998	1,803	1,603	1,403	1,203
18,600	18,650	2,561	2,374	2,186	2,009	1,814	1,614	1,414	1,214
18,650	18,700	2,574	2,386	2,199	2,020	1,825	1,625	1,425	1,225
18,700	18,750	2,586	2,399	2,211	2,031	1,836	1,636	1,436	1,236
18,750	18,800	2,599	2,411	2,224	2,042	1,847	1,647	1,447	1,247

Continued on next page

1977 Tax Table B—MARRIED FILING JOINTLY (Box 2) and QUALIFYING WIDOW(ER)S (Box 5)
(Continued)

(If your income or exemptions are not covered, use Schedule TC (Form 1040), Part I to figure your tax)

If line 34, Form 1040 is—		And the total number of exemptions claimed on line 7 is—							
Over	But not over	2	3	4	5	6	7	8	9
		Your tax is—							
18,800	18,850	2,611	2,424	2,236	2,053	1,858	1,658	1,458	1,258
18,850	18,900	2,624	2,436	2,249	2,064	1,869	1,669	1,469	1,269
18,900	18,950	2,636	2,449	2,261	2,075	1,880	1,680	1,480	1,280
18,950	19,000	2,649	2,461	2,274	2,086	1,891	1,691	1,491	1,291
19,000	19,050	2,661	2,474	2,286	2,099	1,902	1,702	1,502	1,302
19,050	19,100	2,674	2,486	2,299	2,111	1,913	1,713	1,513	1,313
19,100	19,150	2,686	2,499	2,311	2,124	1,924	1,724	1,524	1,324
19,150	19,200	2,699	2,511	2,324	2,136	1,935	1,735	1,535	1,335
19,200	19,250	2,711	2,524	2,336	2,149	1,946	1,746	1,546	1,346
19,250	19,300	2,724	2,536	2,349	2,161	1,957	1,757	1,557	1,357
19,300	19,350	2,736	2,549	2,361	2,174	1,968	1,768	1,568	1,368
19,350	19,400	2,749	2,561	2,374	2,186	1,979	1,779	1,579	1,379
19,400	19,450	2,761	2,574	2,386	2,199	1,990	1,790	1,590	1,390
19,450	19,500	2,774	2,586	2,399	2,211	2,001	1,801	1,601	1,401
19,500	19,550	2,786	2,599	2,411	2,224	2,012	1,812	1,612	1,412
19,550	19,600	2,799	2,611	2,424	2,236	2,023	1,823	1,623	1,423
19,600	19,650	2,811	2,624	2,436	2,249	2,034	1,834	1,634	1,434
19,650	19,700	2,824	2,636	2,449	2,261	2,045	1,845	1,645	1,445
19,700	19,750	2,836	2,649	2,461	2,274	2,056	1,856	1,656	1,456
19,750	19,800	2,849	2,661	2,474	2,286	2,069	1,867	1,667	1,467
19,800	19,850	2,861	2,674	2,486	2,299	2,081	1,878	1,678	1,478
19,850	19,900	2,874	2,686	2,499	2,311	2,094	1,889	1,689	1,489
19,900	19,950	2,886	2,699	2,511	2,324	2,106	1,900	1,700	1,500
19,950	20,000	2,899	2,711	2,524	2,336	2,119	1,911	1,711	1,511
20,000	20,050	2,911	2,724	2,536	2,349	2,131	1,922	1,722	1,522
20,050	20,100	2,924	2,736	2,549	2,361	2,144	1,933	1,733	1,533
20,100	20,150	2,936	2,749	2,561	2,374	2,156	1,944	1,744	1,544
20,150	20,200	2,949	2,761	2,574	2,386	2,169	1,955	1,755	1,555
20,200	20,250	2,961	2,774	2,586	2,399	2,181	1,966	1,766	1,566
20,250	20,300	2,974	2,786	2,599	2,411	2,194	1,977	1,777	1,577
20,300	20,350	2,986	2,799	2,611	2,424	2,206	1,988	1,788	1,588
20,350	20,400	2,999	2,811	2,624	2,436	2,219	1,999	1,799	1,599
20,400	20,450	3,011	2,824	2,636	2,449	2,231	2,010	1,810	1,610
20,450	20,500	3,024	2,836	2,649	2,461	2,244	2,021	1,821	1,621
20,500	20,550	3,036	2,849	2,661	2,474	2,256	2,034	1,832	1,632
20,550	20,600	3,049	2,861	2,674	2,486	2,269	2,046	1,843	1,643
20,600	20,650	3,061	2,874	2,686	2,499	2,281	2,059	1,854	1,654
20,650	20,700	3,074	2,886	2,699	2,511	2,294	2,071	1,865	1,665
20,700	20,750	3,087	2,899	2,711	2,524	2,306	2,084	1,876	1,676
20,750	20,800	3,101	2,911	2,724	2,536	2,319	2,096	1,887	1,687
20,800	20,850	3,115	2,924	2,736	2,549	2,331	2,109	1,898	1,698
20,850	20,900	3,129	2,936	2,749	2,561	2,344	2,121	1,909	1,709
20,900	20,950	3,143	2,949	2,761	2,574	2,356	2,134	1,920	1,720
20,950	21,000	3,157	2,961	2,774	2,586	2,369	2,146	1,931	1,731
21,000	21,050	3,171	2,974	2,786	2,599	2,381	2,159	1,942	1,742
21,050	21,100	3,185	2,986	2,799	2,611	2,394	2,171	1,953	1,753
21,100	21,150	3,199	2,999	2,811	2,624	2,406	2,184	1,964	1,764
21,150	21,200	3,213	3,011	2,824	2,636	2,419	2,196	1,975	1,775
21,200	21,250	3,227	3,024	2,836	2,649	2,431	2,209	1,986	1,786
21,250	21,300	3,241	3,036	2,849	2,661	2,444	2,221	1,999	1,797
21,300	21,350	3,255	3,049	2,861	2,674	2,456	2,234	2,011	1,808
21,350	21,400	3,269	3,061	2,874	2,686	2,469	2,246	2,024	1,819
21,400	21,450	3,283	3,074	2,886	2,699	2,481	2,259	2,036	1,830
21,450	21,500	3,297	3,087	2,899	2,711	2,494	2,271	2,049	1,841
21,500	21,550	3,311	3,101	2,911	2,724	2,506	2,284	2,061	1,852
21,550	21,600	3,325	3,115	2,924	2,736	2,519	2,296	2,074	1,863
21,600	21,650	3,339	3,129	2,936	2,749	2,531	2,309	2,086	1,874
21,650	21,700	3,353	3,143	2,949	2,761	2,544	2,321	2,099	1,885
21,700	21,750	3,367	3,157	2,961	2,774	2,556	2,334	2,111	1,896
21,750	21,800	3,381	3,171	2,974	2,786	2,569	2,346	2,124	1,907
21,800	21,850	3,395	3,185	2,986	2,799	2,581	2,359	2,136	1,918
21,850	21,900	3,409	3,199	2,999	2,811	2,594	2,371	2,149	1,929
21,900	21,950	3,423	3,213	3,011	2,824	2,606	2,384	2,161	1,940
21,950	22,000	3,437	3,227	3,024	2,836	2,619	2,396	2,174	1,951
22,000	22,050	3,451	3,241	3,036	2,849	2,631	2,409	2,186	1,964
22,050	22,100	3,465	3,255	3,049	2,861	2,644	2,421	2,199	1,976
22,100	22,150	3,479	3,269	3,061	2,874	2,656	2,434	2,211	1,989
22,150	22,200	3,493	3,283	3,074	2,886	2,669	2,446	2,224	2,001
22,200	22,250	3,507	3,297	3,087	2,899	2,681	2,459	2,236	2,014
22,250	22,300	3,521	3,311	3,101	2,911	2,694	2,471	2,249	2,026
22,300	22,350	3,535	3,325	3,115	2,924	2,706	2,484	2,261	2,039
22,350	22,400	3,549	3,339	3,129	2,936	2,719	2,496	2,274	2,051

Continued next column

If line 34, Form 1040 is—		And the total number of exemptions claimed on line 7 is—							
Over	But not over	2	3	4	5	6	7	8	9
		Your tax is—							
22,400	22,450	3,563	3,353	3,143	2,949	2,731	2,509	2,286	2,064
22,450	22,500	3,577	3,367	3,157	2,961	2,744	2,521	2,299	2,076
22,500	22,550	3,591	3,381	3,171	2,974	2,756	2,534	2,311	2,089
22,550	22,600	3,605	3,395	3,185	2,986	2,769	2,546	2,324	2,101
22,600	22,650	3,619	3,409	3,199	2,999	2,781	2,559	2,336	2,114
22,650	22,700	3,633	3,423	3,213	3,011	2,794	2,571	2,349	2,126
22,700	22,750	3,647	3,437	3,227	3,024	2,806	2,584	2,361	2,139
22,750	22,800	3,661	3,451	3,241	3,036	2,819	2,596	2,374	2,151
22,800	22,850	3,675	3,465	3,255	3,049	2,831	2,609	2,386	2,164
22,850	22,900	3,689	3,479	3,269	3,061	2,844	2,621	2,399	2,176
22,900	22,950	3,703	3,493	3,283	3,074	2,856	2,634	2,411	2,189
22,950	23,000	3,717	3,507	3,297	3,087	2,869	2,646	2,424	2,201
23,000	23,050	3,731	3,521	3,311	3,101	2,881	2,659	2,436	2,214
23,050	23,100	3,745	3,535	3,325	3,115	2,894	2,671	2,449	2,226
23,100	23,150	3,759	3,549	3,339	3,129	2,906	2,684	2,461	2,239
23,150	23,200	3,773	3,563	3,353	3,143	2,919	2,696	2,474	2,251
23,200	23,250	3,787	3,577	3,367	3,157	2,931	2,709	2,486	2,264
23,250	23,300	3,801	3,591	3,381	3,171	2,944	2,721	2,499	2,276
23,300	23,350	3,815	3,605	3,395	3,185	2,956	2,734	2,511	2,289
23,350	23,400	3,829	3,619	3,409	3,199	2,969	2,746	2,524	2,301
23,400	23,450	3,843	3,633	3,423	3,213	2,981	2,759	2,536	2,314
23,450	23,500	3,857	3,647	3,437	3,227	2,994	2,771	2,549	2,326
23,500	23,550	3,871	3,661	3,451	3,241	3,006	2,784	2,561	2,339
23,550	23,600	3,885	3,675	3,465	3,255	3,019	2,796	2,574	2,351
23,600	23,650	3,899	3,689	3,479	3,269	3,031	2,809	2,586	2,364
23,650	23,700	3,913	3,703	3,493	3,283	3,044	2,821	2,599	2,376
23,700	23,750	3,927	3,717	3,507	3,297	3,057	2,834	2,611	2,389
23,750	23,800	3,941	3,731	3,521	3,311	3,071	2,846	2,624	2,401
23,800	23,850	3,955	3,745	3,535	3,325	3,085	2,859	2,636	2,414
23,850	23,900	3,969	3,759	3,549	3,339	3,099	2,871	2,649	2,426
23,900	23,950	3,983	3,773	3,563	3,353	3,113	2,884	2,661	2,439
23,950	24,000	3,997	3,787	3,577	3,367	3,127	2,896	2,674	2,451
24,000	24,050	4,011	3,801	3,591	3,381	3,141	2,909	2,686	2,464
24,050	24,100	4,025	3,815	3,605	3,395	3,155	2,921	2,699	2,476
24,100	24,150	4,039	3,829	3,619	3,409	3,169	2,934	2,711	2,489
24,150	24,200	4,053	3,843	3,633	3,423	3,183	2,946	2,724	2,501
24,200	24,250	4,067	3,857	3,647	3,437	3,197	2,959	2,736	2,514
24,250	24,300	4,081	3,871	3,661	3,451	3,211	2,971	2,749	2,526
24,300	24,350	4,095	3,885	3,675	3,465	3,225	2,984	2,761	2,539
24,350	24,400	4,109	3,899	3,689	3,479	3,239	2,996	2,774	2,551
24,400	24,450	4,123	3,913	3,703	3,493	3,253	3,009	2,786	2,564
24,450	24,500	4,137	3,927	3,717	3,507	3,267	3,022	2,799	2,576
24,500	24,550	4,151	3,941	3,731	3,521	3,281	3,036	2,811	2,589
24,550	24,600	4,165	3,955	3,745	3,535	3,295	3,050	2,824	2,601
24,600	24,650	4,179	3,969	3,759	3,549	3,309	3,064	2,836	2,614
24,650	24,700	4,193	3,983	3,773	3,563	3,323	3,078	2,849	2,626
24,700	24,750	4,208	3,997	3,787	3,577	3,337	3,092	2,861	2,639
24,750	24,800	4,224	4,011	3,801	3,591	3,351	3,106	2,874	2,651
24,800	24,850	4,240	4,025	3,815	3,605	3,365	3,120	2,886	2,664
24,850	24,900	4,256	4,039	3,829	3,619	3,379	3,134	2,899	2,676
24,900	24,950	4,272	4,053	3,843	3,633	3,393	3,148	2,911	2,689
24,950	25,000	4,288	4,067	3,857	3,647	3,407	3,162	2,924	2,701
25,000	25,050	4,304	4,081	3,871	3,661	3,421	3,176	2,936	2,714
25,050	25,100	4,320	4,095	3,885	3,675	3,435	3,190	2,949	2,726
25,100	25,150	4,336	4,109	3,899	3,689	3,449	3,204	2,961	2,739
25,150	25,200	4,352	4,123	3,913	3,703	3,463	3,218	2,974	2,751
25,200	25,250	4,368	4,137	3,927	3,717	3,477	3,232	2,987	2,764
25,250	25,300	4,384	4,151	3,941	3,731	3,491	3,246	3,001	2,776
25,300	25,350	4,400	4,165	3,955	3,745	3,505	3,260	3,015	2,789
25,350	25,400	4,416	4,179	3,969	3,759	3,519	3,274	3,029	2,801
25,400	25,450	4,432	4,193	3,983	3,773	3,533	3,288	3,043	2,814
25,450	25,500	4,448	4,208	3,997	3,787	3,547	3,302	3,057	2,826
25,500	25,550	4,464	4,224	4,011	3,801	3,561	3,316	3,071	2,839
25,550	25,600	4,480	4,240	4,025	3,815	3,575	3,330	3,085	2,851
25,600	25,650	4,496	4,256	4,039	3,829	3,589	3,344	3,099	2,864
25,650	25,700	4,512	4,272	4,053	3,843	3,603	3,358	3,113	2,876
25,700	25,750	4,528	4,288	4,067	3,857	3,617	3,372	3,127	2,889
25,750	25,800	4,544	4,304	4,081	3,871	3,631	3,386	3,141	2,901
25,800	25,850	4,560	4,320	4,095	3,885	3,645	3,400	3,155	2,914
25,850	25,900	4,576	4,336	4,109	3,899	3,659	3,414	3,169	2,926
25,900	25,950	4,592	4,352	4,123	3,913	3,673	3,428	3,183	2,939
25,950	26,000	4,608	4,368	4,137	3,927	3,687	3,442	3,197	2,952

Continued on next page

1977 Tax Table B—MARRIED FILING JOINTLY (Box 2) and QUALIFYING WIDOW(ER)S (Box 5)

(Continued)

(If your income or exemptions are not covered, use Schedule TC (Form 1040), Part I to figure your tax)

If line 34, Form 1040 is—		And the total number of exemptions claimed on line 7 is—							
Over	But not over	2	3	4	5	6	7	8	9
		Your tax is—							
26,000	26,050	4,624	4,384	4,151	3,941	3,701	3,456	3,211	2,966
26,050	26,100	4,640	4,400	4,165	3,955	3,715	3,470	3,225	2,980
26,100	26,150	4,656	4,416	4,179	3,969	3,729	3,484	3,239	2,994
26,150	26,200	4,672	4,432	4,193	3,983	3,743	3,498	3,253	3,008
26,200	26,250	4,688	4,448	4,208	3,997	3,757	3,512	3,267	3,022
26,250	26,300	4,704	4,464	4,224	4,011	3,771	3,526	3,281	3,036
26,300	26,350	4,720	4,480	4,240	4,025	3,785	3,540	3,295	3,050
26,350	26,400	4,736	4,496	4,256	4,039	3,799	3,554	3,309	3,064
26,400	26,450	4,752	4,512	4,272	4,053	3,813	3,568	3,323	3,078
26,450	26,500	4,768	4,528	4,288	4,067	3,827	3,582	3,337	3,092
26,500	26,550	4,784	4,544	4,304	4,081	3,841	3,596	3,351	3,106
26,550	26,600	4,800	4,560	4,320	4,095	3,855	3,610	3,365	3,120
26,600	26,650	4,816	4,576	4,336	4,109	3,869	3,624	3,379	3,134
26,650	26,700	4,832	4,592	4,352	4,123	3,883	3,638	3,393	3,148
26,700	26,750	4,848	4,608	4,368	4,137	3,897	3,652	3,407	3,162
26,750	26,800	4,864	4,624	4,384	4,151	3,911	3,666	3,421	3,176
26,800	26,850	4,880	4,640	4,400	4,165	3,925	3,680	3,435	3,190
26,850	26,900	4,896	4,656	4,416	4,179	3,939	3,694	3,449	3,204
26,900	26,950	4,912	4,672	4,432	4,193	3,953	3,708	3,463	3,218
26,950	27,000	4,928	4,688	4,448	4,208	3,967	3,722	3,477	3,232
27,000	27,050	4,944	4,704	4,464	4,224	3,981	3,736	3,491	3,246
27,050	27,100	4,960	4,720	4,480	4,240	3,995	3,750	3,505	3,260
27,100	27,150	4,976	4,736	4,496	4,256	4,009	3,764	3,519	3,274
27,150	27,200	4,992	4,752	4,512	4,272	4,023	3,778	3,533	3,288
27,200	27,250	5,008	4,768	4,528	4,288	4,037	3,792	3,547	3,302
27,250	27,300	5,024	4,784	4,544	4,304	4,051	3,806	3,561	3,316
27,300	27,350	5,040	4,800	4,560	4,320	4,065	3,820	3,575	3,330
27,350	27,400	5,056	4,816	4,576	4,336	4,079	3,834	3,589	3,344
27,400	27,450	5,072	4,832	4,592	4,352	4,093	3,848	3,603	3,358
27,450	27,500	5,088	4,848	4,608	4,368	4,107	3,862	3,617	3,372
27,500	27,550	5,104	4,864	4,624	4,384	4,121	3,876	3,631	3,386
27,550	27,600	5,120	4,880	4,640	4,400	4,135	3,890	3,645	3,400
27,600	27,650	5,136	4,896	4,656	4,416	4,149	3,904	3,659	3,414
27,650	27,700	5,152	4,912	4,672	4,432	4,163	3,918	8,673	3,428
27,700	27,750	5,168	4,928	4,688	4,448	4,178	3,932	3,687	3,442
27,750	27,800	5,184	4,944	4,704	4,464	4,194	3,946	3,701	3,456
27,800	27,850	5,200	4,960	4,720	4,480	4,210	3,960	3,715	3,470
27,850	27,900	5,216	4,976	4,736	4,496	4,226	3,974	3,729	3,484
27,900	27,950	5,232	4,992	4,752	4,512	4,242	3,988	3,743	3,498
27,950	28,000	5,248	5,008	4,768	4,528	4,258	4,002	3,757	3,512
28,000	28,050	5,264	5,024	4,784	4,544	4,274	4,016	3,771	3,526
28,050	28,100	5,280	5,040	4,800	4,560	4,290	4,030	3,785	3,540
28,100	28,150	5,296	5,056	4,816	4,576	4,306	4,044	3,799	3,554
28,150	28,200	5,312	5,072	4,832	4,592	4,322	4,058	3,813	3,568
28,200	28,250	5,328	5,088	4,848	4,608	4,338	4,072	3,827	3,582
28,250	28,300	5,344	5,104	4,864	4,624	4,354	4,086	3,841	3,596
28,300	28,350	5,360	5,120	4,880	4,640	4,370	4,100	3,855	3,610
28,350	28,400	5,376	5,136	4,896	4,656	4,386	4,114	3,869	3,624
28,400	28,450	5,392	5,152	4,912	4,672	4,402	4,128	3,883	3,638
28,450	28,500	5,408	5,168	4,928	4,688	4,418	4,143	3,897	3,652
28,500	28,550	5,424	5,184	4,944	4,704	4,434	4,159	3,911	3,666
28,550	28,600	5,440	5,200	4,960	4,720	4,450	4,175	3,925	3,680
28,600	28,650	5,456	5,216	4,976	4,736	4,466	4,191	3,939	3,694
28,650	28,700	5,472	5,232	4,992	4,752	4,482	4,207	3,953	3,708
28,700	28,750	5,489	5,248	5,008	4,768	4,498	4,223	3,967	3,722
28,750	28,800	5,507	5,264	5,024	4,784	4,514	4,239	3,981	3,736
28,800	28,850	5,525	5,280	5,040	4,800	4,530	4,255	3,995	3,750
28,850	28,900	5,543	5,296	5,056	4,816	4,546	4,271	4,009	3,764
28,900	28,950	5,561	5,312	5,072	4,832	4,562	4,287	4,023	3,778
28,950	29,000	5,579	5,328	5,088	4,848	4,578	4,303	4,037	3,792
29,000	29,050	5,597	5,344	5,104	4,864	4,594	4,319	4,051	3,806
29,050	29,100	5,615	5,360	5,120	4,880	4,610	4,335	4,065	3,820
29,100	29,150	5,633	5,376	5,136	4,896	4,626	4,351	4,079	3,834
29,150	29,200	5,651	5,392	5,152	4,912	4,642	4,367	4,093	3,848
29,200	29,250	5,669	5,408	5,168	4,928	4,658	4,383	4,108	3,862
29,250	29,300	5,687	5,424	5,184	4,944	4,674	4,399	4,124	3,876
29,300	29,350	5,705	5,440	5,200	4,960	4,690	4,415	4,140	3,890
29,350	29,400	5,723	5,456	5,216	4,976	4,706	4,431	4,156	3,904
29,400	29,450	5,741	5,472	5,232	4,992	4,722	4,447	4,172	3,918
29,450	29,500	5,759	5,489	5,248	5,008	4,738	4,463	4,188	3,932
29,500	29,550	5,777	5,507	5,264	5,024	4,754	4,479	4,204	3,946
29,550	29,600	5,795	5,525	5,280	5,040	4,770	4,495	4,220	3,960

Continued next column

If line 34, Form 1040 is—		And the total number of exemptions claimed on line 7 is—							
Over	But not over	2	3	4	5	6	7	8	9
		Your tax is—							
29,600	29,650	5,813	5,543	5,296	5,056	4,786	4,511	4,236	3,974
29,650	29,700	5,831	5,561	5,312	5,072	4,802	4,527	4,252	3,988
29,700	29,750	5,849	5,579	5,328	5,088	4,818	4,543	4,268	4,002
29,750	29,800	5,867	5,597	5,344	5,104	4,834	4,559	4,284	4,016
29,800	29,850	5,885	5,615	5,360	5,120	4,850	4,575	4,300	4,030
29,850	29,900	5,903	5,633	5,376	5,136	4,866	4,591	4,316	4,044
29,900	29,950	5,921	5,651	5,392	5,152	4,882	4,607	4,332	4,058
29,950	30,000	5,939	5,669	5,408	5,168	4,898	4,623	4,348	4,073
30,000	30,050	5,957	5,687	5,424	5,184	4,914	4,639	4,364	4,089
30,050	30,100	5,975	5,705	5,440	5,200	4,930	4,655	4,380	4,105
30,100	30,150	5,993	5,723	5,456	5,216	4,946	4,671	4,396	4,121
30,150	30,200	6,011	5,741	5,472	5,232	4,962	4,687	4,412	4,137
30,200	30,250	6,029	5,759	5,489	5,248	4,978	4,703	4,428	4,153
30,250	30,300	6,047	5,777	5,507	5,264	4,994	4,719	4,444	4,169
30,300	30,350	6,065	5,795	5,525	5,280	5,010	4,735	4,460	4,185
30,350	30,400	6,083	5,813	5,543	5,296	5,026	4,751	4,476	4,201
30,400	30,450	6,101	5,831	5,561	5,312	5,042	4,767	4,492	4,217
30,450	30,500	6,119	5,849	5,579	5,328	5,058	4,783	4,508	4,233
30,500	30,550	6,137	5,867	5,597	5,344	5,074	4,799	4,524	4,249
30,550	30,600	6,155	5,885	5,615	5,360	5,090	4,815	4,540	4,265
30,600	30,650	6,173	5,903	5,633	5,376	5,106	4,831	4,556	4,281
30,650	30,700	6,191	5,921	5,651	5,392	5,122	4,847	4,572	4,297
30,700	30,750	6,209	5,939	5,669	5,408	5,138	4,863	4,588	4,313
30,750	30,800	6,227	5,957	5,687	5,424	5,154	4,879	4,604	4,329
30,800	30,850	6,245	5,975	5,705	5,440	5,170	4,895	4,620	4,345
30,850	30,900	6,263	5,993	5,723	5,456	5,186	4,911	4,636	4,361
30,900	30,950	6,281	6,011	5,741	5,472	5,202	4,927	4,652	4,377
30,950	31,000	6,299	6,029	5,759	5,489	5,218	4,943	4,668	4,393
31,000	31,050	6,317	6,047	5,777	5,507	5,234	4,959	4,684	4,409
31,050	31,100	6,335	6,065	5,795	5,525	5,250	4,975	4,700	4,425
31,100	31,150	6,353	6,083	5,813	5,543	5,266	4,991	4,716	4,441
31,150	31,200	6,371	6,101	5,831	5,561	5,282	5,007	4,732	4,457
31,200	31,250	6,389	6,119	5,849	5,579	5,298	5,023	4,748	4,473
31,250	31,300	6,407	6,137	5,867	5,597	5,314	5,039	4,764	4,489
31,300	31,350	6,425	6,155	5,885	5,615	5,330	5,055	4,780	4,505
31,350	31,400	6,443	6,173	5,903	5,633	5,346	5,071	4,796	4,521
31,400	31,450	6,461	6,191	5,921	5,651	5,362	5,087	4,812	4,537
31,450	31,500	6,479	6,209	5,939	5,669	5,378	5,103	4,828	4,553
31,500	31,550	6,497	6,227	5,957	5,687	5,394	5,119	4,844	4,569
31,550	31,600	6,515	6,245	5,975	5,705	5,410	5,135	4,860	4,585
31,600	31,650	6,533	6,263	5,993	5,723	5,426	5,151	4,876	4,601
31,650	31,700	6,551	6,281	6,011	5,741	5,442	5,167	4,892	4,617
31,700	31,750	6,569	6,299	6,029	5,759	5,459	5,183	4,908	4,633
31,750	31,800	6,587	6,317	6,047	5,777	5,477	5,199	4,924	4,649
31,800	31,850	6,605	6,335	6,065	5,795	5,495	5,215	4,940	4,665
31,850	31,900	6,623	6,353	6,083	5,813	5,513	5,231	4,956	4,681
31,900	31,950	6,641	6,371	6,101	5,831	5,531	5,247	4,972	4,697
31,950	32,000	6,659	6,389	6,119	5,849	5,549	5,263	4,988	4,713
32,000	32,050	6,677	6,407	6,137	5,867	5,567	5,279	5,004	4,729
32,050	32,100	6,695	6,425	6,155	5,885	5,585	5,295	5,020	4,745
32,100	32,150	6,713	6,443	6,173	5,903	5,603	5,311	5,036	4,761
32,150	32,200	6,731	6,461	6,191	5,921	5,621	5,327	5,052	4,777
32,200	32,250	6,749	6,479	6,209	5,939	5,639	5,343	5,068	4,793
32,250	32,300	6,767	6,497	6,227	5,957	5,657	5,359	5,084	4,809
32,300	32,350	6,785	6,515	6,245	5,975	5,675	5,375	5,100	4,825
32,350	32,400	6,803	6,533	6,263	5,993	5,693	5,391	5,116	4,841
32,400	32,450	6,821	6,551	6,281	6,011	5,711	5,407	5,132	4,857
32,450	32,500	6,839	6,569	6,299	6,029	5,729	5,424	5,148	4,873
32,500	32,550	6,857	6,587	6,317	6,047	5,747	5,442	5,164	4,889
32,550	32,600	6,875	6,605	6,335	6,065	5,765	5,460	5,180	4,905
32,600	32,650	6,893	6,623	6,353	6,083	5,783	5,478	5,196	4,921
32,650	32,700	6,911	6,641	6,371	6,101	5,801	5,496	5,212	4,937
32,700	32,750	6,930	6,659	6,389	6,119	5,819	5,514	5,228	4,953
32,750	32,800	6,949	6,677	6,407	6,137	5,837	5,532	5,244	4,969
32,800	32,850	6,969	6,695	6,425	6,155	5,855	5,550	5,260	4,985
32,850	32,900	6,988	6,713	6,443	6,173	5,873	5,568	5,276	5,001
32,900	32,950	7,008	6,731	6,461	6,191	5,891	5,586	5,292	5,017
32,950	33,000	7,027	6,749	6,479	6,209	5,909	5,604	5,308	5,033
33,000	33,050	7,047	6,767	6,497	6,227	5,927	5,622	5,324	5,049
33,050	33,100	7,066	6,785	6,515	6,245	5,945	5,640	5,340	5,065
33,100	33,150	7,086	6,803	6,533	6,263	5,963	5,658	5,356	5,081
33,150	33,200	7,105	6,821	6,551	6,281	5,981	5,676	5,372	5,097

Continued on next page

1977 Tax Table B—MARRIED FILING JOINTLY (Box 2) and QUALIFYING WIDOW(ER)S (Box 5)
(Continued)

(If your income or exemptions are not covered, use Schedule TC (Form 1040), Part I to figure your tax)

If line 34, Form 1040 is— Over	But not over	2	3	4	5	6	7	8	9
		Your tax is—							
33,200	33,250	7,125	6,839	6,569	6,299	5,999	5,694	5,389	5,113
33,250	33,300	7,144	6,857	6,587	6,317	6,017	5,712	5,407	5,129
33,300	33,350	7,164	6,875	6,605	6,335	6,035	5,730	5,425	5,145
33,350	33,400	7,183	6,893	6,623	6,353	6,053	5,748	5,443	5,161
33,400	33,450	7,203	6,911	6,641	6,371	6,071	5,766	5,461	5,177
33,450	33,500	7,222	6,930	6,659	6,389	6,089	5,784	5,479	5,193
33,500	33,550	7,242	6,949	6,677	6,407	6,107	5,802	5,497	5,209
33,550	33,600	7,261	6,969	6,695	6,425	6,125	5,820	5,515	5,225
33,600	33,650	7,281	6,988	6,713	6,443	6,143	5,838	5,533	5,241
33,650	33,700	7,300	7,008	6,731	6,461	6,161	5,856	5,551	5,257
33,700	33,750	7,320	7,027	6,749	6,479	6,179	5,874	5,569	5,273
33,750	33,800	7,339	7,047	6,767	6,497	6,197	5,892	5,587	5,289
33,800	33,850	7,359	7,066	6,785	6,515	6,215	5,910	5,605	5,305
33,850	33,900	7,378	7,086	6,803	6,533	6,233	5,928	5,623	5,321
33,900	33,950	7,398	7,105	6,821	6,551	6,251	5,946	5,641	5,337
33,950	34,000	7,417	7,125	6,839	6,569	6,269	5,964	5,659	5,354
34,000	34,050	7,437	7,144	6,857	6,587	6,287	5,982	5,677	5,372
34,050	34,100	7,456	7,164	6,875	6,605	6,305	6,000	5,695	5,390
34,100	34,150	7,476	7,183	6,893	6,623	6,323	6,018	5,713	5,408
34,150	34,200	7,495	7,203	6,911	6,641	6,341	6,036	5,731	5,426
34,200	34,250	7,515	7,222	6,930	6,659	6,359	6,054	5,749	5,444
34,250	34,300	7,534	7,242	6,949	6,677	6,377	6,072	5,767	5,462
34,300	34,350	7,554	7,261	6,969	6,695	6,395	6,090	5,785	5,480
34,350	34,400	7,573	7,281	6,988	6,713	6,413	6,108	5,803	5,498
34,400	34,450	7,593	7,300	7,008	6,731	6,431	6,126	5,821	5,516
34,450	34,500	7,612	7,320	7,027	6,749	6,449	6,144	5,839	5,534
34,500	34,550	7,632	7,339	7,047	6,767	6,467	6,162	5,857	5,552
34,550	34,600	7,651	7,359	7,066	6,785	6,485	6,180	5,875	5,570
34,600	34,650	7,671	7,378	7,086	6,803	6,503	6,198	5,893	5,588
34,650	34,700	7,690	7,398	7,105	6,821	6,521	6,216	5,911	5,606
34,700	34,750	7,710	7,417	7,125	6,839	6,539	6,234	5,929	5,624
34,750	34,800	7,729	7,437	7,144	6,857	6,557	6,252	5,947	5,642
34,800	34,850	7,749	7,456	7,164	6,875	6,575	6,270	5,965	5,660
34,850	34,900	7,768	7,476	7,183	6,893	6,593	6,288	5,983	5,678
34,900	34,950	7,788	7,495	7,203	6,911	6,611	6,306	6,001	5,696
34,950	35,000	7,807	7,515	7,222	6,930	6,629	6,324	6,019	5,714
35,000	35,050	7,827	7,534	7,242	6,949	6,647	6,342	6,037	5,732
35,050	35,100	7,846	7,554	7,261	6,969	6,665	6,360	6,055	5,750
35,100	35,150	7,866	7,573	7,281	6,988	6,683	6,378	6,073	5,768
35,150	35,200	7,885	7,593	7,300	7,008	6,701	6,396	6,091	5,786
35,200	35,250	7,905	7,612	7,320	7,027	6,719	6,414	6,109	5,804
35,250	35,300	7,924	7,632	7,339	7,047	6,737	6,432	6,127	5,822
35,300	35,350	7,944	7,651	7,359	7,066	6,755	6,450	6,145	5,840
35,350	35,400	7,963	7,671	7,378	7,086	6,773	6,468	6,163	5,858
35,400	35,450	7,983	7,690	7,398	7,105	6,791	6,486	6,181	5,876
35,450	35,500	8,002	7,710	7,417	7,125	6,809	6,504	6,199	5,894
35,500	35,550	8,022	7,729	7,437	7,144	6,827	6,522	6,217	5,912
35,550	35,600	8,041	7,749	7,456	7,164	6,845	6,540	6,235	5,930
35,600	35,650	8,061	7,768	7,476	7,183	6,863	6,558	6,253	5,948
35,650	35,700	8,080	7,788	7,495	7,203	6,881	6,576	6,271	5,966
35,700	35,750	8,100	7,807	7,515	7,222	6,900	6,594	6,289	5,984
35,750	35,800	8,119	7,827	7,534	7,242	6,919	6,612	6,307	6,002
35,800	35,850	8,139	7,846	7,554	7,261	6,939	6,630	6,325	6,020
35,850	35,900	8,158	7,866	7,573	7,281	6,958	6,648	6,343	6,038
35,900	35,950	8,178	7,885	7,593	7,300	6,978	6,666	6,361	6,056
35,950	36,000	8,197	7,905	7,612	7,320	6,997	6,684	6,379	6,074
36,000	36,050	8,217	7,924	7,632	7,339	7,017	6,702	6,397	6,092
36,050	36,100	8,236	7,944	7,651	7,359	7,036	6,720	6,415	6,110
36,100	36,150	8,256	7,963	7,671	7,378	7,056	6,738	6,433	6,128
36,150	36,200	8,275	7,983	7,690	7,398	7,075	6,756	6,451	6,146
36,200	36,250	8,295	8,002	7,710	7,417	7,095	6,774	6,469	6,164
36,250	36,300	8,314	8,022	7,729	7,437	7,114	6,792	6,487	6,182
36,300	36,350	8,334	8,041	7,749	7,456	7,134	6,810	6,505	6,200
36,350	36,400	8,353	8,061	7,768	7,476	7,153	6,828	6,523	6,218
36,400	36,450	8,373	8,080	7,788	7,495	7,173	6,846	6,541	6,236
36,450	36,500	8,392	8,100	7,807	7,515	7,192	6,865	6,559	6,254
36,500	36,550	8,412	8,119	7,827	7,534	7,212	6,884	6,577	6,272
36,550	36,600	8,431	8,139	7,846	7,554	7,231	6,904	6,595	6,290
36,600	36,650	8,451	8,158	7,866	7,573	7,251	6,923	6,613	6,308
36,650	36,700	8,470	8,178	7,885	7,593	7,270	6,943	6,631	6,326
36,700	36,750	8,491	8,197	7,905	7,612	7,290	6,962	6,649	6,344
36,750	36,800	8,512	8,217	7,924	7,632	7,309	6,982	6,667	6,362
36,800	36,850	8,533	8,236	7,944	7,651	7,329	7,001	6,685	6,380
36,850	36,900	8,554	8,256	7,963	7,671	7,348	7,021	6,703	6,398
36,900	36,950	8,575	8,275	7,983	7,690	7,368	7,040	6,721	6,416
36,950	37,000	8,596	8,295	8,002	7,710	7,387	7,060	6,739	6,434
37,000	37,050	8,617	8,314	8,022	7,729	7,407	7,079	6,757	6,452
37,050	37,100	8,638	8,334	8,041	7,749	7,426	7,099	6,775	6,470
37,100	37,150	8,659	8,353	8,061	7,768	7,446	7,118	6,793	6,488
37,150	37,200	8,680	8,373	8,080	7,788	7,465	7,138	6,811	6,506
37,200	37,250	8,701	8,392	8,100	7,807	7,485	7,157	6,830	6,524
37,250	37,300	8,722	8,412	8,119	7,827	7,504	7,177	6,849	6,542
37,300	37,350	8,743	8,431	8,139	7,846	7,524	7,196	6,869	6,560
37,350	37,400	8,764	8,451	8,158	7,866	7,543	7,216	6,888	6,578
37,400	37,450	8,785	8,470	8,178	7,885	7,563	7,235	6,908	6,596
37,450	37,500	8,806	8,491	8,197	7,905	7,582	7,255	6,927	6,614
37,500	37,550	8,827	8,512	8,217	7,924	7,602	7,274	6,947	6,632
37,550	37,600	8,848	8,533	8,236	7,944	7,621	7,294	6,966	6,650
37,600	37,650	8,869	8,554	8,256	7,963	7,641	7,313	6,986	6,668
37,650	37,700	8,890	8,575	8,275	7,983	7,660	7,333	7,005	6,686
37,700	37,750	8,911	8,596	8,295	8,002	7,680	7,352	7,025	6,704
37,750	37,800	8,932	8,617	8,314	8,022	7,699	7,372	7,044	6,722
37,800	37,850	8,953	8,638	8,334	8,041	7,719	7,391	7,064	6,740
37,850	37,900	8,974	8,659	8,353	8,061	7,738	7,411	7,083	6,758
37,900	37,950	8,995	8,680	8,373	8,080	7,758	7,430	7,103	6,776
37,950	38,000	9,016	8,701	8,392	8,100	7,777	7,450	7,122	6,795
38,000	38,050	9,037	8,722	8,412	8,119	7,797	7,469	7,142	6,814
38,050	38,100	9,058	8,743	8,431	8,139	7,816	7,489	7,161	6,834
38,100	38,150	9,079	8,764	8,451	8,158	7,836	7,508	7,181	6,853
38,150	38,200	9,100	8,785	8,470	8,178	7,855	7,528	7,200	6,873
38,200	38,250	9,121	8,806	8,491	8,197	7,875	7,547	7,220	6,892
38,250	38,300	9,142	8,827	8,512	8,217	7,894	7,567	7,239	6,912
38,300	38,350	9,163	8,848	8,533	8,236	7,914	7,586	7,259	6,931
38,350	38,400	9,184	8,869	8,554	8,256	7,933	7,606	7,278	6,951
38,400	38,450	9,205	8,890	8,575	8,275	7,953	7,625	7,298	6,970
38,450	38,500	9,226	8,911	8,596	8,295	7,972	7,645	7,317	6,990
38,500	38,550	9,247	8,932	8,617	8,314	7,992	7,664	7,337	7,009
38,550	38,600	9,268	8,953	8,638	8,334	8,011	7,684	7,356	7,029
38,600	38,650	9,289	8,974	8,659	8,353	8,031	7,703	7,376	7,048
38,650	38,700	9,310	8,995	8,680	8,373	8,050	7,723	7,395	7,068
38,700	38,750	9,331	9,016	8,701	8,392	8,070	7,742	7,415	7,087
38,750	38,800	9,352	9,037	8,722	8,412	8,089	7,762	7,434	7,107
38,800	38,850	9,373	9,058	8,743	8,431	8,109	7,781	7,454	7,126
38,850	38,900	9,394	9,079	8,764	8,451	8,128	7,801	7,473	7,146
38,900	38,950	9,415	9,100	8,785	8,470	8,148	7,820	7,493	7,165
38,950	39,000	9,436	9,121	8,806	8,491	8,167	7,840	7,512	7,185
39,000	39,050	9,457	9,142	8,827	8,512	8,187	7,859	7,532	7,204
39,050	39,100	9,478	9,163	8,848	8,533	8,206	7,879	7,551	7,224
39,100	39,150	9,499	9,184	8,869	8,554	8,226	7,898	7,571	7,243
39,150	39,200	9,520	9,205	8,890	8,575	8,245	7,918	7,590	7,263
39,200	39,250	9,541	9,226	8,911	8,596	8,265	7,937	7,610	7,282
39,250	39,300	9,562	9,247	8,932	8,617	8,284	7,957	7,629	7,302
39,300	39,350	9,583	9,268	8,953	8,638	8,304	7,976	7,649	7,321
39,350	39,400	9,604	9,289	8,974	8,659	8,323	7,996	7,668	7,341
39,400	39,450	9,625	9,310	8,995	8,680	8,343	8,015	7,688	7,360
39,450	39,500	9,646	9,331	9,016	8,701	8,362	8,035	7,707	7,380
39,500	39,550	9,667	9,352	9,037	8,722	8,382	8,054	7,727	7,399
39,550	39,600	9,688	9,373	9,058	8,743	8,401	8,074	7,746	7,419
39,600	39,650	9,709	9,394	9,079	8,764	8,421	8,093	7,766	7,438
39,650	39,700	9,730	9,415	9,100	8,785	8,440	8,113	7,785	7,458
39,700	39,750	9,751	9,436	9,121	8,806	8,461	8,132	7,805	7,477
39,750	39,800	9,772	9,457	9,142	8,827	8,482	8,152	7,824	7,497
39,800	39,850	9,793	9,478	9,163	8,848	8,503	8,171	7,844	7,516
39,850	39,900	9,814	9,499	9,184	8,869	8,524	8,191	7,863	7,536
39,900	39,950	9,835	9,520	9,205	8,890	8,545	8,210	7,883	7,555
39,950	40,000	9,856	9,541	9,226	8,911	8,566	8,230	7,902	7,575

Continued next column

1977 Tax Table C—MARRIED FILING SEPARATELY (Box 3)

(For married persons filing separate returns with tax table income of $20,000 or less who claim fewer than 4 exemptions)

To find your tax: Read down the left income column until you find your income as shown on line 34 of Form 1040. Read across to the column headed by the total number of exemptions claimed on line 7 of Form 1040. The amount shown at the point where the two lines meet is your tax. Enter on Form 1040, line 35.

The $1,600 zero bracket amount, your deduction for exemptions and the general tax credit have been taken into account in figuring the tax shown in this table. **Do not take a separate deduction for them.**

Caution: *If you or your spouse itemize deductions, or if you can be claimed as a dependent on your parent's return AND you have unearned income (interests, dividends, etc.) of $750 or more AND your earned income is less than $1,600 you must first use Schedule TC (Form 1040), Part II.*

Over	But not over	1	2	3	Over	But not over	1	2	3	Over	But not over	1	2	3
If $2,600 or less your tax is 0					5,000	5,050	403	227	68	7,800	7,850	980	780	580
					5,050	5,100	413	236	76	7,850	7,900	991	791	591
2,600	2,625	2	0	0	5,100	5,150	422	245	84	7,900	7,950	1,002	802	602
2,625	2,650	5	0	0	5,150	5,200	432	254	92	7,950	8,000	1,013	813	613
2,650	2,675	9	0	0	5,200	5,250	441	264	100	8,000	8,050	1,024	824	624
2,675	2,700	12	0	0	5,250	5,300	451	273	108	8,050	8,100	1,035	835	635
2,700	2,725	16	0	0	5,300	5,350	460	283	116	8,100	8,150	1,046	846	646
2,725	2,750	19	0	0	5,350	5,400	470	292	124	8,150	8,200	1,057	857	657
2,750	2,775	23	0	0	5,400	5,450	479	302	133	8,200	8,250	1,068	868	668
2,775	2,800	26	0	0	5,450	5,500	489	311	141	8,250	8,300	1,079	879	679
2,800	2,825	30	0	0	5,500	5,550	498	321	150	8,300	8,350	1,090	890	690
2,825	2,850	33	0	0	5,550	5,600	508	330	158	8,350	8,400	1,101	901	701
2,850	2,875	37	0	0	5,600	5,650	517	340	167	8,400	8,450	1,114	912	712
2,875	2,900	41	0	0	5,650	5,700	527	349	175	8,450	8,500	1,126	923	723
2,900	2,925	44	0	0	5,700	5,750	536	359	184	8,500	8,550	1,139	934	734
2,925	2,950	48	0	0	5,750	5,800	546	368	192	8,550	8,600	1,151	945	745
2,950	2,975	52	0	0	5,800	5,850	555	378	201	8,600	8,650	1,164	956	756
2,975	3,000	56	0	0	5,850	5,900	565	387	210	8,650	8,700	1,176	967	767
3,000	3,050	61	0	0	5,900	5,950	574	397	219	8,700	8,750	1,189	978	778
3,050	3,100	69	0	0	5,950	6,000	584	406	229	8,750	8,800	1,201	989	789
3,100	3,150	76	0	0	6,000	6,050	593	416	238	8,800	8,850	1,214	1,000	800
3,150	3,200	84	0	0	6,050	6,100	603	425	248	8,850	8,900	1,226	1,011	811
3,200	3,250	91	0	0	6,100	6,150	612	435	257	8,900	8,950	1,239	1,022	822
3,250	3,300	99	0	0	6,150	6,200	622	444	267	8,950	9,000	1,251	1,033	833
3,300	3,350	106	0	0	6,200	6,250	631	454	276	9,000	9,050	1,264	1,044	844
3,350	3,400	114	0	0	6,250	6,300	641	463	286	9,050	9,100	1,276	1,055	855
3,400	3,450	122	0	0	6,300	6,350	650	473	295	9,100	9,150	1,289	1,066	866
3,450	3,500	130	0	0	6,350	6,400	661	482	305	9,150	9,200	1,301	1,079	877
3,500	3,550	138	0	0	6,400	6,450	672	492	314	9,200	9,250	1,314	1,091	888
3,550	3,600	146	0	0	6,450	6,500	683	501	324	9,250	9,300	1,326	1,104	899
3,600	3,650	154	4	0	6,500	6,550	694	511	333	9,300	9,350	1,339	1,116	910
3,650	3,700	162	11	0	6,550	6,600	705	520	343	9,350	9,400	1,351	1,129	921
3,700	3,750	170	19	0	6,600	6,650	716	530	352	9,400	9,450	1,364	1,141	932
3,750	3,800	178	26	0	6,650	6,700	727	539	362	9,450	9,500	1,376	1,154	943
3,800	3,850	186	34	0	6,700	6,750	738	549	371	9,500	9,550	1,389	1,166	954
3,850	3,900	194	41	0	6,750	6,800	749	558	381	9,550	9,600	1,401	1,179	965
3,900	3,950	203	49	0	6,800	6,850	760	568	390	9,600	9,650	1,414	1,191	976
3,950	4,000	211	56	0	6,850	6,900	771	577	400	9,650	9,700	1,426	1,204	987
4,000	4,050	220	64	0	6,900	6,950	782	587	409	9,700	9,750	1,439	1,216	998
4,050	4,100	228	71	0	6,950	7,000	793	596	419	9,750	9,800	1,451	1,229	1,009
4,100	4,150	237	79	0	7,000	7,050	804	606	428	9,800	9,850	1,464	1,241	1,020
4,150	4,200	245	87	0	7,050	7,100	815	615	438	9,850	9,900	1,476	1,254	1,031
4,200	4,250	254	95	0	7,100	7,150	826	626	447	9,900	9,950	1,489	1,266	1,044
4,250	4,300	262	103	0	7,150	7,200	837	637	457	9,950	10,000	1,501	1,279	1,056
4,300	4,350	271	111	0	7,200	7,250	848	648	466	10,000	10,050	1,514	1,291	1,069
4,350	4,400	280	119	0	7,250	7,300	859	659	476	10,050	10,100	1,526	1,304	1,081
4,400	4,450	289	127	0	7,300	7,350	870	670	485	10,100	10,150	1,539	1,316	1,094
4,450	4,500	299	135	0	7,350	7,400	881	681	495	10,150	10,200	1,551	1,329	1,106
4,500	4,550	308	143	0	7,400	7,450	892	692	504	10,200	10,250	1,564	1,341	1,119
4,550	4,600	318	151	0	7,450	7,500	903	703	514	10,250	10,300	1,576	1,354	1,131
4,600	4,650	327	159	6	7,500	7,550	914	714	523	10,300	10,350	1,589	1,366	1,144
4,650	4,700	337	168	14	7,550	7,600	925	725	533	10,350	10,400	1,602	1,379	1,156
4,700	4,750	346	176	21	7,600	7,650	936	736	542	10,400	10,450	1,616	1,391	1,169
4,750	4,800	356	185	29	7,650	7,700	947	747	552	10,450	10,500	1,630	1,404	1,181
4,800	4,850	365	193	36	7,700	7,750	958	758	561	10,500	10,550	1,644	1,416	1,194
4,850	4,900	375	202	44	7,750	7,800	969	769	571	10,550	10,600	1,658	1,429	1,206
4,900	4,950	384	210	52										
4,950	5,000	394	219	60										

Continued next column   Continued next column   Continued on next page

1977 Tax Table C—MARRIED FILING SEPARATELY (Box 3)
(Continued)

(If your income or exemptions are not covered, use Schedule TC (Form 1040), Part I to figure your tax)

If line 34, Form 1040 is—		And the total number of exemptions claimed on line 7 is—			If line 34, Form 1040 is—		And the total number of exemptions claimed on line 7 is—			If line 34, Form 1040 is—		And the total number of exemptions claimed on line 7 is—		
Over	But not over	1	2	3	Over	But not over	1	2	3	Over	But not over	1	2	3
		Your tax is—					Your tax is—					Your tax is—		
10,600	10,650	1,672	1,441	1,219	13,800	13,850	2,627	2,352	2,078	17,000	17,050	3,778	3,453	3,148
10,650	10,700	1,686	1,454	1,231	13,850	13,900	2,643	2,368	2,093	17,050	17,100	3,798	3,471	3,166
10,700	10,750	1,700	1,466	1,244	13,900	13,950	2,659	2,384	2,109	17,100	17,150	3,817	3,490	3,184
10,750	10,800	1,714	1,479	1,256	13,950	14,000	2,675	2,400	2,125	17,150	17,200	3,837	3,509	3,202
10,800	10,850	1,728	1,491	1,269	14,000	14,050	2,691	2,416	2,141	17,200	17,250	3,856	3,529	3,220
10,850	10,900	1,742	1,504	1,281	14,050	14,100	2,707	2,432	2,157	17,250	17,300	3,876	3,548	3,238
10,900	10,950	1,756	1,516	1,294	14,100	14,150	2,723	2,448	2,173	17,300	17,350	3,895	3,568	3,256
10,950	11,000	1,770	1,529	1,306	14,150	14,200	2,739	2,464	2,189	17,350	17,400	3,915	3,587	3,274
11,000	11,050	1,784	1,541	1,319	14,200	14,250	2,755	2,480	2,205	17,400	17,450	3,934	3,607	3,292
11,050	11,100	1,798	1,554	1,331	14,250	14,300	2,771	2,496	2,221	17,450	17,500	3,954	3,626	3,310
11,100	11,150	1,812	1,567	1,344	14,300	14,350	2,787	2,512	2,237	17,500	17,550	3,973	3,646	3,328
11,150	11,200	1,826	1,581	1,356	14,350	14,400	2,804	2,528	2,253	17,550	17,600	3,993	3,665	3,346
11,200	11,250	1,840	1,595	1,369	14,400	14,450	2,822	2,544	2,269	17,600	17,650	4,012	3,685	3,364
11,250	11,300	1,854	1,609	1,381	14,450	14,500	2,840	2,560	2,285	17,650	17,700	4,032	3,704	3,382
11,300	11,350	1,868	1,623	1,394	14,500	14,550	2,858	2,576	2,301	17,700	17,750	4,051	3,724	3,400
11,350	11,400	1,882	1,637	1,406	14,550	14,600	2,876	2,592	2,317	17,750	17,800	4,071	3,743	3,418
11,400	11,450	1,896	1,651	1,419	14,600	14,650	2,894	2,608	2,333	17,800	17,850	4,090	3,763	3,436
11,450	11,500	1,910	1,665	1,431	14,650	14,700	2,912	2,624	2,349	17,850	17,900	4,110	3,782	3,455
11,500	11,550	1,924	1,679	1,444	14,700	14,750	2,930	2,640	2,365	17,900	17,950	4,129	3,802	3,474
11,550	11,600	1,938	1,693	1,456	14,750	14,800	2,948	2,656	2,381	17,950	18,000	4,149	3,821	3,494
11,600	11,650	1,952	1,707	1,469	14,800	14,850	2,966	2,672	2,397	18,000	18,050	4,168	3,841	3,513
11,650	11,700	1,966	1,721	1,481	14,850	14,900	2,984	2,688	2,413	18,050	18,100	4,188	3,860	3,533
11,700	11,750	1,980	1,735	1,494	14,900	14,950	3,002	2,704	2,429	18,100	18,150	4,207	3,880	3,552
11,750	11,800	1,994	1,749	1,506	14,950	15,000	3,020	2,720	2,445	18,150	18,200	4,227	3,899	3,572
11,800	11,850	2,008	1,763	1,519	15,000	15,050	3,038	2,736	2,461	18,200	18,250	4,246	3,919	3,591
11,850	11,900	2,022	1,777	1,532	15,050	15,100	3,056	2,752	2,477	18,250	18,300	4,266	3,938	3,611
11,900	11,950	2,036	1,791	1,546	15,100	15,150	3,074	2,769	2,493	18,300	18,350	4,285	3,958	3,630
11,950	12,000	2,050	1,805	1,560	15,150	15,200	3,092	2,787	2,509	18,350	18,400	4,306	3,977	3,650
12,000	12,050	2,064	1,819	1,574	15,200	15,250	3,110	2,805	2,525	18,400	18,450	4,327	3,997	3,669
12,050	12,100	2,078	1,833	1,588	15,250	15,300	3,128	2,823	2,541	18,450	18,500	4,348	4,016	3,689
12,100	12,150	2,092	1,847	1,602	15,300	15,350	3,146	2,841	2,557	18,500	18,550	4,369	4,036	3,708
12,150	12,200	2,106	1,861	1,616	15,350	15,400	3,164	2,859	2,573	18,550	18,600	4,390	4,055	3,728
12,200	12,250	2,120	1,875	1,630	15,400	15,450	3,182	2,877	2,589	18,600	18,650	4,411	4,075	3,747
12,250	12,300	2,134	1,889	1,644	15,450	15,500	3,200	2,895	2,605	18,650	18,700	4,432	4,094	3,767
12,300	12,350	2,148	1,903	1,658	15,500	15,550	3,218	2,913	2,621	18,700	18,750	4,453	4,114	3,786
12,350	12,400	2,163	1,917	1,672	15,550	15,600	3,236	2,931	2,637	18,750	18,800	4,474	4,133	3,806
12,400	12,450	2,179	1,931	1,686	15,600	15,650	3,254	2,949	2,653	18,800	18,850	4,495	4,153	3,825
12,450	12,500	2,195	1,945	1,700	15,650	15,700	3,272	2,967	2,669	18,850	18,900	4,516	4,172	3,845
12,500	12,550	2,211	1,959	1,714	15,700	15,750	3,290	2,985	2,685	18,900	18,950	4,537	4,192	3,864
12,550	12,600	2,227	1,973	1,728	15,750	15,800	3,308	3,003	2,701	18,950	19,000	4,558	4,211	3,884
12,600	12,650	2,243	1,987	1,742	15,800	15,850	3,326	3,021	2,717	19,000	19,050	4,579	4,231	3,903
12,650	12,700	2,259	2,001	1,756	15,850	15,900	3,344	3,039	2,734	19,050	19,100	4,600	4,250	3,923
12,700	12,750	2,275	2,015	1,770	15,900	15,950	3,362	3,057	2,752	19,100	19,150	4,621	4,271	3,942
12,750	12,800	2,291	2,029	1,784	15,950	16,000	3,380	3,075	2,770	19,150	19,200	4,642	4,292	3,962
12,800	12,850	2,307	2,043	1,798	16,000	16,050	3,398	3,093	2,788	19,200	19,250	4,663	4,313	3,981
12,850	12,900	2,323	2,057	1,812	16,050	16,100	3,416	3,111	2,806	19,250	19,300	4,684	4,334	4,001
12,900	12,950	2,339	2,071	1,826	16,100	16,150	3,434	3,129	2,824	19,300	19,350	4,705	4,355	4,020
12,950	13,000	2,355	2,085	1,840	16,150	16,200	3,452	3,147	2,842	19,350	19,400	4,726	4,376	4,040
13,000	13,050	2,371	2,099	1,854	16,200	16,250	3,470	3,165	2,860	19,400	19,450	4,747	4,397	4,059
13,050	13,100	2,387	2,113	1,868	16,250	16,300	3,488	3,183	2,878	19,450	19,500	4,768	4,418	4,079
13,100	13,150	2,403	2,128	1,882	16,300	16,350	3,506	3,201	2,896	19,500	19,550	4,789	4,439	4,098
13,150	13,200	2,419	2,144	1,896	16,350	16,400	3,525	3,219	2,914	19,550	19,600	4,810	4,460	4,118
13,200	13,250	2,435	2,160	1,910	16,400	16,450	3,544	3,237	2,932	19,600	19,650	4,831	4,481	4,137
13,250	13,300	2,451	2,176	1,924	16,450	16,500	3,564	3,255	2,950	19,650	19,700	4,852	4,502	4,157
13,300	13,350	2,467	2,192	1,938	16,500	16,550	3,583	3,273	2,968	19,700	19,750	4,873	4,523	4,176
13,350	13,400	2,483	2,208	1,952	16,550	16,600	3,603	3,291	2,986	19,750	19,800	4,894	4,544	4,196
13,400	13,450	2,499	2,224	1,966	16,600	16,650	3,622	3,309	3,004	19,800	19,850	4,915	4,565	4,215
13,450	13,500	2,515	2,240	1,980	16,650	16,700	3,642	3,327	3,022	19,850	19,900	4,936	4,586	4,236
13,500	13,550	2,531	2,256	1,994	16,700	16,750	3,661	3,345	3,040	19,900	19,950	4,957	4,607	4,257
13,550	13,600	2,547	2,272	2,008	16,750	16,800	3,681	3,363	3,058	19,950	20,000	4,978	4,628	4,278
13,600	13,650	2,563	2,288	2,022	16,800	16,850	3,700	3,381	3,076					
13,650	13,700	2,579	2,304	2,036	16,850	16,900	3,720	3,399	3,094					
13,700	13,750	2,595	2,320	2,050	16,900	16,950	3,739	3,417	3,112					
13,750	13,800	2,611	2,336	2,064	16,950	17,000	3,759	3,435	3,130					

Continued next column   Continued next column

1977 Tax Table D—HEAD OF HOUSEHOLD (Box 4)

(For unmarried (including certain married persons living apart) or legally separated persons who qualify as heads of household with tax table income of $20,000 or less who claim fewer than 9 exemptions)

To find your tax: Read down the left income column until you find your income as shown on line 34 of Form 1040. Read across to the column headed by the total number of exemptions claimed on line 7 of Form 1040. The amount shown at the point where the two lines meet is your tax. Enter on Form 1040, line 35.

The $2,200 zero bracket amount, your deduction for exemptions and the general tax credit have been taken into account in figuring the tax shown in this table. **Do not take a separate deduction for them.**

If line 34, Form 1040 is— Over	But not over	1	2	3	4	5	6	7	8
		Your tax is—							
If $3,200 or less your tax is 0									
3,200	3,250	4	0	0	0	0	0	0	0
3,250	3,300	11	0	0	0	0	0	0	0
3,300	3,350	18	0	0	0	0	0	0	0
3,350	3,400	25	0	0	0	0	0	0	0
3,400	3,450	32	0	0	0	0	0	0	0
3,450	3,500	39	0	0	0	0	0	0	0
3,500	3,550	46	0	0	0	0	0	0	0
3,550	3,600	53	0	0	0	0	0	0	0
3,600	3,650	60	0	0	0	0	0	0	0
3,650	3,700	67	0	0	0	0	0	0	0
3,700	3,750	74	0	0	0	0	0	0	0
3,750	3,800	81	0	0	0	0	0	0	0
3,800	3,850	88	0	0	0	0	0	0	0
3,850	3,900	95	0	0	0	0	0	0	0
3,900	3,950	102	0	0	0	0	0	0	0
3,950	4,000	109	0	0	0	0	0	0	0
4,000	4,050	117	0	0	0	0	0	0	0
4,050	4,100	125	0	0	0	0	0	0	0
4,100	4,150	133	0	0	0	0	0	0	0
4,150	4,200	141	0	0	0	0	0	0	0
4,200	4,250	149	4	0	0	0	0	0	0
4,250	4,300	157	11	0	0	0	0	0	0
4,300	4,350	165	18	0	0	0	0	0	0
4,350	4,400	173	25	0	0	0	0	0	0
4,400	4,450	181	32	0	0	0	0	0	0
4,450	4,500	189	39	0	0	0	0	0	0
4,500	4,550	197	46	0	0	0	0	0	0
4,550	4,600	205	53	0	0	0	0	0	0
4,600	4,650	213	60	0	0	0	0	0	0
4,650	4,700	221	67	0	0	0	0	0	0
4,700	4,750	229	74	0	0	0	0	0	0
4,750	4,800	236	82	0	0	0	0	0	0
4,800	4,850	243	90	0	0	0	0	0	0
4,850	4,900	250	98	0	0	0	0	0	0
4,900	4,950	257	106	0	0	0	0	0	0
4,950	5,000	264	114	0	0	0	0	0	0
5,000	5,050	272	122	0	0	0	0	0	0
5,050	5,100	280	130	0	0	0	0	0	0
5,100	5,150	288	138	0	0	0	0	0	0
5,150	5,200	296	146	0	0	0	0	0	0
5,200	5,250	304	154	4	0	0	0	0	0
5,250	5,300	312	162	11	0	0	0	0	0
5,300	5,350	320	170	18	0	0	0	0	0
5,350	5,400	328	178	25	0	0	0	0	0
5,400	5,450	336	186	32	0	0	0	0	0
5,450	5,500	344	194	39	0	0	0	0	0
5,500	5,550	352	202	47	0	0	0	0	0
5,550	5,600	360	210	55	0	0	0	0	0
5,600	5,650	368	218	63	0	0	0	0	0
5,650	5,700	376	226	71	0	0	0	0	0
5,700	5,750	384	235	79	0	0	0	0	0
5,750	5,800	392	244	87	0	0	0	0	0
5,800	5,850	400	253	95	0	0	0	0	0
5,850	5,900	408	262	103	0	0	0	0	0
5,900	5,950	416	271	111	0	0	0	0	0
5,950	6,000	424	280	119	0	0	0	0	0

Continued next column

If line 34, Form 1040 is— Over	But not over	1	2	3	4	5	6	7	8
		Your tax is—							
6,000	6,050	432	289	127	0	0	0	0	0
6,050	6,100	440	298	135	0	0	0	0	0
6,100	6,150	448	307	143	0	0	0	0	0
6,150	6,200	456	316	151	0	0	0	0	0
6,200	6,250	464	325	159	4	0	0	0	0
6,250	6,300	472	334	167	12	0	0	0	0
6,300	6,350	480	343	175	20	0	0	0	0
6,350	6,400	488	352	183	28	0	0	0	0
6,400	6,450	496	361	191	36	0	0	0	0
6,450	6,500	504	370	200	44	0	0	0	0
6,500	6,550	512	379	209	52	0	0	0	0
6,550	6,600	520	388	218	60	0	0	0	0
6,600	6,650	528	397	227	68	0	0	0	0
6,650	6,700	536	406	236	76	0	0	0	0
6,700	6,750	544	415	245	84	0	0	0	0
6,750	6,800	552	424	254	92	0	0	0	0
6,800	6,850	560	433	263	100	0	0	0	0
6,850	6,900	568	442	272	108	0	0	0	0
6,900	6,950	576	451	281	116	0	0	0	0
6,950	7,000	584	460	290	124	0	0	0	0
7,000	7,050	593	469	299	132	0	0	0	0
7,050	7,100	601	478	308	140	0	0	0	0
7,100	7,150	610	487	317	148	0	0	0	0
7,150	7,200	618	496	326	156	1	0	0	0
7,200	7,250	627	504	335	165	9	0	0	0
7,250	7,300	635	512	344	174	17	0	0	0
7,300	7,350	644	520	353	183	25	0	0	0
7,350	7,400	652	528	362	192	33	0	0	0
7,400	7,450	661	536	371	201	41	0	0	0
7,450	7,500	669	544	380	210	49	0	0	0
7,500	7,550	678	552	389	219	57	0	0	0
7,550	7,600	686	560	398	228	65	0	0	0
7,600	7,650	695	568	407	237	73	0	0	0
7,650	7,700	703	576	416	246	81	0	0	0
7,700	7,750	712	584	425	255	89	0	0	0
7,750	7,800	720	593	434	264	97	0	0	0
7,800	7,850	729	601	443	273	105	0	0	0
7,850	7,900	737	610	452	282	113	0	0	0
7,900	7,950	746	618	461	291	121	0	0	0
7,950	8,000	754	627	470	300	130	0	0	0
8,000	8,050	763	635	479	309	139	0	0	0
8,050	8,100	771	644	488	318	148	0	0	0
8,100	8,150	780	652	497	327	157	0	0	0
8,150	8,200	788	661	506	336	166	6	0	0
8,200	8,250	797	669	515	345	175	14	0	0
8,250	8,300	805	678	524	354	184	22	0	0
8,300	8,350	814	686	533	363	193	30	0	0
8,350	8,400	822	695	542	372	202	38	0	0
8,400	8,450	831	703	551	381	211	46	0	0
8,450	8,500	839	712	560	390	220	54	0	0
8,500	8,550	848	720	569	399	229	62	0	0
8,550	8,600	856	729	579	408	238	70	0	0
8,600	8,650	865	737	588	417	247	78	0	0
8,650	8,700	873	746	598	426	256	86	0	0
8,700	8,750	882	754	607	435	265	95	0	0
8,750	8,800	890	763	617	444	274	104	0	0

Continued on next page

1977 Tax Table D—HEAD OF HOUSEHOLD (Box 4)
(Continued)

(If your income or exemptions are not covered, use Schedule TC (Form 1040), Part I to figure your tax)

Over	But not over	1	2	3	4	5	6	7	8	Over	But not over	1	2	3	4	5	6	7	8
8,800	8,850	899	771	626	453	283	113	0	0	11,600	11,650	1,462	1,305	1,155	994	803	626	448	277
8,850	8,900	907	780	636	462	292	122	0	0	11,650	11,700	1,472	1,315	1,165	1,005	813	635	458	286
8,900	8,950	916	788	645	471	301	131	0	0	11,700	11,750	1,483	1,325	1,175	1,016	822	645	467	295
8,950	9,000	925	797	655	480	310	140	0	0	11,750	11,800	1,493	1,336	1,185	1,027	832	654	477	304
9,000	9,050	935	805	664	489	319	149	0	0	11,800	11,850	1,504	1,346	1,195	1,038	841	664	486	313
9,050	9,100	945	814	674	498	328	158	0	0	11,850	11,900	1,514	1,357	1,205	1,049	851	673	496	322
9,100	9,150	955	822	683	507	337	167	3	0	11,900	11,950	1,525	1,367	1,215	1,060	860	683	505	331
9,150	9,200	965	831	693	516	346	176	11	0	11,950	12,000	1,536	1,378	1,225	1,071	871	692	515	340
9,200	9,250	975	839	702	525	355	185	19	0	12,000	12,050	1,547	1,388	1,235	1,082	882	702	524	349
9,250	9,300	985	848	712	534	364	194	27	0	12,050	12,100	1,559	1,399	1,245	1,093	893	711	534	358
9,300	9,350	995	856	721	544	373	203	35	0	12,100	12,150	1,570	1,409	1,255	1,104	904	721	543	367
9,350	9,400	1,005	865	731	553	382	212	43	0	12,150	12,200	1,582	1,420	1,265	1,115	915	730	553	376
9,400	9,450	1,015	873	740	563	391	221	51	0	12,200	12,250	1,593	1,430	1,275	1,125	926	740	562	385
9,450	9,500	1,025	882	750	572	400	230	60	0	12,250	12,300	1,605	1,441	1,285	1,135	937	749	572	394
9,500	9,550	1,035	890	759	582	409	239	69	0	12,300	12,350	1,616	1,451	1,295	1,145	948	759	581	404
9,550	9,600	1,045	899	769	591	418	248	78	0	12,350	12,400	1,628	1,462	1,305	1,155	959	768	591	413
9,600	9,650	1,055	907	778	601	427	257	87	0	12,400	12,450	1,639	1,472	1,315	1,165	970	778	600	423
9,650	9,700	1,065	916	788	610	436	266	96	0	12,450	12,500	1,651	1,483	1,325	1,175	981	787	610	432
9,700	9,750	1,075	925	797	620	445	275	105	0	12,500	12,550	1,662	1,493	1,336	1,185	992	797	619	442
9,750	9,800	1,085	935	805	629	454	284	114	0	12,550	12,600	1,674	1,504	1,346	1,195	1,003	806	629	451
9,800	9,850	1,095	945	814	639	463	293	123	0	12,600	12,650	1,685	1,514	1,357	1,205	1,014	816	638	461
9,850	9,900	1,105	955	822	648	472	302	132	0	12,650	12,700	1,697	1,525	1,367	1,215	1,025	825	648	470
9,900	9,950	1,115	965	831	658	481	311	141	0	12,700	12,750	1,708	1,536	1,378	1,225	1,036	836	657	480
9,950	10,000	1,125	975	839	667	490	320	150	0	12,750	12,800	1,720	1,547	1,388	1,235	1,047	847	667	489
10,000	10,050	1,135	985	848	677	499	329	159	0	12,800	12,850	1,731	1,559	1,399	1,245	1,058	858	676	499
10,050	10,100	1,145	995	856	686	509	338	168	0	12,850	12,900	1,743	1,570	1,409	1,255	1,069	869	686	508
10,100	10,150	1,155	1,005	865	696	518	347	177	8	12,900	12,950	1,754	1,582	1,420	1,265	1,080	880	695	518
10,150	10,200	1,165	1,015	873	705	528	356	186	16	12,950	13,000	1,766	1,593	1,430	1,275	1,091	891	705	527
10,200	10,250	1,175	1,025	882	715	537	365	195	25	13,000	13,050	1,779	1,605	1,441	1,285	1,102	902	714	537
10,250	10,300	1,185	1,035	890	724	547	374	204	34	13,050	13,100	1,791	1,616	1,451	1,295	1,113	913	724	546
10,300	10,350	1,195	1,045	899	734	556	383	213	43	13,100	13,150	1,804	1,628	1,462	1,305	1,124	924	733	556
10,350	10,400	1,205	1,055	907	743	566	392	222	52	13,150	13,200	1,816	1,639	1,472	1,315	1,135	935	743	565
10,400	10,450	1,215	1,065	916	753	575	401	231	61	13,200	13,250	1,829	1,651	1,483	1,325	1,146	946	752	575
10,450	10,500	1,225	1,075	925	762	585	410	240	70	13,250	13,300	1,841	1,662	1,493	1,336	1,157	957	762	584
10,500	10,550	1,235	1,085	935	772	594	419	249	79	13,300	13,350	1,854	1,674	1,504	1,346	1,168	968	771	594
10,550	10,600	1,245	1,095	945	781	604	428	258	88	13,350	13,400	1,866	1,685	1,514	1,357	1,179	979	781	603
10,600	10,650	1,255	1,105	955	791	613	437	267	97	13,400	13,450	1,879	1,697	1,525	1,367	1,190	990	790	613
10,650	10,700	1,265	1,115	965	800	623	446	276	106	13,450	13,500	1,891	1,708	1,536	1,378	1,201	1,001	801	622
10,700	10,750	1,275	1,125	975	810	632	455	285	115	13,500	13,550	1,904	1,720	1,547	1,388	1,212	1,012	812	632
10,750	10,800	1,285	1,135	985	819	642	464	294	124	13,550	13,600	1,916	1,731	1,559	1,399	1,223	1,023	823	641
10,800	10,850	1,295	1,145	995	829	651	474	303	133	13,600	13,650	1,929	1,743	1,570	1,409	1,234	1,034	834	651
10,850	10,900	1,305	1,155	1,005	838	661	483	312	142	13,650	13,700	1,941	1,754	1,582	1,420	1,245	1,045	845	660
10,900	10,950	1,315	1,165	1,015	848	670	493	321	151	13,700	13,750	1,954	1,766	1,593	1,430	1,256	1,056	856	670
10,950	11,000	1,325	1,175	1,025	857	680	502	330	160	13,750	13,800	1,966	1,779	1,605	1,441	1,267	1,067	867	679
11,000	11,050	1,336	1,185	1,035	867	689	512	339	169	13,800	13,850	1,979	1,791	1,616	1,451	1,278	1,078	878	689
11,050	11,100	1,346	1,195	1,045	876	699	521	348	178	13,850	13,900	1,991	1,804	1,628	1,462	1,289	1,089	889	698
11,100	11,150	1,357	1,205	1,055	886	708	531	357	187	13,900	13,950	2,004	1,816	1,639	1,472	1,300	1,100	900	708
11,150	11,200	1,367	1,215	1,065	895	718	540	366	196	13,950	14,000	2,016	1,829	1,651	1,483	1,311	1,111	911	717
11,200	11,250	1,378	1,225	1,075	906	727	550	375	205	14,000	14,050	2,029	1,841	1,662	1,493	1,322	1,122	922	727
11,250	11,300	1,388	1,235	1,085	917	737	559	384	214	14,050	14,100	2,041	1,854	1,674	1,504	1,334	1,133	933	736
11,300	11,350	1,399	1,245	1,095	928	746	569	393	223	14,100	14,150	2,054	1,866	1,685	1,514	1,345	1,144	944	746
11,350	11,400	1,409	1,255	1,105	939	756	578	402	232	14,150	14,200	2,066	1,879	1,697	1,525	1,357	1,155	955	755
11,400	11,450	1,420	1,265	1,115	950	765	588	411	241	14,200	14,250	2,079	1,891	1,708	1,536	1,368	1,166	966	766
11,450	11,500	1,430	1,275	1,125	961	775	597	420	250	14,250	14,300	2,091	1,904	1,720	1,547	1,380	1,177	977	777
11,500	11,550	1,441	1,285	1,135	972	784	607	429	259	14,300	14,350	2,104	1,916	1,731	1,559	1,391	1,188	988	788
11,550	11,600	1,451	1,295	1,145	983	794	616	439	268	14,350	14,400	2,116	1,929	1,743	1,570	1,403	1,199	999	799

Continued next column   Continued on next page

1977 Tax Table D—HEAD OF HOUSEHOLD (Box 4)

(Continued)

(If your income or exemptions are not covered, use Schedule TC (Form 1040), Part I to figure your tax)

If line 34, Form 1040 is— Over	But not over	1	2	3	4	5	6	7	8	If line 34, Form 1040 is— Over	But not over	1	2	3	4	5	6	7	8
		Your tax is—										Your tax is—							
14,400	14,450	2,129	1,941	1,754	1,582	1,414	1,210	1,010	810	17,200	17,250	2,877	2,672	2,469	2,267	2,079	1,861	1,643	1,436
14,450	14,500	2,141	1,954	1,766	1,593	1,426	1,221	1,021	821	17,250	17,300	2,891	2,685	2,483	2,280	2,091	1,874	1,655	1,447
14,500	14,550	2,154	1,966	1,779	1,605	1,437	1,232	1,032	832	17,300	17,350	2,905	2,699	2,496	2,294	2,104	1,886	1,666	1,459
14,550	14,600	2,166	1,979	1,791	1,616	1,449	1,243	1,043	843	17,350	17,400	2,919	2,712	2,510	2,307	2,116	1,899	1,678	1,470
14,600	14,650	2,179	1,991	1,804	1,628	1,460	1,254	1,054	854	17,400	17,450	2,933	2,726	2,523	2,321	2,129	1,911	1,689	1,482
14,650	14,700	2,191	2,004	1,816	1,639	1,472	1,265	1,065	865	17,450	17,500	2,947	2,739	2,537	2,334	2,141	1,924	1,701	1,493
14,700	14,750	2,204	2,016	1,829	1,651	1,483	1,276	1,076	876	17,500	17,550	2,961	2,753	2,550	2,348	2,154	1,936	1,714	1,505
14,750	14,800	2,216	2,029	1,841	1,662	1,493	1,287	1,087	887	17,550	17,600	2,975	2,766	2,564	2,361	2,166	1,949	1,726	1,516
14,800	14,850	2,229	2,041	1,854	1,674	1,504	1,299	1,098	898	17,600	17,650	2,989	2,780	2,577	2,375	2,179	1,961	1,739	1,528
14,850	14,900	2,241	2,054	1,866	1,685	1,514	1,310	1,109	909	17,650	17,700	3,003	2,793	2,591	2,388	2,191	1,974	1,751	1,539
14,900	14,950	2,254	2,066	1,879	1,697	1,525	1,322	1,120	920	17,700	17,750	3,017	2,807	2,604	2,402	2,204	1,986	1,764	1,551
14,950	15,000	2,267	2,079	1,891	1,708	1,536	1,333	1,131	931	17,750	17,800	3,031	2,821	2,618	2,415	2,216	1,999	1,776	1,562
15,000	15,050	2,280	2,091	1,904	1,720	1,547	1,345	1,142	942	17,800	17,850	3,045	2,835	2,631	2,429	2,229	2,011	1,789	1,574
15,050	15,100	2,294	2,104	1,916	1,731	1,559	1,356	1,153	953	17,850	17,900	3,059	2,849	2,645	2,442	2,241	2,024	1,801	1,585
15,100	15,150	2,307	2,116	1,929	1,743	1,570	1,368	1,164	964	17,900	17,950	3,073	2,863	2,658	2,456	2,254	2,036	1,814	1,597
15,150	15,200	2,321	2,129	1,941	1,754	1,582	1,379	1,175	975	17,950	18,000	3,087	2,877	2,672	2,469	2,267	2,049	1,826	1,608
15,200	15,250	2,334	2,141	1,954	1,766	1,593	1,391	1,186	986	18,000	18,050	3,101	2,891	2,685	2,483	2,280	2,061	1,839	1,620
15,250	15,300	2,348	2,154	1,966	1,779	1,605	1,402	1,197	997	18,050	18,100	3,115	2,905	2,699	2,496	2,294	2,074	1,851	1,631
15,300	15,350	2,361	2,166	1,979	1,791	1,616	1,414	1,208	1,008	18,100	18,150	3,129	2,919	2,712	2,510	2,307	2,086	1,864	1,643
15,350	15,400	2,375	2,179	1,991	1,804	1,628	1,425	1,219	1,019	18,150	18,200	3,143	2,933	2,726	2,523	2,321	2,099	1,876	1,654
15,400	15,450	2,388	2,191	2,004	1,816	1,639	1,437	1,230	1,030	18,200	18,250	3,157	2,947	2,739	2,537	2,334	2,111	1,889	1,666
15,450	15,500	2,402	2,204	2,016	1,829	1,651	1,448	1,241	1,041	18,250	18,300	3,171	2,961	2,753	2,550	2,348	2,124	1,901	1,679
15,500	15,550	2,415	2,216	2,029	1,841	1,662	1,460	1,252	1,052	18,300	18,350	3,185	2,975	2,766	2,564	2,361	2,136	1,914	1,691
15,550	15,600	2,429	2,229	2,041	1,854	1,674	1,471	1,264	1,063	18,350	18,400	3,199	2,989	2,780	2,577	2,375	2,149	1,926	1,704
15,600	15,650	2,442	2,241	2,054	1,866	1,685	1,483	1,275	1,074	18,400	18,450	3,213	3,003	2,793	2,591	2,388	2,161	1,939	1,716
15,650	15,700	2,456	2,254	2,066	1,879	1,697	1,494	1,287	1,085	18,450	18,500	3,227	3,017	2,807	2,604	2,402	2,174	1,951	1,729
15,700	15,750	2,469	2,267	2,079	1,891	1,708	1,506	1,298	1,096	18,500	18,550	3,241	3,031	2,821	2,618	2,415	2,186	1,964	1,741
15,750	15,800	2,483	2,280	2,091	1,904	1,720	1,517	1,310	1,107	18,550	18,600	3,255	3,045	2,835	2,631	2,429	2,199	1,976	1,754
15,800	15,850	2,496	2,294	2,104	1,916	1,731	1,529	1,321	1,118	18,600	18,650	3,269	3,059	2,849	2,645	2,442	2,211	1,989	1,766
15,850	15,900	2,510	2,307	2,116	1,929	1,743	1,540	1,333	1,129	18,650	18,700	3,283	3,073	2,863	2,658	2,456	2,224	2,001	1,779
15,900	15,950	2,523	2,321	2,129	1,941	1,754	1,552	1,344	1,140	18,700	18,750	3,297	3,087	2,877	2,672	2,469	2,237	2,014	1,791
15,950	16,000	2,537	2,334	2,141	1,954	1,766	1,563	1,356	1,151	18,750	18,800	3,311	3,101	2,891	2,685	2,483	2,250	2,026	1,804
16,000	16,050	2,550	2,348	2,154	1,966	1,779	1,575	1,367	1,162	18,800	18,850	3,325	3,115	2,905	2,699	2,496	2,264	2,039	1,816
16,050	16,100	2,564	2,361	2,166	1,979	1,791	1,586	1,379	1,173	18,850	18,900	3,339	3,129	2,919	2,712	2,510	2,277	2,051	1,829
16,100	16,150	2,577	2,375	2,179	1,991	1,804	1,598	1,390	1,184	18,900	18,950	3,353	3,143	2,933	2,726	2,523	2,291	2,064	1,841
16,150	16,200	2,591	2,388	2,191	2,004	1,816	1,609	1,402	1,195	18,950	19,000	3,368	3,157	2,947	2,739	2,537	2,304	2,076	1,854
16,200	16,250	2,604	2,402	2,204	2,016	1,829	1,621	1,413	1,206	19,000	19,050	3,383	3,171	2,961	2,753	2,550	2,318	2,089	1,866
16,250	16,300	2,618	2,415	2,216	2,029	1,841	1,632	1,425	1,217	19,050	19,100	3,399	3,185	2,975	2,766	2,564	2,331	2,101	1,879
16,300	16,350	2,631	2,429	2,229	2,041	1,854	1,644	1,436	1,229	19,100	19,150	3,414	3,199	2,989	2,780	2,577	2,345	2,114	1,891
16,350	16,400	2,645	2,442	2,241	2,054	1,866	1,655	1,448	1,240	19,150	19,200	3,430	3,213	3,003	2,793	2,591	2,358	2,126	1,904
16,400	16,450	2,658	2,456	2,254	2,066	1,879	1,667	1,459	1,252	19,200	19,250	3,445	3,227	3,017	2,807	2,604	2,372	2,139	1,916
16,450	16,500	2,672	2,469	2,267	2,079	1,891	1,678	1,471	1,263	19,250	19,300	3,461	3,241	3,031	2,821	2,618	2,385	2,151	1,929
16,500	16,550	2,685	2,483	2,280	2,091	1,904	1,690	1,482	1,275	19,300	19,350	3,476	3,255	3,045	2,835	2,631	2,399	2,164	1,941
16,550	16,600	2,699	2,496	2,294	2,104	1,916	1,701	1,494	1,286	19,350	19,400	3,492	3,269	3,059	2,849	2,645	2,412	2,176	1,954
16,600	16,650	2,712	2,510	2,307	2,116	1,929	1,713	1,505	1,298	19,400	19,450	3,507	3,283	3,073	2,863	2,658	2,426	2,189	1,966
16,650	16,700	2,726	2,523	2,321	2,129	1,941	1,724	1,517	1,309	19,450	19,500	3,523	3,297	3,087	2,877	2,672	2,439	2,202	1,979
16,700	16,750	2,739	2,537	2,334	2,141	1,954	1,736	1,528	1,321	19,500	19,550	3,538	3,311	3,101	2,891	2,685	2,453	2,215	1,991
16,750	16,800	2,753	2,550	2,348	2,154	1,966	1,749	1,540	1,332	19,550	19,600	3,554	3,325	3,115	2,905	2,699	2,466	2,229	2,004
16,800	16,850	2,766	2,564	2,361	2,166	1,979	1,761	1,551	1,344	19,600	19,650	3,569	3,339	3,129	2,919	2,712	2,480	2,242	2,016
16,850	16,900	2,780	2,577	2,375	2,179	1,991	1,774	1,563	1,355	19,650	19,700	3,585	3,353	3,143	2,933	2,726	2,493	2,256	2,029
16,900	16,950	2,793	2,591	2,388	2,191	2,004	1,786	1,574	1,367	19,700	19,750	3,600	3,368	3,157	2,947	2,739	2,507	2,269	2,041
16,950	17,000	2,807	2,604	2,402	2,204	2,016	1,799	1,586	1,378	19,750	19,800	3,616	3,383	3,171	2,961	2,753	2,520	2,283	2,054
17,000	17,050	2,821	2,618	2,415	2,216	2,029	1,811	1,597	1,390	19,800	19,850	3,631	3,399	3,185	2,975	2,766	2,534	2,296	2,066
17,050	17,100	2,835	2,631	2,429	2,229	2,041	1,824	1,609	1,401	19,850	19,900	3,647	3,414	3,199	2,989	2,780	2,547	2,310	2,079
17,100	17,150	2,849	2,645	2,442	2,241	2,054	1,836	1,620	1,413	19,900	19,950	3,662	3,430	3,213	3,003	2,793	2,561	2,323	2,091
17,150	17,200	2,863	2,658	2,456	2,254	2,066	1,849	1,632	1,424	19,950	20,000	3,678	3,445	3,227	3,017	2,807	2,574	2,337	2,104

Continued next column

A–3 1977 OPTIONAL STATE SALES TAX TABLES

1977 Optional State Sales Tax Tables

Your itemized deduction for general sales taxes paid can be estimated from these tables plus any qualifying sales taxes paid on the items listed on page 14. The larger of the sales tax estimate from this table or the sales tax your records show that you paid can be entered on Schedule A, line 14.

If your income was more than $19,999 but less than $100,000, compute your deduction as follows:

Step 1.—Find the $19,000–19,999 income line in the table for your state and read across to find the amount of sales tax for your family size.

Step 2.—Subtract $19,999 from the amount of your income. For each $1,000 or fraction of $1,000 that your income is greater than $19,999, but less than $50,000, add 2 percent of the amount you found in step 1, above.

Step 3.—For each $1,000 or fraction of $1,000 that your income is greater than $49,999, but less than $100,000, add 1 percent of the amount you found in step 1, above.

If your income was $100,000 or more, your deduction is 210 percent of the amount determined in Step 1, above.

Alabama [2]

Income [1]	1	2	3&4	5	Over 5
Under $3,000	$45	$53	$66	$71	$72
$3,000–$3,999	55	66	81	89	91
$4,000–$4,999	64	79	95	105	108
$5,000–$5,999	73	90	108	120	124
$6,000–$6,999	81	101	120	134	139
$7,000–$7,999	88	111	131	147	154
$8,000–$8,999	95	121	142	160	168
$9,000–$9,999	102	130	152	172	181
$10,000–$10,999	109	139	162	184	194
$11,000–$11,999	115	148	171	195	207
$12,000–$12,999	121	157	180	206	219
$13,000–$13,999	127	165	189	217	231
$14,000–$14,999	133	173	198	228	243
$15,000–$15,999	139	181	207	238	254
$16,000–$16,999	144	189	215	248	265
$17,000–$17,999	149	197	223	258	276
$18,000–$18,999	154	204	231	268	287
$19,000–$19,999	159	211	238	277	297

Arizona [3]

Income [1]	1	2	3	4	5	Over 5
Under $3,000	$51	$67	$70	$84	$84	$85
$3,000–$3,999	63	82	86	100	101	105
$4,000–$4,999	73	95	101	114	118	123
$5,000–$5,999	82	107	115	127	134	140
$6,000–$6,999	91	118	127	139	149	156
$7,000–$7,999	99	128	139	150	163	171
$8,000–$8,999	107	138	151	161	176	185
$9,000–$9,999	114	147	162	171	189	199
$10,000–$10,999	121	156	172	180	201	212
$11,000–$11,999	128	165	182	189	213	225
$12,000–$12,999	134	174	192	197	224	237
$13,000–$13,999	140	182	201	205	235	249
$14,000–$14,999	146	190	210	213	246	261
$15,000–$15,999	152	197	219	221	256	272
$16,000–$16,999	158	204	228	229	266	283
$17,000–$17,999	164	211	237	237	276	294
$18,000–$18,999	169	218	245	245	286	305
$19,000–$19,999	174	225	253	253	295	315

Arkansas [2]

Income [1]	1	2	3&4	5	Over 5
Under $3,000	$38	$45	$54	$58	$59
$3,000–$3,999	47	56	67	73	74
$4,000–$4,999	54	66	78	86	88
$5,000–$5,999	61	76	88	98	101
$6,000–$6,999	67	85	98	110	114
$7,000–$7,999	73	93	108	121	126
$8,000–$8,999	79	101	117	132	137
$9,000–$9,999	84	109	125	141	148
$10,000–$10,999	89	116	133	151	158
$11,000–$11,999	94	123	141	160	168
$12,000–$12,999	99	130	149	169	178
$13,000–$13,999	104	137	156	178	188
$14,000–$14,999	109	144	163	186	198
$15,000–$15,999	113	151	170	194	207
$16,000–$16,999	117	157	177	202	216
$17,000–$17,999	121	163	184	210	225
$18,000–$18,999	125	169	190	218	234
$19,000–$19,999	129	175	196	226	242

California [4]

Income [1]	1&2	3&4	5	Over 5
Under $3,000	$51	$61	$68	$68
$3,000–$3,999	66	78	87	87
$4,000–$4,999	80	93	104	104
$5,000–$5,999	93	107	120	120
$6,000–$6,999	106	121	135	136
$7,000–$7,999	118	134	149	152
$8,000–$8,999	130	147	163	167
$9,000–$9,999	141	159	176	181
$10,000–$10,999	152	171	189	195
$11,000–$11,999	163	183	202	209
$12,000–$12,999	174	194	214	222
$13,000–$13,999	184	205	226	235
$14,000–$14,999	194	216	238	248
$15,000–$15,999	204	227	249	260
$16,000–$16,999	214	238	260	272
$17,000–$17,999	224	248	271	284
$18,000–$18,999	233	258	282	296
$19,000–$19,999	242	268	293	308

Colorado [3]

Income [1]	1	2	3	4	5	Over 5
Under $3,000	$35	$48	$49	$59	$59	$60
$3,000–$3,999	44	58	61	71	73	75
$4,000–$4,999	51	68	72	82	85	88
$5,000–$5,999	58	76	82	91	97	100
$6,000–$6,999	64	84	91	100	107	112
$7,000–$7,999	70	92	100	109	117	123
$8,000–$8,999	76	99	108	117	127	133
$9,000–$9,999	81	106	116	124	136	143
$10,000–$10,999	86	112	124	131	145	153
$11,000–$11,999	91	118	132	138	154	163
$12,000–$12,999	96	124	139	145	162	173
$13,000–$13,999	101	130	146	151	172	181
$14,000–$14,999	106	136	153	157	178	190
$15,000–$15,999	110	141	160	163	186	198
$16,000–$16,999	114	146	167	169	194	206
$17,000–$17,999	118	151	173	175	201	214
$18,000–$18,999	122	156	179	181	208	222
$19,000–$19,999	126	161	185	186	215	230

Connecticut

Income [1]	1&2	3&4	5	Over 5
Under $3,000	$44	$51	$61	$61
$3,000–$3,999	59	68	79	79
$4,000–$4,999	73	83	96	96
$5,000–$5,999	87	98	112	112
$6,000–$6,999	101	113	127	127
$7,000–$7,999	114	127	142	142
$8,000–$8,999	127	141	156	156
$9,000–$9,999	140	154	170	171
$10,000–$10,999	152	167	183	186
$11,000–$11,999	164	180	196	201
$12,000–$12,999	176	193	209	216
$13,000–$13,999	188	205	222	230
$14,000–$14,999	200	217	235	244
$15,000–$15,999	212	229	247	258
$16,000–$16,999	224	241	259	272
$17,000–$17,999	236	253	271	286
$18,000–$18,999	247	265	283	300
$19,000–$19,999	258	277	294	314

Dist. of Columbia

Income [1]	1	2	3&4	5	Over 5
Under $3,000	$34	$39	$49	$53	$53
$3,000–$3,999	41	50	61	66	66
$4,000–$4,999	48	60	73	78	78
$5,000–$5,999	54	69	83	90	90
$6,000–$6,999	60	78	92	101	101
$7,000–$7,999	66	87	101	111	112
$8,000–$8,999	71	95	110	121	123
$9,000–$9,999	76	103	119	130	134
$10,000–$10,999	81	111	127	139	144
$11,000–$11,999	86	119	135	148	154
$12,000–$12,999	90	127	142	157	164
$13,000–$13,999	94	135	149	166	174
$14,000–$14,999	98	142	156	174	184
$15,000–$15,999	102	149	163	182	194
$16,000–$16,999	106	156	170	190	203
$17,000–$17,999	110	163	177	198	212
$18,000–$18,999	114	170	184	206	221
$19,000–$19,999	118	176	190	213	230

Florida

Income [1]	1&2	3&4	5	Over 5
Under $3,000	$30	$40	$44	$44
$3,000–$3,999	40	51	56	56
$4,000–$4,999	50	62	68	68
$5,000–$5,999	60	72	79	79
$6,000–$6,999	68	81	89	89
$7,000–$7,999	76	90	99	100
$8,000–$8,999	84	99	109	110
$9,000–$9,999	92	108	118	120
$10,000–$10,999	100	116	127	130
$11,000–$11,999	108	124	136	140
$12,000–$12,999	116	132	145	150
$13,000–$13,999	124	140	154	159
$14,000–$14,999	132	148	162	168
$15,000–$15,999	140	155	170	177
$16,000–$16,999	147	162	178	186
$17,000–$17,999	154	169	186	195
$18,000–$18,999	161	176	194	204
$19,000–$19,999	168	183	201	213

Georgia [2]

Income [1]	1	2	3&4	5	Over 5
Under $3,000	$40	$49	$59	$65	$65
$3,000–$3,999	50	61	72	80	80
$4,000–$4,999	58	72	85	94	94
$5,000–$5,999	65	82	96	106	107
$6,000–$6,999	72	91	106	118	120
$7,000–$7,999	79	100	116	129	133
$8,000–$8,999	85	109	125	140	145
$9,000–$9,999	91	117	134	150	157
$10,000–$10,999	96	125	143	159	168
$11,000–$11,999	102	133	151	169	179
$12,000–$12,999	107	140	159	178	190
$13,000–$13,999	112	147	167	187	200
$14,000–$14,999	117	154	174	196	210
$15,000–$15,999	121	160	181	204	220
$16,000–$16,999	125	166	188	212	230
$17,000–$17,999	129	172	195	220	240
$18,000–$18,999	132	178	202	228	250
$19,000–$19,999	136	183	208	235	259

Hawaii

Income [1]	1	2	3&4	5	Over 5
Under $3,000	$69	$87	$91	$101	$101
$3,000–$3,999	85	105	111	123	123
$4,000–$4,999	99	120	129	143	144
$5,000–$5,999	112	135	145	161	163
$6,000–$6,999	123	148	159	178	181
$7,000–$7,999	134	160	173	193	198
$8,000–$8,999	145	172	186	208	215
$9,000–$9,999	155	183	199	222	230
$10,000–$10,999	165	193	213	236	245
$11,000–$11,999	174	203	222	249	260
$12,000–$12,999	183	213	233	261	274
$13,000–$13,999	192	222	244	273	287
$14,000–$14,999	200	231	254	285	300
$15,000–$15,999	208	240	264	296	313
$16,000–$16,999	216	248	274	307	326
$17,000–$17,999	224	256	284	318	338
$18,000–$18,999	232	264	293	329	350
$19,000–$19,999	239	272	302	339	362

See page 582 for notes 1 through 5.

Idaho

Income [1]	Family size (persons)					
	1	2	3	4	5	Over 5
Under $3,000	$34	$45	$47	$57	$57	$58
$3,000–$3,999	42	55	59	69	69	72
$4,000–$4,999	49	64	69	79	82	85
$5,000–$5,999	56	73	79	88	93	97
$6,000–$6,999	62	81	88	97	104	109
$7,000–$7,999	68	88	97	105	113	120
$8,000–$8,999	74	95	105	113	124	130
$9,000–$9,999	79	102	113	120	133	140
$10,000–$10,999	84	109	121	127	142	150
$11,000–$11,999	89	115	129	134	151	159
$12,000–$12,999	94	121	136	140	159	168
$13,000–$13,999	99	127	143	146	167	177
$14,000–$14,999	104	133	150	152	175	186
$15,000–$15,999	109	139	157	158	183	194
$16,000–$16,999	113	145	164	164	191	202
$17,000–$17,999	117	150	170	170	198	210
$18,000–$18,999	121	155	176	176	205	218
$19,000–$19,999	125	160	182	182	212	226

Illinois [5]

Income [1]	Family size (persons)					
	1	2	3	4	5	Over 5
Under $3,000	$54	$70	$80	$92	$92	$97
$3,000–$3,999	66	86	98	111	113	121
$4,000–$4,999	77	100	115	128	133	142
$5,000–$5,999	87	114	131	144	151	162
$6,000–$6,999	97	126	145	158	168	181
$7,000–$7,999	106	138	159	171	184	199
$8,000–$8,999	115	149	171	184	199	216
$9,000–$9,999	123	160	184	196	214	232
$10,000–$10,999	131	170	196	208	228	248
$11,000–$11,999	138	180	207	219	242	263
$12,000–$12,999	145	190	218	230	255	277
$13,000–$13,999	152	199	229	240	268	291
$14,000–$14,999	159	208	240	250	281	305
$15,000–$15,999	166	217	250	260	293	319
$16,000–$16,999	173	226	260	269	305	332
$17,000–$17,999	179	234	270	278	317	345
$18,000–$18,999	185	242	280	287	328	358
$19,000–$19,999	191	250	289	295	339	371

Indiana

Income [1]	Family size (persons)				
	1	2	3 & 4	5	Over 5
Under $3,000	$37	$41	$47	$51	$51
$3,000–$3,999	47	53	60	65	65
$4,000–$4,999	56	63	72	72	78
$5,000–$5,999	65	73	83	90	91
$6,000–$6,999	73	83	94	102	103
$7,000–$7,999	81	92	104	112	115
$8,000–$8,999	89	101	114	122	127
$9,000–$9,999	96	110	124	133	138
$10,000–$10,999	103	118	133	143	149
$11,000–$11,999	110	126	142	153	160
$12,000–$12,999	117	134	151	163	171
$13,000–$13,999	124	142	159	172	182
$14,000–$14,999	130	150	167	181	192
$15,000–$15,999	136	157	175	190	202
$16,000–$16,999	142	164	183	199	212
$17,000–$17,999	148	171	191	208	222
$18,000–$18,999	154	178	199	216	232
$19,000–$19,999	160	185	207	224	242

Iowa

Income [1]	Family size (persons)		
	1 & 2	3, 4 & 5	Over 5
Under $3,000	$30	$35	$35
$3,000–$3,999	39	45	46
$4,000–$4,999	47	54	56
$5,000–$5,999	55	63	66
$6,000–$6,999	62	72	76
$7,000–$7,999	69	81	86
$8,000–$8,999	76	89	95
$9,000–$9,999	83	97	104
$10,000–$10,999	89	105	113
$11,000–$11,999	95	113	122
$12,000–$12,999	101	120	131
$13,000–$13,999	107	127	140
$14,000–$14,999	113	134	149
$15,000–$15,999	119	141	157
$16,000–$16,999	125	148	165
$17,000–$17,999	131	155	173
$18,000–$18,999	137	162	181
$19,000–$19,999	142	168	189

Kansas [2]

Income [1]	Family size (persons)					
	1	2	3	4	5	Over 5
Under $3,000	$41	$51	$56	$64	$64	$67
$3,000–$3,999	50	63	69	78	78	84
$4,000–$4,999	58	74	82	90	92	100
$5,000–$5,999	66	84	93	102	106	114
$6,000–$6,999	73	93	104	112	118	127
$7,000–$7,999	80	102	114	122	130	140
$8,000–$8,999	86	110	124	132	142	153
$9,000–$9,999	92	118	133	141	153	165
$10,000–$10,999	98	125	142	150	163	176
$11,000–$11,999	104	132	151	158	173	187
$12,000–$12,999	109	139	159	166	183	198
$13,000–$13,999	114	146	167	174	193	208
$14,000–$14,999	119	153	175	182	203	218
$15,000–$15,999	124	159	183	189	212	228
$16,000–$16,999	129	165	191	196	221	238
$17,000–$17,999	134	171	198	203	230	248
$18,000–$18,999	138	177	205	210	239	258
$19,000–$19,999	142	183	212	216	247	267

Michigan

Income [1]	Family size (persons)			
	1 & 2	3 & 4	5	Over 5
Under $3,000	$35	$43	$45	$45
$3,000–$3,999	46	55	58	58
$4,000–$4,999	55	66	70	70
$5,000–$5,999	64	76	81	82
$6,000–$6,999	73	86	92	94
$7,000–$7,999	82	96	102	105
$8,000–$8,999	90	105	112	116
$9,000–$9,999	98	114	122	127
$10,000–$10,999	106	123	131	138
$11,000–$11,999	113	131	140	149
$12,000–$12,999	120	139	149	159
$13,000–$13,999	127	147	158	169
$14,000–$14,999	134	155	167	179
$15,000–$15,999	141	163	176	189
$16,000–$16,999	148	171	184	199
$17,000–$17,999	155	179	192	209
$18,000–$18,999	162	186	200	218
$19,000–$19,999	168	193	208	227

Minnesota [2]

Income [1]	Family size (persons)		
	1 & 2	3, 4 & 5	5
Under $3,000	$27	$30	$30
$3,000–$3,999	35	38	39
$4,000–$4,999	42	46	47
$5,000–$5,999	49	54	55
$6,000–$6,999	56	61	63
$7,000–$7,999	62	68	71
$8,000–$8,999	68	75	79
$9,000–$9,999	74	82	86
$10,000–$10,999	80	88	93
$11,000–$11,999	85	94	100
$12,000–$12,999	90	100	107
$13,000–$13,999	95	106	114
$14,000–$14,999	100	112	121
$15,000–$15,999	105	118	128
$16,000–$16,999	110	124	134
$17,000–$17,999	115	130	140
$18,000–$18,999	120	135	146
$19,000–$19,999	125	140	152

Kentucky

Income [1]	Family size (persons)		
	1 & 2	3 & 4	5
Under $3,000	$46	$57	$61
$3,000–$3,999	59	73	78
$4,000–$4,999	72	87	93
$5,000–$5,999	84	100	107
$6,000–$6,999	95	112	121
$7,000–$7,999	106	124	135
$8,000–$8,999	116	135	148
$9,000–$9,999	126	146	161
$10,000–$10,999	136	157	174
$11,000–$11,999	146	167	187
$12,000–$12,999	155	177	200
$13,000–$13,999	164	187	212
$14,000–$14,999	173	197	224
$15,000–$15,999	182	206	236
$16,000–$16,999	191	215	248
$17,000–$17,999	200	224	259
$18,000–$18,999	208	233	270
$19,000–$19,999	216	242	281

Louisiana [2]

Income [1]	Family size (persons)			
	1 & 2	3 & 4	5	Over 5
Under $3,000	$25	$31	$34	$34
$3,000–$3,999	33	40	44	44
$4,000–$4,999	41	49	53	53
$5,000–$5,999	48	57	62	62
$6,000–$6,999	55	64	70	70
$7,000–$7,999	62	71	78	78
$8,000–$8,999	69	78	85	85
$9,000–$9,999	76	85	93	94
$10,000–$10,999	82	92	100	102
$11,000–$11,999	88	98	107	110
$12,000–$12,999	94	104	114	118
$13,000–$13,999	100	110	121	125
$14,000–$14,999	106	116	128	132
$15,000–$15,999	112	122	134	139
$16,000–$16,999	118	128	140	146
$17,000–$17,999	124	134	146	153
$18,000–$18,999	130	140	152	160
$19,000–$19,999	136	145	158	167

Maine

Income [1]	Family size (persons)				
	1 & 2	3	4	5	Over 5
Under $3,000	$40	$48	$56	$57	$57
$3,000–$3,999	52	61	70	72	72
$4,000–$4,999	64	74	83	87	87
$5,000–$5,999	75	86	96	101	101
$6,000–$6,999	86	98	107	114	114
$7,000–$7,999	97	109	118	126	126
$8,000–$8,999	107	120	129	138	139
$9,000–$9,999	117	130	139	150	152
$10,000–$10,999	127	140	149	161	165
$11,000–$11,999	136	150	158	172	177
$12,000–$12,999	145	160	167	183	189
$13,000–$13,999	154	170	176	194	201
$14,000–$14,999	163	179	185	204	212
$15,000–$15,999	172	188	194	214	223
$16,000–$16,999	181	197	203	224	234
$17,000–$17,999	190	206	211	234	245
$18,000–$18,999	199	215	219	244	256
$19,000–$19,999	207	223	227	253	267

Maryland

Income [1]	Family size (persons)			
	1 & 2	3 & 4	5	Over 5
Under $3,000	$37	$47	$51	$51
$3,000–$3,999	48	60	65	65
$4,000–$4,999	58	72	78	78
$5,000–$5,999	68	83	90	90
$6,000–$6,999	78	94	102	102
$7,000–$7,999	87	104	113	114
$8,000–$8,999	96	113	124	126
$9,000–$9,999	105	122	134	138
$10,000–$10,999	114	131	144	149
$11,000–$11,999	122	140	154	160
$12,000–$12,999	130	149	163	171
$13,000–$13,999	138	158	172	182
$14,000–$14,999	146	166	181	193
$15,000–$15,999	154	174	190	203
$16,000–$16,999	161	182	199	213
$17,000–$17,999	168	190	208	223
$18,000–$18,999	175	197	216	233
$19,000–$19,999	182	204	224	243

Massachusetts

Income [1]	Family size (persons)		
	1	2, 3 & 4	5 and over
Under $3,000	$13	$17	$24
$3,000–$3,999	17	22	30
$4,000–$4,999	20	27	36
$5,000–$5,999	24	32	42
$6,000–$6,999	27	37	47
$7,000–$7,999	30	42	52
$8,000–$8,999	33	47	57
$9,000–$9,999	36	52	62
$10,000–$10,999	39	57	67
$11,000–$11,999	42	61	72
$12,000–$12,999	44	65	76
$13,000–$13,999	47	69	80
$14,000–$14,999	50	73	84
$15,000–$15,999	52	77	88
$16,000–$16,999	55	81	92
$17,000–$17,999	57	85	96
$18,000–$18,999	60	89	100
$19,000–$19,999	62	93	104

[1] Total of amount on Form 1040, line 29 and nontaxable receipts such as social security, veterans', railroad retirement benefits, workmen's compensation, untaxed portion of long-term capital gains, dividends exclusion, unemployment compensation and public assistance payments.

[2] Local sales taxes are not included. Add an amount based on the ratio between the local and State sales tax rates considering the number of months the taxes have been in effect.

[3] Local sales taxes are not included. Add the amount paid.

[4] The 1¼ percent local sales tax is included. If the ½ of 1 percent sales tax is paid all year (Alameda, Contra Costa, San Francisco, and Santa Clara counties) add 8 percent to the table amount.

[5] Local sales taxes are included.

1977 Optional State Sales Tax Tables

Your itemized deduction for general sales taxes paid can be estimated from these tables plus any qualifying sales taxes paid on the items listed on page 14. The larger of the sales tax estimate from this table or the sales tax your records show that you paid can be entered on Schedule A, line 14.

If your income was more than $19,999 but less than $100,000, compute your deduction as follows:

Step 1.—Find the $19,000–19,999 income line in the table for your State and read across to find the amount of sales tax for your family size.

Step 2.—Subtract $19,999 from the amount of your income. For each $1,000 or fraction of $1,000 that your income is greater than $19,999, but less than $50,000, add 2 percent of the amount you found in step 1, above.

Step 3.—For each $1,000 or fraction of $1,000 that your income is greater than $49,999, but less than $100,000, add 1 percent of the amount you found in step 1, above.

If your income was $100,000 or more, your deduction is 210 percent of the amount determined in Step 1, above.

Income [1]	Mississippi Family size (persons)				Missouri [2] Family size (persons)						Nebraska [2] Family size (persons)						Nevada [3] Family size (persons)					
	1 & 2	3&4	5	Over 5	1	2	3	4	5	Over 5	1	2	3	4	5	Over 5	1	2	3	4	5	Over 5
Under $3,000	$70	$83	$100	$109 $109	$37	$48	$53	$60	$60	$64	$38	$50	$56	$63	$64	$67	$38	$51	$53	$65	$65	$67
$3,000-$3,999	86	104	124	135 135	46	59	66	73	75	80	47	61	69	76	79	84	47	62	66	78	79	82
$4,000-$4,999	100	123	144	159 159	53	69	77	85	88	94	55	71	80	88	93	99	55	72	77	89	92	96
$5,000-$5,999	113	141	163	181 182	60	78	87	96	100	108	62	81	91	99	105	113	62	81	88	99	104	109
$6,000-$6,999	125	158	181	201 204	67	87	97	106	112	121	69	89	101	110	117	126	69	90	98	108	116	121
$7,000-$7,999	136	173	198	220 225	73	95	106	115	123	133	75	97	111	119	128	139	75	98	107	116	127	133
$8,000-$8,999	147	188	214	238 246	79	102	115	124	133	144	81	105	120	128	137	151	81	105	116	124	137	144
$9,000-$9,999	157	203	230	256 266	84	109	124	132	143	155	87	112	128	137	149	162	87	112	125	132	147	154
$10,000-$10,999	167	217	244	273 285	89	116	132	140	153	166	92	119	136	145	159	173	92	119	133	139	156	164
$11,000-$11,999	176	230	258	289 304	94	123	140	148	162	177	97	126	144	153	168	184	97	126	141	146	165	174
$12,000-$12,999	185	243	272	305 322	99	129	147	155	171	187	102	133	152	161	177	195	102	133	149	153	174	183
$13,000-$13,999	194	256	285	320 340	104	135	154	162	180	197	107	139	160	168	186	205	107	139	156	159	182	192
$14,000-$14,999	202	269	298	335 358	109	141	161	169	189	207	112	145	167	175	195	215	112	145	163	165	190	201
$15,000-$15,999	210	281	311	350 375	114	147	168	176	197	216	117	151	174	182	204	225	117	151	170	171	198	210
$16,000-$16,999	218	293	323	364 392	118	153	175	183	205	225	121	157	181	189	213	234	122	157	177	177	206	219
$17,000-$17,999	226	305	335	378 408	122	159	182	189	213	234	125	163	188	195	220	243	126	163	184	184	214	227
$18,000-$18,999	234	316	347	392 424	126	164	189	195	221	243	129	168	195	201	228	252	130	168	191	191	222	235
$19,000-$19,999	241	327	359	405 440	130	169	195	201	228	251	133	173	201	207	236	261	134	173	197	197	229	243

Income [1]	North Carolina [5] Family size (persons)					North Dakota Family size (persons)				Ohio [2] Family size (persons)				Oklahoma [2] Family size (persons)					
	1	2	3&4	5	Over 5	1&2	3&4	5	Over 5	1&2	3&4	5	Over 5	1	2	3&4	5	Over 5
Under $3,000	$46	$53	$66	$72	$72	$24	$29	$30	$30	$27	$33	$33	$34	$25	$29	$35	$38	$38
$3,000-$3,999	56	67	81	89	90	31	37	39	39	36	43	44	45	31	37	43	47	48
$4,000-$4,999	65	79	95	105	107	38	45	47	47	44	52	54	56	36	44	51	56	58
$5,000-$5,999	74	91	108	120	123	45	52	55	55	52	61	64	66	41	50	58	64	66
$6,000-$6,999	82	102	120	133	138	51	59	63	63	60	70	74	76	45	56	64	72	74
$7,000-$7,999	89	112	131	146	152	57	66	71	71	68	78	83	86	49	61	70	79	82
$8,000-$8,999	96	122	141	159	166	63	73	78	78	75	86	92	96	53	66	76	86	89
$9,000-$9,999	103	131	151	171	179	69	79	85	85	82	94	101	105	57	71	82	93	96
$10,000-$10,999	109	140	161	182	192	75	85	92	92	89	102	110	114	60	76	87	99	103
$11,000-$11,999	115	149	171	193	204	81	91	99	99	96	110	117	123	64	81	92	105	110
$12,000-$12,999	121	158	180	204	216	87	97	106	106	103	117	129	132	68	86	97	111	117
$13,000-$13,999	127	167	189	215	228	92	103	113	113	110	124	136	141	71	91	102	117	123
$14,000-$14,999	133	175	197	225	239	97	109	119	119	117	131	144	150	74	96	107	123	129
$15,000-$15,999	139	183	205	235	250	102	115	125	125	124	138	152	159	77	100	112	129	135
$16,000-$16,999	144	191	213	245	261	107	121	131	131	130	145	160	168	80	104	117	135	141
$17,000-$17,999	149	199	221	254	272	112	126	137	137	136	152	168	177	83	108	121	139	147
$18,000-$18,999	154	207	229	263	282	117	131	143	143	142	159	176	185	86	112	125	145	153
$19,000-$19,999	159	214	237	272	292	122	136	149	149	148	165	184	193	88	116	129	149	159

Income [1]	New Jersey Family size (persons)		New Mexico [2] Family size (persons)						New York [4] Family size (persons)				
	4 or under	5 and over	1	2	3	4	5	Over 5	1&2	3	4	5	Over 5
Under $3,000	$28	$37	$58	$77	$78	$92	$92	$92	$37	$44	$53	$56	$56
$3,000-$3,999	38	47	71	94	96	111	111	113	49	57	66	71	71
$4,000-$4,999	47	57	83	109	113	128	128	134	60	69	79	84	84
$5,000-$5,999	56	67	94	123	129	143	146	153	70	81	90	97	97
$6,000-$6,999	65	76	104	135	144	157	163	171	80	92	101	109	109
$7,000-$7,999	74	85	113	147	158	170	179	188	90	102	111	120	120
$8,000-$8,999	82	94	122	158	171	183	194	204	99	112	121	131	131
$9,000-$9,999	90	102	131	169	184	195	209	220	108	122	130	141	142
$10,000-$10,999	98	110	139	179	196	206	223	235	117	132	139	151	154
$11,000-$11,999	106	118	147	189	208	217	237	250	126	142	148	161	165
$12,000-$12,999	114	126	155	199	220	227	250	264	135	151	157	171	176
$13,000-$13,999	122	134	162	208	231	237	263	278	144	160	165	180	187
$14,000-$14,999	130	141	169	217	242	247	276	291	152	169	173	189	198
$15,000-$15,999	138	148	176	226	253	256	289	304	160	178	181	198	209
$16,000-$16,999	146	155	183	235	263	265	301	317	168	187	189	207	220
$17,000-$17,999	154	162	190	243	273	273	313	330	176	196	196	215	230
$18,000-$18,999	161	169	196	251	283	283	324	342	184	204	204	223	240
$19,000-$19,999	168	176	202	259	293	293	335	354	192	212	212	231	250

See page 584 for notes 1 through 8.

Income [1]	Pennsylvania: Family size (persons) 4 or under	5 and over	Rhode Island: Family size (persons) 4 or under	5	Over 5	South Carolina: Family size (persons) 1	2	3&4	5	Over 5
Under $3,000	$24	$31	$36	$51	$51	$52	$61	$73	$80	$80
$3,000–$3,999	33	40	50	66	66	63	76	90	99	99
$4,000–$4,999	42	49	62	79	79	73	90	105	116	118
$5,000–$5,999	50	58	74	91	91	83	102	119	132	135
$6,000–$6,999	58	67	85	103	103	91	114	132	147	151
$7,000–$7,999	66	75	96	115	115	99	125	144	161	167
$8,000–$8,999	74	83	107	126	126	107	136	156	174	182
$9,000–$9,999	82	91	118	137	138	114	146	167	187	196
$10,000–$10,999	90	99	128	147	150	121	156	178	200	210
$11,000–$11,999	98	107	138	157	161	128	166	188	212	224
$12,000–$12,999	106	114	148	167	172	134	175	198	224	237
$13,000–$13,999	114	121	158	177	183	140	184	208	235	250
$14,000–$14,999	122	128	168	187	194	146	193	217	246	262
$15,000–$15,999	130	135	178	196	205	152	202	226	257	274
$16,000–$16,999	138	142	188	205	216	158	210	235	267	286
$17,000–$17,999	146	149	198	214	227	163	218	244	277	298
$18,000–$18,999	153	156	208	223	238	168	226	252	287	310
$19,000–$19,999	160	163	217	232	248	173	234	260	297	321

Income [1]	South Dakota [6]: Family size (persons) 1	2	3	4	5	Over 5	Tennessee [2]: Family size (persons) 1	2	3&4	5	Over 5	Texas [2]: Family size (persons) 1&2	3&4	5	Over 5
Under $3,000	$52	$66	$71	$81	$81	$83	$54	$62	$76	$84	$84	$32	$41	$44	$44
$3,000–$3,999	64	81	88	99	99	105	66	78	95	104	105	42	52	56	56
$4,000–$4,999	75	95	104	115	117	125	77	93	111	123	125	51	62	67	68
$5,000–$5,999	84	107	118	130	134	144	87	106	126	140	144	59	71	78	79
$6,000–$6,999	93	119	132	144	150	161	97	119	140	156	161	67	80	88	89
$7,000–$7,999	102	130	145	157	165	178	106	131	153	171	178	75	89	98	99
$8,000–$8,999	110	141	157	169	179	194	114	143	165	186	194	83	97	107	109
$9,000–$9,999	118	151	169	181	193	210	122	154	177	200	209	90	105	116	118
$10,000–$10,999	125	161	181	192	207	225	130	165	189	213	224	97	113	125	127
$11,000–$11,999	132	170	192	203	220	240	137	175	200	226	239	104	120	133	136
$12,000–$12,999	139	179	203	213	233	254	144	185	211	239	253	111	127	141	145
$13,000–$13,999	146	188	213	223	245	268	151	195	221	251	267	118	134	149	153
$14,000–$14,999	153	197	223	233	257	281	158	205	231	263	280	125	141	157	161
$15,000–$15,999	159	205	233	242	269	294	164	215	241	275	293	132	148	165	169
$16,000–$16,999	165	213	243	251	280	307	170	224	251	286	306	139	155	173	177
$17,000–$17,999	171	221	253	260	291	320	176	233	260	297	319	145	162	180	185
$18,000–$18,999	177	229	262	269	302	333	182	242	269	308	331	151	168	187	193
$19,000–$19,999	182	236	271	278	313	345	188	251	278	319	343	157	174	194	201

Income [1]	Utah [7]: Family size (persons) 1	2	3	4	5	Over 5	Vermont: Family size (persons) 1	2	3&4	5	Over 5	Virginia [3]: Family size (persons) 1	2	3&4	5	Over 5
Under $3,000	$59	$77	$80	$95	$95	$95	$14	$17	$22	$27	$27	$43	$50	$63	$69	$70
$3,000–$3,999	73	95	99	115	115	118	18	22	28	34	34	52	63	78	86	88
$4,000–$4,999	85	111	117	132	134	140	22	27	34	41	41	61	75	91	101	104
$5,000–$5,999	97	125	134	148	153	160	25	32	39	47	47	69	86	103	115	119
$6,000–$6,999	108	138	149	163	171	179	29	37	44	53	53	76	96	114	128	133
$7,000–$7,999	118	151	163	176	187	197	32	41	49	58	59	83	106	125	141	147
$8,000–$8,999	128	163	177	189	203	215	35	45	54	64	65	90	115	135	153	160
$9,000–$9,999	137	175	191	202	219	232	38	50	59	69	71	96	124	145	164	172
$10,000–$10,999	146	186	204	214	234	248	41	54	64	74	76	102	132	154	175	184
$11,000–$11,999	154	196	216	225	248	264	44	58	68	79	81	108	140	163	186	196
$12,000–$12,999	162	206	228	236	262	279	47	62	72	83	86	114	148	172	196	208
$13,000–$13,999	170	216	240	246	275	294	50	66	76	88	91	119	156	180	206	219
$14,000–$14,999	178	226	251	256	288	308	53	70	80	93	96	124	164	188	216	230
$15,000–$15,999	186	235	262	266	301	322	56	74	84	97	101	129	172	196	225	240
$16,000–$16,999	194	244	273	276	314	336	58	77	88	102	106	134	179	204	234	250
$17,000–$17,999	201	253	284	285	326	350	61	81	92	106	111	139	186	212	243	260
$18,000–$18,999	208	262	294	294	338	363	64	85	96	110	116	144	193	219	252	270
$19,000–$19,999	215	271	304	304	350	376	66	88	100	114	120	149	200	226	261	280

Income [1]	Washington [8]: Family size (persons) 1	2	3	4	5	Over 5	West Virginia: Family size (persons) 1	2	3&4	5	Over 5	Wisconsin: Family size 1&2	3&4	5	Over 5	Wyoming [2]: Family size (persons) 1	2	3	4	5	Over 5
Under $3,000	$59	$79	$81	$98	$98	$98	$36	$42	$52	$57	$57	$40	$47	$48	$48	$39	$51	$53	$62	$62	$62
$3,000–$3,999	74	97	102	118	120	122	45	53	65	71	71	51	60	62	63	48	63	65	75	76	78
$4,000–$4,999	87	114	121	137	142	145	52	63	76	84	85	61	73	75	77	56	73	77	87	89	92
$5,000–$5,999	99	129	138	154	162	167	59	73	86	96	97	71	84	88	91	64	82	88	97	101	106
$6,000–$6,999	110	143	154	169	181	187	66	82	96	107	109	81	95	100	104	71	91	98	107	113	118
$7,000–$7,999	120	156	170	184	199	207	72	90	105	118	121	90	106	112	117	77	99	107	116	124	130
$8,000–$8,999	130	169	185	197	216	225	78	98	114	128	132	99	116	123	129	83	107	116	125	134	141
$9,000–$9,999	140	181	199	210	232	243	84	106	122	138	143	107	126	134	141	89	115	125	133	144	152
$10,000–$10,999	149	193	213	223	248	261	89	113	130	147	153	115	136	145	153	95	122	134	140	154	163
$11,000–$11,999	158	204	226	235	263	278	94	121	138	156	163	123	145	155	165	101	129	142	148	163	173
$12,000–$12,999	167	215	239	247	278	294	99	128	145	165	173	131	154	165	176	106	136	150	155	172	183
$13,000–$13,999	176	225	252	258	293	310	104	135	152	174	183	139	163	175	187	111	142	158	162	181	193
$14,000–$14,999	184	235	265	269	307	326	109	142	159	182	192	147	172	185	198	116	148	165	169	190	202
$15,000–$15,999	192	245	277	279	321	341	114	148	166	190	201	154	181	195	209	121	154	172	175	199	211
$16,000–$16,999	200	255	289	289	334	356	119	154	173	198	210	161	190	205	220	126	160	179	181	207	220
$17,000–$17,999	208	265	301	301	347	371	123	160	180	206	219	168	198	215	231	131	166	186	187	215	229
$18,000–$18,999	216	274	312	312	360	385	127	166	186	214	228	175	206	224	241	136	172	193	193	223	238
$19,000–$19,999	223	283	323	323	373	399	131	172	192	221	236	182	214	233	251	140	177	200	200	231	246

[1] Total of amount on Form 1040, line 29 and nontaxable receipts such as social security, veterans', railroad retirement benefits, workmen's compensation, untaxed portion of long-term capital gains, dividends exclusion, unemployment compensation and public assistance payments.

[2] Local sales taxes are not included. Add an amount based on the ratio between the local and State sales tax rates considering the number of months the taxes have been in effect.

[3] Local sales taxes are included.

[4] Local sales taxes are not included. If paid all year add 25 percent of the table amount for each 1 percent of local sales tax rate. Otherwise use a proportionate amount. For New York City add 103 percent of the table amount to include personal services taxed after February 29, 1976.

[5] Local sales taxes are included. Taxpayers not paying local sales tax should use 75 percent of the amount allowed.

[6] Local sales taxes are not included. Add the amount paid.

[7] Local ¾ percent sales taxes are included. Add 5 percent of the table amount if the ¼ percent county sales tax for transportation is paid all year (Davis, Salt Lake and Weber). Otherwise add a proportionate amount (see footnote 2).

[8] Local ½ percent sales taxes are included. If the 3/10's of 1 percent sales tax for public transportation is paid all year (Grays Harbor and King Counties) add 6 percent to the table amount. Otherwise add a proportionate amount (see footnote 2).

A–4 1977 STATE GASOLINE TAX TABLES

State Gasoline Tax Table

The following list shows the tax rate on a gallon of gasoline in each State based on information available on September 1, 1977. Find the rate for your State. Then use the table below to find how much tax to deduct for the number of miles you drove your car. If your car had 4 cylinders or less, you may deduct only half the table amount. If the rate for your State changed during 1977, find your deduction for the miles you drove at each rate, and add the amounts.

If your records show that you paid more than the amount shown in the table, you can deduct the larger amount.

Alabama 7¢
Alaska 8¢
Arizona 8¢
Arkansas 8.5¢
California 7¢
Colorado 7¢
Connecticut 11¢
Delaware 9¢
  (after June 30, 11¢)
District of Columbia 10¢
Florida 8¢
Georgia 7.5¢

Hawaii 8.5¢
Idaho 9.5¢
Illinois 7.5¢
Indiana 8¢
Iowa 7¢
Kansas 8¢
Kentucky 9¢
Louisiana 8¢
Maine 9¢
Maryland 9¢
Massachusetts 8.5¢
Michigan 9¢

Minnesota 9¢
Mississippi 9¢
Missouri 7¢
Montana 7.75¢
  (after June 30, 8¢)
Nebraska 8.5¢
  (after July 31, 9.5¢)
Nevada 6¢
New Hampshire 9¢
  (after July 31, 10¢)
New Jersey 8¢
New Mexico 7¢

New York 8¢
North Carolina 9¢
North Dakota 7¢
  (after June 30, 8¢)
Ohio 7¢
Oklahoma 6.58¢
  (use deduction for 6.5¢)
Oregon 7¢
Pennsylvania 9¢
Rhode Island 10¢
South Carolina 8¢
  (after June 30, 9¢)

South Dakota 8¢
Tennessee 7¢
Texas 5¢
Utah 7¢
Vermont 9¢
Virginia 9¢
Washington 9¢
  (after June 30, 11¢)
West Virginia 8.5¢
Wisconsin 7¢
Wyoming 8¢

TAX RATE

Nonbusiness miles driven	5¢	6¢	6.5¢	7¢	7.5¢	7.75¢	8¢	8.5¢	9¢	9.5¢	10¢	11¢	Nonbusiness miles driven
Under 3,000	$8	$10	$11	$12	$12	$13	$13	$14	$15	$16	$17	$18	Under 3,000
3,000 under 4,000	14	17	19	20	22	22	23	25	26	27	29	32	3,000 under 4,000
4,000 under 5,000	19	22	24	26	28	29	30	32	33	35	37	41	4,000 under 5,000
5,000 under 6,000	23	27	30	32	34	35	36	39	41	43	46	50	5,000 under 6,000
6,000 under 7,000	27	32	35	38	40	42	43	46	48	51	54	59	6,000 under 7,000
7,000 under 8,000	31	37	40	43	47	48	50	53	56	59	62	68	7,000 under 8,000
8,000 under 9,000	35	42	46	49	53	54	56	60	63	67	70	77	8,000 under 9,000
9,000 under 10,000	39	47	51	55	59	61	63	67	71	75	79	86	9,000 under 10,000
10,000 under 11,000	43	52	56	61	65	67	69	74	78	82	87	95	10,000 under 11,000
11,000 under 12,000	48	57	62	67	71	74	76	81	86	90	95	105	11,000 under 12,000
12,000 under 13,000	52	62	67	72	77	80	83	88	93	98	103	114	12,000 under 13,000
13,000 under 14,000	56	67	73	78	84	86	89	95	100	106	112	123	13,000 under 14,000
14,000 under 15,000	60	72	78	84	90	93	96	102	108	114	120	132	14,000 under 15,000
15,000 under 16,000	64	77	83	90	96	99	102	109	115	122	128	141	15,000 under 16,000
16,000 under 17,000	68	82	89	95	102	106	109	116	123	130	136	150	16,000 under 17,000
17,000 under 18,000	72	87	94	101	108	112	116	123	130	137	145	159	17,000 under 18,000
18,000 under 19,000	76	92	99	107	115	118	122	130	138	145	153	168	18,000 under 19,000
19,000 under 20,000	81	97	105	113	121	125	129	137	145	153	161	177	19,000 under 20,000
20,000*	83	99	107	116	124	128	132	141	149	157	165	182	20,000*

*For over 20,000 miles, use table amounts for total miles driven. For example, for 25,000 miles, add the deduction for 5,000 to the deduction for 20,000 miles.

APPENDIX B
TAX FORMS

B-1   SHORT FORM 1040A   U. S. INDIVIDUAL INCOME TAX RETURN

Form 1040A — Department of the Treasury—Internal Revenue Service
U.S. Individual Income Tax Return   **1977**

Use IRS label. Otherwise, print or type.

First name and initial (if joint return, give first names and initials of both)	Last name	Your social security number
Present home address (Number and street, including apartment number, or rural route)	For Privacy Act Notice, see page 9 of Instructions.	Spouse's social security no.
City, town or post office, State and ZIP code	Occupation Yours ▶ Spouse's ▶	

Presidential Election Campaign Fund
Do you want $1 to go to this fund? .... Yes ☐ No ☐
If joint return, does your spouse want $1 to go to this fund? Yes ☐ No ☐
Note: Checking "Yes" will not increase your tax or reduce your refund.

Filing Status — Check Only One Box

1 ☐ Single   2 ☐ Married filing joint return (even if only one had income)
3 ☐ Married filing separately. If spouse is also filing, give spouse's social security number in the space above and enter full name here ▶.............
4 ☐ Unmarried Head of Household. Enter qualifying name ▶ . See page 6 of Instructions.

Exemptions

Always check the "Yourself" box. Check other boxes if they apply.

5a ☐ Yourself   ☐ 65 or over   ☐ Blind   Enter number of boxes checked on 5a and b ▶
b ☐ Spouse   ☐ 65 or over   ☐ Blind
c First names of your dependent children who lived with you ▶............ Enter number of children listed ▶

d Other dependents: (1) Name	(2) Relationship	(3) Number of months lived in your home	(4) Did dependent have income of $750 or more?	(5) Did you provide more than one-half of dependent's support?

Enter number of other dependents ▶
Add numbers entered in boxes above ▶

6 Total number of exemptions claimed ....

Please Attach Copy B of Forms W-2 Here

7 Wages, salaries, tips, and other employee compensation. (Attach Forms W-2. If unavailable, see page 11 of Instructions)	7	
8 Interest income (see page 4 of Instructions)	8	
9a Dividends............ 9b Less exclusion............ Balance ▶ (See pages 4 and 11 of Instructions)	9c	
10 Adjusted gross income (add lines 7, 8, and 9c). If under $8,000, see page 2 of Instructions on "Earned Income Credit." If eligible, enter child's name ▶	10	
11a Credit for contributions to candidates for public office. Enter one-half of amount paid but do not enter more than $25 ($50 if joint return) 11a		

IF YOU WANT IRS TO FIGURE YOUR TAX, PLEASE STOP HERE AND SIGN BELOW.

b Total Federal income tax withheld (if line 7 is larger than $16,500, see page 12 of Instructions) 11b
c Earned income credit (from page 2 of Instructions) 11c

12 Total (add lines 11a, b, and c)	12	
13 Tax on the amount on line 10. (See Instructions for line 13 on page 12, then find your tax in Tax Tables on pages 14–25.)	13	
14 If line 12 is larger than line 13, enter amount to be **REFUNDED TO YOU** .... ▶	14	
15 If line 13 is larger than line 12, enter **BALANCE DUE**. Attach check or money order for full amount payable to "Internal Revenue Service." Write social security number on check or money order . . ▶	15	

Please Attach Check or Money Order Here

Under penalties of perjury, I declare that I have examined this return, including accompanying schedules and statements, and to the best of my knowledge and belief, it is true, correct, and complete. Declaration of preparer (other than taxpayer) is based on all information of which preparer has any knowledge.

Please Sign

▶ Your signature   Date
▶ Spouse's signature (if filing jointly, BOTH must sign even if only one had income)

▶ Paid preparer's signature and identifying number (see instructions)
▶ Paid preparer's address (or employer's name, address, and identifying number)

B–2   FORM 1040   U. S. INDIVIDUAL INCOME TAX RETURN

Form **1040** Department of the Treasury—Internal Revenue Service
U.S. Individual Income Tax Return **1977**

For the year January 1–December 31, 1977, or other taxable year beginning _____ , 1977 ending _____ , 19 ____ .

Use IRS label. Otherwise, print or type.	First name and initial (if joint return, give first names and initials of both) Last name	Your social security number
	Present home address (Number and street, including apartment number, or rural route)	**For Privacy Act Notice, see page 3 of Instructions.**	Spouse's social security no.
	City, town or post office, State and ZIP code	Occu-pation Yours ▶ Spouse's ▶	

Presidential Election Campaign Fund ▶

Do you want $1 to go to this fund? . . . . Yes ☐ No ☐

If joint return, does your spouse want $1 to go to this fund? . Yes ☐ No ☐

Note: *Checking "Yes" will not increase your tax or reduce your refund.*

Filing Status

Check Only One Box

1 ☐ Single

2 ☐ Married filing joint return (even if only one had income)

3 ☐ Married filing separately. If spouse is also filing, give spouse's social security number in the space above and enter full name here ▶ ....

4 ☐ Unmarried Head of Household. Enter qualifying name ▶ .... See page 7 of Instructions.

5 ☐ Qualifying widow(er) with dependent child (Year spouse died ▶ 19 ____). See page 7 of Instructions.

Exemptions

Always check the "Yourself" box. Check other boxes if they apply.

6a ☐ Yourself   ☐ 65 or over   ☐ Blind   Enter number of boxes checked on 6a and b ▶ ☐

b ☐ Spouse   ☐ 65 or over   ☐ Blind

c First names of your dependent children who lived with you ▶ ....   Enter number of children listed ▶ ☐

d Other dependents: (1) Name	(2) Relationship	(3) Number of months lived in your home.	(4) Did dependent have income of $750 or more?	(5) Did you provide more than one-half of dependent's support?

Enter number of other dependents ▶ ☐

7 Total number of exemptions claimed . . . .   Add numbers entered in boxes above ▶ ☐

Income

(Please Attach Copy B of Forms W-2 Here)

8	Wages, salaries, tips, and other employee compensation. (Attach Forms W-2. If unavailable, see page 5 of Instructions.)	8	
9	Interest income. (If over $400, attach Schedule B.)	9	
10a	Dividends (If over $400, attach Schedule B) ...., 10b less exclusion ...., **Balance** ▶	10c	
	(See pages 9 and 17 of Instructions)		

(If you have no other income, skip lines 11 through 20 and go to line 21.)

11	State and local income tax refunds (does not apply if refund is for year you took standard deduction) . . .	11	
12	Alimony received	12	
13	Business income or (loss) (attach Schedule C)	13	
14	Capital gain or (loss) (attach Schedule D)	14	
15	50% of capital gain distributions not reported on Schedule D	15	
16	Net gain or (loss) from Supplemental Schedule of Gains and Losses (attach Form 4797) . . .	16	
17	Fully taxable pensions and annuities not reported on Schedule E	17	
18	Pensions, annuities, rents, royalties, partnerships, estates or trusts, etc. (attach Schedule E) .	18	
19	Farm income or (loss) (attach Schedule F)	19	
20	Other (state nature and source—see page 9 of Instructions) ▶	20	
21	**Total income.** Add lines 8, 9, and 10c through 20 . . . . ▶	21	

Adjustments to Income   *(If none, skip lines 22 through 27 and enter zero on line 28.)*

(Please Attach Check or Money Order Here)

22	Moving expense (attach Form 3903)	22		
23	Employee business expenses (attach Form 2106)	23		
24	Payments to an individual retirement arrangement (from attached Form 5329, Part III)	24		
25	Payments to a Keogh (H.R. 10) retirement plan	25		
26	Forfeited interest penalty for premature withdrawal	26		
27	Alimony paid (see page 11 of Instructions)	27		
28	**Total adjustments.** Add lines 22 through 27 . . . . ▶		28	
29	Subtract line 28 from line 21		29	
30	Disability income exclusion (sick pay) (attach Form 2440)		30	
31	**Adjusted gross income.** Subtract line 30 from line 29. Enter here and on line 32. If you want IRS to figure your tax for you, see page 4 of the Instructions . . . . ▶		31	

Form 1040 (1977)   Page **2**

<table>
<tr><td rowspan="8">**Tax Computation**</td><td>32 Amount from line 31 . . . .</td><td>32</td><td></td></tr>
<tr><td>33 If you itemize deductions, enter excess itemized deductions from Schedule A, line 41 . . . . }

If you do NOT itemize deductions, enter zero. . . . . }
Caution: *If you have unearned income and can be claimed as a dependent on your parent's
return, check here* ▶ ☐ *and see page 11 of the Instructions. Also see page 11 of
the Instructions if:*
● *You are married filing a separate return and your spouse itemizes deductions, OR*
● *You file Form 4563, OR*
● *You are a dual-status alien.*</td><td>33</td><td></td></tr>
<tr><td>34 Tax Table Income. Subtract line 33 from line 32 . . . .</td><td>34</td><td></td></tr>
<tr><td>**Note:** See Instructions for line 35 on page 11. Then find your tax on the amount on line 34
in the Tax Tables. Enter the tax on line 35. However, if line 34 is more than $20,000
($40,000 if you checked box 2 or 5) or you have more exemptions than those covered in the
Tax Tables for your filing status, use Part I of Schedule TC (Form 1040) to figure your tax. You
must also use Schedule TC if you file Schedule G (Form 1040), Income Averaging.</td><td></td><td></td></tr>
<tr><td>35 Tax. Check if from ☐ Tax Tables or ☐ Schedule TC . . . .</td><td>35</td><td></td></tr>
<tr><td>36 Additional taxes. (See page 12 of Instructions.) Check if from ☐ Form 4970, ☐ Form 4972,
☐ Form 5544, ☐ Form 5405, or ☐ Section 72(m)(5) penalty tax . . . .</td><td>36</td><td></td></tr>
<tr><td>37 **Total.** Add lines 35 and 36 . . . . ▶</td><td>37</td><td></td></tr>
</table>

<table>
<tr><td rowspan="10">**Credits**</td><td>38 Credit for contributions to candidates for public office . . . . . .</td><td>38</td><td></td><td></td><td></td></tr>
<tr><td>39 Credit for the elderly (attach Schedules R&RP) . . . .</td><td>39</td><td></td><td></td><td></td></tr>
<tr><td>40 Credit for child and dependent care expenses (attach Form 2441) .</td><td>40</td><td></td><td></td><td></td></tr>
<tr><td>41 Investment credit (attach Form 3468) . . . .</td><td>41</td><td></td><td></td><td></td></tr>
<tr><td>42 Foreign tax credit (attach Form 1116) . . . .</td><td>42</td><td></td><td></td><td></td></tr>
<tr><td>43 Work Incentive (WIN) Credit (attach Form 4874) . . . .</td><td>43</td><td></td><td></td><td></td></tr>
<tr><td>44 New jobs credit (attach Form 5884) . . . .</td><td>44</td><td></td><td></td><td></td></tr>
<tr><td>45 See page 12 of Instructions . . . .</td><td>45</td><td></td><td></td><td></td></tr>
<tr><td>46 Total credits. Add lines 38 through 45 . . . .</td><td>46</td><td></td><td></td><td></td></tr>
<tr><td>47 **Balance.** Subtract line 46 from line 37 and enter difference (but not less than zero) . . . . ▶</td><td>47</td><td></td><td></td><td></td></tr>
</table>

<table>
<tr><td rowspan="8">**Other Taxes**</td><td>48 Self-employment tax (attach Schedule SE) . . . .</td><td>48</td><td></td></tr>
<tr><td>49 Minimum tax. Check here ▶ ☐ and attach Form 4625 . . . .</td><td>49</td><td></td></tr>
<tr><td>50 Tax from recomputing prior-year investment credit (attach Form 4255) . . . .</td><td>50</td><td></td></tr>
<tr><td>51 Social security tax on tip income not reported to employer (attach Form 4137) . . . .</td><td>51</td><td></td></tr>
<tr><td>52 Uncollected employee social security tax on tips (from Form W–2) . . . .</td><td>52</td><td></td></tr>
<tr><td>53 Tax on an individual retirement arrangement (attach Form 5329) . . . .</td><td>53</td><td></td></tr>
<tr><td>54 **Total tax.** Add lines 47 through 53 . . . . ▶</td><td>54</td><td></td></tr>
</table>

<table>
<tr><td rowspan="9">**Payments**</td><td>55 Total Federal income tax withheld (attach Forms W–2, W–2G, and
W–2P to front) . . . .</td><td>55</td><td></td><td></td><td></td></tr>
<tr><td>56 1977 estimated tax payments (include amount allowed as credit
from 1976 return) . . . .</td><td>56</td><td></td><td></td><td></td></tr>
<tr><td>57 Earned income credit. If line 31 is under $8,000, see page 2 of
Instructions. If eligible, enter child's name ▶. . . . .</td><td>57</td><td></td><td></td><td></td></tr>
<tr><td>58 Amount paid with Form 4868 . . . .</td><td>58</td><td></td><td></td><td></td></tr>
<tr><td>59 Excess FICA and RRTA tax withheld (two or more employers) . . .</td><td>59</td><td></td><td></td><td></td></tr>
<tr><td>60 Credit for Federal tax on special fuels, etc. (attach Form 4136) . .</td><td>60</td><td></td><td></td><td></td></tr>
<tr><td>61 Credit from a Regulated Investment Company (attach Form 2439) . . . . . .</td><td>61</td><td></td><td></td><td></td></tr>
<tr><td>61a See page 13 of Instructions . . . .</td><td>61a</td><td></td><td></td><td></td></tr>
<tr><td>62 **Total.** Add lines 55 through 61a . . . . ▶</td><td>62</td><td></td><td></td><td></td></tr>
</table>

<table>
<tr><td rowspan="4">**Refund or Due**</td><td>63 If line 62 is larger than line 54, enter amount **OVERPAID** . . . . ▶</td><td>63</td><td></td></tr>
<tr><td>64 Amount of line 63 to be **REFUNDED TO YOU** . . . . ▶</td><td>64</td><td></td></tr>
<tr><td>65 Amount of line 63 to be credited on 1978 estimated tax . . . ▶ | 65 |</td><td></td><td></td></tr>
<tr><td>66 If line 54 is larger than line 62, enter **BALANCE DUE.** Attach check or money order for full amount
payable to "Internal Revenue Service." Write social security number on check or money order . . . ▶
(Check ▶ ☐ if Form 2210 (2210F) is attached. See page 14 of Instructions.)</td><td>66</td><td></td></tr>
</table>

Please Sign Here

Under penalties of perjury, I declare that I have examined this return, including accompanying schedules and statements, and to the best of my knowledge and belief, it is true, correct, and complete. Declaration of preparer (other than taxpayer) is based on all information of which preparer has any knowledge.

▶ _____   ▶ Paid preparer's signature and identifying number (see instructions)
Your signature   Date   _____

▶ _____   _____
Spouse's signature (if filing jointly, BOTH must   Paid preparer's address (or employer's name, address, and identifying number)
sign even if only one had income)

☆ U.S. GOVERNMENT PRINTING OFFICE : 1977—O—235-057

SCHEDULES A & B—ITEMIZED DEDUCTIONS AND DIVIDEND AND INTEREST INCOME

Schedules A&B—Itemized Deductions AND Interest and Dividend Income

(Form 1040)
Department of the Treasury
Internal Revenue Service

▶ **Attach to Form 1040.** ▶ **See Instructions for Schedules A and B (Form 1040).**

1977

Name(s) as shown on Form 1040	Your social security number

Schedule A Itemized Deductions (Schedule B is on back)

Medical and Dental Expenses (not compensated by insurance or otherwise) (See page 14 of Instructions.)

1 One-half (but not more than $150) of insurance premiums for medical care. (Be sure to include in line 10 below) . . .

2 Medicine and drugs . . . .

3 Enter 1% of line 31, Form 1040 . . .

4 Subtract line 3 from line 2. Enter difference (if less than zero, enter zero) . .

5 Enter balance of insurance premiums for medical care not entered on line 1 . .

6 Enter other medical and dental expenses:

a Doctors, dentists, nurses, etc. . . . .

b Hospitals . . . .

c Other (itemize—include hearing aids, dentures, eyeglasses, transportation, etc.) ▶

7 Total (add lines 4 through 6c) . . .

8 Enter 3% of line 31, Form 1040 . . .

9 Subtract line 8 from line 7 (if less than zero, enter zero) . . . .

10 Total (add lines 1 and 9). Enter here and on line 33 . . . . ▶

Taxes (See page 14 of Instructions.)

11 State and local income . . . . . .

12 Real estate . . . .

13 State and local gasoline (see gas tax tables)

14 General sales (see sales tax tables) . .

15 Personal property . . . .

16 Other (itemize) ▶

17 Total (add lines 11 through 16). Enter here and on line 34 . . . . . . ▶

Interest Expense (See page 16 of Instructions.)

18 Home mortgage . . . .

19 Other (itemize) ▶

20 Total (add lines 18 and 19). Enter here and on line 35 . . . . ▶

Contributions (See page 16 of Instructions for examples.)

21 a Cash contributions for which you have receipts, cancelled checks or other written evidence . . . .

b Other cash contributions. List donees and amounts. ▶

22 Other than cash (see page 16 of instructions for required statement) . . . .

23 Carryover from prior years . . . . .

24 Total contributions (add lines 21a through 23). Enter here and on line 36 . . ▶

Casualty or Theft Loss(es) (See page 16 of Instructions.)

25 Loss before insurance reimbursement .

26 Insurance reimbursement . . . . .

27 Subtract line 26 from line 25. Enter difference (if less than zero, enter zero) .

28 Enter $100 or amount on line 27, whichever is smaller . . . .

29 Casualty or theft loss (subtract line 28 from line 27). Enter here and on line 37 ▶

Miscellaneous Deductions (See page 16 of Instructions.)

30 Union dues . . . .

31 Other (itemize) ▶

32 Total (add lines 30 and 31). Enter here and on line 38 . . . . ▶

Summary of Itemized Deductions (See page 17 of Instructions.) **A**

33 Total medical and dental—line 10 . .

34 Total taxes—line 17 . . . .

35 Total interest—line 20 . . . . . .

36 Total contributions—line 24 . . . .

37 Casualty or theft loss(es)—line 29 . .

38 Total miscellaneous—line 32 . . . .

39 Total deductions (add lines 33 through 38). ▶

40 If you checked Form 1040, box:
2 or 5, enter $3,200
1 or 4, enter $2,200
3, enter $1,600 . . . .

41 Excess itemized deductions (subtract line 40 from line 39). Enter here and on Form 1040, line 33. (If line 40 is more than line 39 see "Who MUST Itemize Deductions" on page 11 of the Instructions.) . . ▶

Schedules A&B (Form 1040) 1977   **Schedule B—Interest and Dividend Income**   Page **2**

Name(s) as shown on Form 1040 (Do not enter name and social security number if shown on other side)	Your social security number

Part I   Interest Income

1 *If you received more than $400 in interest, complete Part I.* Interest includes earnings from savings and loan associations, mutual savings banks, cooperative banks, and credit unions as well as interest on bank deposits, bonds, tax refunds, etc. Interest also includes original issue discount on bonds and other evidences of indebtedness (see page 17 of Instructions). **(List payers and amounts.)**

Part II   Dividend Income

3 *If you received more than $400 in* **gross dividends** *(including capital gain distributions) and other distributions on stock, complete Part II (see Note below and page 17 of instructions).* **(List payers and amounts**—write (H), (W), (J), for stock held by husband, wife, or jointly.)

4 Total of line 3 . . . .

5 Capital gain distributions (see page 18 of Instructions. Enter here and on Schedule D, line 7). See Note below . . . . .

6 Nontaxable distributions (see page 18 of instructions) . . .

7 Total (add lines 5 and 6) . . . .

8 **Dividends before exclusion (subtract line 7 from line 4).** Enter here and on Form 1040, line 10a . . . .

2 Total interest income. Enter here and on Form 1040, line 9 . . . .

Note: *If you received capital gain distributions and do not need Schedule D to report any other gains or losses or to compute the alternative tax, do not file that schedule. Instead, enter 50 percent of capital gain distributions on Form 1040, line 15.*

B

Part III   Foreign Accounts and Foreign Trusts

If you are required to list interest in Part I or dividends in Part II, **OR** *if you had a foreign account or were a grantor of, or a transferor to a foreign trust, you must answer both questions in Part III. (See page 18 of Instructions.)*

1 Did you, at any time during the taxable year, have any interest in or signature or other authority over a bank, securities, or other financial account in a foreign country (except in a U.S. military banking facility operated by a U.S. financial institution)? . . . . ☐ **Yes** ☐ **No**

If "Yes," see page 3 of instructions.

2 Were you the grantor of, or transferor to, a foreign trust during any taxable year, which foreign trust was in being during the current taxable year, whether or not you have any beneficial interest in such trust? . . . ☐ **Yes** ☐ **No**

If "Yes," you may be required to file Forms 3520, 3520–A, or 926.

SCHEDULE C PROFIT OR (LOSS) FROM BUSINESS OR PROFESSION

SCHEDULE C
(Form 1040)
Department of the Treasury
Internal Revenue Service

Profit or (Loss) From Business or Profession
(Sole Proprietorship)
Partnerships, Joint Ventures, etc., Must File Form 1065.
► Attach to Form 1040. ► See Instructions for Schedule C (Form 1040).

1977

C

Name of proprietor | Social security number

A Principal business activity (see Schedule C Instructions) ►...........................; product ►.............................

B Business name ►...

C Employer identification number ►...

D Business address (number and street) ►..

City, State and ZIP code ►...

E Indicate method of accounting: **(1)** ☐ Cash **(2)** ☐ Accrual **(3)** ☐ Other ►.................................... | Yes | No

F Was an Employer's Quarterly Federal Tax Return, Form 941, filed for this business for any quarter in 1977? . . . .

G Did you own the business at the end of 1977? . . . .

H How many months in 1977 did you own this business? ►..............................

I Check valuation method(s) used for total closing inventory: ☐ cost, ☐ lower of cost or market, ☐ other (if "other," attach explanation).

Was there any substantial change in determining quantities, costs, or valuations between opening and closing inventory? If "Yes," attach explanation.

Income	1 Gross receipts or sales $.................. Less: returns and allowances $.............. Balance ►	**1**
	2 Less: Cost of goods sold and/or operations (Schedule C–1, line 8)	**2**
	3 Gross profit	**3**
	4 Other income (attach schedule)	**4**
	5 **Total income** (add lines 3 and 4)	**5**
Deductions	6 Depreciation (explain in Schedule C–2)	**6**
	7 Taxes on business and business property	**7**
	8 Rent on business property	**8**
	9 Repairs	**9**
	10 Salaries and wages not included on line 3, Schedule C–1 (exclude any paid to yourself) .	**10**
	11 Insurance	**11**
	12 Legal and professional fees	**12**
	13 Commissions	**13**
	14 Amortization (attach statement)	**14**
	15 a Pension and profit-sharing plans (see Schedule C Instructions)	**15a**
	b Employee benefit programs (see Schedule C Instructions)	**b**
	16 Interest on business indebtedness	**16**
	17 Bad debts arising from sales or services	**17**
	18 Depletion	**18**
	19 Other business expenses (specify):	
	a	
	b	
	c	
	d	
	e	
	f	
	g	
	h	
	i	
	j	
	k	
	l	
	m	
	n	
	o	
	p Total other business expenses (add lines 19a through 19o)	**19p**
	20 Total deductions (add lines 6 through 19p)	**20**

21 Net profit or (loss) (subtract line 20 from line 5). Enter here and on Form 1040, line 13. **ALSO** enter on Schedule SE, line 5a . . . . ► | **21**

Did you claim a deduction for expenses of an office in your home? . . . . ☐ Yes ☐ No

Schedule C (Form 1040) 1977   Page **2**

SCHEDULE C–1.—Cost of Goods Sold and/or Operations
(See Schedule C Instructions for Line 2)

1 Inventory at beginning of year (if different from last year's closing inventory, attach explanation) . . .	1	
2 Purchases $......................... Less: cost of items withdrawn for personal use $...................... **Balance ▶**	2	
3 Cost of labor (do not include salary paid to yourself)	3	
4 Materials and supplies	4	
5 Other costs (attach schedule)	5	
6 Add lines 1 through 5	6	
7 Inventory at end of year	7	
8 Cost of goods sold and/or operations (subtract line 7 from line 6). Enter here and on page 1, line 2 .	8	

SCHEDULE C–2.—Depreciation (See Schedule C Instructions for Line 6)
If you need more space, use Form 4562.

a. Description of property	b. Date acquired	c. Cost or other basis	d. Depreciation allowed or allowable in prior years	e. Method of computing depreciation	f. Life or rate	g. Depreciation for this year
1 Total additional first-year depreciation (do not include in items below)———————————————▶						
2 Other depreciation:						
3 Totals			. . . .			
4 Depreciation claimed in Schedule C–1, above						
5 Balance (subtract line 4 from line 3). Enter here and on page 1, line 6						

SCHEDULE C–3.—Expense Account Information (See Schedule C Instructions for Schedule C–3)

Enter information with regard to yourself and your five highest paid employees. In determining the five highest paid employees, expense account allowances must be added to their salaries and wages. However, the information need not be submitted for any employee for whom the combined amount is less than $25,000, or for yourself if your expense account allowance plus line 21, page 1, is less than $25,000.	Name	Expense account	Salaries and Wages
	Owner		
	1		
	2		
	3		
	4		
Did you claim a deduction for expenses connected with:	5		

(1) Entertainment facility (boat, resort, ranch, etc.)? . . ☐ **Yes** ☐ **No**   (3) Employees' families at conventions or meetings? . . ☐ **Yes** ☐ **No**

(2) Living accommodations (except employees on business)? ☐ **Yes** ☐ **No**   (4) Employee or family vacations not reported on Form W–2? ☐ **Yes** ☐ **No**

SCHEDULE D   CAPITAL GAINS AND LOSSES

SCHEDULE D (Form 1040) Department of the Treasury Internal Revenue Service	**Capital Gains and Losses** (Examples of property to be reported on this Schedule are gains and losses on stocks, bonds, and similar investments, and gains (but not losses) on personal assets such as a home or jewelry.) ▶ Attach to Form 1040. ▶ See Instructions for Schedule D (Form 1040).	**1977**

Name(s) as shown on Form 1040 | Social security number

Part I   Short-term Capital Gains and Losses—Assets Held Not More Than 9 Months   **D**

a. Kind of property and description (Example, 100 shares of ''Z'' Co.)	b. Date acquired (Mo., day, yr.)	c. Date sold (Mo., day, yr.)	d. Gross sales price	e. Cost or other basis, as adjusted (see Instruction F) and expense of sale	f. Gain or (loss) (d less e)
1					

2   Enter your share of net short-term gain or (loss) from partnerships and fiduciaries . . . . . | 2 |
3   Enter net gain or (loss), combine lines 1 and 2 . . . . | 3 |
4   Short-term capital loss carryover attributable to years beginning after 1969 (see Instruction I) . | 4 | (|) |
5   Net short-term gain or (loss), combine lines 3 and 4 . . . . | 5 |

Part II   Long-term Capital Gains and Losses—Assets Held More Than 9 Months

6					

7   Capital gain distributions . . . . | 7 |
8   Enter gain, if applicable, from Form 4797, line 4(a)(1) (see Instruction A) . . . . . . | 8 |
9   Enter your share of net long-term gain or (loss) from partnerships and fiduciaries . . . . . | 9 |
10   Enter your share of net long-term gain from small business corporations (Subchapter S) . . . | 10 |
11   Net gain or (loss), combine lines 6 through 10 . . . . | 11 |
12   Long-term capital loss carryover attributable to years beginning after 1969 (see Instruction I) . | 12 | (|) |
13   Net long-term gain or (loss), combine lines 11 and 12 . . . . | 13 |

Part III   Summary of Parts I and II (If You Have Capital Loss Carryovers From Years Beginning Before 1970, Do Not Complete This Part. See Form 4798 Instead.)

14   Combine lines 5 and 13, and enter the net gain or (loss) here . . . . | 14 |
15   If line 14 shows a gain—
   a Enter 50% of line 13 or 50% of line 14, whichever is smaller (see Part IV for computation of alternative tax). Enter zero if there is a loss or no entry on line 13 . . . . | 15a |
     Note: If the amount you enter on line 15a is other than zero, you may be liable for minimum tax. See Form 4625 and instructions.
   b Subtract line 15a from line 14. Enter here and on Form 1040, line 14 . . . . | 15b |
16   If line 14 shows a loss—
   a Enter one of the following amounts:
     (i)   If line 5 is zero or a net gain, enter 50% of line 14;
     (ii) If line 13 is zero or a net gain, enter line 14; or,
     (iii) If line 5 and line 13 are net losses, enter amount on line 5 added to 50% of amount on line 13 . . . . | 16a |
   b Enter here and enter as a (loss) on Form 1040, line 14, the smallest of:
     (i)   The amount on line 16a;
     (ii) $2,000 ($1,000 if married and filing a separate return); or,
     (iii) Taxable income, as adjusted (see Instruction J) . . . . | 16b | (|) |

   Note: If the amount on line 16a is larger than the loss shown on line 16b, complete Part V to determine Post-1969 Capital Loss Carryovers from 1977 to 1978.

[B7084]

Schedule D (Form 1040) 1977   Page **2**

Part IV Computation of Alternative Tax (See Instruction S to See if the Alternative Tax Will Benefit You)

17 Enter amount from Schedule TC (Form 1040), Part I, line 3 . . . . **17**

18 Enter amount from line 15a (or Form 4798, Part I, line 8(a)) **18**

19 Subtract line 18 from line 17 (if line 18 exceeds line 17, do not complete the rest of this part. The
    Alternative Tax will not benefit you) **19**

    Note: *If line 18 does not exceed $25,000 ($12,500 if married filing separately), skip lines 20
    through 23 and enter zero on line 24.*

20 Enter $25,000 ($12,500 if married filing separately) **20**

21 Add lines 19 and 20 . . . . **21**

22 Tax on amount on line 17 (use Tax Rate Schedule in instructions) .   **22**

23 Tax on amount on line 21 (use Tax Rate Schedule in instructions) .   **23**

24 Subtract line 23 from line 22 . . . . **24**

25 Tax on amount on line 19 (use Tax Rate Schedule in instructions) **25**

26 Enter 50% of line 18 but not more than $12,500 ($6,250 if married filing separately) **26**

27 Alternative Tax—add lines 24, 25, and 26. If smaller than the tax figured on the amount on
    Schedule TC (Form 1040), Part I, line 3, enter this alternative tax on Schedule TC (Form 1040),
    Part I, line 4. Also check the Schedule D box on Schedule TC (Form 1040), Part I, line 4 . . . . **27**

Part V Computation of Post-1969 Capital Loss Carryovers from 1977 to 1978
(Complete this part if the amount on line 16a, is larger than the loss shown on line 16b.)

Section A.—Short-term Capital Loss Carryover

28 Enter loss shown on line 5; if none, enter zero and ignore lines 29 through 33—then go to line 34 . **28**

29 Enter gain shown on line 13. If that line is blank or shows a loss, enter zero **29**

30 Reduce any loss on line 28 to the extent of any gain on line 29 . . . . **30**

31 Enter amount shown on line 16b **31**

32 Enter smaller of line 30 or 31 . . . . **32**

33 Excess of amount on line 30 over amount on line 32 . . . . **33**

    Note: *The amount on line 33 is the portion of your short-term capital loss carryover from 1977 to 1978 that is attributable to
    years beginning after 1969.*

Section B.—Long-term Capital Loss Carryover

34 Line 31 less line 32 **(Note:** *If you skipped lines 29 through 33, enter amount from line 16b)* . . . **34**

35 Enter loss from line 13; if none, enter zero and ignore lines 36 through 39 . . . . **35**

36 Enter gain shown on line 5. If that line is blank or shows a loss, enter a zero **36**

37 Reduce any loss on line 35 to the extent of any gain on line 36 . . . . **37**

38 Multiply amount on line 34 by 2 . . . . **38**

39 Excess of amount on line 37 over amount on line 38 . . . . **39**

    Note: *The amount on line 39 is the portion of your long-term capital loss carryover from 1977 to 1978 that is attributable to
    years beginning after 1969.*

SCHEDULE E   SUPPLEMENTAL INCOME SCHEDULE

SCHEDULE E
(Form 1040)
Department of the Treasury
Internal Revenue Service

Supplemental Income Schedule

(From pensions and annuities, rents and royalties, partnerships, estates and trusts, etc.)
▶ Attach to Form 1040.   ▶ See Instructions for Schedule E (Form 1040).

1977

Name(s) as shown on Form 1040 | Your social security number

Part I **Pension and Annuity Income.** If fully taxable, do not complete this part. Enter amount on Form 1040, line 17. For one pension or annuity not fully taxable, complete this part. If you have more than one pension or annuity that is not fully taxable, attach a separate sheet listing each one with the appropriate data and enter combined total of taxable portions on line 5.

1 Name of payer
2 Did your employer contribute part of the cost? . . . . ☐ Yes ☐ No
  If "Yes," is your contribution recoverable within 3 years of the annuity starting date? . . . . ☐ Yes ☐ No
  If "Yes," show: Your contribution $......................, Contribution recovered in prior years . . . | 2 |
3 Amount received this year . . . . | 3 |
4 Amount excludable this year . . . . | 4 |
5 Taxable portion (subtract line 4 from line 3) . . . . | 5 |

Part II **Rent and Royalty Income.** If you need more space, use Form 4831.
Have you claimed expenses connected with your vacation home rented to others? ☐ Yes ☐ No

(a) Kind and location of property if residential, also write "R"	(b) Total amount of rents	(c) Total amount of royalties	(d) Depreciation (explain below) or depletion (attach computation)	(e) Other expenses (Repairs, etc.— explain below)

6 Totals . . . .
7 Net income or (loss) from rents and royalties (column (b) plus column (c) less columns (d) and (e)) . | 7 |
8 Net rental income or (loss) (from Form 4831) . . . . | 8 |
9 Net farm rental profit or (loss) (from Form 4835) . . . . | 9 |
10 Total rent and royalty income (add lines 7, 8, and 9) . . . . | 10 |

Part III **Income or Losses from Partnerships, Estates or Trusts, Small Business Corporations.**

Enter in column (b): P for Partnership, E for Estate or Trust, or S for Small Business Corp.

(a) Name	(b)	(c) Employer identification number	(d) Your share of gross farming or fishing income	(e) Income or (loss)	(f) Additional 1st year depreciation (applicable only to partnerships)

11 Totals .
12 Income or (loss). Total of column (e) less total of column (f) . . . . | 12 |

13 **TOTAL (add lines 5, 10, and 12). Enter here and on Form 1040, line 18** . . . . ▶ | 13 |

Explanation of Column (e), Part II

Item	Amount	Item	Amount	Item	Amount

Schedule for Depreciation Claimed in Part II above. If you need more space use Form 4562.

(a) Description of property	(b) Date acquired	(c) Cost or other basis	(d) Depreciation allowed or allowable in prior years	(e) Method of computing depreciation	(f) Life or rate	(g) Depreciation for this year	**E**
1 Total additional first-year depreciation (do not include in items below) ────────▶							
2 Totals							

☆ U.S. GOVERNMENT PRINTING OFFICE :1977—O—235-062

SCHEDULE F FARM INCOME AND EXPENSES

SCHEDULE F
(Form 1040)

Department of the Treasury
Internal Revenue Service

Farm Income and Expenses
(Compute social security self-employment tax on Schedule SE)
► Attach to Form 1040 or Form 1065. ► See Instructions for Schedule F (Form 1040).
► If rental income, see instructions before using this schedule.

1977

Name of proprietor(s)

Social security number

Business name and address ►

Location of farm(s) and number of acres in each farm ►

Employer identification number (See Instructions)

Part I Farm Income—Cash Receipts and Disbursements Method		
Do not include sales of livestock held for draft, breeding, sport, or dairy purposes; report such sales on Form 4797.		
Sales of Purchased Livestock and Other Items Purchased for Resale		
a. Description	b. Amount received	c. Cost or other basis
1 Livestock:	$	$
2 Other items:		
3 Totals	$	$
4 Profit or (loss), subtract line 3, column c from line 3, column b . . . . ►		$

Sales of Market Livestock and Produce Raised and Held Primarily for Sale and Other Farm Income

Kind	Quantity	Amount
5 Cattle		$
6 Calves		
7 Sheep		
8 Swine		
9 Poultry		
10 Dairy products . . .		
11 Eggs		
12 Wool		
13 Cotton		
14 Tobacco		
15 Vegetables		
16 Grain		
17 Fruits and nuts . . .		
18 Other (specify):		

OTHER FARM INCOME

19 Machine work		
20 (a) Patronage dividends (See Sch. F instructions) . .		
(b) Per-unit retains (See Sch. F instructions)		
21 Nonpatronage distributions from exempt cooperatives .		
22 Agricultural program payments:		
(a) Cash		
(b) Materials and services		
23 Commodity credit loans under election (or forfeited) . .		
24 Federal gasoline tax credit		
25 State gasoline tax refund		
26 Other (specify):		
27 Add lines 5 through 26		$
28 Gross profits* (add lines 4 and 27) . . . . ►		$

Part II Farm Deductions—For Cash and Accrual Method Taxpayers		**F**
Do not include personal or living expenses not attributable to production of farm income, such as taxes, insurance, repairs, etc., on your dwelling.		
Items	Amount	
29 Labor hired	$	
30 Repairs, maintenance . .		
31 Interest		
32 Rent of farm, pasture . .		
33 Feed purchased . . .		
34 Seeds, plants purchased .		
35 Fertilizers, lime, chemicals .		
36 Machine hire		
37 Supplies purchased . . .		
38 Breeding fees		
39 Veterinary fees, medicine .		
40 Gasoline, fuel, oil		
41 Storage, warehousing . .		
42 Taxes		
43 Insurance		
44 Utilities		
45 Freight, trucking		
46 Conservation expenses . .		
47 Land clearing expenses . .		
48 Pension and profit-sharing plans (see Sch. F instructions)		
49 Employee benefit programs other than line 48 (see Sch. F instructions)		
50 Other (specify):		
51 Add lines 29 through 50 ►	$	
52 Depreciation (from line 57, Part III) . . . . . ►		
53 Total deductions. Add lines 51 and 52 . . . . . ►	$	

54 Net farm profit or (loss) (subtract line 53 from line 28). Enter here and on Form 1040, line 19 or on Form 1065, line 9. **ALSO** enter on Schedule SE, Part I, line 1a . . . . ► $

* Use amount on line 28 for optional method of computing net earnings from self-employment. (See Schedule SE, Part I, line 3.)

Schedule F (Form 1040) 1977

Page 2

Part III — Depreciation

(Do not include property you and your family occupy as a dwelling, its furnishings, and other items used for personal purposes.)
If you need more space, use Form 4562.

a. Description of property	b. Date acquired	c. Cost or other basis	d. Depreciation allowed or allowable in prior years	e. Method of computing depreciation	f. Life or rate	g. Depreciation for this year
55 Total additional first-year depreciation (do not include in items below) ——————→						
56 Other depreciation:						
57 Totals			Enter here and in Part II, line 52 . ▶			

Part IV — Farm Income—Accrual Method

(Do not include sales of livestock held for draft, breeding, sport, or dairy purposes;
report such sales on Form 4797 and omit them from "On hand at beginning of year" column)

Description (Kind of livestock, crops, or other products)	On hand at beginning of year		Purchased during year		Raised during year	Consumed or lost during year	Sold during year		On hand at end of year	
	Quantity	Inventory value	Quantity	Amount paid	Quantity	Quantity	Quantity	Amount received	Quantity	Inventory value
		$		$				$		$
58 Totals (enter here and in Part V below)	$ (Enter on line 68)		$ (Enter on line 69)				$ (Enter on line 60)		$ (Enter on line 59)	

Part V — Summary of Income and Deductions—Accrual Method

59 Inventory of livestock, crops, and products at end of year . . . . $

60 Sales of livestock, crops, and products during year . . . . $

61 Agricultural program payments: (a) Cash . . . .

(b) Materials and services . . . .

62 Commodity credit loans under election (or forfeited) . . . .

63 Federal gasoline tax credit . . . .

64 State gasoline tax refund . . . .

65 Other farm income (specify): ....

66 Add lines 60 through 65 . . . .

67 Total (add lines 59 and 66) . . . . $

68 Inventory of livestock, crops, and products at beginning of year . . . . $

69 Cost of livestock and products purchased during year . . . .

70 Gross profits* (subtract the sum of lines 68 and 69 from line 67) . . . . ▶ $

71 Total deductions from Part II, line 53 . . . . $

72 Net farm profit or (loss) (subtract line 71 from line 70). Enter here and on Form 1040, line 19 or on Form 1065, line 9. **ALSO** enter on Schedule SE, Part I, line 1a. . . . . ▶ $

* Use amount on line 70 for optional method of computing net earnings from self-employment. (See Schedule SE, Part I, line 3.)

SCHEDULE G   INCOME AVERAGING

SCHEDULE G (Form 1040) Department of the Treasury Internal Revenue Service	**Income Averaging** ▶ See instructions on pages 3 and 4. ▶ Attach to Form 1040.	**1977**

Name(s) as shown on Form 1040	Your social security number

Base Period Income and Adjustments

	(a) 1st preceding base period year **1976**	(b) 2d preceding base period year **1975**	(c) 3rd preceding base period year **1974**	(d) 4th preceding base period year **1973**
1 Taxable income				
2 Income earned outside of the United States or within U.S. possessions and excluded under sections 911 and 931				
3 If you checked, on {2 or 5 enter $3,200} in your 1977 Form {1 or 4 enter $2,200} each 1040, box {3 enter $1,600} column .				
4 Base period income (add lines 1, 2 and 3). If less than zero, enter zero				

Computation of Averageable Income

5 Taxable income for 1977 from Schedule TC (Form 1040), Part I, line 3 . .	**5**
6 Certain amounts received by owner-employees subject to a penalty under section 72(m)(5)	**6**
7 Subtract line 6 from line 5	**7**
8 Excess community income	**8**
9 Adjusted taxable income (subtract line 8 from line 7). If less than zero, enter zero	**9**
10 30% of the sum of line 4, columns (a) through (d)	**10**
11 Averageable income (subtract line 10 from line 9)	**11**

Complete the remaining parts of this form only if line 11 is more than $3,000. If $3,000 or less, you do not qualify for income averaging. Do not fill in rest of form.   **G**

Computation of Tax

12 Amount from line 10	**12**	
13 20% of line 11	**13**	
14 Total (add lines 12 and 13)	**14**	
15 Excess community income from line 8	**15**	
16 Total (add lines 14 and 15)	**16**	
17 Tax on amount on line 16	**17**	
18 Tax on amount on line 14 . . . . **18**		
19 Tax on amount on line 12 . . . . **19**		
20 Subtract line 19 from line 18 . . . . **20**		
21 Multiply the amount on line 20 by 4	**21**	
Note: If no entry was made on line 6 above, skip lines 22 through 24 and go to line 25.		
22 Tax on amount on line 5 . . . . **22**		
23 Tax on amount on line 7 . . . . **23**		
24 Subtract line 23 from line 22	**24**	
25 Tax (add lines 17, 21, and 24). Enter here and on Schedule TC (Form 1040), Part I, line 4. Also check Schedule G box on Schedule TC (Form 1040), Part I, line 4	**25**	

Computations on this page are not needed unless you used the optional tax tables for 1975, 1974 or 1973.

Computation of Taxable Income for 1975 if You Used the Optional Tax Tables

1 Enter amount from:
Form 1040 (1975), line 15 }
Form 1040A (1975), line 12 } **1**

2 a Enter 16% of line 1:
but not more than $2,400 if you were married filing jointly (or a qualifying widow(er)) }
but not more than $2,300 if you were single (or a head of household) . . . . }
but not more than $1,300 if you were married filing separately . . . . } **2a**

b Enter:
$1,900 if you were married filing jointly (or a qualifying widow(er)) }
$1,600 if you were single (or a head of household) . . . . . } **2b**
$950 if you were married filing separately . . . . }

c Standard deduction. Enter line 2a or b whichever is greater. (If you were married and filed separately and your spouse used the percentage standard deduction (line 2a), then you must use it.) . . . **2c**

3 Subtract line 2c from line 1 . . . . **3**

4 Multiply total number of exemptions claimed by $750 . . . . **4**

5 Taxable income (subtract line 4 from line 3). Enter here and on page 1, line 1, column (b) **5**

Computation of Taxable Income for 1974 and 1973 if You Used the Optional Tax Tables

		1974	1973
1 Enter amount from: Form 1040 (1974 and 1973), line 15 . } Form 1040A (1974 and 1973), line 12 }	**1**		
2 a Enter 15% of line 1 (limited to $1,000 if you were married and filed separately)	**2a**		
b Enter $1,300 ($650 if you were married and filed separately)	**2b**		
c Standard deduction. Enter line 2a or b whichever is greater. (If you were married and filed separately and your spouse used the percentage standard deduction (line 2a), then you must use it.)	**2c**		
3 Subtract line 2c from line 1	**3**		
4 Multiply total number of exemptions claimed by $750	**4**		
5 Taxable income (subtract line 4 from line 3). Enter here and on page 1, line 1, in the applicable column(s) (c) or (d)	**5**		

SCHEDULES R & RP—CREDIT FOR THE ELDERLY

Schedules R & RP—Credit for the Elderly

(Form 1040)   (Public Retirees Under 65 See Schedule RP on Back)   **1977**

Department of the Treasury
Internal Revenue Service

▶ **Attach to Form 1040.** ▶ **See Instructions for Schedules R and RP (Form 1040).**

Name(s) as shown on Form 1040 | Your social security number

Important:

● Use Schedule R if you are 65 or over (or if married filing jointly and either spouse is 65 or over) and have any type of income.

● Use Schedule RP (on back) if you are under 65 and have pension or annuity income from a public retirement system such as a federal, state, or local government system.

● You may elect to use Schedule RP (on back) if you are married filing jointly, one of you is 65 or over and the other is under 65, and the one who is under 65 has pension or annuity income from a public retirement system. Unless you both elect to use Schedule RP, you must use Schedule R.

Schedule R Credit for the Elderly—Individual(s) 65 or Over Having Any Type of Income   **R**

Filing Status and Age (check only one)		
A ☐	Single, 65 or over	
B ☐	Married filing joint return, only one spouse 65 or over	
C ☐	Married filing joint return, both spouses 65 or over	
D ☐	Married filing separate return, 65 or over, and have not lived with your spouse at any time during the taxable year	

1 Initial amount of income for credit computation:
   If box A or B checked—enter $2,500
   If box C checked—enter $3,750
   If box D checked—enter $1,875 . . . . **1**

2 Deduct:

   a Amounts received as pensions or annuities under the Social Security Act, the Railroad Retirement Acts (but not supplemental annuities), and certain other exclusions from gross income (see instructions) . . . . . .

   b Enter one-half the excess of your adjusted gross income (Form 1040, line 31) over: $7,500 if box A checked; $10,000 if box B or C checked; or $5,000 if box D checked . . . .

3 Total of lines 2a and 2b **3**

4 Balance (subtract line 3 from line 1). If line 3 is larger than line 1, do not file this schedule **4**

5 Tentative credit. Enter 15% of line 4 . . . . **5**

6 Amount of tax shown on Form 1040, line 37 . . . . **6**

7 **Credit for the Elderly.** Enter here and on Form 1040, line 39, the amount on line 5 or 6 whichever is smaller . . . . ▶ **7**

Schedules R&RP (Form 1040) 1977

Name(s) as shown on Form 1040

Your social security number

Schedule RP Credit for the Elderly—Individual(s) Under 65 Having Gross Income from a Public Retirement System as a Result of His (Her) Services or Services of His (Her) Deceased Spouse **RP**

Name of public retirement system of spouse(s) under 65

Filing Status and Age (check only one)

A ☐ Single, under 65

B ☐ Married filing joint return, one spouse under 65 and having public retirement system income and other spouse 65 or over. By checking this box and completing Schedule RP, you and your spouse elect to compute your credit under this schedule. If you checked this box and live in a community property State, see Schedule RP instructions

C ☐ Married filing joint return, both spouses under 65. If you checked this box and live in a community property State, see Schedule RP instructions

D ☐ Married filing separate return, under 65, and have not lived with your spouse at any time during the taxable year

Joint return filers use column A for wife and column B for husband. All other filers use column B only.

Exception: *If you checked Filing Status and Age box B, the spouse under 65 should use column B.*

	A	B
1 Maximum amount of retirement income for credit computation: If box A checked—enter $2,500 If box B or C checked—enter $3,750 (**Note:** *The $3,750 must be divided between you and your spouse, but not more than $2,500 may be allocated to either. It will generally be more advantageous to allocate the greater amount to the spouse with the most retirement income*) If box D checked—enter $1,875		
2 **Deduct:**		
a Amounts received as pensions or annuities under the Social Security Act, the Railroad Retirement Acts (but not supplemental annuities), and certain other exclusions from gross income (see instructions)		
b Earned income such as wages, salaries, fees, etc. received (does not apply to persons 72 or over):		
(i) If you are under 62, enter earned income in excess of $900 . . .		
(ii) If you are 62 or over but under 72, enter amount determined as follows: If earned income is $1,200 or less, enter zero . . . . If earned income is over $1,200 but not over $1,700, enter one-half of amount over $1,200; or if earned income is over $1,700, enter amount over $1,450		
3 Total of lines 2a and 2b		
4 Balance (subtract line 3 from line 1). If column A or B is more than zero, complete this schedule. If both columns are zero or less, do not file this schedule		
5 Retirement income: a **If under 65—** Enter only income from pensions and annuities under public retirement systems (e.g. Federal, State Governments, etc.) received as a result of your services or services of your deceased spouse that is included in gross income (but not Social Security, Railroad Retirement or certain other payments excluded from gross income)		
b **If 65 or older—** Enter total of pensions and annuities, interest, dividends, proceeds of retirement bonds, and amounts received from individual retirement accounts and individual retirement annuities that are included in gross income, and gross rents from Schedule E, Part II, column (b); Form 4831, line 3; or Form 4835, line 22. Also include your share of gross rents from partnerships and your proportionate share of taxable rents from estates and trusts		
6 Line 4 or line 5, whichever is smaller		

7 Total (add amounts on line 6).	7	
8 Tentative credit. Enter 15% of line 7.	8	
9 Amount of tax shown on Form 1040, line 37	9	
10 **Credit for the Elderly.** Enter here and on Form 1040, line 39, the amount on line 8 or line 9, whichever is smaller . . . . ▶	10	

SCHEDULE SE   COMPUTATION OF SOCIAL SECURITY
SELF–EMPLOYMENT TAX

| SCHEDULE SE (Form 1040) Department of the Treasury Internal Revenue Service | **Computation of Social Security Self-Employment Tax** ► Each self-employed person must file a Schedule SE. ► Attach to Form 1040. ► See Instructions for Schedule SE (Form 1040). | **1977** |

● If you had wages, including tips, of $16,500 or more that were subject to social security or railroad retirement taxes, do not fill in this schedule (unless you are eligible for the Earned Income Credit). See Instructions.

● If you had more than one business, combine profits and losses from all your businesses and farms on this Schedule SE.

Important.—The self-employment income reported below will be credited to your social security record and used in figuring social security benefits.

| NAME OF SELF-EMPLOYED PERSON (AS SHOWN ON SOCIAL SECURITY CARD) | Social security number of self-employed person ► | |

● If you have only farm income complete Parts I and III.   ● If you have only nonfarm income complete Parts II and III.
● If you have both farm and nonfarm income complete Parts I, II, and III.

Part I   Computation of Net Earnings from FARM Self-Employment

You may elect to compute your net farm earnings using the OPTIONAL METHOD, line 3, instead of using the Regular Method, line 2, if your gross profits are: (1) $2,400 or less, or (2) more than $2,400 and net profits are less than $1,600. However, lines 1 and 2 must be completed even if you elect to use the FARM OPTIONAL METHOD.

REGULAR METHOD	a Schedule F, line 54 (cash method), or line 72 (accrual method)	1a	
1 Net profit or (loss) from:	b Farm partnerships	1b	
2 Net earnings from farm self-employment (add lines 1a and b)		2	

FARM OPTIONAL METHOD
3 If gross profits from farming [1] are:
    a Not more than $2,400, enter two-thirds of the gross profits . .
    b More than $2,400 and the net farm profit is less than $1,600, enter $1,600

| | 3 | |

[1] Gross profits from farming are the total gross profits from Schedule F, line 28 (cash method), or line 70 (accrual method), plus the distributive share of gross profits from farm partnerships (Schedule K–1 (Form 1065), line 14(b)) as explained in instructions for Schedule SE.

4 Enter here and on line 12a, the amount on line 2, or line 3 if you elect the farm optional method .

| | 4 | |

Part II   Computation of Net Earnings from NONFARM Self-Employment

REGULAR METHOD
5 Net profit or (loss) from:

a Schedule C, line 21. (Enter combined amount if more than one business.)	5a	
b Partnerships, joint ventures, etc. (other than farming)	5b	
c Service as a minister, member of a religious order, or a Christian Science practitioner. (Include rental value of parsonage or rental allowance furnished.) If you filed Form 4361, check here ► ☐ and enter zero on this line	5c	
d Service with a foreign government or international organization	5d	
e Other structions for line 20.) (See Form 1040 in- Specify ►	5e	

6 Total (add lines 5a through e) . . . .

| | 6 | |

7 Enter adjustments if any (attach statement) . . . .

| | 7 | |

8 Adjusted net earnings or (loss) from nonfarm self-employment (line 6, as adjusted by line 7) . .

| | 8 | |

If line 8 is $1,600 or more OR if you do not elect to use the Nonfarm Optional Method, omit lines 9 through 11 and enter amount from line 8 on line 12b, Part III.

Note: You may use the nonfarm optional method (line 9 through line 11) only if line 8 is less than $1,600 and less than two-thirds of your gross nonfarm profits,[2] and you had actual net earnings from self-employment of $400 or more for at least 2 of the 3 following years: 1974, 1975, and 1976. The nonfarm optional method can only be used for 5 taxable years.

SE

NONFARM OPTIONAL METHOD

9 a Maximum amount reportable, under both optional methods combined (farm and nonfarm) . | 9a | $1,600 | 00
   b Enter amount from line 3. (If you did not elect to use the farm optional method, enter zero) . | 9b | |
   c Balance (subtract line 9b from line 9a) . . . . | 9c | |

10 Enter two-thirds of gross nonfarm profits [2] or $1,600, whichever is smaller . . . . | 10 | |

11 Enter here and on line 12b, the amount on line 9c or line 10, whichever is smaller . . . . | 11 | |

[2] Gross profits from nonfarm business are the total of the gross profits from Schedule C, line 3, plus the distributive share of gross profits from nonfarm partnerships (Schedule K–1 (Form 1065), line 14(b)) as explained in instructions for Schedule SE. Also, include gross profits from services reported on line 5c, d, and e, as adjusted by line 7.

Part III   Computation of Social Security Self-Employment Tax

12 Net earnings or (loss): a From farming (from line 4) . . . . | 12a | |
   b From nonfarm (from line 8, or line 11 if you elect to use the Nonfarm Optional Method) . . . | 12b | |

13 Total net earnings or (loss) from self-employment reported on line 12. (If line 13 is less than $400, you are not subject to self-employment tax. Do not fill in rest of schedule.) . . . . | 13 | |

14 The largest amount of combined wages and self-employment earnings subject to social security or railroad retirement taxes for 1977 is . . . . | 14 | $16,500 | 00

15 a Total "FICA" wages (from Forms W–2) and "RRTA" compensation . . . | 15a | |
   b Unreported tips subject to FICA tax from Form 4137, line 9 or to RRTA . . | 15b | |
   c Total of lines 15a and b . . . . | 15c | |

16 Balance (subtract line 15c from line 14) . . . . | 16 | |

17 Self-employment income—line 13 or 16, whichever is smaller . . . . | 17 | |

18 Self-employment tax. (If line 17 is $16,500, enter $1,303.50; if less, multiply the amount on line 17 by .079.) Enter here and on Form 1040, line 48 . . . . | 18 | |

B–3   FORM 1040–ES   ESTIMATED TAX DECLARATION AND
VOUCHER FOR INDIVIDUALS

1977 Estimated Tax Worksheet (Keep for your records—Do Not File)

Name	Social Security Number

1 Enter amount of Adjusted Gross Income expected in taxable year . . . .

2 (a) If you expect to itemize deductions, enter the estimated total of those deductions . . . .

    (b) Standard deduction—If you do not expect to itemize deductions and you are:

        (i) Married filing a joint return or a qualifying widow(er), enter the greater of $2,100 **OR** 16% of line 1—but not more than $2,800 . . . .

        (ii) Single or head of household, enter the greater of $1,700 **OR** 16% of line 1—but not more than $2,400 . . . .

        (iii) Married filing a separate return, enter the greater of $1,050 **OR** 16% of line 1—but not more than $1,400 . . . .

3 Line 1 less line 2 . . . .

4 Exemptions ($750 for each, including additional exemptions for age and blindness) . . . .

5 Line 3 less line 4. This is your estimated taxable income . . . .

6 Tax. (Figure the tax on the amount on line 5 using the Tax Table or Tax Rate Schedule X, Y, or Z. See instruction 13) . . . .

7 General tax credit (see instruction 14) . . . .

8 Line 6 less line 7 . . . .

9 Credits (credit for the elderly, credit for child care expenses, investment credit, etc.) . . . .

10 Line 8 less line 9 . . . .

11 Tax from recomputing a prior year investment credit and work incentive (WIN) credit . . . .

12 Estimate of 1977 self-employment income $.................................; if $16,500 or more, enter $1,303.50, if less, multiply the amount by .079. If joint declaration and both have self-employment income, make separate computations . . . .

13 Tax on premature distributions from a self-employed retirement plan or an individual retirement arrangement

14 Add lines 10 through 13 . . . .

15 (a) Earned income credit (see instruction 15) . . . .

    (b) Estimated income tax withheld and to be withheld during 1977 . . . . .

    (c) Credit for Federal tax on gasoline, special fuels, and lubricating oil (see Form 4136)

16 Total (add lines 15(a), (b) and (c)) . . . .

17 Estimated tax (line 14 less line 16). Enter here and in Block A on declaration-voucher. If $100 or more, file the declaration-voucher, if less, no declaration is required . . . .

18 Computation of installments— **If declaration is due to be filed on:**

April 15, 1977, enter ¼	of line 17 here and	
June 15, 1977, enter ⅓	on line 1 of original	. .
September 15, 1977, enter ½ . .	and subsequent	
January 16, 1978, enter amount .	declaration-vouchers	

Note: *If your estimated tax should change during the year, you may use the amended computation on page 1 to determine amended amounts to enter on your declaration-voucher.*

Page **2**

Detach here

Form **1040-ES**	Estimated Tax Declaration–Voucher	
Department of the Treasury Internal Revenue Service	for Individuals—1977	Voucher **4**
	(To be used for making declaration and payment)	(Calendar year—Due Jan. 16, 1978)

*A. Estimated tax or amended estimated tax for the year ending (month and year)	*B. Overpayment from last year credited to estimated tax for this year	If fiscal year taxpayer, see Instruction 11.

* Complete only if this is an original or amended declaration and your total estimated tax for the year is $100.00 or more.

$ _____ $ _____

Return this voucher with check or money order payable to the Internal Revenue Service. For where to file your declaration–voucher, see Instruction 4.

1. Amount of this installment . . . ▶ $ _____
2. Amount of any unused overpayment credit applied to this installment (See Instruction 9) . . . .
3. Amount of this installment payment (line 1 less line 2) . . . . . . ▶ $ _____

If this is an original declaration–voucher, file even if line 3 is zero.

*Sign ▶ here ▶

Your Signature _____

Spouse's signature (if joint declaration) _____

Your social security number	Spouse's number, if joint declaration
First name and middle initial (of both spouses if joint declaration)	Last name
Address (Number and street)	
City, State, and ZIP code	

Please type or print

Form 1040-ES
Department of the Treasury
Internal Revenue Service

Estimated Tax Declaration—Voucher for Individuals—1977
(To be used for making declaration and payment)

Voucher **3**
(Calendar year—Due Sept. 15, 1977)

A. Estimated tax or amended estimated tax for the year ending (month and year)	**B. Overpayment from last year credited to estimated tax for this year**
$	$

If fiscal year taxpayer, see Instruction 11.

* Complete only if this is an original or amended declaration and your total estimated tax for the year is $100.00 or more.

Return this voucher with check or money order payable to the Internal Revenue Service. For where to file your declaration–voucher, see Instruction 4.

1. Amount of this installment . . . ▶ $
2. Amount of any unused overpayment credit applied to this installment (See Instruction 9) . . . .
3. Amount of this installment payment (line 1 less line 2) . . . . ▶ $

If this is an original declaration–voucher, file even if line 3 is zero.

Sign here ▶
Your Signature

Spouse's signature (if joint declaration)

Your social security number	Spouse's number, if joint declaration
First name and middle initial (of both spouses if joint declaration)	Last name

Address (Number and street)

City, State, and ZIP code

Detach here

Form 1040-ES
Department of the Treasury
Internal Revenue Service

Estimated Tax Declaration—Voucher for Individuals—1977
(To be used for making declaration and payment)

Voucher **2**
(Calendar year—Due June 15, 1977)

A. Estimated tax or amended estimated tax for the year ending (month and year)	**B. Overpayment from last year credited to estimated tax for this year**
$	$

If fiscal year taxpayer, see Instruction 11.

* Complete only if this is an original or amended declaration and your total estimated tax for the year is $100.00 or more.

Return this voucher with check or money order payable to the Internal Revenue Service. For where to file your declaration–voucher, see Instruction 4.

1. Amount of this installment . . . ▶ $
2. Amount of any unused overpayment credit applied to this installment (See Instruction 9) . . . .
3. Amount of this installment payment (line 1 less line 2) . . . . ▶ $

If this is an original declaration–voucher, file even if line 3 is zero.

Sign here ▶
Your Signature

Spouse's signature (if joint declaration)

Your social security number	Spouse's number, if joint declaration
First name and middle initial (of both spouses if joint declaration)	Last name

Address (Number and street)

City, State, and ZIP code

Detach here

Form 1040-ES
Department of the Treasury
Internal Revenue Service

Estimated Tax Declaration—Voucher for Individuals—1977
(To be used for making declaration and payment)

Voucher **1**
(Calendar year—Due April 15, 1977)

A. Estimated tax for the year ending (month and year)	**B. Overpayment from last year credited to estimated tax for this year**
$	$

If fiscal year taxpayer, see Instruction 11.

* Do not file this declaration–voucher if your total estimated tax for the year is less than $100.00.

Return this voucher with check or money order payable to the Internal Revenue Service. For where to file your declaration–voucher, see Instruction 4.

1. Amount of this installment . . . ▶ $
2. Amount of overpayment credit from last year (all or part) applied to this installment (See Instruction 9) . ▶
3. Amount of this installment payment (line 1 less line 2) . . . . ▶ $

File this original declaration–voucher even if line 3 is zero.

Sign here ▶
Your Signature

Spouse's signature (if joint declaration)

Your social security number	Spouse's number, if joint declaration
First name and middle initial (of both spouses if joint declaration)	Last name

Address (Number and street)

City, State, and ZIP code

B-4 FORM 1120 U. S. CORPORATION INCOME TAX RETURN

Form **1120**	**U.S. Corporation Income Tax Return**	**1977**
Department of the Treasury Internal Revenue Service	For calendar year 1977 or other taxable year beginning ...., 1977, ending ...., 19........ (PLEASE TYPE OR PRINT)	

Check if a—
A Consolidated return ☐
B Personal Holding Co. ☐
C Business Code No. (See Page 8 of instructions)

Use IRS label. Otherwise print or type.

Name

Number and street

City or town, State, and ZIP code

D Employer identification number

E Date incorporated

F Enter total assets from line 14, column (D), Schedule L (See specific Instructions)
$

IMPORTANT—Fill in all applicable lines and schedules. If the lines on the schedules are not sufficient, see instruction N.

GROSS INCOME

1	Gross receipts or gross sales.................................**Less:** Returns and allowances...........................	1
2	**Less:** Cost of goods sold (Schedule A) and/or operations (attach schedule)	2
3	Gross profit	3
4	Dividends (Schedule C)	4
5	Interest on obligations of the United States and U.S. instrumentalities	5
6	Other interest	6
7	Gross rents	7
8	Gross royalties	8
9	(a) Capital gain net income (attach separate Schedule D)	9(a)
	(b) Net gain or (loss) from line 9, Part II, Form 4797 (attach Form 4797)	9(b)
10	Other income (see instructions—attach schedule)	10
11	TOTAL income—Add lines 3 through 10	11

DEDUCTIONS

12	Compensation of officers (Schedule E)	12
13	Salaries and wages (not deducted elsewhere)	13
14	Repairs (see instructions)	14
15	Bad debts (Schedule F if reserve method is used)	15
16	Rents	16
17	Taxes (attach schedule)	17
18	Interest	18
19	Contributions (**not over 5% of line 30 adjusted per instructions—attach schedule**) . . .	19
20	Amortization (attach schedule)	20
21	Depreciation from Form 4562 (attach Form 4562) ...., less depreciation claimed in Schedule A and elsewhere on return ...., Balance ▶	21
22	Depletion	22
23	Advertising	23
24	Pension, profit-sharing, etc. plans (see instructions) (enter number of plans ▶ ....)	24
25	Employee benefit programs (see instructions)	25
26	Other deductions (attach schedule)	26
27	TOTAL deductions—Add lines 12 through 26	27
28	Taxable income before net operating loss deduction and special deductions (line 11 less line 27)	28
29	**Less:** (a) Net operating loss deduction (see instructions—attach schedule) . .	29(a)
	(b) Special deductions (Schedule I)	29(b)
30	Taxable income (line 28 less line 29)	30

TAX

31	TOTAL TAX (Schedule J)	31
32	**Credits:** (a) Overpayment from 1976 allowed as a credit . . .	
	(b) 1977 estimated tax payments	
	(c) Less refund of 1977 estimated tax applied for on Form 4466 . ( )	
	(d) Tax deposited with Form 7004 (attach copy)	
	(e) Tax deposited with Form 7005 (attach copy)	
	(f) Credit from regulated investment companies (attach Form 2439) .	
	(g) U.S. tax on special fuels, nonhighway gas and lubricating oil (attach Form 4136) . .	
33	TAX DUE (line 31 less line 32). See instruction G for depositary method of payment	33
34	OVERPAYMENT (line 32 less line 31)	34
35	Enter amount of line 34 you want: Credited to 1978 estimated tax ▶ Refunded ▶	35

Under penalties of perjury, I declare that I have examined this return, including accompanying schedules and statements, and to the best of my knowledge and belief it is true, correct, and complete. Declaration of preparer (other than taxpayer) is based on all information of which the preparer has any knowledge.

▶ Signature of officer   Date   ▶ Paid preparer's signature and identifying number (see instructions)

▶ Title   ▶ Paid preparer's address (or employer's name, address and identifying number)

235–106–1

Form 1120 (1977)   Page **2**

Schedule A Cost of Goods Sold (See instruction 2)

1 Inventory at beginning of year . . . .
2 Merchandise bought for manufacture or sale . . . .
3 Salaries and wages . . . .
4 Other costs (attach schedule) . . . .
5 Total . . . .
6 Less: Inventory at end of year . . . .
7 Cost of goods sold—Enter here and on line 2, page 1 . . . .
8 (a) Check valuation method(s) used for total closing inventory:
     ☐ Cost   ☐ Lower of cost or market   ☐ Other (if "other," attach explanation)
  (b) Check if this is the first year LIFO inventory method was adopted and used . . . . ☐
     If checked, attach Form 970.
  (c) If the LIFO inventory method was used for this taxable year, enter percentage (or amounts) of closing in-
     ventory computed under LIFO . . . . |
  (d) If you are a manufacturer, check if you valued your inventory in accordance with regulations section 1.471–11 . . . . . ☐
  (e) Was there any substantial change in determining quantities, cost, or valuations between opening and closing inventory? . . . . ☐ Yes   ☐ No
     If "Yes," attach explanation.

Schedule C Dividends (See instruction 4)

1 Domestic corporations subject to 85% deduction . . . .
2 Certain preferred stock of public utilities . . . .
3 Foreign corporations subject to 85% deduction . . . .
4 Dividends from wholly-owned foreign subsidiaries subject to 100% deduction (section 245(b)) . . .
5 Other dividends from foreign corporations . . . .
6 Includable income from controlled foreign corporations under subpart F (attach Forms 3646) . . . . . .
7 Foreign dividend gross-up (section 78) . . . .
8 Qualifying dividends received from affiliated groups and subject to the 100% deduction (section 243(a)(3)) .
9 Qualifying dividends received from affiliated groups and subject to the provisions of section 1564(b) . . .
10 Taxable dividends from a DISC or former DISC not included in line 1 (section 246(d)) . . . .
11 Other dividends . . . .
12 Total—Enter here and on line 4, page 1 . . . .

Schedule E Compensation of Officers (See instruction 12)

1. Name of officer	2. Social security number	3. Time devoted to business	Percent of corporation stock owned		6. Amount of compensation	7. Expense account allowances
			4. Common	5. Preferred		

Total compensation of officers—Enter here and on line 12, page 1 . . . .

Schedule F Bad Debts—Reserve Method (See instruction 15)

1. Year	2. Trade notes and accounts receivable outstanding at end of year	3. Sales on account	Amount added to reserve		6. Amount charged against reserve	7. Reserve for bad debts at end of year
			4. Current year's provision	5. Recoveries		
1972						
1973						
1974						
1975						
1976						
1977						

Schedule I Special Deductions

1 (a) 85% of line 1, Schedule C . . . .
  (b) 60.208% of line 2, Schedule C . . . .
  (c) 85% of line 3, Schedule C . . . .
  (d) 100% of line 4, Schedule C . . . .
2 Total—See instructions for limitation . . . .
3 100% of line 8, Schedule C . . . .
4 Enter dividends-received deduction allowed for dividends reported on line 9, Sch. C. See section 1564(b) for computation . . . .
5 Dividends paid on certain preferred stock of public utilities (see instructions) . . . .
6 Western Hemisphere trade corporations (see instructions) . . . .
7 Total special deductions—Add lines 2 through 6. Enter here and on line 29(b), page 1 . . . .

235–106–**2**

Form 1120 (1977)   Page **3**

Schedule J   Tax Computation

1 Taxable income (line 30, page 1) . . . .
2 Enter line 1 or $25,000, whichever is lesser. (Members of a controlled group, see instructions) . . . .
3 Line 1 less line 2 . . . .
4 Enter line 3 or $25,000, whichever is lesser. (Members of a controlled group, see instructions) . . . .
5 Line 3 less line 4 . . . .
6 20% of line 2 . . . .
7 22% of line 4 . . . .
8 48% of line 5 . . . .
9 Income tax (Sum of lines 6, 7 and 8 or alternative tax from separate Schedule D, whichever is lesser).
10 (a) Foreign tax credit (attach Form 1118) . . . .
   (b) Investment credit (attach Form 3468) . . . .
   (c) Work incentive (WIN) credit (attach Form 4874) . . . . .
   (d) New jobs credit (attach Form 5884) . . . .
11 Total of lines 10(a), (b), (c), and (d) . . . .
12 Line 9 less line 11 . . . .
13 Personal holding company tax (attach Schedule PH (Form 1120)) . . . .
14 Tax from recomputing a prior year investment credit (attach Form 4255) . . . . .
15 Tax from recomputing a prior year WIN credit (see instructions—attach computation) . . . .
16 Minimum tax on tax preference items (see instructions—attach Form 4626) . . . . .
17 Total tax—Add lines 12 through 16. Enter here and on line 31, page 1 . . . .

Schedule K   Record of Federal Tax Deposits Tax Class Number 503
(List deposits in order of date made—See instruction G)

Date of deposit	Amount	Date of deposit	Amount	Date of deposit	Amount

		Yes	No
G	Did you claim a deduction for expenses connected with:		
	(1) Entertainment facility (boat, resort ranch, etc.)?		
	(2) Living accommodations (except for employees on business)? .		
	(3) Employee's families at conventions or meetings?		
	(4) Employee or family vacations not reported on Form W–2? . .		

Enter total amount of deduction(s) on Form 1120 that are claimed under section 274 (entertainment, gifts, etc.) ▶

H (1) Did you at the end of the taxable year own, directly or indirectly, 50% or more of the voting stock of a domestic corporation? (For rules of attribution, see section 267(c).) . . . .
If "Yes," attach a schedule showing:
  (a) name, address, and identifying number;
  (b) percentage owned; and
  (c) taxable income or (loss) (e.g., if a Form 1120: from line 28, page 1, Form 1120) of such corporation for the taxable year ending with or within your taxable year.
(2) Did any individual, partnership, corporation, estate or trust at the end of the taxable year own, directly or indirectly, 50% or more of your voting stock? (For rules of attribution, see section 267(c).) . . . .
If "Yes:"
  (a) Attach a schedule showing name, address, and identifying number.
  (b) Enter percentage owned ▶
  (c) Was the owner of such voting stock a person other than a U.S. person? (See instruction S.) . . . .
    If "Yes," enter owner's country ▶

I Did you ever declare a stock dividend? . . . .

J Taxable income or (loss) from line 28, page 1, Form 1120 for your taxable year beginning in:
1974............, 1975..........., 1976...........

		Yes	No
K	Were you a member of a controlled group subject to the provisions of section 1561?		

If "Yes," check the type of relationship:
(1) ☐ parent-subsidiary   (2) ☐ brother-sister
(3) ☐ combination of (1) and (2) (See section 1563.)

L Refer to page 8 of instructions and state the principal:
Business activity.....................
Product or service.....................

M Did you file all required Forms 1087, 1096 and 1099? . . .

N Were you a U.S. shareholder of any controlled foreign corporation? (See sections 951 and 957.) . . . .
If "Yes," attach Form 3646 for each such corporation.

O Was this firm in business at the end of 1977? . . . . .

P How many months in 1977 was this firm in business?............

Q During this taxable year, did you pay dividends (other than stock dividends and distributions in exchange for stock) in excess of your current and accumulated earnings and profits? (See sections 301 and 316.) . . . .
If "Yes," file Form 5452. If this is a consolidated return, answer here for parent corporation and on Form 851, Affiliation Schedule, for each subsidiary.

R If you are a farmers' cooperative, check type:
☐ purchasing   ☐ marketing   ☐ service
☐ other (explain) ▶

S Did you, at any time during the taxable year, have any interest in or signature or other authority over a bank, securities or other financial account in a foreign country (except in a U.S. military banking facility operated by a U.S. financial institution)? If "Yes," see Instruction V . . . .

T Were you the grantor of, or transferor to, a foreign trust during any taxable year, which foreign trust was in being during the current taxable year, whether or not you have any beneficial interest in such trust? If "Yes," you may be required to file Forms 3520, 3520–A, or 926 . . . .

235–106–1

Form 1120 (1977)   Page **4**

Schedule L   Balance Sheets

ASSETS	Beginning of taxable year		End of taxable year	
	(A) Amount	(B) Total	(C) Amount	(D) Total
1 Cash				
2 Trade notes and accounts receivable				
(a) Less allowance for bad debts				
3 Inventories				
4 Gov't obligations: (a) U.S. and instrumentalities				
(b) State, subdivisions thereof, etc.				
5 Other current assets (attach schedule)				
6 Loans to stockholders				
7 Mortgage and real estate loans				
8 Other investments (attach schedule)				
9 Buildings and other fixed depreciable assets				
(a) Less accumulated depreciation				
10 Depletable assets				
(a) Less accumulated depletion				
11 Land (net of any amortization)				
12 Intangible assets (amortizable only)				
(a) Less accumulated amortization				
13 Other assets (attach schedule)				
14 Total assets				
LIABILITIES AND STOCKHOLDERS' EQUITY				
15 Accounts payable				
16 Mtges., notes, bonds payable in less than 1 yr.				
17 Other current liabilities (attach schedule)				
18 Loans from stockholders				
19 Mtges., notes, bonds payable in 1 yr. or more				
20 Other liabilities (attach schedule)				
21 Capital stock: (a) Preferred stock				
(b) Common stock				
22 Paid-in or capital surplus				
23 Retained earnings—Appropriated (attach sch.)				
24 Retained earnings—Unappropriated				
25 Less cost of treasury stock		( )		( )
26 Total liabilities and stockholders' equity				

Schedule M–1   Reconciliation of Income Per Books With Income Per Return

1 Net income per books

2 Federal income tax

3 Excess of capital losses over capital gains

4 Income subject to tax not recorded on books this year (itemize) _____

_____

5 Expenses recorded on books this year not deducted in this return (itemize)

  (a) Depreciation . . . . $_____

  (b) Depletion . . . . . $_____

_____

6   Total of lines 1 through 5

7 Income recorded on books this year not included in this return (itemize)

  (a) Tax-exempt interest $_____

_____

8 Deductions in this tax return not charged against book income this year (itemize)

  (a) Depreciation . . $_____

  (b) Depletion . . $_____

_____

9   Total of lines 7 and 8

10 Income (line 28, page 1)—line 6 less 9

Schedule M–2   Analysis of Unappropriated Retained Earnings Per Books (line 24 above)

1 Balance at beginning of year

2 Net income per books

3 Other increases (itemize) _____

_____

_____

_____

4   Total of lines 1, 2, and 3

5 Distributions: (a) Cash

              (b) Stock

              (c) Property

6 Other decreases (itemize) _____

_____

7   Total of lines 5 and 6

8 Balance at end of year (line 4 less 7)

B–5   FORM 1120S   U. S. SMALL BUSINESS CORPORATION INCOME TAX RETURN

Form 1120S
Department of the Treasury
Internal Revenue Service

U.S. Small Business Corporation
Income Tax Return for calendar year 1977 or

1977

other taxable year beginning ...., 1977, ending ...., 19........

A Date of election as small business corporation

Use IRS label. Otherwise, print or type.

Name

Number and street

City or town, State, and ZIP code

B Business Code No. (see page 7 of instructions)

C Employer identification no.

D Date incorporated

E Enter total assets from line 14, column (D), Schedule L (See instruction R)
$

IMPORTANT—All applicable lines and schedules must be filled in. If the lines on the schedules are not sufficient, see instruction N.
Note: *If section 465 (deductions limited to amount at-risk) applies, see instruction for line 28.*

GROSS INCOME	1 Gross receipts or gross sales .... **Less:** Returns and allowances	1
	2 **Less:** Cost of goods sold (Schedule A) and/or operations (attach schedule)	2
	3 Gross profit	3
	4 **(a)** Domestic dividends	4(a)
	(b) Foreign dividends	4(b)
	5 Interest on obligations of the U.S. and U.S. instrumentalities . .	5
	6 Other interest	6
	7 Gross rents	7
	8 Gross royalties	8
	9 Gains and losses (attach separate Schedule D (Form 1120S) and/or Form 4797):	
	(a) Net short-term capital gain reduced by any net long-term capital loss	9(a)
	(b) Net capital gain (if more than $25,000, see instructions)	9(b)
	(c) Ordinary gain or (loss) from Part II, Form 4797	9(c)
	10 Other income (see instructions—attach schedule)	10
	11 TOTAL income—Add lines 3 through 10	11

DEDUCTIONS	12 Compensation of officers (Schedule E)	12
	13 Salaries and wages (not deducted elsewhere)	13
	14 Repairs (see instructions)	14
	15 Bad debts (Schedule F if reserve method is used)	15
	16 Rents	16
	17 Taxes (attach schedule)	17
	18 Interest	18
	19 Contributions (**not over 5% of line 28 adjusted per instructions—attach schedule**)	19
	20 Amortization (attach schedule)	20
	21 Depreciation from Form 4562 (attach Form 4562) ...., less depreciation claimed in Schedule A and elsewhere on return ...., Balance ▶	21
	22 Depletion (attach schedule)	22
	23 Advertising	23
	24 Pension, profit-sharing, etc. plans (see instructions) (enter number of plans ▶................)	24
	25 Employee benefit programs (see instructions)	25
	26 Other deductions (attach schedule)	26
	27 TOTAL deductions—Add lines 12 through 26	27
	28 Taxable income (line 11 less line 27) (see instructions)	28

TAX	29 Income tax on capital gains (Schedule J)	29
	30 Minimum tax (see instructions—attach Form 4626)	30
	31 Total tax (add lines 29 and 30)	31
	32 **Credits: (a)** Tax deposited with Form 7004 (attach copy) . . . 32(a)	
	(b) Tax deposited with Form 7005 (attach copy) . . . 32(b)	
	(c) Credit for U.S. tax on special fuels, nonhighway gas, and lubricating oil (attach Form 4136) . . . 32(c)	
	33 **TAX DUE** (line 31 less line 32). See instruction G for depositary method of payment ——▶	33
	34 **OVERPAYMENT** (line 32 less line 31)	34

Under penalties of perjury, I declare that I have examined this return, including accompanying schedules and statements, and to the best of my knowledge and belief it is true, correct, and complete. Declaration of preparer (other than taxpayer) is based on all information of which the preparer has any knowledge.

▶ Signature of officer   Date

▶ Paid preparer's signature and identifying number (see Instructions)

▶ Title

235–125–1

Paid preparer's address (or employer's name, address, and identifying number)

Schedule A Cost of Goods Sold (See instruction 2)

1 Inventory at beginning of year . . . . _____
2 Merchandise bought for manufacture or sale . . . . _____
3 Salaries and wages . . . . _____
4 Other costs (attach schedule) . . . . _____
5 Total of lines 1 through 4 . . . . _____
6 **Less:** Inventory at end of year . . . . _____
7 Cost of goods sold—Enter here and on line 2, page 1 . . . . _____
8 **(a)** Check valuation method(s) used for total closing inventory:
   ☐ Cost
   ☐ Lower of cost or market
   ☐ Other (attach explanation)
   (b) Check if this is the first year LIFO inventory method was adopted and used . . . . ☐
   If checked, attach Form 970.
   (c) If the LIFO inventory method was used for this taxable year, enter percentage (or amounts) of closing
   inventory computed under LIFO . . . . _____
   (d) If you are a manufacturer, check if you valued your inventory in accordance with section 1.471–11 of the
   regulations . . . . ☐
   (e) Was there any substantial change in determining quantities, cost, or valuations between opening and closing inventory? . . . . ☐ Yes ☐ No
   If "Yes," attach explanation.

Schedule E Compensation of Officers (See instruction 12)

1. Name of officer	2. Social security number	3. Time devoted to business	4. Percentage of corporation stock owned	5. Amount of compensation	6. Expense account allowances

Total compensation of officers—Enter here and on line 12, page 1 . . . .

Schedule F Bad Debts—Reserve Method (See instruction 15)

| 1. Year | 2. Trade notes and accounts receivable outstanding at end of year | 3. Sales on account | Amount added to reserve | | 6. Amount charged against reserve | 7. Reserve for bad debts at end of year |
			4. Current year's provision	5. Recoveries		
1972						
1973						
1974						
1975						
1976						
1977						

Schedule J Tax Computation (See instructions)

1 Taxable income (line 28, page 1) . . . . _____
2 Enter $25,000. (Members of a controlled group, see instructions) . . . . _____
3 Line 1 less line 2 . . . . _____
4 Enter line 3 or $25,000, whichever is lesser. (Members of a controlled group, see instructions) . . . . . _____
5 Line 3 less line 4 . . . . _____
6 Enter 20% of line 2 . . . . _____
7 Enter 22% of line 4 . . . . _____
8 Enter 48% of line 5 . . . . _____
9 Add lines 6, 7, and 8 . . . . _____
10 Net capital gain (from line 9(b), page 1) . . . . _____
11 Subtract $25,000. (Statutory minimum) $25,000.00
12 Balance (line 10 less line 11). (See instructions) . . . . _____
13 Enter 30% of line 12. (See instructions) . . . . _____
14 Income tax on capital gains (line 9 or line 13, whichever is lesser). Enter here and on line 29, page 1 . . . . _____

235–125–1

Form 1120S (1977)   Page **3**

Schedule K Computation of Undistributed Taxable Income and Summary of Distributions and Other Items

Computation of Corporation's Undistributed Taxable Income

1 Taxable income (line 28, page 1) . . . .

2 Less: **(a)** Money distributed as dividends out of earnings and profits of the taxable year

(b) Tax imposed on certain capital gains (line 31, page 1) . . . . .

3 Corporation's undistributed taxable income . . . .

4 Actual dividend distributions taxable as ordinary income. (Do not include amounts shown on line 6) . .

5 Actual dividend distributions taxable as long-term capital gains (after tax) . . . .

6 Actual dividend distributions taxable as ordinary income and qualifying for dividend exclusion . . .

7 Nondividend distributions . . . .

8 Undistributed taxable income—taxable as ordinary income or (loss) . . . .

9 Undistributed taxable income—taxable as long-term capital gain (after tax) . . . .

10 Investment credit property   Cost or basis

Basis of new investment property	**(a)** 3 or more but less than 5 years		
	(b) 5 or more but less than 7 years		
	(c) 7 or more years		
Qualified progress expenditures	1974, 1975 and 1976	**(d)** 7 or more years	
	1977	**(e)** 7 or more years	
Cost of used investment property	**(f)** 3 or more but less than 5 years		
	(g) 5 or more but less than 7 years		
	(h) 7 or more years		

Property Qualified for Investment Credit

11 Interest on investment indebtedness:

(a) *(1)* Interest on investment indebtedness incurred prior to December 17, 1969 . . . .

(2) Interest on investment indebtedness incurred prior to September 11, 1975, but after December 16, 1969 . . .

(3) Interest on investment indebtedness incurred after September 10, 1975 . . . .

(b) Net investment income or (loss) . . . .

(c) Excess expenses from "net lease property" . . . .

(d) Net capital gain attributable to investment property . . . .

12 Item of tax preference (see instructions): **(a)** Accelerated depreciation on—

(1) Low income rental housing . . . .

(2) Other real property . . . .

(3) Personal property subjected to a lease . . . .

(b) Amortization: *(1)* ...., *(2)* ...., *(3)* ...., *(4)* ....

(c) Reserve for losses on bad debts of financial institutions . . . .

(d) Depletion . . . .

(e) Intangible drilling costs . . . .

(f) Net capital gain (after tax) . . . .

13 New jobs credit (see instructions) . . . .

Additional Information Required

	Yes	No
F Did you at the end of the taxable year own, directly or indirectly, 50% or more of the voting stock of a domestic corporation? .		

(For rules of attribution, see section 267(c).) If the answer is "Yes," attach a schedule showing: (a) name, address, and employer identification number and (b) percentage owned.

G Taxable income or (loss) from line 28, Page 1, Form 1120S for your taxable year beginning in: 1974 ....;

1975 ....; 1976 ....

H Refer to page 7 of instructions and state the principal:

Business activity ....-...........................

Product or service ....

	Yes	No
I Were you a member of a controlled group subject to the provisions of section 1561?		

J Did you claim a deduction for expenses connected with:

	Yes	No
(1) Entertainment facility (boat, resort, ranch, etc.)? . . .		
(2) Living accommodations (except for employees on business)?		
(3) Employees' families at conventions or meetings? . . .		
(4) Employee or family vacations not reported on Form W–2? .		

	Yes	No
Enter total amount of deduction(s) on Form 1120S that are claimed under section 274 (entertainment, gifts, etc.) ▶		
K Did you file all required Forms 1087, 1096, and 1099?. . .		
L Answer only if (1) this is the first 1120S return filed since your election to be treated as a small business corporation and (2) the corporation was in existence for the taxable year prior to the election and had investment credit property: Was an agreement filed under section 1.47–4(b) of the regulations?		
M Did you, at any time during the taxable year, have any interest in or signature or other authority over a bank, securities, or other financial account in a foreign country (except in a U.S. military banking facility operated by a U.S. financial institution)? If "Yes," see Instruction R .		
N Were you the grantor of, or transferor to, a foreign trust during any taxable year, which foreign trust was in being during the current taxable year, whether or not you have any beneficial interest in such trust? If "Yes," you may be required to file Forms 3520, 3520–A, or 926		
O Was this firm in business at the end of 1977?		
P How many months in 1977 was this firm in business? . .		

235–125–1

Form 1120S (1977)

Schedule L   Balance Sheets

Assets	Beginning of Taxable year		End of Taxable year	
	(A) Amount	(B) Total	(C) Amount	(D) Total
1 Cash				
2 Trade notes and accounts receivable				
(a) Less allowances for bad debts				
3 Inventories				
4 Gov't obligations: (a) U.S. and instrumentalities				
(b) State, subdivisions thereof, etc.				
5 Other current assets (attach schedule)				
6 Loans to shareholders				
7 Mortgage and real estate loans				
8 Other investments (attach schedule)				
9 Buildings and other fixed depreciable assets				
(a) Less accumulated depreciation				
10 Depletable assets				
(a) Less accumulated depletion				
11 Land (net of any amortization)				
12 Intangible assets (amortizable only)				
(a) Less accumulated amortization				
13 Other assets (attach schedule)				
14 Total assets				
Liabilities and Shareholders' Equity				
15 Accounts payable				
16 Mtges., notes, bonds payable in less than 1 year				
17 Other current liabilities (attach schedule)				
18 Loans from shareholders				
19 Mtges., notes, bonds payable in 1 year or more				
20 Other liabilities (attach schedule)				
21 Capital stock				
22 Paid-in or capital surplus				
23 Retained earnings—appropriated (attach schedule)				
24 Retained earnings—unappropriated				
25 Shareholders' undistributed taxable income previously taxed				
26 Less cost of treasury stock		( )		( )
27 Total liabilities and shareholders' equity				

Schedule M-1   Reconciliation of Income Per Books With Income Per Return

1 Net income per books		7 Income recorded on books this year not included	
2 Federal income tax		in this return (itemize)	
3 Excess of capital losses over capital gains		(a) Tax-exempt interest $	
4 Income subject to tax not recorded on books this			
year (itemize)		8 Deductions in this tax return not charged against	
5 Expenses recorded on books this year not deducted		book income this year (itemize)	
in this return (itemize)			
		9 Total of lines 7 and 8	
6 Total of lines 1 through 5		10 Income (line 28, page 1)—line 6 less line 9	

Schedule M-2   Analysis of Unappropriated Retained Earnings Per Books (line 24 above)

1 Balance at beginning of year		5 Distributions out of current or accumulated earn-	
2 Net income per books		ings and profits: (a) Cash	
3 Other increases (itemize)		(b) Stock	
		(c) Property	
		6 Current year's undistributed taxable income or net	
		operating loss (total of lines 8 and 9, Schedule K)	
		7 Other decreases (itemize)	
		8 Total of lines 5, 6, and 7	
4 Total of lines 1, 2, and 3		9 Balance at end of year (line 4 less line 8)	

B–6 FORM 2106 EMPLOYEE BUSINESS EXPENSES

Form **2106**	**Employee Business Expenses**	**1977**

Department of the Treasury
Internal Revenue Service

▶ Attach to Form 1040.

Your name

Social security number

Occupation in which expenses were incurred

Employer's name ▶

Employer's address ▶

Instructions

Include all expenses you paid as an employee, or expenses you charged to your employer (for example, through use of credit cards), or expenses for which you received an advance, allowance, or reimbursement.

Travel and Transportation.—You can deduct bus, taxi, plane, train fares, and the cost of using your car in your work.

If you use your own car for business reasons, you can deduct what it cost you for business use. Instead of figuring your actual expenses such as gas, oil, repairs, license tags, insurance, and depreciation, you may prefer to take a standard mileage rate.

This is figured at 17 cents a mile (15 cents a mile for taxable years beginning after 1973 and before 1977) for the first 15,000 miles and 10 cents for each mile over 15,000. Add to this amount the business portion of automobile interest and State and local taxes (other than gasoline), parking fees, license tags, insurance, and depreciation. For automobiles that have been or are considered fully depreciated under the straight-line method of depreciation, the standard mileage rate is 10 cents a mile for all business mileage.

To determine if your automobile has been fully depreciated under the straight-line method of depreciation, apply the following rule.

If you use the optional method of computing operating cost of an automobile for the entire length of time that you use the automobile for business purposes, such period of time is the actual useful life of the automobile to you. The automobile will not be considered to have become fully depreciated until the end of such useful life. However, if at any time during the period that you use the automobile for business purposes you computed and deducted the actual costs of all operating and fixed cost of the automobile for business purposes, the useful life of the automobile to you will be the estimated period on which you based your computation of the allowable straight-line depreciation deduction for the year. Thereafter, regardless of whether you use the actual cost method or the optional method for subsequent taxable years, the automobile will be considered fully depreciated at the end of the period estimated to be its useful life to you.

The use of the optional method is limited to a self-employed individual or an employee who operates only one automobile at a time for business purposes. If you alternate in using different automobiles on different occasions for business purposes or replace your automobile during the year, the standard mileage rate applies to the combined total business mileage of the automobiles, as if they were one, to arrive at a deduction.

The optional method cannot be used if you have claimed depreciation in a prior year using a method other than straight-line (or if you have claimed additional first-year depreciation), use the automobile for hire, such as taxicabs, or two or more automobiles used at the same time, such as in fleet operations.

Use of the optional method will not prevent you from claiming an investment credit so long as you can properly establish that the useful life of the automobile is at least 3 years (see Form 3468).

Meals and Lodging.—You can deduct these if you were temporarily away from home on business. Your "home" for this purpose is your principal or regular post of duty. You cannot deduct the cost of meals on daily trips where you did not need sleep or rest.

Outside Salesperson.—In addition to the above, an outside salesperson can generally deduct other expenses necessary in sales work, for example, selling expenses, stationery, and postage. An outside salesperson is one who does all selling away from the employer's place of business. If your main duties are service and delivery, such as a milk driver-salesperson, you are not considered an outside salesperson.

Other Business Expenses.—If you itemize deductions on Schedule A, you can also deduct other business expenses under the heading "Miscellaneous deductions." Examples of these expenses are dues to unions and professional organizations and the cost of tools, materials, etc., that your employer did not pay for.

Limitations apply to deductions relating to the use of your home for business purposes. Under these rules, you must use a portion of your home as an office exclusively on a regular basis in connection with your employer's trade or business and for the convenience of your employer to be able to deduct the expenses allocable to that portion. For more information, see **Publication 587**, Business Use of Your Home.

There is a limitation on the amount of expenses that can be deducted for transportation, meals, lodging, etc. for attending no more than two foreign conventions during the taxable year.

For a detailed explanation of the rules for deductions for travel, entertainment, and gift expenses, see **Publication 463**, Travel, Entertainment, and Gift Expenses.

Use Form 3903 to compute any moving expense deduction.

PART I.—Employee Business Expenses Deductible in Computing Adjusted Gross Income on Form 1040, Line 31

1 Airplane, boat, railroad, etc., fares
2 Meals and lodging
3 Automobile expenses (from Part IV)
4 Other (specify) (Include expenses not listed on lines 1 through 3 to extent of reimbursement) ▶

5   Total of lines 1 through 4
6 Less: Employer's payments for above expenses (other than amounts included on Form W–2)
7 Excess expenses (line 5 less line 6). Enter here and include on Form 1040, line 23
8 Excess payments (line 6 less line 5). Enter here and include on Form 1040, line 20

PART II.—Employee Business Expenses which are Deductible if You Itemize Deductions on Schedule A (Form 1040)

1 Business expenses other than those included above (specify) ▶

2   Total
If you itemize your deductions, deduct under Miscellaneous Deductions, Schedule A (Form 1040).

PART III.—Additional Information to be Furnished When Claiming a Deduction for Educational Expenses

1 Name of educational institution or activity ▶
2 Address ▶
3 Were you required to undertake this education to meet the minimum educational requirements to qualify in your employment, trade or business? ☐ Yes ☐ No
4 Will the study program undertaken qualify you for a new trade or business? ☐ Yes ☐ No
5 If your answer to question 3 or 4 is No, state the reason for obtaining the additional education and show the relationship between the courses taken and your employment during the period ▶

6 List the principal subjects studied at the educational institution or describe your educational activity ▶

235–131–1   Form **2106** (1977)

Form 2106 (1977)   **Page 2**

PART IV.—Automobile Expenses (Use either the regular or the optional method.)

	Automobile 1	Automobile 2	Automobile 3
A. Months automobile held for business use	_____ months	_____ months	_____ months
B. Total mileage for months in A	_____ miles	_____ miles	_____ miles
C. Portion of total mileage applicable to business	_____ miles	_____ miles	_____ miles

Regular Method: (Include expenses only for the number of months indicated in A above.)

	Automobile 1	Automobile 2	Automobile 3
1 Gasoline, oil, lubrication, etc.			
2 Repairs			
3 Tires, supplies, etc..			
4 Other: (a) Insurance			
(b) Taxes			
(c) Tags and licenses			
(d) Interest.			
(e) Miscellaneous.			
5 Total			
6 Percentage of expense applicable to business (line C above divided by line B above)	%	%	%
7 Business portion (line 5 multiplied by line 6)			
8 Depreciation from Part VI, column (h)			
9 Line 8 divided by 12 months			
10 Multiply line 9 by A, above			
11 Total (line 7 plus line 10) (see line 19)			

Optional Method:

12 Enter 15,000 miles or the combined mileage on line C above, whichever is smaller		_____ miles
13 Multiply line 12 by 17¢ and enter result		
14 Any excess of the combined mileage of line C over 15,000 miles		_____ miles
15 Multiply line 14 by 10¢ and enter result		
16 Total mileage rate expense (line 13 plus line 15)		
17 Business portion of automobile interest and State and local taxes (other than gasoline)		
18 Total (line 16 plus line 17)		

Summary:

19 Enter the combined total from line 11 or the amount on line 18, whichever is used	
20 Add parking fees and tolls	
21 Total. Enter here and in Part I, line 3	

PART V.—Computation of Automobile Basis

Old Car Traded In:

1 (a) Total mileage accumulated   _____ miles
   (b) Portion applicable to business   _____ miles
   (c) Percentage applicable to business
      (line (b) divided by line (a))   _____ %
2 Purchase price or other basis
3 Less: Trade-in allowance
4 Difference (line 2 less line 3)
5 Line 4 multiplied by percentage on line 1(c)
6 Less gain or plus (loss) on previous trade-in.
7 Difference (line 5 less line 6)
8 Depreciation allowed or allowable
9 Gain (line 8 less line 7) or (loss) (line 7 less line 8) on business portion of car

Present Car:

10 Purchase price or other basis
11 Less: Estimated salvage value
12 Balance (line 10 less line 11)
13 Line 12 multiplied by percentage on line 6 of Part IV
14 Less gain or plus (loss) on line 9
15 Basis for computing depreciation

Note: *If you acquired the vehicle for cash only, or by trade-in of another vehicle not used in business, complete only lines 10 through 15. If acquired by trade-in of another vehicle previously used in business, complete lines 1 through 15. (Recompute the basis for depreciation each succeeding year if the percentage of business use changes.)*

PART VI.—Depreciation of Automobile

Make and style of vehicle (a)	Date acquired (b)	Basis (From line 15, Part V) (c)	Age when acquired (d)	Depreciation allowed in prior years (e)	Method of computing depreciation (f)	Rate (%) or life (years) (g)	Depreciation for a year (h)

B–7 FORM 2119 SALE OR EXCHANGE OF PERSONAL RESIDENCE

Form **2119**	**Sale or Exchange of Personal Residence**	Taxable year

(Rev. Oct. 1977)
Department of the Treasury
Internal Revenue Service

▶ Attach to Form 1040.

Note: *Do not include expenses which are deductible as moving expenses on Form 3903.*

Name(s) as shown on Form 1040 | Your social security number

1(a) Date former residence sold

(b) Have you ever deferred any gain on the sale or exchange of a personal residence? . . . . | Yes | No

(c) Have you ever claimed a credit for purchase or construction of a new principal residence? . (If "Yes," see Form 5405.)

2(a) Date new residence bought

(b) If new residence was constructed for or by you, date construction began

(c) Date you occupied new residence

(d) Were both the old and new properties used as your principal residence? . . . . . . | Yes | No

(e) Were any rooms in either residence rented or used for business purposes at any time? . . | Yes | No
(If "Yes," explain on separate sheet and attach.)

(f) If you were married, do you and your spouse have the same proportionate ownership interest in your new residence as you had in your old residence? . . . .
(If "No," see the Consent on other side.)

3(a) Were you 65 or older on date of sale? . . . .
(If "Yes," see Note below.)

(b) If you answered "Yes" to 3(a), did you use the property sold as your principal residence for a total of at least 5 years (except for short temporary absences) of the 8-year period preceding the sale? . . . .

(c) If you answered "Yes" to 3(b), do you want to elect to exclude gain on the sale from your gross income? . . .

Computation of Gain and Adjusted Sales Price

4 Selling price of residence. (Do not include selling price of personal property items.)	**4**	
5 Less: Commissions and other expenses of sale (from Schedule I on other side)	**5**	
6 Amount realized	**6**	
7 Less: Basis of residence sold (from Schedule II on other side) . . . . . /	**7**	
8 Gain on sale (subtract line 7 from line 6). If line 7 is more than line 6, there is no gain, so you should not make further entries on this form. A loss on the sale of a personal residence is nondeductible	**8**	
9 Fixing-up expenses (from Schedule III on other side)	**9**	
10 Adjusted sales price (subtract line 9 from line 6)	**10**	

If you answered "No" to question 3(a) or 3(c), complete lines 11 through 14.
If you answered "Yes" to question 3(c), complete lines 15 through 17, or 15 through 20, whichever is applicable.

Computation of Gain to be Reported and Adjusted Basis of New Residence—General Rule

11 Cost of new residence	**11**	
12 Gain taxable this year (line 10 less line 11, but not more than line 8). If line 11 is more than line 10, enter zero. Enter here and on Schedule D (Form 1040), in column f, line 1, or line 6, whichever is applicable .	**12**	
13 Gain on which tax is to be deferred (subtract line 12 from line 8)	**13**	
14 Adjusted basis of new residence (subtract line 13 from line 11)	**14**	

Computation of Exclusion, Gain to be Reported, and Adjusted Basis of New Residence—Special Rule
(For use of taxpayers 65 years of age or over who checked "Yes," in 3(c) above.)

15 If line 10 above is $35,000 or less, the entire gain shown on line 8 is excludable from gross income. If line 10 is over $35,000, determine the excludable portion of the gain as follows:

(a) Divide amount on line 10 into $35,000 . . . . |15(a)|

(b) Excludable portion of gain (multiply amount on line 8 by figure on line 15(a) and enter result here) . | **15(b)** |

16 Nonexcludable portion of gain (subtract line 15(b) from line 8) . . . . | **16** |

17 Cost of new residence. If a new personal residence was not purchased, enter "None," and do not complete the following lines. Then enter the amount shown on line 16 on Schedule D (Form 1040), in column f, line 6 . . . . | **17** |

18 Gain taxable this year. (Subtract the sum of lines 15(b) and 17 from line 10. But this amount may not exceed line 16.) If line 17 plus line 15(b) is more than line 10, enter zero. Enter here and on Schedule D (Form 1040), in column f, line 6 . . . . | **18** |

19 Gain on which tax is to be deferred (subtract line 18 from line 16) . . . . | **19** |

20 Adjusted basis of new residence (subtract line 19 from line 17) . . . . | **20** |

Note: If you were 65 or older when you sold or exchanged your principal residence, and if that was your principal residence for 5 of the 8 years preceding the sale or exchange, you may elect to exclude part or all of the gain. If the property is held by you and your spouse as joint tenants, tenants by the entirety, or community property and you and your spouse file a joint return, only you or your spouse need meet the age requirement. You are only eligible for the exclusion once. This is true regardless of your marital status at the time you made the election.

Form 2119 (Rev. 10-77)   Page **2**

Consent of You and Your Spouse to Apply Separate Gain on Sale of Old Residence to Basis of New Residence

Note: *The following Consent need not be completed if there was no gain on the sale of the old residence. If, however, there was a gain, and if the ownership interests of you and your spouse in the old and new residences were not in the same proportion, the separate gain on the sale of the old residence will be separately taxable to you and your spouse unless this Consent is filed.*

	Your portion	Spouse's portion
Adjusted sales price of old residence (from line 10)	$	$
Cost of new residence (from line 11 or 17)	$	$

The undersigned taxpayers, you and your spouse, consent to have the basis of the joint or separate interest in the new residence reduced by the amount of the joint or separate gain on the sale of the old residence which is not taxable solely by reason of the filing of this Consent.

Your signature	Date
Spouse's signature	Date

SCHEDULE I—Commissions and Other Expenses of Sale (Line 5)

This includes sales commissions, advertising expenses, attorney and legal fees, etc., incurred to effect the sale of the old residence. Enter the name and address of the payee and the date of payment for each item.

Item explanation	Amount
	$

SCHEDULE II—Basis of Old Residence (Line 7)

This includes the original cost of the property to the taxpayer, commissions, and other expenses incurred in its purchase, the cost of improvements, etc., less the total of the depreciation allowed or allowable (if any), all casualty losses previously allowed (if any), and the nontaxable gain (if any) on the sale or exchange of a previous personal residence.

Item explanation	Amount
	$

SCHEDULE III—Fixing-up Expenses (Line 9)

These are decorating and repair expenses which were incurred solely to assist in the sale of the old property, and which are not ordinarily deductible in computing taxable income nor taken into account in computing the basis of the old residence or the amount realized from its sale. Fixing-up expenses must have been incurred for work performed within 90 days before the contract to sell was signed, and must have been paid for not later than 30 days after the sale.

Item explanation	Date work performed	Date paid	Amount
			$

For more information obtain Publication 523, Tax Information on Selling or Purchasing Your Home, from your local IRS office.

B-8 FORM 2210 UNDERPAYMENT OF ESTIMATED TAX BY INDIVIDUALS

Form **2210** Department of the Treasury Internal Revenue Service	**Underpayment of Estimated Tax by Individuals** ▶ Attach this form to Form 1040.	**1976**

Name(s) as shown on Form 1040	Social security number

How to Figure Your Underpayment (Complete lines 1 through 15)

If you meet any of the exceptions (see Instruction D) which avoid the underpayment penalty for ALL quarters, omit lines 1 through 15 and go directly to line 16.

1 1976 tax (from Form 1040, line 22) . . . .

2 Earned income credit (from Form 1040, line 23c) . . . . .

3 Tax credit claimed for special fuels, nonhighway gasoline and lubricating oil (from Form 1040, line 64) . . . .

4 Minimum tax (from Form 1040, line 56) . . . .

5 Social security tax on unreported tip income (from Form 1040, line 59) . . . .

6 Uncollected employee social security tax on tips reported on Forms W–2 (from Form 1040, line 60) . . . .

7 Excess contribution tax (from Form 1040, line 61) . . . . .

8 Total (add lines 2 through 7) . . . .

9 Balance (line 1 less line 8) . . . .

10 Enter 80% of the amount shown on line 9 . . . . .

	Due Dates of Installments			
	Apr. 15, 1976	June 15, 1976	Sept. 15, 1976	Jan. 15, 1977
11 Divide amount on line 10 by the number of installments required for the year (see Instruction B). Enter the result in appropriate columns				
12 Amounts paid on estimate for each period and tax withheld (see Instruction E)				
13 Overpayment of previous installment (see Instruction F) .				
14 Total (add lines 12 and 13)				
15 Underpayment (line 11 less line 14) OR Overpayment (line 14 less line 11)				

Exceptions Which Avoid the Penalty (See Instruction D)
(Farmers and fishermen see Instruction H for special exception)

16 Total amount paid and withheld from January 1 through the installment date indicated				
17 Exception 1.—Prior year's tax. 1975 tax . . . . ▶ $	25% of 1975 tax	50% of 1975 tax	75% of 1975 tax	100% of 1975 tax
18 Exception 2.—Tax on prior year's income using 1976 rates and exemptions	Enter 25% of tax	Enter 50% of tax	Enter 75% of tax	Enter 100% of tax
19 Exception 3.—Tax on annualized 1976 income	Enter 20% of tax	Enter 40% of tax	Enter 60% of tax	Not applicable
20 Exception 4.—Tax on 1976 income over 3, 5, and 8-month periods.	Enter 90% of tax	Enter 90% of tax	Enter 90% of tax	Not applicable

How to Figure the Penalty (Complete lines 21 through 25 for installments not avoided by an exception)

21 Amount of underpayment (from line 15)				
22 Date of payment or April 15, 1977, whichever is earlier (see Instruction G)				
23 Number of days from due date of installment to date shown on line 22				
24 Penalty (7 percent a year on the amount shown on line 21 for the number of days shown on line 23)				

25 Penalty (add amounts on line 24). Check the box on Form 1040, line 25, and show this amount in the bottom margin as "Penalty for underpayment." Then increase the "Balance Due IRS" or decrease the amount "Overpaid" accordingly . . . .

Form **2210** (1976)

B–9 FORM 3468 COMPUTATION OF INVESTMENT CREDIT

Form **3468**	**Computation of Investment Credit**	19**77**

Department of the Treasury
Internal Revenue Service

▶ Attach to your tax return.

Name	Identifying number as shown on page 1 of your tax return

1 Use schedule below to list qualified investment in new and used property acquired or constructed and placed in service during the taxable year; and also list qualified progress expenditures made during the 1977 taxable year and qualified progress expenditures made in 1974, 1975, and 1976 taxable years providing a proper election as prescribed in section 46(d)(6) was made for such prior years. If progress expenditure property is placed in service during the taxable year, do not list qualified progress expenditures for this property. See instruction for line 1.

If 100% investment credit is being claimed on certain ships, check this block. ▶ ☐ See Instruction K for details.

Note: *Include your share of investment in property made by a partnership, estate, trust, small business corporation, or lessor.*

Type of property		Line	(1) Life years	(2) Cost or basis (See instruction G)	(3) Applicable percentage	(4) Qualified investment (Column 2 x column 3)
New property		(a)	3 or more but less than 5		$33\frac{1}{3}$	
		(b)	5 or more but less than 7		$66\frac{2}{3}$	
		(c)	7 or more		100	
Qualified progress expenditures	1974, 1975 and 1976	(d)	7 or more		20	
	1977	(e)	7 or more		60	
Used property (See instructions for dollar limitation)		(f)	3 or more but less than 5		$33\frac{1}{3}$	
		(g)	5 or more but less than 7		$66\frac{2}{3}$	
		(h)	7 or more		100	

2 Qualified investment—add lines 1(a) through (h) . . . .

3 10% of line 2 . . . .

4 7% (4% for public utility property) of certain property (see instruction for line 1) . . . .

5 Corporations electing the additional investment credit for contributions to Employee Stock Ownership Plans—Attach election statement. (See Instruction I and instruction for line 5.)

    (a) Additional 1% credit—Enter 1% of line 2 . . . .

    (b) Additional credit not to exceed .5%—Enter allowable percentage times adjusted line 2 (attach schedule) . . . .

6 Carryback and carryover of unused credit(s). See Instruction F—attach computation . . . . .

7 Tentative investment credit—Add lines 3 through 6 . . . .

Limitation

8 (a) Individuals—Enter amount from line 37, page 2, Form 1040 . . . .

    (b) Estates and trusts—Enter amount from line 26 or 27, page 1, Form 1041 . . . .

    (c) Corporations—Enter amount from line 9, Schedule J, page 3, Form 1120 . . . . . .

9 (a) Credit for the elderly (individuals only) . . . .

    (b) Foreign tax credit . . . .

    (c) Tax on lump-sum distributions (see instruction for line 9(c)) . . . .

    (d) Possession Tax Credit (corporations only) . . . .

    (e) Section 72(m)(5) penalty tax . . . .

10 Total—Add lines 9(a) through (e) . . . .

11 Line 8 less line 10 . . . .

12 (a) Enter amount on line 11 or $25,000, whichever is lesser. (Married persons filing separately, controlled corporate groups, estates, and trusts, see instruction for line 12.) . . . .

    (b) If line 11 exceeds line 12(a), enter 50% of the excess. (Public utilities, railroads, and airlines, see Instruction J.) . . . .

13 Total—Add lines 12(a) and (b) . . . .

14 Investment credit—Amount from line 7 or line 13, whichever is lesser. Enter here and on line 41, Form 1040; line 10(b), Schedule J, page 3, Form 1120; or the appropriate line on other returns . . . . .

Schedule A	If any part of your investment in line 1 or 4 above was made by a partnership, estate, trust, small business corporation, or lessor, complete the following statement and identify property qualifying for the 7% or 10% investment credit.

Name (Partnership, estate, trust, etc.)	Address	Property			
		Progress expenditures	New	Used	Life years
		$	$	$	

If property is disposed of prior to the life years used in computing the investment credit, see Instruction E.

B–10   FORM 3903   MOVING EXPENSE ADJUSTMENT

Form **3903** Department of the Treasury Internal Revenue Service	**Moving Expense Adjustment** ▶ Attach to Form 1040.	19**77**

Name(s) as shown on Form 1040 | Social security number

(a) What is the distance from your **former** residence to your **new** business location? .... miles

(b) What is the distance from your **former** residence to your **former** business location? .... miles

(c) If the distance in (a) is 35 or more miles farther than the distance in (b), complete the rest of this form. If the distance is less than 35 miles, you are not entitled to a moving expense deduction. (See instruction A.) This rule is not applicable to members of the armed forces.

1 Transportation expenses in moving household goods and personal effects	1	
2 Travel, meals, and lodging expenses in moving from former to new residence	2	
3 Pre-move travel, meals, and lodging expenses in searching for a new residence after obtaining employment . . .	3	
4 Temporary living expenses in new location or area during any 30 consecutive days after obtaining employment . .	4	
5 Total (Add lines 3 and 4.)	5	
6 Enter the lesser: Line 5 or $1,500 ($750 if married, filing a separate return, and you resided with your spouse who also started work during the taxable year) . .	6	
7 Expenses incident to: (Check one.) **(a)** ☐ sale or exchange of your former residence; or, **(b)** ☐ if nonowner, settlement of your unexpired lease on former residence .	7	
8 Expenses incident to: (Check one.) **(a)** ☐ purchase of a new residence; or, **(b)** ☐ if renting, acquiring a new lease	8	
9 Total (Add lines 6, 7, and 8.)	9	

Note: Amounts on lines 7(a) and 8(a) not deducted because of the $3,000 (or $1,500) limitation may generally be used either to decrease the gain on the sale of your residence, or to increase the basis of your new residence.

10 Enter the lesser: Line 9 or $3,000 ($1,500 if married, filing a separate return, and you resided with your spouse who also started work during the taxable year). (See instruction C(2).)	10	
11 Total moving expenses (Add lines 1, 2, and 10.)	11	
12 Reimbursements and allowances received for this move (other than amounts included on Form W–2) (See instruction L.)	12	
13 If line 12 is less than line 11, enter the difference here and on Form 1040, line 22	13	
14 If line 12 is larger than line 11, enter the excess here and on Form 1040, line 20, as "Excess moving reimbursement"	14	

B–11 FORM 4684 CASUALTIES AND THEFTS

Form **4684** Department of the Treasury Internal Revenue Service	**Casualties and Thefts** ▶ See separate instructions. ▶ Attach to Form 1040.	**19****77**

Name(s) as shown on Form 1040	Social Security Number

Use Part I to determine the amount of a deductible casualty or theft loss of property, other than trade, business, rental, or royalty property, provided only one casualty or theft occurred during the taxable year and any related insurance or other compensation did not exceed the property's cost or other basis, as adjusted.

Use Part II to determine the amount of a casualty or theft loss or gain if the circumstances mentioned in Part I are not applicable. For example: (1) if there is more than one casualty or theft occurrence; (2) if there are both casualty or theft losses and gains; or (3) trade, business, rental, or royalty property is involved. If Part II is used, go to Part III, on page 2, first.

Part I Casualty or Theft Loss (Use if One Loss Occurred)	Item or article	Item or article	Item or article
1 Description of property			
2 Cost or other basis, as adjusted (see instruction H) . . .			
3 Decrease in fair market value (see instruction I)			
a. Value before casualty or theft			
b. Value after casualty or theft			
c. Excess of line 3a over line 3b			
4 Lesser of line 2 or line 3c			
5 Insurance recovery or other compensation			
6 Excess of line 4 over line 5			
7 Total of amounts on line 6			
8 Amounts on line 6 attributable to income-producing property			
9 Subtract line 8 from line 7			
10 Enter $100, or amount on line 9, whichever is smaller (see instruction J)			
11 Excess of line 9 over line 10			
12 Casualty or theft loss. Add line 8 and line 11, enter here and on Schedule A (Form 1040), line 29—identify as "4684"			

Part II Summary of Gains and Losses (Use if More Than One Loss Occurred)	(B) Losses from casualties or thefts		(C) Gains from casualties or thefts includible in income
(A) Identify casualty or theft loss from Part III	(i) Property other than trade, business, rental, or royalty property	(ii) Trade, business, rental, or royalty property	

Casualty or Theft of Property Held 9 Months or Less

	(B)(i)	(B)(ii)	(C)
1			
2 Totals, add amounts on line 1 for each column			
3 Combine line 2, columns (B)(ii) and (C). Enter here and on Form 4797, Part II, line 8, column g (Note: if Form 4797 is not required for other transactions, enter amount on Form 1040, line 16—identify as "4684")			
4 Enter amount from line 2, column (B)(i) here and on Schedule A (Form 1040), line 29—identify as "4684" .			

Casualty or Theft of Property Held More Than 9 Months (See instruction G)

	(B)(i)	(B)(ii)	(C)
5 Any casualty or theft gains from Form 4797, Part III, line 23			
6			
7 Total losses, add amounts on line 6, columns (B)(i) and (B)(ii) . . .			/////////
8 Total gains, add lines 5 and 6, column (C)			
9 Combine line 7, columns (B)(i) and (B)(ii)			
10 If line 9 is more than line 8: **a.** Combine line 7, column (B)(ii) and line 8. Enter here and on Form 4797, Part II, line 8, column g (Note: if Form 4797 is not required for other transactions, enter amount on Form 1040, line 16—identify as "4684")			
b. Enter amount from line 7, column (B)(i) here and on Schedule A (Form 1040), line 29—identify as "4684"			
11 If line 9 is equal to or less than line 8, enter the difference here and on Form 4797, Part I, line 3, column g—identify as "Gain from Form 4684, Part II, line 11"			

235–162–1   Form **4684** (1977)

Form 4684 (1977)

Page 2

Part III — Applicable if Part II is used

(A) Description of property	(B) Cost or other basis, as adjusted. See Instruction H.	(C) Insurance recovery or other compensation. If col. (C) exceeds col. (B), skip to col. (I).	(D) Fair market value before casualty or theft. See Instruction I.	(E) Fair market value after casualty or theft. See Instruction I.	(F) Decrease in fair market value. Col. (D), less col. (E)—if no decrease, enter zero. See Instruction I.	(G) Lesser of col. (B) or col. (F).	(H) LOSS — (i) Property other than trade, business, rental or royalty property.	(H) LOSS — (ii) Trade, business, rental or royalty property. Excess of col. (G) over col. (C).	(I) GAIN — Excess of col. (C) over col. (B). See Instruction K.

Property Held 9 Months or Less

Casualty or Theft Occurrence Number 1

1

2 Total of amounts on line 1, column (H)(i)

3 Amount on line 2 attributable to income-producing property

4 Subtract line 3 from line 2

5 $100 limitation, or portion of limitation used, see instruction J

6 Excess of line 4 over line 5

7 Total of amounts on lines 3 and 6, column (H)(i) and line 1, column (H)(ii) and column (I)—enter here and in Part II, line 1, and identify as "Casualty or theft occurrence number 1"

Property Held More Than 9 Months

8

9 Total of amounts on line 8, column (H)(i)

10 Amount on line 9 attributable to income-producing property

11 Subtract line 10 from line 9

12 Portion of $100 limitation not used on line 5

13 Excess of line 11 over line 12

14 Total of amounts on lines 10 and 13, column (H)(i) and line 8, column (H)(ii) and column (I)—enter here and in Part II, line 6, and identify as "Casualty or theft occurrence number 1"

Casualty or Theft Occurrence Number 2

Property Held 9 Months or Less

15

16 Total of amounts on line 15, column (H)(i)

17 Amount on line 16 attributable to income-producing property

18 Subtract line 17 from line 16

19 $100 limitation, or portion of limitation used, see instruction J

20 Excess of line 18 over line 19

21 Total of amounts on lines 17 and 20, column (H)(i) and line 15, column (H)(ii) and column (I)—enter here and in Part II, line 1, and identify as "Casualty or theft occurrence number 2"

Property Held More Than 9 Months

22

23 Total of amounts on line 22, column (H)(i)

24 Amount on line 23 attributable to income-producing property

25 Subtract line 24 from line 23

26 Portion of $100 limitation not used on line 19

27 Excess of line 25 over line 26

28 Total of amounts on lines 24 and 27, column (H)(i) and line 22, column (H)(ii) and column (I)—enter here and in Part II, line 6, and identify as "Casualty or theft occurrence number 2"

☆ U.S. GOVERNMENT PRINTING OFFICE : 1977—O-235-162

235-162-2

B–12   FORM 4797   SUPPLEMENTAL SCHEDULE OF GAINS AND LOSSES

Form **4797**	**Supplemental Schedule of Gains and Losses**	
Department of the Treasury Internal Revenue Service	Sales, Exchanges and Involuntary Conversions under Sections 1231, 1245, 1250, 1251, 1252, and 1254 To be filed with Form 1040, 1041, 1065, 1120, etc.—See Separate Instructions	**1977**

Name(s) as shown on return	Identifying number as shown on page 1 of your tax return

Part I   Sales or Exchanges of Property Used in Trade or Business, and Involuntary Conversions (Section 1231)

SECTION A.—Involuntary Conversions Due to Casualty and Theft (See Instruction E)

a. Kind of property (if necessary, attach additional descriptive details not shown below)	b. Date acquired (mo., day, yr.)	c. Date sold (mo., day, yr.)	d. Gross sales price	e. Depreciation allowed (or allowable) since acquisition	f. Cost or other basis, cost of subsequent improvements (if not purchased, attach explanation) and expense of sale	g. Gain or loss (d plus e less f)
1						

2 Combine the amounts on line 1. Enter here, and on the appropriate line as follows . . . .

  (a) For all except partnership returns:
    (1) If line 2 is zero or a gain, enter that amount in column g, line 3.
    (2) If line 2 is a loss, enter the loss on line 5.
  (b) For partnership returns: Enter the amount shown on line 2 above, on Schedule K (Form 1065), line 6.

SECTION B.—Sales or Exchanges of Property Used in Trade or Business and Certain Involuntary Conversions (Not Reportable in Section A) (See Instruction E)

3						

4 Combine the amounts on line 3. Enter here, and on the appropriate line as follows . . . .

  (a) For all except partnership returns:
    (1) If line 4 is a gain, enter the gain as a long-term capital gain on Schedule D (Form 1040, 1120, etc.) that is being filed. See instruction E.
    (2) If line 4 is zero or a loss, enter that amount on line 6.
  (b) For partnership returns: Enter the amount shown on line 4 above, on Schedule K (Form 1065), line 7.

Part II   Ordinary Gains and Losses

a. Kind of property (if necessary, attach additional descriptive details not shown below)	b. Date acquired (mo., day, yr.)	c. Date sold (mo., day, yr.)	d. Gross sales price	e. Depreciation allowed (or allowable) since acquisition	f. Cost or other basis, cost of subsequent improvements (if not purchased, attach explanation) and expense of sale	g. Gain or loss (d plus e less f)
5 Amount, if any, from line 2(a)(2)						
6 Amount, if any, from line 4(a)(2)						
7 Gain, if any, from page 2, line 22						
8						

9 Combine amounts on lines 5 through 8. Enter here, and on the appropriate line as follows . . . .

  (a) For all except individual returns: Enter the gain or (loss) shown on line 9, on the line provided for on the return (Form 1120, etc.) being filed. See instruction F for specific line reference.
  (b) For individual returns:
    (1) If the gain or (loss) on line 9, includes losses which are to be treated as an itemized deduction on Schedule A (Form 1040) (see instruction F), enter the total of the loss(es) here and include on Schedule A (Form 1040), line 29—identify as "loss from Form 4797, line 9(b)(1)" . . . .
    (2) Redetermine the gain or (loss) on line 9, excluding the loss (if any) entered on line 9(b)(1). Enter here and on Form 1040, line 16 . . . .

Form 4797 (1977)

Part III — Gain From Disposition of Property Under Sections 1245, 1250, 1251, 1252, 1254—Assets Held More than Nine Months (See Separate Instructions)

Disregard lines 18 and 19 if there are no dispositions of farm property or farmland, or if this form is filed by a partnership.

10 Description of sections 1245, 1250, 1251, 1252, and 1254 property:

	Date acquired (mo., day, yr.)	Date sold (mo., day, yr.)
(A)		
(B)		
(C)		
(D)		

Relate lines 10(A) through 10(D) to these columns ► ► ► ►	Property (A)	Property (B)	Property (C)	Property (D)
11 Gross sales price				
12 Cost or other basis and expense of sale				
13 Depreciation (or depletion) allowed (or allowable)				
14 Adjusted basis, subtract line 13 from line 12				
15 Total gain, subtract line 14 from line 11				
16 If section 1245 property:				
(a) Depreciation allowed (or allowable) after applicable date (see instructions)				
(b) Enter smaller of line 15 or 16(a)				
17 If section 1250 property:				
(a) Additional depreciation after 12/31/75				
(b) Applicable percentage times the smaller of line 15 or line 17(a) (see instruction G.4)				
(c) Excess, if any, of line 15 over line 17(a) (If line 15 does not exceed line 17(a), skip lines 17(d) through 17(h), and enter the amount from line 17(b) on line 17(i))				
(d) Additional depreciation after 12/31/69 and before 1/1/76 . . .				
(e) Applicable percentage times the smaller of line 17(c) or line 17(d) (see instruction G.4)				
(f) Excess, if any, of line 17(c) over line 17(d) (If line 17(c) does not exceed line 17(d), skip lines 17(g) and 17(h), and combine the amounts on lines 17(b) and 17(e) on line 17(i))				
(g) Additional depreciation after 12/31/63 and before 1/1/70 . .				
(h) Applicable percentage times the smaller of line 17(f) or 17(g) (see instruction G.4)				
(i) Add lines 17(b), 17(e), and 17(h)				
18 If section 1251 property:				
(a) If farmland, enter soil, water, and land clearing expenses for current year and the four preceding years				
(b) If farm property other than land, subtract line 16(b) from line 15; if farmland, enter smaller of line 15 or 18(a) (see instruction G.5)				
(c) Excess deductions account (see instruction G.5)				
(d) Enter smaller of line 18(b) or 18(c)				
19 If section 1252 property:				
(a) Soil, water, and land clearing expenses made after 12/31/69 . .				
(b) Amount from line 18(d), if none enter a zero				
(c) Excess, if any, of line 19(a) over line 19(b)				
(d) Line 19(c) times applicable percentage (see instruction G.5) . .				
(e) Subtract line 19(b) from line 15				
(f) Enter smaller of line 19(d) or 19(e)				
20 If section 1254 property:				
(a) Intangible drilling and development costs deducted after 12/31/75 (see instruction G.6)				
(b) Enter smaller of line 15 or 20(a)				

Summary of Part III Gains (Complete Property columns (A) through (D) through line 20(b) before going to line 21)

21 Total gains for all properties (add columns (A) through (D), line 15) . . . .

22 Add columns (A) through (D), lines 16(b), 17(i), 18(d), 19(f), and 20(b). Enter here and on line 7 . . . .

23 Subtract line 22 from line 21. Enter here and in appropriate Section in Part I (see instructions E and G.2) . . .

☆ U.S. GOVERNMENT PRINTING OFFICE: 1977—O—235-167

*

APPENDIX C

GLOSSARY OF TAX TERMS

[NOTE: The words and phrases appearing below have been defined to reflect their conventional use in the field of taxation. Such definitions may, therefore, be incomplete for other purposes.]

–A–

Accelerated depreciation. Various methods of depreciation that yield larger deductions in the earlier years of the life of an asset than the straight-line method. Examples include the double declining-balance and the sum of the years' digits methods of depreciation. § 167(b)(2) and (3).

Accident and health benefits. Employee fringe benefits provided by employers through the payment of health and accident insurance premiums or the establishment of employer funded medical reimbursement plans. Employers generally are entitled to a deduction for such payments whereas employees generally exclude the fringe benefits from gross income.

Accounting income. The accountants' concept of income is generally based upon the realization principle. Financial accounting income may differ from taxable income e. g., accelerated depreciation might be used for Federal income tax and straight-line depreciation for financial accounting. Differences are included in a reconciliation of taxable and accounting income on Schedule M of Form 1120 for corporations.

Accounting method. The method under which income and expenses are determined for tax purposes. Major accounting methods are the cash basis and the accrual basis. Special methods are available for the reporting of gain on installment sales, recognition of income on construction projects (i. e., the completed-contract and percentage-of-completion methods), and the valuation of inventories (i. e., last-in-first-out and first-in-first-out). §§ 446–472. See *accrual method, cash basis, completed-contract method, percentage-of-completion method,* etc.

Accounting period. The period of time, usually a year, used by a taxpayer for the determination of tax liability. Unless a fiscal year is chosen, taxpayers must determine and pay their income tax liability by using the calendar year (i. e., January 1 through December 31) as the period of measurement. An example of a fiscal year is July 1 through June 30. A change in accounting periods (e. g., from a calendar year to a fiscal year) generally requires the consent of the IRS. New taxpayers, such as a newly formed corporation or an estate created upon the death of an individual taxpayer, are free to select either a calendar or a fiscal year without the consent of the IRS. §§ 441–443.

Accrual method. A method of accounting that reflects expenses incurred and income earned for any one tax year. In contrast to the cash basis of accounting, expenses do not have to be paid to be deductible nor

627

does income have to be received to be taxable. Unearned income (e. g., prepaid interest and rent) generally is taxed in the year of receipt regardless of the method of accounting used by the taxpayer. § 446 (c)(2). See *accounting method, cash method,* and *unearned income.*

Accumulated earnings tax. A special tax imposed on corporations that accumulate (rather than distribute) their earnings beyond the reasonable needs of the business. The tax is imposed on accumulated taxable income in addition to the corporate income tax.

Additional first-year depreciation. Taxpayers may elect to deduct additional depreciation equal to 20 percent of the cost of new or used tangible depreciable property which has a useful life of 6 or more years. The maximum additional depreciation is $10,000 and the basis for regular depreciation is reduced by the amount of depreciation claimed under this rule. § 179.

Adjusted basis. The cost or other basis of property reduced by depreciation allowed or allowable and increased by capital improvements. See *basis.*

Adjusted gross income. A determination peculiar to individual taxpayers. Generally, it represents gross income less business expenses, expenses attributable to the production of rent or royalty income and the long-term capital gain deduction.

Ad valorem tax. A tax imposed on the value of property. The more common ad valorem tax is that imposed by states, counties, and cities on real estate. Ad valorem taxes, can, however, be imposed upon personal property e. g., a motor vehicle tax may be imposed upon the value of an automobile and is therefore deductible as a tax.

Advance payments. In general, prepayments for services or goods are includible in gross income upon receipt of the advance payment (for both accrual and cash basis taxpayers). However, Revenue Procedure 71–21 provides guidelines for the deferral of tax on certain advance payments providing specific conditions are met.

Alimony payments. Alimony and separate maintenance payments are includible in the gross income of the recipient and are deductible (for AGI after 1976) by the payor. The payments must be periodic and made in discharge of a legal obligation arising from a marital or family relationship. Child support and voluntary payments are not treated as alimony. § 71.

All events test. For accrual method taxpayers, income is earned when (1) all the events have occurred which fix the right to receive the income and (2) the amount can be determined with reasonable accuracy. Accrual of income cannot be postponed simply because a portion of the income may have to be returned in a subsequent period.

Allowance for depreciation. See *reserve for depreciation.*

Alternative tax. An option allowed taxpayers in computing the tax on net long-term capital gains. Generally, the alternative tax rate applicable to non-corporate taxpayers is 25 percent, while the corporate rate is 30 percent. Under the alternative tax method, 25 percent (30 percent for corporations) of the net long-term capital gain is added to the tax liability computed without including the net long-term capital gains. If the alternative tax method is not used, non-corporate tax-payers may claim a 50 percent long-term capital gain deduction. In such case, the remaining 50 percent of such gains are includible in the computation of taxable or tax table income. If a corporate taxpayer does not use the alternative tax, all of the long-term capital gain is includible in taxable income under the regular tax computation.

Amortization. The allocation (and charge to expense) of the cost or other basis of an intangible asset over its estimated useful life. Intangible assets which have an indefinite life e. g., goodwill are not amortizable. Examples of amortizable intangibles include patents, copyrights and leasehold interests.

Amount realized. The amount received by a taxpayer upon the sale or exchange of property. The measure of the amount received is the sum of the cash and the fair market value of any property or services received. Determining the amount realized is the starting point for arriving at realized gain or loss. The amount realized is defined in § 1001(b) and the Regulations thereunder. See *realized gain or loss* and *recognized gain or loss.*

Annuities. A fixed sum payable to a person at specified intervals for a specific period of time or for life. Payments represent a partial return of capital and a return (interest) on the capital investment. There-fore, an exclusion ratio must generally be used to compute the amount of taxable income. Special rules apply to employee retirement plan annuities.

Arm's length transaction. The standard under which unrelated parties would determine an exchange price pursuant to a transaction. Sup-pose, for example, X Corporation sells property to its sole shareholder for $10,000. In testing whether the $10,000 is an "arm's length" price, one would ascertain the price which would have been negotiated between the corporation and an unrelated party in a bargained exchange.

Assignment of income. A procedure whereby a taxpayer attempts to avoid the recognition of income by assigning the property that gen-erates the income to another. Such a procedure will not avoid the recognition of income by the taxpayer making the assignment if it can be said that the income was earned at the point of the transfer. In this case, usually referred to as an anticipatory assignment of income, the income will be taxed to the person who earns it.

Association. An organization treated as a corporation for Federal tax purposes even though it may not qualify as such under applicable state law. What is designated as a trust or a partnership, for example, may be classified as an association if it clearly possesses corporate attributes. Corporate attributes include: centralized management, continuity of existence, free transferability of interests, and limited liability. § 7701(a)(3).

Attribution. Under certain circumstances, the tax law applies attribu-tion rules to assign to one taxpayer the ownership interest of another taxpayer. If, for example, the stock of X Corporation is held 60 per-cent by M and 40 percent by S, M may be deemed to own 100 percent of X Corporation if M and S are mother and son. In such case, the stock owned by S is attributed to M.

Audit. Inspection and verification of a taxpayer's return or other transactions possessing tax consequences. An "office audit" is an audit by the IRS which is conducted in the agent's office. A "field audit" is conducted by the IRS on the business premises of the tax-payer or in the office of the tax practitioner representing the tax-payer.

Automobile expenses. Automobile expenses are generally deductible only to the extent the automobile is used in business or for the produc-tion of income. Personal commuting expenses are not deductible. The taxpayer may deduct actual expenses including depreciation or a stand-ard mileage rate may be used (15 cents per mile for the first 15,000 miles and 10 cents thereafter during any one year). Automobile ex-penses relative to charitable activities and travel incurred for medical purposes are deductible to the extent of actual out-of-pocket expenses or 7 cents per mile.

–B–

Bad debts. A deduction is permitted if a business account receivable subsequently becomes worthless providing the income arising from the debt was previously included in income. The deduction is allowed only in the year of worthlessness. If a reserve method is used, partial or totally worthless accounts are charged to the reserve.

Basis. The amount assigned to an asset for income tax purposes. For assets acquired by purchase, basis would be cost (§ 1012). Special rules govern the basis of property received by virtue of another's death (§§ 1014, 1023) or by gift (§ 1015), the basis of stock received on a transfer of property to a controlled corporation (§ 358), the basis of the property transferred to the corporation (§ 362), and the basis of property received upon the liquidation of a corporation (§ 334).

Book value. The net amount of an asset after reduction by a related reserve. The book value of accounts receivable, for example, would be the amount of the receivables less the reserve for bad debts.

Boot. Cash or property of a type not included in the definition of a non-taxable exchange. The receipt of boot will cause an otherwise tax-free transfer to become taxable to the extent of the lesser of: the fair market value of such boot or the realized gain on the transfer. For example, see transfers to controlled corporations under § 351(b) and like kind exchanges under § 1031(b). See *realized gain or loss*.

Bribes and illegal payments. § 162 denies a deduction for bribes or kickbacks; for fines and penalties paid to a government for violation of law; and two-thirds of the treble damage payments made to claim-ants under violation of the the antitrust law. Denial of a deduction for bribes and illegal payments is based upon the judicially established principle that such payments are in violation of public policy and are, therefore, not a necessary expense.

Burden of proof. The requirement in a lawsuit to show the weight of evidence and, thereby, gain a favorable decision. Except in cases of tax fraud, the burden of proof in a tax case generally will be on the taxpayer.

Business gifts. Business gifts are deductible only to the extent that each gift does not exceed $25 per person per year. Exceptions are made for gifts costing $4 or less and for certain employee awards that are under $100.

Business investigation expenses. See *investigation of a new business.*

–C–

Capital asset. Broadly speaking, all assets are capital except those specifically excluded. Major categories of non-capital assets include: property held for resale in the normal course of business (i. e., inventory), trade accounts and notes receivable, depreciable property and real estate used in a trade or business (i. e., "§ 1231 assets"). § 1221.

Capital contribution. Various means by which a shareholder makes additional funds available to the corporation (i. e., placed at the risk of the business) without the receipt of additional stock. Such contributions are added to the basis of the shareholder's existing stock investment and do not generate income to the corporation. § 118.

Capital expenditure. An expenditure which should be added to the basis of the property improved. For income tax purposes, this generally precludes a full deduction for the expenditure in the year paid or incurred. Any cost recovery in the form of a tax deduction would have to come in the form of depreciation. § 263.

Capital gain deduction. See *alternative tax.*

Capital gain. The gain from the sale or exchange of a capital asset. See *capital asset.*

Capital gain or loss holding period. The requirements for long-term treatment are more than 6 months for 1976, more than 9 months for 1977, and more than one year for 1978 and subsequent years.

Capital loss. The loss from the sale or exchange of a capital asset. See *capital asset.*

Canons of taxation. Tax criteria used in the selection of a tax base originally discussed by Adam Smith in his Wealth of Nations. Canons of taxation include the following: equality; convenience; certainty; and economy.

Cash basis. See *accounting methods.*

Cash equivalent doctrine. Generally, a cash basis taxpayer does not report income until cash is constructively or actually received. Under the cash equivalent doctrine, cash basis taxpayers are required to report income even though no cash is actually received in a transaction if the equivalent of cash is received e. g., property is received instead of cash in a taxable transaction.

Casualty loss. A casualty is defined as "the complete or partial destruction of property resulting from an identifiable event of a sudden, unexpected or unusual nature" e. g., floods, storms, fires, auto accidents. Individuals may deduct a casualty loss only if the loss is incurred in a trade or business; in a transaction entered into for profit; or is a loss arising from fire, storm, shipwreck, or other casualty or from theft. Individuals deduct personal casualty losses as itemized deductions subject to a $100 nondeductible amount. Special rules are provided for the netting of casualty gains and losses. See *Chapter 15*.

Change in accounting method. A change in the taxpayer's method of accounting e. g., from FIFO to LIFO generally requires prior approval from the IRS. Generally, a request must be filed within 180 days after the beginning of the taxable year of the desired change. In some instances, the permission for change will not be granted unless the taxpayer agrees to certain terms or adjustments which are prescribed by the IRS.

Changes in Accounting Period. A taxpayer must obtain the consent of the IRS before changing his tax year. Income for the short period created by the change is required to be annualized.

Charitable contributions. Contributions are deductible (subject to various restrictions and ceiling limitations) if made to qualified non-profit charitable organizations. A cash basis taxpayer is entitled to a deduction solely in the year of payment. Accrual basis corporations may accrue contributions at year-end if payment is authorized by the Board of Directors prior to the end of the year and payment is made within $2\frac{1}{2}$ months from the end of the year.

Child and dependent care credit. A tax credit of 20 percent of employment related expenses (child and dependent care expenses) for amounts up to $4,000 is available to individuals who are employed on a full-time basis and maintain a household for a dependent child or disabled spouse or dependent.

Child support payments. Payments for child support do not constitute alimony and are, therefore, not includible in gross income by the recipient or deductible as alimony by the payor. None of the amounts paid are regarded as child support unless the divorce decree or separation agreement specifically calls for child support payments.

Claim of right doctrine. A judicially imposed doctrine applicable to both cash and accrual basis taxpayers which holds that an amount is includible in income upon actual or constructive receipt if the taxpayer has an unrestricted claim to such amounts.

Classification of employee expenses. The deductions *for* adjusted gross income include travel, transportation, moving expenses, expenses of an outside salesman and other reimbursed expenses. All other employee expenses are deductible *from* adjusted gross income.

Clear reflection of income. The IRS has the authority to redetermine a taxpayer's income using a method which clearly reflects income if the taxpayer's method does not do so. § 446(b). In addition, the IRS may apportion or allocate income among various related business if income is not "clearly reflected." § 482.

Closely-held corporation. A corporation, the stock ownership of which is not widely dispersed. Instead, a few shareholders are in control of corporate policy and are in a position to benefit personally from such policy.

Completed contract method. A method of reporting gain or loss on certain long-term contracts. Under this method of accounting, gross income and expenses are recognized in the tax year in which the contract is completed. Reg. § 1.451–3. For another alternative, see *percentage of completion method.*

Condemnation. The taking of property by a public authority. The property is condemned as the result of legal action and the owner is compensated by the public authority. The power to condemn property is known as the right of eminent domain.

Conduit concept. An approach the tax law assumes in the tax treatment of certain entities and their owners. Specific tax characteristics pass through the entity without losing their identity. For example, items of income and expense, capital gains and losses, tax credits etc., pass through a partnership (a conduit) and are subject to taxation at the partner level. In a Subchapter S corporation, certain items pass through (e. g., undistributed taxable income) and are treated as taxable income to the shareholders.

Constructive ownership. See *attribution.*

Constructive receipt. If income is unqualifiedly available, it will be subject to the income tax although not physically in the taxpayer's possession. An example would be accrued interest on a savings account. Under the constructive receipt of income concept, such interest will be taxed to a depositor in the year it is available rather than the year actually withdrawn. The fact that the depositor uses the cash basis of accounting for tax purposes makes no difference. See Reg. § 1.451–2.

Convention expenses. Travel expenses incurred in attending a convention are deductible if the meetings are related to a taxpayer's trade or business or job related activities. If, however, the convention trip is primarily for pleasure, no deduction is permitted. Specific limitations are provided for foreign convention expenses. In general, an individual may not attend more than two foreign conventions during the taxable year.

Contributions to the capital of a corporation. See *capital contribution.*

Court of Appeals. Any of eleven Federal courts which consider tax matters appealed from the U. S. Tax Court or a U. S. District Court. Appeal from a U. S. Court of Appeals is to the U. S. Supreme Court by Writ of Certiorari.

Court of Claims. One of three Federal trial courts that considers Federal tax controversy. Appeal from the U. S. Court of Claims is directly to the U. S. Supreme Court.

–D–

Death benefits. A payment made by an employer to the beneficiary or beneficiaries of a deceased employee on account of the death of the employee. Under certain conditions, the first $5,000 of such payment will not be subject to the income tax. § 101(b)(1).

Declaration of estimated tax. A procedure whereby individuals and corporations are required to make quarterly installment payments of estimated tax. Individuals are required to make the declaration and file quarterly payments of the estimated tax if certain requirements are met e. g., if gross income exceeds $20,000 for a married taxpayer filing jointly; if more than $500 is from sources other than wages. A declaration is not required for an individual if the estimated tax can reasonably be expected to be less than $100.

Deductions for adjusted gross income. See *adjusted gross income.*

Deferred compensation. Compensation which will be taxed when received or upon the removal of certain restrictions upon receipt and not when earned. An example would be contributions by an employer to a qualified pension or profit-sharing plan on behalf of an employee. Such contributions will not be taxed to the employee until the funds are made available or distributed to the employee (e. g., upon retirement). See *qualified pension or profit-sharing plan.*

Deficiency. Additional tax liability owed by a taxpayer and assessed by the IRS.

Depletion. The process by which the cost or other basis of a natural resource (e. g., an oil and gas interest) is recovered upon extraction and sale of the resource. The two ways to determine the depletion allowance are the cost and percentage (or statutory) methods. Under the cost method, each unit of production sold is assigned a portion of the cost or other basis of the interest. This is determined by dividing the cost or other basis by the total units expected to be recovered. Under the percentage (or statutory) method the tax law provides a special percentage factor for different types of minerals and other natural resources. This percentage is multiplied by the gross income from the interest to arrive at the depletion allowance. §§ 613 and 613A.

Depreciation. The write-off for tax purposes of the cost or other basis of a tangible asset over its estimated useful life. As to intangible assets, see *amortization.* As to natural resources, see *depletion.* Also see *estimated useful life.*

Determination letter. Upon the request of a taxpayer, a District Director will pass upon the tax status of a completed transaction. Determination letters are most frequently used to clarify employee status, to determine whether a pension or profit-sharing plan "qualifies" under the Code, and to determine the tax exempt status of certain non-profit organizations.

Direct charge-off method. A method of accounting for bad debts whereby a deduction is permitted only when an account becomes partially or completely worthless. See *reserve for bad debts.*

Disability pay. A partial exclusion from income is permitted for payments from employers to former employees who are under 65 and are permanently and totally disabled. The exclusion is limited to $100 per week and is reduced on a dollar for dollar basis if the taxpayer's adjusted gross income is more than $15,000.

Disaster loss. If a casualty is sustained in an area designated as a disaster area by the President of the U.S., the casualty is designated a disaster loss. In such an event, the disaster loss may be treated as having occurred in the taxable year immediately preceding the taxable year in which the disaster actually occurred. Thus, immediate tax benefits are provided to victims of a disaster. See *casualty loss*.

District court. A Federal District Court is a trial court for purposes of litigating Federal tax matters. It is the only trial court where a jury trial can be obtained.

Dividend exclusion. The $100 exclusion allowed individuals for dividends received from certain qualifying domestic corporations. § 116.

Dividends received deduction. A deduction allowed a corporate shareholder for dividends received from a domestic corporation. The deduction usually is 85 percent of the dividends received but could be 100 percent if an affiliated group is involved. §§ 243–246.

–E–

Earned income. Income from personal services as distinguished from income generated by property. See § 911 and the Regulations thereunder. Also see *maximum tax on earned income*.

Earned income credit. A 10 percent refundable tax credit on earned income up to $4,000 for low income workers who maintain a household for dependent children. The amount of credit is reduced on a dollar for dollar basis if earned income (or adjusted gross income) is greater than $4,000.

Earnings and profits. A tax concept peculiar to corporate taxpayers which measures economic capacity to make a distribution to shareholders that is not a return of capital. Such a distribution will result in dividend income to the shareholders to the extent of the corporation's current and accumulated earnings and profits.

Education expenses. Employees may deduct education expenses if such items are incurred either (1) to maintain or improve existing job related skills or (2) to meet the express requirements of the employer or the requirements imposed by law to retain employment status. Such expenses are not deductible if the education is (1) required to meet the minimum educational requirements for the taxpayer's job or (2) the education qualifies the individual for a new trade or business.

Employee expenses. See *classification of employee expenses*.

Entertainment. Such expenses are deductible only if they are directly related or associated with business. Various restrictions and documentation requirements have been imposed upon the deductibility of entertainment expenses to prevent abuses by business executives and employees.

Estate tax. A tax imposed on the right to transfer property by death. Thus, an estate tax is levied on the decedent's estate and not on the heir receiving the property.

Estimated useful life. The period over which an asset will be used by a particular taxpayer. Although such period cannot be longer than the estimated physical life of an asset, it could be shorter if the taxpayer does not intend to keep the asset until it wears out. Assets such as goodwill do not have an estimated useful life. The estimated useful life of an asset is essential to measuring the annual tax deduction for depreciation and amortization and in determining the amount of any investment tax credit allowable.

Excise tax. A tax on the manufacture, sale, or use of goods or on the carrying on of an occupation or activity. Also a tax on the transfer of property. Thus, the Federal death and gift taxes are, theoretically, excise taxes.

–F–

Fair market value. The amount at which property would change hands between a willing buyer and a willing seller, neither being under any compulsion to buy or sell and both having reasonable knowledge of the relevant facts. Reg. § 20.2031–1(b).

First-in first-out (FIFO). An accounting method for determining the cost of inventories. Under this method the inventory on hand is deemed to be the sum of the cost of the most recently acquired units.

Foreign earned income exclusion. A U. S. citizen who is either a bona fide resident or is present in a foreign country for 510 days during a period of 18 consecutive months may exclude up to $15,000 per year of foreign earned income in computing the U.S. tax liability. U.S. citizens are generally subject to the U.S. tax on total income regardless of the origin of such income. See *foreign tax credit or deduction.*

Foreign tax credit or deduction. Both individual taxpayers and corporations may claim a foreign tax credit on income earned and subject to tax in a foreign country or U.S. possession. As an alternative to the credit, a deduction may be taken for the foreign taxes paid. §§ 33,-164, and 901–905.

Franchise. A franchise is an agreement which gives the transferee the right to distribute, sell, or provide goods, services, or facilities, within a specified area. The cost of obtaining a franchise may be amortized over the life of the agreement. In general, a franchise is a capital asset and results in capital gain or loss if all significant powers, rights or continuing interests are transferred pursuant to the sale of a franchise.

Fringe benefits. Compensation or other benefits received by an employee which are not in the form of cash. Some fringe benefits (e. g., accident and health plans, group-term life insurance) may be excluded from the employee's gross income and, therefore, not subject to the Federal income tax.

Fruit and the tree doctrine. The courts have held that an individual who earns income from his property or services cannot assign that income to another. For example, a father cannot assign his earnings from commissions to his son and escape income tax on such amount.

–G–

Gasoline tax. See *state and local taxes.*

General tax credit. Individual taxpayers are allowed a general tax credit equal to the greater of (a) 2 percent of taxable income up to $9,000 or (b) $35 for each personal and dependency exemption.

Gift. A transfer of property for less than adequate consideration. Gifts usually occur in a personal setting (such as between members of the same family).

Gift tax. A tax imposed on the transfer of property by gift. Such tax is imposed upon the donor of a gift and is based upon the fair market value of the property on the date of the gift.

Goodwill. The ability of a business to generate income in excess of a normal rate on assets due to superior managerial skills, market position, new product technology etc. In the purchase of a business, goodwill represents the difference between the purchase price and the value of the net assets. Goodwill is an intangible asset which possesses an indefinite life and cannot, therefore, be amortized for Federal income tax purposes. Reg. § 1.167(a)–3.

Government bonds issued at a discount. Certain U. S. Government bonds (Series E) are issued at a discount and do not pay interest during the life of the bond. Instead, the bonds are redeemable at increasing fixed amounts. Thus, the difference between the purchase price and the amount received upon redemption represents interest income to the holder. A cash basis taxpayer may defer recognition of taxable income until such bonds are redeemed. As an alternative the taxpayer may elect to include the annual increase in the value of the bond in gross income on an annual basis.

Gross income. Income subject to the Federal income tax. Gross income does not include income such as interest on municipal bonds. In the case of a manufacturing or merchandising business, gross income means gross profit (i. e., gross sales or gross receipts less cost of goods sold). § 61 and Reg. § 1.61–3(a).

Group-term life insurance. Life insurance coverage permitted by an employer for a group of employees. Such insurance is renewable on a year-to-year basis and does not accumulate in value (i. e., no cash surrender value is built up). The premiums paid by the employer on such insurance are not taxed to an employee on coverage of up to $50,000 per year. § 79 and Reg. § 1.79–1(b).

–H–

Head of household. An unmarried individual who maintains a household for another and satisfies certain conditions set forth in § 2(b). Such status enables the taxpayer to use a set of income tax rates [see § 1 (b)] that are lower than those applicable to other unmarried individuals [§ 1(c)] but higher than those applicable to surviving spouses and married persons filing a joint return [§ 1(a)]. See *tax rate schedules.*

Hobby loss. A nondeductible loss arising from a personal hobby as contrasted with an activity engaged in for profit. Generally, the law provides a presumption that an activity is engaged in for profit if gross profits are earned during any 2 or more years during a 5 year period. § 183.

Holding period. The period of time property has been held for income tax purposes. The holding period is of crucial significance in determining whether or not gain or loss from the sale or exchange of a capital asset is long- or short-term. § 1223.

–I–

Imputed interest. In the case of certain long-term sales of property, the IRS has the authority to convert some of the gain from the sale into interest income if the contract does not provide for a minimum rate of interest to be paid by the purchaser. The application of this procedure has the effect of forcing the seller to recognize less long-term capital gain and more ordinary income (i. e., interest income). The interest element is currently being imputed at 7 percent. § 483 and the Regulations.

Income Averaging. A special method whereby the income tax of an individual is determined by taking into account the taxable income of the past four years. The income averaging procedure provides relief from the annual accounting period concept where a taxpayer goes from a "rags to riches" income position and has a relatively large amount of income "bunched" in a particular year. See Schedule G of Form 1040 and §§ 1301–1305.

Individual retirement account. Employees not covered by qualified pension or profit-sharing plans are permitted to set aside up to 15 percent of their salary per year (generally not to exceed $1,500) for a retirement account. The amount set aside can be deducted by the employee and will be subject to income tax only upon withdrawal. Specific requirements are established for the withdrawal of such amounts and penalties are provided for failure to comply.

Installment method. A method of accounting enabling a taxpayer to spread the recognition of gain on the sale of property over the payout period. Under this elective procedure, the seller computes the gross profit percentage from the sales (i. e., the gain divided by the selling price) and applies it to each payment received to arrive at the gain to be recognized. § 453.

Intangible drilling and development costs. Taxpayers may elect to expense or capitalize (subject to amortization) intangible drilling and development costs. However, ordinary income recapture provisions now apply to oil and gas properties upon a sale or other disposition if the expense method is elected. § 263(c) and § 1254(a).

Interest on life insurance proceeds. Interest of up to $1,000 per year earned on insurance proceeds, which are retained by an insurance company for making periodic payments to a surviving spouse, are exempt from Federal income tax. § 101(d).

Investigation of a new business. See *business investigation expenses.*

Investment indebtedness. If funds are borrowed by noncorporate tax-payers for the purpose of purchasing or continuing to hold investment property, some portion of the interest expense deduction may be disallowed. Interest is generally limited to $10,000 plus net investment income. Amounts which are disallowed may be carried forward and treated as investment interest of the succeeding year. § 163(d).

Investment tax credit. A special tax credit usually equal to 10 percent of the qualified investment in tangible personalty used in a trade or business. If the tangible personalty has an estimated useful life of 7 years or more the full cost of the property qualifies for the credit. Only two-thirds qualifies for 5 years or more but less than 7 years and only one-third for 3 years or more but less than 5 years. No credit is available if the property has an estimated useful life of less than 3 years. §§ 38, 46–50. See *estimated useful life* and *recapture of investment tax credit.*

Investment tax credit recapture. See *recapture of investment tax credit.*

Involuntary conversion. The loss or destruction of property through theft, casualty, or condemnation. Any gain realized on an involuntary conversion can, at the taxpayer's election, be considered non-recognizable for Federal income tax purposes if the owner reinvests the proceeds within a prescribed period of time in property that is similar or related in service or use. § 1033.

IRA. See *individual retirement account.*

Itemized deductions. Certain personal expenditures allowed by the Code as deductions *from* adjusted gross income if an individual taxpayer chooses not to use the standard deduction and total itemized deductions exceed the standard deduction (zero bracket amount). Examples include certain medical expenses, interest on home mortgages, state sales taxes, and charitable contributions. Itemized deductions are reported on Schedule A of Form 1040.

–K–

Keogh plans. See *self-employed retirement plan.*

–L–

Last-in first-out (LIFO). An accounting method for valuing inventories for tax purposes. Under this method it is assumed that the inventory on hand is valued at the cost of the earliest acquired units. § 472 and the Regulations thereunder.

Lessee. One who rents property from another. In the case of real estate, the lessee is also known as the tenant.

Lessor. One who rents property to another. In the case of real estate, the lessor is also known as the landlord.

Life insurance proceeds. Generally, life insurance proceeds paid to a beneficiary upon the death of the insured are exempt from Federal income tax. An exception is provided where a life insurance contract has been transferred for valuable consideration to another individual who assumes ownership rights. In such case the proceeds are income to the assignee to the extent that the proceeds exceed the amount paid for the policy plus any subsequent premiums paid. Insurance proceeds may be subject to the Federal estate tax if the decedent retained any incidents of ownership in the policy prior to death or if the proceeds are payable to his estate. §§ 101 and 2042.

Like-kind exchange. An exchange of property held for productive use in a trade or business or for investment (except inventory and stocks and bonds) for property of the same type. Unless different property is received (i. e., "boot") the exchange will be nontaxable. § 1031. See *boot*.

Liquidation of a corporation. In a complete or partial liquidation of a corporation, amounts received by the shareholders in exchange for their stock are usually treated as a sale or exchange of the stock resulting in capital gain or loss treatment. Special rules apply to one month liquidations—§ 333, twelve month liquidations—§ 337, and the liquidation of a subsidiary—§ 332.

Lump-sum distribution. Payment of the entire amount due at one time rather than in installments. Such distributions often occur from qualified pension or profit-sharing plans upon the retirement or death of a covered employee. The recipient of a lump-sum distribution may recognize both long-term capital gain and ordinary income upon the receipt of the distribution. The ordinary income portion is subject to a special 10-year income averaging provision.

–M–

Marital deduction. A deduction allowed upon the transfer of property from one spouse to another. The deduction is allowed under the Federal gift tax for lifetime (i. e., inter vivos) transfers or under the Federal death tax for death (i. e., testamentary) transfers. §§ 2056 and 2523.

Maximum tax on earned income. The tax law places a 50 percent ceiling tax rate on personal service income, e. g., wages, salaries, professional fees, pensions, deferred compensation and other forms of compensation for personal services. § 1348.

Medical expenses. Medical expenses of an individual and his dependents are allowed as an itemized deduction to the extent that such amounts (less insurance reimbursements) exceed 3 percent of adjusted gross income. Special rules are provided for medicines and drugs and health insurance premiums. § 213.

Minimum tax. A 15 percent minimum tax is imposed on certain tax preference items. The tax is in addition to the regular income tax and is designed to further tax certain preferentially treated income of higher bracket taxpayers. Examples of tax preference items include accelerated depreciation on real property and 50 percent of long-term capital gains. §§ 56–58.

Mitigation of the annual accounting period concept. Various tax provisions that provide relief from the effect of the finality of the annual accounting period concept. For example, income averaging provisions provide relief for taxpayers with a large and unusual amount of income concentrated in a single tax year. See *accounting periods*.

Moving expenses. A deduction *for* AGI is permitted to employees and self-employed individuals providing certain tests are met e. g., the taxpayer's new job must be at least 35 miles farther from the old residence than the old residence was from the former place of work. In addition, the employee must be employed on a full-time basis at the new location for 39 weeks. Ceiling limitations are placed upon direct moving expenses (e. g., expenses of moving personal belongings and traveling) and upon indirect expenses such as house-hunting trips and temporary living expenses. § 217.

–N–

Necessary. Appropriate and helpful in furthering the taxpayer's business or income producing activity. §§ 162(a) and 212. See *ordinary*.

Net operating loss. In order to mitigate the effect of the annual accounting period concept, § 172 allows taxpayers to use an excess loss of one year as a deduction for certain past or future years. In this regard, a carryback period of three years and a carryforward period of seven years is allowed. See *mitigation of the annual accounting period concept*.

Net worth method. An aproach used by the IRS to reconstruct the income of a taxpayer who fails to maintain adequate records. Under this approach, the gross income for the year is the increase in net worth of the taxpayer (i. e., assets in excess of liabilities) with appropriate adjustment for nontaxable receipts and nondeductible expenditures. The net worth method often is used when tax fraud is suspected.

Nonbusiness bad debts. A bad debt loss not incurred in connection with a creditor's trade or business. Such loss is deductible as a short-term capital loss and will only be allowed in the year the debt becomes entirely worthless. In addition to family loans, many investor losses fall into the classification of nonbusiness bad debts. § 166(d). See *bad debts*.

Nonqualified deferred compensation plans. Compensation arrangements which are frequently offered to executives. Such plans may include stock options, restricted stock etc. Generally, an executive may defer the recognition of taxable income to future periods and the employer does not receive a tax deduction until the employee is required to include the compensation in income.

Normal tax. A normal tax applies to all taxable income at the same rate. Currently, the normal tax on corporations is 20 percent on taxable income up to $25,000 and 22 percent on taxable income in excess of $25,000. § 11(b). See *surtax*.

–O–

Office in home expenses. Employment and business related expenses attributable to the use of a residence (e. g., den or office) are allowed only if the portion of the residence is exclusively used on a regular basis as the taxpayer's principal place of business or as a place of business which is used by patients, clients, or customers. If the expenses are employment related, the use must be for the convenience of the employer as opposed to being merely appropriate and helpful.

Open transaction. A judicially imposed doctrine which allows the taxpayer to defer all gain until he or she has collected an amount equal to the adjusted basis of assets transferred pursuant to an exchange transaction. This doctrine, although generally not accepted by the IRS, has been applied where the property received in an exchange has no ascertainable fair market value due to the existence of contingencies.

Options. The sale or exchange of an option to buy or sell property results in capital gain or loss if the property is a capital asset. Generally, the closing of an option transaction results in short-term capital gain or loss to the writer of the call and the purchaser of the call option. § 1234.

Ordinary. Common and accepted in the general industry or type of activity in which the taxpayer is engaged. It comprises one of the tests for the deductibility of expenses incurred or paid in connection with a trade or business; for the production or collection of income; for the management, conservation, or maintenance of property held for the production of income; or in connection with the determination, collection, or refund of any tax. §§ 162(a) and 212. See *necessary.*

Organization expenses. A corporation may elect to amortize certain organizational expenses over a period of 60 months or more. Certain expenses of organizing a company do not qualify for amortization e. g., expenditures connected with issuing or selling stock or other securities. § 248.

Outside salesmen. An "outside salesman" is one who solicits business away from the employer's place of business on a full-time basis. If an employee qualifies as an "outside salesman", all employment related expenses are deductible *for* AGI.

–P–

Partnerships. Partnerships are treated as a conduit and are, therefore, not subject to taxation. The various items of partnership income, loss, gains and losses etc. flow through to the individual partners and are reported on their personal income tax returns.

Passive investment income. As defined in § 1372(e)(5)(C), "passive investment income" means gross receipts from royalties, certain rents, dividends, interest, annuities, and gains from the sale or exchange of stock and securities. With certain exceptions, if the passive investment income of a corporation exceeds 20 percent of its gross receipts, Subchapter S status is not available or is lost.

Patents. A patent is an identifiable intangible asset which may be amortized over the remaining life of the patent. The sale of a patent usually results in favorable long-term capital gain treatment. § 1235.

Penalties. Penalty taxes are not deductible expenses e. g., underpayment penalties on estimated taxes. See *bribes and illegal payments.*

Percentage of completion method. A method of reporting gain or loss on certain long-term contracts. Under this method of accounting, the gross contract price is included in income as the contract is completed. Reg. § 1.451–3. See *completed contract method.*

Personal expenses. Expenses of an individual for personal consumption which are not deductible unless specifically provided for under the tax law. § 262.

Personal property. Generally, all property other than real estate. It is sometimes designated as personalty when real estate is termed realty. Personal property also can refer to property which is not used in a taxpayer's trade or business or held for the production or collection of income. When used in this sense, personal property could include both realty (e. g., a personal residence) and personalty (e. g., personal effects such as clothing and furniture).

Personal residence. The sale of a personal residence generally results in the recognition of capital gain (but not loss). However, the gain may be deferred if the adjusted sales price of the old residence is re-invested in the purchase of a new residence within certain prescribed time periods. Also, taxpayers age 65 or over may exclude all or part of the gain from tax providing certain requirements are met. §§ 1034 and 121.

Personal and dependency exemptions. The tax law provides a $750 exemption for each individual taxpayer and an additional $750 exemption for his or her spouse if a joint return is filed. Additional personal exemptions are provided for old age (65) and blindness. An individual may also claim a $750 dependency exemption for each dependent providing certain tests are met. § 151.

Points. Loan origination fees which are generally deductible as interest by a buyer of property. A seller of property who pays "points" is required to reduce the selling price and does not, therefore, receive an interest deduction.

Political contributions. Individuals may elect to take a tax credit equal to one-half of certain qualifying political contributions. The credit is limited to $25 ($50 on a joint return). As an alternative, a taxpayer may claim a deduction *from* AGI up to $100 ($200 on a joint return).

Pollution control facilities. A certified pollution control facility the cost of which may be amortized over a 60 month period if elected by the taxpayer. § 169.

Prepaid expenses. Cash basis as well as accrual basis taxpayers are generally required to capitalize prepayments for rent, insurance etc. that cover more than one year. Deductions are taken during the period the benefits are received. See *prepaid interest.*

Prizes and awards. The fair market value of a prize or award is generally includible in gross income. Certain exceptions are provided where the prize or award is made in recognition of religious, charitable, scientific, educational, artistic, literary, or civic achievement providing certain other requirements are met. § 74.

Public policy limitation. See *bribes and illegal payments.*

-Q-

Qualified pension or profit-sharing plan. An employer-sponsored plan that meets the requirements of § 401. If these requirements are met, none of the employer's contributions to the plan will be taxed to the employee until distributed to him or her [§ 402]. The employer will be allowed a deduction in the year the contributions are made [§ 404].

–R–

Realized gain or loss. The difference between the amount realized upon the sale or other disposition of property and the adjusted basis of such property. § 1001. See *basis*.

Reasonable needs of the business. See *accumulated earnings tax*.

Recapture. To recover the tax benefit of a deduction or a credit previously taken. See *recapture of depreciation* and *recapture of the investment tax credit*.

Recapture of depreciation. Upon the disposition of depreciable property used in a trade or business, gain or loss is determined measured by the difference between the consideration received (i. e., the amount realized) and the adjusted basis of the property. Prior to the enactment of the recapture of depreciation provisions of the Code, any such gain recognized could be § 1231 gain and usually qualified for long-term capital gain treatment. The recapture provisions of the Code (e. g., §§ 1245 and 1250) may operate to convert some or all of the previous § 1231 gain into ordinary income. The justification for recapture of depreciation is that it prevents a taxpayer from converting a dollar of deduction (in the form of depreciation) into fifty cents of income (§ 1231 gain taxed as a long-term capital gain). The recapture of depreciation rules do not apply when the property is disposed of at a loss. See *section 1231 gains and losses*.

Recapture of investment tax credit. When investment credit property is disposed of or ceases to be used in the trade or business of the taxpayer, some of the investment tax credit claimed on such property may be recaptured as additional tax liability. The amount of the recapture is the difference between the amount of the credit originally claimed and what should have been claimed in light of the length of time the property was actually held or used for qualifying purposes. See *investment tax credit*.

Recapture potential. Reference is to property which, if disposed of in a taxable transaction, would result in the recapture of depreciation [§§ 1245 or 1250] and/or of the investment tax credit [§ 47].

Recognized gain or loss. The portion of realized gain or loss that is subject to income taxation. See *realized gain or loss*.

Regulations. Treasury Department Regulations represent the position of the IRS as to how the Internal Revenue Code is to be interpreted. Their purpose is to provide taxpayers and IRS personnel with rules of general and specific application to the various provisions of the tax law. Regulations are published in the Federal Register and in all tax services.

Rehabilitation expenditures. A special 5 year amortization election is provided for rehabilitation expenditures on low-income housing. The expenditures must exceed $3,000 per dwelling unit over 2 consecutive years and in the aggregate may not exceed $20,000 per dwelling unit. § 167(k).

Related party transactions. The tax law places restrictions upon the recognition of gains and losses between related parties due to the potential for abuse. For example, restrictions are placed upon the deduction of losses from the sale or exchange of property between related parties. A related party includes a corporation which is controlled by the taxpayer. § 267.

Research and experimental expenditures. Three alternative methods are provided in the Code. The expenditures may be expensed in the year paid or incurred; deferred subject to amortization; or capitalized. If an election is not made to expense such costs or to defer the expenditures subject to amortization (over 60 months), the research and experimental costs must be capitalized. § 174.

Reserve for bad debts. A method of accounting whereby an allowance is permitted for estimated uncollectible accounts. Actual write-offs are charged to the reserve and recoveries of previously written off amounts are credited to the reserve.

Reserves for estimated expenses. Except in the case of bad debts, reserves for estimated expenses e. g., warranty service costs, are not permitted for tax purposes even though such reserves are appropriate for financial accounting purposes.

Restricted property. See *nonqualified deferred compensation plans.*

Restrictions upon depreciation methods. Certain restrictions are placed upon the depreciation of new and used real property. Generally, only straight-line depreciation may be claimed for used real property. In addition, 200 percent D.B. and S.Y.D. are not available for nonresidential real estate.

Retirement of corporate obligations. The retirement of corporate and certain government obligations is considered to be a sale or exchange. Gain or loss, therefore, is treated as capital gain or loss upon the retirement of a corporate obligation rather than ordinary income or loss. § 1232.

Return of capital doctrine. See *open transaction.*

Revenue Procedure. A matter of procedural importance to both taxpayers and the IRS concerning the administration of the tax laws is issued as a Revenue Procedure (abbreviated as "Rev.Proc."). A Revenue Procedure is first published in an Internal Revenue Bulletin (I. R. B.) and later transferred to the appropriate Cumulative Bulletin (C. B.). Both the Internal Revenue Bulletins and the Cumulative Bulletins are published by the U. S. Government.

Revenue Ruling. A Revenue Ruling (abbreviated "Rev.Rul.") is issued by the National Office of the IRS to express an official interpretation of the tax law as applied to specific transactions. Unlike a Regulation, it is more limited in application. A Revenue Ruling is first published in an Internal Revenue Bulletin (I. R. B.) and later transferred to the appropriate Cumulative Bulletin (C. B.). Both the Internal Revenue Bulletins and the Cumulative Bulletins are published by the U. S. Government.

–S–

Salvage value. The estimated value which will be realized upon the sale or other disposition of an asset at the end of its useful life. Salvage value is not changed merely because of fluctuations in price levels although the salvage value may be changed upon a redetermination of the useful life of the asset. No salvage is used if the declining balance method is employed. Further, a taxpayer may disregard salvage value up to 10 percent of the basis for tangible depreciable property which has an estimated life of three years or more.

Sales taxes. State and local taxes are deductible if such taxes are separately stated and imposed upon the taxpayer (consumer). Unless business related, sales taxes are deductible *from* AGI. The IRS issues optional state sales tax tables which may be used by individuals.

Scholarships and fellowships. Scholarships and fellowships are generally excluded from gross income of the recipient unless the payments are a disguised form of compensation for services rendered. Special rules apply where the payments are for dual motives i. e., to aid the recipient and to benefit the grantor. § 117.

Section 1231 assets. § 1231 assets are depreciable assets and real estate used in a trade or business and held for more than six months (more than nine months in 1977 and more than twelve months in 1978 and thereafter). Under certain circumstances, the classification also includes: timber, coal, domestic iron ore, livestock (held for draft, breeding, dairy, or sporting purposes), and unharvested crops. § 1231(b). See *section 1231 gains and losses.*

Section 1231 gains and losses. If the combined gains and losses from the taxable dispositions of § 1231 assets plus the net gain from involuntary conversion (of both § 1231 assets and long-term capital assets) is a gain, such gains and losses are treated as long-term capital gains and losses. In arriving at § 1231 gains, however, the depreciation recapture provisions (e. g., §§ 1245 and 1250) are first applied to produce ordinary income. If the net result of the combination is a loss, such gains and losses from § 1231 assets are treated as ordinary gains and losses. § 1231(a). See *section 1231 assets.*

Section 38 property. Property which qualifies for the investment tax credit. Generally, this includes all tangible property (other than real estate) used in a trade or business. § 48.

Section 1245 property. Property which is subject to the recapture of depreciation under § 1245. For a definition of § 1245 property see § 1245(a)(3). See *recapture of depreciation* and *section 1245 recapture.*

Section 1250 property. Real estate which is subject to the recapture of depreciation under § 1250. For a definition of § 1250 property see § 1250(c). See *recapture of depreciation* and *section 1250 recapture.*

Section 1245 recapture. Upon a taxable disposition of § 1245 property, all depreciation claimed on such property after 1963 will be recaptured as ordinary income (but not to exceed recognized gain from the disposition).

Section 1250 recapture. Upon a taxable disposition of § 1250 property, some of the excess depreciation (amounts in excess of straight-line) claimed on the property may be recaptured as ordinary income. Various recapture rules apply depending upon the type of property i. e., residential or commercial real estate and the date acquired. Generally, the excess depreciation (amounts in excess of what would have been claimed under the straight-line method) is recaptured in full to the extent of the gain recognized.

Section 1244 stock. Stock issued under § 1244 by qualifying small business corporations. If § 1244 stock becomes worthless, the shareholders may claim an ordinary loss rather than the usual capital loss.

Self-employment tax. A tax of 7.9 percent up to $16,500 in 1977 is levied on individuals with net earnings from self-employment to provide social security benefits for such individuals. If a self-employed individual also receives wages from an employer which are subject to FICA, the self-employment tax is reduced.

Self-employment retirement plan. Also known as HR 10 or Keogh plans. Under such plans a taxpayer may deduct each year up to either 15 percent of net earnings from self-employment or $7,500, whichever is less.

Short sales. A short sale occurs where a taxpayer sells borrowed property (usually stock) and repays the lender with substantially identical property either held on the date of the short sale or purchased after the sale. No gain or loss is recognized until the short sale is closed and such gain or loss is generally short term. § 1233.

Small business corporation. A corporation which satisfies the definition of § 1371(a), § 1244(c)(2) or both. Satisfaction of § 1371(a) permits a Subchapter S election, while satisfaction of § 1244 enables the shareholders of the corporation to claim an ordinary loss on the worthlessness of the stock.

Standard deduction. Also referred to as the zero bracket amount. The standard deduction is built into the rate tables and rate schedules for years after 1976. Therefore, if an individual itemizes his or her deductions, only the amounts in excess of the standard deduction are deducted. The standard deduction is a flat $3,200 for married taxpayers filing jointly and $2,200 for single taxpayers.

State and local taxes. See *sales tax*.

Stock options. Stock options are generally used to compensate executives and key employees. Qualified stock options may not be granted after May 20, 1976. If a nonqualified stock option has a readily ascertainable market value, the difference between the fair market value and the option price must be included in the employee's gross income at the date of grant. Thereafter, capital gain or loss is recognized upon the disposition of the optioned stock. If the optioned stock has no readily ascertainable fair market value, the excess of the fair market value over the option price is taxable on the date of exercise. The employer receives a corresponding tax deduction at the time and for the same amount that is includible in the employee's income. § 422 and Reg. § 1.-421–6.

Stock redemptions. The redemption of the stock of a shareholder by the issuing corporation is generally treated as a sale or exchange of the stock unless the redemption is a dividend. §§ 301 and 302.

Subchapter S corporation. An elective provision permitting certain small business corporations (§ 1371) and their shareholders to elect (§ 1372) to be treated for income tax purposes in accordance with the operating rules of §§ 1373–1379. Of major significance is the fact that Subchapter S status usually avoids the corporate income tax, and corporate losses can be claimed by the shareholders.

Surtax. An additional tax on what is already subject to tax. The current surtax on corporations is 26 percent on the taxable income in excess of $50,000. When combined with the normal tax of 22 percent, such excess taxable income is, therefore, taxed at a rate of 48 percent. § 11(c). See *normal tax* and *surtax exemption*.

Surtax exemption. The portion of taxable income not subject to the surtax. At present, the surtax exemption for corporations is the first $50,000 of taxable income. § 11(d). See *surtax*.

–T–

Tax avoidance. The minimization of one's tax liability by taking advantage of legally available tax planning opportunities. Tax avoidance may be contrasted with tax evasion which entails the reduction of tax liability by using illegal means.

Tax benefit rule. A rule which limits the recognition of income from the recovery of an expense or loss properly deducted in a prior tax year to the amount of the deduction that generated a tax benefit. Assume for example, that last year T (an individual) had medical expenses of $1,200 and adjusted gross income of $30,000. Due to the 3 percent limitation, T was able to deduct only $300 of these expenses [i. e., $1,200 − (3 percent × $30,000)]. If, in this year, T is reimbursed by his insurance company for $400 of these expenses, the tax benefit rule limits the amount of income from the reimbursement to $300 (i. e., the amount previously deducted with a tax benefit).

Tax credit for elderly. Elderly taxpayers (age 65 and over) may receive a tax credit amounting to 15 percent of $2,500 or $3,750 for married individuals filing jointly. This amount is reduced by social security benefits, excluded pension benefits and one-half of the taxpayer's adjusted gross income in excess of $7,500 ($10,000 for married taxpayers filing jointly). § 37.

Tax court. The U. S. Tax Court is one of three trial courts of original jurisdiction which decides litigation involving Federal income, death, or gift taxes. It is the only trial court where the taxpayer must not first pay the deficiency assessed by the IRS. The Tax Court will not have jurisdiction over a case unless the statutory notice of deficiency (i. e., "90-day letter") has been issued by the IRS and the taxpayer files the petition for hearing within the time prescribed.

Tax-free exchange. Transfers of property specifically exempted from Federal income tax consequences. Examples are a transfer of property to a controlled corporation under § 351(a) and a like-kind exchange under § 1031(a). The term "tax-free exchange" is a misnomer which is, in reality, a deferral of tax.

Tax home. Since travel expenses of an employee are deductible only if the taxpayer is away from home, the deductibility of such expenses rests upon the definition of "tax home". The IRS position is that "tax home" is the business location, post or station of the taxpayer. If an employee is temporarily reassigned to a new post for a period of one year or less, the taxpayer's home should be his personal residence and the travel expenses should be deductible. The courts are in conflict regarding what constitutes a person's "home" for tax purposes.

Tax preference items. Those items set forth in § 57 which may result in the imposition of the 15 percent minimum tax. See *minimum tax.*

Tax rates—corporations. See *normal tax* and *surtax.*

Tax rate schedules. Rate schedules appearing in Appendix A–1 which are used by upper income taxpayers. Separate rate schedules are provided for married individuals filing jointly, unmarried individuals who maintain a household, single taxpayers, and estates and trusts and married individuals filing separate returns.

Tax tables. Tax tables appearing in Appendix A–2 are provided for middle and lower income taxpayers. Separate columns are provided for single taxpayers, married taxpayers filing jointly, head of household, and married taxpayers filing separately.

Thin corporation. When debt owed by a corporation to its shareholders is large in relationship to its capital structure (i. e., stock and shareholder equity), the IRS may contend that the corporation is thinly capitalized. In effect, this means that some or all of the debt will be reclassified as equity. The immediate result is to disallow any interest deduction to the corporation on the reclassified debt. To the extent of the corporation's earnings and profits, interest payments and loan repayments are treated as dividends to the shareholders. § 385.

Timber. Special rules apply to the recognition of gain from the sale of timber. A taxpayer may elect to treat the cutting of timber, which is held for sale or use in a trade or business, as a sale or exchange. If the holding period requirements are met, the gain is recognized as § 1231 gain and may, therefore, receive favorable long-term capital gain treatment. § 631.

Trade or business expenses. Deductions *for* AGI which are attributable to a taxpayer's business or profession. Some employee expenses may also be treated as trade or business expenses. See *employee expenses.*

Transportation expenses. Transportation expenses for an employee include only the cost of transportation (taxi fares, automobile expenses etc.) in the course of employment where the employee is not "away from home" in a travel status. Commuting expenses are not deductible. See *automobile expenses.*

Travel expenses. Travel expenses include meals and lodging and transportation expenses while away from home in the pursuit of a trade or business (including that of an employee). See *tax home.*

654   Appendix D

TAX REFORM ACT

(26 U.S.C.A.)

APPENDIX E
CITATOR EXAMPLE

ILLUSTRATION OF THE USE OF THE P–H CITATOR

Background

The Prentice-Hall *Federal Tax Citator* is a separate four-volume service with a loose-leaf current matters section. Cases that are reported by the *Citator* are divided into the various issues involved. Since the researcher may be interested in only one or two issues, only those cases involving the particular issue need to be checked.

The four volumes of the P–H *Federal Tax Citator* and the period of time covered by each are:

Volume 1 for AFTR Series (1919–1941)

Volume 2 for AFTR Series (1941–1948)

Volume 3 for AFTR Series (1948–1954)

Volume 1 for AFTR Second Series (1954–1967)

Loose-leaf volume for AFTR Second Series (1967 to present)

Through the use of symbols, the *Citator* indicates whether a decision is followed, explained, criticized, questioned, or overruled by a later court decision. These symbols are reproduced in Figure 1.

Figure 1

Prentice-Hall Citator Symbols

COURT DECISIONS

Judicial History of the Case

a   affirmed (by decision of a higher court)

d   dismissed (appeal to a higher court dismissed)

m   modified (decision modified by a higher court, or on rehearing)

r   reversed (by a decision of a higher court)

s   same case (e. g., on rehearing)

rc   related case (companion cases and other cases arising out of the same subject matter are so designated)

x   certiorari denied (by the Supreme Court of the United States)

(C or G)   The Commissioner or Solicitor General has made the appeal

(T)   Taxpayer has made the appeal

(A)   Tax Court's decision acquiesced in by Commissioner

(NA)   Tax Court's decision nonacquiesced in by Commissioner

sa   same case affirmed (by the cited case)

sd   same case dismissed (by the cited case)

sm   same case modified (by the cited case)

sr   same case reversed (by the cited case)

sx   same case-certiorari denied

Syllabus of the Cited Case

iv   four (on all fours with the cited case)

f   followed (the cited case followed)

e   explained (comment generally favorable, but not to a degree that indicates the cited case is followed)

k   reconciled (the cited case reconciled)

n   dissenting opinion (cited in a dissenting opinion)

g   distinguished (the cited case distinguished either in law or on the facts)

l   limited (the cited case limited to its facts. Used when an appellate court so limits a prior decision, or a lower court states that in its opinion the cited case should be so limited)

c   criticized (adverse comment on the cited case)

q   questioned (the cited case not only criticized, but its correctness questioned)

o   overruled

Example

Determine the background and validity of *Adda v. Comm.*, 37 AFTR 654, 171 F.2d 457 (CA–4, 1948).

Solution

Turning directly to the case itself (reproduced as Figure 2), note the two issues involved (i. e., "1." and "2."). For purposes of emphasis, these issues have been bracketed and identified as such by a marginal notation added to Figure 2. The reason for the division of the issues becomes apparent when the case is traced through the *Citator*.

Figure 2

ADDA v. COMMISSIONER OF INTERNAL REVENUE 457
Cite as 171 F.2d 457

ADDA v. COMMISSIONER OF INTERNAL REVENUE

No. 5796.

United States Court of Appeals
Fourth Circuit.

Dec. 3, 1948.

ISSUE 1.

1. Internal revenue ☞792

Where nonresident alien's brother residing in United States traded for alien's benefit on commodity exchanges in United States at authorization of alien, who vested full discretion in brother with regard thereto, and many transactions were effected through different brokers, several accounts were maintained, and substantial gains and losses realized, transactions constituted a "trade or business," profits of which were "capital gains" taxable as income to the alien. 26 U.S.C.A. § 211(b).

See Words and Phrases, Permanent Edition, for other judicial constructions and definitions of "Capital Gains" and "Trade or Business".

ISSUE 2.

2. Internal revenue ☞792

The exemption of a nonresident alien's commodity transactions in the United States provided for by the Internal Revenue Code does not apply where alien has agent in United States using his own discretion in effecting transactions for alien's account. 26 U.S.C.A. § 211(b).

On Petition to Review the Decision of The Tax Court of the United States.

Petition by Fernand C. A. Adda to review a decision of the Tax Court redetermining a deficiency in income tax imposed by the Commissioner of Internal Revenue.

Decision affirmed.

Rollin Browne and Mitchell B. Carroll, both of New York City, for petitioner.

Irving I. Axelrad, Sp. Asst. to Atty. Gen. (Theron Lamar Caudle, Asst. Atty. Gen., and Ellis N. Slack and A. F. Prescott, Sp. Assts. to Atty. Gen., on the brief), for respondent.

Before PARKER, Chief Judge, and SOPER and DOBIE, Circuit Judges.

PER CURIAM.

[1, 2] This is a petition by a non-resident alien to review a decision of the Tax Court. Petitioner is a national of Egypt, who in the year 1941 was residing in France. He had a brother who at that time was residing in the United States and who traded for petitioner's benefit on commodity exchanges in the United States in cotton, wool, grains, silk, hides and copper. This trading was authorized by petitioner who vested full discretion in his brother with regard thereto, and it resulted in profits in the sum of $193,857.14. The Tax Court said: "While the number of transactions or the total amount of money involved in them has not been stated, it is apparent that many transactions were effected through different brokers, several accounts were maintained, and gains and losses in substantial amounts were realized. This evidence shows that the trading was extensive enough to amount to a trade or business, and the petitioner does not contend, nor has he shown, that the transactions were so infrequent or inconsequential as not to amount to a trade or business." We agree with the Tax Court that, for reasons adequately set forth in its opinion, this income was subject to taxation, and that the exemption of a non-resident alien's commodity transactions in the United States, provided by section 211(b) of the Internal Revenue Code, 26 U.S.C.A. § 211 (b), does not apply to a case where the alien has an agent in the United States using his own discretion in effecting the transactions for the alien's account. As said by the Tax Court, "Through such transactions the alien is engaging in trade or business within the United States, and the profits on these transactions are capital gains taxable to him." Nothing need be added to the reasoning of the Tax Court in this connection, and the decision will be affirmed on its opinion.

Affirmed.

Refer to Volume 3 for the AFTR Series (covering the period from October 7, 1948, through July 29, 1954) of the P–H *Federal Tax*

Citator. Reference to the case is located on page 5505. This page is reproduced in Figure 3.

Figure 3

» Adamson — Adler «   5505

ADAMSON, JAMES H. & MARION C. v U. S., — F Supp —, 36 AFTR 1529, 1946 P.-H. ¶ 72,418 (DC Calif) (See Adamson v U. S.)

ADAMSON, R. R., MRS., — BTA —, 1934 (P.-H.) BTA Memo. Dec. ¶ 34,370

ADAMSON v U. S., 26 AFTR 1188 (DC Calif, Sept 8, 1939)
iv—Coggan, Linus C., 1939 (P.-H.) BTA Memo. Dec. page 39—806

ADAMSON; U. S. v, 161 F(2d) 942, 35 AFTR 1404 (CCA 9)
1—Lazier v U. S., 170 F(2d) 524, 37 AFTR 545, 1948 P.-H. page 73,174 (CCA 8)
1—Grace Bros., Inc. v Comm., 173 F(2d) 178, 37 AFTR 1014, 1949 P.-H. page 72,433 (CCA 9)
1—Briggs; Hofferbert v, 178 F(2d) 744, 38 AFTR 1219, 1950 P.-H. page 72,267 (CCA 4)
1—Rogers v Comm., 180 F(2d) 722, 39 AFTR 115, 1950 P.-H. page 72,531 (CCA 3)
1—Lamar v Granger, 99 F Supp 41, 40 AFTR 270, 1951 P.-H. page 72,945 (DC Pa)
1—Herbert v Riddell, 103 F Supp 383, 41 AFTR 975, 1952 P.-H. page 72,383 (DC Calif)
1—Hudson, Galvin, 20 TC 737, 20-1953 P.-H. TC 418

ADAMSON v U. S., — F Supp —, 36 AFTR 1529, 1946 P.-H. ¶ 72,418 (DC Calif, Jan 28, 1946)

ADAMS-ROTH BAKING CO., 8 BTA 458
1—Gunderson Bros. Engineering Corp., 16 TC 129, 16-1951 P.-H. TC 72

ADAMSTON FLAT GLASS CO. v COMM., 162 F(2d) 875, 35 AFTR 1579 (CCA 6)
4—Forrest Hotel Corp. v. Fly, 112 F Supp 789, 43 AFTR 1080, 1953 P.-H. page 72,856 (DC Miss)

ADDA v COMM., 171 F(2d) 457, 37 AFTR 654, 1948 P.-H. ¶ 72,655 (CCA 4, Dec 3, 1948)
Cert. filed, March 1, 1949 (T)
No cert. (G) 1949 P-H ¶ 71,050
x—Adda v Comm., 336 US 952, 69 S Ct 883, 93 L Ed 1107, April 18, 1949 (T)
sa—Adda, Fernand C. A., 10 TC 273 (No. 33), ¶ 10.33 P.-H. TC 1949
iv—Milner Hotels, Inc., N. Y., 173 F (2d) 567, 37 AFTR 1170, 1949 P.-H. page 72,528 (CCA 6)
1—Nubar; Comm. v, 185 F(2d) 588, 39 AFTR 1315, 1950 P.-H. page 73,423 (CCA 4)
g-1—Scottish Amer. Invest. Co., Ltd., The, 12 TC 59, 12-1949 P.-H. TC 32
g-1—Nubar, Zareh, 13 TC 579, 13-1949 P.-H. TC 318

ADDA, FERNAND C. A., 10 TC 273 (No. 33), ¶ 10.33 P.-H. TC 1948 (A) 1948-2 CB 1
a—Adda v Comm., 171 F(2d) 457, 37 AFTR 654, 1948 P.-H. ¶ 72,655 (CCA 4)
1—Nubar; Comm. v, 185 F(2d) 588, 39 AFTR 1315, 1950 P.-H. page 73,423 (CCA 4)
g-1—Scottish Amer. Invest. Co., Ltd., The, 12 TC 59, 12-1949 P.-H. TC 32
g-1—Nubar, Zareh, 13 TC 579, 13-1949 P.-H. TC 318

ADDA, FERNAND C. A., 10 TC 1291 (No. 168), ¶ 10.168 P.-H. TC 1948 (A) 1953-1 CB 3, 1953 P.-H. ¶ 76,453 (NA) 1948-2 CB 5, 1948 P.-H. ¶ 76,434 withdrawn
1—Scottish Amer. Invest. Co., Ltd., The, 12 TC 59, 12-1949 P.-H. TC 32

ADDA INC., 9 TC 199 (A) 1949-1 CB 1, 1949 P.-H. ¶ 76,260 (NA) 1947-2 CB 6 withdrawn
a—Adda, Inc.; Comm. v, 171 F(2d) 367, 37 AFTR 641, 1948 P.-H. ¶ 72,654 (CCA 2)
a—Adda, Inc.; Comm. v, 171 F(2d) 367, 37 AFTR 641, 1949 P.-H. ¶ 72,303 (CCA 2)
e-1—G.C.M. 26069, 1949-2 CB 38, 1949 P.-H. page 76,226
3—Koshland, Execx.; U.S. v, 208 F(2d) 640, — AFTR —, 1953 P.-H. page 73,597 (CCA 9)
4—Kent, Otis Beall, 1954 (P. H.) TC Memo. Dec. page 54—47

ADDA, INC.; COMM. v, 171 F(2d) 367, 37 AFTR 641, 1948 P.-H. ¶ 72,654 (CCA 2, Dec 6, 1948)
sa—Adda, Inc., 9 TC 199
s—Adda, Inc.; Comm. v, 171 F(2d) 367, 37 AFTR 641, 1949 P.-H. ¶ 72,303 (CCA 2) reh. den.
e-1—G.C.M. 26069, 1949-2 CB 39, 1949 P.-H. page 76,227
e-2—G.C.M. 26069, 1949-2 CB 39, 1949 P.-H. page 76,227

ADDA, INC.; COMM. v, 171 F(2d) 367, 37 AFTR 641, 1949 P.-H. ¶ 72,303 (CCA 2, Dec 6, 1948) reh. den.
sa—Adda, Inc., 9 TC 199
s—Adda, Inc.; Comm. v, 171 F(2d) 367, 37 AFTR 641, 1948 P.-H. ¶ 72,654 (CCA 2)

ADDISON-CHEVROLET SALES, INC. v CHAMBERLAIN, L. A. & NAT. BANK OF WASH., THE, — F Supp —, AFTR —, 1954 P.-H. ¶ 72,550 (DC DC) (See Campbell v Chamberlain)

ADDISON v COMM., 177 F(2d) 521, 38 AFTR 821, 1949 P.-H. ¶ 72,637 (CCA 8, Nov 3, 1949)
sa—Addison, Irene D., — TC —, 1948 (P.-H.) TC Memo. Dec. ¶ 48,177
1—Roberts, Supt. v U. S., 115 Ct Cl 439, 87 F Supp 937, 38 AFTR 1314, 1950 P.-H. page 72,292
1—Cold Metal Process Co., The, 17 TC 934, 17-1951 P.-H. TC 512
1—Berger, Samuel & Lillian, 1954 (P.-H.) TC Memo. Dec. page 54—232
2—Urquhart, George Gordon & Mary F., 20 TC 948, 20-1953 P.-H. TC 536

ADDISON, IRENE D., — TC —, 1948 (P.-H.) TC Memo. Dec. ¶ 48,177
App (T) Jan 14. 1949 (CCA 8)
a—Addison v Comm., 177 F(2d) 521, 38 AFTR 821, 1949 P.-H. ¶ 72,637 (CCA 8)
1—Urquhart, George Gordon & Mary F., 20 TC 948, 20-1953 P.-H. TC 536

ADDITON, HARRY L. & ANNIE S., 3 TC 427
1—Lum, Ralph E., 12 TC 379, 12-1949 P.-H. TC 204
1—Christie, John A. & Elizabeth H., — TC —, 1949 (P.-H.) TC Memo. Dec. page 49—795

ADDRESSOGRAPH - MULTIGRAPH CORP., 1945 (P.-H.) TC Memo. Dec. ¶ 45,058
f-10—Rev. Rul. 54-71, 1954 P.-H. page 76,453

ADDRESSOGRAPH-MULTIGRAPH CORP. v U. S., 112 Ct Cl 201, 78 F Supp 111, 37 AFTR 53, 1948 P.-H. ¶ 72,504 (June 1, 1948)
No cert (G) 1949 P.-H. ¶ 71,041
1—New Oakmont Corp., The v U. S., 114 Ct Cl 686, 86 F Supp 901, 38 AFTR 924, 1949 P.-H. page 73,181

ADELAIDE PARK LAND, 25 BTA 211
g—Amer. Security & Fidelity Corp., — BTA —, 1940 (P.-H.) BTA Memo. Dec. page 40—571

ADELPHI PAINT & COLOR WORKS, INC., 18 BTA 436
1—Neracher, William A., — BTA —, 1939 (P.-H.) BTA Memo. Dec. page 39—69
1—Lyman-Hawkins Lumber Co., — BTA —, 1939 (P.-H.) BTA Memo. Dec. page 39—350

ADEMAN v U. S., 174 F(2d) 283, 37 AFTR 1406 (CCA 9, April 25, 1949)

ADICONIS, NOELLA L. (PATNAUDE), 1953 (P.-H.) TC Memo. Dec. ¶ 53,305

ADJUSTMENT BUREAU OF ST. LOUIS ASSN., OF CREDIT MEN, 21 BTA 232
1—Cook County Loss Adjustment Bureau, — BTA —, 1940 (P.-H.) BTA Memo. Dec. page 40—331

ADKINS, CHARLES I., — BTA —, 1933 (P.-H.) BTA Memo. Dec. ¶ 33,457

ADLER v COMM., 77 F(2d) 733, 16 AFTR 162 (CCA 5)
g-2—McEuen v Comm., 196 F(2d) 130, 41 AFTR 1172, 1952 P.-H. page 72,604 (CCA 5)

Correlating the symbols reproduced in Figure 3 with the shaded portion of Figure 3, reveals the following information about *Adda v. Comm.*:

Application for certiorari (i. e., appeal to the U.S. Supreme Court) filed by the taxpayer (T) on March 1, 1949.

Certiorari was denied (x) by the U.S. Supreme Court on April 18, 1949.

The trial court decision is reported in 10 T.C. 273 and was affirmed on appeal (sa) to the Fourth Court of Appeals.

During the time frame of Volume 3 of the *Citator* (October 7, 1948, through July 29, 1954), one decision (*Milner Hotels, Inc.*) has agreed "on all fours with the cited case" (iv). One decision (*Comm. v. Nubar*) has limited the cited case to its facts (1) and two decisions (*The Scottish American Investment Co., Ltd.* and *Zareh Nubar*) have distinguished the cited case on issue number one (g–1).

Reference to Volume 1 for the AFTR Second Series (covering the period from 1954 through 1967) of the P–H *Federal Tax Citator* does not show *Adda v. Comm.* This means, of course, that the case was not cited or referred to during the period covered (i. e., 1954–1967).

Reference to the loose-leaf volume for the AFTR Second Series (covering the period from 1967 to the present) of the P–H *Federal Tax Citator* shows the case named on page 10,007. This page is reproduced in Figure 4.

Correlating the symbols reproduced in Figure 3 with the shaded portion of Figure 4 reveals the following *additional* information about *Adda v. Comm.*:

Another decision (*Ralph E. Purvis*) has distinguished the cited case on issue number one (g–1).

One decision (*Piedad Alvarado deKrause*) has reconciled the cited case on issue number one (k–1).

Except as otherwise noted, it would appear that *Adda v. Comm.* has withstood the test of time.

Figure 4

ADAMS—contd

e—El-Sabban, Mohamed Z. & Effat I., 1971 P-H TC Memo 71-475 [See 46 TC 358]

e-1—Hechavarria, Orlando v U.S., 33 AFTR2d 74-1168, 374 F Supp 131 (DC Ga)

e-1—Rynowiecki, Kajetan, 1968 P-H TC Memo 68-179 [See 46 TC 361]

e-1—DeLauzirika, Angel & Norma, 1971 P-H TC Memo 71-800 [See 46 TC 352]

ADAMS, WILLIAM W. v U.S., 34 AFTR2d 74-5962 (USCA 7, 10-3-74)

sr—Adams, William W. v U.S., 31 AFTR2d 73-1087, 353 F Supp 333 (DC Wis)

ADAMS, WILLIAM W. v U.S., 31 AFTR2d 73-1087, 353 F Supp 333 (DC Wis, 1-5-73)

r—Adams, William W. v U.S., 34 AFTR2d 74-5962 (USCA 7)

ADAMSON, LARRY R. & FLORENCE A., 1973 P-H TC Memo ¶ 73,107

ADDA v COMM., 171 F2d 457, 37 AFTR 654 (USCA 4)

g-1—Purvis, Ralph E. & Patricia Lee, 1974 P-H TC Memo 74-669

k-1—deKrause, Piedad Alvarado, 1974 P-H TC Memo 74-1291

ADDA, FERNAND C. A., 10 TC 273, ¶ 10.133 P-H TC 1948

g-1—Purvis, Ralph E. & Patricia Lee, 1974 P-H TC Memo 74-669

k-1—deKrause, Piedad Alvarado, 1974 P-H TC Memo 74-1291

ADDA, INC., 9 TC 199

4— Midler Court Realty, Inc., 61 TC 597, 61 P-H TC 368

ADDA, INC.; COMM. v, 171 F2d 367, 37 AFTR 641 (USCA 2)

2—Midler Court Realty, Inc., 61 TC 597, 61 P-H TC 368

ADDISON v COMM., 177 F2d 521, 38 AFTR 821 (USCA 8)

g-1—Galewitz, Samuel & Marian, 50 TC 113, 50 P-H TC 79

n-2—Woodward, Fred W. & Elsie M., 49 TC 385, 49 P-H TC 270

ADDRESSOGRAPH-MULTIGRAPH CORP., 1945 P-H TC Memo ¶ 45,058

f-2—Vulcan Materials Co. v U.S., 25 AFTR2d 70-446, 308 F Supp 57 (DC Ala)

f-3—Marlo Coil Co. v U.S., 1969 P-H 58,133 (Ct Cl Comr Rep)

ADDRESSOGRAPH-MULTIGRAPH CORP. v U.S., 112 Ct Cl 201, 78 F Supp 111, 37 AFTR 53

e-1—Central & South West Corp. v U.S., 1968 P-H 58,175 (Ct Cl Comr Rep)

ADELBERG, MARVIN & HELEN, 1971 P-H TC Memo ¶ 71,015

ADELMAN v U.S., 27 AFTR2d 71-1464, 440 F2d 991 (USCA 9, 5-3-71)

sa—Adelman v U.S., 24 AFTR2d 69-5769, 304 F Supp 599 (DC Calif)

ADELMAN v U.S., 24 AFTR2d 69-5769, 304 F Supp 599 (DC Calif, 9-30-69)

a—Adelman v U.S., 27 AFTR2d 71-1464, 440 F2d 991 (USCA 9)

ADELSON v U.S., 15 AFTR2d 046, 342 F2d 332 (USCA 9)

f-1—Cochran, Carol J., 1973 P-H TC Memo 73-459

f-2—Krist, Edwin F. v Comm., 32 AFTR2d 73-5663, 483 F2d 1351 (USCA 2)

f-2—Roy, Leo J. & Concetta C., 1969 P-H TC Memo 69-653, 69-655

f-2—Rosenberg, Esther M., 1969 P-H TC Memo 69-1285

f-2—Statton, Zella V., 1969 P-H TC Memo 69-1390

f-2—Postman, Arthur D., 1974 P-H TC Memo 74-612

ADELSON v U.S., 12 AFTR2d 5010, 221 F Supp 31 (DC Calif)

f-1—Roy, Leo J. & Concetta C., 1969 P-H TC Memo 69-653, 69-655

ADER, SPECIAL AGENT; DeGROSA, PRESIDENT OF DeGROSA TRUCKING CO., v, 23 AFTR2d 69-402, 405 F2d 926 (USCA 3) (See DeGrosa; U.S. v)

ADIRONDACK LEAGUE CLUB, 55 TC 796, ¶ 55.83 P-H TC

a—Adirondack League Club v Comm., 29 AFTR2d 72-1083, 458 F2d 506 (USCA 2)

e—Iowa State University of Science & Technology v U.S., 34 AFTR2d 74-5551 (Ct Cl) 500 F2d 521 [See 55 TC 808, n. 5, 808-809, 815-819]

ADIRONDACK—contd

French, R. T., Co., The, 60 TC 849, 60 P-H TC 519 [See 55 TC 813-814]

f-1—Five Lakes Outing Club v U.S., 30 AFTR2d 72-5664, 72-5665 (USCA 8) [See 55 TC 807, 808-809]

g-1—Mountain Lake Corp. v U.S., 27 AFTR2d 71-988 (DC Fla)

n-1—Internat. Trading Co., 57 TC 468, 57 P-H TC 317

ADIRONDACK LEAGUE CLUB v COMM., 29 AFTR2d 72-1083, 458 F2d 506 (USCA 2, 5-5-72)

sa—Adirondack League Club, 55 TC 796, ¶ 55.83 P-H TC

f-1—Five Lakes Outing Club v U.S., 30 AFTR2d 72-5664, 72-5665, 468 F2d 444 (USCA 8)

e-1—Iowa State University of Science & Technology v U.S., 34 AFTR2d 74-5551 (Ct Cl) 500 F2d 521

1—French, R. T., Co., The, 60 TC 849, 60 P-H TC 519

ADKINS, BUHL NORMA JEAN, 51 TC 957, ¶ 51.96 P-H TC (A) 1970-1 CB xviii (See Adkins, Leland & Bernice)

ADKINS, LELAND & BERNICE, 51 TC 957, ¶ 51.96 P-H TC (A) 1970-1 CB xviii

f—Gap Anthracite Co., 1972 P-H TC Memo 72-971 [See 51 TC 965]

e-1—Costantino, Florence, 1970 P-H TC Memo 70-223 [See 51 TC 967]

ADKINS-PHELPS, INC.; U.S. v, 22 AFTR2d 5637, 400 F2d 737 (USCA 8, 9-30-68)

No cert (G) 1969 P-H ¶ 61,000

sa—Adkins-Phelps, Inc. v U.S., 19 AFTR2d 663 (DC Ark)

e-1—Coast Quality Constr. Corp. & Subsidiaries v U.S., 30 AFTR2d 72-5149, 463 F2d 510 (USCA 5)

1—Wortham Machinery Co. v U.S., 34 AFTR2d 74-5003, 375 F Supp 838 (DC Wyo)

ADKINS-PHELPS, INC. v U.S., 19 AFTR2d 663 (DC Ark)

a—Adkins-Phelps, Inc.; U.S. v, 22 AFTR2d 5637, 400 F2d 737 (USCA 8)

ADLER, ABE B. & LEONA M., 1968 P-H TC Memo ¶ 68,100

App (T) 11-12-68 (USCA 6)

f-7—McManus, Herbert C. & Myrtle G., 1972 P-H TC Memo 72-1053

ADLER, ARTHUR, 1959 P-H TC Memo ¶ 59,115

f—Aldridge, Harry D. & Virgil, 51 TC 482, 51 P-H TC 337

ADLER v COMM., 13 AFTR2d 1175, 330 F2d 91 (USCA 9)

f—Carpenter, Meade A., Jr. v U.S., 34 AFTR2d 74-5085, 495 F2d 184 (USCA 5) [See 13 AFTR2d 1177, 330 F2d 93]

f—Green, Thomas J., Jr. & Ellen S., 59 TC 458, 59 P-H TC 309 [See 13 AFTR2d 1176-1177, 330 F2d 93]

f-1—Altman, Leon S. & Olga H., 53 TC 490, 53 P-H TC 351

f-1—Aldridge, Harry D. & Virgil, 51 TC 482, 51 P-H TC 337

e-1—Peterson, Arthur William & Dorothy E., 1970 P-H TC Memo 70-890

e-1—Boerner, Gerhard F. B & Shirley A., 1971 P-H TC Memo 71-255

ADLER v COMM., 25 AFTR2d 70-692, 422 F2d 63 (USCA 6, 2-20-70)

f-1—McManus, Herbert C. & Myrtle G., 1972 P-H TC Memo 72-1053

ADLER, ERNEST, 8 TC 726

g-1—Benichou, Chantoub, 1970 P-H TC Memo 70-1271

ADLER, EST. OF, v U.S., 25 AFTR2d 70-1608 (DC Fla) (See Miami Beach First Nat. Bk., The, Adm. v U.S.)

ADLER, EXECX. v U.S., 27 AFTR2d 71-1812, 443 F2d 116 (USCA 5) (See Miami Beach First Nat. Bank, The, Adm. v U.S.)

ADLER, EXECX. v U.S., 25 AFTR2d 70-1608 (DC Fla) (See Miami Beach First Nat. Bk., The, Adm. v U.S.)

ADLER, IRVING A., 1963 P-H TC Memo ¶ 63,196

f-1—Altman, Leon S. & Olga H., 53 TC 490, 53 P-H TC 351

e-1—Peterson, Arthur William & Dorothy E., 1970 P-H TC Memo 70-890

ADLER, LOUIS, REALTY CO., INC., 6 TC 778

e-1—Metropolitan Invest. Co., The v U.S., 31 AFTR2d 73-340 (DC Ohio)

1—Bixby, Mark & Hudythe, 58 TC 780, 58 P-H TC 529

ADLER v NICHOLAS, 166 F2d 674, 36 AFTR 827 (USCA 10)

7—Adams v U.S., 28 AFTR2d 71-5092, 328 F Supp 232 (DC Neb)

APPENDIX F

COMPREHENSIVE TAX RETURN PROBLEM

In January 1977, O. B. Allen received a B.S. Degree in Marketing at L.S.U. (Baton Rouge) and immediately accepted a position with the Wipe Corporation as an outside salesman and local sales manager in the Houston area.

O. B. Allen is 23 years of age and has been a full-time student at L.S.U. since his graduation from Baton Rouge High School four years ago. He was married to the former Nancy Hebert during his junior year in college. Nancy, age 25, has two children by a former marriage: Marcus, age 2, and Belinda, age 3. Both children live with O. B. and Nancy but neither has been formally adopted by O. B. Under the divorce decree, Nancy receives $100 a month from her ex-husband for the support of the children.

During 1977 the Allens received the following receipts:

1) Commissions from the sale of Wipe of $10,400 and regular salary as sales manager of $12,800. These gross amounts were reduced by Federal income tax withholdings of $3,663, FICA of $908.40 and hospitalization insurance of $450 (the employee's 50% contribution to a group policy carried by the employer with Ajax Medical Insurance Co.).

2) Income of $4,900 from rental property located at 240 Alaska Street, Baton Rouge, Louisiana. The property was inherited from O. B.'s aunt, who, at the time of her death on December 28, 1976, was using it as her personal residence. The property cost the aunt $24,000 in 1960 and had a fair market value of $50,000 on the date of her death and on the date it was first rented. The property was rented on February 1, 1977 under a two-year lease for $400 per month, rent due on the first with the last month's rent payable in advance. In addition, O. B. required a deposit of $100 which would be refunded in the event the property was undamaged upon the termination of the lease. A local real estate broker estimates that one-fourth of the cost and value of the property is attributable to the lot. Assume the house has an estimated useful life of 20 years remaining and no salvage value.

3) $8,790.70 from a garage sale held on January 3, 1977 at the Alaska Street property in which the following items were disposed of:

Wedding rings and other personal effects (used clothing, etc.)	$ 820.70
Household furnishings	900.00
Second-hand refrigerator	70.00
LaSalle automobile (12-cylinder 1937 sedan)	7,000.00

All items except the refrigerator were inherited by O. B. Allen from his aunt. O. B. has no idea what the cost of each item was or when it was acquired by his aunt. He does believe, however, that each item has not changed in value from the date of his aunt's death to the time of the sale. The refrigerator was acquired by the Allens in November 1974 from a junk dealer for $5 and in inoperative condition. O. B. rebuilt the motor himself spending $45 for parts. He estimates that this work would have cost $120 (including parts) if performed by a regular repair service. The refrigerator was used by the Allens in their Baton Rouge apartment.

4) $242.50 received from Wipe Corporation on March 3, 1977 representing reimbursement for a visit O. B. made to the home office in New York in early December 1976 on a job interview. The sum represents out-of-pocket costs deducted by the Allens on their 1976 joint income tax return. It is not reflected in the Form W–2 O. B. received from the company covering his 1977 earnings.

5) $175 paid to O. B. on September 8, 1977 by the Ajax Medical Insurance Company. This was the amount due under the policy as a pregnancy benefit. Nancy Allen delivered her third child (a male named Julius Allen) on August 3, 1977 at Memorial Baptist Hospital in Houston. O. B. paid all the medical expenses incurred by his wife, then subsequently filed a claim with Ajax.

6) $2,252.50 withdrawn by mail on July 6, 1977 from a savings account with Louisiana National Bank of Baton Rouge, Louisiana. Of this amount, $252.50 represents interest ($52.50 accrued during 1977) none of which has ever been reported on the tax returns previously filed by the Allens.

7) During late August and all of September and October of 1977 Nancy worked as a hostess at various conventions held in Houston. For this work she received $8,980, none of which was subject to withholdings (either Federal income tax or FICA). In these activities she was recommended by the Bell Captain of the headquarters hotel and paid by the group sponsoring the convention or by some of the more appreciative participants.

8) Proceeds of $2,475 from the redemption of U.S. Savings Bonds (Series E) on January 6, 1977. These bonds were purchased by Nancy for $2,250 with cash funds received from her ex-husband as a community property settlement. None of the interest on these bonds has been reported on any of the tax returns filed by Nancy either separately or jointly with O. B.

9) Refund of $45 from the State of Louisiana received on July 13, 1977. During 1976 Nancy held a part-time job and this was the amount withheld from her wages. On May 15, 1977 the Allens filed a state income tax return and, as no tax was due, claimed the $45 as a refund. On their 1976 Federal income tax return the Allens claimed the standard deduction.

During 1977 the Allens had the following stock sales and purchases:

Asset	Date Acquired	Date Sold	Purchase Price	Selling Price	Sale Brokerage Commission
R Corp. (100 Sh.)	1/ 5/72	2/ 3/77	$3,000	$2,025	$25
S Corp. (100 Sh.)	6/ 5/71	2/10/77	——	1,020	20
T Corp. (75 Sh.)	12/ 2/75	2/17/77	——	5,050	50
R Corp. (50 Sh.)	2/27/77	——	900	——	——

All of the stock is common and none paid any dividends during 1977. The purchase price listed includes brokerage commission but the selling price does not. Thus, in the case of the R Corporation sale on 2/3/77, O. B. received a check from his broker for $2,000 ($2,025 less $25).

The S Corporation stock was acquired by O. B. as a gift from his uncle on June 5, 1971. The uncle paid $8,000 for the stock and it possessed a date of gift value of $4,500. The uncle paid a gift tax on the transfer of $150.

The T Corporation stock was acquired by gift from Nancy's father who purchased it in 1963 at a cost of $1,000. The stock had a value of $4,000 on December 2, 1976 and the father paid a gift tax on the transfer of $100.

During 1977 the Allens had the following disbursements and losses:

A) $280 paid to the District Director of Internal Revenue on April 15, 1977. This represents the balance due over withholdings on the Allen's joint return for calendar year 1976.

B) $1,200 sent to the District Director on September 15, 1977 accompanied by a Form 1040–ES. At this time the Allens were concerned that, as a result of Nancy's unusual financial success as a hostess, O. B.'s withholdings would be severely inadequate to cover their income tax liability for 1977. No other declaration of estimated taxes was filed during the year nor was any other prepayment made before or after September 15.

C) Ordinary repairs made to the Alaska Street property (after its rental) as follows:

Plumbing	$84.00
New screen door	32.45
Paint touch-up	18.50
Fix fence	24.25

D) Other costs involving the Alaska Street property:

Interest on mortgage	$620.00
Property taxes	560.00

E) Funeral expenses of $299 paid on January 3, 1977 and incurred in connection with the interment of O. B.'s aunt.

F) Interest expense as follows:

Sears revolving account	$389.52
GMC Acceptance Corporation	550.00
HFC	352.50
Finger's Furniture	246.89

The Sears account was used for the purchase of clothes, toys, and certain household items. The $550 amount represents the interest portion of installments for the purchase of a Bonneville on January 6, 1977. Amounts borrowed from HFC were used by the Allens to pay moving expenses in January and to take a short vacation during the same month. In February the Allens purchased new furniture from Finger's Furniture Co. on credit. The $246.89 is the interest element of the monthly payments.

G) On January 13, 1977 the Allens leased a three-bedroom unfurnished apartment (occupancy as of February 1) for $350 per month and located on Bellaire Blvd. During 1977 they paid the following amounts for this facility:

Rent	$3,850.00
Utilities	557.46
Telephone	132.50

On May 1, 1977 O. B. converted one of the bedrooms in his apartment into an office for use in his business. This procedure is typical with Wipe Corporation personnel as the company provides no office facilities in the Houston area. The area converted comprises approximate 30% of the living space in the apartment and was furnished with rented equipment (paid for by O. B.'s employer). The office and all of its facilities is used exclusively for business purposes. O. B. estimates that he uses the telephone 60% of the time for business.

H) Charitable contributions for the year were as follows:

Date	Name of Organization	Item	Cost	Value
Jan. 17	Goodwill Industries	Used furniture	$2,400	$600
Oct. 1	Salvation Army	Maternity clothes	300	100
Nov. 1	United Fund	Cash	10	10

I) On January 12, 1977 the Allens drove to Houston to find a suitable place to live. They returned to Baton Rouge the next day after leasing the apartment on Bellaire Boulevard. They returned to Houston with all of their belongings on January 31 arriving there on February 1 but were unable to move in until the morning of February 4 because the premises were not vacated until then. Expenses incurred (besides mileage) on these trips were as follows:

	January 12 trip	February 1 trip
Meals on the road	$ 2.80	$ 16.90
Meals in Houston	14.80	48.00
Lodging on the road	—	18.50
Lodging in Houston	22.00	66.00
Trailer rental	—	162.00

None of these expenses were reimbursed by the Wipe Corporation. Assume the mileage from Baton Rouge to Houston (one way) is 282.

J) Not counting the two trips described in I), the Allens drove their Bonneville as follows:

	Miles
Business	17,865
Medical	340
Personal	8,527

As all gasoline purchases were for cash, they have no records to prove the number of gallons purchased. They did, however, purchase new tires for $164.75 and paid $48 for parking during business use. No major repairs were made on the automobile during 1977.

K) The Allens do not keep track of the amount they spend on state and local sales taxes. They can prove, however, that $352 was spent on the purchase of the Bonneville.

L) Medical expenses paid during 1977 were as follows:

Payee	Amount
Dr. John L. Abner (obstetrician)	$500.00
Dr. Lucius Jones (dentist)	600.00
Dr. Anne Brown (pediatrician)	140.00
Ajax Medical Insurance Co. (the employee's 50% contribution)	450.00
Memorial Baptist Hospital	287.50
Internal Medicine Clinic of Houston	320.00
St. Luke's Hospital	218.76
Drugs	314.91
Sanitary Diaper Service	68.40
Maternity clothing	300.00

Except as otherwise noted, none of the above expenses were reimbursed in 1977 under the hospitalization insurance carried by the Allens. The expenditures for the Internal Medicine Clinic and St. Luke's Hospital were for diagnosis and treatment O. B. received in early December for an enlarged liver. O. B. filed a claim for $438.76 ($538.76 less deductible of $100) on December 30, 1977 and received reimbursement from Ajax in this amount on January 14, 1978.

M) On October 3, 1977, while working for a convention at the Marriott Motor Hotel, Nancy's purse was stolen. The theft was immediately reported to the police but no trace of it was ever uncovered. The purse had a value of $40, contained $500 in cash, and a wedding ring worth $35.

N) On March 1, 1976, O. B. loaned $400 to a friend. The friend signed a note promising to repay $500 one year later. On March 9, 1977 O. B. sent the note to a Baton Rouge attorney for collection. Several days later he received the following reply: "Your friend owes money to everybody in town and has long since left for parts unknown—I am enclosing a bill for my services in the amount of $125." O. B. did not pay the bill and has no intention of doing so unless legal action is instituted against him (which he seriously doubts).

Requirements

Based on the assumptions appearing below, prepare a joint income tax return for the Allens for calendar year 1977. The return should be in good form, signed by you as preparer, and should include all necessary supporting schedules.

Assumptions and Additional Requirements

I. The Allens contribute over 50% of the support received by Marcus and Belinda.

II. The Allens use the cash method of accounting for tax purposes.

III. To simplify matters assume all gasoline purchases occurred in Texas.

IV. Assume the sales tax is the same in Baton Rouge as in Houston, Texas. For 1977 the local sales tax was 25% of the State sales tax.

V. Disregard any possible penalties for underpayment of estimated taxes.

VI. Do not prepare a Louisiana nonresident income tax return. Texas has no state income tax.

VII. In determining depreciation deductions use whatever proper method provides the larger benefit for 1977.

VIII. Nancy is self-employed. O. B. is not.

IX. Do not make assumptions not supported by the facts. For example, under J) you must use the automatic mileage method allowed by the IRS as you cannot compute actual depreciation (the cost of the Bonneville is not given) or determine all of the operating expenses (gasoline purchases are unknown). As another example, under I) you cannot presume that the trips to Houston involved any personal vacation.

X. Unless otherwise noted, none of O. B.'s business expenses are reimbursed by Wipe Corporation.

XI. In preparing the Form 1040–ES for 1978 make the following assumptions:

—Use the actual estimate method.

—Presume the 1977 tax law changes (including credit for dependents) is extended.

—The payments will be made quarterly.

—Nancy's income is expected to triple.

—O. B. expects to earn an extra $5,000. His withholdings for Federal income taxes will be $4,940.

—Medical insurance premiums will remain constant. Other medical expenses will decrease so as to provide no tax benefit because of the 1% and 3% limitations.

—Contributions will be negligible and can be disregarded.

—Eliminate non-recurring income items such as 3), 4), 8), and 9).

—No dividend or interest income is anticipated.

—No stock will be sold.

—Eliminate non-recurring expenses such as E), I), K), M), and N).

—Estimate home office expenses on an annual basis.

—Everything else should remain approximately the same.

XII. In Baton Rouge the Allens lived at 1268 Nicholson Drive (Apt. 12–C) 70808 and in Houston at 3689 Bellaire Blvd. (Apt. 186) 77025.

XIII. Nancy's Social Security No. is 458–32–6406 and O. B.'s is 460–31–9201.

XIV.   Include a statement for services rendered reflecting what you would have charged for preparing these materials.

  XV.   Disregard the income averaging provisions of Code Sections 1301–1304.

XVI.   Include a statement describing what, if any, the Allens have done wrong on tax returns filed for calendar years prior to 1977. Do not file amended returns for these years, even if appropriate, but express yourself as to whether or not such action is advisable and why.

*

APPENDIX G

TABLE OF CASES CITED

*

INDEX

DATE DUE